Y0-BEE-675

THE UNITED STATES IN WORLD AFFAIRS 1953

SOME PUBLICATIONS OF THE

COUNCIL ON FOREIGN RELATIONS

FOREIGN AFFAIRS (quarterly), edited by Hamilton Fish Armstrong.

THE UNITED STATES IN WORLD AFFAIRS (annual). Volumes for 1931, 1932, and 1933 by Walter Lippmann and William O. Scroggs; for 1934–1935, 1936, 1937, 1938, 1939 and 1940 by Whitney H. Shepardson and William O. Scroggs; for 1945–1947, 1947–1948 and 1948–1949 by John C. Campbell; for 1949, 1950, 1951, 1952, and 1953 by Richard P. Stebbins.

DOCUMENTS ON AMERICAN FOREIGN RELATIONS (annual). Volume for 1952 edited by Clarence W. Baier and Richard P. Stebbins; for 1953 and 1954, edited by Peter V. Curl.

POLITICAL HANDBOOK OF THE WORLD (annual), edited by Walter H. Mallory.

FOREIGN AFFAIRS BIBLIOGRAPHY, 1942–1952, by Henry L. Roberts.

JAPANESE AND AMERICANS: A Century of Cultural Relations, by Robert S. Schwantes.

THE FUTURE OF UNDERDEVELOPED COUNTRIES: Political Implications of Economic Development, by Eugene Staley.

THE UNDECLARED WAR, 1940–1941, by William L. Langer and S. Everett Gleason.

THE CHALLENGE TO ISOLATION, 1937–1940, by William L. Langer and S. Everett Gleason.

MIDDLE EAST DILEMMAS: The Background of United States Policy, by J. C. Hurewitz.

BRITAIN AND THE UNITED STATES: Problems in Cooperation, a joint report prepared by Henry L. Roberts and Paul A. Wilson.

TRADE AND PAYMENTS IN WESTERN EUROPE: A Study in Economic Cooperation, 1947–1951, by William Diebold, Jr.

THE ECONOMICS OF FREEDOM: The Progress and Future of Aid to Europe, by Howard S. Ellis.

WAR AND THE MINDS OF MEN, by Frederick S. Dunn.

PUBLIC OPINION AND FOREIGN POLICY, by Lester Markel and Others.

THE PRICE OF POWER, by Hanson W. Baldwin.

OUR FARM PROGRAM AND FOREIGN TRADE, by C. Addison Hickman.

THE FOREIGN AFFAIRS READER, edited by Hamilton Fish Armstrong.

THE STUDY OF INTERNATIONAL RELATIONS IN AMERICAN COLLEGES AND UNIVERSITIES, by Grayson Kirk.

THE PROBLEM OF GERMANY, by Hoyt Price and Carl E. Schorske.

FOREIGN AFFAIRS BIBLIOGRAPHY, 1932–1942, by Robert Gale Woolbert.

THE UNITED STATES IN A MULTI-NATIONAL ECONOMY, by Jacob Viner and Others.

THE FAR EASTERN CRISIS, by Henry L. Stimson.

THE STRUGGLE FOR AIRWAYS IN LATIN AMERICA, by William A. M. Burden.

LIMITS OF LAND SETTLEMENT, prepared under the direction of Isaiah Bowman.

SURVEY OF AMERICAN FOREIGN RELATIONS (in four volumes, 1928–1931), prepared under the direction of Charles P. Howland.

DOLLARS IN LATIN AMERICA, by Willy Feuerlein and Elizabeth Hannan.

NEW DIRECTIONS IN OUR TRADE POLICY, by William Diebold, Jr.

INTERNATIONAL AIR TRANSPORT AND NATIONAL POLICY, by Oliver J. Lissitzyn.

THE UNITED STATES IN WORLD AFFAIRS 1953

By Richard P. Stebbins

With the assistance of

Grant S. McClellan

Introduction by Grayson Kirk

Published for the

COUNCIL ON FOREIGN RELATIONS

by

HARPER & BROTHERS

NEW YORK

1955

The Council on Foreign Relations is a non-profit institution devoted to study of the international aspects of American political, economic and strategic problems. It takes no stand, expressed or implied, on American policy.

The authors of books published under the auspices of the Council are responsible for their statements of fact and expressions of opinion. The Council is responsible only for determining that they should be presented to the public.

THE UNITED STATES IN WORLD AFFAIRS, 1953

Printed in the United States of America

For information address Council on Foreign Relations 58 East 68th Street, New York 21

FIRST EDITION

American Book–Stratford Press, Inc., New York

Library of Congress catalog card number: LC 32-26065

COUNCIL ON FOREIGN RELATIONS

ACKNOWLEDGMENTS

THIS volume has been produced by a cooperative effort entailing obligation to a large number of co-workers. Grant S. McClellan directed the project throughout its early stages and supervised the preparation of an initial draft. Considerable portions of the text are based on material prepared by outside specialists, including important manuscripts on the U.S.S.R. by Whitman Bassow and Robert H. McNeal, on the Far East by Herbert Spielman, on the Near East, South Asia, and Africa by William W. Wade, and on Latin America by Olive Holmes Blum. Peter V. Curl prepared the bibliography, chronology, and index as well as the indispensable documentation provided in *Documents on American Foreign Relations, 1953*. The maps and charts are the work of Gustav Schweizer of the American Geographical Society. Elaine P. Adam has done more than any other individual to keep the ship afloat in all weathers. To all these collaborators the author expresses his thanks, together with his apologies for the alterations entailed in adapting their work to the general scheme of the volume. For the text as it stands he assumes full responsibility.

Grateful acknowledgment is also made of the support extended by the Committee on Studies and by my immediate associates at the Council, especially Walter H. Mallory, George S. Franklin, Jr., and William Diebold, Jr. The library staff under Ruth Savord and the business office headed by Frank D. Caruthers, Jr., have likewise met the project's many requirements with their usual good humor and skill.

The editors of the *Current Digest of the Soviet Press* (published by the Joint Committee on Slavic Studies appointed by the American Council of Learned Societies and the Social Science Research Council) have kindly authorized the use of copyright material translated from Soviet sources.

R. P. S.

INTRODUCTION

BY GRAYSON KIRK

I AM happy to write a few words of introduction to *The United States in World Affairs, 1953*. This is a volume which deals with a subject of crucial importance to the future security and welfare of our own country and of the entire world as well. A book such as this deserves to be read by all thoughtful citizens who have come to recognize their role in the determination of national policy.

Today, as never before in our history, we are beginning to realize that the study of international relations is not merely a matter of professional concern to diplomatists and scholars; it affects the ordinary citizen in a deep and meaningful way. The contemporary clash of global ideologies and the accelerating rivalry in nuclear weapons seem destined to have a dramatic and lasting influence on the course of human development in the second half of the twentieth century. As our dissension-ridden world grows smaller and smaller, men must, for their own safety, know more about the processes and problems of international intercourse. If they fail to do so, their apprehensions—and not their hopes—are likely to be realized.

Whether it is understandingly motivated or not, popular interest does grow. Frequently, it produces vast differences in individual and group reactions. Some demand that diplomacy be made more directly responsive to popular control. Others, bewildered by the magnitude and complexity of the problems involved, take refuge in an assumed indifference or in sheer escapism. In the case of still other persons, emotions far outrun understanding and produce a clamor for courses of action which, though plausible, may be completely opposed to the requirements of over-all national policy. Our conclusion must be that, as a people, we have not yet developed a national public opinion sufficiently informed and discriminating as to provide sound policy guidance for our national representatives. And yet such an opinion is precisely what is demanded by the imperatives of our political organization in face of the great issues of our time.

To contribute to the development of such a mature and discriminating outlook on world affairs is the preeminent aim of the series in which this volume appears. Since the publication of its first volume nearly a quarter-century ago, *The United States in World Affairs* has been distinguished by three features which are of inestimable value in our present situation and which so far as I know make it unique in the political literature of this country. First, these volumes present the essential facts relating to the course of American world relations in any given year, and the presentation is made in a carefully digested and coherent narrative which can be read with pleasure as well as enlightenment. Second, the series offers a broad analysis and interpretation of the year's developments which are of immeasurable assistance in appraising both their immediate and their long-term significance. Finally, each volume treats our American role in world affairs from a national rather than an official or partisan standpoint. Though based largely on official sources, its conclusions are drawn independently and may or may not coincide with the official viewpoint. Though respectful toward all genuine conviction, the author avoids uncritical acceptance of claims put forward on behalf of any political party or group. So far as humanly possible, the effort is made to maintain an attitude of objectivity and impartiality which will merit the confidence of all who turn to these books either now or in the future.

Such qualities are particularly to be welcomed in a study of the international developments of 1953, a year in which our foreign relations were unusually affected by considerations of domestic politics as well as by the significant changes which were occurring in the internal life of our principal adversary and in the pattern of international military power and potential. The processes set in motion by the death of

Stalin, the armistice in Korea, and the concurrent developments in military technology have not even yet developed to a point at which anything in the nature of a definitive appraisal is possible. Enough information is available, however, to warrant at least a preliminary attempt at setting the multitudinous and sensational events of this period in their proper perspective. To this effort the author and his associates have brought both skill and sincerity of a high order, and I am confident that the result of their labors will be of lasting value to all who seek a clearer insight into matters of concern to every American.

PREFACE

THE year 1953 witnessed some relaxation of the global tensions associated with the postwar East-West struggle but brought no assurance of durable peace between the Communist powers and the Western democracies. Changes of leadership in the United States and the Soviet Union, followed by an armistice in the Korean war, facilitated a limited shift of emphasis from military preparations to increased civilian benefits in both opposed camps. But the policy aims of the Communist and Western governments still appeared basically incompatible, and meanwhile the increasing nuclear potential on both sides accentuated the long-run hazards to civilization. While the United States extended its world-wide network of mutual security arrangements, it tended to limit somewhat its direct participation in the affairs of the free world and was only partially successful in dealing with economic, political, and psychological weaknesses among the non-Communist nations. Some threatening situations were remedied, others were permitted to deteriorate. The lack of a unified and effective Western policy toward Communist China was a source of continuing diplomatic embarrassment.

The present volume attempts to portray these tendencies in terms consistent with the general aim of presenting a dispassionate, nonpartisan analysis of American world policy as it develops from year to year. Like earlier volumes in the series, it makes no pretense at definitive history nor at exhaustive treatment of any particular segment of our national foreign relations. What it does attempt is to aid in the understanding of current affairs through a balanced interpretation that brings recent happenings into focus and relates them to the broad underlying tendencies that are reshaping the modern world.

Although the interval of nearly eighteen months since the close of the year under review is longer than customary, it makes possible the inclusion of some additional information as well as the achievement of what I hope is a more accurate perspective than would be possible in dealing with events only a few weeks old. These advantages have been of special value in attempting to grapple with developments so complex in themselves and, in addition, so deeply involved in political controversies toward which the author is obligated to maintain an attitude of judicial impartiality. A good many readers will doubtless share my dissatisfaction with some features of the present text, especially the long introductory chapter which attempts to survey a rapidly changing world situation from the special viewpoint of the United States during a period of internal transition. Those of us who have worked on the project can only hope that the detailed information presented will be adequate for reference purposes while not unduly cluttering the narrative for those who prefer to read it as a whole.

A word may be appropriate as to the practice followed in regard to documentary footnotes. When a statement or document appears in one of the volumes of the annual *Documents on American Foreign Relations,* the reference is to that standard collection. Other official material is taken where possible from the *Department of State Bulletin,* which provides convenient texts of documents of foreign as well as American origin. For Soviet material we have relied on the authoritative translations of the *Current Digest of the Soviet Press.* The *New York Times* has once again served as an indispensable source of information and documentation on all phases of American foreign relations.

R. P. S.

New York, June 1, 1955.

CONTENTS

MAPS AND CHARTS

THE
UNITED STATES
IN
WORLD AFFAIRS
1953

CHAPTER ONE

NEW ERA IN WASHINGTON

FOUR PRINCIPAL events will distinguish the year 1953 in the history of the United States and of mankind. In Washington, on January 20, General of the Army Dwight D. Eisenhower took the oath as thirty-fourth President of the United States, the first to head an incoming Republican administration since 1929. In Moscow, probably on March 5, Premier Joseph V. Stalin died after nearly twenty years of personal rule in the Soviet Union during which his name had come to epitomize the malignant tendencies of international Communism. In Panmunjom, Korea, on July 27, a military armistice was signed by representatives of the United Nations, the Republic of Korea, and Communist authorities of North Korea and mainland China, thus ending the military phase of a collective struggle against Communist aggression which had begun in June 1950 and developed into one of the largest and most devastating localized wars in history. And on August 12, less than ten months after the achievement by the United States of a successful thermonuclear explosion of staggering force in the remote Pacific, the Soviet Union likewise exploded "one of the types of the hydrogen bomb." [1]

In the long perspective of history, there seems no doubt that the last of these developments will rank as the most important. The changes of leadership in the United States and the Soviet Union, chief protagonists in the global power and ideological struggle of the mid-twentieth century, were to occasion minor modifications in the international demeanor of each but would lead to no discernible change in fundamental policy on either side. The armistice in Korea, while it

[1] *New York Times,* August 21, 1953.

eliminated a source of bloodshed and possible general war, likewise failed to influence the roots of the East-West antagonism or to safeguard the non-Communist world against the continuation and intensification of Communist aggressive efforts on both the military and political levels. But the developing Soviet command of nuclear processes—fission in 1949, fusion in 1953—deprived the Western world of what had been its main element of military superiority over its Communist enemies. Henceforth the people of the United States, in common with those of virtually all other nations, would be compelled to live with the possibility of instantaneous mass destruction on a scale that no human imagination could adequately conceive.

The outlook for the generation of human beings which had unlocked the secrets of the atom had appeared sufficiently problematical even before it was realized that Soviet scientists were pressing so close upon the heels of their American and British competitors. In his last major pronouncement as Chief Executive of the United States, President Harry S. Truman had grimly summarized the implications of the successful thermonuclear experiment already carried out by this country at Eniwetok Atoll on November 1, 1952:

". . . We have entered another stage in the world-shaking development of atomic energy. From now on, man moves into a new era of destructive power, dwarfing the mushroom clouds of Hiroshima and Nagasaki. . . .

"The war of the future would be one in which man could extinguish millions of lives at one blow, demolish the great cities of the world, wipe out the cultural achievements of the past—and destroy the very structure of a civilization that has been slowly and painfully built up through hundreds of generations.

"Such a war is not a possible policy for rational men. We know this, but we dare not assume that others would not yield to the temptation science is now placing in their hands. . . ." [2]

Though the United States still retained a massive preponderance in the field of nuclear weapons, this advantage could no longer be fully relied upon to protect this country and its allies from overwhelming attack. Already the Russians pos-

[2] Message on the State of the Union, January 7, in *Documents on American Foreign Relations, 1953*, 14.

sessed a growing number of atomic bombs, each with a destructive power equal to many thousands of tons of TNT. As soon as they had accumulated a sufficient stockpile of these formidable weapons together with the means of delivering them, nothing except their own calculation of the probable gains and losses could prevent them from striking with devastating force against their principal antagonist. No warning or defensive system this country might devise could keep some hostile bombers from getting through to rain death and destruction on American cities. Unless some means could be found for effectively barring the use of atomic weapons in warfare—or, preferably, for eliminating war itself—a future collision with the U.S.S.R. would almost certainly result in millions of American casualties and crippling damage to the material and spiritual fabric of American life.

Even if both sides should choose to refrain from the use of nuclear weapons and thus minimize the possibility of mutual annihilation, the non-Communist powers would still find themselves at a heavy disadvantage. Thus far, their defenses against Communist aggression had rested primarily on a superiority in air and atomic power which served to counterbalance the superiority of the Communist bloc in trained and mobilized manpower. With this superiority neutralized, it was difficult to see how the Communist armies could be prevented from overrunning the remaining defenses of free Europe and Asia, thus placing themselves in a most favorable position for a final life-and-death struggle with the United States. This was the harsh background against which the nation's foreign relations would in future have to be conducted.

But most people's minds recoiled from a subject so forbidding to contemplate, so difficult to comprehend, and so shrouded in official secrecy. Men and women in all countries continued for the most part to think in the more familiar terms of the pre-atomic age—quite baffling enough, with its multifarious political and social problems all permeated by the influence of the "cold war" between East and West. When the new force entered consciously into their calculations, the reaction differed in different countries. In the United States a certain number of people still looked on the A-bomb or the H-bomb as a quick and decisive means of settling all outstanding international differences to the advantage of this country. Abroad, many indulged in thoughtless condemnation of United States policy for its supposed readiness to act on such views, held in reality by only a few extremists. For the vast majority of humankind, however, the atom figured mainly as a vague portent of increased instability and insecurity, a further incentive to enjoy as many of the good things of life as possible while time and opportunity remained.

Partly for this reason, perhaps, the problems of nuclear warfare had played little direct part in the stirring political campaign which preceded the election of General Eisenhower to the presidency. So far as foreign affairs were concerned, the leaders of the victorious party had concentrated on exploiting the past shortcomings, real or alleged, of their Democratic opponents in the struggle with world Communism, rather than on trying to strike out any fundamentally new line of policy which would embrace the rapidly developing potentialities of the atomic age. Implicit in the Republican program, perhaps, was a tendency toward still greater reliance on air power and atomic weapons as the main element in the national defense. But no precise policy deductions could be drawn from the language of the Republican campaign platform, which had merely promised

> "the quickest possible development of appropriate and completely adequate air power and the simultaneous readiness of coordinated air, land and sea forces, with all necessary installations, bases, supplies and munitions, including atomic energy weapons in abundance." [3]

This, in fact, was but one of numerous features in the Republican program whose significance could not be rightly assessed until the new administration had taken office and had an opportunity to begin applying its own philosophy of government. General Eisenhower and, with him, the Republican party had engaged themselves to pursue the struggle with world Communism by methods which would be both more effective and more economical than those used hitherto. Their only detailed commitment in this area, however, was to try to end the war in Korea. Beyond that, the Republican

[3] Republican platform, July 10, 1952, *ibid., 1952,* 84.

leaders had voiced aims and displayed attitudes which would undoubtedly introduce a change in the spirit and tempo of American policy, but whose detailed expression could not be clearly forecast. The 1952 election had been primarily a national vote of confidence in General Eisenhower, rather than an unqualified endorsement of the Republican party as such. Only time would show how far the new President's own views on world affairs, formed as they had been in long years of professional service under Democratic administrations, would be influenced by one or another shade of opinion within the party which had chosen him as its candidate.

Widely though Republican leaders had differed in past years on the details of national foreign policy, the general Republican approach to international affairs was governed by a conviction that American national interests had suffered during the past two decades as the result of an overindulgent attitude toward foreign nations whose long-term aims and interests did not necessarily coincide with those of the United States. That the Roosevelt administration had been instrumental in the overthrow of aggressive totalitarianism in Germany and Japan, and that the Truman administration had successfully blocked the postwar advance of Soviet Communism in Western Europe and the Near East, was admitted by most Republicans. But these achievements were held to be offset by such tragic facts as the Soviet domination of Eastern Europe after 1945, the Communist conquest of China in 1948–1949, the Communist aggression in Korea in 1950, and the continuance of a struggle in that country which by the beginning of 1953 had been going on for eighteen months and had cost the United States no fewer than 128,238 casualties, including 22,556 killed. Some Republicans went further and charged the Roosevelt and Truman administrations with undue "softness" toward Communism both at home and abroad. Many maintained that American lives and wealth had been squandered in the pursuit of policies which were unsuited to attain their objectives and which, especially in recent years, had been inspired by an undue deference to the opinions of allied democracies like Great Britain and France or international bodies like the United Nations.

All this the recently victorious party had promised to set right. American policy was to be guided henceforth not by misplaced benevolence but by the principle of "enlightened self-interest," rigorously applied. Relations with friends and allies, and with international bodies, would be placed on a basis of reciprocal advantage and mutual self-respect. No longer would Europe be favored at the expense of Asia. Waste of funds on "give-away" foreign aid programs would cease. Economic policy would be consciously directed to maintaining and increasing the national prosperity of the United States, the best and only guarantee of a prosperous world economy. Substantial savings would be achieved within the government and the defense establishment even while the national defense was being strengthened. Disloyal and questionable individuals would be removed from government service. "Appeasement" of Communism would cease. The "negative, futile and immoral" policy of containment—the Truman administration's answer to Communist expansionism—would be superseded by a "dynamic" policy aimed at the liberation of the "captive" peoples held in the grip of Soviet Communism and at the ultimate disintegration of the Communist empire itself.

These, certainly, were objectives with which no loyal American who abhorred the repression and cruelty of the Soviet system could quarrel. Yet some of them would obviously be difficult to accomplish; and many of those outside the Republican party were fearful lest overzealous efforts along such lines result in doing more harm than good. How was the doctrine of "enlightened" self-interest to be construed in practice? Narrowly applied, it could demolish the whole structure of American world relations, founded as it was on the belief that a large measure of support for other friendly countries was in itself a matter of national interest. What, in reality, was to be the concrete form of our new policies, in Europe and Asia? What would be the future of the program for mutual security, of trade policy? Above all, what was to be the practical application of the "liberation" or "roll-back" doctrine which General Eisenhower and Mr. John Foster Dulles had put forward during the campaign, and how was the aim of "liberating" the captive peoples or "rolling back"

Soviet dominance to be reconciled with its proponents' unquestionable dedication to the cause of peace? Was liberation of the captive peoples a mere campaign slogan, or did it represent a genuine objective of the incoming administration? And if it was a genuine objective, was there really some way to accomplish it without making war on the Soviet Union? Such were some of the questions that were being asked, not only in America but all over the world, as Washington prepared to receive its first Republican administration in twenty years.

Surprisingly, the months that followed were to provide few definite answers. Although Mr. Eisenhower as President was to demonstrate an unshakable attachment to the cause of honorable peace and would frequently act as a restraining influence on associates, the general orientation of United States policy under Republican leadership was destined for many months to remain something of an enigma, a set of formulas without precise content. Through most of 1953, diverse influences within the Republican party would continue the competition for mastery which had been going on for years before 1952. The ultimate direction of Republican policy could not be gauged until means had been found for harmonizing or balancing such divergent views as those associated with Messrs. Eisenhower and Dulles, Henry Cabot Lodge, Jr., Robert A. Taft, John W. Bricker, and Joseph R. McCarthy. Meanwhile the tendency of our foreign relations could only be appraised in terms of the degree to which it appeared to conform to, or deviate from, the experience of past years. In general, the instinct of the new President seemed to lie predominantly in the direction of continuity; that of many of his supporters, in the direction of greater or less innovation. The interplay of these conflicting tendencies was to be a major influence on the development of United States policy and international affairs throughout 1953.

1. MR. TRUMAN HANDS OVER

To say that the Republicans were taking control at a difficult moment in the nation's history would be a gross understatement. Apart from the complexities and dissonances of the domestic scene, some of which must presently be considered in their relation to our international position, the whole field of foreign relations had been for months in a state of confusion and uncertainty. Since the early autumn of 1952, when the likelihood of a change of administration had first become apparent, neither the United States nor other governments had shown much eagerness to take important actions on the international plane. In Korea, armistice negotiations had been suspended since October 8, 1952; the United Nations Command was still awaiting a constructive move by the North Korean and Chinese Communist representatives toward solution of the one issue nominally remaining in dispute, the disposition of prisoners of war unwilling to return to their Communist homelands. In Europe, the movement toward military and political integration among the Western European democracies which had culminated in May 1952 in the signature of the Treaty Constituting the European Defense Community (E.D.C.) had once again slackened off, raising a prospect that France and perhaps other countries might after all refuse to go through with the plan. Such an eventuality would threaten the whole program of multilateral defense against possible Soviet aggression in Europe, in which the United States was intimately involved through its responsibilities as an occupying power in Germany and a key member of the North Atlantic Treaty Organization.

But while the momentum of international diplomacy had been running down, there had been no slackening in the divisive psychological currents that exert so strong an influence in contemporary world affairs. If anything, ideological antagonisms and emotional sensibilities had been accentuated by the events of recent months. The Nineteenth Congress of the Communist Party of the Soviet Union, held in Moscow in October 1952, had produced a broad reaffirmation of the U.S.S.R.'s ambitions in world affairs together with a reminder that the Kremlin relied heavily for the achievement of its aims on the operation of internal cleavages and "contradictions" in the non-Communist world. Such conflicts and cleavages, moreover, had been perceptibly growing in acuteness, to a point where they unquestionably menaced the strength and solidarity of the free community. For years the Western democracies had been concentrating their main efforts and resources on the attempt to erect defenses against Communist aggression, primarily in Europe; but they themselves, meanwhile, had been under sharp attack by formerly subordinate peoples, principally in Asia, who demanded the speedy concession of all sorts of advantages which to them meant national independence and self-respect. In most of these "colonial" conflicts the United States was not directly involved, except as a powerful country that sought to do justice to all non-Communist points of view. But there were other momentous questions in which the United States, as the strongest non-Communist power, was most directly implicated and in which, unhappily, it lacked the full sympathy of even its closest friends and allies. On some of the most vital international problems of the 1950's, a distinct cleavage could be traced between the outlook prevailing in the United States and the attitude which tended to predominate elsewhere in the free world.

Three questions, in particular, found the United States in a state of open or latent disagreement with many of its associates. Since all of them were key questions whose ramifications extended into every area of international relations, the consequences were necessarily far-reaching even when not dramatic.

First was the all-important question of the prospects for peace or war, and the corollary problem of possible peaceful accommodation of international differences with the U.S.S.R. The United States, while insisting on its own sincerely peaceful intentions and vigorously pressing its defense preparations, had sought to avoid fundamental discussion with the U.S.S.R. until such time as the free nations might together be in a position to negotiate with their antagonists from a "position of strength." But many people abroad seemed to feel that the Soviet Union was not really likely to begin a major war, that American military preparations actually increased rather than lessened the danger of an all-out conflict—probably with atomic weapons—and that the possibilities for negotiated settlement of existing differences ought to be more thoroughly explored.

Closely related was a broader question concerning the relative emphasis to be given to military and nonmilitary lines of action in the whole policy of the free world. The United States, looking at the problem of East-West relations primarily in military terms, had lately been putting most of the emphasis on purely military preparedness and giving correspondingly less weight to measures concerned with the economic, social, and political strength of the free world. But there were millions of people who claimed, or felt, that the real danger to the free world was not so much its military unpreparedness as the prevalence of inadequate living standards, social tensions, governmental instability, and similar conditions which made many of the free nations good targets for Communist tactics of division and subversion. The United States, they maintained, ought to take more account of these conditions and make more adequate provision for them, even at the cost of some slackening in strictly military preparations.

A source of special difficulty in this connection was the divergence between the attitude of the United States and that of most other non-Communist countries toward Communist China. To the United States, the Communist conquest of China in 1948–1949 had signified the imposition of an essentially alien domination upon an unwilling people; and we had steadily refused to acquiesce in this development by according the new regime diplomatic recognition or agreeing to its representation in the United Nations. Still less were we willing to consider any change in the control of the islands of Formosa and the Pescadores, which were still held by the defeated government of the Republic of China under Generalissimo Chiang Kai-shek. Basing our stand on both moral principle and strategic interest, we had at times appeared willing even to risk general war in the Far East—which might develop into global war—rather than make any concessions to Chinese Communist demands. Yet it was impossible to overlook the fact that few countries shared this national appraisal of the China situation. To most it seemed that the Communists had come to power in mainland China largely as a result of internal factors; that once in, they could not easily be turned out; and that it was better, on the whole, to let bygones be bygones and try to find some way of making the best of the situation that now existed. This inability on the part of some of our closest allies to share our moral indignation about the China situation had been the source of many acute difficulties in recent years in connection with the conduct of the Korean war, trade with Communist China, the Treaty of Peace with Japan, and other Far Eastern matters.

Seldom put into words, but perhaps most important of all, was an underlying question relating to the general spirit of American foreign policy as reflected in these and other, subordinate matters. Was this spirit wholly in tune with the fundamental aspirations of free humanity, as Americans usually claimed and as most foreigners were anxious to believe? Or had the spirit of American policy undergone a change under the stress of recent world events? Whatever deficiencies might have been found in its international action in past years, the United States had undeniably rendered incalculable services to the cause of freedom—services that were widely acknowledged and gratefully remembered. This country's armed might was still the only substantial guarantee of freedom in those countries that still enjoyed it. Yet there was now abroad in the world considerable uncertainty as to the real outlook of this country in both domestic and foreign affairs. "Today," Secretary of State Dulles was to remark a few months later, "some seem to feel that Americanism means being tough and 'hard-boiled,' doing nothing unless we are quite sure that it is to our immediate short-term advantage; boasting of our own merit and seeing in others only demerit." That, Mr. Dulles added, was only a caricature of America." [4] But did our leadership in the free world reflect a true community of beliefs and sentiments, or were we beginning to rely on coercion in those instances where persuasion proved difficult? Again, people in foreign lands had found themselves increasingly answering such questions in the affirmative—occasionally with malign satisfaction, more often with genuine grief. It was this aspect of the international scene in the winter of 1952–1953 that would, perhaps, have justified the deepest concern on the part of all Americans, irrespective of political party. Too many people, uncertain of the real aims of the United States, confused in some cases by Communist propa-

[4] Address of June 16, in *Department of State Bulletin,* XXVIII, June 29, 1953, 897.

ganda, and confronted by sensational developments in this country which they had no means of properly evaluating, were moving toward the conclusion that the United States was almost as disturbing an influence in world affairs as was the Soviet Union itself.

It is not the purpose in this brief survey to try to pass judgment on these interpretations of the American role in world affairs. The point of this discussion is that such attitudes did exist and did play a vital role in the life of the free world—as the highest American authorities were to recognize on more than one occasion. For many observers, moreover, the differences between the United States and its friends seemed likely to be increased, rather than lessened, by the advent of a Republican administration. It had never been a secret that Republicans, generally speaking, attached rather less importance to the outside world and its opinions than recent Democratic administrations had done. Though many Republicans had shown a lively interest in the possibilities of "psychological warfare" or "psychological strategy" as a technique for the achievement of foreign policy objectives, this was not always accompanied by an appreciation of popular or national psychology as a factor in day-to-day international affairs. What many foreigners feared, therefore, was that the Republicans, being in general strongly attached to the specifically "American" view on the controversial questions noted above, would commit the United States to a course so uncompromising that latent differences would be forced into the open and such solidarity as still existed among the non-Communist nations would be further shaken.

State of the Union, January 7

A consciousness of these possibilities seemed evident in the message on the State of the Union which President Truman delivered to Congress on January 7, thirteen days before the new administration took office.[5] This final pronouncement of the outgoing President was both a review of past experience and an appeal to fundamental principles which would remain as applicable under the new administration as they had been under the old. The shadow of the atomic cloud

[5] *Documents on American Foreign Relations, 1953,* 1-19.

hung over this message as it was to hang over few public pronouncements in the months to come. The most widely noted passage was a direct warning to Premier Stalin not to underestimate the impact of recent nuclear developments:

"You claim belief in Lenin's prophecy that one stage in the development of communist society would be war between your world and ours. But Lenin was a pre-atomic man, who viewed society and history with pre-atomic eyes. Something profound has happened since he wrote. War has changed its shape and its dimension. It cannot now be a 'stage' in the development of anything save ruin for your regime and your homeland."

There was also an admonition for any in America who still declined to recognize their nation's peril in a world in which both of the contending sides were now capable of using atomic weapons:

". . . war has undergone a technological change which makes it a very different thing from what it used to be. War today between the Soviet empire and the free nations might dig the grave not only of our Stalinist opponents, but of our own society, our world as well as theirs."

Beyond this, Mr. Truman undertook to reemphasize certain aspects of the world situation to which the critics of his administration had sometimes given only limited attention. The Communist threat, he once more pointed out, was not a mere military menace but "a challenge partly military and partly economic, partly moral and partly intellectual, confronting us at every level of human endeavor and all around the world."

"It has been and must be the free world's purpose not only to organize defenses against aggression and subversion, not only to build a structure of resistance and salvation for the community of nations outside the iron curtain, but in addition to give expression and opportunity to the forces of growth and progress in the free world, to so organize and unify the cooperative community of free men that we will not crumble but grow stronger over the years, and the Soviet empire, not the free world, will eventually have to change its ways or fall."

To this end, the President intimated, two things in particular were needful. One was unity of action among the free nations of the world—"a condition essential not only to their progress, but to their survival as free people." The other was a willingness on the part of Americans to persevere in the unprecedented efforts and sacrifices they had been called upon to make in recent years—and, Mr. Truman warned, would still be called upon to make in the future:

"Were we to grow discouraged now, were we to weaken and slack off, the whole structure we have built, these past eight years, would come apart and fall away. Never then, no matter by what stringent means, could our free world regain the ground, the time, the sheer momentum, lost by such a move. There can and should be changes and improvements in our programs, to meet new situations, serve new needs. But to desert the spirit of our basic policies, to step back from them now, would surely start the free world's slide toward the darkness that the communists have prophesied—toward the moment for which they watch and wait.

"If we value our freedom and our way of life and want to see them safe, we must meet the challenge and accept its implications, stick to our guns and carry out our policies."

A final warning against the effects of the fear, intolerance, and enforced conformity which had gained ground in America as a concomitant of the anti-Communist struggle concluded President Truman's valedictory.

In the expectant January atmosphere, with all ears strained for the first utterances of the incoming leaders, these observations received less attention than they perhaps merited; while Mr. Truman's very substantial budget estimates for the fiscal year 1953–54, sent up to the newly elected Congress on January 9, excited incredulity rather than serious study. To the historian and the student, nevertheless, such utterances by an outgoing chief executive present a valuable summary of the underlying considerations in American foreign policy as it had developed since the close of World War II. As such, they offer one of the best means of assessing the degree of continuity or change introduced under the new administration which was taking office.

2. SEIZING THE INITIATIVE

One of the leading Republican complaints against the conduct of foreign policy under President Truman's administration was to the effect that the United States had yielded "the initiative" to the Communist powers and been placed in the position of dancing to the Communist tune instead of forcing the Communists to adjust themselves to United States policy moves. The charge was partly true. The nation had never felt much zeal for undertaking anti-Communist policies of global scope, and its leaders had seldom tried to enlist public support for measures that lacked the stimulus of an immediate emergency. At the same time, the United States had not entirely failed to take the initiative, in concert with its allies, in many areas of policy where the Soviet bloc had actually been obliged to remain on the defensive. To an impartial eye, many of the most significant acts of Soviet policy in recent years were most readily understood as responses to the American effort to devise a broad, militarily powerful defensive coalition based on the allied nations of Western Europe together with Western Germany and Japan.

Many Republicans, however, had not been satisfied with this comparatively undramatic form of initiative. It was their professed aim to "seize" the initiative at every point, to exploit all the resources of "psychological warfare," and to keep the national adversary in a perpetual state of anxious uncertainty as to the next move scheduled by the partisans of freedom. Only in this way, they argued, could a beginning be made at reversing the tide of Communist conquest and compelling the Communist rulers to disgorge their ill-gotten gains.

Any plans for action along these lines that might have been developed by Mr. Eisenhower and his advisers could obviously not be disclosed in advance; nor could even the broad philosophy of the new administration be fully set forth at this early date. Mr. Eisenhower's personal convictions about the role which the United States was called upon to play in world affairs were to be eloquently stated in his inaugural address on January 20, and would actually impress most observers by their similarity to the views of his predecessor. But there was not to be any one systematic and detailed exposition of Republican foreign policy plans. These were put forward gradually in a series of pronouncements which gave some indication both of issues on which the new administration entered office with strong opinions and of others on which it had not yet taken a firm position.

Mr. Dulles on Liberation

The first official or quasi-official foreign policy statement from responsible Republican quarters was made not by Mr. Eisenhower but by Mr. Dulles, whose diplomatic and party services had earned his designation as the first Republican Secretary of State since Henry L. Stimson. In the course of his pre-confirmation testimony before the Senate Foreign Relations Committee on January 15, Mr. Dulles was given the opportunity to restate the opinions on a "dynamic" foreign policy and on the "liberation" of captive peoples which had loomed so large in the campaign just concluded. His reply offered a reassurance to those observers, particularly in Europe, who had feared possible warlike implications in the "liberation" doctrine. The reassurance was coupled, however, with an uncompromising reassertion of Mr. Dulles' belief that the peoples suffering under Communist tyranny in Europe and Asia must, and could, be liberated by peaceful means:

". . . We shall never have a secure peace or a happy world so long as Soviet communism dominates one-third of all the peoples that there are, and is in the process of trying at least to extend its rule to many others. . . . Therefore, a policy which only aims at containing Russia where it now is, is, in itself, an unsound policy; but it is a policy which is bound to fail because a purely defensive policy never wins against an aggressive policy. If our only policy is to stay where we are, we will be driven back. It is only by keeping alive the hope of liberation, by taking advantage of that wherever opportunity arises, that we will end this terrible peril which dominates the world. . . . But all of this can be done and must be done in ways which will not provoke a general war, or in ways which will be and can be a peaceful process, but those who do not believe that results can be accomplished by moral pressures, by the weight of propaganda, just do not know what they are talking about. . . ."[6]

On various other points touched by the committee, Mr. Dulles avoided prejudging the position of the new administration. But he left no doubt as to the seriousness with which it would regard the threat of Soviet Communism—"not only the gravest threat that ever faced the United States, but the gravest threat that has ever faced what we call western civilization, or, indeed, any civilization which was dominated by a spiritual faith." So long as "Soviet Communism" held to its present views, Mr. Dulles did not see how there could be "any permanent reconciliation" with it—although, he said, he did not exclude "the possibility of coming to working agreements of a limited character." Nor could he envisage any acquiescence on the part of the United States in the Communist domination of China:

"The present tie between China and Moscow is an unholy arrangement which is contrary to the traditions, the hopes, the aspirations of the Chinese people. Certainly we cannot tolerate a continuance of that, or a welding of the 450 million people of China into the servile instruments of Soviet aggression."[7]

It was not suggested that the United States should take any specific action to eliminate these conditions—only that the conditions themselves were unacceptable in the long run.

The Eisenhower Inaugural

How far President Eisenhower shared the detailed opinions of the new Secretary of State was not made clear by his inaugural address,[8] in which he confined himself to the enunciation of broad principles rather than concrete policies. The emphasis was peaceful but firm:

"Abhorring war as a chosen way to balk the purposes of those who threaten us, we hold it to be the first task of statesmanship to develop the strength that will deter the forces of aggression

[6] *Nomination of John Foster Dulles, Secretary of State-Designate: Hearings*, Senate Committee on Foreign Relations, 83d Congress, 1st Session, January 15, 1953 (Washington, 1953), 5-6.

[7] *Ibid.*, 10, 5.

[8] *Department of State Bulletin*, XXVIII, February 2, 1953, 167-170.

and promote the conditions of peace. . . . Realizing that common sense and common decency alike dictate the futility of appeasement, we shall never try to placate an aggressor by the false and wicked bargain of trading honor for security. . . ."

That was as near as the President came to forecasting the future course of relations with the Communist world. More revealing—and decidedly heartening to persons of internationalist views—were his comments on the interdependence of free peoples and on the general spirit in which American policy would be conducted:

". . . It is proper that we assure our friends once again that . . . we Americans know and observe the difference between world leadership and imperialism; between firmness and truculance; between a thoughtfully calculated goal and spasmodic reaction to the stimulus of emergencies."

Because we honored "the identity and heritage of each nation of the world," we would "never use our strength to try to impress upon another people our own cherished political and economic institutions." We rejected "any insinuation that one race or another, one people or another, is in any sense inferior or expendable"; we held "all continents and peoples in equal regard and honor." We were "persuaded by necessity and by belief that the strength of all free peoples lies in unity, their danger in discord."

In conformity with this basic attitude, Mr. Eisenhower intimated, the United States would continue to work with other free nations in the task of building world peace and prosperity. We would "strive to foster everywhere, and to practice ourselves, policies that encourage productivity and profitable trade." Within the framework of the United Nations, we hoped to strengthen "regional groupings of free peoples . . . the world over." Respecting the United Nations itself "as the living sign of all people's hope for peace," we would strive to make it "not merely an eloquent symbol but an effective force."

But the emphasis in such common efforts was to be somewhat different in future. Preeminent importance would be given to safeguarding America's own strength and security—"a trust upon which rests the hope of free men everywhere."

While desirous of helping "proven friends of freedom . . . to achieve their own security and well-being," we would also "count upon them to assume, within the limits of their resources, their full and just burdens in the common defense of freedom." Descending for a moment to the level of practical policy, the President admonished the leaders of Western Europe to "strive with renewed vigor to make the unity of their peoples a reality" and thus fulfill one of the long-standing objectives of American policy.

Americans, too, were called upon to rededicate themselves to the cause the President had outlined:

> "We must be ready to dare all for our country. . . . We must be willing, individually and as a nation, to accept whatever sacrifices may be required of us. . . . No person, no home, no community can be beyond the reach of this call. We are summoned to act in wisdom and in conscience; to work with industry, to teach with persuasion, to preach with conviction, to weigh our every deed with care and with compassion. For this truth must be clear before us: Whatever America hopes to bring to pass in the world must first come to pass in the heart of America."

These declarations were greeted with special enthusiasm by those at home and abroad who had feared that a Republican administration might tend to revert to a policy of isolationism or, at least, of severely limited cooperation with the rest of the free world. In this key pronouncement, the new President sounded not too much unlike the old; his abhorrence of the notion of preventive war against the Soviet Union was manifest, and he evidently retained a strong preference for collective rather than unilateral forms of international action. To be sure, there were a few questions still remaining. Where would the balance be struck between (a) the preeminent claims of national security and prosperity, and (b) the continuing need of other non-Communist nations for American military, economic, and political support? How would the new administration go about redeeming its pledge to realize drastic economies at a time when, as the President had said, "forces of good and evil are massed and armed and opposed as rarely before in history"? What practical innovations of policy would be introduced with a view to "seizing the initiative" or achieving success in areas where success had eluded the grasp of the former administration? Would American policy be conducted entirely in the broadly humane spirit of the President's address, or would it be influenced to an important degree by the more combative attitudes which had found expression during the campaign?

Not very much light was thrown on these matters by the administration's next official foreign policy pronouncement, an informal radio and television talk by Secretary Dulles on January 27, his sixth day in office.[9] Again the Secretary of State repudiated the idea of preventive war, at the same time reiterating his belief that if the love of freedom could be maintained among the 800 millions "swallowed" by the "Russian Communists," the latter might eventually succumb to "indigestion." "Perhaps," he added, "in time the indigestion will become so acute that it might be fatal." Most of the Secretary's remarks, however, were devoted to the thesis that "enlightened self-interest" made it necessary for the United States to have "friends and allies in the world" in order to frustrate what he described as the Soviet aim of encircling this country militarily all round the globe, from Kamchatka to Europe.

Mr. Dulles made no mention in this speech of the United Nations nor of the problems of colonial and underdeveloped areas, except for a reference to the role of Communist agitation in the unrest prevalent in Asia, Africa, and Latin America. Nor did he go into the problem of the two Chinese governments, the Communist "People's Republic" on the Chinese mainland and the American-supported "Republic of China" in Formosa. He did, however, earnestly reaffirm the desire of the United States for rapid progress toward unity in Western Europe, and particularly for prompt ratification of the six-nation treaty establishing the European Defense Community. Together with Harold Stassen, the new Director for Mutual Security, Mr. Dulles was about to leave for a quick survey of European conditions before the Mutual Security program for the next fiscal year was drawn up for submission to Congress. Europeans detected a note of warning in Mr. Dulles' comment:

[9] *Department of State Bulletin,* XXVIII, February 9, 1953, 212-216.

"The United States has made a big investment in Western Europe on the theory that there could be unity there. Of the 40 billion dollars which we have sent abroad since the end of the Second World War, almost 30 billions have gone into Western Europe. If, however, there were no chance, and that I just refuse to believe, but if it appeared there were no chance of getting effective unity, and if in particular France, Germany, and England should go their separate ways, then certainly it would be necessary to give a little rethinking to America's own foreign policy in relation to Western Europe."

Such plain speaking by an American Secretary of State was something new in the history of the Atlantic partnership. It suggested that despite an avowed preference for proceeding in concert with this country's allies, the new administration did not consider itself bound in case our allies failed to live up to our expectations.

State of the Union, February 2

Mr. Dulles and Mr. Stassen were already in Europe when the President released his first detailed pronouncement involving foreign affairs, a fresh message concerning the State of the Union which Mr. Eisenhower delivered personally to Congress on February 2.[10] In office almost a fortnight, the President declared that his administration had "begun the definition of a new, positive foreign policy"—one which, he indicated, would involve "application of America's influence in world affairs with such fortitude and such foresight that it will deter aggression and eventually secure peace." This policy would be governed by certain basic ideas: among them, that foreign policy must be "clear, consistent, and confident"; produced by "genuine, continuous cooperation" between the executive and the legislature; and "developed and directed in the spirit of true bipartisanship." It must be "a coherent global policy," because "the freedom we cherish and defend in Europe and in the Americas is no different from the freedom that is imperiled in Asia." Dedicated to making the free world secure, our policy would "envision all peaceful methods and devices—except breaking faith with our friends." We would "never acquiesce in the enslavement of any people in

[10] *Documents on American Foreign Relations, 1953,* 19-26.

order to purchase fancied gain for ourselves." In an obvious reference to the Yalta and other wartime agreements with the Soviet Union, the President added that he would ask Congress at a later date "to join in an appropriate resolution making clear that this Government recognizes no kind of commitment contained in secret understandings of the past with foreign governments which permit this kind of enslavement."

As for relations with the non-Communist world, the President declared that our policy would "recognize the truth that no single country, even one so powerful as ours, can alone defend the liberty of all nations threatened by Communist aggression from without or subversion within." Thus we would "give help to other nations," but only "in the measure that they strive earnestly to do their full share of the common task." Once again, the President stressed the need for "practical unity" in Western Europe as a basic principle of American policy.

Not much had been heard as yet concerning the policies the new administration would adopt in the field of foreign trade, which had come to play an increasingly important role in the world economy as our direct economic assistance to other nations had dwindled. Many had apprehended a revival of the protectionist tendencies with which the Republican party was historically identified; but those concerned primarily for the economic health of the free world could draw considerable comfort from the President's assurance that our foreign policy would "recognize the importance of profitable and equitable world trade." Not content with making this generalization or with pointing out that our friends could do much to improve their own trading positions, the President went on to enumerate a whole series of steps by which his administration desired to assist them through legislative or executive action—always, of course, on the understanding that our own efforts would be matched by satisfactory action on their part.[11]

Concerning national defense the President said little except that the effort "to achieve adequate military strength within the limits of endurable strain upon our economy" would require substantial overhauling of the defense establishment; that the Secretary of Defense would be responsible

[11] For details cf. below, pp. 92-93.

for planning "to give our Nation maximum safety at minimum cost"; that domestic, foreign, and military policies would be closely coordinated under the National Security Council; that defensive power as well as retaliatory power was an important deterrent to enemy attack, and that, "because we have incontrovertible evidence that Soviet Russia possesses atomic weapons," civil defense preparedness was "sheer necessity." He also promised a stronger international information policy, a review of existing legislation in the field of immigration, and a careful screening of Federal employees "to make certain that this Nation's security is not jeopardized by false servants" and "to clear the atmosphere of that unreasoned suspicion that accepts rumor and gossip as substitutes for evidence."

"Deneutralizing" Formosa

So much of the President's message concerned the broad lines of action—not so very different, apparently, from those pursued by the former administration—which he and his coadjutors planned to follow in the months ahead. But he also had some announcements of immediate importance with respect to the war in the Far East. During the campaign, Mr. Eisenhower as the Republican candidate had promised not only to do his utmost to secure peace in Korea but also to see to it that the armed forces of the Korean Republic were built up so that United States troops could be gradually withdrawn from the front lines. He now revealed that the new administration was in fact "giving immediate increased attention to the development of additional Republic of Korea forces." Furthermore—and this was the really sensational feature of the message—he announced that he had decided to alter a military arrangement of long standing which had come to be looked upon as one of the unwritten "ground rules" of the Korean conflict. This was President Truman's order of June 27, 1950 by which the United States Seventh Fleet had been charged with preventing either a Chinese Communist attack on the island of Formosa or Chinese Nationalist air and sea operations directed from Formosa against the mainland.

The purpose of this order, issued immediately after the North Korean Communist aggression of June 25, 1950, had been to protect Formosa against a possible Chinese Communist attack at a time when the full extent of the Communist aggression in the Far East could not be gauged. The corollary limitation on action by the Chinese Government on Formosa had originated not in any desire to make things easy for the Communists but in the belief that, under the circumstances then prevailing, any other course would have amounted to direct intervention in China's unfinished civil war.[12] Since that time, however, the Chinese Communists had themselves invaded Korea and had consistently refused to conclude an armistice on the terms offered them; yet the order to the Seventh Fleet had remained formally unchanged. In President Eisenhower's view, this "meant, in effect, that the United States Navy was required to serve as a defensive arm of Communist China." There was, he said, "no longer any logic or sense in a condition that required the United States Navy to assume defensive responsibilities on behalf of the Chinese Communists" —and, the President added, "permitted those Communists, with greater impunity, to kill our soldiers and those of our United Nations allies in Korea." Consequently, he said, he was "issuing instructions that the Seventh Fleet no longer be employed to shield Communist China." He wished to make crystal clear that "this order implies no aggressive intent on our part." But, he said, "we certainly have no obligation to protect a nation fighting us in Korea."

Though Democrats might not be flattered by this interpretation of President Truman's order, Republicans could not fail to be elated by the intimation that "the wraps" were at last to be taken off Chiang Kai-shek and his seasoned veterans. Use of the Chinese Nationalists for hit-and-run raids against the Communist mainland, if not for a full-scale invasion of continental China, was a Republican demand of long standing and had been one element in General Douglas MacArthur's famous 1951 prescription for victory in Korea. Chiang Kai-shek himself had grumbled for years at the restrictions imposed by the United States, and had seemed to live for the

[12] Cf. *The United States in World Affairs, 1950,* 207-208; also the testimony of Admiral Forrest P. Sherman, Chief of Naval Operations, and Dean G. Acheson, Secretary of State, in *Military Situation in the Far East: Hearings,* Senate Armed Services and Foreign Relations Committees, 82d Congress, 1st Session (Washington, 1951), II, 1620 and III, 1970.

day when his forces could commence a war of liberation by reinvading the mainland with United States naval and air support. But always hitherto the United States had shrunk from underwriting such ventures, partly because of the likelihood of political complications with allied governments but mainly from a belief that the military consequences would be impossible to control and might easily result in involving American forces on the mainland of China. Now, so it appeared, these inhibitions were to be cast aside. Strengthened by the equipment and training the United States had long been providing, Chiang's army of 300,000 or more would be free to do its utmost.

In Taipei, Formosa, President Chiang expressed high satisfaction, at the same time assuring his "friends abroad" that he would not ask for additional aid in ground forces. In New York, the official Nationalist Chinese news service deflated the sensation somewhat by revealing that Nationalist forces had already been operating against the mainland on a considerable scale despite the Seventh Fleet order. During 1952, anti-Communist raiders had "temporarily occupied" twenty-one Communist cities, 350 villages, and nine islands, and had captured or destroyed considerable equipment and facilities.[13]

But, in that case, what was actually new in the Eisenhower order? Was it merely the formal recognition of a *de facto* situation long in existence? Did it presage expanded operations, intensification of the Nationalist hit-and-run raids, or an all-out invasion of the mainland? Would we provide air and naval cover for Chinese Nationalist raids? And what did the United States propose to do in case Nationalist actions resulted in a Communist attack upon Formosa, the Pescadores, or the Seventh Fleet itself? What if there should be an unsuccessful attempt to invade the mainland on a large scale and the invading forces seemed about to be thrown back into the sea? If Chinese Nationalist losses in attacks against the mainland were so great as to endanger seriously the security of Formosa, who could or would defend the island?

[13] *New York Times*, February 4, 1953. Legal sanction for such activities, if required, lay in the fact that they had been launched not from Formosa or the adjacent Pescadores Islands but from smaller Nationalist-held islands such as Quemoy which lay much closer to the mainland.

Official and semiofficial comment in Washington did little to dispel the mystery. Some reference was made to an increase of military pressure on the Chinese Communists which ought, it was argued, to make them more amenable to conclude an armistice in Korea. In this way, what looked on the surface like a warlike move would actually be serving the ends of peace. For the most part, however, administration circles were content to describe the "deneutralizing" of Formosa—or the "unleashing" of Chiang Kai-shek, as it was often called—as an example of that "psychological warfare" by which the national adversaries were henceforth to be kept on the defensive and guessing about America's next move. To reveal the full implications or possible consequences of the Eisenhower decision, it was claimed, would defeat its main purpose.

Unfortunately, however, a move apparently designed to embarrass and alarm the enemy also had the effect of alarming and embarrassing various friends. The deneutralization order gave rise to considerable misgivings in Great Britain, India, and other non-Communist nations which had long feared that any large-scale operations against Communist China would involve a general enlargement of Far Eastern hostilities and possible danger of a third world war. Such apprehensions were particularly keen in the United Kingdom. The day after the presidential message, Foreign Secretary Anthony Eden told an alarmed House of Commons that the British Government, when informed of the proposed action three days in advance, had immediately advised American authorities that they feared it "would have unfortunate political repercussions without compensating military advantages." He added that Great Britain possessed "no information whatever" as to what action might follow from the decision, but advised the House to avoid "extremist views" until there was evidence on which to base them.[14] Two days later, after con-

[14] *Parliamentary Debates, Weekly Hansard,* House of Commons, February 3, 1953, 1674-1680. Mr. Eden also mentioned that a series of small Nationalist raids beginning in November 1952 had led the British Government to take up the general problem with both the old and the new administrations and to advise that "the ending of the neutralisation policy would have important political repercussions." In his statement two days later (see below), he added that the possibility of a deneutralization of Formosa had been discussed informally in January between Prime Minister Churchill and representatives of the incoming administration.

versations with Secretary Dulles in London, Mr. Eden assured the Commons that he perceived no reason for panic concerning American Far Eastern policy, that the President's decision did "not mean that grave events will necessarily follow," and that he anticipated such close Anglo-American collaboration in future as to make it unlikely that any step which could have far-reaching international reactions would be taken without London having an opportunity to express its views beforehand.[15]

In the course of his European conversations Mr. Dulles undoubtedly heard a good deal about the uneasiness which had accompanied the change of government, and which the "deneutralization" bombshell had done nothing to diminish. In a second report to the American people on his return to Washington (February 12), the Secretary admitted that together with "good will and friendliness," he and Mr. Stassen had also encountered "some fear that the United States is not qualified to give the free world the kind of leadership which it needs at this critical moment."

> "It is conceded that we have the material power, but it is questioned whether we have the accumulated wisdom to make the best use of that power. . . . It is important for us all to remember that we do carry a tremendous responsibility. Any false step could mean disaster not only for us but for our friends. Possibly our friends would suffer even more than we ourselves. Therefore, we must be sober and restrained in our national conduct. . . . In order to win and hold the confidence of those whom we need as friends and allies, we must at all times play the part of a Nation that is fully aware of the grave responsibility which it carries." [16]

Subsequent implementation of America's "new" policy in the Far East appeared, indeed, fully to meet the tests of soberness and restraint. Although the United States initiated stepped-up deliveries to Formosa of modern weapons and equipment—including the first deliveries of jet aircraft—it was soon evident that Nationalist operations for the present would still be limited to the familiar pattern of hit-and-run attacks against Communist-held offshore islands. The United States

[15] *Ibid.*, February 5, 1953, 2061-2067.
[16] *Department of State Bulletin*, XXVIII, February 23, 1953, 289.

showed no disposition either to incite Chiang Kai-shek to play his cards prematurely or to court international complications on its own account by seeking to impose a naval blockade or apply other novel forms of pressure against the Chinese Communists.[17] Although plans were also announced for increasing the Republic of Korea's active forces from twelve to fourteen divisions,[18] there was no intensification of military operations in the Korean theater. The administration seemed willing to concentrate its main effort in the Far East on tightening controls over the shipment of strategic goods to Communist China in accordance with the United Nations resolution of May 18, 1951. This was a field in which much apparently remained to be done; but it was not one in which it seemed profitable to look for early or spectacular results.[19]

The "Captive Peoples" Resolution

A somewhat similar destiny awaited the administration's second major initiative in the field of foreign affairs, likewise foreshadowed in the State of the Union message. This was the so-called "Captive Peoples" resolution, which the President had said would amount to a disavowal by Congress and the administration of past secret commitments involving the United States and permitting "enslavement" of other peoples. A logical sequel to campaign denunciations of American diplomacy at the Tehran, Yalta, and Potsdam conferences,[20] such a declaration was also regarded in Republican quarters as a positive foreign policy step of great importance—an opening gun in the campaign for what Secretary Dulles and others envisaged as the ultimate "liberation" of the captive peoples by peaceful means.

It is true that the most criticized product of United

[17] On the question of blockade see the statement of Secretary Dulles, February 18, *ibid.*, March 2, 1953, 335.

[18] *New York Times*, February 8, 1953.

[19] Cf. below, pp. 61-62.

[20] Cf. the language of the Republican campaign platform: "The Government of the United States, under Republican leadership, will repudiate all commitments contained in secret understandings such as those of Yalta which aid Communist enslavements. It will be made clear, on the highest authority of the President and the Congress, that United States policy, as one of its peaceful purposes, looks happily forward to the genuine independence of those captive peoples." *Documents on American Foreign Relations, 1952*, 83.

States wartime diplomacy, the so-called Yalta agreement regarding Japan of February 11, 1945, had already been disavowed once by the Senate in an action which Mr. Dulles had characterized at the time as recognizing "our total freedom from any obligations that stem from Yalta." [21] The present effort, however, was expected to be much wider in scope and amount to a repudiation of the whole wartime policy of seeking accommodation with the U.S.S.R. through the various territorial and other arrangements agreed upon between 1943 to 1945. In thus repudiating the ill-fated diplomatic bargains of the past, it was felt, we would be reassuring those who labored under the yoke of Communism that we would never reconcile ourselves to their permanent enslavement.

But here again the administration found difficulty in reconciling the expectations of its supporters with the requirements of world policy. Repudiation of wartime agreements was not so simple as it looked at first sight. For practical purposes most of these agreements were already dead, having been persistently violated by the Soviet Union in letter and spirit over a period of years. Yet outright repudiation would have carried the United States much farther, in a legal and political sense, than it could advantageously go. Documents like the Yalta Declaration on Liberated Europe and the Potsdam Declaration on Germany had failed to limit substantially the extension of Soviet-Communist control in Eastern and Central Europe, but they were still the only documents in existence which imposed clear-cut, specific obligations on the U.S.S.R. to respect the rights of neighboring peoples. If denounced, the United States would not only be violating its own longstanding objection to unilateral abrogation of international agreements (most of the wartime agreements with Russia were actually tripartite instruments to which Great Britain was also a party) but would also be depriving itself of a basis for protesting Soviet actions.

Thus the resolution introduced into both houses of Congress on behalf of the administration on February 20 [22] was a

[21] Cf. *The United States in World Affairs, 1952,* 60-61.

[22] H.J. Res 200, 83d Congress; text in *Documents on American Foreign Relations, 1953,* 188-189. Cf. also Secretary Dulles' comments in *Department of State Bulletin,* XXVIII, March 2, 1953, 330.

much tamer document than most Republicans had looked for. It was intended, Mr. Dulles explained, not as a "domestic political pronouncement" but as "a pronouncement in relation to foreign policy." While deploring "the forcible absorption of free peoples into an aggressive despotism," it put the blame not on the wartime agreements (or on the Democratic administration which had concluded them) but rather on the failure of the Soviet Government to live up to their "clear intent." Far from denouncing, it came close to endorsing the agreements by declaring that the United States rejected "any interpretations or applications" which had been "perverted" in such a way as to "bring about the subjugation of free peoples." Mr. Dulles' text also proclaimed the hope (though not the promise) that peoples subjected to Soviet despotism would again enjoy the right of self-determination "within a framework which will sustain the peace," and that they would again have the right to choose their form of government and exercise sovereign rights of self-government "in accordance with the pledge of the Atlantic Charter."

Since this draft presented a carefully worded and effective statement of American feelings and yet refrained from even indirect criticism of past Presidents, Democratic opinion in Congress favored it. Democratic congressional leaders, speaking for nearly half the membership of both houses, had already signified their readiness to support the administration in a spirit of "true bipartisanship" in those foreign policy actions that proved to be consistent with established national aims. They were understandably gratified to find the administration tacitly disowning the politically inspired clamor against Yalta and Potsdam. Yet the very feature that commended the resolution to Democrats made it unacceptable to many Republicans who considered it important to censure the diplomatic record of the Roosevelt-Truman era. The administration found itself in the embarrassing position of being sustained by Democrats while opposed by many of the party with which it had taken office—the first appearance of an alignment that was to become increasingly familiar during the next two years. A serious dilemma ensued. The Democrats would not vote for a resolution that condemned their party; few Republicans would endorse a resolution that refrained from such condemnation. Yet if the resolution was to have any significance as a positive act of American policy and an encouragement to the captive millions behind the Iron Curtain, it was essential that it be carried by a large majority. Secretary Dulles, supported by the President, warned that a resolution which reflected disunity between Republicans and Democrats "would be worse than no resolution at all."

A compromise amendment, aimed at rescuing the administration from its plight, was offered by Senator Taft of Ohio and approved by the Senate Foreign Relations Committee on March 3. By its terms, the Congress would have refrained from open denunciation of the wartime agreements but would have declared that the resolution did not "constitute any determination" as to their validity or invalidity. This text most Democrats declined to support, since it called in question the status of agreements which, they insisted, had been made in good faith and, moreover, were still apparently regarded as binding on the Russians. But with this refusal there disappeared the possibility of anything but a closely divided vote. On March 7, Republican leaders were constrained to shelve the matter. Two days earlier had come the news of Stalin's death, and Republican spokesmen argued that any "rocking of the boat" should be avoided at such a critical juncture.

Like the "deneutralization" of Formosa, the debate on the "Captive Peoples" resolution occasioned great though temporary excitement in the United States and abroad but had little substantive effect on the world situation. Happily, however, the attempt to convey a message of hope and comfort to those behind the Iron Curtain did not entirely miscarry. On February 27 the Senate unanimously adopted a separate resolution denouncing the "vicious and inhuman campaigns" against religious and ethnic minority groups conducted by the Soviet and satellite governments in Europe and Asia, and urging the President to take appropriate steps to stimulate action in their behalf by the United Nations.[23] Such a declaration might fall short of rolling back the Iron Curtain, but at least gave evidence that Americans had not become so engrossed in their domestic controversies as to lose interest in

[23] S. Res. 84, 83d Congress, adopted February 27, 1953; text (with letter of transmittal to the U.N. Secretary-General) *ibid.*, April 6, 1953, 506.

the plight of fellow creatures who presently lacked the blessings of political freedom.

Back to Diplomacy

The general orientation of American policy under the nation's new guides was naturally a matter of deep concern to the governments of allied and friendly nations, several of whose leaders took the earliest opportunity to visit Washington in order to sound out the views of the new administration and seek enlightenment as to its concrete intentions. Even before the inauguration, Prime Minister Winston Churchill of Great Britain had paid a private visit to New York (January 5-7) during which he had three conferences with the President-elect and undoubtedly did his best to acquaint the latter with current British views on the world situation—including, no doubt, both the prevalent concern over Far Eastern developments and his own frequently expressed desire for a fuller exchange of information on atomic matters. In return, the Prime Minister was presumably assured of the incoming administration's strong interest in a revival of the movement toward European unity and particularly in the early ratification of the treaty establishing the European Defense Community, to which Great Britain was not a party but whose acceptance by the continental nations seemed to hinge largely on the assurance of British support.

A few weeks later there were other British visitors in Washington. Foreign Secretary Eden and Chancellor of the Exchequer R. A. Butler paid an official visit to the national capital on March 4-7, days which were to be made forever memorable by the dramatic news of Stalin's illness and death. Trade policy and problems of currency convertibility were the chief topics of official conversation, but discussions in this field did not go very much beyond the general principles outlined in President Eisenhower's State of the Union message. The administration had already decided to conduct "an intensive examination and review" of the whole field of foreign economic policy before it attempted to formulate any specific courses of action. Thus the British, who had feared a return to protectionism by this country more perhaps than any other possibility except an extension of the Korean war, had to content themselves with the broad assurance that Washington shared their intention to work in the direction of "a better balanced, growing world trade and . . . the restoration of a multilateral system of trade and payments." [24]

On the political side, Mr. Dulles and Mr. Eden had an opportunity to exchange views on the possible implications of Stalin's death and to agree once again on the importance of early establishment of the European Defense Community, constructive solutions of Middle East problems, and prevention of the shipment of strategic materials to the Communist aggressors in China. Mr. Eden outlined certain measures by which his government had decided to strengthen the existing trade controls in the Far East, and it was agreed that the two governments would jointly seek the cooperation of other maritime and trading nations to this end. Mr. Dulles, on his part, indicated that the latest British proposals for settling the affairs of the expropriated British oil company in Iran seemed "reasonable and fair," thus in effect assuring the British that no attempt would be made to undermine the firm position they had adopted toward the ultranationalist Iranian government of Dr. Mohammad Mosaddeq.[25] Not less valuable to the Foreign Secretary was an assurance that the use of United States strategic air bases in the United Kingdom in any emergency was still regarded in Washington as a matter for joint decision "in the light of the circumstances prevailing at the time." [26] This understanding would help to reassure those elements in the British Parliament which feared, or professed to fear, that the United States might use its United Kingdom bases unilaterally to launch an atomic bomb attack on the Soviet Union and thus provoke Soviet atomic retaliation against Great Britain.

It is noteworthy that the joint communiqué which stressed the urgency of setting up the European Defense Community made no reference to any direct British participation in Western European affairs, but spoke only of the need for "further *continental* unity." Although the American advice

[24] Communiqué, March 7, in *Documents on American Foreign Relations, 1953*, 249-251. For further discussion of trade policy see below, pp. 91-102.
[25] On the Iranian situation cf. below, pp. 304-309.
[26] Communiqué, March 7, cited.

tendered on this occasion presumably was a factor in the subsequent decision of the United Kingdom to defer its planned withdrawal from the European Payments Union, there were indications that the United States had renounced any intention of trying to induce its ally to join the continental countries in any political or military ventures of a supranational character. Great Britain, apparently, was to be treated as a partner with a permanent and irreducible identity of its own, not as one of the nations that were being urged to surrender at least a portion of their sovereignty and national individuality to an integrated European community. From the standpoint of traditional British policy, this in itself was an achievement of no small importance, one which would help to console the British ministers for their inability to influence official thinking in Washington on the large policy issues of the Far East and particularly the attitude to be adopted toward Communist China.

French Statesmen in Washington

France, whose leaders of the moment were the next great power representatives to visit Washington, occupied a somewhat different position in the world-wide scheme of resistance to Communist aggression. In Indochina, France was engaged almost single-handed (with American material aid) in military resistance to a movement which had begun as a struggle for national independence but had fallen under complete Communist control and now constituted one of the two main prongs of Communist aggression in the Far East. In Europe, meanwhile, France had emerged under Premier René Mayer as the principal obstacle to the establishment of the European Defense Community and thus to the whole American and allied program of Western European consolidation.

Both aspects of the French problem were intensively discussed at the end of March when M. Mayer visited Washington in company with Foreign Minister Georges Bidault and other high French officials. On the European side of France's responsibilities, no full agreement could be reached despite the recognition by both delegations of the necessity for establishing the Defense Community "with minimum delay." M. Mayer, who had persuaded the other five parties to the E.D.C.

treaty to accept a series of interpretative protocols designed to attenuate the French commitment,[27] had also insisted that there must be a settlement of the long-standing Franco-German quarrel over the Saar territory before France itself could ratify the treaty. In the conferences at the State Department he argued this view at length, repeating his contentions in an address to the National Press Club in Washington on March 27. Mr. Dulles, on his side, publicly intimated that to his mind the French position had no valid legal basis.[28]

The talks on the Far East, and on the related question of the financial burden France was carrying there and in Europe, went somewhat better. Like their British predecessors, the French ministers pledged increased efforts to prevent the shipment of strategic materials to Communist China. They also promised that France would do its utmost to increase the effectiveness of the French and indigenous forces fighting in Indochina "with a view to destroying the organized Communist forces and bringing peace and prosperity to her free associates within the French Union" (the Associated States of Cambodia, Laos, and Vietnam). Although the ambassadors of the nominally independent governments of Vietnam and Cambodia were present at this phase of the discussions, nothing was said publicly about any pressure on France to move faster in making the independence of the Associated States a reality. There was also no definite commitment by the United States as to the scope of its future material and financial support, but it was clearly indicated that such aid would be forthcoming as soon as appropriate plans for military action in Indochina had been developed and analyzed.

In addition, the United States fully and publicly endorsed the French contention that the struggles against Communist aggression in Indochina and Korea were "parts of the same pattern" and required frequent consultation between the two governments if the operations were to be successfully carried out. Anticipating the possibility of an armistice in Korea (the Communists had just proposed a renewal of the truce talks at Panmunjom),[29] the two governments joined in a veiled warn-

[27] Cf. below, pp. 158-160.
[28] *New York Times,* March 28, 1953.
[29] Cf. below, pp. 219-220.

ing to Communist China not to plan on using the Chinese forces thus freed for any operations against Indochina or Southeast Asia. "It was the view of both Governments," they said, "that should the Chinese Communist regime take advantage of such an armistice to pursue aggressive war elsewhere in the Far East, such action would have the most serious consequences for the efforts to bring about peace in the world and would conflict directly with the understanding on which any armistice in Korea would rest." [30]

Reconciliation with Germany

Bilateral conversations with the leaders of Great Britain and France, as members of the Western "Big Three," were nothing new in postwar American diplomacy. A greater air of novelty surrounded the visit to Washington of Chancellor Konrad Adenauer of the Federal Republic of Germany, which took place on April 7-9. In effect the meeting of the West German Chancellor and his aides with President Eisenhower and Secretary Dulles put the finishing touches on America's official reconciliation with a nation that had figured as the primary aggressor of World War II but had now become an associate in superior standing, thanks to the dramatic reversal of American policies which had taken place under the pressure of the cold war. Federal Germany, unlike France, was by this time well on the way toward acceptance of the European Defense Community. The Bundestag or lower house had already approved the treaty (March 19),[31] and there was thus no obstacle to a clear-cut endorsement of this project together with an expression of hope for an early agreement on the Saar and a promise that the German government, too, would tighten up on strategic exports to the Communist bloc.

Possibly more remarkable were the various advantages which the United States declared itself ready to concede to the Federal Republic: military equipment for the German contingents to be formed within the European Defense Community, economic aid to Berlin, assistance in resettling refugees from Communism, reconsideration of the status of war

[30] U.S.-French communiqué, March 28, in *Documents on American Foreign Relations, 1953,* 269-272.
[31] Cf. below, p. 161.

criminals, restoration of German trademarks, negotiation of a new friendship treaty, placement of "offshore procurement" orders, intensified cultural relations, and return of 350 former German vessels were among those singled out for mention. Equally important was the assurance that Western Germany's adherence to the Western community had not caused the United States to lose interest in the eventual reunification of *all* Germany—"by peaceful means and on a free and democratic basis." [32] Such assurances were indispensable to the Chancellor in his continuing effort to persuade a skeptical parliament and public that integration with the West did not mean "selling out" more than 18,000,000 inhabitants of Communist-controlled East Germany.

3. Security or Strait Jacket?

While the administration was thus engaged in clarifying its position in relation to the principal members of the Western community, it was also struggling with immense problems connected with the reorganization of the government and with the elimination of those Communist influences which many believed to have infected the national body politic. The rather emotional character of the debate on the "Captive Peoples" resolution had been due less to its potential importance as an act of foreign policy than to its close involvement with these more specialized issues which grew directly out of the domestic political experience of the past several years. The era of the "cold war" and of sharpening antagonism to Moscow had witnessed the growth among the American people of a tremendous concern with the problem of Communist espionage and subversion at home. Stimulated by such developments as the disclosure that atomic secrets had been transmitted to the U.S.S.R., the perjury conviction of Alger Hiss, and the charges of Communist infestation brought by Senator McCarthy of Wisconsin against the State Department and other government agencies, the issue had swelled to a point at which it had tended to overshadow most aspects of foreign relations both in the national consciousness and in the political strategy of the Republican party. Encouraged in greater or less

[32] Communiqué, April 9, *ibid.*, 278-282.

degree by Republican sources, there had developed a widespread impression not only that the national interest had been misconceived or even sabotaged under the former administrations, but that the national government was still permeated with untrustworthy individuals and un-American tendencies. Inevitably, the Republican administration which had now taken office found that its work was affected in many ways by this belief and by the emotional manifestations that accompanied it.

There is no need to justify in these pages either the abhorrence of Communism which animated the overwhelming majority of the American people or their insistence that Communist influence must be rigorously excluded from their government. The utter barbarity of Communist methods (evidenced anew during 1953 in official revelations concerning the "brainwashing" techniques and other atrocities practiced against Communist victims, including American prisoners of war in Korea) [33] had long been familiar to informed Americans and fully warranted the national revulsion against Communism and all its works. But without in any way minimizing the evils in question, it must be pointed out that the reaction against them sometimes took forms that rendered the task of government more difficult and even interfered with the orderly pursuit of an anti-Communist policy at home and abroad. It must also be admitted that some of the impressions current with regard to subversive or pro-Communist influences in the United States were grossly exaggerated, and that the way in which the issue had been discussed for some years before 1953 had brought about a perceptible degeneration of the moral and intellectual atmosphere of the nation and an unhealthy prevalence of what President Eisenhower had called "that unreasoned suspicion that accepts rumor and gossip as substitutes for evidence."

In promising a prompt and thorough overhaul of the Federal employee loyalty program, the President had expressed the hope that the nation's internal security would thus be

[33] Cf. especially the speech of Allen W. Dulles, Director of the Central Intelligence Agency, April 10, in *U.S. News & World Report,* XXXIV, No. 19, May 8, 1953, 54-58; also the address of Charles W. Mayo to the First (Political and Security) Committee of the U.N. General Assembly, October 26, in *Department of State Bulletin,* XXIX, November 9, 1954, 641-647.

fully safeguarded and the atmosphere cleared of these unwholesome tendencies. This hope, however, was not destined for early fulfillment. Ingrained habits of thought and political agitation could not be changed overnight. Furthermore, the issue was kept alive not merely by disclosures or purported disclosures of past mismanagement but also by new developments in several cases originating in earlier years. Thus on January 21, a New York Federal court found thirteen "second-string" American Communist leaders guilty of conspiring to teach and advocate the overthrow of the United States Government by force and violence. On February 4 a former Department of Commerce economist, William W. Remington, was sentenced to three years' imprisonment for perjury in denying the wartime transmittal of secret information to a confessed Communist. On May 2 a sensational development of an opposite kind occurred in the case of Owen Lattimore, the Far Eastern expert whom Senator McCarthy had once designated as the "top Russian espionage agent in the United States." In one of the high points of a case that is still unsettled as this is written, a Federal judge dismissed four counts of a government perjury indictment against Mr. Lattimore and expressed "serious doubt" as to the materiality of the other three counts.

Rather more violent were the emotional storms that raged at home and abroad around the figures of Julius and Ethel Rosenberg, convicted of conspiring in wartime to give defense secrets (actually, secrets relating to the atomic bomb) to Soviet Russia. Sentenced to death in March 1951—the first such sentence imposed in the United States in peacetime—the Rosenbergs and their Communist attorneys had resorted to a long series of delaying actions and pleas for clemency which kept their plight continuously in the public eye and succeeded in delaying their execution until June 19, 1953. Meanwhile their cause was embraced not only by some well-meaning individuals who thought the sentence too severe but also by the entire apparatus of the international Communist movement, which dramatized it as a reflection of alleged "fascist" tendencies in the United States and sponsored innumerable petitions and manifestoes demanding that the result of American judicial processes be nullified. Abroad, especially in Europe, the effect of this campaign was to strengthen an already widespread impression that civil liberties in the United States had been seriously undermined and the country subjected to a minor reign of terror. At home, the successive crises of the Rosenberg story reinforced the popular sense of fear and hostility toward anything that could be made to look remotely like Communism.

State Department and Foreign Service

This was the rather unhealthy atmosphere in which it was now proposed to set the nation's house in order and repair deficiencies in its foreign policy and relations. There were differing views among Republicans as to how this task should be undertaken and how far it should be carried. It was normal that an incoming administration should plan to displace a certain number of high officials, lay down new rules and standards for the conduct of the public business, and make alterations of substance or emphasis in many aspects of public policy. But the situation in 1953 was far from normal. Quite aside from the continuing tensions of the "cold war," the Republicans had been out of power for twenty years; and they had convinced themselves and much of the electorate that the Federal establishment, while expanding out of all proportion to real needs, had also become permeated with disloyalty and perpetrated acts of substantive policy which could not be repudiated too soon. In particular, the great majority of Republicans had been agreed on the necessity for a thorough reorganization or "clean-up" of the State Department and the Foreign Service as a counterpart to the disavowal of past policies which was contemplated by the "Captive Peoples" resolution.

To carry out such a reorganization without some impairment of efficiency and morale within the nation's foreign affairs services would have been difficult under the best of circumstances and proved impossible under the conditions of early 1953. Contrary to some impressions, the Department of State was not found to be heavily infiltrated with disloyal individuals; up to September 30, only 306 citizen employees and 178 aliens had been terminated on any type of security grounds,[34] and no indication was given that any of these had been actively disloyal. But meanwhile total personnel of the Department was reduced from 42,154 to 20,321 in the seven months from February to August, partly through transfer to other agencies (16,000) and partly through outright termination (5,000).[35] Most individuals involved in the process were badly shaken by the successive reductions in force, investigations and reinvestigations, and above all by the incomprehension and contempt with which these generally loyal and able public servants seemed to be regarded not only by outsiders but by some of the newly appointed officials of the Department.

The designation of experienced diplomats like Secretary Dulles and Under-Secretary Walter Bedell Smith as the new "top command" within the Department of State had seemed to preclude any reckless attack on people whom the former had described as "the 'shock troops' in the cold war which is being waged against us." [36] Nevertheless, the Secretary declared early in his tenure that while prepared to defend what he knew to be "sound and defensible," he was "not prepared blindly to defend a situation which was created under my predecessors and which I have taken office with a mandate to change." "I frankly concede," he said, "that the present months are months of difficulty, since it will necessarily take considerable time before the new administration through its own orderly processes can correct the accumulated errors of the last 20 years." [37]

For the great majority of the nation's foreign affairs personnel the operation of these "orderly processes" turned out to be something of a nightmare. Direct responsibility for personnel security matters was entrusted to a former senatorial assistant with a strongly developed sense of security and a background of investigative police work but limited experience in international affairs. "Economies, a severe reduction

[34] Departmental announcement, November 5, in *Department of State Bulletin,* XXIX, 689, November 16, 1953.

[35] Statement of Under-Secretary W. B. Smith, *ibid.,* September 21, 1953, 375. Of the original 42,154, about 10,000 were employed in the U.S. and 32,000 abroad. *Ibid.,* July 6, 1953, 29-30.

[36] Remarks of January 28, *ibid.,* XXVIII, February 9, 1953, 240.

[37] Press conference statement, February 27, *ibid.,* March 9, 1953, 390-391.

in force, accelerated 'selection out' and forced retirements, a halt in promotions, altered rules regarding leaves—all combined to dislocate plans and frustrate expectations. On top of these came the stringent revised security program, which was committed to political appointees whose words and acts justified doubts as to their judicial impartiality." [38] This comment on the situation in the career Foreign Service, from a source by no means disposed to ignore the shortcomings of the State Department, was equally applicable to the other groups affected.

A quite special problem, but one which touched the national interest as closely as it did that of the individuals involved, concerned the responsibility for objective reporting and interpretation by government experts of those foreign situations which were of interest to the United States. Sound foreign policy, obviously, presupposed a sound understanding of foreign conditions. There had, however, been recent instances in which individual Foreign Service officers had been publicly criticized on the ground that their reports had leaned too much to one side in dealing with controversial issues, especially in China. Some of this criticism had seemed to be politically motivated; and some fears had been expressed that under the new administration our official observers might be inhibited in reporting any facts that might differ from the administration's view.

Mr. Dulles in his first message to his new associates had assured them that although nothing less than "positive loyalty" to the administration's policies could be tolerated, this did "not, of course, call for any one to practice intellectual dishonesty or to distort his reporting to please superiors." [39] Yet doubts persisted as to how far it was safe or practicable to ignore official sensibilities. They were not wholly dispelled by Mr. Dulles' action in the long-standing case of John Carter Vincent, a Career Minister whose record of diplomatic service in the Far East had figured prominently in Republican charges of a "sell-out" to the Chinese Communists, and whose

[38] Henry M. Wriston, "Young Men and the Foreign Service," *Foreign Affairs,* XXXIII, October 1954, 37.

[39] Message of January 21, in *Department of State Bulletin,* XXVIII, February 2, 1953, 170.

loyalty had subsequently been called in question by the Loyalty Review Board of the Civil Service Commission.[40] Assuming personal responsibility for settling an issue inherited from his predecessor, Mr. Dulles found that Mr. Vincent was in fact neither a loyalty nor a security risk, but that his "reporting of the facts, evaluation of the facts, and policy advice during the period under review show a failure to meet the standard which is demanded for a Foreign Service Officer of his experience and responsibility at this critical time." [41] Critics of this stand argued that there would be little incentive for other Foreign Service officers to submit unpalatable reports if it entailed a risk of being subsequently pronounced loyal but incompetent. How seriously the morale of the service was affected was a subject of differing opinions within the Foreign Service itself.

Diplomatic Appointments

Possibly of wider public interest were the changes the new administration was making in the occupancy of major diplomatic posts. As was natural under the circumstances, the bipartisan character which had marked such Truman appointments as those of Warren J. Austin to the United Nations, John J. McCloy as High Commissioner in Germany, and John Foster Dulles as an adviser to the Department of State was generally absent from the new designations. The early appointees of the Eisenhower administration were almost uniformly Republicans: Henry Cabot Lodge, Jr. to the United Nations, Winthrop W. Aldrich to London, C. Douglas Dillon to Paris, Mrs. Clare Booth Luce to Rome. President James B. Conant of Harvard, who had not been active in party politics, was designated as High Commissioner and future Ambassador to the German Federal Republic. A lone Democrat, retiring Under-Secretary of State David K. E. Bruce, was named to the unglamorous but potentially important post of American representative to the European Coal and Steel Community and observer to the Interim Committee of the European Defense Community.

[40] *Ibid.,* XXVIII, January 19, 1953, 121-122; cf. *ibid.,* February 9, 1953, 241.

[41] Memorandum released March 4, *ibid.,* March 23, 1953, 454-455. Pursuant to his own application submitted after a conversation with the Secretary, Mr. Vincent was retired effective March 31, 1953.

None of these were primarily diplomatists by training or experience; but the career Foreign Service was also not overlooked in the new appointments. Chester W. Bowles, Democratic appointee who had achieved an extraordinary personal success as Ambassador to India, was replaced by George V. Allen, a career diplomat who had achieved extraordinary success as Ambassador to Iran and later to Yugoslavia. And on February 27 another outstanding career diplomat was named to represent the United States at the critical post in Moscow. The incumbent ambassador, George F. Kennan—one of the earliest exponents of the "containment" policy—had been declared *persona non grata* by the Soviet Government months earlier and now, at forty-nine, was permitted to retire as a sequel to expressions of disagreement with prevailing views on peaceful "liberation." To replace him the President nominated Charles E. Bohlen, another outstanding authority on the Soviet Union who, among other distinctions, had served as President Roosevelt's personal interpreter at wartime conferences with Stalin.

Ironically, Mr. Bohlen's nomination reached the Senate just when that body was considering how sharply it wished to repudiate the wartime agreements which had been negotiated with Mr. Bohlen's assistance. His close connection with these transactions, even though only in a technical capacity, made him a symbol for the critics of President Roosevelt's diplomacy—all the more so when he refused, in testimony before the Senate Foreign Relations Committee, to condemn the agreements made at Yalta or the motives of the men who negotiated them.[42] But the repercussions of the Bohlen appointment extended far beyond the matter of evaluating the Yalta agreements. A more important consequence was the emergence of open divisions within the Republican party and the revelation that one element in that party continued to look at diplomatic problems with far different eyes from those of the President and Secretary of State. Already substantial elements in the Republican party had voiced their disappointment over the circumspect attitude of the adminis-

[42] *Nomination of Charles E. Bohlen: Hearings,* Senate Foreign Relations Committee, 83d Congress, 1st Session, March 2 and 18, 1953 (Washington, 1953).

tration and their preference for a more sharply defined attack both on Communism abroad and on the political opposition at home. What had not come out so clearly was that one section of the party would not merely withhold support from the administration in cases of disagreement but would oppose it by the same unorthodox methods that had been developed in the course of several years of political warfare against the Truman administration.

A good many Americans had imagined that with a Republican administration installed in Washington there would be no further scope for the particular variety of anti-Communist tactics by which Senator McCarthy had achieved national and international prominence. His past activities in connection with the exposure of Communists in government had derived much of their political effectiveness from the fact that he was in opposition. With the advent of an administration pledged to stringent scrutiny and methodical removal of all who were found unfit or untrustworthy, his personal function as a kind of self-appointed watchdog over the government had seemed likely to disappear. Not many had realized that the Senator's special brand of anti-Communism was not subject to the normal restraints of party loyalty or discipline, that he would continue to rely exclusively on his own opinions in all matters involving Communism, and that he would continue to set his judgment against that of the State Department and the White House as readily as he had done in the days of Secretary of State Dean Acheson and President Truman. In fact, Senator McCarthy's actions during the Republican year 1953 were to differ from those of past years only in the broader scope made possible by his new position as chairman of the Committee on Government Operations and its Permanent Subcommittee on Investigations. Acting mainly in this capacity but apparently recognizing no definable limit to his responsibilities, the Senator had lost no time in undertaking investigations of various phases of State Department activities, some of which were to make front-page news for months to come. His first overt challenge to the Department's top authorities came, however, in connection with the Bohlen nomination.

On March 18 the Senate Foreign Relations Committee

unanimously approved Mr. Bohlen's appointment—though not before Secretary Dulles had gone to somewhat extraordinary lengths to dispel their misgivings, assuring them (a) that he had personally examined a Federal Bureau of Investigation file on Mr. Bohlen and found no reason to doubt his loyalty or security, and (b) that while it was not desired to keep the nominee in the "policy-making position" he had hitherto occupied in the Department, he was felt to be "a reliable contact with the Russians" and thus the most suitable man for the Moscow post.[43] These assurances were not enough either for Senator McCarthy or for Senator Pat McCarran, the Democratic Senator who came nearest to sharing Mr. McCarthy's views. Stalin had died while the appointment was before the Foreign Relations Committee, and there was some feeling in Washington that the United States should lose no time in sending a permanent representative to Moscow. But it was another nine days before a vote could be taken. Claims were made that Secretary Dulles had overruled the judgment of the State Department's new security officer; Senator McCarthy charged the Secretary with falsification,[44] urged that he be recalled with his subordinate to testify under oath, and called on Mr. Bohlen to take a "lie detector" test. After two members of the Foreign Relations Committee had received permission to examine the F.B.I. file and reported that it contained nothing not already known, Senator McCarthy continued to insist on the nominee's unfitness because of his association with what the Senator called the "Acheson-Truman policies" and the "Hiss-Acheson gang." Ten Republicans and two Democrats joined him when the Senate voted on March 27, by 74 to 13, to confirm the new Ambassador and let him proceed to Moscow.

Investigating the Information Services

This was a passing sensation, soon crowded out of memory by the rush of other developments. Quite different was Senator McCarthy's multiform investigation of the Voice of America and its parent body, the International Information Administration of the State Department, which held the

[43] *Nomination of Charles E. Bohlen,* cited, 101-112.
[44] *New York Times,* March 21, 1953.

headlines for several months and, among other effects, definitely intensified the revulsion abroad against those aspects of American life which had come to be known as "McCarthyism." During the tense weeks that followed the death of Stalin, the agency responsible for America's world-wide "psychological offensive" and for broadcasting in forty-six languages to a potential audience in one hundred countries [45] was not only beset by paralyzing uncertainty about its own future but grievously shaken by the public hunt for subversives carried on by the Wisconsin Senator and his staff.[46] The investigation brought to light a number of bureaucratic grudges but little that looked like subversion; and in the opinion of most authorities on the subject it impaired the effectiveness of the foreign information program for a long time to come. While some observers laid most of the blame on the tactics of the McCarthy committee, others reproached the State Department with a lack of resolution and intelligence in meeting the McCarthy challenge.

Probably the most widely publicized aspect of the assault on the information program—for as such it was regarded by most persons familiar with the subject—concerned the contents of the American information libraries which the agency maintained in 189 foreign centers. Stung by charges that the Information Agency's facilities were actually being used for the dissemination of Communist propaganda, the State Department itself had issued a directive ordering that "no material by any Communists, fellow-travelers, et cetera [*sic*] will be used under any circumstances by any IIA media." When the difficulty of applying such loose designations in specific instances had become obvious, a new order was sub-

[45] Wilson Compton (I.I.A. Administrator), "Information and U.S. Foreign Policy," *Department of State Bulletin,* XXVIII, February 16, 1953, 252-256.

[46] For details see especially *State Department Information Program—Voice of America: Hearings,* Senate Permanent Subcommittee on Government Operations, 83d Congress, 1st Session (Washington, 1953); also the personal narrative of Martin Merson, who was second in command of I.I.A., published under the title of "My Education in Government" in *Reporter,* XI, No. 6, October 7, 1954, 15-27; and the report of Administrator Robert L. Johnson on "The Book and Library Program of the IIA" in *Documents on American Foreign Relations, 1953,* 84-93. A brief, informed account of the Voice of America investigation appears in Edward W. Barrett, *Truth Is Our Weapon* (New York, Funk & Wagnalls, 1953), 101-114.

stituted which called for the removal of works by persons "who obviously follow the Communist line or participate in Communist front organizations"—as well as of any magazine issues containing "any material detrimental to U.S. objectives." [47] No clarifying interpretation of these terms was provided, with the result that works by various authors of high repute were removed from the library shelves along with some thirty-nine individual copies of works by known Communist adherents.

The McCarthy organization was wholly unsatisfied with these accomplishments. In April two of the Senator's young assistants made a whirlwind inspection tour of American information establishments in Europe, where their "frivolous and irresponsible" behavior—to quote the later verdict of a Republican Senator—

> "caused amazement that led to serious doubts as to the seriousness, responsibility, and intelligence of this Government as represented by emissaries of its upper legislative chamber. No one can know the dismay which was spread among our friends abroad unless he has heard it from those friends at first hand." [48]

So far as the I.I.A. was concerned, the immediate sequel was a charge by Senator McCarthy (May 5) that the agency was still harboring 30,000 to 40,000 books by "Communists and fellow-travelers" on its library shelves. Later investigation disclosed that the authors in question actually included "some of the most respected names in our literature." [49]

These developments were extensively and unfavorably reported in the world press, and obvious parallels were drawn with the "book-burnings" practiced by Nazis and other enemies of freedom. The analogy was reinforced by the disclosure that amid the general confusion a few books actually had been burned by harassed I.I.A. librarians. Unfortunately the technical question of what literature was suited for sponsorship by the United States Government in "special-purpose" libraries in foreign lands became widely confused

[47] Merson, *loc. cit.,* 18. A slightly different text, dated March 17, appears in *Department of State Bulletin,* XXIX, July 13, 1953, 58-59.

[48] Speech of Senator Ralph E. Flanders of Vermont, in *Congressional Record* (Daily Edition), July 30, 1954, 12112.

[49] Merson, *loc. cit.,* 23-24.

with the general question of intellectual freedom. Few critics of "McCarthyism," especially abroad, stopped to reflect that in reviewing its official policies in the field of international information the United States was not necessarily engaged in an attack on freedom of thought as such. It must be added, however, that in the somewhat overexcited atmosphere that characterized the proceedings the distinction was not always easy to keep in mind.

In June, believers in intellectual freedom were heartened by President Eisenhower's admonition to a commencement audience at Dartmouth College. "Don't join the book burners," he said, and went on to urge his hearers to read about Communism in order to know what it was they wished to defeat. But by that time Senator McCarthy had involved himself in so many other aspects of national and international affairs that the specific issues raised by his attack on the I.I.A. had begun to wane in prominence. A few weeks later I.I.A.'s functions were taken over by a new, independent bureau, the United States Information Agency, which assumed responsibility for most of the government's foreign information activities and might prove less vulnerable to domestic attack than the old State Department-directed program had been.[50]

Relations with the U.N.

The acute concern with the "Communist menace" that made these activities possible also had a powerful impact on American relations with the United Nations, an institution whose location in New York City made it peculiarly susceptible to the fluctuations of American opinion. During late 1952, congressional and grand jury investigations of possible Communist penetration of the United Nations Secretariat and the Specialized Agencies had led to the identification of several apparent Communists or ex-Communists among American staff members of those organizations. In itself this development had raised serious issues regarding the mutual obligations of the world organization and its member states; and the hostile tone and spirit of the investigations had helped to produce a rather serious crisis in the relations between the United Nations and the host country. Since many of the United Na-

[50] On the later history of the information program cf. below, pp. 75-76.

tions' harshest critics were associated with the Republican party, there had been some apprehension lest the advent of a Republican administration might even lead to a further deterioration. These fears proved exaggerated. President Eisenhower, sensing no doubt that the public was still basically favorable to the United Nations despite dissatisfaction with some phases of its record,[51] had promised to strive to make the world organization "not merely an eloquent symbol but an effective force." Henry Cabot Lodge, Jr., the new United States Representative to the United Nations, had forecast that there would be a new vigor and determination in United States action within the world organization. But aside from some passing disregard of diplomatic amenities, delegates to the Seventh Regular Session of the General Assembly, which reconvened on February 24 after a recess taken to permit the new administration to find its bearings, perceived no radical departure from the policies of the Truman administration either at United Nations headquarters or in the conduct of the United Nations resistance to aggression in Korea.

"Security" problems which had become acute in recent months did nevertheless cause a certain amount of continuing tension between the United States and the United Nations, and competed for public attention with the work of the spring Assembly session in regard to disarmament, collective security, and Far Eastern matters.[52] The concrete issue raised by the refusal of certain staff members of United States nationality to testify as to their alleged Communist affiliations had already been largely settled by Secretary-General Trygve Lie's dismissal of the uncommunicative officials.[53] Many delegates, however, had expressed misgivings about the merits of this procedure and also about the rigorous security clear-

[51] An opinion poll taken in February 1953 by the National Opinion Research Center of the University of Chicago (see its "Occasional Reports," Series FA, No. 1) indicated that 84 percent of the respondents endorsed continuing membership in the U.N., while only 10 percent favored withdrawal and 6 percent were undecided. The comparable pro-U.N. figure was 78 percent in January 1951, 85 percent in May 1952, and 84 percent in May 1953.

[52] Cf. below, pp. 117-124.

[53] Cf. *The United States in World Affairs, 1952,* 376-384 and *Documents on American Foreign Relations, 1952,* 347-359; also the comments of Ambassador Lodge in *Department of State Bulletin,* XXVIII, May 4, 1953, 658-660.

ances which the United States was establishing for those of its nationals who were employed by the United Nations and other international organizations.[54] Legitimate concern for American security, it was felt, was taking a form in which it threatened to compromise the independence of the United Nations. This apprehension was rather plainly evident behind a smoothly worded resolution in which the Assembly expressed confidence that future personnel policy would be conducted in conformity with the principles of the United Nations Charter and called on all member states to assist the Secretary-General in this endeavor.[55]

Apart from its effects on the morale and general state of mind of the Secretariat, the current American attitude on security also created certain practical difficulties for the functioning of the United Nations. American members of the Secretariat who were assigned to duties outside the country discovered that they could not obtain passports until an overburdened F.B.I. had completed their security checks. More startling were the difficulties experienced by certain foreign members of nongovernmental organizations in securing permission to enter the United States to attend meetings of the Economic and Social Council. In the past, American officials had sometimes availed themselves of technicalities in order to deny entry to representatives of Communist-dominated organizations which were accredited to the United Nations. In April 1953 they for the first time openly invoked security considerations in refusing visas to a Frenchman and a Cana-

[54] Security screening of U.S. employees of the U.N. and other international organizations was instituted by President Truman on January 9 and extended by President Eisenhower on June 2, 1953. See the executive orders and related documents, *ibid.*, January 12, 1953, 61-63 and June 22, 1953, 882-883. A potentially more drastic action was that of the U.S. Senate in passing a bill (S. 3, 83d Congress, June 8, 1953) providing heavy fines or imprisonment for any U.S. citizen who accepted U.N. employment without prior security clearance.

[55] General Assembly Resolution 708 (VII), adopted April 1, in *Documents on American Foreign Relations, 1953*, 419-420. A twelve-power draft resolution which would have prevented the Secretary-General from taking further action pending a thorough review of the problem by the Assembly was defeated as a result of "strenuous" efforts by the U.S. delegation. *US Participation in the UN: Report by the President to the Congress for the Year 1953* (Department of State Publication 5459, Washington, 1954), 206. For further developments, cf. below, pp. 397-398.

dian woman affiliated respectively with the World Federation of Trade Unions and the Women's International Democratic Federation. This action rested on an interpretation of American rights under the United Nations Headquarters Agreement which was not endorsed by United Nations legal authorities. Negotiations subsequently carried on with the Secretary-General produced no more than "a measure of agreement" which, it was suggested, might "help to remove difficulties over the matter in the future." [56]

The Bricker Amendment

How far these actions contributed to enhance the security or the dignity of the United States might be a matter of opinion, but there was no possibility of doubt that those Americans who feared the subversive potentialities of the United Nations were in deadly earnest. Indeed, if the world organization had demonstrated half the power for good that some of its American critics believed it to possess for evil, world peace and prosperity would have been assured. The suspicion with which a vocal if numerically limited segment of the American public continued to regard the United Nations had been demonstrated many times in recent years. It was to be demonstrated once again during 1953 in connection with the second appearance of that most dignified manifestation of American security consciousness, the Bricker Amendment.

The Bricker Amendment differed in important respects from most efforts at protecting the United States from the insidious operations of foreign and domestic enemies. Where most such efforts were concerned with protection against specific evils like espionage, sabotage, or hostile propaganda, this one was regarded by many of its advocates as a necessary protection against all those tendencies toward "internationalism," "world government," and the like which were felt to be threatening the "American way of life." Where most security precautions were designed to inhibit the operations of disloyal individuals or groups, the Bricker Amendment

[56] Text of U.S. statement (April 9) in *Department of State Bulletin*, XXVIII, April 27, 1953, 625; cf. U.N. Press Release PM/2558, July 27, 1953, quoted in "Issues Before the Eighth General Assembly," *International Conciliation*, No. 493, September 1953, 121-122.

sought primarily to guard against a possible betrayal of national interest by the President himself. This it proposed to do by amending the Constitution in such a way as to (a) limit the scope of international treaties to which the United States could be a party, and (b) impose novel controls on the power of the President to negotiate treaties and executive agreements. The former limitation was designed primarily to prevent the intrusion of international bodies like the United Nations, under cover of international treaties, into matters of domestic interest such as those envisaged by the United Nations-sponsored draft international covenants of human rights. The latter provision was directed mainly toward preventing the national executive from making international commitments which might be out of harmony with national or congressional feeling. Discussion at the last session of Congress had made it clear that both aims reflected a general reaction against what were considered the internationalist excesses of recent years. The extent of this reaction might be guessed from the fact that sixty-three Senators of both parties were inscribed as cosponsors when the amendment's author, Senator John W. Bricker of Ohio, introduced his latest text in the form of a Joint Resolution on January 7, 1953.[57]

The belief that some modification of the constitutional provisions regarding the treaty power would be desirable under modern conditions was not confined to so-called isolationist circles. Mr. Dulles himself had publicly warned (in a speech of April 12, 1952) of the "great dangers" inherent in the existing powers of the executive in this field. But Secretary Dulles was hardly more enthusiastic than Secretary Acheson had been over the drastic remedies provided by the Bricker resolution. As introduced in January 1953, the proposed amendment nullified not only any treaty provision which was in conflict with the Constitution but also any treaty which conferred upon an international organization or foreign power any authority in matters "essentially within the jurisdiction of the United States." It further provided

[57] S. J. Res. 1, 83d Congress, 1st Session, in *Documents on American Foreign Relations, 1953,* 101-102. For background cf. *The United States in World Affairs, 1952,* 98-99 and *Documents on American Foreign Relations, 1952,* 66-70.

that treaties and executive agreements could become effective as internal law in the United States "only through the enactment of appropriate legislation by the Congress," and that executive agreements could be made "only in the manner and to the extent prescribed by law." Even less welcome to the State Department was a substitute text offered by Republican Senator Arthur V. Watkins of Utah (and subsequently incorporated into the Bricker Amendment as the so-called "which clause") which specified that a treaty or executive agreement could become effective as internal law "only through legislation which would be valid in the absence of a treaty."[58] Since Congress was debarred by the Constitution from enacting legislation in fields reserved to the States, this meant in effect that a treaty involving matters in any such field would require the concurrence of all forty-eight States before it could become effective.

Even before Secretary Dulles went up to testify before the Senate Judiciary Committee on April 6, a decision had been reached within the executive branch to modify one of the well-established American policies which had in the past been most disturbing to many who favored the Bricker Amendment. These groups had, over the years, been among the most dubious observers of the many-sided effort to establish through the United Nations a wider respect for and observance of human rights and fundamental freedoms. Despite its active support by their own government, they felt that this effort was characterized by an unhealthy tendency to establish principles and practices on the international level that were not fully acceptable within the United States itself. In this way, they feared, it created a danger that some international authority would circumvent the duly constituted State and national authorities in this country.

Largely for this reason, the atmosphere in the Senate had in recent years become so unfavorable to endeavors of this kind that it had begun to seem unlikely that the United Nations would succeed in evolving any human rights treaties to which the United States could become a party. And now Mr. Dulles announced that the United States was in fact desisting

[58] S.J. Res. 43 (Watkins amendment), *ibid.*, 103; revised Bricker amendment, *ibid.*, 102.

from the whole effort to strengthen the observance of human rights by international compact:

". . . while we shall not withhold our counsel from those who seek to draft a treaty or covenant on human rights, we do not ourselves look upon a treaty as the means which we would now select as the proper and most effective way to spread throughout the world the goals of human liberty to which this nation has been dedicated since its inception." [59]

Next day it was revealed that the new United States representative to the United Nations Human Rights Commission, Mrs. Oswald B. Lord, would present an alternative proposal in the form of "positive U.N. action programs" which were held to constitute a more promising approach. The proposals presently unfolded, involving world-wide studies, annual reports, and special "advisory services" on specific aspects of human rights,[60] were meritorious in themselves but would probably have made a better impression in United Nations quarters if brought forward under different circumstances.

The Administration Objects

Having made this conciliatory gesture to the Bricker forces, Secretary Dulles went on to give his frank opinion that the pending resolutions, despite the "good intentions" which prompted them, "actually could be dangerous to our peace and security." They would, he said, "basically change the Constitution of the United States relative to the making of treaties and executive agreements," and would "subject the current, day-by-day, conduct of foreign affairs to impediments which might be stifling." The provision respecting international organizations might prevent this country from making effective treaty arrangements for the international control of atomic energy, not to mention such commonplace fields of international supervision as aviation, radio, narcotics, and quarantine regulation. The requirement that treaties be implemented by congressional legislation, over

[59] *Department of State Bulletin,* XXVIII, April 20, 1953, 592. Cf. also an earlier statement, *ibid.,* March 16, 1953, 404.

[60] *Ibid.,* April 20, 1953, 579-582; June 15, 1953, 842-848. On the reaction in the Human Rights Commission, cf. *International Conciliation,* No. 493, September 1953, 82-83.

and above the normal consent to ratification by the Senate, "would make it much more difficult to consummate effective treaties" and "gravely" impair our nation's ability to deal with other nations. As to the additional restriction embodied in the Watkins amendment or "which clause," this "would require the concurrence of all 48 States to make effective such common treaties as treaties of Friendship, Commerce and Navigation, extradition, reciprocal inheritance taxation, migratory birds, collection of foreign debts, and status of foreign troops." [61]

With respect to the limitations on executive agreements, Secretary Dulles pointed out that such agreements when of major importance already were normally made pursuant to congressional or treaty authorization, or required congressional action for their implementation. "But every day," he went on, "the President, directly or through his agents, makes minor agreements of some kind or description with other governments or officials. There are masses of agreements made, and changed, almost daily with relation to the development of foreign bases and disposition of our troops abroad. There are many agreements with other governments to impose restrictions upon trade with areas unfriendly to us. There are daily agreements regarding a host of matters." To "subject this entire process to Congressional prescription" would "gravely embarrass the President in dealing currently with foreign affairs." Mr. Dulles brought an assurance from the White House that in doubtful cases the executive branch was determined to consult with appropriate congressional leaders and committees. But he warned against this method of attempting to regulate matters which should be dealt with "by friendly cooperation between the three Departments of Government which are involved." "Our Constitution, as it is, has served us well in the field of foreign relations," he concluded. "There is no actual experience to demonstrate the need of the far-reaching changes here proposed. The fears are hypothetical. Therefore, I suggest that this constitutional area is one which deserves to be kept under constant ob-

[61] Statement of April 6, as excerpted in *Documents on American Foreign Relations, 1953,* 103-108.

servation and study, but that there is no present need for constitutional change." [62]

But the advocates of constitutional change were not prepared to follow this advice. Defenders of the amendment argued that situations might arise in which the executive could conclude treaties or agreements that contravened the Constitution itself, perhaps even striking at the American form of government. The new policy on human rights had quite failed to allay their apprehensions. Various legal authorities and public groups were rallying to their support with a fervor extraordinary in so abstruse a matter. Thus by mid-June, when the Senate Judiciary Committee reported a simplified version of the Bricker Amendment that also embodied the "which clause" of the Watkins resolution,[63] it was apparent that the debate had only just begun.

The President himself had thus far taken little part in the discussion except to express his confidence that the matter could be ironed out by an appropriate use of words. Nevertheless it was quite evident that the administration would feel unable to accept the language proposed by the Senate committee. Conferences of Republican leaders with Senator Bricker only made the impasse more obvious. Once again, as with the "Captive Peoples" resolution, the President and his supporters seemed unable to achieve agreement within their own party on a major policy issue. At length, on July 22, a new proposal was offered on behalf of the administration by Senator William F. Knowland of California, who had succeeded the ailing Senator Taft as majority leader. This substitute amendment, for which the President quickly expressed unqualified support, eliminated both the "which clause" and the congressional regulation of executive agreements; instead it (a) empowered the courts to review the constitutionality of treaties and international agreements, and (b) gave the Senate explicit authority when considering the ratification of treaties to stipulate that they should not become effective without appropriate legislation by the Congress.[64]

[62] *Ibid.*

[63] *Ibid.*, 102.

[64] The Knowland amendment also provided for a record vote in the Senate on ratification of treaties. *Ibid.*, 108-110.

The pressure for adjournment of Congress prevented a vote on either the Knowland amendment or on any of the texts it was designed to replace. It seemed clear, however, that the features which commended the Knowland version to the White House would make it unacceptable to many of those who had backed the more radical project. Senator Bricker, unmoved by the President's admonition that "probably as never before in our history it is essential that our country be able effectively to enter into agreements with other nations," appeared determined that the next Congress should deal with his plan in its integrity. Those who shared his outlook seemed unlikely to modify their convictions. In the meantime their efforts had produced at least two significant results: they had stimulated the process of national self-education in some of the complexities of governmental and foreign affairs; and they had elicited from the nation's leaders renewed avowals of their belief that the security of the United States did not require the assumption of a national strait jacket.[65]

Refugee Legislation

A minor application of this principle on which the administration and Congress were able to agree was embodied in the Refugee Relief Act of 1953, which provided for the permanent entry into the United States, on an emergency basis outside the regular immigration quota, of 186,000 escapees from Communist persecution as well as selected persons in other groups up to a total of 214,000.[66] This legislation did not affect the alleged injustices and discriminatory features of the basic Immigration and Nationality Act of 1952, to which the President had drawn attention in his State of the Union message and which he had since vainly

[65] This expression appears (without specific reference to the Bricker Amendment) in an address by Assistant Secretary of State Thruston B. Morton in *Department of State Bulletin*, XXVIII, June 1, 1953, 772. For a further expression of Secretary Dulles' views in the matter cf. *ibid.*, XXIX, September 7, 1953, 307-310.

[66] Public Law 203, 83d Congress, approved August 7, 1953. Since 5,000 visas were set aside for nonimmigrants already in the U.S., the number of new arrivals would be limited to 209,000. For details cf. *ibid.*, XXVIII, June 15, 1953, 857-859; XXIX, August 24, 1953, 231-235 and December 21, 1953, 859-862; XXX, January 4, 1954, 23-24.

asked Congress to correct.[67] It did not go all the way to meet his recommendation that 240,000 special immigrants be admitted to this country over a two-year period, primarily in order to alleviate the conditions brought about by the mass flight of refugees from behind the Iron Curtain.[68] It would be of only limited assistance in the efforts undertaken by the United States and twenty-one other governments in the Intergovernmental Committee for European Migration, which sought to move up to 3,500,000 persons, mainly from European countries, to underpopulated areas.[69] But it would at least offer a new life to as many of the lucky 214,000 as could meet the stringent security requirements of the act before the opportunity expired on December 31, 1956.

4. ALONE OR WITH OTHERS?

Possibly even more significant than the specific points at issue in the Bricker Amendment and the refugee legislation were certain implicit questions about the general tendency of contemporary American life and foreign policy. The positions people took in such controversies were usually determined less by their technical merits than by individual convictions about the whole nature of America's relationship to the outside world. Should our action among the nations in the crisis of the twentieth century be guided primarily by the notion that we were "all in the same boat" or by preparedness to go it "alone, if necessary"? This was the fundamental question around which practically all debate on foreign policy matters in the postwar years ultimately revolved.

In a country whose overwhelming majority was opposed both to Soviet Communism as such and to the notion of attempting to force the issue with the Soviets by recourse to

[67] Message of February 2, *ibid.*, XXVIII, February 9, 1953, 211; letter of April 6, *ibid.*, May 18, 1953, 731. Cf. also the excerpts from the report of President Truman's Commission on Immigration and Naturalization, *ibid.*, January 19, 1953, 97-102.

[68] Letter of April 22, *ibid.*, May 4, 1953, 639; cf. also the President's correspondence with Queen Juliana of the Netherlands, *ibid.*, 639-641.

[69] Cf. Hugh Gibson, "Migration from Western Europe under the I.C.E.M.," *ibid.*, XXIX, July 27, 1953, 117-121; also George L. Warren, "International Efforts to Solve Refugee Problem," *ibid.*, XXX, January 4, 1954, 26-30.

arms, it was inevitable that most of the practical issues of foreign policy should concern the kind of relationship to be sought with the other nations of the "free" or non-Communist world. Was it really necessary, under the conditions of the postwar years, for this country to have strong and faithful friends and allies? If so, what price could and should we pay to secure and retain them? How far must we, as the strongest non-Communist power, consider their interests and opinions, and how far must they rather defer to ours? In formulating our own approach to foreign policy, was it sufficient to rely on our own sense of fitness or must we, as some claimed, make a special effort to take into account the frequently differing preconceptions of other peoples? Must we ourselves begin to readjust our own way of looking at and doing things in order to meet the new challenges with which modern world conditions confronted us? In an abstract and theoretical way, these were the questions that were being fought out in the struggle over the Bricker Amendment and many another act of foreign policy legislation. Meanwhile similar questions were being fought out on other emotional levels in connection with the day-to-day conduct of foreign relations. A brief review of some salient foreign policy developments of the first half of 1953 will illustrate the variety of national attitudes which left their mark on concrete foreign policy decisions.

Ever since the beginning of the United Nations action in Korea in 1950, the situation in the Far East had presented itself to many Americans as the ultimate test of a foreign policy professedly based on a fundamental solidarity of interest between the United States and its allies of the free world. The limited contribution of other United Nations members to the resistance in Korea, their objections to any intensification of military action against the aggressors by this country, the refusal of Great Britain and various other friendly governments to second our views on the nonrecognition of Communist China, their insistence on maintaining at least limited trade relations with the Chinese Communist aggressors, were felt in some American quarters to invalidate the whole theory on which we claimed to be operating. Others who took a more lenient view had maintained that our allies and friends were doing what they could to support the principles we held in common, and that their friendship, in any case, was too important to us in global terms to warrant any undue display of impatience on our part.

As the fighting in Korea dragged on through the early months of 1953, these issues continued to agitate American opinion and inter-allied relations. Their significance was enhanced during this period by two new factors which were gradually introducing a significant change in the international picture. One was the presence of the new administration in Washington, whose position on some of the specific problems of the Far Eastern war was still in process of clarification. The other was the disappearance of Stalin and the beginning of a new trend in Communist policies which apparently held out a real hope for the settlement of the difficulties in Korea and possibly elsewhere. This, in brief, was the background against which Americans continued to debate the fundamentals of their own international policy.

Curbing the China Trade

In their conversations with British, French, and German leaders, the spokesmen of the new administration had laid particular stress on the necessity for further restricting the shipment of strategic goods to Communist China. This emphasis had various motivations. In the foreground was the conviction of Washington officials that increased effort along these lines was doubly necessary in view of the decision not to resort to a naval blockade or other intensified military action against Communist China. It was true that the trade controls available to the West could at best affect only a limited portion of total Chinese Communist foreign trade, which was being increasingly reoriented toward the Soviet bloc. In 1952, 72 percent of all Communist China's foreign trade had been with Communist countries, in contrast to a 1950 figure of only 25 percent.[70] Nevertheless, a good deal had been accomplished in the denial of strategic materials to Communist China under the United Nations General Assembly resolution of May 18,

[70] *World-Wide Enforcement of Strategic Trade Controls—Mutual Defense Assistance Control Act of 1951 (the Battle Act): Third Report to Congress, First Half of 1953* (Washington, G.P.O., 1953), 36.

1951; and there was also in existence a special committee of governments interested in East-West trade whose members, while unwilling to imitate the example of the United States in banning *all* trade with continental China, had undertaken to embargo the shipment of several hundred items over and above those they were already denying to the European Communist bloc.[71]

In February 1953 this country tightened its own embargo on shipments to Communist China and barred any vessels carrying United States aid goods to Formosa (later, to any destination) from calling at Communist ports for sixty days after discharging their cargoes. In June, the administration virtually barred the refuelling or provisioning of foreign ships or aircraft scheduled to visit mainland China. Simultaneously, efforts were made to strengthen the United Nations embargo on strategic goods to the Chinese mainland. Not only did the major participants in the embargo agree to include additional items in the "strategic" category, but Great Britain and France agreed (a) to screen cargoes carried by their merchant vessels in order to ensure that such ships were not carrying materials on the strategic list, and (b) to deny their bunkering facilities to ships of any nationality which were carrying such cargoes to China.[72]

A sharp distinction was made in these negotiations between "strategic" goods, as defined by the United Nations resolution of 1951, and the "nonstrategic" goods which Great Britain and other countries continued to send to Communist China with the consent, if not the approval, of the authorities in Washington. Trade of this latter type, the administration felt, was of considerable economic importance to friendly nations, helped to relieve their economic dependence on the United States, and, furthermore, made no identifiable contribution to Chinese military potential. To a limited extent, such nonstrategic trade had actually increased even while strategic trade was being cut down. According

[71] *Ibid.*, 20-21 and 33-34.

[72] *Ibid.*, 38-41; see also the Washington communiqués of March 7 and March 28, cited above, and the statements of Mutual Security Director Stassen, March 3 and 30, printed respectively in *Department of State Bulletin*, XXVIII, March 23, 1953, 435 and *Documents on American Foreign Relations, 1953*, 93-99.

to one later estimate, total exports from the free world to Communist China, after decreasing from $446 million in 1951 to $268 million in 1952, increased again to $275 million in 1953.[73] The increase in nonstrategic trade could be attributed primarily to a change in the attitude of the Communists themselves, who had "dropped their reluctance to deal with the West and were placing more and bigger orders for the kind of goods that the free governments would have been willing to ship all along." [74]

The distinction between strategic and nonstrategic goods, though of great importance to the countries concerned, was sometimes a little difficult to grasp for those Americans whose primary concern was with the fortunes of the Korean battlefront. It was also largely ignored by Senator McCarthy and his Investigations Subcommittee, which selected this issue for one of its most vigorous demonstrations against Communism and, by implication at least, against this country's allies and the foreign policy of the United States. In contrast to the attitude of the administration, the McCarthy committee appeared to take the position that not merely strategic trade but *all* allied trade with Communist China was harmful. Through the labeling of such commerce with opprobrious terms like "blood trade" and "blood traffic," the inference was suggested that these allied shipments were directly responsible for the American (and allied) casualty lists in Korea.

On March 9, only two days after Foreign Secretary Eden and Mr. Butler had finished making their new commitments in Washington, the McCarthy committee disclosed that it planned to investigate why ninety-six merchant vessels which were owned by Greek, Italian, and French concerns, but on which the United States still held $25 million in mortgages, continued to carry materials destined for Communist China and other Communist countries. Before the issues raised by this accusatory announcement had been clarified, the Senator announced on March 27 that in view of the "dismal failure"

[73] *East-West Trade: Hearing,* House Foreign Affairs Committee, Subcommittee on Foreign Economic Policy, 83d Congress, 2d Session, February 16, 1954 (Washington, G.P.O., 1954), 17.

[74] *World-Wide Enforcement of Strategic Trade Controls,* cited, 38.

of the executive branch to put a stop to such activities his own organization had been forced to take action independently. Representatives of his subcommittee, he said, had themselves negotiated a secret pact with the Greek owners of 242 merchant ships who had pledged themselves to break off all trade with North Korea, Communist China, and the Soviet Far East.

On the surface, at least, this was a substantial achievement. Greek-owned vessels, many of which operated under other flags, accounted for a substantial part of China's waterborne trade and had been notoriously difficult to control. True, it was later asserted that few ships involved in the McCarthy arrangement had actually engaged in the Communist trade in recent years. But this, in any case, was the least of the issues raised by the McCarthy action. In Washington it was widely felt that Mr. McCarthy's method of dealing with the problem not only went beyond the recognized responsibilities of a member of Congress but threatened to interfere with the efforts of the executive branch itself. Mutual Security Director Stassen, the first prominent administration representative to take a public stand against the Senator's activities, told him plainly on March 30 that he was "in effect undermining" the work of the Mutual Security Agency in this field and that his activities were "harmful to our objective" of curbing shipments to Communist ports.[75] This use of words Mr. Stassen presently retracted at the instance of the President, and the incident was temporarily smoothed over in a series of intimate conferences. Secretary Dulles, whose responsibilities included general policy guidance of Mutual Security Agency operations, lunched with the Senator on April 1 and won his assent to the proposition that the conduct of foreign relations was, after all, the province of the State Department and that the McCarthy subcommittee should furnish it with all relevant data in its possession.[76]

By no means the least disturbing aspect of this affair was the additional strain it imposed on our relations with Great Britain, France, India, and other countries through the broad and derogatory terms in which the Senator character-

[75] *New York Times,* March 31, 1953.

[76] *Department of State Bulletin,* XXVIII, April 13, 1953, 533.

ized their role in what he called the Far Eastern "blood traffic." Accusations of perfidy and greed were particularly resented in Great Britain, where American hostility toward Communist China was considered somewhat indiscriminate in any case and where it was felt that American sources were sometimes too quick to criticize the lawful actions of an ally who was making a substantial contribution in Korea. British spokesmen strenuously defended their country's compliance with all agreements pertaining to the strategic embargo against Communist China. They did not, however, deny that the general attitude of their government in matters involving the Peking regime differed considerably from that of the United States.

Far Eastern Difficulties

These broader differences, in fact, were becoming steadily more prominent as the result of the death of Stalin, the renewed prospects of an armistice in Korea, and the simultaneous revival in the West of proposals for an attempt to reduce international tension through a high-level meeting with the new leaders of the U.S.S.R. As usual, the appearance of a more conciliatory demeanor on the part of the Soviet Government, noticeable in the weeks after Stalin's death, found opinion in Western Europe much more eager to plunge into renewed negotiations with the Kremlin than Washington appeared to be—although Chancellor Adenauer, when he visited Washington on April 7-9, agreed that any attempt at holding an East-West conference would be premature to say the least.[77] American views on the conditions which must be met before any such meeting could be held with expectation of success were set forth in an important address by the President (April 16) which must be considered more fully in connection with the general problem of East-West relations after the death of Stalin.[78]

But meanwhile affairs had moved rapidly in the Far East. In Korea, an agreement had been reached on an exchange of sick and wounded prisoners of war, and formal armistice

[77] Communiqué, April 9, in *Documents on American Foreign Relations, 1953*, 278-279.
[78] Cf. below, pp. 128-130.

negotiations were on the point of resuming. The United Nations General Assembly, which had remained in session primarily to deal with the Korean issue, adopted a resolution on April 18 in which it expressed the hope of an early armistice and decided to recess its session as soon as its current agenda was completed.[79] This optimism, however, was not widely shared in American quarters, where a good many flaws were still detected in the Communists' behavior. The exchange of sick and wounded prisoners was duly carried out during the second half of April; but there was evidence that the Communists had failed to return a considerable number of prisoners who were sick or wounded but able to travel. The stories brought back by returning Americans, moreover, abundantly confirmed the reports that American captives had been gravely mistreated and in some cases massacred by their Communist captors. Such disclosures could hardly predispose the public to take a more indulgent view of Far Eastern Communism.

Moreover, such improvement as might have occurred in the prospects in Korea was balanced by a deteriorating situation in Indochina. There, an act of "straight aggression" had occurred on April 12 when Vietminh rebels from within the state of Vietnam invaded the sister Kingdom of Laos with the avowed object of creating a revolution in Laos and Cambodia and bringing about the union of those states with a Communist Vietnam. In the ensuing crisis, the United States rushed military supplies to neighboring Thailand, loaned six military transport planes with civilian pilots to the French defenders, and consulted its allies about possible United Nations action.[80] No action was called for, as the invading forces presently withdrew; but it was apparent that this "new act of aggression" might have had "serious consequences for Thailand and the whole of Southeast Asia" and was bound to "cast doubt on Communist intentions." [81]

[79] Resolution 705 (VII), in *Documents on American Foreign Relations, 1953,* 431-432. For the detailed story of the Korean armistice negotiations cf. below, pp. 217-232.

[80] *Department of State Bulletin,* XXVIII, May 4, 1953, 641; May 11, 1953, 678; May 18, 1953, 708, 709.

[81] U.S.-Canadian communiqué, May 8, in *Documents on American Foreign Relations, 1953,* 402-404. The two-day Washington visit of Canadian Prime Minister Louis St. Laurent and Secretary for External Affairs Lester B. Pearson also brought reaffirmation of the need for vigorous and coordinated defense

The discontent of some Americans with the course of events in the Far East and, indeed, with the whole concept of a Far Eastern policy conducted under the limitations imposed by the attitudes of other countries, found increasingly vigorous expression during these weeks when the world was waiting to find out whether the Communists really did contemplate a Korean armistice and a new departure in East-West relations. Late in April, General MacArthur, now speaking in a private capacity, restated his well-known thesis that the proper way to end the Korean war was to threaten direct and vigorous military action against Communist China:

". . . We still possess the potential to destroy Red China's flimsy industrial base and sever her tenuous supply lines from the Soviet. . . . A warning of action of this sort provides the leverage to induce the Soviet to bring the Korean struggle to an end without further bloodshed. It would dread risking the eventuality of a Red China debacle, and such a hazard might well settle the Korea war and all other pending global issues on equitable terms just as soon as it realizes we have the will and the means to bring them to a prompt and definite determination." [82]

This prescription for direct action by the United States had, of course, been fully considered during the famous "MacArthur hearings" of 1951, when the nation's accredited military and political leaders had unanimously rejected it on the grounds that (a) it would cost this country the support of its allies, (b) it might precipitate full-scale war with the Soviet Union, and (c) it was unlikely to be militarily decisive against China.[83] Nevertheless the General's views continued to commend themselves to a large section of American opinion, primarily among those who had become disillusioned over the

---

preparations, an exchange of views concerning progress toward expanded world trade, and a disclosure that the administration had decided, despite previous inaction by the Congress, to recommend U.S. participation in the building of the St. Lawrence-Great Lakes Seaway. For the background of this recommendation, which was favorably acted upon by Congress in 1954, cf. *Documents on American Foreign Relations, 1953,* 406-407 and *Department of State Bulletin,* XXVIII, June 8, 1953, 824-826.

82 Letter of April 19, as published in *New York Times,* April 25, 1953.

83 Cf. *The United States in World Affairs, 1951,* 108-111.

achievements of the United Nations and favored stronger American measures, "alone, if necessary," in the Far East. Persons of this turn of mind were especially irritated by suggestions now being made in British and other foreign quarters that it might be wise to make some concessions to the Chinese Communists in order to stimulate their desire for a Korean armistice—and that once this aim had been achieved there would be no further obstacle to admitting the Peking government to representation in the United Nations.

McCarthy vs. Attlee

The strength of the emotions involved, both in the United States and abroad, could be gauged by an exchange of transatlantic discourtesies which now took place in connection with a debate on foreign affairs in the British House of Commons. On May 11 Prime Minister Churchill delivered an important speech in which he not only proposed a conference of great powers "on the highest level" to explore the possibilities of a relaxation of tension but also uttered a warning against an attitude of intransigence—presumably by the United States—on Far Eastern matters.[84] Next day the leader of the Laborite Opposition, former Prime Minister Clement R. Attlee, brought forward a lengthy critique of American attitudes on foreign affairs, observing among other things that under the American system of government the administration was "not really master in their own house" and that one sometimes wondered "who is more powerful, the President or Senator McCarthy." Mr. Attlee personally believed that both "the Chinese" and "the United States Administration" wanted a settlement in the Far East. But, he said, "There are elements in the United States that do not want a settlement. . . . There are people who want an all-out war with China and against Communism in general, and there is the strong influence of the Chiang Kai-shek lobby." Any high-level conference, Mr. Attlee went on, would need to be most carefully prepared: "It would be possible for President Eisenhower to attend a conference and, on his return to the United States, to be thrown over, as President Wilson was after the discussions at Versailles. It is, therefore, essential

[84] Cf. below, pp. 132-134.

that whoever goes to this conference should go with full authority." [85]

The wisdom and propriety of such observations by a responsible opposition leader at a moment when Anglo-American relations were not of the best might be questioned; but it is unlikely that anyone present in the House of Commons on that day foresaw the violence of the reaction in the United States Senate. Two days later Senator McCarthy brought to the Senate floor an inaccurate newspaper account of the Attlee speech [86] on the basis of which he proceeded to attack both the speaker and all those who had unprotestingly listened to him. "Comrade Attlee [*sic*]," he said, had "deliberately insulted the United States and insulted the American people." Did he not know that "the American people repudiated his pals—the Achesons, the Lattimores, and the Vincents—by the most resounding vote by which they have ever repudiated any clique"? Another Senator (Mr. Knowland) had said, in Senator McCarthy's paraphrase, "that Britain is trying to blackmail us into accepting the Communist plan [in Korea] on the ground that if we do not accept it Britain will withdraw from the Korean war." "Mr. President," Senator McCarthy went on, "I say to them that if that be true, if they are trying to blackmail us into accepting a Communist peace on the ground that if we do not they will withdraw, I say, 'Withdraw and be damned.' And then, Mr. President, let us sink every accursed ship carrying materials to the enemy and resulting in the death of American boys, regardless of what flag those ships may fly." [87]

Though this outburst met with few signs of disapprobation in the Senate, the resulting furor on both sides of the Atlantic represented a temporary high water mark in Senator McCarthy's influence on international affairs. While his committee continued to develop data purporting to illustrate the

[85] *Parliamentary Debates, Weekly Hansard,* House of Commons, May 12, 1953, 1068-1069, 1074.

[86] Senator McCarthy quoted the *Washington Times-Herald* as saying: "Attlee said he welcomed Churchill's proposal Monday for an immediate meeting of heads of state, but he doubted the wisdom of President Eisenhower's attendance. He hinted the presence of any American would only hinder talks." (*Congressional Record, Daily Edition,* May 14, 1953, 4909.)

[87] *Ibid.,* 4909-4912.

nefarious role of the British in trade with China, the feeling was growing in Washington that this kind of approach to foreign relations was fundamentally incompatible with the policies of collective international action which the administration had undertaken to carry forward. Disagreement with Senator McCarthy did not, however, imply readiness to make concessions on Far Eastern policy. The more talk there was abroad about Peking's claim to representation in the United Nations, the more strongly congressional opposition stiffened against it—the more so because there were recurrent reports that the administration was itself exploring possible ways of breaking the diplomatic impasse on China policy.[88] Various proposals were offered for a reaffirmation of congressional sentiment in the matter, some of them more drastic than anything seriously considered in the past. Senator Knowland introduced a pair of resolutions[89] calling for this country's withdrawal from the United Nations if Communist China was admitted. The Senate Appropriations Committee determined on May 27 to recommend that the United States discontinue making financial contributions to the United Nations if Communist China or its representatives gained a seat on the Security Council.[90]

Taft vs. Eisenhower

But it was Senator Taft who gave the most comprehensive expression to such feelings, in a statement significant both as the last major utterance of the Ohio Senator and as the stimulus to one of President Eisenhower's most distinct repudiations of the "go-it-alone" philosophy. Already stricken with the fatal illness to which he succumbed a few weeks later, Mr. Taft was unable to deliver in person the speech of May 26[91] in which he virtually wrote off the United Nations as an instrument for dealing with aggression and went on to cast grave doubt on the practicability of this country's attempt at maintaining a "world-wide alliance" against Soviet Russia:

[88] E.g., *New York Times,* April 9, 1953.

[89] S. Res. 112 and S. Con. Res. 29, 83d Congress, introduced May 19, 1953.

[90] S. Rept. 309 on H.R. 4974 (Departments of State, Justice, and Commerce Appropriation Bill, 1954), May 28, 1953, 7.

[91] *Documents on American Foreign Relations, 1953,* 110-114.

"I believe we might as well forget the United Nations as far as the Korean war is concerned. I think we should do our best now to negotiate this truce, and if we fail, then let England and our Allies know that we are withdrawing from all further peace negotiations in Korea. Even the best truce under present conditions will be extremely unsatisfactory. It will divide Korea along an unnatural line and create an unstable condition likely to bring war again at any moment. . . . I believe we might as well abandon any idea of working with the United Nations in the East and reserve to ourselves a completely free hand. . . ."

No one should be shocked by this view, Senator Taft continued, because in Europe we had already "practically abandoned [the United Nations] entirely" in concluding the North Atlantic Treaty, an instrument which he regarded as "the complete antithesis" of the United Nations Charter. And even NATO filled him with doubts, both as to its military practicability and as to the attitudes of this country's allies:

"We have to have not only the written word, but the real sympathetic support of our allies in that job. Recent events in France and England indicate that they are more than anxious to settle with Russia, and resume as much trade as possible, which means that as long as Russia talks nicely, the whole military alliance against Russia is weak, even though military preparations behind the lines continue unabated. . . . The present Administration has the job of trying to maintain this worldwide alliance against Soviet Russia. . . . I have no doubt about the desirability of the policy if it does not go beyond our economic strength, but I do doubt its possibility."

Undoubtedly Senator Taft here pointed to basic weaknesses in the international position of the United States. Disappointed in the record of the United Nations as a peacekeeping agency, he may have underestimated its value as a means of mobilizing world support for those American objectives that were held in common with other free world nations. Probably he overstated the readiness of this country's allies to succumb to Soviet blandishments. He certainly gave insufficient emphasis to the part played by some of this country's own actions in undermining confidence in our intentions and purposes. But it was undeniable that to maintain this type of "world-wide alliance against Soviet Russia" under the conditions prevailing in 1953 was an effort that strained this country's diplomatic resources to the utmost. And it was significant, to say the least, that an American of Senator Taft's stature and experience should respond to the situation by advocating virtual abandonment of the United Nations if not of the Atlantic alliance. Of what significance were President Eisenhower's repeated endorsements of those institutions if such views could be advanced by one of the most respected figures in his own party? Could foreign policy be conducted on the basis of such conflicting opinions, people asked, or had the time arrived for a "showdown" between the divergent tendencies symbolized by the President and the most influential Republican member of the Senate?

Characteristically, the President refrained from precipitating a showdown; yet he spoke with unusual vigor and earnestness when asked to comment on the Taft thesis at his press conference on May 28. He assured his listeners that he shared "the irritations and the sense of frustration that comes to everybody who is working for what he believes to be a decent purpose and finds himself balked by what he thinks is the ignorance, or the errors, of someone who is otherwise his friend." But, he insisted, our whole policy was based on the theory that "No single free nation can live alone in the world. We have to have friends. Those friends have got to be tied to you, in some form or another." And this meant, in effect, that the Taft approach was unworkable:

"... You can't have cooperative action in these great developments and processes in just the spots of the globe, or in just the particular problems that you would like to select. If you are going to go it alone one place, you of course have to go it alone everywhere. If you are going to try to develop a coalition of understanding based upon decency, on ideas of justice, common concepts of governments, established by the will of free men, then you have got to make compromises. You have got to find the way in between the conflicting partisan considerations that will serve the best good of all. . . . We have to have that unity in basic purposes that comes from a recognition of common interests. That is what we are up against."

The President closed this remarkable statement by voicing the conviction that "only patience, only determination, only optimism and a very deep faith can carry America forward. ... I earnestly believe we cannot desert the great purpose for which we are seeking—for which we are working." [92]

In such terms the President rejected the "go-it-alone" doctrine as a principle of diplomacy.[93] Four days later he gave a practical illustration of his attitude by persuading Republican leaders to drop the attempt at putting pressure on the United Nations to exclude Communist China—at the same time assuring them, however, that the administration "not only was opposed to the admission of Red China" but would "take an active part in the leadership in opposing admission." [94] As in the days of President Truman and Secretary Acheson, the United States was determined to keep an aggressive Communist China out of the United Nations.[95] But it was determined to do this by the exercise of a positive diplomacy and not by methods which, if anyone had attempted them against this country, would rightly have been denounced as "blackmail."

Psychological Strategy and Foreign Policy

In taking this position the President might easily have been influenced by the thinking of a special presidential Committee on International Information Activities, headed by William H. Jackson, which was just completing a broad reappraisal of the government's informational and "psychological warfare" policies.[96] The Jackson committee recommended a number of organizational changes which were carried out in the course of the summer, notably the replacement of the

[92] Verbatim text as published in *New York Times,* May 29, 1953. For a more finished statement of the President's views see his address of June 10 in *Department of State Bulletin,* XXVIII, June 22, 1953, 863-865.

[93] In a clarifying statement issued on June 5, Senator Taft pointed out that he had nowhere used the words "go it alone," and added that "the United Nations serves a very useful purpose as a town meeting of the world where disputes can be brought out in the open and peaceful means urged to prevent war, but it is an impossible weapon against forcible aggression."

[94] Statement by Senator Knowland, in *New York Times,* June 3, 1953.

[95] Cf. *The United States in World Affairs, 1951,* 118-119.

[96] A summary of its report, dated June 30, appears in *Documents on American Foreign Relations, 1953,* 80-84; see also the implementing measures set forth in *Department of State Bulletin,* XXIX, September 28, 1953, 420-421.

existing Psychological Strategy Board by a high-level Operations Coordinating Board under the National Security Council which would "coordinate the development by departments and agencies of detailed operational plans to carry out national security policies." A more noteworthy contribution was a redefinition of the whole problem of informational and "psychological" policy, in its relationship to national policy and behavior generally.

"Cold war" and "psychological warfare," the Jackson Committee suggested, were terms that did not adequately reflect the real aims of the United States and its allies. For the basic aim of all these countries was to build a world of peace and freedom. United States informational policies should be shaped accordingly:

> "The primary and over-riding purpose of the information program should be to submit evidence to the peoples of other nations that their own aspirations for freedom, progress and peace are supported and advanced by the objectives and policies of the United States. The efforts of all media . . . should be directed to this end: to show the identity of our goals with those of other peoples. These goals and desires which we hold in common must be explained in ways that will cause others to join with us in achieving them."

Equally noteworthy was the rejection of the standard opinion "that 'psychological activities' and 'psychological strategy' somehow exist apart from official policies and actions and can be dealt with independently by experts in this field." The reality, the committee pointed out, was quite different:

> ". . . There is a 'psychological' aspect or implication to every diplomatic, economic, or military policy and action. . . . Every significant act of virtually every department and agency of Government has its effect, either positively or negatively, in the global struggle for freedom. The important task is to build awareness throughout the entire Government of the impact of day-to-day governmental actions and to coordinate and time such actions so as to derive from them the maximum advantages."

In other words, "psychological" operations in the narrow, technical sense were likely to prove rewarding only if (a) they were consistent with, and supported by, the general trend of American policy, and (b) they could show that American objectives and policies were in harmony with the aspirations of other peoples for freedom, progress, and peace. This was practically the same thing as saying that only those American policies which were consonant with the aspirations of other peoples would be psychologically effective—undoubtedly a profound truth which, if adequately understood, would go far to explain both the successes and the failures of American foreign policy in the postwar years.

How far the subsequent development of American policy would be influenced by this insight still remained somewhat uncertain as the administration completed its first half year in office. The new United States Information Agency under Theodore C. Streibert, which had been designated to take over the battered remains of the International Information Administration,[97] adopted the Jackson report as its basic text and laid plans to "emphasize the community of interest that exists among freedom-loving peoples and show how American objectives and policies advance the legitimate interests of such peoples." Partly for budgetary reasons, however—the funds available for the next year were reduced to $75 million as compared with $105 million in 1952–53, thus necessitating a reduction of personnel from 8,200 to 6,200 and the abolition of 500 unfilled positions—the agency was forced to limit its services to free world countries and to concentrate most of its effort on programs directed to the lands behind the Iron Curtain. Broadcasts in French, Portuguese, Spanish (to Latin America), Hebrew, Malayan, and Thai had been discontinued, and English-language broadcasts reduced, as early as April while the program was still under the State Department. The U.S.I.A. later eliminated Finnish and six more Eastern languages, limiting the total number of broadcast languages to thirty-four. "The 'Voice'," Mr. Streibert said in August, "will hammer away at the uncertainties, the doubts,

[97] Under Reorganization Plan No. 8 of 1953, which became effective August 1, the U.S.I.A. was established as an independent agency responsible for the Voice of America and all other phases of the information program except for educational exchange, which remained in the State Department. For the relevant texts cf. *ibid.*, XXVIII, June 15, 1953, 849-856; XXIX, July 6, 1953, 27-30 and August 24, 1953, 238-242.

and suspicions behind the Iron and Bamboo Curtains." In October he added that every effort would also be made "to show the mutuality of our interests and goals with legitimate goals of other peoples." [98]

The question still left unanswered by these arrangements was a more basic one. What the world needed most to know in 1953 was not simply whether the United States would be able to secure international acceptance of its policies by more skillful psychological management. What the world needed to know was how far the United States intended to pursue a foreign policy which was *in itself* attuned to the views and sympathies of other nations, and how far, on the other hand, it planned to seek its own objectives on its own terms, independently of the climate of world opinion. The early utterances of the administration had suggested a genuine concern for developing policies which responded to the aspirations of other nations as well as our own. On the other hand, the administration itself could not overlook the existence of competing pressures, including an influential body of opinion which seemed wholly preoccupied with one or two specialized aspects of the Communist problem, was disinclined to respect any point of view except its own, and evidently hoped to remold American policy in its own image. Until this situation was clarified it would be risky to speculate as to the quality of America's future participation in world affairs.

In the meantime, some of the other limitations on American action had become clearer as the administration began to define its objectives in the fields of national defense and economy.

5. THE ECONOMICS OF WORLD POLICY

The first months of the Eisenhower administration produced numerous declarations about preserving the strength and solidarity of the free world by the combined efforts of the United States and its non-Communist friends and allies. Such expressions, however, were invariably qualified in one sig-

[98] I.I.A. announcement, April 22, *ibid.*, XXVIII, May 11, 1953, 699; U.S.I.A. announcement, August 27, *ibid.*, XXIX, September 7, 1953, 321-322; letter of Mr. Streitbert to the President, October 27, *ibid.*, November 30, 1953, 756-757.

nificant respect. Nothing was to be done in the sphere of world policy that threatened to undermine the national economy of the United States itself, the ultimate safeguard of freedom both at home and abroad. The Truman administration, most Republicans felt, had been less than careful of the foundations of American strength. Not only had it been addicted to undesirable economic practices at home, but it had allowed its economic policies to be unduly influenced by foreign policy considerations, thus doubly neglecting its responsibility for husbanding the national wealth and maintaining a vigorous free enterprise system. Under the Eisenhower administration, the emphasis was to be reversed. The welfare of the national economy would be its primary concern; for only an economically healthy nation would be capable of discharging the responsibilities of America's world position. At the moment the nation was, to be sure, spectacularly prosperous; but the new administration was pledged to introduce a new type of prosperity which could not possibly be identified with the continuance of bloodshed in Korea or the perpetuation of what was sometimes hyperbolically referred to as a "garrison state." If there were any external objectives that conflicted with this central aim, they would have to be reexamined.

As a matter of abstract logic, there might seem to be some conflict between the two goals of a flourishing national economy and a strong role in world affairs. If too much emphasis on external obligations might overstrain the domestic economy, an excessive tenderness for the economy might also result in an inadequate discharge of world responsibilities. The two administrations chose different ways of resolving this dilemma. Many Democrats, pointing to the constant rise in national productivity, asserted that the national economy was actually quite capable of meeting the demands placed upon it and did not, in reality, impose significant limitations on the nation's external policy. Republicans, concerned by high taxes, unbalanced budgets, and a huge national debt, were doubtful of this analysis. Retrenchment, many of them felt, had become essential. Continuance of tremendous outlays for defense, foreign aid, international information, and the like would not stop the Communists but might actually play into their hands. Had not Lenin and Stalin asserted that the way to overcome an "imperialist" nation was to force it into bankruptcy? The beginning of a strong world policy was to be strong at home.

It was not surprising that such views should be especially prevalent in a Republican administration which was to a large extent composed of businessmen and imbued with a "business" philosophy. It was all the more understandable in view of the pre-election assurances of such authorities as General Eisenhower and Mr. Dulles that governmental economy was perfectly consistent with both a sound defense and a "dynamic" foreign policy. Nor was any serious reason discovered for modifying this approach after the new administration took office. Tax reduction and progress toward a balanced budget represented political commitments of the first order; and new developments were constantly occurring which seemed to bear out the expectation that substantial economies could be achieved without impairing the nation's world position.

For one thing, the United States was making spectacular progress in the military application of atomic energy, which many regarded as the key to a simpler and cheaper national defense. The practicability of the hydrogen or "super" bomb had been positively demonstrated in the autumn of 1952; through the spring of 1953 a series of test explosions in the southwestern United States gave evidence that the development of atomic weapons for both strategic and tactical uses was not being neglected. Then there was the apparent relaxation of international tension that set in with the death of Stalin and the resumption of armistice negotiations in Korea. Although the administration steadily maintained that these events had brought no evidence of genuine change in Soviet intentions, the majority in Congress could hardly be blamed for taking them into account when called upon to vote the still formidable appropriations for the next fiscal year. All in all, budgetary retrenchment seemed so desirable an objective that only secondary consideration was given to the way in which our economies might affect the world position of our own or other nations whose strength was considered important to American security.

The financial policies of the former administration, which

had aroused such strong Republican objection, had been the fiscal expression of a general foreign policy of global resistance to Soviet-Communist aggression through collective arrangements entered into with other nations and international groupings. Retrenchment, conversely, would involve some measure of "disengagement" from this network of overseas commitments, both military and economic. On the military side, it would presumably mean lessened emphasis on direct participation by United States forces in local defensive efforts around the periphery of the Communist world, and increased reliance on the concept of a central reserve or "striking force" which might serve to deter aggression or at least to back up the defensive efforts of allied countries. Some such idea had been crystallized by Mr. Dulles as far back as December 29, 1950, in a speech which had stressed the impracticability of building "static defensive forces" to protect each nation threatened by Soviet aggression and had referred to "the capacity to counter-attack . . . by action of our own choosing" as "the ultimate deterrent" and the only "effective defense, for us and for others." [99] Phrases like "the arsenal of retaliation" which Mr. Dulles had used at that time were destined to figure largely in the strategic thinking of the administration in which he had become Secretary of State.

On the economic side, budgetary retrenchment would necessarily imply a redistribution of burdens as between the United States and the countries receiving American aid, with greater reliance on those countries' determination to build up their own strength and a commensurate reduction in the United States foreign aid or "Mutual Security" program. In the related field of trade policy, a similar shift of emphasis might be expected. Where the Truman administration had laid primary stress on the need to increase United States imports in order to alleviate world balance-of-payments problems, the Eisenhower administration would postpone definite action. But its refusal of an unqualified reaffirmation of existing policies in this field would in itself prolong the uncertainty about the ultimate direction of United States trade policy and would cast some doubt on the readiness of the

[99] *Department of State Bulletin,* XXIV, January 15, 1951, 85-89.

United States to participate actively in the building of a healthier world economy.

Trimming the Budget

For many Republicans, and for not a few Democrats, a degree of disengagement from the concerns of the free world was fully justified if it enabled the United States to balance the budget and revert to an orthodox policy of living within its means. But they were soon compelled to realize that the process would not be easy or rapid. Even budget-cutting proved far more difficult in practice than it had seemed in anticipation. President Truman's budget proposals for the fiscal year 1953–54, envisaging total expenditures of $78.6 billion and an over-all deficit of $9.9 billion, had not been taken very seriously even as a point of departure; yet it required only a little analysis to see that not many items could be cut substantially without really serious impairment of the national position. Of the total estimated expenditure, not less than $57.3 billion, or 73 percent, was allocated to what were described as "major national security programs"—military services, international security and foreign relations, atomic energy development, and related activities. Much of the remainder represented fixed charges for interest and veteran's programs. Ordinary activities of government accounted for only $10.3 billion or 13 percent of the total.[100]

Any really substantial reductions, therefore, would have to be achieved in the area of "major national security programs" and, more specifically, in the $46.3 billion that had been tentatively allocated to expenditure on the Air Force, Army, Navy, and defense-supporting activities during the twelve months from July 1, 1953 to June 30, 1954. From a financial point of view, President Truman had explained, the post-Korean defense program was just reaching its peak; by the end of the fiscal year, expenditures should begin to decline. Once the armed forces had been stabilized at their approved goals, military expenditure might be expected to level off (if there were no new aggressions) at the amounts needed to maintain them with the best available equipment—perhaps

[100] Budget message for the fiscal year ending June 30, 1954, in *New York Times*, January 10, 1953.

at around $35 to $40 billion a year. Of the defense expenditure proposed for the next fiscal year, not much could be eliminated if only because most of the funds had already been committed for items of military equipment ordered two or three years previously and only now scheduled for delivery. As regards new appropriations or "obligational authority," however, Mr. Truman's request for a fresh $41.2 billion for 1953–54 already represented a sharp decline from the corresponding figures for 1951–52 ($61.7 billion) and 1952–53 ($52.4 billion).

The Eisenhower administration made no attempt to prepare a complete new budget to replace President Truman's blueprint, but went vigorously to work investigating the possibilities of trimming his estimates in detail. There was obviously no possibility of avoiding the anticipated heavy deficit for the fiscal year 1953 (June 30 was to find the government almost $9.4 billion in the red); but it was hoped that with good management the $9.9 billion deficit predicted by Mr. Truman for fiscal 1954 could at least be substantially reduced even if it could not be wiped out altogether. On April 30 President Eisenhower reported that as a result of "three months' hard work" in reconciling military and economic logic, he would be able to ask Congress "to appropriate at least $8.5 billion dollars less new money for fiscal year 1954 than had been asked for by the previous Administration." "The great bulk of it," he added, "of course, relates to security programs." But he assured the nation that this would "not reduce the effective military strength we will deliver to ourselves and our allies during fiscal 1954." [101]

National Defense

The basic problem in regard to the defense program, the President explained, had been to bring economic and military necessities "into some kind of realistic focus"; to devise a long-term program which took account of the fact "that a very real danger not only exists this year, but may continue to exist for years to come; that our strength, which is already very real, must now be made stronger, not by inefficient and

101 *Ibid.*, May 1, 1953.

expensive starts and stops, but by steady continuous improvement." The essence of the change, he continued, was this:

"We reject the idea that we must build up to a maximum attainable strength for some specific date theoretically fixed for a specified time in the future. Defense is not a matter of maximum strength for a single date. It is a matter of adequate protection to be projected as far into the future as the actions and apparent purposes of others may compel us. It is a policy that can if necessary be lived with over a period of years." [102]

With this analysis the President apparently buried the philosophy which had underlain the emergency expansion of United States and NATO armed forces in the period since the Korean aggression while he himself had been Supreme Allied Commander, Europe. In that capacity he, of course, had often drawn attention to the undiminished military threat from the East and insisted on the necessity of a maximum effort to build up the defenses of the Western allies. But experience in NATO had shown how difficult it was to carry out overambitious plans for military expansion such as those which had been developed at the NATO conference in Lisbon in February 1952, only to be shelved within a few months.[103] Apparently the President had been led to the conclusion that in the United States, as well as in Europe, it was a mistake to push defense preparations too rapidly: it was better to build slowly and steadily, even though it meant slackening the rate of expansion and perhaps having less strength available on some arbitrarily selected date which might not be the date of Soviet aggression at all.

If this calculation was influenced in any way by developments in the Soviet Union and the vague prospect of a relaxation in global tensions, the President did not say so. Conceivably the death of Stalin may actually have reduced the likelihood of an early armed clash with the U.S.S.R. and thus provided an additional, *a posteriori* justification of the change of policy. In the minds of the President and his supporters, however, the change seemed fully justified by other factors: the comparatively high level of rearmament already achieved,

[102] *Ibid.*

[103] Cf. *The United States in World Affairs, 1952,* 126-127 and 401-405.

steady progress in the field of atomic weapons, and, above all, the overriding commitment to reduce expenditures.[104]

Despite the emphasis on economy, the most remarkable feature of the revised defense plans submitted by Defense Secretary Charles E. Wilson in May was neither the reduction in total appropriation requests from $41.2 billion to $36.04 billion (later reduced again to $35.8 billion), nor the reduction in planned expenditure of the Defense Department from $45.5 billion to $43.2 billion. It was, rather, the change in the proposed allocation of funds within the defense establishment itself and the corresponding change in the relative strength envisaged for the three fighting services.

President Truman's budget had been drawn for an establishment of slightly over 3,600,000 uniformed men and women organized into twenty-one Army divisions, three Marine divisions, a Navy with 408 combatant ships plus air support, and an Air Force which had attained a paper strength of 103 wings and was building toward an ultimate strength of 143 wings, supposedly to be attained by the middle of 1955. Under the Eisenhower-Wilson budget, the Army, Navy, and Marine Corps were to be maintained at roughly their existing strength; but the projected rate of growth of the Air Force was to be sharply curtailed and the available funds redistributed accordingly. The new Air Force targets announced by Secretary Wilson—pending an intensive and detailed "new look at the entire defense picture" which he said would take place during the summer and autumn—involved nothing less than the abandonment of the proposed 143-wing Air Force in favor of an "interim" goal of 120 wings, with 114 wings to be "activated and substantially well equipped" by the middle of 1954.[105]

For an administration that prided itself on its sensitivity to congressional sentiment, the determination to trim the budget

[104] Additional justification for reducing defense expenditure could, of course, be found in the conclusion of the Korean armistice on July 27. This, however, was a development that could not be counted upon until the last moment. Furthermore, President Eisenhower indicated in his radio report of May 19 (*New York Times*, May 20, 1953) that the Truman budget had also appeared to assume a cessation of hostilities in Korea or, at any rate, had made "no specific budgetary provision for continuance of this conflict."

[105] Statement to the House Appropriations subcommittee, May 11, in *Documents on American Foreign Relations, 1953*, 52-62.

at the expense of the Air Force was presented in a manner that seemed to take little account of legislative partiality for that service. Many congressmen, not all of them Democrats, professed themselves unable to understand the arguments by which administration spokesmen endeavored to show that a reduction in Air Force appropriations would actually produce more air power rather than less. How did it happen that the process of military retrenchment was being begun by cutting back the very force that was so often depicted as the most dependable and economical safeguard of American and world security? Was this the work of General Omar N. Bradley and the old, Truman-appointed Joint Chiefs of Staff, who were just now being replaced (to the audible relief of Senator Taft and other Republicans) by a new group named by the new President? [106] General Hoyt S. Vandenberg, the retiring Chief of Staff of the Air Force, made it clear that he at least was by no means favorable to the proposed reduction. Was it possible, then, that General Eisenhower, who insisted that all major particulars of the revised defense budget had his personal endorsement, was still looking at defense problems through the eyes of a ground commander? Had he concluded that it was unwise to put too many of our defense eggs in the air-atomic basket? If so, why did he limit himself to cutting down the Air Force while offering no proposals on broad manpower policy, such as had been envisaged by the Universal Training Act of 1951? Or was it the fact, as the administration claimed, that the Air Force expansion program initiated under President Truman had so far outrun immediate possibilities that its overestimates and potential extravagances could be curbed without sacrificing real effectiveness? The new authorities in the Pentagon had laid great stress on their determination to trim "fat" while sparing "muscle" throughout the military establishment. Conceivably an Air Force expansion program that already had a backlog of $28.5 billion in unspent funds contained its proportionate share of fat.

At all events, it was soon clear that the apparent de-empha-

[106] On May 12 the President announced the designations of Admiral Arthur W. Radford as Chairman of the Joint Chiefs of Staff, Gen. Matthew B. Ridgway as Chief of Staff of the Army, and Admiral Robert B. Carney as Chief of Naval Operations. Gen. Nathan F. Twining had previously been nominated as Chief of Staff of the Air Force.

sis on air power represented at most a temporary expedient dictated by budgetary and management considerations, not a reversal of fundamental strategic policy. President Eisenhower hastened to assure an air-minded nation that the Air Force would still have over $40 billion to work with, and that almost sixty cents out of every defense dollar would be "devoted to air power and air defense." More than half of the Navy's budget, he pointed out, was also allocated to air power —"which daily becomes a more important factor in war." [107] Members of both houses eventually swallowed their misgivings and even undertook some further economizing on their own account, trimming the total defense appropriation to $34.4 billion in the final measure passed July 29, two days after the guns ceased firing in Korea.

The long-range military and strategic implications of this shift in the pattern of defense expenditures were not easy to assess. Admittedly it represented only an interim plan, a kind of holding operation pending restudy of the whole defense program. To the extent that military policy under the new estimates contemplated the continued, coordinated development of all phases of national military power, it would be consistent with the global defensive pattern laid down in earlier years and with the continuing fulfillment of obligations the United States had assumed under the United Nations, the North Atlantic Treaty, and other regional security arrangements. To the extent, however, that it continued to place the primary emphasis on the development of strategic air power in conjunction with a heavy reliance on atomic weapons, it would also be consistent with a gradual reorientation of military policy toward greater reliance on "retaliatory" or "deterrent" power and diminishing participation in the physical defense of areas directly exposed to Soviet-Communist aggression. Which of these two directions the United States would ultimately take was, of course, a matter of considerable consequence not only at home but throughout the world. Meanwhile, some further indication of the trend of thinking about America's role among the nations could be found in the actions being taken with reference to the Mutual Security Program.

[107] Radio report, May 19, in *New York Times,* May 20, 1953.

The Mutual Security Program

Critics of American world policy as it had developed in recent years were almost unanimous in deprecating what seemed to them an overemphasis on military preparedness to the detriment of possible measures for world-wide economic and social improvement. Now, under a new administration, the military budget was being cut back, although the new leaders had given the most solemn assurances that military preparedness would not be lessened. Nor was the reduction in defense expenditure to be balanced by increased attention to possible nonmilitary needs in the free world. On the contrary, expenditure for the direct benefit of other non-Communist nations was also to be reduced, and such expenditure as was still found necessary was to be given a sharper military application than ever before.

The continuing justification for a broad program of assistance to friendly nations was vigorously pointed out in one of the early reports issued on behalf of the Eisenhower administration:

"It is no longer realistic to consider America's security position solely in terms of our national defense facilities. . . . The adequacy of our protection can only be measured by assessing the total strength of the free world. Therefore, where America can contribute to building the strength of other free nations without serious sacrifice of its own strength, the net result is to enhance the overall security of the American people." [108]

For purposes such as these the United States had already furnished, in the seven and one-half years since World War II, a total of $37.6 billion (net) in grants and loans to foreign countries.[109] For the fiscal year 1953–54 the Truman administration had recommended the appropriation of a further $7.6 billion in new money, a considerable increase over the

[108] *Report to Congress on the Mutual Security Program,* June 30, 1953 (Washington, G.P.O., 1953), 4.

[109] According to figures compiled by the Department of Commerce, U.S. gross foreign aid (grants and credits) from July 1, 1945 through December 31, 1952 totaled $41,034 million; net foreign aid (after deduction of reverse grants, returns on grants, and principal collected on credits) totaled $37,612 million. The corresponding figures for Western Europe were $30,128 million (gross) and $27,915 million (net). Cf. E. S. Kerber, "United States Foreign Aid in 1952," *Survey of Current Business,* XXXIII, No. 3, March 1953, 13-19.

$6 billion appropriated the year before. As with the defense appropriation, this recommendation took account of the long "lead time" involved in the manufacture of complicated items of military equipment, a factor which sometimes led to the accumulation of substantial funds which had been appropriated but not yet spent. The Eisenhower administration, after reviewing the status of the Mutual Security Program and ascertaining that no less than $9.5 billion would be left over from previous appropriations, reduced the request for new money first to $5.8 billion,[110] then to $5.5 billion, and ultimately to $5.1 billion. Congress in turn appropriated, at the beginning of August, a total of $4.5 billion in new money, together with $2.1 billion of the funds available from previous appropriations. In this substantial reduction it disregarded a strong plea by the President to refrain from trying to go below his own estimates.[111] Even so, the cuts were less drastic than might have been expected at a time when the dollar position of most foreign aid recipients was improving as it was during the first half of 1953.

Possibly more significant than the reduced size of the total appropriation was the strengthened military emphasis in what had originally been conceived as an economic aid program but in recent years had become predominantly a mutual defense effort.[112] Of the total new appropriation ($4,531 million),

110 Cf. the message of the President and statements by Messrs. Dulles and Stassen, May 5, in *Department of State Bulletin,* XXVIII, May 25, 1953, 735-742.

111 Letter of July 22, *ibid.*, XXIX, August 3, 1953, 158-159. As usual, the Mutual Security Program was continued by two separate enactments: the Mutual Security Act of 1953, or authorization measure (Public Law 118, 83d Congress, approved July 16, 1953); and the Mutual Security Appropriation Act, 1954 (Public Law 218, 83d Congress, approved August 7, 1953). A convenient tabular presentation of the administration estimates and congressional authorizations and appropriations for the year appears in *Survey of Activities of the Committee on Foreign Affairs, House of Representatives, 83d Congress (January 3, 1953-August 20, 1954)* (Committee Print, Washington, G.P.O., 1954), 9-10.

112 Appropriations for military aid had begun to overshadow those for economic assistance with the official end of the European Recovery Program in 1951. Because of the delays in production, actual deliveries of military aid shipments did not begin to exceed economic aid deliveries on a global basis until the last quarter of 1952. Cf. Kerber, *loc. cit.*, 13-19. The chart on p. 88, adapted from *Report to Congress on the Mutual Security Program,* June 30, 1953, 10, illustrates the changing composition of foreign aid shipments through fiscal year 1952, with estimates for fiscal years 1953 and 1954.

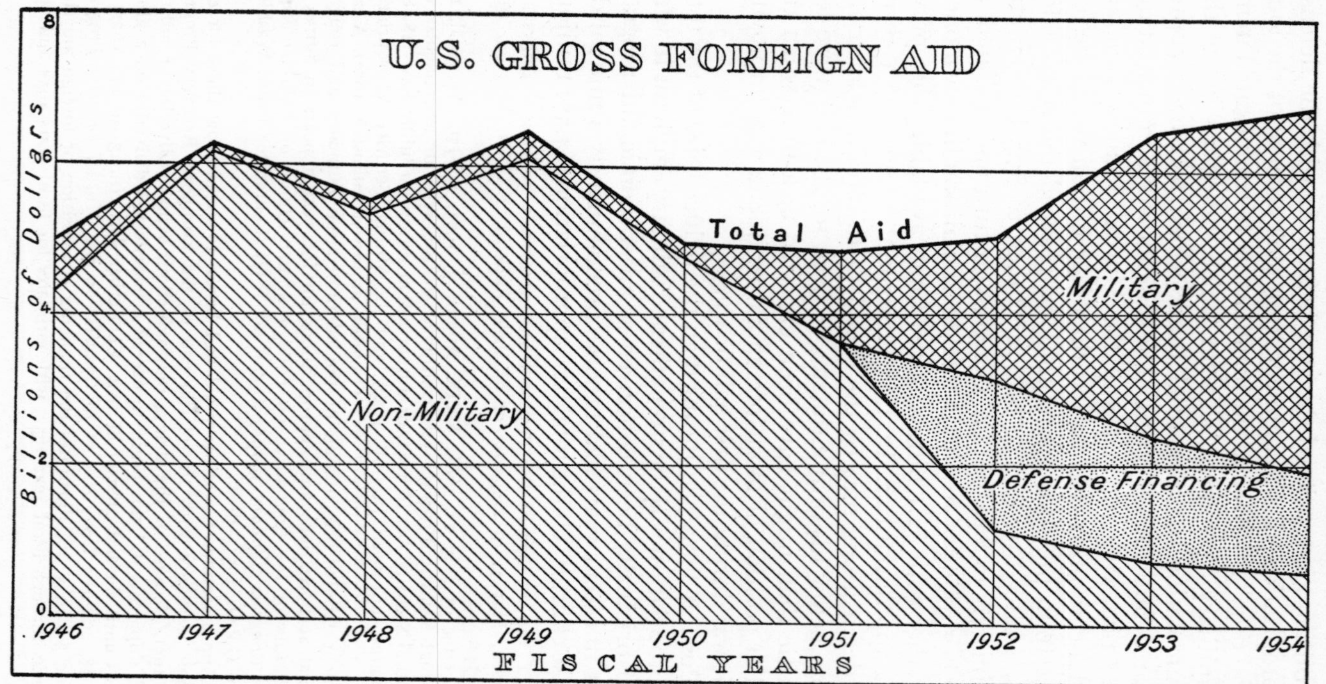
U.S. GROSS FOREIGN AID
Total Aid
Military
Defense Financing
Non-Military
Billions of Dollars
0
2
4
6
8
1946
1947
1948
1949
1950
1951
1952
1953
1954
FISCAL YEARS

70 percent or $3,180 million was allocated to direct military assistance and another 20 percent ($924 million) to related activities identified as mutual defense financing, defense support, economic and technical assistance directly related to defense, and "mutual special weapons planning." [113] The remaining 10 percent was split between ordinary technical assistance programs and basic materials development ($126.4 million), special economic aid for the Near East and Africa ($147 million) and India and Pakistan ($75 million), and contributions to the United Nations Korean Reconstruction Agency ($50.7 million) and other multilateral economic programs ($28.4 million).[114] Although the new administration was no less assiduous than its predecessor in pointing out that mutual defense required sound economies as well as strong armies, the practical weight of the program thus fell heavily on the military side.

The geographic distribution of the new funds also departed somewhat from the pattern of previous years, in line with the universal Republican insistence that more must be done in the Far East even if less was done elsewhere. Europe's share of the total appropriation sank from nearly three-fourths to not much more than half, largely through a drastic reduction in military aid and the near elimination of economic or "defense support" assistance, which had become less essential than in earlier years. In contrast, the total of the various types of aid apportioned to Asia and the Pacific ($1.6 billion) represented approximately twice the figure for the previous year and more than one-third of the entire appropriation. In straight military assistance alone the Far East was allocated $1,035 million, as compared with $1,860 million for Europe, $270 million for the Near East and Africa, and $72 million

[113] Included in this latter figure were $85 million for manufacture in France of artillery, ammunition, and semiautomatic weapons required by French forces for NATO defense; $85 million for manufacture in the United Kingdom of military aircraft required by U.K. forces for NATO defense; $50 million for furnishing "special weapons" to appropriate countries or organizations; and $400 million for procurement of equipment, materials, and services for the native and French forces in Indochina.

[114] In separate legislation Congress appropriated another $200 million for Korean rehabilitation (Supplemental Appropriation Act, 1954; Public Law 207, 83d Congress) and made various provisions for the gift or sale of surplus agricultural commodities; cf. below, pp. 100-101, 250.

for Latin America. This distribution reflected not only a warmer solicitude for the Far East on the part of the dominant political party but also a realization that the most immediate military dangers to Western Europe had already been largely overcome, thus making it possible to shift the emphasis in the program toward areas that were still notoriously weak and exposed.

The new allocation for European military aid was limited in one important respect which the administration had not foreseen and apparently did not find helpful, despite its consonance with Mr. Dulles' January hint about "a little rethinking" of our European policy unless there was progress toward effective unity in that area. Congressional impatience over the slow progress toward ratification of the European Defense Community had revived the old temptation to use the appropriating power of Congress as a means of pressure on allied countries. When the bill to authorize the Mutual Security Program for the coming year went to the White House, it was buttressed by an amendment (named for Democratic Representative James P. Richards of South Carolina) which stipulated that half of the funds provided for European military aid could be made available only to the European Defense Community or to its member countries. If the Community failed to come into existence, the funds could not be made available unless Congress changed its mind on recommendation of the President.[115] Outside the realm of "psychological strategy" this stipulation would have no immediate effect, since arms deliveries to Europe would for some time to come be financed from earlier appropriations. It might prove embarrassing if ratification of E.D.C. failed to take place before the backlog was used up.

Under a reorganization plan prepared in the White House, administration of the new Mutual Security Program was to be entrusted to a brand-new agency, the Foreign Operations Administration (F.O.A.), which was being established under Mr. Stassen's leadership to take over the functions of the old Mutual Security Agency plus the management of the Technical Cooperation (Point Four) Program and various specialized relief and reconstruction operations formerly adminis-

[115] Sec. 101, Mutual Security Act of 1953.

tered by the Department of State. This arrangement paralleled the establishment of the United States Information Agency as a separate entity and was designed, according to the President, to enable the State Department to concentrate on its basic tasks of foreign policy formulation and general guidance of the nation's international activities.[116]

International Economic Policy

By various expedients, among which the reductions in the defense and Mutual Security appropriations loomed largest, the administration and Congress managed between them to reduce total appropriations for the new fiscal year by about $12 billion below the Truman estimates and to trim the prospective deficit from $9.9 billion to a figure which ultimately turned out to be only a little over $3 billion.[117] True, some of these were mere paper savings of funds which would need to be appropriated or expended later for obligations already foreseen. The ultimate results of the economy effort would not be apparent for some time to come, either in dollars and cents or in the effects on national and mutual security. For the next year or two, the United States and its allies, so far as the latter still depended on this country, would still be coasting along essentially on appropriations and other arrangements made during the Truman administration. The full impact of the Eisenhower economies would not be felt before 1954 or 1955, if then.

In the meantime their main significance was that of indicators useful in gauging the general attitude prevailing in Washington. In fiscal matters, that attitude seemed to consist in a general acceptance of established world policies, subject, however, to an overriding concern for national solvency as expressed in prospects for a balanced budget and tax reductions. In military and mutual security matters, as in most other phases of foreign relations, there had been no radical shift to new policies tailored to the economy concept, although

116 Cf. Reorganization Plan No. 7 of 1953 and related documents in *Department of State Bulletin,* XXVIII, June 15, 1953, 849-855 and XXIX, August 24, 1953, 240-242.

117 Final figures for the fiscal year 1954 showed receipts of $64.6 billion, expenditures of $67.6 billion, and a deficit of $3,029 million. *New York Times,* July 23, 1954.

a real attempt was being made to get better value for each dollar spent. The main difference seemed to be that the old policies were being carried on with a reduced budget. Left in abeyance was the question whether these limitations would increase or undermine the effectiveness of the policies themselves.

Much the same might be said of the important field of international trade and financial policy. In this area there was no formal repudiation of the liberal approach embodied in the Reciprocal Trade Agreements Program—no official substitution of protectionism for the free-trade policies with which a good many Republicans professed a lack of sympathy. On the contrary, the Trade Agreements Act was extended for another year, as a "temporary" measure designed to enable the administration to study matters afresh and try to reconcile divergent viewpoints within the majority party. In this respect the technique was similar to that followed in respect to the defense program. Yet the very fact that the positive action so often urged on the United States was put off in favor of another "thorough and comprehensive reexamination" of our entire foreign economic policy showed that the old bases and assumptions of that policy were no longer as firm as they had been. Presidential references to "profitable and equitable world trade" had to be read with the realization that this was a field in which the President would be disinclined to dogmatize and in which his influence on his own party might be less than it was in military matters. Whatever the economists might say about the obligations of a creditor nation and the urgent need for foreign countries to increase their exports to the United States, there were plenty of businessmen and legislators who saw the matter in more local terms and whose own calculations led them to opposite policy conclusions.

In his State of the Union message the President had not only endorsed the general principle of trade expansion but also mentioned several lines of action by which the United States could supplement the efforts being made by friendly nations to create broader markets and more dependable currencies. In addition to the proposed extension of the Trade Agreements Act (originally recommended without time limit), he had spoken of revision of customs regulations, encouragement of private American investment abroad, use of overseas facilities for the manufacture of mutual defense items (offshore procurement), and increased acquisition of important raw materials from abroad.[118]

Action—rarely of a conclusive nature—was taken during 1953 along each of these lines. The enactment of a Customs Simplification Bill, which in previous years had twice been blocked by the Democratic-controlled Senate Finance Committee, ranked as one of the noteworthy legislative victories of the new administration despite the fact that most of the bill's more controversial features were omitted pending further study.[119] Efforts to encourage the flow of private foreign investment, primarily through the fostering of a more attractive investment "climate" abroad, were pursued on various levels by the Mutual Security (Foreign Operations) Agency, though not effectively enough to prevent a decline in the net outflow of American investment capital compared to the previous year.[120] The same organization continued and speeded up the placement of "offshore procurement" contracts, mainly in Europe, as an integral part of the Mutual Security Program; by mid-1953 the total of such contracts already signed had reached $2.2 billion and the actual flow of dollars to participating countries in payment for the manufacture of mutual defense items was expected to reach some $500 million during the fiscal year.[121] Purchases of foreign raw materials failed, however, to increase in accordance with presidential expectations, partly because the national stockpile goals were nearing fulfillment and world market prices of raw materials had fallen off. In the long run, this country's

118 *Documents on American Foreign Relations, 1953*, 22.

119 Public Law 243, 83d Congress, approved August 8, 1953; presidential comment in *Department of State Bulletin*, XXIX, August 17, 1953, 202.

120 Cf. *Report to Congress on the Mutual Security Program*, June 30, 1953, 12, 60-61. The net outflow of direct investment capital from the U.S. was $528 million in 1951, $850 million in 1952, and $722 million in 1953 (over 80 percent of it to Western Hemisphere countries). Reinvestment of earnings by foreign subsidiaries brought the total increase in U.S. direct investment abroad during 1953 to $1.5 billion. Cf. Samuel Pizer and Frederick Cutler, "Foreign Investments and Income," *Survey of Foreign Business*, XXXIV, No. 11, November 1954, 6-9.

121 *Report to Congress on the Mutual Security Program*, June 30, 1953, 16-18; same, December 31, 1953 (Washington, G.P.O., 1954), 14.

need for foreign raw materials might be an important factor in establishing a better balanced world economy. But as a short-run factor its effect was less than expected.[122]

Foreign Trade and the Dollar Gap

But even maximum accomplishment along such lines would leave the matter of general tariff and trade policy as the central unsolved issue of American foreign economic relationships. Year after year, as economic conditions abroad became more nearly normal and United States foreign aid dwindled, one simple fact had stood out more starkly: The United States was not buying as much from other countries as it wanted to sell to them. This, moreover, was a situation that could not very well go on indefinitely. In the long run, we should either have to buy more or be prepared to sell less—even though the latter alternative might hurt our own economy as well as our foreign partners.

For the moment, this dilemma was still somewhat obscured by two factors: (1) the continuance of large United States military aid shipments, through which we in effect gave away rather than sold a considerable portion of our annual exports; and (2) the substantial expenditures of our military forces abroad, which were equivalent to three or four billion dollars a year in extra imports. These two factors together were sufficient to enable most European countries to improve their foreign exchange and balance-of-payments positions during 1953 despite their failure to make a significant dent in the regular import market. But neither type of expenditure was intended to last forever; and if these extraordinary items were disregarded, there was already apparent a potential adverse trend in the export position of the United States. European and other trading countries, unable to earn all the dollars they needed in trade with this country, had no recourse but

[122] U.S. imports of "crude materials" amounted to $2,937 million in calendar 1952, $2,603 million in calendar 1953, and $1,238 million (or an annual rate of $2,476 million) in the first half of calendar 1954 (*Foreign Commerce Weekly,* March 29, 1954, 32; September 27, 1954, 27). The President's budget message for fiscal 1955 estimated stockpile purchases of foreign and domestic materials, which had amounted to $919 million in fiscal 1953, at $770 million in fiscal 1954 and $585 million in fiscal 1955 (*New York Times,* January 22, 1954). Actual expenditure in fiscal 1954 fell $120 million below this estimate (*ibid.,* July 23, 1954).

to restrict their purchases in the American market and look elsewhere for the satisfaction of their import needs. Thanks to the general improvement in economic conditions in many parts of the free world, they were able to meet their requirements from other sources much more successfully than would have been true a few years earlier.

Largely as a result of these factors, United States exports (exclusive of military aid shipments) fell from $13.2 billion in 1952 to $12.2 billion in 1953. This rather sharp decline was even more remarkable when viewed in relation to the expanding productivity of the national economy as a whole. In 1951, this country's commercial merchandise exports had been equivalent to 4.2 percent of the gross national product. In 1952, the figure was only 3.8 percent; in 1953, it was 3.3 percent. Our imports, too, were beginning to decline in relation to the gross national product, even when they increased somewhat in value. In 1952, merchandise imports amounted to $10.7 billion or 3.1 percent of gross national product; in 1953, they rose to $10.9 billion but sank to 3.0 percent of the larger gross national product of that year.[123] Limited imports, no longer offset by large-scale grants and loans, meant continued dollar shortages abroad, reduced demand for American manufactures and farm products, and therefore limited or declining exports.

The causes and implications of these phenomena had been examined in recent years by an imposing number of expert groups, both European and American.[124] With impressive regularity they had concluded that while the illness demanded a variety of medicines, the most important and in fact indispensable one was an increase in United States imports, principally from Europe. This objective, which admittedly would necessitate strenuous efforts by Europeans to improve their position in the American market, also presupposed additional action by the United States to reduce the barriers still operating to keep out foreign products. This was generally felt to involve not only a streamlining of our perplexing customs

[123] "U.S. Imports Rise and Exports Level Off in 1953," *Foreign Commerce Weekly*, LI, No. 12, March 22, 1954, 16-19. In 1954, commercial exports (exclusive of military aid) recovered to $12.8 billion while imports declined to $10.2 billion. *Ibid.*, LIII, No. 15, April 11, 1955, 13-15.

[124] Cf. *The United States in World Affairs, 1952*, 407-412.

procedures but also a resolute continuation of the process of mutual tariff reduction initiated twenty years earlier under the original Trade Agreements Act. Some authorities held that even this might not fully suffice and that unilateral tariff reductions by the United States, even without matching concessions by other parties, might be desirable in some instances.

These views, which had become commonplace under the old administration, were emphasized once again in one of the first official reports made to the new President—a document prepared at the request of President Truman by the Public Advisory Board for Mutual Security under the chairmanship of Daniel W. Bell. Entitled *A Trade and Tariff Policy in the National Interest,* the Bell report warned that "if this country does not soon take measures to facilitate an increase in imports, U.S. exports will decline and American industry and agriculture will be seriously affected." Appended was a series of specific recommendations calculated to "enable foreign countries to expand their sales to us by 700 million to 1 billion dollars annually within 3 to 5 years." The basic recommendation was, "That decisions on trade policy be based on national interest, rather than the interest of particular industries or groups." It was also suggested that specific industries be helped, if necessary, to adjust themselves to the new conditions brought about by foreign competition rather than being permitted to block tariff reductions which were in the interest of the nation as a whole.[125]

If this general line of thought had been as acceptable in Republican as it was in many Democratic circles, the President would presumably have seen no need to defer action until there had been still another reassessment of the problem by still another distinguished study group. The recommendations of any group that was not specifically committed to a high-tariff policy could be pretty accurately forecast in advance, though they might be more likely to carry weight with a Republican Congress if formulated under Republican auspices. Republicans, like Democrats, generally recognized

[125] *A Trade and Tariff Policy in the National Interest: A Report to the President by the Public Advisory Board* (Washington, Mutual Security Agency, February 1953), as summarized in *Department of State Bulletin,* XXVIII, March 23, 1953, 436-438.

that our agriculture and industry were dependent on continued large export markets, and that exports presupposed imports. But with this recognition went an insistent demand for protection from foreign competition on the part of influential producer groups—a number of which, moreover, could argue convincingly that their continued prosperity was vital to the national defense. Thus the administration found it advisable, in the words of Secretary Dulles, to urge "that there be in effect a 'standstill' until this problem can be studied under fresh auspices in its relation to the complex problems into which tariff policy must be fitted." [126]

Extending the Trade Agreements Act

Even a "standstill," by which the administration meant a one-year extension of the existing Trade Agreements Act, was not easy to extract from the protection-minded group of congressmen. Led by Representative Richard Simpson, Republican of Pennsylvania, many of these preferred to rally behind a substitute bill which proposed a whole series of increased tariff rates and import quotas as well as limiting the President's authority in relation to matters dealt with by the Tariff Commission. Before the administration could be assured of its "standstill" it was obliged to make various concessions, among them a promise that no new trade agreements of importance would be signed during the year ahead. This undertaking, which compelled the United States to postpone scheduled trade negotiations with Japan as well as a fresh round of tariff negotiations under the General Agreement on Tariffs and Trade (GATT), resembled the administration's dropping of the covenants on human rights at the commencement of hearings on the Bricker Amendment. In addition, the administration accepted certain modifications in the procedure of the Tariff Commission which were frankly designed to ensure that requests for protection on the part of particular industries would receive fuller consideration than in the past. Attempts by the protectionists to increase the membership of the Tariff Commission from six to seven, thus giving it a partisan majority, delayed passage

[126] Statement to the House Ways and Means Committee, May 4, *ibid.*, May 25, 1953, 745.

of the extension bill [127] until August but were eventually dropped after the President had filled two vacancies on the commission by the appointment of Republicans acceptable to the protectionist wing.

The matter of appointments also promised to play a crucial role in relation to the promised "broad-gauge study ... of what our foreign economic policy should be." At the President's suggestion,[128] Congress provided in the new Trade Agreements Act for the establishment of a bipartisan Commission on Foreign Economic Policy which would consist of (a) seven public members appointed by the President, and (b) ten members of Congress, half of whom were to be appointed by the presiding officer of each house.[129] Commission Chairman Clarence B. Randall, chairman of the board of directors of the Inland Steel Corporation, commented at the group's first meeting later in the year that its members held "strong convictions somewhat at variance." While the seven presidential nominees (two industrialists, two bankers, one cotton broker, one trade-union representative, and one economist) seemed to include few advocates of protection, the presence in the ten-man congressional group of such high-tariff Republicans as Representative Simpson, Representative Daniel A. Reed of New York, and Senator Eugene D. Millikin of Colorado ensured a vigorous representation of the protectionist viewpoint. The commission was directed to report to the next regular session of Congress early in 1954. Meanwhile the President commended to its attention both the Bell report and a special report, embodying similar conclusions, which had been prepared by former Ambassador Lewis W. Douglas as an outgrowth of the Anglo-American financial and economic conversations held in Washington in March.[130]

While Congress awaited the deliberations of the Randall

[127] Public Law 215, 83d Congress, approved August 7, 1953.

[128] Letter of May 2, in *Department of State Bulletin*, XXVIII, May 25, 1953, 747-748.

[129] On the establishment of the commission cf. *ibid.*, XXIX, August 31, 1953, 279-280.

[130] "The Dollar-Sterling Relationship and its Effect on U.S. Foreign Economic Policy: Report of the Douglas Mission," *ibid.*, XXIX, August 31, 1953, 275-279; reprinted in part in *Documents on American Foreign Relations, 1953*, 251-257.

Commission and the evolution of national opinion, various actions were being taken (or omitted) in Washington which were aimed primarily at other objectives but had at least an indirect effect on the general trade and payments problem. Controls on strategic trade with the Soviet bloc, which from an economic viewpoint represented a significant though doubtless unavoidable limitation on Western European export possibilities, were being sharpened and enforced with more zeal than was applied to seeking alternative markets for Western European goods.[131] At the same time, legislation designed to strengthen the competitive position of various segments of the American economy was kept in force and in some instances developed further.

The new administration refrained from making any request for repeal of the old "Buy American Act," despite the view expressed by the State Department that this relic of the depression era was "not in accord with the . . . basic policy of increasing the strength of the free world to withstand aggression." [132] Similarly, the Mutual Security legislation for the year reaffirmed the usual requirement that at least half of all foreign aid cargoes shipped from the United States must be carried in American-flag vessels. In addition, it carried a new requirement inspired by growing concern over this country's huge surplus of unsold agricultural products—namely, that not less than $100 million nor more than $250 million of the funds appropriated for Mutual Security should "be used, directly or indirectly, to finance the purchase of surplus agricultural commodities, or products thereof, produced in the United States." [133]

[131] Cf. *World-Wide Enforcement of Strategic Trade Controls—Mutual Defense Assistance Control Act of 1951 (the Battle Act): Third Report to Congress, First Half of 1953* (Washington, G.P.O., 1953). Like his predecessor, President Eisenhower found it necessary to invoke the discretionary provisions of the Battle Act in determining that the shipment of specified strategic commodities from Western countries to the Soviet bloc (in this case, $3,260,286 in industrial goods from Western Germany, France, Norway, and Great Britain) did not warrant the termination of U.S. aid to those countries. See the President's letter of August 1, 1953, and enclosure, *ibid.*, 73-77.

[132] Quoted by Richard M. Boeckel, "Record of 83d Congress (First Session)," *Editorial Research Reports,* II, Nos. 4-6, August 4, 1953, 551.

[133] Section 706 (h), Public Law 118, 83d Congress; details in *Department of State Bulletin,* XXIX, November 9, 1953, 638-640.

Farm Policy

A few years earlier a similar proposal to use foreign aid funds for the disposal of agricultural surpluses had brought from Senator Taft the comment, "I don't think we ought to be enacting a farm-relief program in this bill." [134] But the problem of dealing with excess agricultural production was growing ever more acute as foreign agriculture recovered while the United States continued, in accordance with what had originally been emergency policies developed under Democratic leadership, to subsidize the production of a larger volume of farm products than could be profitably disposed of through commercial channels either at home or abroad. Already the Commodity Credit Corporation was holding over $3 billion in surplus stocks of agricultural commodities. This was another field where domestic and foreign policy had yet to be brought "into some kind of realistic focus," possibly by discouraging excess production through some modification of the existing system of farm price supports. In the meantime various expedients were being tried with a view to promoting the disposition of greater quantities of farm products through sales or even gifts to foreign countries, thus reducing the surplus stocks on hand and perhaps establishing new markets for the future.

In April, the renewal of the International Wheat Agreement guaranteed the United States an annual market for 270 million bushels of wheat within fixed price limits over a three-year period.[135] Altruistic impulses, though carefully excluded from the Mutual Security Program,[136] were also invoked in the interest of reducing agricultural surpluses. To avert a threat of famine, Congress in June authorized the gift to Pakistan of one million tons of surplus wheat at

[134] *The United States in World Affairs, 1949,* 86.

[135] Great Britain considered the maximum import price too high and refrained from adhering to the new International Wheat Agreement, which was signed in Washington April 13. For details cf. *Department of State Bulletin,* XXVIII, May 18, 1953, 714-715; XXIX, July 13, 1953, 61-62; July 27, 1953, 115-116; August 24, 1953, 245. The U.S. was also a signatory (as an importing rather than an exporting country) to the International Sugar Agreement signed in London August 24, 1953; details *ibid.,* XXIX, October 26, 1953, 542-546.

[136] Cf. the testimony of Secretary Dulles, *ibid.,* XXVIII, May 25, 1953, 736.

an estimated cost of $102 million.[137] A few weeks later the President received authority to give up to $100 million in surplus farm products not only to friendly countries but also to "friendly peoples" behind the Iron Curtain, where it was hoped that such a manifestation of American generosity would help to weaken Communist control.[138] Under this legislation about 18,000 tons of American food products were distributed in packaged form to residents of Soviet-controlled East Germany; Christmas food parcels were delivered to needy families in Western Europe, the Near East, and Latin America; and 57,200 tons of surplus wheat were provided to alleviate serious shortages in Bolivia, Jordan, and Libya.[139]

One device that was *not* applied to the solution of the national farm problem was the spur of foreign competition. Even the limitations on the importation of fats, oils, and dairy products which had been instituted under the well-known "Cheese Amendment" (Section 104 of the Defense Production Act of 1951) were retained in modified form, despite the fact that such restrictions had been formally condemned by the contracting parties to the General Agreement on Tariffs and Trade and had called forth sharp protests from Canada, New Zealand, Australia, Denmark, Sweden, the Netherlands, and other countries. The State Department had found that this type of protectionism, instituted in disregard of prior commitments to friendly countries, was "seriously undermining efforts to build confidence in our leadership along the whole front of our foreign policy." [140] But there was other legislation on the books which, it was hoped, would make it possible to afford due protection to the dairy industry while perhaps avoiding these unpleasant consequences. Before the "Cheese Amendment" expired on June 30 a presidential proclamation was issued bringing the prod-

137 Public Law 77, 83d Congress, approved June 25, 1953; cf. below, p. 310 f.

138 Public Law 216, 83d Congress, approved August 7, 1953; details in *Department of State Bulletin,* XXIX, July 13, 1953, 61-62 and August 3, 1953, 159-160.

139 *Report to Congress on the Mutual Security Program,* December 31, 1953, 7-9; on the East German food program cf. also below, p. 143.

140 Testimony of Harold F. Linder, Assistant Secretary of State for Economic Affairs, before the Senate Banking and Currency Committee, April 1, in *Department of State Bulletin,* XXVIII, April 13, 1953, 554-558.

ucts in question under appropriate provisions of the Agricultural Adjustment Act.[141]

Some of these actions were provisional or even experimental in character, and did not necessarily prefigure whatever new trade policy was destined to emerge from the deliberations of the Randall Commission. Nevertheless, the balance of the year's achievements proved disappointing to those at home and abroad who had hoped the presidential generalizations on trade policy would be given a more positive content. There had been little visible willingness on the part of Congress to treat the problem of America's trade relations as one of genuine international concern. On the contrary, there was an obvious parallel between the air of aloofness adopted by this country in economic matters and its apparent tendency—perhaps stronger in appearance than in reality—toward reduced participation in the free world's military, political, and emotional concerns.

If it was possible to speak of a trend toward partial dissociation from the rest of the non-Communist world, the matter was of special significance at this particular moment because it happened to coincide with the disappearance of Stalin and the emergence of new leaders in the Soviet Union who evidently took great interest in encouraging and exploiting whatever centrifugal tendencies existed among the non-Communist nations. It is now necessary for us to look more closely at this latter development as it affected the broad course of East-West relations and the fortunes of the anti-Communist coalition.

[141] Proclamations of June 8 and 30, *ibid.*, XXVIII, June 29, 1953, 918-920 and XXIX, July 13, 1953, 62. Sec. 22 of the Agricultural Adjustment Act enables the President to impose quotas for the protection of products benefiting by Federal price supports.

CHAPTER TWO

NEW ERA IN MOSCOW

From the glare of publicity in which the United States conducts its national business, we pass to the mysterious and impenetrable darkness that enshrouds the operations of the Soviet Government. So deeply hidden are the secrets of this more than medieval despotism that no outsider can claim more than a severely limited insight into its vital processes. On some of the most momentous questions of Soviet life and government, we cannot hope to penetrate to the unvarnished truth; we can only elaborate provisional hypotheses which it may never be possible finally to confirm or disprove. Fortunately, however, these limitations do not apply in equal degree to all aspects of Soviet policy, particularly in the international sphere. Though we cannot always identify the inner motivations of Soviet behavior, we can at least discern its general tendency and effects and endeavor to shape our own conduct accordingly.

Typical of the enigmatic qualities of the Soviet system is the fact that even the occurrences surrounding the death of Stalin—surely a key event in Soviet and world history—remain subject to widely differing interpretations. All that we know for certain is that early on Wednesday, March 4, 1953, the Soviet Government suddenly announced that its leader was gravely ill in consequence of a brain hemorrhage and stroke suffered the preceding Sunday night; that two days later a further bulletin, accompanied by a detailed medical certificate, declared that Stalin had died at 9:50 P.M. on Thursday, March 5; and that by the evening of March 6 the highest surviving Soviet authorities were in a position to announce a far-reaching rearrangement of governmental and party functions as well as numerous individual appointments and reassignments. According to some interpretations, this series of events represented no more than the efficient execution of plans made long in advance, perhaps by Stalin himself. Others suspect that the seventy-three-year-old dictator had actually died some time earlier, the announcement being withheld until his successors had reached at least provisional agreement on the succession to his authority. Some even maintain that one or more of the successors may have been directly responsible for Stalin's death, either because he represented a bar to their ambitions or because the reckless obstinacy of his domestic and foreign policies was felt to be endangering the permanent interests of the Soviet state.

Speculation on these developments is further complicated by the urge to relate them in some fashion to the melodramatic "doctors' plot" incident of January 1953, one of the more lurid manifestations of the anti-Semitic trend which prevailed in much of the Communist world in late 1952 and early 1953. On January 13, a group of Soviet medical authorities, several of them Jewish and all of them allegedly acting on behalf of an international Jewish charitable organization and American and British "intelligence services," had been publicly accused of planning to murder some of the highest party and military officials of the U.S.S.R., including Marshals Alexander M. Vasilevsky and Ivan S. Konev, in continuation of a series of crimes which allegedly had already cost the lives of two Politburo members—one of them no less a figure than the late Andrei A. Zhdanov. These charges were accompanied by sharp criticism of the Soviet security services for allegedly failing to discover the doctors' machinations in time; thus they were widely construed as a typically indirect attack on Lavrenti P. Beria, chief authority in the Soviet security system. Although it seemed probable at the time that the affair had been set in motion either by Stalin himself or by Georgi M. Malenkov, his protégé and heir apparent, later developments suggested that other elements in the Communist party apparatus and the Soviet military hierarchy might also have been involved.[1]

[1] An alternative interpretation held that the "doctors' plot" story was really directed against Malenkov as a former enemy of Zhdanov.

Whatever the correct solution of the "doctors' plot" enigma, Beria as well as Malenkov figured prominently in the new appointments announced immediately after Stalin's death. Malenkov succeeded to Stalin's position as Chairman of the U.S.S.R. Council of Ministers; Beria was named a First Deputy Chairman as well as Minister of Internal Affairs. Appointed to serve with him as First Deputy Chairmen were Vyacheslav M. Molotov (Foreign Minister), Nikolai A. Bulganin (War Minister), and Lazar M. Kaganovich. All of the foregoing were also named to the supreme Communist party organ, the Presidium of the Central Committee, where they shared honors with Marshal Kliment Y. Voroshilov, Nikita S. Khrushchev, Anastas I. Mikoyan, Maxim Z. Saburov, and M. G. Pervukhin. Voroshilov was awarded, in addition, the top honorific post of Chairman of the Presidium of the Supreme Soviet (Parliament), succeeding N. M. Shvernik, who had held the post since 1946.

Though history had waited almost thirty years for the end of Stalin's dictatorial rule, it was soon evident that a further wait was in store before any final appraisal of its significance could be attempted. While some observers hopefully stressed the possible sources of weakness in the post-Stalin regime, the general consensus was that the transfer of power had not shaken the Soviet state in any significant degree. Especially in the early days of their power, Malenkov and his associates repeatedly stressed the need for "monolithic unity," thus indicating that they were aware of the possibility of a debacle; yet they apparently succeeded in warding off serious internal disturbances and continued to manipulate the instruments of power with the authority of the experienced administrators they were. Even the life-and-death struggle which was apparently going forward within the new leadership itself was carried on with due concern for the maintenance of outward serenity.

Nor could serious weakness be detected in the international position of the new government. While maintaining and enhancing its existing strength in conventional fields of warfare, it was also to announce in August that the hydrogen bomb as well as the atomic bomb had been added to the Soviet repertory. In the satellite areas of Eastern Europe, and especially in Eastern Germany, the new rulers were to be faced in June with the eruption of open resistance to the puppet Communist regimes. But the summary repression of these riots would not only prove the Soviets' ability to maintain their iron hold over the satellites; it would also lead to the virtual shelving of American hopes for the early liberation of captive peoples by peaceful means.

As to the implications of Stalin's death for the long-term development of Soviet foreign policy, there were differences of opinion not only among experts but among governments. Especially significant and characteristic were the variations that developed between the predominant Western European and American interpretations. On the European side, what might be called the "hopeful" view was ably expounded by Isaac Deutscher, the noted biographer of Stalin.[2] For this school of thought, Stalinism had been a product of the primitive economic and social conditions of post-revolutionary Russia. The system had found its most characteristic expression in the iron discipline of the police state and in mystical reverence for the party and its leader. But Stalinism itself, the argument ran, by freeing the Russian masses from poverty and superstition, had made its own eventual disappearance inevitable. An educated, "modernized" populace would not accept such tyranny and ritualism but would push the state eventually toward some form of democratic socialism. Such a state, it was reasoned, was not far away in Russia. With its arrival a policy of accommodation toward the rest of the world would be possible. Perhaps this would also include a withdrawal from Eastern Europe and genuine efforts to achieve international disarmament.

Observers anxious to find evidence of such a process could soon cite a variety of novel trends: an attack on the cult of individual leadership, considerable official talk of individual and minority rights, and a lessened discrimination against the ordinary consumer in the development of internal economic policies. It was such manifestations that prompted Prime Minister Churchill to refer on May 11 to the possibil-

[2] Cf. Isaac Deutscher, *Russia: What Next?* (New York, Oxford University Press, 1953).

ity that a "spontaneous and healthy evolution" inside Russia might point the way to "a generation of peace." [3]

In the United States, however, most observers agreed that despite various new departures in internal policy, neither the essential makeup of the Soviet regime nor its long-term aims abroad had altered.[4] The cult of the leader had perhaps given way to a new emphasis on "collective leadership," but Russia was still a tight dictatorship under the control of a small group of men with enormous power. Possibly there were fewer restrictions on personal liberty than under the Stalinist dictatorship, but this seemed more a device to let off steam than a genuine application of democratic principles. The proposed revision of the criminal code, verbal deference to the rights of individuals, and a widely heralded amnesty for certain categories of prisoners could be interpreted as means of rallying support to the new rulers rather than an indication that the totalitarian principles of Communism were about to be abandoned. Any plan to increase the supply of consumers' goods, most American analysts believed, could be similarly explained; at most, it might reflect a recognition that chronic privation had reduced the working efficiency of the Soviet population to a level that menaced the continued rapid growth of the national economy and military potential. A greater abundance of consumers' goods would tend to increase the nation's over-all strength on a long-term basis without significantly affecting the still overwhelming priority of heavy industry.

But even if the long-term Soviet ambition to achieve world domination stood unaltered, it was not to be expected that Soviet external policies should long be confined to the rigid Stalinist mold. For ten years past, as Secretary Dulles observed in hailing the end of the "Stalin era" and the beginning of the "Eisenhower era," world affairs had been dominated by the "malignant power" of the defunct dictator.[5] His obtusely methodical attacks on the liberties of free nations

[3] *Documents on American Foreign Relations,* 1953, 245, 247; cf. further below, pp. 132-134.

[4] Cf. Philip E. Mosely, "The Kremlin's Foreign Policy Since Stalin," *Foreign Affairs,* XXXII, October 1953, 20-33.

[5] Statement of March 9, in *Department of State Bulletin,* XXVIII, March 23, 1953, 430.

had contributed, more than any other single factor, to the consolidation of the free world and the growing strength of the military coalition which was now ranged against the Soviet Union. His successors, whatever their individual ambitions, could have no interest in forwarding this process. Their obvious interest lay in slowing or even reversing it—in promoting not the unity, but the disunity, of the non-Communist world. They could not afford, perhaps, to slacken the Soviet Union's own precautions against the possibility of an armed clash with the West. But there were many avenues by which, without sacrificing any of the real advantages they held, they could hope to encourage the doubts and dissensions already so evident in the opposite camp. Their attempts to exploit these opportunities, and the efforts of the West to comprehend and frustrate them, would constitute the main substance of international history in 1953 and later. The initial trials of the new tactics would take place even while the struggle for power within the Soviet world was going forward.

1. FROM STALIN TO MALENKOV

At home, Stalin's heirs dealt with the problem of transferring power from one absolute regime to another with what history will doubtless pronounce a model of despatch. The crucial initial phase was completed after no more than a single day of interregnum, during which the Central Committee nervously appealed to the populace to avoid "panic and disarray." By March 7 the Soviet public could read the edict establishing a new order in both the Soviet state and the Communist party. By the middle of the month, this new equilibrium had been approved by the Central Committee of the party and the Supreme Soviet.

Governmental and Party Reorganization

The decisions initially announced in March 1953 entailed a remodeling of the topmost organs in both the Communist party and the Soviet Government. The changes in party organization seemed especially remarkable because they virtually undid the work of the Nineteenth Party Congress of October 1952, which had abolished the old Politburo and

Orgburo and replaced them with a single Party Presidium of thirty-six members. Either this arrangement had proved unmanageable in practice or it was felt to be unsuited to the new conditions; in any case, the decree of March 6 reduced the membership of the Presidium to fourteen (ten members and four alternates) and thus restored it to a position comparable to that of the old Politburo.[6]

The top echelons of state power underwent a similar change through the establishment within the Council of Ministers of a single, five-member Presidium—consisting of the Chairman of the Council of Ministers (Malenkov) and the four First Deputy Chairmen (Beria, Molotov, Bulganin, and Kaganovich)—to replace the two coordinating organs previously in existence. In the Council of Ministers as a whole, a further streamlining was effected by combining a number of ministries; especially important here were the merger of the War and Navy Ministries into a single Ministry of Defense under Bulganin and the consolidation of all police powers under the single Ministry of Internal Affairs, headed initially by Beria.

Who were these men who had so quickly remade Stalin's edifice of political power? Without doubt the leading figure at this early stage was Georgi Maximilianovich Malenkov, a man of unmistakable physical characteristics but one whose career, political and private, was veiled in greater obscurity even than that of Stalin. Since he was born in 1904 and joined the Bolshevik party only in 1920, Malenkov could not be classed as an "Old Bolshevik" or a venerable "Man of October." Like Stalin, his rise to power had been achieved mainly by his skill as a party bureaucrat, a successful organizer and intriguer, rather than as a colorful public figure or weighty theoretician. Formerly Stalin's personal secretary, he had emerged in 1934 as chief of the personnel department of the Central Committee of the Party, a key position from which he could manipulate party patronage. Between 1939 and 1946 he had worked his way into all three of the top

[6] The joint party and government announcement of March 6 is printed in *New York Times,* March 7, 1953. For a general survey of Soviet internal and foreign affairs in the months after Stalin's death cf. "La Politique de l'U.R.S.S. depuis le décès de Staline," *Chronique de politique étrangère,* VI, July 1953, 426-473.

party organs as then constituted, the Secretariat, the Politburo, and the Orgburo. In 1944 he was made a vice-premier in the Council of Ministers and played an important role in gearing the Soviet armaments industry to the war effort. Later Malenkov had apparently triumphed over Andrei Zhdanov in a bitter political battle which many observers looked upon as an early phase of the struggle for Stalin's succession. His role as Stalin's heir presumptive had appeared to be confirmed in October 1952 when he delivered the major report to the Nineteenth Party Congress, a ponderous task formerly reserved to the leader himself. Thus it was in no way surprising that he should emerge as Premier, receive first listing among the members of the newly consolidated party Presidium, and deliver the principal oration at Stalin's funeral on March 9.

To Beria, as First Deputy Premier and Minister of Internal Affairs, apparently belonged the second place in the new equilibrium. In the official lists of precedence, such as the order of eulogists at Stalin's funeral, Beria's name followed Malenkov's. Since his position as official boss of all police forces had made him a powerful figure in his own right, there was immediate speculation as to the possibility that he would come into conflict with the new premier. Who more likely than Malenkov to have been behind Beria's discomfiture in the recent matter of the doctors' plot? On the surface, however, the relations of the two men were idyllic, as the mid-March session of the Supreme Soviet conspicuously demonstrated. It was Beria who, to the "stormy applause" of the assembled deputies, officially nominated Malenkov to his new position and lauded him as "a talented disciple of Lenin and a faithful comrade-in-arms of Stalin." [7]

Third in the official ranking, apparently, stood Vyacheslav M. Molotov, one of the few surviving "Old Bolsheviks" and now a First Deputy Premier as well as the new head of the Ministry of Foreign Affairs, which he had relinquished to Andrei Y. Vyshinsky in 1949. (Vyshinsky, attending the General Assembly in New York, was made a First Deputy Foreign Minister and permanent Soviet representative at the United

[7] *Pravda,* March 15, 1953; English translation in *Current Digest of the Soviet Press,* V, No. 8, April 4, 1953, 3.

Nations.) Among Molotov's political assets could be listed seniority as a Politburo member, a close relationship to Stalin dating from pre-revolutionary times, service as Premier from 1930 to 1941, and wide experience and considerable reputation in the field of foreign affairs. On the other hand, the death of Stalin found Molotov without control of any specific instrument of internal power, thus placing him at a distinct disadvantage as compared with several younger men.

Another old Bolshevik who could claim almost three decades of membership in the Politburo and long-standing personal ties with Stalin was the new Chairman of the Presidium of the Supreme Soviet, Marshal Kliment Y. Voroshilov. It seemed probable, however, that Voroshilov's duties were mainly decorative, since his principal task was to preside over that unfailing source of praise and approval which took the place of a parliament in the Soviet scheme of things.

Three other appointments were specially noted at the time. Marshal Nikolai A. Bulganin, another old party man, was named a First Deputy Premier and given the vital portfolio of Defense. Also appointed as a First Deputy Premier was Lazar M. Kaganovich, an expert in economic matters and the only remaining Jew among the leading Bolsheviks; while the U.S.S.R.'s leading authority on foreign trade questions, Anastas I. Mikoyan, received the special title of Deputy Premier.

The last vital question to be settled was the disposition of Stalin's party post as Secretary of the Central Committee of the Communist Party. This was announced on March 20 with the belated publication of a decision allegedly reached at a Central Committee meeting on March 14. Many observers had expected Malenkov to occupy first place in the party Secretariat as well as the Council of Ministers; but the announcement stated that Malenkov, on the contrary, had resigned from the Secretariat entirely and that its new leader was Nikita S. Khrushchev, a member of the Party Presidium.[8] Although Khrushchev held no post in the Council of Minis-

[8] Khrushchev's primacy was at first indicated only by the fact that his name was listed first among the members of the Secretariat. His real importance in the Secretariat was formally acknowledged in September 1953 when he received the official title of First Secretary.

ters, neither had Stalin between 1924 and 1941, and as the year progressed it became increasingly clear that he must be ranked very near the top if, indeed, he was not actually Malenkov's chief rival. To later analysis the Central Committee meeting of March 14 would mark an initial check to Malenkov's ambitions and an important stage in the rise of Khrushchev to a position of commanding influence.

Novel Internal Trends

The equilibrium thus established remained ostensibly unchanged until July. Despite innumerable harangues on the solidarity of the regime, however, there were a number of indications that all was not yet fully serene. One of the most tantalizing indications of a struggle behind the scenes occurred on April 4 with the official disavowal and denunciation of the charges brought against the Soviet doctors on January 13. Far from having plotted the deaths of Soviet officials, said the new announcement, investigation by Beria's Ministry of Internal Affairs disclosed that the doctors, fifteen in all, had actually been arrested "incorrectly without any legal basis whatsoever," incriminated by false documentation, and forced to confess by "the use of impermissible means of investigation which are strictly forbidden under Soviet law." Now they had been "completely rehabilitated" and released. The finger of accusation now pointed not at any of Beria's men but at Semyon D. Ignatiev, who had been Minister of State Security at the time and was generally looked upon as a Malenkov protégé. Was Beria trying to get back at Malenkov by discrediting persons who had been his own nominal subordinates? If so, his triumph was to be short-lived.

Another indication of possible trouble within the ruling clique was the rapid turnover of personnel in the middle echelons of the party and state hierarchies, particularly at the level of the Union Republic (state) administrations. Although these displacements could not always be related to specific antagonisms at the top, a series of sweeping personnel changes in the Republic of Georgia during April seemed clearly to represent an attempt by Beria to strengthen his individual position in his native region. Such an interpretation seemed validated by the equally drastic countermeasures which were to occur in Georgia and elsewhere after Beria's disgrace in July.

One of the noteworthy aspects of the reversal in the doctors' plot affair was the indirect and deprecatory admission that the victims had been subjected to "impermissible" techniques of investigation which were now stated to be "strictly forbidden by Soviet law"—notwithstanding the fact that mental if not physical torture was known by all the world to constitute an integral part of the Communist system of jurisprudence. This sudden emphasis on the protection of the individual against an inhuman bureaucratic machine was one of several devices by which the new leadership was apparently seeking to earn the good will of the Soviet public. Beria himself, than whom no one then living was more closely identified with the methods of police terror that had shaped the Soviet Union, had seized the occasion of Stalin's funeral to enunciate a policy of respect for the civil rights guaranteed by the Soviet Constitution. In the following weeks a trend toward relaxation of some of the repressive features of the Soviet system was evidenced in various ways, most notably in an amnesty for certain classes of offenders which was issued over Voroshilov's signature on March 27.

Another repellent feature of the Stalin era that seemed destined for liquidation was the personal cult of Stalin and of the single leader. The hypocritical veneration of Stalin himself, which had, of course, reached nauseating proportions during Stalin's later career, was abruptly dropped shortly after the close of the brief official mourning period. Malenkov led the trend toward limitation of such reverential references, which before long reached the point of direct condemnation of one-man government and "un-Marxist" exaggeration of the importance of individuals. Particularly significant in this regard was the publication in *Pravda* on July 26 of a treatise entitled "Fifty Years of the Communist Party of the Soviet Union, 1903–1953"—apparently designed to supersede Stalin's own well-known work on that subject—which not only minimized the historical role of the late dictator but sharply criticized "the idealistic cult of the individual leader" as "alien to the spirit of Marxism-Leninism."

With these manifestations of concern for popular feeling went a considerable show of solicitude for popular welfare. As yet there was no talk of any massive reorientation of Soviet economic policies for the benefit of the common man, but already scattered measures, such as the announcement of important price reductions on April 1, seemed aimed at alleviating the lot of the ordinary consumer. Even if limited in scope, concessions of this kind would help to placate the Soviet population and minimize the likelihood of internal disturbances while the struggle for power among Stalin's lieutenants was being fought out. Meanwhile the new leaders were also engaged in a comparable effort on the international plane. Here, too, apparently, their immediate concern was to mitigate the most offensive features of the Stalinist heritage, thus establishing an atmosphere favorable to a relaxation of tensions and perhaps more conducive to realization of their long-term objective of dividing their enemies.

2. NEW TENDENCIES IN FOREIGN POLICY

Had there been any truth in the notion that authoritative circles in the West thought seriously of attempting by a preventive attack to eliminate the aggressive potential of the U.S.S.R., the confusion consequent on Stalin's death offered an opportunity that was presumably unlikely to occur a second time. No such attempt was made or even suggested in any responsible quarter, in the United States or abroad. Instinctively rather than by calculation, the allied statesmen and peoples preferred to sit tight and await the actions of the new Soviet leaders.

The earliest Western contacts with the post-Stalinist empire could not be considered reassuring. Four successive incidents involving military aircraft in different parts of the world suggested that if anything the Communist rulers intended to maintain or even heighten the existing state of international tension.

Probably by mere coincidence, the Danish island of Bornholm was electrified on the very day of Stalin's death by the arrival of a Russian MIG-15 jet fighter whose Polish pilot demanded asylum as a political refugee. Angry notes were exchanged between the Polish and Danish governments before the request was granted and the plane examined and released.[9]

More serious, on March 10 an American jet fighter was shot down over Western Germany by two MIG-15-type Czechoslovak aircraft which entered the United States occupation zone from Czechoslovakia and opened fire without warning. In reply to the American protest, the Czechoslovak Foreign Office truculently asserted that the destroyed plane was one of two which had been guilty of violating Czechoslovak territory—an assertion which the United States was able to deny categorically, though vainly so far as the Czechoslovak authorities were concerned, on the basis of radar records.[10]

The pilot of the destroyed American jet was able to parachute to safety in Germany, but the occupants of a British bomber which Soviet jet fighters shot down over Germany on March 12 were less fortunate. The entire seven-man crew was killed in what Prime Minister Churchill called a "cruel and wanton" attack on an unarmed aircraft—which, he conceded, might have innocently strayed into the Soviet occupation zone, though hardly to the distance of 120 miles as claimed by the Russians. At least two other British aircraft were threatened by Soviet fighters on the same day.

Three days later, on March 15 (Pacific time), two Soviet MIG's attacked a United States Air Force weather patrol plane twenty-five miles off the Kamchatka Peninsula in the North Pacific. The American plane returned the fire but escaped undamaged. As usual in such cases, the Soviet Government produced a diametrically opposite version of the facts, asserting that the plane had twice violated the "state frontier" of the U.S.S.R. and opened fire when the Soviet fighters approached.[11]

[9] A second Polish flier landed on Bornholm May 22 and also received asylum.

[10] U.S. notes of March 10 and 13 and Czechoslovak note of March 11, in *Department of State Bulletin,* XXVIII, March 30, 1953, 474-475; further correspondence *ibid.,* XXIX, August 10, 1953, 180-183. A claim for indemnity in the amount of $271,384 was filed by the U.S. in the International Court of Justice on March 22, 1955. *Ibid.,* XXXII, April 18, 1955, 648-650.

[11] U.S. note of March 18, Soviet note of March 22, and U.S. comments, *ibid.,* XXVIII, April 20, 1953, 577-578. Another, similar attack occurred July 29; cf. below, p. 235.

Such occurrences did not seem to reflect a specially pacific disposition on the part of Stalin's heirs; yet there were various indications that they did not fully typify the new Soviet leaders' approach to international relations. Communist authorities had always been peculiarly sensitive about the operations of foreign military aircraft anywhere near their "state frontiers," and were not overscrupulous in the measures they took against any plane they might think was venturing too close. Possibly a sense of crisis in the Communist world had made their fliers unusually suspicious at this particular time; or perhaps they were only exercising their usual excessive and indiscriminate caution. At all events, the Soviet Government apparently saw no reason why a vigilant, not to say provocative, defense of "state frontiers" should not be combined with a conciliatory tone in general foreign policy. Already, Premier Malenkov had taken the opportunity of Stalin's funeral to reassert Leninist-Stalinist doctrine about the possibility of "peaceful coexistence" between the "capitalist" and "socialist" systems. Now, within a day of the incident in the Pacific, he declared to the Supreme Soviet:

> "At the present time there is no disputed or unresolved question that cannot be settled peacefully by mutual agreement of the interested countries. This applies to our relations with all states, including the United States of America." [12]

Subsequent developments were to show that this language, rather than the language of the MIG's, reflected what was to be the dominant emphasis in Soviet foreign policy during the period ahead. And why, indeed, should it have been otherwise? Side by side with the expectation of an eventual clash between Communist and "capitalist" nations, there had always been embedded in the Soviet outlook the notion that the Soviet Union could derive benefit from a foreign policy based on "prolonged coexistence and peaceful competition" between the two systems. Such a conception did not rule out the possibility that an armed clash might eventually prove unavoidable, but it did testify to the fact that the Soviet Government did not require a continuously warlike

[12] Statement of March 15, in *Pravda,* March 16, 1953; *Current Digest of the Soviet Press,* V, No. 8, April 4, 1953, 5.

atmosphere in order to advance its interests. Stalin himself, in his last major pronouncement, had laid down the thesis that the post-World War II "contradictions" in the capitalist world were on the increase and presented a favorable opportunity for exploitation.[13] Stalin's own disappearance made it that much the easier for his successors to withdraw from an overextended diplomatic position and concentrate on efforts to foment disunity in the non-Communist camp—at the same time, of course, maintaining and consolidating the numerous advantages the U.S.S.R. already possessed.

Developments at the U.N.

If Soviet foreign policies were to be modified in any significant way as a result of Stalin's death, it was reasonable to look for some premonitory adjustments in that sensitive barometer of world politics, the United Nations General Assembly. But it was some time before any improvement could be detected in the atmosphere of the Assembly's Seventh Regular Session, which had been resumed in New York a few days before Stalin's death. The debates on Korea had been marked by the usual bitter East-West exchanges, and other developments had tended to throw the intransigence of the U.S.S.R. into high relief. Secretary-General Trygvie Lie told the Assembly on March 10 that his resignation, announced earlier in the session, had been motivated largely by the three-year boycott maintained against him by the Soviet bloc in reprisal for his stand on the Korean issue—an attitude which he characterized as "the crudest form of pressure" and the "most serious violation" to date of the pertinent article of the United Nations Charter.[14]

Next day Mr. Lodge enlivened the Assembly by taunting the Soviet representative with "the fear which seems to motivate everyone in an official position in your country." This fear, said the American delegate, was not a rational fear of

[13] "Economic Problems of Socialism in the U.S.S.R." (October 2, 1952); excerpts in *Documents on American Foreign Relations, 1952,* 105-110.

[14] U.N. General Assembly, *Official Records, Seventh Session, Plenary Meetings* (U.N. Document A/PV. 413, March 10, 1953), 535. General summaries of the second part of the Assembly's Seventh Session appear in *International Organization,* VII, May 1953, 243-254 and August 1953, 380-385, and in *Chronique de politique étrangère,* VI, July 1953, 437-446.

attack from outside, for the Soviet leaders knew there was no cause to fear aggression by the free world:

"It must be a fear of their own people, a fear that stems from the tyranny which they impose on the Soviet people. It is this fear which motivates Soviet imperialism and which gives to the Kremlin leaders these dreams of world dominion. . . . The more I study the subject, the more I am convinced that fear is at the bottom of all the violent words and violent deeds which distinguish the foreign policy of the Soviet Union." [15]

A psychologist might have found considerable justification for this view in the extreme sensitivity of Communist representatives, at the United Nations and elsewhere, about the possibility of hostile actions which might be undertaken in or near their territory. This peculiarity, so evident in their behavior toward foreign aircraft, was equally apparent in their persistent rejection of disarmament proposals based on international inspection and control and in their violent objections to American efforts in behalf of the oppressed millions behind the Iron Curtain.

Both of these latter issues were represented once again on the Assembly's current agenda; but their discussion during March revealed as little change in the general Soviet attitude as had the course of other debates such as those on collective security [16] or on the repatriation of the Greek soldiers detained in Communist countries since the end of the Greek civil war in 1949.[17] During the debate on the disarmament item, Ernest A. Gross of the United States recalled Malenkov's recent declarations and asked the Soviet representatives point-blank whether their government was willing to discuss

15 Statement in plenary session, March 11, in *Department of State Bulletin*, XXVIII, March 23, 1953, 446.

16 By Resolution 703 (VII) of March 17 (*Documents on American Foreign Relations, 1953*, 420) the Assembly requested the Collective Measures Committee to continue its studies directed toward strengthening the collective security potential of the U.N. in line with the "Uniting for Peace" resolution of 1950. The vote was 50 in favor, 5 opposed (Soviet bloc), and 3 abstentions.

17 Resolution 702 (VII), adopted March 17 by a vote of 54-5 (Soviet bloc)-0, appealed to the detaining governments to release those who wished to go home and provided for consultations to this end. For details and text cf. Harry N. Howard, "Greek Questions in the Seventh Session of the General Assembly, Part II," *Department of State Bulletin*, XXIX, August 31, 1953, 293-298.

disarmament "constructively" in the United Nations and thus "give tangible form . . . to what the Soviet rulers claim is their 'tried and tested policy of peace'." [18] Other delegates expressed the keenest interest in the Soviet reply, but could only concur in Mr. Gross's later comment that he found nothing in the statements of the Communist representatives which would "reveal any true purpose toward reaching a solution" of the problem.[19]

The matter of alleged American support of espionage and subversive activities behind the Iron Curtain had become a major diplomatic issue as early as 1951, when the Communist governments had staged a spectacular demonstration against a provision of that year's Mutual Security Act in which the sum of $100 million was somewhat ambiguously set aside for expenditure on selected persons who were "residing in or escapees from" the U.S.S.R. or Communist-dominated countries.[20] Continuing objections by the Communist governments to the American interest in such persons had lately involved the State Department in lengthy controversies with the U.S.S.R. and Hungary,[21] with Poland,[22] and with Czecho-

[18] Statement in the First (Political and Security) Committee, March 18, *ibid.*, XXVIII, March 30, 1953, 476.

[19] Statement of March 21, *ibid.*, April 6, 1953, 503. By Resolution 740 (VII), adopted April 8 by a vote of 52-5 (Soviet bloc)-3, the Assembly requested the Disarmament Commission to continue its effort to develop disarmament plans embracing both atomic and conventional weapons—the whole program "to be carried out under effective international control in such a way that no State would have cause to fear that its security was endangered." (Text in *Department of State Bulletin*, XXVIII, April 20, 1953, 584). The First Committee rejected on March 21 a Soviet draft resolution (U.N. Document A/C.1/L.31, March 19, 1953) repeating the standard Soviet demand for a one-third reduction in conventional armaments and a prohibition of weapons of mass destruction, and censuring the Western powers for their alleged attempts to divert the Disarmament Commission from the question of armaments reduction to "that of illegally obtaining intelligence reports on the armaments of individual states."

[20] *The United States in World Affairs, 1951,* 396-401.

[21] Since December 1952 the U.S. had been engaged in diplomatic correspondence with Hungary and the U.S.S.R. in an endeavor to recover possession of a military aircraft forced down in Hungarian territory on November 19, 1951 after allegedly violating the Rumanian and Hungarian frontiers for the purpose of dropping "spies and saboteurs." Formal damage claims in the amount of $637,894.15 were preferred against the two governments on March 17, 1953; these claims having been rejected, the U.S. on February 16, 1954 took the case to the International Court of Justice. Cf. *ibid.*, 398-401; *Department of State*

slovakia,[23] whose government was now asking the Assembly to condemn the Mutual Security Act and recommend abrogation of the section concerned with Iron Curtain fugitives. The Czechoslovak charges were ridiculed by Mr. Lodge, who explained that 95.7 percent of the fund in question was actually being spent for "regular military and economic aid," while the balance of $4,300,000 had been set aside to assist in providing escapees with reception and living quarters and other necessities while awaiting the opportunity to emigrate.[24] The Czechoslovak proposal was decisively rejected by the Political Committee (March 26) and, in due course, by the full Assembly (April 8); but the discussion did nothing to mitigate the mutual antagonism habitually displayed by spokesmen of the respective camps.

Equally unpromising was the debate which began on March 27 on a United States proposal, co-sponsored by sixteen governments, calling for an impartial investigation of Communist charges concerning the alleged use of bacteriological warfare by the United Nations command in Korea. These accusations, which despite authoritative denials had provided one of the main themes of Communist "hate" propaganda through most of 1952, had been revived by the

---

Bulletin, XXVII, December 22, 1952, 980-984; XXVIII, January 12, 1953, 51-52; February 16, 1953, 257-259; April 6, 1953, 496-498; XXX, March 22, 1954, 449-451. No judgment could be obtained because the respondents failed to accept the Court's jurisdiction. *Ibid.,* XXXI, July 26, 1954, 130-131.

[22] On January 16, 1953 Poland protested in a 19-page note against various alleged anti-Polish acts by the U.S., including a "brutal violation" of Polish territory by an American military aircraft on November 4, 1952 and the "organizing of aggressive intelligence and subversion on Polish territory." The U.S. denied the allegations in a note of February 9, printed *ibid.,* XXVIII, February 23, 1953, 304-305.

[23] Czechoslovakia in a note of January 30 complained of various acts of alleged espionage and subversion supposedly carried out by U.S. agents financed by the Mutual Security Act. The U.S. rejected the charges in a note of March 4. See the Czechoslovak note in *Department of State Bulletin,* XXVIII, March 16, 1953, 410-411, and the U.S. reply *ibid.,* 409-410 and in *Documents on American Foreign Relations, 1953,* 179-180. In a related move, the U.S. in a note to Rumania on February 20 refuted charges of espionage and sabotage brought against certain former Rumanian employees of American oil companies in a "show trial" held at Ploesti, Rumania between February 9 and 12. See *Department of State Bulletin,* XXVIII, March 2, 1953, 333-335.

[24] Statement in the First Committee, March 23, in *Department of State Bulletin,* XXVIII, April 13, 1953, 539-541.

Communists in February 1953 and were accompanied by new "evidence" in the form of sworn statements by two captured American officers who were supposed to have admitted receiving special training as a preliminary to participation in bacteriological warfare missions. To those familiar with Communist "brainwashing" techniques it seemed obvious that these false confessions had been extracted through the same kind of "impermissible" methods whose use against Soviet citizens the new Soviet rulers were now beginning to decry.[25] As the best means of convincing world opinion of the falsity of the charges, the United States had renewed its demand for an impartial investigation under international auspices. But the Communist authorities had invariably refused to cooperate in such an investigation, and they evinced undiminished hostility to the resolution now before the Assembly. Although fifty-one delegates eventually joined in requesting "all the governments and authorities concerned" to cooperate with a five-power investigating group to be set up on behalf of the Assembly,[26] few of them can have expected their action to yield practical results.

Thus, almost a fortnight after Malenkov's statement to the Supreme Soviet, there had been no sign whatever of a change in Soviet aims or attitudes, Mr. Vyshinsky had returned from a quick trip to Moscow with nothing that could be made to look like a concession or even a novel tactic. The Security Council had devoted fruitless meetings to the search for a new Secretary-General to replace Mr. Lie, only to find itself as hopelessly deadlocked as when it had last tried to deal with the issue in 1950.[27] Secretary Dulles had reported that the State Department drew no great comfort from the speeches of

[25] Cf. Allen W. Dulles, "Brain Warfare: Russia's Secret Weapon," *U.S. News and World Report,* XXXIV, No. 19, May 8, 1953, 58; also the denial issued by Gen. Mark W. Clark, February 24, in *Department of State Bulletin,* XXVIII, March 23, 1953, 451; and the statement of Mr. Gross in the First Committee, March 27, *ibid.,* April 27, 1953, 612-616.

[26] Resolution 706 (VII), April 23, in *Documents on American Foreign Relations, 1953,* 436-437. The investigating commission was not set up because the Communist governments failed to signify acceptance of the investigation. Cf. further below, pp. 404-405.

[27] Cf. *The United States in World Affairs, 1950,* 372-373. The Security Council's deliberations are briefly summarized in *International Organization,* VII, May 1953, 256-257.

Soviet leaders, and that no overtures had been received through diplomatic channels.[28] In Korea, the Chinese Communists had captured the position known as "Old Baldy" in the course of their strongest attack in five months.

The Tune Changes

Then, all at once, the log jam began to break—first in the Far East, then at the United Nations. The North Korean and Chinese Communist military commanders, replying on March 28 to a weeks-old communication from the United Nations command, unexpectedly signified their agreement to an exchange of sick and wounded prisoners of war and suggested a resumption of the formal armistice negotiations at Panmunjom. Chou En-lai, the Chinese Communist Premier and Foreign Minister, declared two days later that Communist China and North Korea, "in order to satisfy the desire of the people of the world for peace," were prepared "to take steps to eliminate the differences" on the sole remaining obstacle to conclusion of a full armistice, the question of repatriation of healthy prisoners of war. With this welcome announcement went a practical suggestion which pointed the way to the solution eventually reached.[29] That this was more than a casual propaganda gesture became evident with its immediate endorsement by Foreign Minister Molotov, who stated on April 1 that the Soviet Government fully supported "this noble act," had no doubt that it would "find ardent support among peoples throughout the world," and was confident that it would "be correctly understood" by the United States Government. Molotov added the characteristic comment that the United Nations could, "naturally," do more toward a Korean armistice if the Chinese and Korean peoples were admitted to "lawful representation" in the world body.[30]

In the meantime the problem of a successor to Secretary-General Lie had unexpectedly been solved. When the Security Council held its third closed meeting of the month

[28] Statement of March 20, in *Department of State Bulletin,* XXVIII, March 30, 1953, 467.

[29] *Ibid.,* XXVIII, April 6, 1953, 494-495 and April 13, 1953, 526-527; Mark W. Clark, *From the Danube to the Yalu* (New York, Harper, 1954), 240-244. For details cf. below, pp. 219-220.

[30] *Department of State Bulletin,* XXVIII, April 13, 1953, 528-529.

on March 31, the representative of France proposed the name of Dag Hammarskjold, Swedish Minister of State, who had briefly headed his country's delegation to the General Assembly. The Soviet representative, who had already vetoed or rejected Lester B. Pearson of Canada, Carlos P. Romulo of the Philippines (the preferred candidate of the United States), Luis Padilla Nervo of Mexico, and Nasrollah Entezam of Iran, indicated that Mr. Hammarskjold would be acceptable to his government. There being no strong objection from other quarters, the Security Council decided by a vote of ten to nothing, with the abstention of Nationalist China, to recommend the choice of Mr. Hammarskjold. This recommendation the Assembly gratefully followed on April 7, electing Mr. Hammarskjold for a five-year term as Secretary-General by a vote of 57 to 1, with one abstention. Again Nationalist China represented practically the only opposition, presumably because Sweden had recognized the Communist Chinese government.

Other conciliatory-looking gestures from the Soviet camp were now coming thick and fast. At the end of March, British and Soviet officers in Germany met on Soviet initiative to consider improved safety measures which might obviate further tragedies like that of the bomber shot down on March 12; this led to the resumption on April 7 of four-power contact on at least one phase of the German problem. At the United Nations, Soviet comments took on a noticeably milder tone. In the disarmament discussion, Mr. Vyshinsky continued to oppose the Western concept but refrained from formally repeating the stock Soviet demand for prohibition of the atomic bomb and a one-third armaments cut. "Life goes forward," he said. "Life changes relations, relations change with events"; and he urged the West to respond to Soviet overtures in kind and "begin to dig the tunnel of friendship from both ends." [31] During the next fortnight the Communist delegations went so far as to make possible the unanimous approval of two political resolutions relating

[31] U.N. General Assembly, *Official Records, Seventh Session, Plenary Meetings* (U.N. Document A/PV.424, April 8, 1953), 691. In committee debate on a related Polish resolution, Vyshinsky continued to reassert the traditional Soviet position on disarmament.

to the Far East, one of which suspended consideration of the Korean problem until the conclusion of an armistice or "other developments" required the Assembly's attention [32] while the other called for the evacuation or internment of some 12,000 fugitive Chinese Nationalist troops in Burma whose depredations and lawless conduct had been causing concern in that country.[33]

3. MEETING AT THE TOP?

What was the true significance of these and other Soviet gestures which soon became too numerous to be recorded individually? To some, they added up to an impressive demonstration of Soviet good will which, if properly received, could lead to a solution of larger issues. Others pointed out that many of the Soviet "concessions" represented no more than the correction of gross breaches of normal international usage. Such gestures as the permission accorded several Russian women who had married Americans to leave the Soviet Union cost practically nothing and could hardly be interpreted as indicating a major policy reversal. A more significant test would be the progress of armistice negotiations at Panmunjom; but even the conclusion of a Korean armistice might be ascribed to special factors which would leave the question of general Soviet intentions unanswered. Yet obviously this was a question of the most vital significance to the entire non-Communist world, whose collective life had for so long been dominated by the specter of Soviet ambitions. If the new Soviet leaders were really prepared to leave the free world in peace, or even to relax for a time the expansionist pressure that had been maintained through Stalin's later years, humanity might look forward to an era of much-needed tranquility and fruitful labor. If, on the other hand, the Soviet overtures were merely a disguise or a Machiavellian device to disarm the suspicions of antagonists, those who took them seriously might be walking into a trap of colossal dimensions.

[32] Resolution 705 (VII), April 18, in *Documents on American Foreign Relations, 1953*, 431-432.

[33] Resolution 707 (VII), April 23, 1953, adopted by a vote of 59-0-1 (China). For details cf. below, pp. 280-281.

The Problem of Interpretation

Hardly less significant than the true aim of the Soviet leaders was the reaction their behavior might evoke in the United States. As the strongest and most influential member of the non-Communist bloc, this country was likely to exercise a powerful influence not only on the attitude of allied countries but perhaps on that of the Soviet Government itself. A great deal would hinge, therefore, on the correctness with which the Soviet moves were appraised in Washington. One error that American statesmen seemed unlikely to make was that of overestimating the significance of the Soviet gestures and abandoning the attitude of caution ingrained by years of bitter experience. But it was also possible to fall into the opposite error of *under*valuing the Soviet moves and thus forfeiting what might be a chance for real improvement in the international situation. If the United States was sufficiently impressed by the Soviet demonstrations to attempt a really serious exploration of the possibilities for better East-West relations, there might develop—assuming that the Russians were prompted by similar aims—a considerable relaxation of the rigidities which had characterized international affairs in recent years. Such a development might have advantages for all concerned. If, on the other hand, this country should appear indifferent to such possibilities it was unlikely that the Soviet overtures, sincere or not, would produce beneficial results. More probably they would have the effect of accentuating the differences already existing between this country and its allies on broad questions of East-West policy.[34]

President Eisenhower seemed conscious of this broader responsibility when he told the press on April 2 that while not ignoring the frustrations of the past, he believed we should take at face value every offer that was made to us until it was proved unworthy of confidence. The United States, he said, stood ready to meet any honest advance.[35] Mr. Dulles, who felt that the administration's "vigorous, positive policies" were now beginning to bear fruit, warned that nothing had oc-

[34] Cf. the analysis of Ridgway B. Knight, Deputy Director of the State Department's Office of Western European Affairs, May 7, in *Department of State Bulletin,* XXVIII, June 1, 1953, 773-774.

[35] *New York Times,* April 3, 1953.

curred to change "the basic situation of danger in which we stand"; but this, he said, did not prevent "accommodations from time to time which may be useful," and he mentioned Korea and Austria as typifying "a whole series of outstanding questions which can be a matter of accommodation." [36] In the meantime, as President Eisenhower and Chancellor Adenauer agreed on April 9, "the free nations of the West must not relax their vigilance nor diminish their efforts to increase their unity and common strength." [37]

Those who sought to gauge the likelihood of a genuine new departure in East-West relations were aware of various fundamental difficulties, irrespective of the real intentions of the Soviet leaders. Most serious, perhaps, was the deep and perhaps invincible distrust which had developed between the two camps and would continue to condition the attitude of the Russians as well as the West. Complete lack of faith in each other's intentions would make a real meeting of minds almost impossible even if both parties genuinely desired it—which was as yet by no means certain. How, in practice, was the sincerity of the Soviet leaders' desire for peace to be established? They could hardly be expected to come hat in hand to the West, apologizing for past faults and offering to surrender all the advantages the Soviet Union had gained in Stalin's time. Possibly they *would* find it convenient to settle a few outstanding issues like Korea and Austria; but would even this constitute an adequate proof of future good intentions? Hostility to the "imperialist" West was of the very essence of the Soviet system. Was this hostility now going to be abandoned? And if not, was there any point in striving for partial agreements which would leave the basic antagonism undiminished?

Perhaps there was. Even if a fundamental transformation of the Soviet outlook was unlikely, there might be advantages in fostering an improvement in East-West relations through "accommodations" of the type mentioned by Secretary Dulles. Such settlements could at least be expected to benefit the people immediately concerned. But here a further difficulty

36 Press conference statement, April 3, in *Department of State Bulletin*, XXVIII, April 13, 1953, 524-525.

37 *Documents on American Foreign Relations, 1953*, 279; cf. above, pp. 36-37.

arose. "Accommodation" in diplomacy is usually obtained through mutual concessions by both sides; whereas in the special situation now existing, most of the concessions would necessarily have to come from the Soviet side alone. There were plenty of areas in which the Western powers and their friends would have welcomed concessions by the U.S.S.R., but very few in which they would have felt able to make comparable concessions themselves. Their present policies were a direct reflection of what had seemed the radical and unlimited hostility of the Soviet Union to democratic or "capitalist" government and society. To modify those policies in any significant degree might fatally endanger the democratic cause.

Yet was there any valid reason to expect that the Soviet Government would be willing to make all the concessions while allowing the West to reap all the benefits? All governments are reluctant to surrender their advantages unilaterally. For the Soviet Government, which was at least as suspicious of the West as the West was of it, such surrenders would be peculiarly difficult. Unless the Soviet Union was crippled by internal weaknesses which had remained hidden from the West, it seemed unlikely that its leaders would consider any large-scale retreat from positions they now held. At most they might settle for some kind of "stand-still" agreement whereby both parties would undertake to rest on their present lines.

For the United States, there were special difficulties which lay primarily in the moral and psychological rather than in the strictly political realm. No country was more skeptical than the United States of Soviet intentions, or more apprehensive of being inveigled into some act of "appeasement." No country, moreover, had been so outspoken in condemning Communist domination of non-Soviet peoples, or had gone so clearly on record as refusing to acquiesce in such "enslavement." Although domestic political factors had intervened to prevent the formal adoption of the "Captive Peoples" Resolution, American leaders had declared again and again that we would never "break faith with our friends" or lend ourselves to "any international 'deal' or 'trade' confirming the rule of Soviet despotism over the alien peoples it dominates in Europe and Asia." [38] This did not mean, apparently, that

[38] Statement by Secretary Dulles, February 26, *ibid.*, 190.

we intended to try to liberate these captive peoples by force, even though we meant to do our best to keep their hope of liberation alive. To most Americans it did mean that we would consider no action—even in relation to such a matter as representation in the United Nations—which could be construed as approving the Communist rule over any peoples who had been our friends. Yet this attitude, however high-minded, was an undeniable obstacle to negotiations with the other camp. If the Communists were to make concessions in the interest of abating the tension, they would presumably want at least some assurance that they need not worry about the security of their own possessions. Yet how could such an assurance be given by a country which remained so enthusiastically committed to the "liberation" doctrine? [39]

The President Speaks

These limitations on the Western negotiating position came out rather clearly in the important foreign policy address which President Eisenhower delivered before the American Society of Newspaper Editors on April 16.[40] What he said, in effect, was that the United States would welcome a reversal of Soviet policies but intended to pursue its own policies unchanged. In humanity's present tragic situation, the free nations would "welcome sincerely any genuine evidence of peaceful purpose enabling all peoples again to resume their common quest of a just peace." "We welcome every honest act of peace. We care nothing for mere rhetoric. We are only for sincerity of peaceful purpose attested by deeds." Even a few "clear and specific acts," said the President—such as the signature of an Austrian treaty, or the release of thousands of prisoners still held from World War II—would be "impressive signs of sincere intent."

But this, Mr. Eisenhower went on to suggest, would be only a beginning. The real test of Soviet intentions was set

[39] Secretary Dulles remarked in a speech in Chicago on November 29, 1954: "Our policies do not exclude international conferences, even with those who are hostile to us. . . . *The scope of conferences with the Soviet Government is necessarily limited by our attitude toward the captive peoples,* for the Soviets know that we will not make any deal which would condone and perpetuate the captivity of men and nations." (Emphasis supplied.)

[40] *Documents on American Foreign Relations, 1953,* 27-34.

out in three questions relating respectively to peace in Asia, freedom for captive peoples, and disarmament:

"Is the new leadership of the Soviet Union prepared to use its decisive influence in the Communist world, including control of the flow of arms, to bring not merely an expedient truce in Korea but genuine peace in Asia?

"Is it prepared to allow other nations, including those of Eastern Europe, the free choice of their own forms of government?

"Is it prepared to act in concert with others upon serious disarmament proposals to be made firmly effective by stringent U.N. control and inspection?

"If not, where then is the concrete evidence of the Soviet Union's concern for peace?"

To students of Soviet politics it was evident that a satisfactory response to these questions would have implied a revolutionary change in the Soviet concept of international affairs. A Communist government which was willing to renounce its dominion over Eastern Europe and submit its military arrangements to international control might easily have found it possible to accept still other elements of the President's program, which included (1) "immediate" cessation of hostilities in Korea and "prompt initiation of political discussions leading to . . . free elections in a united Korea"; (2) "an end to the direct and indirect attacks upon the security of Indochina and Malaya"; (3) speedy conclusion of an Austrian treaty "which will free that country from economic exploitation and from occupation by foreign troops"; (4) extension of the existing unity of Western Europe to embrace a "broader European community" (including "a free and united Germany, with a government based upon free and secret elections," and buttressed by "the full independence of the East European nations"); and (5) limitation of both conventional and atomic armaments.[41] Such a government might even have accepted the President's contention that "the defense of West-

[41] The President's specific disarmament proposals, which generally paralleled the position adopted by the Western powers in the U.N. Disarmament Commission, were unanimously endorsed by the Senate in S. Res. 150, 83d Congress, adopted July 29. Text and comment appear in *Department of State Bulletin*, XXIX, August 31, 1953, 299-300.

ern Europe imperatively demands the unity of purpose and action made possible by the North Atlantic Treaty Organization, embracing a European Defense Community"—which, moreover, must include Western Germany.

A Communist government which could accept such stipulations as these would have had little if any objection to the final phase of the President's program: "the dedication of the energies, the resources, and the imaginations of all peaceful nations to a new kind of war . . . not upon any human enemy but upon the brute forces of poverty and need." It might even have seconded the pledge with which the President climaxed his speech, in language reminiscent of President Truman's address to the United Nations General Assembly in 1950:[42]

"This Government is ready to ask its people to join with all other nations in devoting a substantial percentage of the savings achieved by disarmament to a fund for world aid and reconstruction. The purposes of this great work would be to help other peoples to develop the underdeveloped areas of the world, to stimulate profitable and fair world trade, to assist all peoples to know the blessings of productive freedom."

Unfortunately, the government headed by Mr. Malenkov was not of this accommodating mind, and its reaction eliminated any prospect that world conditions would admit of an early congressional appropriation for special "world aid and reconstruction." Although the President's speech was widely acclaimed in the free world (Mr. Churchill called it "a massive and magnificent statement of our case," and even Mr. Attlee termed it a "great" speech), and although the Soviet authorities thought it important enough to reprint in full in *Pravda* and *Izvestia* of April 25, it did not provide a basis for the kind of negotiations that might have interested the Soviet leadership. Accompanying the publication in the Soviet press was a lengthy commentary[43] professing sympathy with the idea of peaceful settlement but strongly objecting to both the manner and the content of the President's proposals. Mr. Eisenhower, it said, "deemed it possible for some reason to

[42] Cf. *The United States in World Affairs, 1950,* 368.

[43] *Current Digest of the Soviet Press,* V, No. 14, May 16, 1953, 5-8.

link his proposals for peace with a whole series of preliminary conditions imposed by him on the Soviet Union, although these claims in his speech were not strengthened by corresponding obligations on the part of the U.S.A." The Soviet Union, it said, had always been ready for friendly discussion and settlement of "immediate international questions." But this was true only on the condition "that proposals for their settlement . . . are to some extent acceptable and do not run counter either to the fundamental interests of the Soviet people or the interests of other peace-loving peoples."

Through detailed analysis of the President's proposals, in language moderate in tone but uncompromising in substance, the statement made clear that few of them met the Soviet test of acceptability even if they could be reconciled with the President's own professed desire for peace. "The appeals for peace in the President's speech will of course, receive our due support. . . . Soviet leaders feel that proposals truly aimed at peace can serve as a basis for improving international relations. This, however, does not mean that Soviet leaders are ready to accept new versions of old methods as such proposals." The President had said nothing about "the [Communist] Chinese People's Republic, the restoration of China's national rights in the United Nations, or of its legal territorial rights, including the island of Taiwan [Formosa]. Does not this question relate to the urgent international problems of our times?" And how was the President's address to be harmonized with a speech which Mr. Dulles had made to the same audience on April 18, in which the authors of the Soviet statement professed to find a "belligerence" quite at variance with the President's more pacific utterances?[44]

Although President Eisenhower was quoted by his intimates as feeling that the "milder tone" of the Soviet statement might be "a first step toward something concrete," [45] it seemed more likely that it closed the door on concrete developments of a favorable nature. The President had made clear in his speech that the United States, while eager to grasp at

[44] Secretary Dulles' speech, a review of foreign policy developments during the first ninety days of the Eisenhower administration, is printed in *Department of State Bulletin,* XXVIII, April 27, 1953, 603-608; cf. below, p. 247.
[45] White House statement, April 25, *ibid.,* May 11, 1953, 678.

realistic prospects for improvement, had not altered its fundamental views and aims in international affairs. The Soviet leaders had now made clear that their views and aims in essential matters were equally unchanged. There would be no lack of further Soviet moves,[46] speculations about Soviet intentions, and proposals for capitalizing on the peaceful aspirations proclaimed by both sides. The fundamental question, however, had already been answered for those who had eyes to read. The change in Soviet demeanor did *not* betoken either an abandonment of traditional Soviet objectives or a readiness to yield power positions which were still tightly under Soviet control. At most it was a tactical shift designed to procure a breathing space and, perhaps, to promote Soviet interests by encouraging false hopes, relaxation, and division in the free world.

This interpretation of Soviet moves did not preclude the possibility that international tension would continue to abate, nor did it prevent the Western powers from making advantageous use of the opportunities provided by a relaxation of the "cold war." It did confront them with the danger that if they relaxed their strength or allowed their solidarity to be impaired, they might be playing into the hands of an adversary whose basic hostility remained as implacable as ever.

The Prime Minister's Proposals

Notwithstanding the well-founded skepticism of most responsible Western statesmen, the feeling was widespread among the Western peoples and their governments that it would be a grave mistake to foreclose the possibility of useful contacts with the Soviet leaders. At least one of the Communist "moves and gestures" had, after all, possessed real practical import; the exchange of sick and wounded prisoners in Korea had begun on schedule, and formal armistice negotiations were to resume on April 26th. True, there had also been the invasion of Laos by the Vietminh, maintained in flagrant disregard of the President's appeal for peace in the

[46] One such move was a repetition by Molotov of the familiar Soviet demand for a "peace pact" of the Big Four and Communist China, which was conveyed in a message of April 28 to the Communist-controlled "Congress of the Peoples for Peace." The State Department reaction appears *ibid.*, May 18, 1954, 714.

Far East.[47] But this might prove to be a purely local affair. No one, as Mr. Churchill pointed out to the House of Commons on April 20, could yet measure "the extent or purpose of the change which has become apparent in the Soviet mood or even perhaps in their policy." "No single hope, however slender, should be cast away," the Prime Minister insisted; and he went on to express the daring hope that "the processes of good will which may be at work . . . may presently lead to conversations on the highest level, even if informal and private, between some of the principal Powers concerned." [48]

This idea of a high-level meeting was developed more fully by the Prime Minister—now Sir Winston Churchill—in a major speech in the House of Commons on May 11.[49] Two additional thoughts distinguished this important presentation, which took into account both the President's address of April 16 and the more recent Soviet comments upon it. First, Sir Winston suggested, in a situation of this kind it would be a mistake to lay down too many conditions in advance, "to assume that nothing can be settled . . . unless or until everything is settled." Even one or two achievements, such as a peace in Korea and an Austrian treaty, "might lead to an easement in our relations for the next few years, which might in itself open new prospects to the security and prosperity of all nations and every continent." Above all, he said, "it would be a pity if the natural desire to reach a general settlement of international policy were to impede any spontaneous and healthy evolution which may be taking place inside Russia" —if statements by the NATO powers should "supersede or take the emphasis out of what may be a profound movement of Russian feeling."

Second, the Prime Minister offered the bold suggestion that the Russians, like the Western peoples, might feel some concern about their own security, and that this should be taken into account in Western planning. "I do not believe," he said, "that the immense problem of reconciling the security of Russia with the freedom and safety of Western Europe

[47] Cf. above, p. 66.

[48] *Parliamentary Debates, Weekly Hansard,* House of Commons, April 20, 1953, 649-650.

[49] *Ibid.,* May 11, 1953, 887-902; excerpts in *Documents on American Foreign Relations, 1953,* 244-247.

is insoluble." To indicate one possible approach, he recalled the Locarno Treaty of 1925, under which Great Britain (and Italy) had promised to defend the frontier separating Germany from France and Belgium against aggression from either side. "The master thought which animated Locarno," Sir Winston seemed to suggest, might be adapted to the new situation that was now emerging in Central Europe, thus relieving Russia's fear of Germany as well as Germany's fear of Russia. It must be added that this reference to Locarno proved somewhat puzzling and even disturbing to Sir Winston's hearers and thus served to divert attention from what was apparently his main idea, the need to take Russian security interests into account.

Finally, Sir Winston repeated his proposal for a high-level conference:

"I must make it plain that, in spite of all the uncertainties and confusion in which world affairs are plunged, I believe that a conference on the highest level should take place between the leading Powers without long delay. This conference should not be overhung by a ponderous or rigid agenda, or led into mazes and jungles of technical details, zealously contested by hoards [*sic*] of experts and officials drawn up in vast, cumbrous array. The conference should be confined to the smallest number of Powers and persons possible. It should meet with a measure of informality and a still greater measure of privacy and seclusion. It might well be that no hard-faced agreements would be reached, but there might be a general feeling among those gathered together that they might do something better than tear the human race, including themselves, into bits."

Disagreement in the West

If one of the objectives of recent Soviet moves had been to cause divisions in the West, the effort was already beginning to bear fruit. Although Sir Winston warned earnestly at the conclusion of his speech that "this would be the most fatal moment for the free nations to relax their comradeship and preparations," the speech itself set forth a philosophy widely different from that prevailing in Washington. The warning against an "all-or-nothing" type of approach inevitably recalled the carefully formulated and comprehensive program set forth in the presidential address; the reference to Locarno reawakened old suspicions of British diplomatic perfidy and seemed, moreover, to rule out any idea of liberating the captive peoples; while the demand for a face-to-face meeting with the Russians ran directly counter to a well-established American preference for avoiding further encounters of a type that had yielded such unsatisfactory results at Tehran, Yalta, and Potsdam. In recent years the Truman administration had resolutely set its face against such proposals, even when its opposition made it possible to question the sincerity of this country's devotion to peace. The Eisenhower administration, for all its emphasis on "dynamic" diplomacy, had shown no greater eagerness to grapple with the Russians at close quarters at a time when it had no concessions to make and no prospect of extracting concessions from the adversary.

One of the unintended sequels to the Churchill speech was the violent exchange between Mr. Attlee and Senator McCarthy which was described in the preceding chapter.[50] But even on the executive side of the American government, the reaction to current British thinking was hardly enthusiastic. The State Department recalled that President Eisenhower had already stressed his willingness "to meet the other side halfway when and if there is concrete evidence that such a meeting would produce positive results." The President himself pointed out on May 14 that the heads of state were very busy men. Though he personally was ready to do anything, he believed the dignity and self-respect of the United States demanded that we have some reasonable indication that progress could be made. He had no objection to Sir Winston's proposal; but he would like, before committing this government, something that would be evidence of good faith all round.[51] The most the United States would agree to at the moment, therefore, was a French suggestion for a preliminary high-level meeting *without* the Russians. Plans for an informal get-together of American, British, and French leaders, aimed at developing "common viewpoints . . . on the many problems that must be solved cooperatively so that the cause of world peace may be advanced," were revealed on May 21

[50] Above, pp. 68-69.

[51] *Department of State Bulletin,* XXVIII, May 25, 1953, 748.

and the meeting was scheduled to take place in Bermuda in the course of June.[52]

From the standpoint of predominant European opinion, this expedient would make sense only if it laid the groundwork for a later four-power meeting. In Europe, reaction to the Prime Minister's proposals had been much more positive than in the United States. Profiting by this incipient division, *Pravda* returned to the attack on May 24 with a long, illuminating, and for the most part cordial appraisal of the Churchill speech. While observing that some of the Prime Minister's ideas—notably the attempt to revive Locarno, which Russians traditionally regarded as an attempt to turn German expansionism eastward—would meet with "criticism and serious objections" on the part of Soviet public opinion, the party organ called the idea of a top-level meeting "timely" and "important" and noted that Churchill, "unlike certain other statesmen of the West," did not "tie his proposal . . . to any preliminary obligations for one or the other side." *Pravda* showed no enthusiasm for the proposed Bermuda meeting, to which the Russians were not invited and which they accordingly viewed as a retreat from the spirit of Churchill's offer. However, the article concluded:

> "The Soviet Union is always ready to consider with complete seriousness and conscientiousness any proposals directed to ensuring peace and the broadest possible economic and cultural relations among states." [53]

Diplomatic Developments

Whether aimed at real improvement of the international atmosphere (for Soviet purposes) or only at dividing the West, Soviet activities during this period were not confined to rhetoric; there was also going forward a continuous display of "deeds" by the Soviet and satellite governments which made a considerable impression in the aggregate even if they were of limited significance in detail. One of the most noteworthy was Czechoslovakia's release on May 16 of William N. Oatis,

[52] *Ibid.*, June 1, 1953, 778; "La Conférence de Washington," *Chronique de politique étrangère*, VI, September 1953, 595-596. Cf. below, p. 175.

[53] *Pravda*, May 24; *Current Digest of the Soviet Press*, V, No. 18, June 13, 1953, 9.

the Associated Press correspondent who had been imprisoned in 1951 following an enforced confession of so-called "espionage" activities.[54] In a wider field, the Soviet Government appeared to renounce at least one of the aggressive aims of Stalinism when it informed Turkey that it was withdrawing the claims to Turkish territory put forward in 1945 as well as its demand for bases in the neighborhood of the Turkish Straits.[55] These claims had been among the first unmistakable evidences of the postwar expansionist policies of the Soviet Union; thus their nominal withdrawal (publicly repeated on July 19) could hardly fail to encourage the hope that these expansionist ambitions had waned.

But the acid test of Soviet intentions, as American authorities from President Eisenhower down had frequently declared, lay in Korea and Austria. In Korea, apparently, the Chinese and North Korean Communists were genuinely desirous of a truce; a succession of minor crises failed to mask the progress that was being made toward substantial agreement between the United Nations and Communist commands.[56] Austria, however, was another matter. Here the U.S.S.R. was being asked not to renounce objectives that were beyond its reach in any case, but to surrender solid advantages that it now held. Signature of the Austrian State Treaty, virtually completed in draft form as long ago as 1949, would obligate the Soviet Union to withdraw its occupation forces from Austria, renounce its right to maintain line-of-communication troops in Hungary and Rumania (a matter of legal rather than practical significance), relinquish its control of important economic assets in eastern Austria, and permit the reintegration of this strategically situated and democratically minded little country into the Western camp, politically and economically if not militarily. For years, the Russians had been dodg-

[54] *The United States in World Affairs, 1951*, 131; cf. *Department of State Bulletin*, XXVIII, June 1, 1953, 785. Shortly thereafter the U.S. withdrew the ban on private travel to Czechoslovakia which it had imposed soon after Oatis' arrest. Two months later Hungary moved to correct a comparable injustice by releasing Edgar Sanders, a British businessman imprisoned since 1949; cf. *The United States in World Affairs, 1949*, 273 n.

[55] Soviet statement, May 30, in *Documents on American Foreign Relations, 1953*, 165-166; for background cf. *The United States in World Affairs, 1945–1947*, 149-151.

[56] Cf. below, pp. 217-232.

ing this prospect on one specious pretext after another, despite continuous prodding by the Western powers, the United Nations General Assembly, and Austria itself;[57] and it now appeared that the course of Soviet procrastination was to be still further drawn out.

Two meetings of the Austrian Treaty Deputies (representing the United States, Great Britain, France, and the U.S.S.R.) had taken place in London as recently as February 6 and 9, 1953, but had produced no result since the Soviet deputy had refused to begin discussions until the West had formally withdrawn a proposal advanced the year before to scrap the existing treaty text and substitute an abbreviated treaty which sidestepped most of the issues still in dispute but also deprived the U.S.S.R. of certain material advantages.[58] Since then the issue had lain dormant; but on May 11 the Soviet Ambassador in London (Yakov A. Malik), who served as Soviet representative at meetings of the Big Four deputies, was invited on Western initiative to attend a session of the group in London on May 27. This would be the 261st such meeting since the deputies undertook their assignment in 1947. Mr. Malik delayed his reply until two days before the meeting; then he put forward the unlooked-for and unwarranted assertions that (a) the deputies possessed no independent authority to hold meetings, (b) there was no reason to suppose a meeting now would produce better results than in the past, and (c) it would be "more expedient" to exchange views on the Austrian question through diplomatic channels.[59]

This seemed the most transparent evasion yet; apparently the Kremlin had run out of more plausible pretexts. Yet if the Western powers wanted a treaty and Mr. Malik would not attend meetings, there was no alternative but to accept the Soviet proposal to explore the matter "through diplomatic channels." After all, as the three Western govern-

[57] Cf. "Review of the Austrian Treaty Question," *Department of State Bulletin,* XXVIII, June 8, 1953, 805-814.

[58] The relevant correspondence appears in *Documents on American Foreign Relations, 1953,* 230-234 and (with explanatory comments) in *Department of State Bulletin,* XXVIII, January 26, 1953, 135; February 16, 1953, 259-261; February 23, 1953, 305. For text of the proposed abbreviated treaty, dated March 13, 1952, see *Documents on American Foreign Relations, 1952,* 263-266.

[59] *Ibid., 1953,* 234-235.

ments pointed out in notes to the Kremlin on June 11, the conclusion of an Austrian treaty was "not a question of procedure but of good will." They themselves were "prepared to accept any treaty which would ensure Austria's political and economic independence." Since the Soviet Government had refused to sign any of the drafts evolved thus far, they now asked it to specify "the exact text" which it would be prepared to sign. But no answer to this communication was received until July 30; and when it came, it merely repeated the demand that the Western powers formally withdraw their proposed abbreviated treaty before discussion was resumed.[60]

Refusal to negotiate on the simplest and most straightforward of all East-West issues cast an ironic light on the pleas for negotiation of international differences which were more and more becoming the main theme of world-wide Communist propaganda. This transmutation of the perennial Soviet "peace" campaign was crystallized in the meeting of the Communist-dominated World Peace Council which took place in Budapest on June 15-20, and was dubbed by *Pravda* the "Opening of a World Campaign for Negotiations." During this coming campaign, the Communist organ declared, "the peoples will voice, in various, organized forms, their demand for a peaceful settlement of all the conflicts and issues which exist among states." [61]

But meanwhile there was one grave issue on which the people must immediately concerned were already voicing their feelings, though in a manner quite spontaneous and unorganized and wholly out of keeping with Soviet aims.

4. THE BERLIN RISING AND THE FALL OF BERIA

It might have been expected that the efforts of the new Soviet leaders to placate internal opposition in the U.S.S.R. should find some reflection in the satellite countries of Eastern Europe and in the East German regions which were administered by the Communist puppet government of the

60 *Ibid.*, 236-238; cf. further below, pp. 194-195.

61 *Pravda*, June 21, 1953; *Current Digest of the Soviet Press*, V, No. 25, August 1, 1953, 23.

"German Democratic Republic." During the first months of the new leadership, however, there were few signs of relaxation in the draconian policies of these police governments, which continued their ruthless repression of personal and political freedom even while contriving to show an ever so slightly less forbidding face to the outside world. Concessions of some magnitude were to come at a later stage, but not before a section of the oppressed inhabitants had demonstrated that years of Communist tyranny had failed to extinguish either the love of freedom or the courage to fight for it.

The troubles began late in the spring in Czechoslovakia, the only one of the satellite countries to have undergone a change of government as an immediate sequel to Stalin's demise. President Klement Gottwald died on March 14, having supposedly contracted pneumonia at Stalin's funeral, and was replaced by Antonín Zápotocký; another strong Communist figure, Viliám Široký, moved up to fill Zápotocký's vacant post as Premier, while a third, Antonín Novotný, took over the dominant position in the Communist party secretariat. A number of unpopular measures imposed by the new government culminated on May 31 in the proclamation of a currency reform which not only struck a blow against the former bourgeoisie and wealthier peasants but also came close to wiping out the savings and purchasing power of the urban working classes. Rather serious protest demonstrations occurred in Czechoslovakia on June 1, centering in the industrial city of Plzeň, where the rioters—many of them young people who had been exposed to the full weight of Communist indoctrination—invaded the city hall, manhandled the city council, and destroyed busts of Stalin, Gottwald, and Zápotocký. The disorders were suppressed with great severity and arrests numbered in the thousands.[62]

Ferment in Eastern Germany

In Eastern Germany, conditions had been building toward a more spectacular outburst, in keeping with that region's greater susceptibility to the anti-Communist influences which

[62] Cf. "La Situation en Tchécoslovaquie," *Chronique de politique étrangère,* VI, September 1953, 641-642.

radiated from Western Germany and especially West Berlin. Signs of tension in the "German Democratic Republic" had been conspicuous during the months before June 1953.[63] The Communist-dominated regime aggressively attacked the churches, conducted a minor party purge, and tried to tighten its economic control while food supplies grew leaner and the exodus of refugees to the West increased, reaching an all-time high of 50,000 in the month of Stalin's death. On May 28 the Soviet Union attempted to bolster the standing of its Communist puppets by replacing the Soviet Control Commission, headed by General Vassily I. Chuikov, with a civilian agency under a High Commissioner, Vladimir Semyenov—a move which might have been more impressive if it had not duplicated similar action taken by the Western powers as early as 1949.

More important to the hard-pressed populace of Eastern Germany and East Berlin was an increase of "work norms" —equivalent to a cut in wages—which was announced on May 28 and brought on a series of minor strikes the following week. Sensing a crisis, the government tried to placate the masses by admitting that it had gone too far and making a number of concessions, aimed particularly at helping farmers and small businessmen who were suffering under forced collectivization and nationalization. Far from achieving the desired result, however, this retreat apparently raised popular hopes that the regime was weakening and was taken as an opportunity to press for further concessions.

A spontaneous demonstration of Berlin workers started on June 16 and grew to formidable size the following day. Estimates of the number of demonstrators varied from ten to fifty thousand. Storming through the streets, disarming Peoples' Police, releasing political prisoners and calling for the Communist leaders, the demonstrators were dispersed only after Soviet tanks and troops, possibly three divisions, had been called in. Martial law was declared by the Soviet commander in Berlin, and even official Communist sources admitted that twenty-five persons had been killed in the course

63 Cf. the speech of May 7 by U.S. High Commissioner Conant in *Department of State Bulletin*, XXVIII, June 1, 1953, 767-769; also Geoffrey W. Lewis, "Soviet Germany: The Unruly Satellite," *ibid.*, XXIX, December 28, 1953, 883-891.

of June 17. Nor did the uprising end here. Similar demonstrations occurred in most East German cities as well as in some rural areas. Even after the demonstration, the Berlin workers continued to express their discontent by absenteeism and sit-down strikes.[64]

Although this demonstration decisively discredited Communist claims of popular support in Eastern Germany, its force was soon stifled—notwithstanding the fact that it was not until July 12 that the Russians felt sufficiently secure to abolish martial law. In the meantime, the leaders of the "Democratic Republic" had wit enough to see that Russian tanks, though potent against the fists of unarmed demonstrators, were not an adequate means of restoring their authority. In late June and early July, they admitted that they had erred in setting production quotas too high and pushing collectivization too fast. A wide variety of concessions was offered, including wage, price, and ration adjustments and the suspension of the struggle against the churches, small businessmen, and independent farmers. Wilhelm Pieck, Otto Grotewohl, and Walter Ulbricht, the big three of the "Democratic Republic," managed to retain their own jobs, but lesser heads rolled throughout July.

From the beginning of the riots, the official Soviet explanation had consisted in shrilly accusing the Western powers, particularly the United States, of having planned and fomented them. To bolster this charge the authorities arrested a number of "agents," whose "confessions," however, were obviously spurious and were promptly repudiated by the Western commandants in Berlin.[65]

An even more convincing refutation of the charges, however, was the surprise and bewilderment with which official Washington reacted to the uprising. Here, it seemed, was the beginning of that long-promised disintegration of Soviet-Communist rule by the indomitable spirit of freedom. Yet although the spirit was undeniably there, it seemed unable to prevail against the Soviet tanks; and the President, it is said, remained firmly opposed to the "bold" policy urged by

[64] For details cf. "Les Evénements de Berlin-Est des 16 et 17 Juin 1953," *Chronique de politique étrangère*, VI, September 1953, 635-640.
[65] Cf. *Documents on American Foreign Relations, 1953*, 170-174.

his "psychological warfare" experts.[66] The June 17 riots offered an encouraging demonstration of man's capacity to resist tyranny, and proved beyond doubt that the German Democratic Republic was not a popularly supported regime. But they also revealed that the unarmed captive peoples could not expel their Soviet rulers unaided and that even the United States, short of threatening total war, could do comparatively little to assist them.

Yet if the Berlin riots served to quash American hopes for the early or facile liberation of captive peoples, they at least pointed the way to more modest methods by which help and encouragement could still be brought to Communist victims. The most dramatic and successful response to the East German unrest was President Eisenhower's program—inspired by a suggestion from Chancellor Adenauer—for distribution of American food supplies to the East German population through the Western sector of Berlin. The President's initial offer to the Russians to provide food for them to distribute (July 10) was contemptuously dismissed as a "propaganda maneuver," [67] whereupon the responsibility for the program was turned over to the Foreign Operations Administration and German authorities in the Federal Republic and West Berlin. Between July 27 and October 10, nearly 18,000 tons of food products were distributed in more than 5,500,000 individual parcels to East German residents who slipped into West Berlin to obtain them despite heavy pressure from their Communist rulers.[68]

Nor were the universal implications of the Berlin rising completely overlooked in official Washington. In August, after some legislative delays, Congress completed action on a Concurrent Resolution which commended the "heroic resistance" throughout Eastern Europe, expressed "friendship and sympathy" for the people of Eastern Germany, denounced Communist reprisals against the demonstrators, and

[66] James Reston, "An Inquiry into Foreign Policy," *New York Times Magazine,* January 16, 1955, 62.

[67] *Documents on American Foreign Relations, 1953,* 174-176; further documentation in *Department of State Bulletin,* XXIX, July 20, 1953, 67-68; August 3, 1953, 147; August 17, 1953, 208-210; October 5, 1953, 457-459.

[68] *Report to Congress on the Mutual Security Program,* December 31, 1953 (Washington, G.P.O., 1954), 20-21.

asserted that "this sacrifice for freedom will aid the cause of freedom in all Communist enslaved nations and will inspire freedom-loving people everywhere." [69]

"New Course" in Eastern Europe

The Berlin insurrection marked a turning point in Communist policies both in Germany and throughout the Soviet orbit, though it was not certain how far the "new course" was precipitated by this event and how far it resulted from decisions taken previously. Even before the Berlin riots, the East German Communists had outlined on June 9 a series of measures involving the cessation of various harsh and discriminatory practices in the fields of business, agriculture, education, justice, and religion.[70] After the June riots, other steps were taken in the endeavor to rebuild the shattered prestige of the "Democratic Republic." The previous concessions were confirmed and extended; and on August 20-22, the three top leaders of East German Communism were received in Moscow by the highest authorities of the Soviet Union and presented with a number of material prizes, including an increase in Soviet credits to the puppet republic, a nominal end to reparations as of January 1, 1954, the return of some expropriated industries, a reduction in occupation costs, and the promised release of many of the German prisoners of war still detained in the Soviet Union.[71] These concessions, while doubtless aimed primarily at influencing the West German parliamentary elections scheduled for September 6, left the U.S.S.R. in a position to continue extracting a sizable part of East German production, and fell far short of putting the puppet regime on an equal footing with the Bonn government. But they showed that to the Soviet Government the economic and military advantages of maintaining their German puppet, even though discredited, clearly outweighed the disadvantages.

Meanwhile comparable adjustments were being made in the Eastern European satellite states, where numerous showy concessions to consumer welfare were announced during

[69] S. Con. Res. 36, 83d Congress, adopted August 3, 1953.

[70] *Chronique de politique étrangère*, VI, September 1953, 635-637.

[71] Communiqué, August 22, in *Documents on American Foreign Relations, 1953*, 176-178; cf. below, p. 198.

July, August, and September. In Hungary, dictator Mátyás Rákosi was removed from the Premiership; his successor, Imre Nagy, announced that the five-year plan would be redrawn to place less emphasis on developing heavy industry and more on meeting agricultural and consumer needs.[72] By late October all of the satellite regimes had embarked on a similar policy of slowing the impossible pace of industrialization marked out in the late 1940's.

At the same time the satellite regimes continued to display a more moderate demeanor in their external relations, not only toward the Western powers but also toward Yugoslavia, whose leaders they had been furiously denouncing ever since Marshal Tito's break with the Cominform in 1948. The concessions now offered to Tito's government, such as the negotiation of border disputes and the renewal of full diplomatic relations, were of limited scope but sufficed to cause some uneasiness in the West despite Tito's assurances that he would never allow his country to fall back under Soviet domination.

The End of Beria

The change of pace in Eastern European affairs coincided, at least in timing, with one of the most sensational developments in the struggle for power among Stalin's heirs. For some authorities, the uprisings in Eastern Germany signified a further blow to the prestige of Mr. Beria, whose dependents among the East German Communists could be considered directly responsible for failing to forestall the outbreaks. Others attach more weight to Beria's actions during June in removing important supporters of Mr. Khrushchev from positions of authority, especially in the Ukraine, the Party secretary's principal base of operations. At all events, it was now evident that Beria's star had set. On June 27, tanks and soldiers were seen in the streets of Moscow—suggesting Army participation in the move against Beria—and it was noticed that the Minister of Internal Affairs was absent from an appearance of Soviet notables at the Bolshoi

[72] "La Situation en Hongrie," *Chronique de politique étrangère*, VI, September 1953, 650-657. Rákosi continued to head Hungary's Communist organization as First Secretary of the party.

Theater. A fortnight later (July 10) came the news that the man who had so recently stood at Malenkov's elbow had actually been dismissed from the Communist party and arraigned before the Supreme Court as "an enemy of the party and of the Soviet people." Ambition, it appeared, was Beria's crime, for he was accused not only of long-continued efforts "to undermine the Soviet State in the interest of foreign capital" but also of attempting, by various reprehensible machinations, "to place the Ministry of Internal Affairs above the government and the Communist Party of the Soviet Union."

Inevitably, the fall of this mighty potentate signaled an all-out assault against the following he had built up in the course of his long party career. A widespread purge ensued, centering in the Transcaucasian Republics and especially Georgia, where Beria's power had been most firmly established, but extending into all parts of the Soviet Union. Not all of the purgees were necessarily Beria men; some of them may even have been adherents of Premier Malenkov. Among the survivors, meanwhile, various shifts in political standing occurred. Some of the victims of previous purges, such as S. D. Ignatiev, the scapegoat in the "doctors' plot," were rehabilitated and given new jobs. In September Mr. Khrushchev, who seemed to have played an active part in the purges in cooperation with Soviet military leaders, received public recognition as First Secretary of the Communist Party Central Committee.

The public had to wait until December for a full statement of the grounds for Beria's dethronement. The official indictment, made public on December 16, made the remarkable claim that this high priest of the police state had in reality been an anti-Communist conspirator as early as 1919 and had culminated a career of assassination and sabotage by attempted "seizure of power" following Stalin's death. Six other high officials with a background of police activity were linked to this "conspiracy." Between December 18 and 23, the accused were tried in a special secret session of the Supreme Court of the U.S.S.R., condemned to death, and shot. The most noteworthy features of the trial were, first, that there were no public confessions such as had characterized the notorious purge trials of the late 1930's; and second, that the eight-member court included a number of military men, one of whom, Marshal Ivan S. Konev, served as chairman. Analysts of Soviet politics would later infer that the elimination of Beria and the secret police as an internal power factor had left the Army, the Party organization under Khrushchev, and the state administration under Malenkov as the chief elements still competing for the decisive voice in Soviet affairs.

Soviet Policy After Beria

How far these obscure internal struggles might be connected with the changing orientation of Soviet domestic and foreign policy, no outsider could say. From the point of view of world affairs, the most significant aspect of Beria's removal would seem to have been the fact that it was accomplished with virtually no public commotion and no apparent weakening of the Soviet Government's position at home or abroad. If, as seemed possible, Beria's elimination betokened a more influential role for the military in Soviet affairs, this would reinforce the prospect (already sufficiently evident) that the U.S.S.R.'s armed strength would not be neglected even if there was some retreat from the diplomatic excesses of the Stalinist period. Thus the net effect for the West would be a continuance of the Soviet military threat, coupled, perhaps, with a somewhat greater adroitness in capitalizing on political opportunities both at home and abroad. Beria had not been a Western agent, despite the cynical allegations of his former associates. His removal left the West facing essentially the same problem it had faced before.

The details of Soviet home and foreign policy also seemed not to be greatly affected by Beria's disappearance. If any change was to be detected in internal policy, it lay in the replacement of civil liberties by economic concessions as the central theme of government propaganda. Increased production of food and consumers' goods was the burden of innumerable addresses and resolutions, which took their cue from a report by Premier Malenkov to the Supreme Soviet on August 8:

"Today on the basis of the progress we have made in the development of heavy industry, we have all the necessary conditions for bringing about a sharp rise in the production of consumers' goods.

"We have every possibility to do this and we must do it." [73]

To encourage larger crop yields, the farming population was offered a variety of inducements, including lower taxes, higher farm prices, and reduced quotas for compulsory deliveries to the state. Khrushchev indicated in September that to offset the stagnation of agricultural growth in preceding years it had been found necessary to resort to economic incentives or appeals to "the principle of material interest," as well as sizable investment in fertilizer and other technical improvements. Here was an early intimation of what would later be recognized as the "crisis" of Soviet agriculture.

How would the new emphasis on meeting individual and popular needs affect the U.S.S.R.'s long-term influence in world affairs? Would a radical shift to consumer production—if the shift should turn out to be as radical in reality as it was portrayed in Soviet propaganda—retard the growth of Soviet war potential in terms of heavy industry and armaments? Or was Soviet economic expansion reaching a point where consumer and military needs could *both* be satisfied? Responsible officials in Washington were not reassured as they pored over the intelligence estimates that showed how the basic elements of the Soviet economy had developed since 1940. During that period Soviet coal production had doubled; steel output had increased nearly twofold; petroleum production had grown from an annual figure of 31 million tons to 47 million; electric power had increased by 69 billion kilowatt hours.

It is true that such figures were not especially impressive when measured against comparable statistics for the United States. It was when they were matched against the economic potential of Western Europe that they became alarming. "If the rate of increase continues," said Samuel C. Waugh, Assistant Secretary of State for Economic Affairs, "it

[73] *Pravda,* August 9, 1953; *Current Digest of the Soviet Press,* V, No. 30, September 5, 1953, 4; cf. further below, pp. 192-194.

is highly probable that sometime in the 1960's the economic strength of the Soviet Union will intersect and pass that of Western Europe." [74]

Despite its new preoccupation with consumer needs, the Soviet Government seemed loath to permit any slackening in the over-all rate of industrial progress. Malenkov explicitly stated that the current Five-Year Plan (1950–1955) would be retained, even though its goals for consumer production would apparently be raised somewhat. Later analysis showed that although investment in light industry was scheduled to increase from 7.6 billion rubles in 1953 to an estimated 14 billion in 1954, the latter figure had to be matched against a total of over 90 billion rubles (nominally $22.5 billion) for heavy industry. "All that really happened . . . is that a small marginal shift of resources was effected to strengthen light industry somewhat. Even in 1954, however, the rate of growth in heavy industry was far higher than that in light industry, as it has been ever since 1928." [75]

Still less did the Soviet leaders appear inclined to slacken the rate of direct military preparations, as the Western governments were doing even while they disclaimed belief in the U.S.S.R.'s peaceful gestures. Already the Soviet Government was devoting a far larger proportion of its heavy industry to armaments than any of the Western countries. Furthermore, the Russians were not as crippled by scientific and technical backwardness as many in the West liked to imagine. Their success in producing first the atomic and then the hydrogen bomb was not made possible entirely, or even primarily, by the theft of atomic secrets from the West. Captured MIG-15 jet fighters in Korea bore witness to Soviet technical improvements that were *not* based on allied designs, and even Soviet hydrogen bomb development was reported to be in some ways ahead of this country's. Other aspects of Soviet military preparedness were equally difficult to discount. Allied naval authorities knew that Soviet submarines outnumbered American submarines more than three

[74] Address of July 18, in *Department of State Bulletin,* XXIX, August 3, 1953, 143.

[75] Philip E. Mosely, "How 'New' is the Kremlin's New Line?" *Foreign Affairs,* XXXIII, April 1955, 381.

to one, and that in cruisers Russia's operational fleet outranked the British Navy and was second only to that of the United States. Soviet numerical superiority in tanks, fighter planes, and heavy artillery as well as trained manpower was equally unmistakable.

This did not necessarily mean that the Soviet Union was going to attack the West, either immediately or after the lapse of a few years during which its nuclear stockpile and strategic air force would be built up to optimum size. It did not mean that the Soviet leaders would not still prefer to pursue their aims by nonmilitary methods, which would be far less damaging in a material sense both to the U.S.S.R. and to the countries they hoped to conquer. The grand design of Soviet strategy was still, apparently, to use any and all means of breaking up the Western coalition and isolating the United States from its allies, as a preliminary to the achievement of world domination. But a "soft" policy might very well promote these aims more effectually than would an openly bellicose policy. Initial Soviet soundings of the West, though they had produced few practical results, had at least indicated a discrepancy between American and European attitudes which might be capable of further exploitation. Thus the months ahead might well witness a still further intensification of the more conciliatory tactics initiated soon after Stalin's death.

For the West, several important conclusions seemed to emerge. (1) The Soviet Union had come through the crisis of Stalin's death without serious impairment of either its basic internal strength or its military striking power. (2) Soviet military strength exceeded that of the West in some important respects, and its general level was such that there was probably no sure way of eliminating it which would not expose the centers of Western civilization to grievous and perhaps prohibitive damage. About all the West could reasonably hope to do in this field was to maintain its own military strength in such condition that the Soviets would be unlikely to challenge it. (3) The apparent Soviet preference for nonviolent methods had potential advantages for the West. As long as there was no total war, the possibility would remain that such a catastrophic denouement could be avoided altogether. Meanwhile the West was given an opportunity to compete with the Soviets in a field in which it had many and undoubted advantages provided only that it could summon the wisdom and fortitude to use them. (4) Soviet tactics could also be extremely dangerous to the Western peoples if the latter were induced to relax their vigilance and neglect the weaknesses that needed remedying throughout the free world. In that case the post-Stalin "peace offensive" might prove to have been the penultimate stage in the dissolution of the non-Communist world, a prelude to virtual Soviet domination of the free nations through the threat of hydrogen bombardment.

The reaction of the Western powers to this combination of perils and opportunities will be the main theme of the following chapters.

CHAPTER THREE

THE UNITED STATES AND WESTERN EUROPE

THE MEMBERS of the Atlantic alliance had not awaited the death of Stalin to relax the rhythm of their defense preparations. After laying down an ambitious three-year program of military expansion at the Lisbon meeting of the North Atlantic Council in February 1952, they had been forced to recognize ten months later that there was no realistic prospect of reaching their targets for 1953 and 1954, and that even the 1952 goal for Western Europe (twenty-five active divisions, twenty-five reserve divisions, and 4,000 operational aircraft, exclusive of Greek and Turkish forces) would not be fully attained. One European country after another had announced that the sights had been set too high, and had modified its national defense plans accordingly. The United States, which had signally failed to meet its own commitments for shipping military equipment to its allies, had confirmed the trend by electing an administration and Congress that gave top priority to the objective of budgetary retrenchment and made no secret of their intention to reduce expenditure both on the national armed forces and on foreign military aid.[1]

These economizing tendencies were not dictated by any sudden change in the international military situation or in the presumed intentions of the U.S.S.R. Nevertheless, they were not too difficult to justify by military calculations of a sort. It could be argued that the defensive power of the Atlantic allies, which was constantly growing as guns, tanks, planes, and vehicles continued to roll from the production lines, was already approaching a level sufficient to fulfill its

[1] Cf. *The United States in World Affairs, 1952,* 126-127, 401-405, 417-418.

main purpose of deterring a Soviet attack in Europe. No Western authority had ever thought of trying to equal the strength of one hundred divisions, more or less, which the Soviet Union and its satellites maintained in Eastern Europe. The objective, rather, had been to establish a force sufficiently powerful to discourage a Soviet attack or, if it came, to delay the Soviet advance while reserves were mobilized and American strategic air power was brought into play. Thanks to the superior armament of the Western divisions, such a force might perhaps be considered to exist in Western Europe already; at any rate, it would presumably exist as soon as the twelve German divisions provided for in connection with the European Defense Community had been recruited, trained, and brought into the allied line of battle. Meanwhile American air and atomic power would continue to constitute the ultimate deterrent which, it was hoped, would restrain the Soviets from seeking their aims through military aggression.

These arguments, though not fully accepted at NATO's Supreme Headquarters in Europe (SHAPE), were quite convincing to those who already favored a defense slowdown for other reasons. For the real motives of the slowdown—or "stretch-out," as it came to be called—were economic and political, not military. Both in Europe and the United States, the peoples and the governments which represented them had simply not been willing to continue their defense preparations on the scale that their military planners thought desirable. On both sides of the Atlantic, the decisive argument had been that military requirements were claiming too large a portion of the total wealth and thus endangering economic and, in Europe, even political stability. Offhand there might seem little comparability between the situation in the United States, with its tremendous productivity and unique standard of living, and that of a group of European countries that were just struggling back to prewar levels of consumption, still confronted manifold economic and social problems, and in some cases faced a sizable internal Communist threat. But popular reactions had been similar throughout the Western community. Everywhere there was a demand for lighter taxes, better food, and more houses, automobiles, and television sets even if it meant fewer rifles, airfields, planes, and tanks.

Concessions to this popular pressure were made easier by the fact that the Western governments had recently perfected, in the plan for a European Defense Community, a project which with good luck might make it possible to overcome most of the remaining obstacles to the establishment of a viable Europe which would be strong enough to resist the pressure from the East for an indefinite period. As a result of a variety of factors, the proposed European Defense Community had come to be looked upon as a virtual panacea for Europe's difficulties, a symbol of its regeneration and a touchstone of its future. To its original sponsors, the basic purpose behind this remarkable project had been the comparatively simple military one of plugging a gap in the ground defenses of Western Europe. Assuming that a peaceful resolution of the difficulties between East and West was unlikely and that military aggression against Western Europe was a serious possibility, the statesmen of the Atlantic alliance had reasoned that an adequate defense of Western Europe required the participation of German forces; and the proposed community had seemed the only form in which such participation could be made acceptable to all the parties concerned. In addition, they felt that it was only reasonable for Western Germany to play its proportionate role in the defense of the West rather than devoting all its energies to an economic resurgence which was already threatening to put most Western European countries in the shade.

These military and economic arguments were closely intertwined with that complex of ideas and emotions which constituted the European unity movement and had already given rise to such intra-European endeavors as the European Payments Union, the Council of Europe, and the European Coal and Steel Community or Schuman Plan. Advocates of European union insisted that Europe's very survival as an influence in world affairs demanded an amalgamation of its national economic, military, and political potentialities in the interests of (a) expanded production, (b) adequate defense, and (c) spiritual renewal. Europe without Germany, it was further argued, would be incomplete; inclusion of Western

Germany in the developing structure of Western European economic, political, and military union would not only strengthen Western Europe as a whole but would be the surest means of extinguishing the ancient antagonisms between Germany and its Western neighbors. In forming the Defense Community, the Western European states would not only be safeguarding their security against the U.S.S.R.; they would also be safeguarding their security against each other, thus eliminating the conditions which Secretary Dulles had often referred to as constituting "historically the world's worst fire hazard."

A further impetus toward European union in all these fields derived from the special interest of the United States in seeing Western Europe restored to a condition of strength and independence. Desire for European unity was not confined to those who tended to think of Europe as the area of primary American concern outside the Western hemisphere. It was especially noticeable among some Americans of rather isolationist tendency who had questioned the utility of American aid to Europe in the past and particularly bemoaned the policy of keeping the equivalent of six American divisions on the European Continent on a more or less permanent basis. European unification and German rearmament, these Americans hoped, would make it possible for the United States to discontinue these policies and keep its wealth and its young manhood at home. Rather paradoxically, some of these same Americans tended to take the position that a *failure* of Europe to unify would also justify the United States in withdrawing its support, even though this would presumably mean leaving a military vacuum which only the U.S.S.R. would be in a position to fill.

The single answer devised for this multitude of problems had been the laboriously drafted treaty signed at Paris on May 27, 1952, establishing a European Defense Community of six nations (France, Germany, Italy, Belgium, the Netherlands, and Luxembourg) which would provide the framework of an integrated European army and would be tightly interlocked with the institutions of the European Coal and Steel Community, the North Atlantic Treaty Organization, and a proposed European Political Community as well as with the so-called Contractual Agreements restoring sovereignty to the German Federal Republic.[2] On paper and in a legal sense it was a well-nigh perfect answer, even if doubt persisted in some quarters about its practical workings as well as its relevance to the rapidly changing defense problems of the atomic age. Its one defect—though it was to prove a fatal one—was the fact that it failed to harmonize sufficiently with the mood prevailing in one or more of the countries most directly involved in its establishment and operation. The many ingenious compromises embodied in the E.D.C. treaty and related instruments had disguised but could not remove the basic psychological obstacles to putting the plan into operation. France, to take the most prominent example, had suffered too heavily under successive German invasions and occupations to want the Germans rearmed under this or any other plan. Germans, by and large, were not enthusiastic about being rearmed either—especially if, as seemed likely, rearmament carried out against the frequently expressed wishes of the Soviet Union meant perpetuating the division of their own country and the continuing subjection of its eastern portion to Soviet control. German doubts about the E.D.C. arrangement found their most characteristic expression in the demand for additional concessions by the Western powers; and these in turn invariably served to heighten French misgivings about the whole plan. Mainly because of this basic popular resistance in the two key member countries of the prospective community, none of the six governments concerned had ratified the E.D.C. treaty up to the end of 1952 and there was reason to fear that it would be many months, at best, before its provisions could be put into effect.

The utterances of President Eisenhower and Secretary Dulles after their assumption of office had shown that they were well aware of these difficulties, with which Mr. Dulles was able to acquaint himself in greater detail during his post-inaugural trip to Europe.[3] But the outlook was not judged bad enough to warrant a reexamination of the United States commitment in favor of E.D.C.; instead, the administration undertook in this instance to try to reinvigo-

[2] Cf. *ibid.*, 158-167.

[3] Cf. above, pp. 20-21, 27.

rate a policy worked out by its Democratic predecessor. Unfortunately, however, American attempts to induce the Europeans to adopt a line of action which many of them found unpalatable did not in this instance produce the desired effect. If anything, they seemed rather to stiffen the resistance that was gradually building up in Europe to something that the Europeans were beginning to look upon as an American much more than a European policy objective. Accentuated by the change of tone in the Soviet Union, which was felt by many Europeans to make the whole E.D.C. project less urgent, this division between European and American purposes was to grow increasingly glaring as the months went by. By September the London *Economist* would remark that "the conductors of American policy have allowed a dangerous degree of estrangement to grow up between their own people and their allies by what has seemed to be the inflexibility of their methods and the belligerence of their words." [4]

This estrangement was to appear especially marked in the case of Western Germany and France, the two key countries which E.D.C. was supposed to yoke together in one harness. In Western Germany, resistance to the E.D.C. concept for a time bade fair to destroy the coalition government of Chancellor Adenauer, which had staked its political life on integration with the West and on which the West, in turn, had staked its own hopes for the permanent defense of Western Europe. In France, the widespread hostility to E.D.C. was one factor in a generally tense and disturbed condition which at times threatened virtually to nullify the country's influence in world affairs. For France was not only beset by fear of Germany but also distracted by internal strife, weakened by the long war in Indochina, and confronted by heavy pressure for independence on the part of its North African populations, backed by their self-appointed guardians among the Arab and Asian nations. The generally doubtful prospect was to be relieved in part by the unexpected success of the Adenauer coalition in the West German elections of September 6, as well as by the development of what seemed a firmer defensive basis in the Eastern Mediterranean. But all through 1953 the central issue of E.D.C. was to remain un-

[4] *Economist,* CLXVIII, September 26, 1953, 831.

solved, together with all the grave issues of Western defense and East-West relations that had become linked with it.

1. WATERING DOWN E.D.C.

Though the E.D.C. project was generally looked upon as an essential element in the defense of the West, it was perhaps natural that its fortunes should be affected by the same influences that were making for a degree of retrenchment in Western defense efforts generally. The reaction against E.D.C. which had become noticeable in France and elsewhere within weeks after the treaty was signed had coincided with various other developments—notably the Nineteenth Communist Party Congress in the U.S.S.R.—which even before the death of Stalin were felt by many observers to portend a lessened danger of war and a diminished need for haste in completing the Western defense structure.[5] By the end of 1952 it was possible to question whether a treaty so unsatisfactory to its principal signatories would ever be ratified in its original form. By early 1953 it was certain that France, at any rate, would not ratify before an attempt had been made to secure substantial modifications of the commitments undertaken eight months earlier.

France Raises New Conditions

The French government which had signed the E.D.C. treaty—a right-center coalition headed by Antoine Pinay, with the veteran "European" Robert Schuman at the Foreign Ministry—had resigned on December 23, 1952 for reasons unconnected with foreign policy. The successor government formed by the Radical leader René Mayer, which took office January 7, 1953, appeared rather less favorable to E.D.C. than its predecessor had been. Georges Bidault, the new Foreign Minister, belonged like M. Schuman to the Catholic and internationalist Mouvement Républicain Populaire (M.R.P.), but was personally uncommitted to the program of European unification and Franco-German conciliation for which M. Schuman had labored through so many cabinets. More noteworthy was the fact that the Mayer gov-

[5] Cf. *The United States in World Affairs, 1952,* 385-401.

ernment took office with the open support of the nationalist Rassemblement du Peuple Français (R.P.F.), which had refrained from backing earlier coalition governments and was known for its dislike of the E.D.C. concept and its responsiveness to the nationalist opinions of General Charles de Gaulle.

In the address in which he sought the backing of the Assembly on January 6, M. Mayer gave notice that the E.D.C. treaty and the accompanying treaty and agreements ending the occupation of Germany would be formally submitted for ratification at an early date. But, he said, the government intended meanwhile to seek certain modifications or "clarifications" of the E.D.C. treaty by means of additional protocols which, he hinted, would aim at retaining for France a larger measure of control over the French army than was contemplated in the original document. An effort would also be made, M. Mayer went on, to associate Great Britain more closely with the E.D.C.—an idea calculated to appeal to the many Frenchmen who looked on the United Kingdom as an essential counterweight to a rearmed Germany and were not satisfied with the commitments Great Britain had already undertaken when the E.D.C. treaty was signed. Finally, M. Mayer told the Assembly that the treaties should not be ratified until there had been a definite settlement of the Franco-German dispute over the Saar territory through an agreement which would definitely assure that area a "European" status free from German control.[6]

Given the temper of the French Assembly, this declaration seemed to mean that E.D.C. could not come into being until (1) the treaty was revised, (2) Great Britain made new pledges of continental involvement, and (3) Western Germany renounced its contention that the Saar was properly German territory. Considering the difficulty with which the various interests at issue had been compromised in the original treaties of May 1952, this was not a small order. However, the new government went rapidly to work, submitting the treaties in their original form for the consideration of

6 "Les Protocoles additionels au Traité Instituant la Communauté Européenne de Défense" *Chronique de politique étrangère,* VI, September 1953, 593.

the Assembly[7] and also getting in touch with the other E.D.C. governments about the additional protocols on which France proposed to seek their agreement. A text of the protocols was laid before the Interim Committee of the E.D.C. governments, discussed by the Foreign Ministers of the six countries at a meeting in Rome on February 24-25,[8] and ultimately published in revised form on June 18. In their final version these highly technical protocols, six in number, provided safeguards for the unity of France's army within the European forces of the E.D.C., facilitated the withdrawal of French forces from E.D.C. for emergency use within the French Union, and included other reservations concerning mobilization plans, war matériel, European military schools, and the timing of the establishment of the first echelon of the European forces.[9]

Agreement on these abstruse matters was easier to secure than a reversal of fundamental British and German policies such as would be required for the fulfillment of France's other two conditions. At the moment not much could be accomplished in either direction, although discussions were initiated with the French-oriented government of the Saar territory and led eventually to a new French-Saar agreement (May 20) establishing the Saar's nominal political autonomy while reaffirming its economic dependence on France. French insistence on a Saar settlement as a precondition to E.D.C. was, it will be recalled, one of the sources of disagreement between the French and American governments when Messrs. Mayer and Bidault visited Washington late in March.[10] Yet it was already becoming evident that American exhortations to get ahead with E.D.C. would not move the French more rapidly than they considered their vital interests to allow.

Germany Ratifies

From an American point of view, the unsatisfactory performance of France in relation to E.D.C. was rendered all

[7] See the government statement of January 29, in *Documents on American Foreign Relations, 1953,* 257-269.
[8] *Ibid.,* 408-409.
[9] *Chronique de politique étrangère, loc. cit.,* 594; texts *ibid.,* 690-693.
[10] Cf. above, pp. 34-35.

the more noticeable by the comparatively compliant behavior of the German Federal Republic. An important section of West German opinion, it is true, remained vociferously hostile to the E.D.C. program, if not to rearmament in any form. The Germans were as anxious as the French to take no step that could make an East-West understanding more difficult; their exposed position and the division of their country gave them a uniquely important stake in the general state of East-West relations; their patriotic sensibilities were affronted by the French determination to keep the German-speaking Saar territory detached from Germany. Yet there were differences in the situation of the two countries that made it easier for the Federal Republic to create a favorable impression in Washington. Germany had not suffered at the hands of France in the way that France had suffered under the German occupation. With nothing to fear from its Western neighbors, it had every reason to desire the speedy termination of the few remaining controls exercised by the Western occupying powers. With its strong executive supported by a solid parliamentary coalition, the Federal Republic had demonstrated marked political stability and a firm official, if not popular, attachment to the principles embodied in the E.D.C. treaty.

These elements of superiority were brought conspicuously to the fore on March 19 when the West German Bundestag or lower house became the first parliamentary body in continental Europe to give final approval to the E.D.C. treaty and the accompanying Contractual Agreements. The vote for E.D.C., which climaxed a bitter and even hysterical debate, was 224 to 165; for the Contractuals, which could not become effective without E.D.C., it was 226 to 164. In both cases, the favoring vote fell short of the two-thirds majority which some authorities held to be necessary under Western Germany's Fundamental Law; and the same difficulty was to recur again when the Bundesrat or upper house, after much hesitation and maneuvering, accepted the treaties on May 15 by a vote of 23 to 15. A decision on this constitutional issue, requested by the Social Democratic opposition in 1952, was still pending in the Federal Constitutional

Court. It was clear from the circumstances surrounding the vote, moreover, that formal ratification was a very different thing from wholehearted acceptance of the E.D.C. program, and that German views concerning the disposition of the Saar territory still differed widely from those entertained in France. Nevertheless the Bundestag's action was hailed as a shining example and went far to assure the success of Chancellor Adenauer's April visit to Washington.[11]

Other advances toward European unity had not been entirely lacking. During this same period the six-nation European Coal and Steel Community planned in 1950 was getting under way at its Luxembourg headquarters,[12] and representatives of the same six nations were evolving plans for a European Political Community which would provide an over-all framework for these more specialized endeavors.[13] It was generally conceded, however, that these efforts would have only limited value unless and until the European Defense Community became a reality. That project still seemed a long way from materializing, and meanwhile the gap in Western defenses remained. The situation gave point to a warning by General Matthew B. Ridgway, NATO'S Supreme Allied Commander in Europe, in a ceremony that marked the second anniversary of SHAPE on April 2. The threat to the free world from the military capability of the "potential aggressors," said General Ridgway, "has not diminished an iota in the last two years. Instead, they have increased and continue to increase this capability. . . . At this moment, the forces at our disposal would prove gravely inadequate if put to a test." [14]

[11] Cf. Secretary Dulles' comment, March 19, in *Department of State Bulletin,* XXVIII, March 30, 1953, 470. The Adenauer visit is described above, p. 36 f.

[12] The common market for coal began functioning on February 10 and that for steel on May 1, 1953. Cf. Raymond Vernon, "Launching the European Coal and Steel Community," *ibid.,* June 8, 1953, 799-804. For discussion of a possible U.S. loan to the Community, cf. *ibid.* XXVIII, June 29, 1953, 927-929 and XXIX, July 27, 1953, 107-108.

[13] A draft treaty embodying a statute for the proposed European Community was adopted at Strasbourg on March 10 by the Ad Hoc Assembly established for this purpose in 1952. Cf. "L'Intégration politique européenne," *Chronique de politique étrangère,* VI, May 1953, 277-320, and text of the draft treaty, *ibid.,* 366-388.

[14] *New York Times,* April 3, 1953.

2. THE NATO "STRETCH-OUT"

Though General Ridgway's analysis was admittedly based on a purely military estimate of Soviet capabilities, uninfluenced by speculation as to possible Soviet intentions, a glance at the figures lent weight to his conclusion. Whatever the plans of Stalin's successors in the Kremlin, the fact remained that they could count upon nearly six million armed men to carry out any orders they might see fit to issue. The Soviet Union still maintained its well-trained army of 175 divisions, some thirty of them in Eastern Europe, with twenty-two highly mechanized divisions in Eastern Germany. Satellite forces had been built up to around seventy divisions, numbering more than 1,300,000 men. East Germany had its paramilitary police formations amounting to another 100,000. In the air, the Soviets possessed an operational air force of not less than 20,000 planes, a large proportion of them jet-propelled, plus large reserves. The Soviet undersea fleet, which could be counted upon to attack the transatlantic supply lines in the event of war, was known to number not less than 300 units.[15]

Allied military authorities were hesitant to state exactly what forces they could make available to match that portion of the Soviet strength that might be hurled against Western Europe. Estimates of allied front-line strength in Europe, including the American and British divisions in Germany and the Greek and Turkish formations at the far end of the Mediterranean, commonly ran in the neighborhood of forty divisions—not necessarily comparable to Soviet divisions in numbers or equipment—and perhaps 3,500 operational aircraft. Reserve divisions at 50 percent or less of full combat effectiveness might run to another forty. But even if all these units had been at full strength, which they were not, numbers would have been only a part of the allied defense problem. The strategic and political conditions of European defense raised baffling problems. An elastic defense of ma-

[15] See especially the Annual Report of the Supreme Allied Commander, Europe to the Standing Group, North Atlantic Treaty Organization (Paris, SHAPE Public Information Division, May 30, 1953); excerpts in *Documents on American Foreign Relations, 1953,* 195-203 and (more fully) in *Department of State Bulletin,* XXVIII, June 29, 1953, 899-904.

neuver and counterattack—in other words, a war of movement—was out of the question because SHAPE was obligated for political reasons to try to protect every foot of allied territory against even temporary occupation by the Communists. Even without this factor, it was questionable whether the terrain of Western Europe offered sufficient space for an elastic defense under modern conditions. All the more reason, it seemed, to bring Western Germany into the NATO defense scheme as promptly as possible, thus at least making possible a "forward strategy" based somewhere east of the Rhine.

One factor that might eventually make a considerable difference in European defense planning was the prospect of acquiring tactical atomic weapons such as were being tested in the New Mexico desert. As yet, however, these devices were not ready to be put into the hands of combat troops, and their ultimate effect on the conduct of military operations could only be guessed at. Planning in this field was all the more difficult because those American officers assigned to NATO who knew something about the potentialities of the new weapons were forbidden by law to share the knowledge with their Canadian and European colleagues. Although SHAPE had begun to establish "atomic indoctrination courses" designed to give key NATO commanders and staff officers at least an inkling of the new possibilities, official planning necessarily remained geared to the use of conventional weapons.

There was, however, a more cheerful side to the story of NATO's defense effort. If the Western military position still disclosed grave shortcomings when measured against Soviet capabilities, it also reflected great advances when measured against the situation that had existed three years, two years, or even one year earlier. In 1949, the European members of NATO had had approximately 2,450,000 men under arms; by 1953 the figure had jumped to nearly 3,300,000. Equipment, quality, and training of the forces under arms had steadily improved. The rate of delivery of American military aid shipments had practically doubled within the past year. Even under existing plans, the air forces of the European allies were scheduled to attain a total of more than

4,000 planes, mostly of modern jet types, by the end of 1953. This would be more than twice the air strength that had been available at the beginning of 1952. The number of minesweepers available to European forces at the end of 1953 would exceed the mid-1952 figure by almost 75 percent. Expenditures on airfields and other ground installations (infrastructure) in 1953 would total almost $700 million, two and one-half times the expenditure in any previous year. During 1953, new airfields were due to be completed in Western Europe at the rate of approximately one every week.[16]

These achievements, past and prospective, had not been brought about without effort and sacrifice by all the countries concerned. Since 1949–50, the European NATO countries had increased their defense expenditures by 120 percent. Each year had seen a marked increase over the year preceding—the margin was 20 percent in 1950–51, 47 percent in 1951–52, and 24 percent in 1952–53. Total annual defense expenditures in the four years of NATO's life had come to $5.4 billion the first year, $6.5 billion the second, $9.5 billion the third, and $11.8 billion the fourth; if the United States and Canada were included, the figures swelled respectively to $18.6 billion, $29.2 billion, $54.6 billion, and $63.5 billion.[17] In the situation of early 1953, it was perhaps inevitable that the accomplishments and burdens of the existing program should loom larger in the eyes of NATO statesmen than the military deficiencies which that program left unremedied. As Secretary Dulles later stated to a congressional committee:

"... we came face to face with the fact that the NATO countries had just about reached the upper limit of their ability to maintain the past rapid rate in the buildup of forces, while at the same time improving the quality of their existing forces. The strain on the economies of both ourselves and our European allies was becoming too great." [18]

[16] Speech by Lord Ismay, NATO Secretary-General, Washington, March 12, *ibid.*, March 23, 1953, 427-430.

[17] *Ibid.*

[18] Statement to the Senate Appropriations Committee, July 9, *ibid.*, XXIX, July 20, 1953, 89.

The NATO Council

Thus, when the North Atlantic Council met in Ministerial Session in Paris on April 23-25, its main business was to rationalize a further slowing-down of the allied defense build-up—not a halt or a reduction in the over-all program, but a change of pace whereby any further build-up would be spread over a longer period of years. The philosophy invoked by Mr. Dulles, who was accompanied by the Secretaries of Defense and Treasury and by Mutual Security Director Stassen, was identical to that which was being put forward in justification of reduced defense expenditure in the United States. No longer, it was argued, should the NATO countries exhaust themselves in frantic preparation for some hypothetical year of danger. No one knew when the year of greatest danger would come. "President Eisenhower," as Mr. Dulles later explained, "believes that it is safest to adopt a pace which can be maintained with growing strength, rather than run the risk of dropping exhausted by the wayside before the haven is reached." [19]

Thus the emphasis at the NATO meeting was directed to "getting greater strength by less costly methods," stressing "quality, rather than . . . quantity," and making NATO "compact and hard rather than . . . big and soft." The agreement on force goals for 1953 and the provisional program for 1954 involved some increase in the size of NATO's standing and support forces—perhaps six new divisions in 1953. But the main effort was to be directed to improving the combat effectiveness of existing forces, by a margin which Mr. Dulles estimated as high as 30 percent.[20] There was also a final agreement on the fourth yearly installment or "slice" of the $1.3 billion infrastructure program, to which the United States was contributing about 36 percent or $470 million on a net basis, together with a tentative

[19] Radio-television report, April 29, *ibid.*, 671.

[20] *Ibid.* See also the Council's final communiqué, April 25, in *Documents on American Foreign Relations, 1953*, 192-194, and the interpretive statements in *Report to Congress on the Mutual Security Program*, June 30, 1953 (Washington, G.P.O., 1953), 14-15. Further details on the Council meeting and related developments appear in "Activités dans le cadre du Traité de l'Atlantique Nord: La Conférence de Paris," *Chronique de politique étrangère*, VI, November 1953, 744-759.

understanding on further installments which might reach a total of $700 million during the period 1954–1956. Problems of correlating military production programs in the various NATO countries were extensively canvassed, and a special resolution, introduced by Mr. Dulles and adopted unanimously, stressed the "paramount importance" attached by the Atlantic Community to the speedy ratification of the E.D.C. treaty.[21] In a later exposition of the "long-haul" concept developed at this meeting, Mr. Dulles made it clear that in its estimate of local defense requirements in Europe the Council had not overlooked the factor of American air power. The planned development of defensive strength in Europe, he emphasized, was to be "reinforced by the striking power of a strategic air force based on internationally agreed positions." [22]

In deciding to develop their defensive strength at a rate which would "preserve and not exhaust" their economic strength, the NATO statesmen apparently were not moved by any overconfidence in the intentions of the U.S.S.R. Their communiqué stated that although "recent Soviet moves and gestures" found their governments ready, as always, to welcome "any genuine efforts to reduce international tension," there "had not yet in fact been any change in the fundamental threat to the security of free peoples." The most striking evidence of this continued threat, they went on, "is the huge and constantly strengthened military force maintained by those nations whose policies have been responsible for the present tension." Those nations were "still promoting aggressive war in several parts of the world," the most recent example being the extension of hostilities in Laos—a "serious development" which had "increased the burden of France in the struggle against aggression" and occasioned "deep concern on the part of other Member Governments." Thus the Council "reaffirmed the policy of collective defense," even while looking forward "to the day when a greater share of the resources of their countries would be devoted to national and international reconstruction and de-

[21] *Documents on American Foreign Relations, 1953*, 207.

[22] Address to the Council on Foreign Relations, January 12, 1954, *ibid., 1954*, 12.

velopment." The spokesmen of the fourteen NATO governments therefore resolved to "broaden their cooperation in every field . . . and so . . . make the Atlantic Community a lasting reality." [23]

General Ridgway Dissents

Such phrases had a reassuring ring, even when they warned of dangers still to be surmounted. To General Ridgway, however, and presumably to his associates at SHAPE, they were not a satisfactory substitute for the material exertions the NATO Council had preferred to evade. Back in the United States to testify on the Mutual Security legislation, General Ridgway made a speech on May 21 before the new American Council on NATO which seemed to mark a sharp dissent from the philosophy which had prevailed in Paris. Speaking as the military representative of fourteen nations, he reminded his hearers that responsibility for the defense of Western Europe was not something that could be "deferred to some future day when adequate forces to ensure success might be available." This responsibility, he said, "exists today, if the dread volcano of war should again erupt." The present, in his view, was no time to relax. Despite steady progress during the past year, his command still faced "major deficiencies in manpower, support units, arms and equipment, logistical establishments, stockades of ammunition, and, above all, planes." To slow down now, in the face of the U.S.S.R.'s growing strength and "implacable hostility," would be a gamble "with all that is precious—with human lives and spiritual principles as well as with earthly treasures." Though NATO's military commanders would accept the decisions of civilian authorities "with complete loyalty," General Ridgway said, they would also continue, "loyally yet fearlessly, to point out the military consequences, as in the light of military reasons they see such consequences, of any failures to provide the requirements they consider essential." [24]

In an official report released on June 10, General Ridgway reasserted the same views in greater detail. Surveying the three sectors into which his command was divided, he found

[23] Communiqué, April 25, 1953, cited.

[24] *Department of State Bulletin,* XXVIII, June 22, 1953, 869-873.

that Northern Europe still lacked "within its own resources the minimum forces required to give adequate chances of success against a major attack," and would require assistance from outside. In Central Europe, he was convinced that "the basic elements of strength to attain a capability for defense . . . can be found"—especially if an early German contribution was provided. In Southern Europe, too, the land forces were steadily improving and a successful defense appeared "attainable in the foreseeable future." Viewing the military problem as a whole, however, General Ridgway warned that he found "the disparity between our available forces and those which the Soviet rulers could bring against us so great as to warrant no other conclusion than that a full-scale Soviet attack within the near future would find Allied Command Europe critically weak to accomplish its mission." The potential aggressor retained the initiative, he averred. If NATO was to accomplish its purpose, it "should have the means which can be committed to action within a short time and which can give us the capability of withstanding an initial attack and gaining time to gather our strength." To this end, he concluded, it was imperative to sustain the momentum developed over the past two years and "to maintain our faith in the values we strive to defend." [25]

Organizational Arrangements

General Ridgway had already been designated as the next Chief of Staff of the United States Army, and his views were sure to play a part in the "new look" at the global defense picture which the administration had promised. By that time there might also be a clearer indication as to how soon the E.D.C. was going to materialize. Meanwhile NATO's command had to be reorganized and a few technical details in the relationship of the United States to NATO straightened out. General Alfred M. Gruenther of the United States, who had served as Chief of Staff to both General Eisenhower and General Ridgway, was moved up to the post of Supreme Allied Commander, with Field Marshal Viscount Montgomery of Great Britain continuing to serve as deputy. Their team of subcommanders would include Admiral William M.

[25] *Ibid.*, June 29, 1953, 899-904.

Fechteler (United States) in the Southeast, Marshal Alphonse-Pierre Juin (France) in the Center, and General Lauris Norstad (United States) as Air Deputy.

Concurrently, the United States civilian representation in NATO was reorganized with the establishment of a United States Mission to NATO and European Regional Organizations, headed by John C. Hughes, who would be permanent United States Representative on the North Atlantic Council.[26] And on July 15 the Senate gave its approval to three international agreements of a technical and legal nature to regulate (a) the status of NATO forces stationed in member countries,[27] (b) the status of NATO national representatives and international staff,[28] and (c) the status of NATO's various international military headquarters.[29] Only the first of these was especially controversial, chiefly because it provided that military personnel accused of ordinary, off-duty criminal offenses could be tried in the courts of the country in which the offense took place. A reservation offered by Senator Bricker, forbidding the trial of American servicemen in foreign courts, was defeated and the agreement was approved by 72 votes to 15 after the President had stated that its rejection would undermine "the entire United States military position in Europe." [30]

3. EUROPEAN POLITICAL TRENDS

There was considerable merit in the contention that NATO's defense burdens, however necessary from a military point of view, imposed a critical strain on the economic and political fabric of Western Europe. Notwithstanding

[26] *Ibid.*, XXIX, July 13, 1953, 47-48.

[27] NATO Status of Forces Agreement, signed at London, June 19, 1951 (S. Exec. T, 82d Congress, 2d Session); entered into force August 23, 1953.

[28] Signed at Ottawa, September 20, 1951 (S. Exec. U, 82d Congress, 2d Session); entered into force May 18, 1954.

[29] Protocol to the Status of Forces Agreement, signed at Paris, August 28, 1952 (S. Exec. B, 83d Congress, 1st Session); entered into force April 10, 1954. For background on the three agreements cf. *Department of State Bulletin,* XXVIII, April 27, 1953, 628-634.

[30] *New York Times,* July 16, 1953. Cf. also the statements by Under-Secretary Smith, September 5, in *Department of State Bulletin,* XXIX, September 21, 1953, 374-375, and by Herman Phleger, Legal Adviser, *ibid.*, XXX, February 8, 1954, 198-199.

the remarkable recovery of the past five or six years, few European nations had yet reached a point at which they could sustain both a fully adequate military effort and a standard of living high enough to ensure full productivity and a stable political life. If the psychological atmosphere had been different—if the European nations had been able to maintain the drive and the sense of partnership with the United States that had worked such miracles in the later 1940's—the peoples of Western Europe might have found it easier to accept the continued deferment of material benefits that NATO's military requirements demanded of them. As things stood, however, there was little inclination to rise above the limiting conditions that still operated on both the economic and political planes.

The continued vulnerability of Western European economies was vividly illustrated by the effect of disastrous storms and floods that struck the Netherlands, Belgium, and southeastern England at the end of January 1953, claiming some 2,000 lives and inflicting material damage estimated at many millions of dollars. The Netherlands, which had just joined the growing list of countries able to dispense with further United States economic aid,[31] was forced to appeal for emergency assistance, and the over-all situation was judged grave enough in Washington to warrant the establishment of a special Cabinet Committee under Secretary Dulles to coordinate American relief efforts.[32] Aside from such disasters, economic advance was continuing in most countries, though at a slower rate than in previous years. Various aspects of the American Mutual Security Program—"offshore procurement" of military equipment for the use of NATO forces, "defense support" in the form of raw materials, machinery, and equipment, and a new "productivity program" cosponsored by the Organization for European Economic Cooperation—supplemented direct American mili-

31 By mid-1953 the U.S. had suspended economic aid to Belgium, Denmark, Iceland, Ireland, the Netherlands, Luxembourg, Portugal, and Sweden. *Report to Congress on the Mutual Security Program,* June 30, 1953, 8-9; cf. also *Department of State Bulletin,* XXVIII, February 9, 1953, 217; June 1, 1953, 778; June 22, 1953, 873.

32 The committee's interim report of February 12 appears *ibid.,* March 2, 1953, 335; cf. also *ibid.,* XXX, February 1, 1954, 142.

tary aid and expenditure and were helping most Western European countries to begin rebuilding their depleted gold and dollar reserves.[33]

Yet it was clear to any qualified observer that this improvement, achieved in a period of declining American aid and static American trade policy, rested on insecure foundations. The negative aspects of the situation were so sharply characterized in the *Economic Survey of Europe Since the War* which the United Nations Economic Commission for Europe released in February that an American spokesman found it necessary to reproach the authors with undue pessimism.[34] But similar preoccupations colored the outlook of almost all European experts, such as a group of high O.E.E.C. officials who came to Washington in April and assured American authorities that the European economic situation, despite the great progress achieved during the last five years, remained "far from satisfactory" and needed further urgent action by the United States (principally in lowering trade barriers) as well as by the countries of Western Europe.[35] Paradoxically, the death of Stalin and the prospect of a Korean armistice failed to brighten the over-all economic prospect but actually introduced a new source of uneasiness. By mid-April, when delegates to the United Nations Economic and Social Council (ECOSOC) began their annual discussion of the world economic situation, there was evidence of widespread preoccupation with the effects of declining military expenditure and possible dangers of a world recession.[36]

The impact of these factors varied as widely from country to country as did the social and psychological trends associated with them. Possibly least affected in any adverse sense was the United Kingdom, where eighteen months of Conservative rule had virtually buried the recollections of post-

[33] For details cf. *Report to Congress on the Mutual Security Program,* June 30, 1953, especially pp. 13-27.

[34] *Economic Survey of Europe Since the War: A Reappraisal of Problems and Prospects* (U.N. Publication 1953.II.E.4, Geneva, 1953); U.S. comment in *Department of State Bulletin,* XXVIII, April 13, 1953, 534-538.

[35] Communiqué, April 16, *ibid.,* May 18, 1953, 719-720.

[36] Cf. the summary of the debate in *United Nations Bulletin,* XIV, May 15, 1953, 363-365 and 379-381.

war "austerity." Britain during the spring of 1953 was enjoying something of a rebirth of imperial pomp and grandeur. A series of colorful pageants, which began with the conferring of the Order of the Garter on the Prime Minister on April 24 and culminated in the coronation of Queen Elizabeth II on June 2, helped the public to forget the slow erosion of Britain's position in the Middle East and elsewhere. Behind these stirring events, however, the situation of the United Kingdom left much to be desired, as thoughtful Britons readily acknowledged and as special Ambassador Lewis W. Douglas confirmed in part when he advised the President that Britain's sterling currency, though greatly strengthened in the last year or two, could not yet stand the strain of full convertibility with the dollar and other world currencies.[37]

France in Crisis

In France, with its antiquated physical plant, rigid social system, quarreling political parties, and large Communist minority, the negative aspects were even more conspicuous than the important advances which had been achieved since liberation. The free world had a large interest in the French situation, not only because of France's long-time intellectual and cultural leadership but also because of its key position in the military and political affairs of Europe, Asia, and Africa. Unfortunately the French nation, which two or three years earlier had offered so promising a lead in the twin conceptions of the Schuman Plan and the European Defense Community, was entering one of those periods of irresolution and instability which were the despair of its admirers and a priceless asset to the Communist enemies of freedom. Already France had balked at the original E.D.C. treaty, worked out with such solicitous concern for its natural apprehensions in proximity to a rearming Germany. During the next eighteen months it was to offer the free world a series of bitter disappointments as successive governments bowed to the caprices of the National Assembly and failed

[37] Letter of July 14, in *Documents on American Foreign Relations, 1953*, 253-254; cf. above, p. 98.

to cope with the deteriorating situation in Europe, North Africa, and Indochina.

France's "essential trouble," as one American official remarked, lay in the fact that the country was "over-extended populationwise, economically, and financially"—in other words, that the human and material resources on which the nation was able to draw no longer sufficed to maintain a world position inherited from a more fortunate era. Alone among the European great powers, France had attempted to perpetuate in the postwar era an imperial system that was no longer in harmony either with its own strength or with the spirit of the times. At home, there had been a lack of resolution to carry through the drastic reforms that would have been needed to support France's European and world pretensions. Accentuating the social tensions which French internal policies had failed to allay were the negative emotions generated by the E.D.C. and the prospect of German rearmament—a reaction which, to quote the same American observer,

> "stemmed from the heart of the vast majority of the French people who instinctively revolted against the thought of any kind of union with the traditional enemy of yesterday, and against the thought of the disappearance of the French Army of which the most outspoken antimilitaristic Frenchman remains proud deep down in his heart." [38]

At a particular moment, the predominant issue in France might nominally concern either domestic or foreign policy. At bottom, French affairs were governed by a complex tangle of interests and emotions in which all phases of the French position played a part.

In the weeks that followed the NATO conference, France was among the countries that displayed most eagerness to explore the prospects for a four-power meeting of Eastern and Western leaders, if only because such moves could offer a further excuse for postponing action on the E.D.C. treaty. Yet it was France's own National Assembly that forced the initial postponement of any moves in this direction by turn-

[38] Address by Ridgway B. Knight, Deputy Director, Office of Western European Affairs, May 7, in *Department of State Bulletin*, XXVIII, June 1, 1953, 774-775.

ing the Mayer cabinet out of office on May 21 and leaving the country without a government precisely when the French and British Prime Ministers had been scheduled to meet with President Eisenhower at Bermuda.[39] M. Mayer had taken office with the support of the Gaullists, who were opposed to E.D.C.; and it was the withdrawal of their support that occasioned the fall of his cabinet, technically through the rejection of a request for special financial powers. The ensuing cabinet crisis, the eighteenth since France's liberation, lasted for five incredible weeks before a candidate was found who could muster the requisite 314 Assembly votes and form a new cabinet. Of the many politicians interviewed by President Vincent Auriol, not all of whom were favorable to the E.D.C., only five ventured to present themselves before the Assembly: Paul Reynaud (Independent), Pierre Mendès-France (Radical), Georges Bidault (M.R.P.), who missed by one vote; André Marie (Radical), and Joseph Laniel (Independent), who eventually secured a favorable vote of 398–206 on June 26.[40] By that time the illness of Sir Winston Churchill had necessitated a further postponement of the Bermuda conference. Mr. Eden was also unwell, and on June 30 it was announced that three-power contacts for the moment would be limited to a meeting at the Foreign Secretaries' or Acting Foreign Secretaries' level to be held in Washington on July 10.[41]

Although M. Laniel had promised to maintain the continuity of French foreign policy and decided to retain M. Bidault in the post of Minister of Foreign Affairs, the presence of four Gaullists and of other lukewarm E.D.C. supporters in his cabinet suggested that continuity in European affairs would probably mean further delay for E.D.C., based on the preliminary conditions which M. Mayer had set out and M. Laniel had reaffirmed. Concerning Indochina, M. Laniel indicated a strong inclination to try to end the conflict by negotiation with the Communists, presumably through some sort of compromise. Like every French premier, he also

39 Cf. above, p. 135-136.

40 "De la Chute du gouvernement Mayer à l'avènement du cabinet Laniel," *Chronique de politique étrangère,* VI, September 1953, 626-634.

41 *Department of State Bulletin,* XXIX, July 13, 1953, 49; cf. below, p. 186 ff.

promised to undertake "structural" reforms of economic life, restore the "dynamism" of the national economy, and improve the housing situation. But none of these desirable objectives could be pursued until the national finances were brought into better order and measures taken to curb the yawning budgetary deficit. This would be even more difficult than in the past because the Laniel government, a coalition of the Center and Right, was opposed by the entire Left, including Socialists as well as Communists. Its proposed economy measures, which necessarily would affect the standard of living of wage earners (especially those in the government and nationalized industries), presently brought on the most serious strike wave France had experienced since the Popular Front days of 1936. Through most of August the country was tied up by strikes of postal and public service workers, railwaymen, and others, supported by the Socialist Workers' Force (*Force Ouvrière*) as well as the Communist-led General Confederation of Labor (C.G.T.). This was not a good augury for France's success in coping with the many urgent internal and foreign problems that pressed upon it.

Stagnation in Italy

In Italy, too, the forces of social discontent were threatening to break through the crust of political stability which the successive governments of Premier Alcide De Gasperi had imposed on the country over a period of years. Here, also, there was substantial resistance to the E.D.C. concept, stemming both from the dedicated opposition of Communists and left-wing Socialists and from the attitude of nationalist and monarchist elements which were more concerned with vindicating Italy's historic claims to Trieste than with participating in a new supranational organization. But in Italy, even more than in France, the roots of the disorder could be traced directly to economic and social factors—overpopulation, low productivity, and glaring inequalities in the distribution of wealth. In combination with an alert and disciplined Communist movement enjoying broad mass support, these factors had presented a basic threat to the survival of democratic government in Italy. In the crucial parliamentary elections of 1948, the danger had been averted and the

Christian Democratic party had been placed in a commanding position. But five years later, as the time for general national elections rolled round again, they still constituted a serious limitation on Italy's international role and held a threat of possible political paralysis.

Extraordinary precautions were taken to minimize any danger that might threaten the De Gasperi coalition as a result of the new elections, scheduled for June 7-8. A special electoral law, forced through Parliament on the assumption that the governing coalition could at least count on an absolute majority of the popular vote, provided that any group gaining such a majority would receive a bonus in the form of extra seats sufficient to give it undisputed control of the Chamber. The ardent desire of the United States for such an outcome was made unmistakably clear by Ambassador Luce, though it was to remain debatable among Italian experts whether Signor De Gasperi and the Christian Democrats actually gained or lost votes as the result of her warm endorsement. The Vatican, likewise, threw all its influence behind the anti-Communist cause. But when the official count of the 27 million ballots was completed, it appeared that the coalition had failed by 55,000 votes to qualify for the extra seats and would have to content itself with a scant 303 places in a Chamber of 593. The Christian Democrats, who alone had held an absolute majority in the old Chamber, sank to 262 seats and thus became totally dependent on the support of the smaller parties affiliated with them.

Analysis of the popular vote showed how far the centrist position represented by De Gasperi had weakened since the last national election. The coalition parties, which had captured 61.9 percent of the national vote in 1948, sank to 49.8 percent in 1953—a loss of more than one-fifth. The Communists and left-wing Socialists advanced from 31 percent in 1948 to 35.5 percent in 1953, a net increase of more than one-seventh. More impressive still was the advance of the Monarchists and the neo-Fascist Italian Social Movement (M.S.I.), which had been negligible quantities five years earlier but now accounted together for 12.7 percent of the popular vote and 69 seats in the Chamber. Of the 237 Senate seats at stake, the coalition parties won 125, the Left opposition 82, the Extreme Right 25, and others 5.

Months later it was to be claimed that a more accurate count would have given the coalition parties the extra votes they needed to gain firm control of the Chamber. The actual situation when the Chamber met, however, was such that the center coalition could not be reconstituted unless De Gasperi could gain the support not only of the Liberals and Republicans but also of Giuseppe Saragat and his right-wing Socialists—a group which, though steadfastly opposed to Communism, had never shown much enthusiasm for De Gasperi's policies either at home or abroad. In this crisis their support was not forthcoming, and De Gasperi felt compelled to resign on June 29. A new government which he formed in July (his eighth) was overturned by a vote of no confidence on July 28—the first such occurrence in Italy in more than thirty years.

De Gasperi's system of coalition government, Saragat had said, "was dead and buried." Further attempts to resuscitate it with rightist or leftist aid were rendered fruitless by divisions among the Christian Democrats themselves as well as by the virtual veto power held by Saragat's Democratic Socialists on one side and the Monarchists on the other. Eventually, in near-desperation, the Chamber approved on August 24 a cabinet formed by Christian Democrat Giuseppe Pella and comprising fifteen Christian Democrats and two nonparliamentary figures. Explicitly introduced as a stopgap, the Pella cabinet was to remain in office for want of an alternative until the very end of the year, a living witness to Italy's political and social deadlock.[42]

The German Resurgence

To such spectacles of instability and parliamentary impotence, the situation in Western Germany had offered a refreshing contrast. Here there were no strikes, no cabinet crises, few Communists, no economic disappointments, no marked evasions of American pressure on behalf of E.D.C. True, Germany also faced a general parliamentary election,

[42] Cf. "Les Crises gouvernementales en Italie," *Chronique de politique étrangère,* VII, May 1954, 292-298.

scheduled for September 6, which could conceivably place Chancellor Adenauer in the same uncomfortable predicament as his friend Signor De Gasperi. There were in Germany large elements which though anything but Communistically inclined were bitterly opposed to E.D.C. and many other aspects of allied policy, and who viewed the Chancellor and his aims with undisguised antipathy. These groups, of which the Social Democratic party was by far the largest and best organized, might yet prove to offer a clearer reflection of German national attitudes than the four-party coalition on which the United States had preferred to pin its hopes. For the moment, however, Americans could derive ample comfort from contemplating Western Germany's dramatic recovery from the material and political collapse of 1945.

The impressiveness of the postwar German achievement was not to be gainsaid, greatly assisted though it had been by American aid and by the exemption from rearmament burdens. Amid the omnipresent ruins that still defaced the national scene, the people of Western Germany together with the eight million Eastern refugees and expellees had rebuilt for themselves a thriving, bustling life in sharp contrast to the relative stagnation prevailing in France and Italy. Conditions in Germany could not yet be termed luxurious, except perhaps for those few who had known how to derive individual profit from the upheavals of recent years. The new wealth was not particularly well distributed; hardship as well as affluence was readily discernible.

Still, the changing face of the country confirmed the overall improvement registered in the economic indexes. The most populous state in continental Europe, Western Germany was also rising to first place in coal and steel production and in the volume of its foreign trade. Industrial output and exports were rising steadily. Despite a liberal import policy, the Federal Republic was rapidly becoming Europe's major creditor nation. Its credit balance with the European Payments Union grew from month to month. Nor was the expansion of German exports confined to Europe; its inroads in other world markets, especially in the Near East, were causing growing concern to Great Britain and other traditional competitors. Small wonder if London as well as Washington was eager to see Western Germany included in the European Defense Community, thus equalizing its national responsibilities as well as strengthening the defense of the West.

So far as the United States was concerned, with the advent of the new administration in Washington the Federal Republic seemed to have been taken back into favor virtually without reservation. The United States had been the original promoter of the idea of German rearmament, preferably though not necessarily within a framework of Western European union. From the beginning, the project had been favored in America even among persons not markedly sympathetic to this country's older allies. The action of the Bundestag in approving the E.D.C. treaty, and the favorable impression created by Dr. Adenauer on his April visit to Washington,[43] dissipated any misgivings that might have lingered in official quarters. The Federal Republic had already taken steps to liquidate Germany's accumulated foreign indebtedness [44] and to provide some indemnity to Jewish victims of Nazi persecution; [45] and the United States, on its side, was fully prepared to welcome Germany back into the international family. Among the results of Dr. Adenauer's visit were the return of 350 German vessels taken over by the United States in 1946,[46] discontinuance of the vesting of German-owned properties in this country,[47] an agreement to further cultural exchange between the United States and Germany,[48] and an agreement to revive the old American-German Treaty of Friendship, Commerce, and Consular Rights pending the negotiation of a modern and

[43] Cf. above, pp. 36-37.

[44] *The United States in World Affairs, 1952,* 152; cf. especially Martha M. Black, "The German Debt Settlement," *Department of State Bulletin,* XXIX, October 12, 1953, 479-481.

[45] *The United States in World Affairs, 1952,* 152; cf. "Le Traité de réparations israélo-allemand du 10 Septembre 1952," *Chronique de politique étrangère,* VII, May 1954, 313-331, and Frederick Honig, "The Reparations Agreement Between Israel and the Federal Republic of Germany," *American Journal of International Law,* XLVIII, October 1954, 564-578.

[46] *Department of State Bulletin,* XXVIII, April 20, 1953, 566-567.

[47] *Ibid.,* May 18, 1953, 720.

[48] *Ibid.,* April 20, 1953, 567-568.

more comprehensive friendship treaty.[49] Although Germany would not regain its formal sovereignty until the E.D.C. Treaty and the accompanying Contractual Agreements went into effect, we had, as one State Department official phrased it, "gradually moved from the occupation era to the era of cooperative action." [50]

Amid so much optimism and good will, it was difficult to face the fact that Western Germany still lacked many of the attributes of a strong and dependable partner. Its economic prospects apparently remained reasonably good, notwithstanding the distortion of economic life occasioned by the division of the country. As one authority wrote: "Given time for readjustment, with, say, ten years of good export markets, West Germany will survive the shock of partition" —although, paradoxically, he questioned whether it could withstand as easily "the shock of reunification" with the Eastern zone, where economic developments had been so different.[51] The problem of the original refugees and expellees likewise seemed on the way to gradual solution as more and more of them found a place in the economic life of Western Germany—although this group, constantly augmented by new arrivals from the East, would probably long remain a source of explosive political tendencies and of continuing outcries for the recovery of Germany's lost territories in the East.

Nor were most American observers unduly disturbed by the reemergence of ultranationalist and pro-Nazi tendencies, frequently as these were dramatized by such misadventures as the inadvertent release of a United States public opinion poll (January 17) which pointed to a surprisingly favorable opinion of National Socialism in the generation that had gone through the Hitler Youth. Although Chancellor Adenauer himself was firmly committed to combating any mani-

[49] The text of the agreement to revive the 1923 friendship treaty, signed at Bonn on June 3, approved by the Senate as Executive N, 83d Congress, 1st Session, on July 21, and proclaimed by the President with effect from October 22, appears with related documents, *ibid.*, XXIX, July 20, 1953, 93-94; see also *ibid.*, August 17, 1953, 224-226.

[50] Richard Straus, "America's Changing Relationship with Germany," *ibid.*, July 6, 1953, 12.

[51] Percy W. Bidwell, "How Strong Is the New Germany?" *Yale Review*, XLII, Summer, 1953, 491.

festations of reviving Nazism, the anti-Nazi zeal of his government was rated somewhat less highly. It was the British, not the German authorities, who on January 14 dramatically arrested Dr. Werner Naumann, a former Goebbels aide, and six associates who were charged with plotting a Nazi comeback and intriguing with highly placed members of the coalition parties. At the time, this action seemed almost deliberately calculated to undermine the prestige of the Adenauer government as well as the confidence of France and other nations in the intentions of the new Germany. The government, moreover, showed no taste for strong action when the arrested men were eventually handed over to German jurisdiction. Most of them were individually released, although Naumann and one confederate were belatedly indicted in June 1954 on the comparatively mild charge of "associations subversive of the constitution." In the meantime the government took steps to dissolve the newly formed and openly pro-Nazi German Reich party, with which Naumann had been affiliated.

Such incidents clouded the view of those who sought to peer into Germany's future, and provided a steady stream of arguments to the French opponents of E.D.C. For the present, however, problems of this order seemed quite subordinate to the glaring issues that arose from Germany's partition between East and West, a state of affairs that overshadowed every other aspect of German life and went far to explain the instability and uncertainty of German popular attitudes. Whatever the innermost feelings of the average West German about the plight of his fellow countrymen in the East, the existing situation was both disagreeable and disquieting. There was a general feeling that the division of the country at the line of the Iron Curtain was something too artificial, too absurd to last. Either Germany would be reunited, in which case all existing political arrangements would have to be completely refashioned, or it would become an East-West battleground, in which case nothing that had been accomplished to date would save Germany from almost certain catastrophe. Few Germans could seriously envisage a third possibility, namely that the existing division would continue for years, with the two parts of the country growing farther and farther apart politically, economically, and in fundamental outlook.

This was the situation that primarily determined German attitudes toward E.D.C. and all aspects of the movement toward integration with the West. In the eyes of most Germans, such integration would possess real value only if it promised to forward, and not to impede, the supreme aim of reunifying the country. And it was on precisely this point that German opinions clashed most violently. The Western powers, notably the United States, had been telling Germany for years that the way to achieve reunification was to join up with the West, thus creating a "situation of strength" in which the Western world would be able to negotiate on an equal footing with the Russians—or in which the Russians would bow to the attractive forces of freedom and voluntarily renounce their rule over Eastern Germany. But the Russians themselves had for years been telling them exactly the opposite. According to Moscow, if Western Germany aligned itself with the West—especially if it allowed itself to be rearmed under Western auspices—unification would be made impossible. The way to reunify Germany, the Russians said, was through immediate negotiation between East and West Germans under the auspices of the four occupying powers—in other words, through a "deal" to be worked out on terms dictated from Moscow.[52]

Some Germans inclined more to one view, some to the other. Chancellor Adenauer and many of his supporters, perceiving that negotiation on the basis of any Soviet proposals offered to date could never lead to their goal of "unity in freedom," had preferred to associate themselves with the Western position. European union, they felt, was a good thing in itself; who could be sure that all Germany might not some day find a place in a united Europe? But other Germans, not only the powerful and anti-Communist Social Democrats but many of conservative views or without party affiliation, were skeptical of the Western assurances and believed the Russians meant what they said about rearmament being incompatible with reunification. Without in most instances being deceived by Communist proposals for reunifi-

[52] Cf. *The United States in World Affairs, 1952,* 138-149 and 283-284.

cation on Soviet terms, they still felt that it would be a mistake to commit themselves irrevocably to the West before the possibility of agreement with the East had been fully explored. This feeling was naturally strengthened by the death of Stalin and the intimations of a new mood in Moscow, accompanied as they were by a series of moves obviously aimed at stirring new hopes and thus delaying the consolidation of Western Europe's unity.[53]

There were other factors which contributed to German opposition to the official Western policy—the spirit of party rivalry, the collapse of a military spirit after World War II, fear of reviving militarism at home, patriotic grievances over the Saar, fear of invasion, skepticism about allied defense plans, the desire of German businessmen to expand their trade with the East. All such considerations, together with irrational factors and private concerns of all sorts, were certain to play a role in the September elections, which would determine whether the Adenauer policy of integration first could continue or whether some new approach to the German problem must be sought. If power passed to Erich Ollenhauer and the Social Democrats, or if the Chancellor lost his present working majority, it was unlikely that matters would run as smoothly as in the past even if it was conceded that the Social Democrats, in the last analysis, were not less loyal to Western democratic values than their opponents. Each of the great powers of East and West had a large stake in the outcome, and their collective control over the prospects of unification gave them a powerful leverage. As the Big Four continued through the summer to explore each others' intentions by diplomatic notes, proposals, and counterproposals, each word would be weighed in the light of its effect on the precarious internal balance in Germany.

4. EAST-WEST RELATIONS AND THE GERMAN ELECTION

The reviving prospect of a Big Four meeting or, at least, of a renewal of the long dormant East-West debate on the German issue, had occasioned lively excitement in the Fed-

[53] Cf. the comment of Secretary Dulles, June 15, in *Department of State Bulletin,* XXVIII, June 29, 1953, 896.

eral Republic and led Chancellor Adenauer to send a special emissary to Washington at the beginning of June as well as communicating with the heads of the British and French governments. From President Eisenhower he received the fullest assurance that American policy toward Germany had not changed and that no decisions concerning the German question would be taken at the Bermuda conference or elsewhere without consulting the Chancellor. Sir Winston Churchill and M. Mayer likewise indicated that their governments continued to adhere to the well-established allied policy of insisting on free elections throughout Germany as a necessary first step toward reunification and the conclusion of an all-German peace treaty.[54] The subsequent postponement of the Bermuda conference and the substitution of a meeting of Foreign Secretaries in Washington reduced the likelihood of important developments affecting Germany before the end of the summer; but the West German government and Bundestag proceeded to record once again their own insistence on a democratic solution for all Germany and busied themselves with plans for the holding of nationwide free elections as soon as the great powers gave the word. Chancellor Adenauer sent a special message to Mr. Dulles urging that a four-power conference on the German question be scheduled for the autumn, at latest, and added the suggestion that a general security system be worked out within the framework of the United Nations which would take account of Russian as well as Western security needs.

All of this presupposed that the Russians had modified their own policies on Germany sufficiently to permit free elections to be held throughout the entire country—despite the fact that such elections would almost certainly result in an overwhelming repudiation of the Soviet-controlled East German government. Up to now, however, there had been no firm indication that Moscow was ready to consider such a drastic change of policy; and the Western powers as yet had not even reached agreement on how to go about discovering what was in the minds of the Soviet leaders.

[54] Adenauer-Eisenhower correspondence, June 21-25, in *Department of State Bulletin,* XXIX, July 6, 1953, 10-11. Further details on this section in "La Conférence de Washington (10-14 juillet 1953)," *Chronique de politique étrangère,* VI, September 1953, 598-625.

Despite the frequently expressed reluctance of the United States to consider a face-to-face meeting with the Russians before the latter had given more convincing demonstrations of "sincerity," British policy was still dominated by the hope of a high-level consultation between Soviet and Western leaders such as Prime Minister Churchill had suggested in his speech of May 11.[55] Sir Winston had been "most anxious" to see the President and "set before him personally" the argument he had advanced on that occasion. With the agreement of the Cabinet, he had "prepared in every way" for a conference with Mr. Eisenhower, at which he had "hoped to persuade him to arrange with me to invite a three-Power conference"—from which, apparently, France would have been excluded. But before any meeting could take place, the Prime Minister had been "struck down by a very sudden illness which paralyzed me completely, physically." [56] Since Foreign Secretary Eden was also ill, it was the Marquess of Salisbury, Lord President of the Council and acting Foreign Secretary, who eventually sat down in Washington on July 10 with Mr. Dulles and M. Bidault, Minister of Foreign Affairs in the new Laniel government.

The "Little Bermuda" Conference

Although the Prime Minister later declared that Lord Salisbury had "raised all the arguments which [he himself] would have used in favor of a meeting of the heads of Government," such a project went considerably beyond the immediate interest of the American or even the French representatives. Personalities apart, there was not much chance for fruitful negotiation with the Russians unless the latter should voluntarily come forward with concessions to the Western viewpoint. As we have already seen, the Western governments were of the opinion that on most of the specific issues in dispute they could not afford to make concessions of substance to their unscrupulous rival.[57] In reaffirming the principle of free all-German elections, for example, they

[55] Cf. above, pp. 132-134.
[56] Statements by Sir W. Churchill in *Parliamentary Debates, Weekly Hansard,* House of Commons, March 2, 1955, 2120 and March 14, 1955, 962.
[57] Cf. above, pp. 126-128.

had already declared in effect that the German problem would have to be solved their way or not at all.

In the United States in particular, the tendency at this period was not to offer concessions or even conversations to the adversary but to hold firm in the expectation that the Soviet Union itself would soon be forced to back down. To Secretary Dulles, the recent Berlin rising had offered fresh confirmation of his belief "that the Soviet Communist leaders would come to recognize the futility of trying to hold captive so many peoples who, by their faith and their patriotism, can never really be consolidated into a Soviet Communist world." [58] On the opening day of the Washington conference came the further news of Beria's disgrace. "Freedom is again in the air," Mr. Dulles told the conferees. "A new convulsion is underway. The old system may remain and may continue to threaten, but inherent weakness is disclosed. Totalitarian states always seem hard and united when they are looked upon from without. But their very rigidity is a basic defect." [59]

This optimistic appraisal, even if not fully shared by Lord Salisbury and M. Bidault, helped to define the intellectual framework within which the conference would operate as well as the concrete proposals which would result from its deliberations. There would be no move to bring about a meeting of heads of state such as Sir Winston Churchill had urged, nor would there be any change of position on essential issues. To quote the Prime Minister's later report:

"The idea of a top-level four-Power meeting . . . with a fluid or flexible agenda, was presented forcefully to the Americans and to the French. They could only be brought to agree to an invitation to the Russians for a meeting of the four Foreign Ministers to discuss specifically free elections in Germany, German reunification, and the conclusion of the Austrian Treaty. This was duly

[58] Statement of June 30, in *Department of State Bulletin,* XXIX, July 13, 1953, 40.

[59] Statement to the opening session, July 10, *ibid.,* July 20, 1953, 72. Later information indicated that an unprecedented wave of strikes involving many thousands of slave laborers in Soviet work camps was taking place at this very time. See especially the account of John H. Noble in *New York Times,* April 6, 1955.

conveyed to the Soviet Government. It was the utmost we could get." [60]

The chief result of the Washington conference, therefore, was an invitation to the Soviet Government to join in a fresh attempt to solve the German and Austrian problems on the old basis—specifically, to schedule a meeting of the four Foreign Ministers, which might take place in the early autumn, to discuss the organization of free elections throughout Germany, the establishment of a free all-German government, and the conclusion of the Austrian treaty.[61] If Mr. Molotov should come to such a meeting prepared to defer to allied views, that would be all to the good; if not, the Western powers would at least have done their duty, paid another tribute to the principle of free elections (which, Mr. Dulles had declared, was now capturing the imagination of the captive peoples), and put the issue safely on ice until after the forthcoming elections in Western Germany.

A number of compromises went into the making of this proposal. For Mr. Dulles it represented a considerable departure from his earlier view that no four-power conference should be held until the U.S.S.R. had given concrete proof of its peaceful intentions. The Secretary of State did not even insist, as he would doubtless have preferred to do, that the holding of a conference be made contingent on prior ratification of the E.D.C. treaty. On the other hand, a conference of Foreign Ministers limited to the German and Austrian questions fell far short of Sir Winston Churchill's desire for a general discussion at the highest level. The detailed proposal of the three governments made it quite plain, moreover, that they had no intention of retreating from the substance of the established Western position on Germany. Not only would they continue to insist on all of their previous conditions, starting with "necessary guarantees for freedom of movement, freedom of action for political parties, freedom of the press, and the enjoyment of the basic free-

[60] *Parliamentary Debates, Weekly Hansard,* House of Commons, March 14, 1955, 962-963.

[61] Conference communiqué, July 14, in *Documents on American Foreign Relations, 1953,* 213.

doms by all Germans before, during and after elections."[62] They also reiterated in their communiqué the determination to maintain the defensive strength of NATO and support the growth of a "stable, secure European Community" including the European Defense Community and a rearmed Western Germany. That community, they said, was "peaceful by its very nature," and "not directed against anyone." It could not be scrapped merely because the U.S.S.R. objected to it.

Not less urgent to the Washington conferees than the question of a four-power meeting was the need to try to smooth out the many other differences which had developed among the Western powers in the months since Stalin's death. Great Britain was especially anxious to reestablish some degree of harmony with this country in Far Eastern affairs, which would soon be entering a new phase with the signature of the Korean armistice agreement.[63] France was eager to find out what support could be expected from the United States if it was decided to continue the war in Indochina. The United States would have been glad of some assurance that the European Defense Community would be ratified by France without further delay. Until such problems had been thrashed out and a measure of basic unity reestablished within the Western camp, it would be hazardous to think in terms of broad-scale negotiation with the Russians even if the latter showed unexpected willingness to meet the minimum Western terms.

The discussion of Far Eastern matters at Washington was noteworthy as a first collective attempt by the Western powers to look beyond the impending armistice in Korea. Here, too, there was apparently no disposition to make unwarranted concessions to the Communists. Despite the widespread feeling in Europe that a settlement in Korea should pave the way for a general settlement with Communist China, Mr. Dulles persuaded his two colleagues "that, in existing circumstances and pending further consultation, the common policies of the three Powers towards Communist China should be maintained." This meant continued re-

[62] U.S. note to the U.S.S.R., July 15, *ibid.*, 218-220.

[63] Cf. below, pp. 229-231.

strictions on China trade and continued exclusion of Communist China from the United Nations. Equally important was a renewed warning to the Communists not to think of any further aggression in the Far East, either in Korea or elsewhere. If the aggression in Korea were renewed after an armistice, it was stated, the three governments "would as members of the United Nations again support the restoration of peace and security." An armistice in Korea, moreover, "must not result in jeopardizing the restoration or the safeguarding of peace in any other part of Asia." With specific reference to Indochina, Mr. Dulles and Lord Salisbury commended the intention recently expressed by the French to hasten the sovereignty and independence of the Associated States within the French Union. This, they declared, was one of the most promising steps toward "a satisfactory outcome and the restoration of peace" in that war-torn land. Nothing was said for publication about the growing desire in France to settle the Indochina problem by some kind of direct negotiation with the Communists.[64]

The main achievement of the Washington conference, in the opinion of most observers, had been to reaffirm the unity of the Western allies in the face of Soviet efforts to divide them. The unity, however, was based more on phrases than on fundamental objectives, as seemed evident from the varying interpretations of the conference offered by the participants themselves. M. Bidault and especially Lord Salisbury were at pains to point out to their parliamentary bodies that the door to a four-power conference on a higher level was still open, and that a change in policy toward Communist China was likewise not excluded. Mr. Dulles laid more stress on the reaffirmation of existing policies, which, he said, were now "showing their worth" as crisis increasingly rocked the Soviet world.[65] With reference to Eastern Europe, the conference had expressed only a general desire "to see true liberty restored"; whereas the State Department in its independent utterances was formally reaffirming "the firm and abiding purpose of the United States" to bring about condi-

[64] Communiqué, July 14, cited; for details on Indochina cf. below, pp. 271 ff.
[65] Broadcast, July 17, in *Department of State Bulletin*, XXIX, July 27, 1953, 99-102.

tions which would make this possible.[66] Regarding Germany, the President assured Chancellor Adenauer in a letter of July 23 that the policy outlined in the Washington communiqué was merely the "diplomatic confirmation" of earlier statements by President, Chancellor, and Bundestag. He went on to picture possible future developments in Germany in terms of prompt formation of E.D.C., eventual "liquidation of the present Communist dictatorship and of the Soviet occupation," and the emergence of a reunited Germany—which, he said, would be wise enough to avoid "complete and premature disarmament" and "defenseless neutralization" at a time when other nations might remain heavily armed.[67]

Such an outcome was, of course, exactly what the Soviet Union had for years been devoting all its energies to preventing. Unless it had radically altered its views, the Kremlin was not likely to look very favorably on Western proposals which pointed in the direction of the President's vision. Even before the President's letter was written, the French neutralist organ *Le Monde* had commented that if the Big Three had wanted to be sure of a Soviet refusal they could not have done better than to repeat, as they had done, the terms for Germany which the U.S.S.R. had already found totally unacceptable.[68] Soviet reaction to the allied overture would presently strengthen the view that Moscow, while unwilling to reject the Western concept in so many words, was by no means ready to agree to free elections in Germany under any conditions that could cost the U.S.S.R. its position in the country. Instead, the Kremlin set itself to play upon the still obvious differences among the allies while keeping German (and Western European) opinion in ferment by hinting at other possibilities than those envisaged in Washington.

66 Letter of Livingston T. Merchant, Assistant Secretary for European Affairs, July 16, *ibid.*, August 10, 1953, 183-184. The same point was made by implication in a note of July 31 to Czechoslovakia, rejecting a Czechoslovak protest (July 20) against the release in Germany of propaganda balloons intended for the Czechoslovak people by the American "Crusade for Freedom" organization. *Ibid.*, August 17, 1953, 210-211.

67 *Ibid.*, August 3, 1953, 147-149.

68 *Le Monde*, July 17, quoted in *Chronique de politique étrangère*, VI, September 1953, 622.

Malenkov on World Policy

To understand the diplomatic exchanges which were initiated by the Western note of July 15 and continued up to the opening of the Berlin conference in January 1954, it is useful to consider the general outlook which apparently colored Moscow's approach to international relations in the second half of 1953. A full-dress presentation of the Soviet "line" on domestic and foreign policy was offered by Premier Malenkov in a report delivered before the Supreme Soviet on August 8—a document which ranks with President Eisenhower's address of April 16 and Prime Minister Churchill's speech of May 11 as one of the major policy declarations of the post-Stalin phase of the "cold war." [69] Its most notable features, apart from its promise of greater benefits for Soviet consumers, were its comparatively moderate, "reasonable" tone and an air of assured self-confidence that seemed to belie the weakness Washington claimed to have discerned in the Soviets' position. For Malenkov, Beria's recent treachery was not worth mentioning. The Korean armistice (signed July 27) represented not a decisive setback for Communist aims but a great and noteworthy victory for the "peace-loving forces." Even the liquidation of the Berlin riots was "an important victory for the cause of peace." The international position of the U.S.S.R., Malenkov averred, was actually "firmer than ever before"; and he was able to cite at least one important asset which Washington had overlooked in its calculation of relative strength. For this was the occasion on which Malenkov revealed the most shattering news of the entire year. "The government considers it necessary to report," he declared, "that the United States has no monopoly of production of the hydrogen bomb."

In his general discussion of international affairs, Malenkov asserted that "a clear improvement in the international situation" had become apparent. "After a long period of growing tension, a certain relaxation in the international atmosphere can now be felt for the first time in the postwar years." The Soviet Union, he said, was doing everything possible to forward this healthy process, true to its long-established

[69] Extensive excerpts appear in *Documents on American Foreign Relations, 1953,* 136-149; cf. also pp. 147-148, above.

policy of "preserving and strengthening peace" and developing "cooperation and business ties with states which desire this." Unfortunately, he claimed, these efforts had been impeded by the attitude of "aggressive circles" which were "stubbornly opposed to a relaxation of international tension" and whose greed for war profits was producing actions in direct conflict with President Eisenhower's statement about resolving international problems with respect for the rights of all countries. Nevertheless, said Malenkov, "It would be a crime before mankind if the certain relaxation in the international atmosphere were to yield to a fresh increase in tension." The U.S.S.R. continued to believe that there was no issue—even among those in dispute between the United States and the U.S.S.R.—that could not be solved peacefully "on the basis of mutual agreement of the interested parties." The U.S.S.R. still stood for "peaceful coexistence of the two systems," considered that there was "no objective basis for conflict" between the United States and the Soviet Union, and was confident that the security interests of both countries, as well as international security (and United States-Soviet trade development) could be ensured "on the basis of normal relations between the two countries." All that was needed for a solution of international problems, he implied, was a complete change in the attitude of the United States.

Having thus attempted to place on the United States the full responsibility for the existing unsatisfactory state of international affairs, Malenkov went on to indicate that the Soviet position on all matters of substance was still completely unchanged. Talks among the great powers could be useful, he said, provided "suitable prerequisites" were created. But these "prerequisites" would have involved a change in American (and Western) policy hardly less revolutionary than President Eisenhower had appeared to ask of the Soviet Union in his speech of April 16. Among them were not only the renunciation of an "aggressive policy" but also the restoration of (Communist) China to "its rightful place both in the United Nations and in the whole system of international relations"; renunciation of a "prejudiced approach" to the Soviet proposals for a peace pact among the "five great powers"; renunciation of the policy of "dragging Germany into an aggressive military bloc" and "reviving an aggressive militarist Germany"; withdrawal of the "abbreviated treaty" for Austria; [70] and a reversal of policy in the United Nations which would return that body "to the path determined by the U.N. Charter." As usual, these demands were set forth in language calculated to appeal strongly to all who differed with one aspect or another of the official United States-North Atlantic policy. Especially noteworthy was the appeal to French fears of a new militarist Germany, "the mortal enemy of France and other neighboring states." Any attempt to link France with E.D.C., said Malenkov, "would mean handing over France to the German revanchists."

East-West Dialogue

But if the U.S.S.R. felt strong enough to continue insisting on its previous position on all these fundamental issues, it was difficult to see much chance for progress even if a four-power conference was held—unless, of course, the West should see fit to modify its own position in the light of what Malenkov had said about Soviet possession of the hydrogen bomb. This startling disclosure was to be confirmed within a few days.[71] Meanwhile, the U.S.S.R.'s official reply to the Western notes of July 15, delivered on August 4,[72] offered no particular hope of agreement on Germany or anything else. While perfectly ready to discuss the German question, it said, the Soviet Government found the Western proposals defective from both a procedural and a substantive point of view. Procedurally, the German question ought not to be taken up in isolation but should be considered as part of the general question of "measures which promote a general lessening of tension in international relations, including questions of reduction of armaments and impermissibility of foreign military bases on territory of other states." Because of the importance of Asian problems in international affairs, the participation of the (Communist) Chinese People's

[70] Cf. below at note 73.
[71] Cf. below, pp. 348-349.
[72] *Department of State Bulletin,* XXIX, September 14, 1953, 352-353; excerpts in *Documents on American Foreign Relations, 1953,* 220-222.

Republic was also said to be "necessary" in any such discussion. As to the detailed proposals of the West regarding free elections in Germany, these were dismissed as a mere delaying tactic aimed at perpetuating the division of the country and delaying the conclusion of a peace treaty. With respect to Austria, the U.S.S.R. recalled once again its demand for withdrawal of the "abbreviated treaty" [73] and suggested that "possible successes in settlement of the German problem could also contribute to a decision of the Austrian treaty as well."

Not many years earlier, the Soviet Government itself had been demanding a big-power conference on the German problem and the Western powers, *per contra*, had been insisting that the scope of any such discussions be broadened to encompass the general sources of international tension.[74] Now the positions were reversed, and it was the West which sought to limit the discussions. Of all the contentious issues of international affairs in 1953, Germany and Austria were those on which the Soviet case was weakest and the allies were most nearly in agreement. If they were not actually the only issues on which the United States was then prepared to engage in East-West discussions, they were undoubtedly those on which it could negotiate most comfortably. But for just these reasons, the Soviet Union found it preferable to try to bring in additional issues on which it could inveigh against the United States position and perhaps develop further cleavages in the solidarity of its Western opponents. Nothing, for instance, could have been better calculated to cause renewed dissension in the West than a proposal to include Communist China in discussion of international problems—an idea for which there was considerable non-Communist support, especially now that the fighting in Korea was ended, but to which the United States remained unalterably opposed. Meanwhile, the Russians had given no sign that they meant to moderate their own claims regarding the treatment of Germany; and by suggesting that the Austrian and German issues were in some way interlinked, they had

[73] Cf. the Soviet note of July 30, *ibid.*, 237-238, and above, pp. 137-139.
[74] *The United States in World Affairs, 1950,* 434-436.

laid a basis for further delaying the signature of an Austrian treaty as well.

Apparently Moscow, like Washington, had reached the conclusion that negotiation at this stage was unlikely to produce acceptable results and that any advantages to be gained would lie in the domain of political warfare, not that of practical diplomacy. Most of the diplomatic notes exchanged during the next few months thus seemed directed more toward the gallery of world opinion than toward their nominal recipients.

One possible exception, however was the note on Austria which the Western powers presented in Moscow on August 17, in which they proposed a new meeting of the Deputies and for the first time definitely promised not to reintroduce their "abbreviated treaty" if only the U.S.S.R. would refrain from raising "extraneous issues" and would really conclude the treaty promptly and not try to tie it up with the German question. To this the Russians replied on August 28 with a restatement of all their earlier arguments, together with an intimation that they would conclude no treaty with Austria that was not based on the harsh provisions agreed upon by all four powers back in 1949.[75] Though their representatives in Austria had meanwhile imitated a number of steps taken by the allies in earlier years to lighten Austria's occupation burden, they clearly had no intention of surrendering their position in the country unless they could gain other advantages more solid than the West seemed likely to offer them.[76]

On the more vital question of Germany, the Russians themselves took the initiative in a new note to the Western powers on August 15 [77] which was clearly composed with an eye to the West German elections, by that time only three weeks away. In its earlier note of August 4 the U.S.S.R. had offered to discuss Germany at a general conference on international tensions. Without withdrawing this offer, it now

[75] U.S. note, August 17, in *Documents on American Foreign Relations, 1953,* 238-239; Soviet note (here dated August 29) in *New York Times,* August 30, 1953.

[76] Cf. "La Question du Traité d'Etat Autrichien," *Chronique de politique étrangère,* VI, November 1953, 734-742.

[77] *Department of State Bulletin,* XXIX, September 14, 1953, 354-356; excerpts in *Documents on American Foreign Relations, 1953,* 223-225.

proposed a different procedure ostensibly calculated to produce quicker and better results. After denouncing the allied proposals regarding free elections in Germany as well as the plans for including Western Germany in E.D.C.—a step which, it reiterated, would make the reunification of Germany "impossible"—the Kremlin offered three concrete proposals: (1) the convocation of a German peace conference within six months; (2) the formation of a provisional all-German government, and "the carrying out of free all-German elections" under its supervision and that of the four powers; and (3) the easing of Germany's financial and economic obligations growing out of the war and the postwar occupation.

When closely analyzed, points (1) and (2) proved to be no more than an updating of earlier Soviet proposals aimed at appealing to German opinion while safeguarding essential Soviet interests in Germany. Their key feature was the composition of the provisional all-German government which was to speak for Germany in both domestic and foreign affairs. Far from being formed on the basis of prior, genuinely free elections, as the allies and the Federal Republic insisted, this body was to be formed by agreement between the democratic government of the Federal Republic and the Communist shadow government of Eastern Germany. Only after this highly artificial government had been set up would elections be held, and then only under conditions to be worked out with the aid of the four powers. Although the Soviet note did not explicitly say so, its tone and language left the impression that care would be taken at each stage of this procedure to prevent any clear expression of German anti-Communist opinion and ensure that the Communists would emerge stronger than ever.

As to point (3), the easing of financial and economic obligations, several measures to alleviate the economic position in the two parts of Germany were proposed: discontinuance of reparation payments after 1953; cancellation of postwar noncommercial indebtedness to the four powers; limitation of current occupation costs to 5 percent of the respective state budgets, or to the 1949 level; and cancellation of indebtedness arising out of occupation costs since 1945. What this meant in practice would depend on clearer definition, although it was worth noting that the Western powers, on their side, had ceased exacting reparations from their zone of Germany as far back as 1949. That the proposed concessions would not involve serious economic sacrifice by the U.S.S.R. seemed all the more probable when Moscow, without awaiting a reply from the West, unilaterally conferred these and other supposed advantages on the East German government leaders who visited the Soviet capital on August 20-22.[78] "It remains to be seen," commented the State Department's skeptical spokesman, "whether the lot of the individual East Zone inhabitant will improve." [79]

But the main weakness of the Soviet note was its failure to deal frankly with the allied proposal for an early four-power conference. As an alternative to this clear-cut initiative it had offered nothing better than "a series of devices which could result in postponing to some indeterminate date the holding of free elections in the Federal Republic, in the East Zone of Germany, and in Berlin." This was a disappointment to Western opinion on which the allies still had time to capitalize before the German election. After consulting among themselves and with Chancellor Adenauer's government, they got off a new note on September 2 in which they endeavored to drive home their point. Omitting "sterile discussion" of the many argumentative points raised by the Soviet Union, they confined themselves to reasserting their interest in an early four-power meeting to discuss free elections in Germany and the status of the future German government. Such a meeting, they said, could take place in Lugano on October 15; the Swiss Government had already agreed. While regretting the Soviet evasions on Austria (which they took care to characterize as a quite distinct problem), they hoped an agreement on the Austrian treaty would also be reached at the same meeting.[80]

[78] Communiqué August 22, *ibid.*, 176-178; cf. above, p. 144.
[79] *Department of State Bulletin*, XXIX, September 7, 1953, 311.
[80] U.S. note, September 2, in *Documents on American Foreign Relations, 1953*, 225-227. Cf. "L'Echange de notes avec l'U.R.S.S. à propos du problème allemand," *Chronique de politique étrangère*, VI, November 1953, 727-733; and for later developments see below, pp. 382-387.

Dr. Adenauer's Triumph

In thus maintaining the pressure for early action on the German question, the Western powers contrived to accentuate the dissatisfaction which the latest Soviet note had aroused in Western Germany. In the days before the election, the allies took other steps which were at least partly designed to convince West Germany's electorate that its best hopes lay with them and with the Adenauer government. On August 27 the Western High Commissioners in Germany urged their Soviet opposite to agree on a relaxation of the irksome restrictions affecting travel between Eastern and Western occupation areas; [81] five days later they announced that at Dr. Adenauer's request they were providing for German representation on the mixed consultative boards whose function was to recommend clemency or parole in the cases of convicted German war criminals.[82] From the American side the pressure was particularly strong. Secretary Dulles told his press conference on September 3 that the continued partition of Germany imposed by the U.S.S.R. was "a scandal" and, more than that, "a crime" and "a menace to the peace." Forsaking the custom of avoiding comment on other countries' internal politics, he went on to say that a defeat for the Adenauer coalition in the forthcoming elections would be disastrous to Germany and its hopes of unity.[83]

A Social Democratic spokesman in Germany, speaking on behalf of those Germans who regarded the Adenauer policy as itself prejudicial to German unity, criticized the Secretary's statement as "an unheard-of twisting of the facts, and a malicious effort of the United States Government to intervene in the German elections." [84] But the Social Democrats and those who shared their views were fighting a losing battle, as became evident when the ballots were counted on September 6. In a record turnout of more than 27 million voters, the coalition parties (Christian Democrats, Free Democrats, and German party) not only retained their control of the Bundestag but gained enough additional seats to

[81] *Department of State Bulletin,* XXIX, September 21, 1953, 391-392.
[82] *Ibid.,* 391.
[83] *New York Times,* September 4, 1953.
[84] *Ibid.*

command a two-thirds majority in conjunction with the new refugee group known as the All-German Bloc. Adenauer's own Christian Democratic and Christian Social Union, the strongest of the coalition parties, won 45.2 percent of the vote and 244 seats, a majority of one in the 487-seat chamber. The Social Democrats, with 28.8 percent of the popular vote and 150 seats, remained as a strong opposition force but lost any hope of effecting a reversal of official policy. Possibly even more noteworthy than the vote of confidence in Dr. Adenauer, whom the British Prime Minister had described as "perhaps the wisest German statesman since the days of Bismarck," was the repudiation of extremist groups, both leftist and rightist. The Communists secured only 2.2 percent of the popular vote; the neo-Nazi Socialist Reich party gained only 1.1 percent. Under a new electoral law adopted earlier in the year, these and other splinter groups representing less than 5 percent of the electorate were denied representation in the new Bundestag. The triumph of the coalition appeared complete.

Not unnaturally, these results were hailed in Washington as an overwhelming endorsement of the Adenauer policies "of German membership in the European community, of democratic reconstruction and of uncompromising opposition to Soviet designs." [85] An endorsement they certainly were, though perhaps rather of the man than of his policies. That the outcome was a great victory for American aims and a severe setback to those of the U.S.S.R. was beyond question; in fact, it represented one of the three principal foreign policy successes of the first year of the Eisenower administration, the others being the Korean armistice and the disappearance of the Mosaddeq government in Iran. Possibly, however, the success could be better measured in terms of the perils it averted than in terms of concrete advance toward American objectives. A defeat of the coalition undoubtedly would have produced a state of dangerous confusion and perhaps dealt a crippling blow to the cause of European unity. How far Dr. Adenauer's victory would speed the advance toward unity in Europe was still a ques-

[85] State Department comment, September 7, in *Department of State Bulletin*, XXIX, September 14, 1953, 356.

tion. E.D.C. had not yet been finally ratified by any other Western country, and considerable time would certainly have to pass before Germany's reluctant youth could be summoned to the recruitment centers.

Some observers of the German scene went so far as to cast serious doubt on the interpretation of Adenauer's victory as a favorable plebiscite on Western policies for Germany. The great issues of foreign policy had perhaps not weighed as heavily with the average German voter as they had done in Washington and other Western capitals. Possibly more telling was the fact that under Dr. Adenauer's leadership the ordinary German had regained a considerable measure of personal security and well-being. A booming economy, rather than preoccupation with the great questions of East and West, was felt by some to be the source of his success. Large political conceptions were somewhat out of fashion in postwar Germany; even Dr. Adenauer's own party was more a coalition of interest groups than the embodiment of any political or religious principle. One German writer said of the election: "The great mass of the little people felt entitled to demand first of all security and prosperity." Another, looking back some sixteen months later, denied that it represented "a decision in favor of Europe" and called it "an election of 'full stomachs' . . . a personal message to the great Chancellor that he should 'go on the way he had done.' "[86]

If Germany's orientation was indeed determined mainly by individual interests and by confidence in a particular personality, one could hardly fail to ask what would happen when the personality disappeared (Dr. Adenauer was seventy-seven) and interests changed. Meanwhile, however, the free world was at liberty to make the best of the opportunities presented by the existing state of affairs. At the very least, the election of September 6 assured the West additional time to work out a common position on the great questions that still awaited resolution—especially those affecting the broad East-West relationship in both Europe and Asia.

[86] *Die Gegenwart,* September 12, 1953; Claus Jacobi, "Germany's Great Old Man," *Foreign Affairs,* XXXIII, January 1955, 244-245.

5. MEDITERRANEAN DEVELOPMENTS

While world attention was fixed on the dialogue between East and West and the prospects for unity in Europe, developments had been occurring along NATO's southern flank which would also have an important bearing on future Western security calculations. At the southeastern extremity of the NATO defense area, the solidarity of the non-Soviet world had been materially strengthened, for the moment at least, by a treaty of friendship and cooperation between Yugoslavia, Greece, and Turkey. At the head of the Adriatic, which was likewise an essential sector from the standpoint of NATO's defensive strategy, that solidarity was still gravely impaired by the perennial rivalry between Italy and Yugoslavia over the Free Territory of Trieste. In the Western Mediterranean, however, the United States and Spain were at long last preparing to sign an agreement whereby this country would secure the use of Spanish air and naval bases while furnishing economic and military aid to the Franco government.

Among the countries of this entire area, the heterogeneity of political aims and doctrines was extreme. Such incidental similarity as their policies had exhibited in recent years grew directly out of their common dislike and fear of the U.S.S.R., a factor which had first brought them into direct relationship with the United States and more recently had assured them a place in the mushrooming edifice of general free world defense.

Yugoslavia and the Balkan Entente

From both a strategic and a political point of view the key problems in relation to the defense of the eastern Mediterranean and the Adriatic were bound up with the status of Yugoslavia, a country that enjoyed the unique distinction of having a Communist government at least provisionally aligned with the West. Yugoslavia had come a long way since the days of Marshal Tito's break with Stalin and the Cominform countries in 1948. Tito now bore the title of "President" and headed a government which, though based on a Communist monopoly of political power, had begun to relax its iron grip in nonessential matters long before the men in the Kremlin had begun to employ similar tactics. From a country that behaved like a hunted animal and growled with equal ferocity at East and West, Yugoslavia had become a recipient of Western economic aid and a beneficiary of the United States military assistance program. The Eisenhower administration, for all its emphasis on anti-Communism, had shown no disposition to question this status or to number the peoples of Yugoslavia among the "captives" whom it purposed to liberate. Nor did the subsequent change of government in Moscow seem likely to have any immediate effect on Yugoslavia's international orientation, despite an evident desire on both sides to move toward a more "normal" form of relations than had prevailed during the past five years.

Toward the end of 1952 there had been evidence that Yugoslavia's leaders were tiring of their country's military isolation in the Balkans and inclining toward a *rapprochement* with Greece and Turkey, two countries which had already become parties to the North Atlantic Treaty in consequence of the United States desire to round out NATO's commitment on the southeast.[87] The primary motive on each side was not political sympathy but a common apprehension of the U.S.S.R. and its satellites. Warmly favored for strategic reasons by the United States, the movement was crowned by the conclusion of a five-year treaty of friendship and collaboration which was signed in Ankara on February 28 and ratified on May 18, 1953.[88] In it the three governments affirmed their resolution "to unite their efforts to make more effective the organization of their defense against all external aggression" and "to consult and cooperate on all questions of common interest and, in particular, on questions regarding their defense." They further agreed that their Foreign Ministers would confer regularly at least once a year, that their general staffs would cooperate in submitting joint recommendations on defense matters "with a view to reaching coordinated decisions," and that their collaboration would

[87] Cf. *The United States in World Affairs, 1952,* 422-424.
[88] Text in *Documents on American Foreign Relations, 1953,* 286-288.

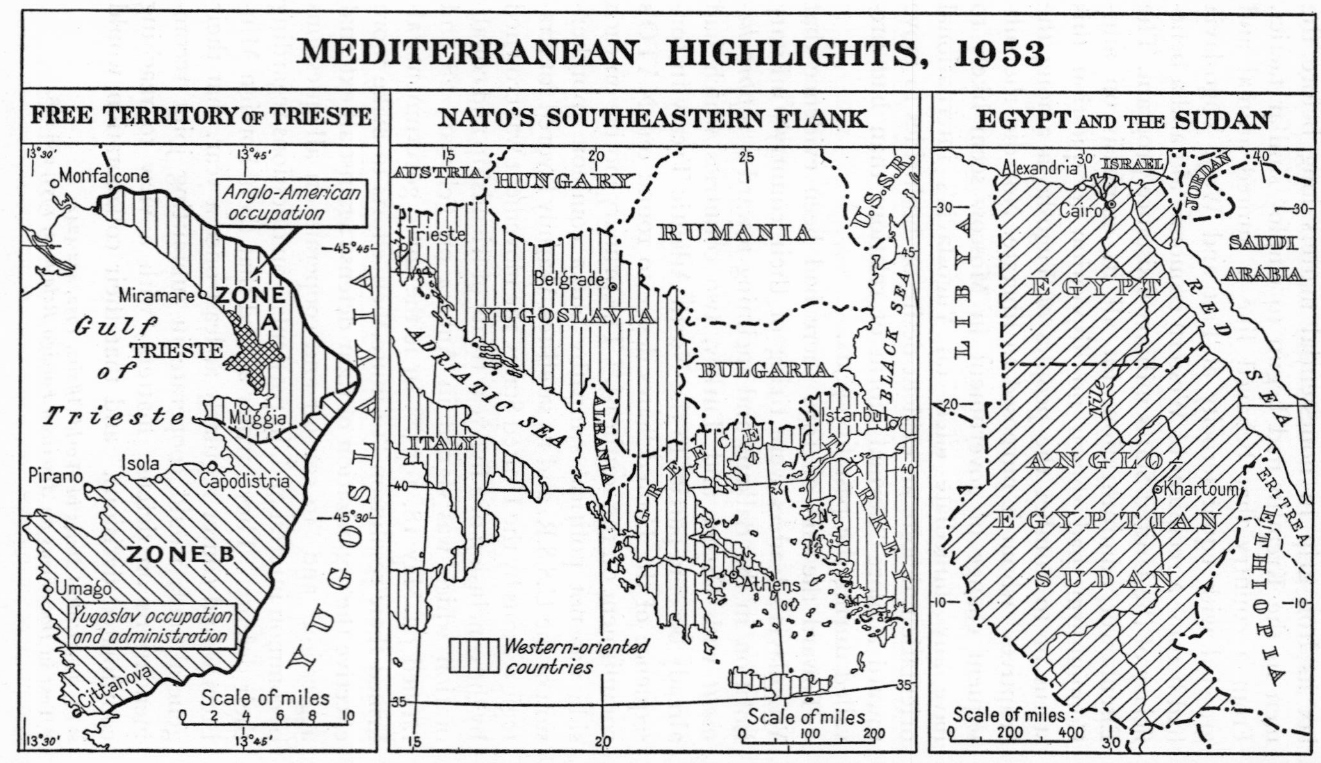
MEDITERRANEAN HIGHLIGHTS, 1953
FREE TERRITORY OF TRIESTE
Monfalcone
Anglo-American occupation
Miramare
ZONE A
Gulf of Trieste
TRIESTE
Muggia
Isola
Pirano
Capodistria
ZONE B
Umago
Yugoslav occupation and administration
Cittanova
YUGOSLAVIA
Scale of miles
0 2 4 6 8 10
NATO'S SOUTHEASTERN FLANK
AUSTRIA
HUNGARY
RUMANIA
U.S.S.R.
Trieste
Belgrade
YUGOSLAVIA
ADRIATIC SEA
BLACK SEA
BULGARIA
ALBANIA
ITALY
GREECE
Istanbul
TURKEY
Athens
Western-oriented countries
Scale of miles
0 100 200
EGYPT AND THE SUDAN
Alexandria
ISRAEL
JORDAN
Cairo
SAUDI ARABIA
LIBYA
EGYPT
RED SEA
Nile
ANGLO-EGYPTIAN SUDAN
Khartoum
ERITREA
ETHIOPIA
Scale of miles
0 200 400

also be extended into the fields of "economy, technology and culture."

Although based, like the North Atlantic Treaty, on the inherent right of individual and collective self-defense set forth in Article 51 of the United Nations Charter, the Balkan treaty was independent of NATO and its text explicitly declared that the rights and obligations of Greece and Turkey under NATO were in no way affected. Unlike the North Atlantic Treaty, moreover, it did not specifically commit any of the parties to come to each other's aid if attacked. Nevertheless, NATO interests were clearly affected in the sense that the new ties now being created made it all the more probable that an attack on Yugoslavia would involve not only Greece and Turkey but also their NATO allies, just as an attack on some NATO country would be likely to involve not only Greece and Turkey but also Yugoslavia. As Tito and the British government leaders agreed shortly afterward when the Yugoslav President paid a state visit to London (March 16-20), "in the event of aggression in Europe, the resulting conflict could hardly remain local in character."

Under these circumstances the question was bound to arise whether it would not be better to bring Yugoslavia into a more direct relationship with NATO, either by including the country among the NATO partners, by broadening the new Balkan pact to include Italy as well, or by using both methods together. In this way a gap in the NATO defense system would be closed and the seventy-odd divisions of the Balkan entente would be enabled to act in full co-ordination with NATO strategy. Military authorities in Washington were strongly in favor of such an arrangement, perhaps recalling that if an Austrian treaty should be concluded and the occupation troops withdrawn from Austria, the allied position in southern Europe would become more than ever dependent upon Yugoslavia and Italy. Greece and probably Turkey were also well disposed to the idea; but nothing could be done about it immediately because of the existence of unclarified issues involving Yugoslavia's general orientation as well as its relations to specific Western countries. For the time being, therefore, the new allies confined themselves to establishing the machinery for consultation and clarifying the problems of common action in the defensive field.

The Trieste Imbroglio

Apart from the difficulties inherent in Yugoslavia's political system and outlook—which still diverged widely from that of the Western powers on practically every question except the danger of Soviet aggression—there would be an insuperable obstacle to Yugoslavia's inclusion in any Western defense plan as long as the Yugoslav-Italian quarrel over Trieste remained unresolved. Yugoslav policy on the Trieste front had been notably less accommodating than it was in the southeast, and Italy too had given no sign of readiness to settle the long-standing Trieste issue on other than its own terms. While Anglo-American troops remained in uneasy occupation of the Italian-administered Trieste city and Zone A and Yugoslavia continued to occupy and administer the southern, mainly rural portion of the Free Territory (Zone B), the turbulence of the Trieste population and the conflicting ambitions of Rome and Belgrade created a dangerously explosive situation in the heart of NATO's southern command area. Local disorders and angry speeches on both sides were of practically everyday occurrence, and in late August a really serious crisis occurred. Yugoslavia, protesting against what it called Italy's "cold annexation" of Zone A, announced a "reexamination" of its policy which Italian authorities interpreted as a threat to annex the Yugoslav-controlled Zone B. Italian troops were moved up to the Yugoslav border, and the Big Three representatives in Rome and Belgrade were compelled to make very earnest representations before the tension subsided and the situation was restored to its previous unsatisfactory state.

The Trieste quarrel not only threatened the tranquility of the Adriatic and the *rapprochement* with Yugoslavia but tended to diminish even the value of Italy's own participation in Western defense efforts. In cultivating warmer relations with Belgrade, the Western powers found themselves in some danger of alienating their older friends in Rome. During Italy's midsummer cabinet crises it became apparent that the feeling on Trieste and Italian-Yugoslav relations could develop to a point at which it would seriously prejudice Italy's future role in NATO and Western Europe. Signor De Gasperi, addressing the Chamber of Deputies on July 21, told Italy's allies they must realize that "certain miscalculations" they were in danger of making might have "repercussions on the solidity of the common alliance itself." [89] His successor, Signor Pella, endorsed this statement and, moreover, showed marked disinclination to press for ratification of the E.D.C. treaty until Italian interests in Trieste were more clearly protected. By October the three Western powers would feel it necessary to intervene directly with a vigorous diplomatic step aimed at settling the issue once for all and thereby flattening the obstacles to a *rapprochement* between Italy and the Balkan allies. But the story of the allied "miscalculation" on that occasion belongs to the later history of allied and NATO policies in 1953.[90]

The Spanish Payoff

Unlike most other endeavors relating to the common defense in Europe, the connection between the United States and Spain was a purely bilateral attachment, brought about by the parallel preoccupations of the two governments without the participation or even the sympathy of most other European countries. In its political aspect, it mirrored the sentiments of those Americans who preferred the forthright anti-Communism of the Franco government to the more subtle outlook of the European democracies. From a military point of view, it fitted in with the growing emphasis on the predominant role of American air and sea power, aimed directly at the Soviet Union, as an alternative to the dependence on localized ground forces which still loomed so large in defense planning for Western Europe proper. Although advocates of the Spanish connection liked to point to Franco's large army as a conclusive argument for their point of view, it seemed rather unlikely that the twenty-two or more Spanish divisions would be sent to join the defense of the Elbe or the Rhine. Had they been available for this purpose, there

[89] *Relazioni internazionali,* XVII, August 1, 1953, 737.

[90] Cf. below, pp. 372-374.

would have been less need for the twelve West German divisions that Washington was so anxious to raise. What really interested United States defense planners was not the Spanish army but the prospect of developing Spanish air and naval bases which could be used, in conjunction with those already available in Great Britain and North Africa, to project American air-atomic power for purposes of deterring and/or retaliating against Soviet aggression.

Negotiations to this end had been in progress in Madrid since April 1952 and finally led to the conclusion on September 26, 1953 of three agreements covering (a) the construction and use of military facilities in Spain by the United States and (b) the economic and military assistance which would be rendered to Spain by this country.[91] These documents stated general principles rather than detailed plans; the long delay in negotiating them had been caused not by any technical complexities but mainly by the extreme concern of the Spanish Government to conserve its national sovereignty unimpaired and ensure that its own territory would be adequately protected in case of trouble. The defense agreement, concluded for a period of ten years with provision for two five-year extensions, would enable the United States to begin construction for the development of certain Spanish military airfields and to modernize certain naval facilities; additional ones might be developed as future conditions required. All such facilities would be open to joint use by Spanish and United States forces, and would remain under Spanish flag and command. Under the economic and military aid agreements, the United States planned to furnish Spain with $141 million in military end-items and $85 million in defense support assistance (raw materials, commodities, equipment, and technical assistance) during the fiscal year 1953–54.[92] Although this fell considerably short of the estimate of Spain's economic needs made by an Amer-

[91] Texts in *Department of State Bulletin*, XXIX, October 5, 1953, 436-442. The main defense agreement appears also in *Documents on American Foreign Relations, 1953*, 283-285.

[92] *Department of State Bulletin*, XXIX, October 5, 1953, 435. Of the total of $226 million, $125 million had been appropriated in 1951 and reappropriated in 1952.

ican expert in 1951,[93] it did not include amounts that would be spent directly by the United States in Spain as the bases were built and manned.

These arrangements had been in the making so long that their completion occasioned comparatively little stir in other parts of Europe, although they were sharply denounced by left-wing Laborite Aneurin Bevan in Great Britain and, of course, by *Pravda,* which assured the French that the "ruling hierarchy" in the United States was about to "grip France in a vice between fascist Spain and revanchist Western Germany." [94] The general tendency in Paris, London, and other capitals was rather to minimize the importance of these new bilateral agreements, which might conceivably add more to Franco's prestige than to the over-all strength of the West. Even American officials pointed out that the arrangements did not constitute a military alliance, that the commitments involved were less extensive than those of NATO, and that no attempt was being made to bring Spain into NATO or the United Nations "by the back door."

But authorities in the Pentagon were sure that the new bases and installations would add greatly to the potential effectiveness of American forces deployed in the Mediterranean area. Undoubtedly their availability would figure prominently in the "new look" at defense problems being undertaken by the Joint Chiefs of Staff.[95] With the U.S.S.R. in possession of the hydrogen bomb and with the consummation of E.D.C. still months away at best, there was no danger that their importance would be underrated.

[93] *The United States in World Affairs, 1951,* 339-340.

[94] *Pravda,* September 25; *Current Digest of the Soviet Press,* V, No. 40, November 18, 1953, 28.

[95] Cf. below, pp. 353-366.

CHAPTER FOUR

FAR EASTERN PANORAMA

WHATEVER THE difficulties of coordinating allied policy in Europe, the Western governments at least were in no doubt as to the identity of their principal antagonist in that part of the world. In Asia they were not so sure. There they were confronted not with a closely knit political and military system centered in Moscow but with a bewildering variety of regimes and movements, all of which partook of the distinctive Communist coloration yet which were impossible to arrange in any clear hierarchical pattern. Exactly who, for instance, had been responsible for the original aggression in Korea, the subsequent intervention of the Chinese Communists, and the still later offer to begin the armistice negotiations, which by now had been going on intermittently for nearly two years? What part had been played in these moves by the North Korean "People's Democratic Republic," the Chinese Communist authorities at Peking, or the Soviet Government itself? Was Pyongyang dependent on Peking, and Peking on Moscow? Or did both Peking and Moscow compete for control of the North Korean puppet government? Did Communist leaders in the Far East take action on their own initiative, trusting to Moscow to back them up after the fat was in the fire, or was each important move planned in the Soviet capital and entrusted to local forces for execution? Allied authorities could only guess at the answers to such questions.

Similar uncertainties arose in connection with the Communist offer to resume armistice negotiations on a new basis in April 1953. It would have been decidedly helpful to the nations resisting aggression in Korea to know whether this move was produced entirely by local circumstances or was undertaken as a part of Moscow's general post-Stalin "peace offensive." Generally speaking, official American quarters inclined to the former view. General Mark W. Clark, the United Nations commander in Korea, claimed that the Communists eventually yielded "only because the military pressure on them was so great they had to yield. . . . In the end we got the cease-fire only because the enemy had been hurt so badly on the field of battle." [1] Secretary Dulles later declared that hostilities had been arrested in Korea "because the aggressor, already thrown back to and behind his place of beginning, was faced with the possibility that the fighting might, to his own great peril, soon spread beyond the limits and methods he had selected." [2] Yet there were indications that Communist calculation in the Far East might also be influenced by other factors besides the fact or threat of military pressure. The "unleashing" of Chiang Kai-shek in January [3] had not, after all, produced any perceptible tremors at Communist headquarters. In February Mr. Lodge had told the General Assembly that what really kept the war going was Soviet military assistance:

> "The whole world knows the truth: That except for the active aid furnished to the North Korean and Chinese Communist aggressors by the Soviet Union, the war in Korea would now be over. . . .
>
> "The rulers of the Soviet Union can stop the war whenever they want to—and Mr. Vyshinsky knows it." [4]

And it was undeniably after the new set of rulers had been installed in the Soviet Union that the war first began to show signs of stopping.

In Indochina and Southeast Asia, the determining influences on Communist policy were even more difficult to

1 Mark W. Clark, *From the Danube to the Yalu* (New York, Harper, 1954), 103, 109. Elsewhere, however (p. 241), General Clark associates the armistice with the Soviet "peace offensive," calling it "the main showpiece in the Communist propaganda array."

2 Address to the Council on Foreign Relations, January 12, 1954, in *Documents on American Foreign Relations, 1954,* 10.

3 Cf. above, pp. 23-26.

4 Statement to the First Committee, February 25, in *Department of State Bulletin,* XXVIII, March 9, 1953, 383.

identify. Here there seemed even less reason to suspect the U.S.S.R. of direct involvement; such aid and counsel as were available to the Vietminh and similar rebel groups seemed almost certainly to originate with Communist China. The question remained, however, how far these rebel activities formed part of an over-all Communist plan, perhaps directed from Peking or ultimately from Moscow, and how far they might be determined by merely local considerations. Resistance to Communism in this area was hampered by the fact that Communism as such formed no more than a part of the rebels' stock in trade. Leaders like Ho Chi Minh in Indochina, though undoubtedly firm devotees of the Communist program, put themselves forward primarily as apostles of national independence and social reform, a device which helped to disarm potential opposition both in their own countries and in other Asian lands like India. It was very difficult to convince an Indian, or a Vietnamese, that Ho Chi Minh was merely a tool of Chinese or Soviet Communism; and even in the West, it was difficult to be sure that his moves invariably reflected the intentions of Peking or Moscow. The Vietminh invasion of Laos in April–May 1953, which coincided with the opening of the Soviet "peace offensive," was widely construed in Western capitals as evidence of Soviet bad faith. Yet so responsible an observer as Sir Winston Churchill had felt justified in questioning this interpretation. The invasion movement, he had suggested, "might well have arisen from local circumstances and impulses, and from plans made many months ago and now, perhaps, reversed." [5] Since the invaders soon afterward withdrew to a remote corner of Laos to wait out the rainy season, it was impossible to determine how far, if at all, such reservations were warranted.

But however mysterious the background of Far Eastern politics, the foreground was all too unmistakably occupied by the huge and forbidding bulk of Communist China. After making every allowance for the possible influence of the Soviet Union, the decisive factor in Far Eastern matters was the largest country in the Far East itself—a country for

[5] *Parliamentary Debates, Weekly Hansard,* House of Commons, May 11, 1953, 890; cf. above, pp. 66, 122-123.

whose acceptance as a great power the United States had labored hard for years, only to see its government usurped and its prerogatives exercised by forces intrinsically hostile to the West and with which no accommodation was felt possible. Whether Communist China was now regarded as a great power in its own right or as the Far Eastern executant of Soviet Communism, its sheer overwhelming size and population, galvanized as it seemed to have been by the dynamic force of the Communist revolution, had made it the inescapably determining force in Far Eastern affairs. Korea, Japan, Formosa, Indochina, Burma, Thailand, Malaya, Indonesia, Nepal, even India felt the oppressive weight of this influence, which, moreover, seemed likely to go on increasing from year to year with the progress of Chinese industrialization and economic development. An ambitious five-year plan of industrial and agricultural expansion, to be carried out with Soviet technical aid and equipment, was announced in 1953 and called for large increases in steel, coal, and nonferrous metals output, doubled power production, and construction of an oil refinery, a synthetic rubber plant, and several fertilizer and pharmaceutical plants.[6] But China's rulers had not awaited the expansion of their economic base to claim the leading voice in Far Eastern affairs. Virtually every Far Eastern problem already was inextricably intermeshed with questions relating to the status of Communist China, its expansionist pressure, and its reiterated demand for international recognition, a seat in the United Nations, and freedom to eliminate the Nationalist Chinese regime encamped in the offshore stronghold of Formosa and the Pescadores Islands.

It would have been easier for the United States and its allies to cope with this situation if they had seen eye to eye concerning the merits of Chinese Communist ambitions. As things stood, however, there was no real unity among them on these matters that in fact made up the central issue of the Far East. Of the major non-Communist powers, only the United States opposed the Chinese Communist political claims with full conviction. Great Britain was the leading

[6] U.N. Economic Commission for Asia and the Far East, *Economic Bulletin for Asia and the Far East,* IV, No. 3, November 1953, 30-31.

representative of an alternative trend which, while willing to contend against Communist aggression outside of China's historic frontiers, was not fundamentally opposed to the Communist political demands as such and even felt that the Chinese Communists might be less aggressively inclined and easier to manage if a means could be found of satisfying at least a portion of their basic political claims.

Whatever the merits of these contrasting viewpoints, their divergence was a basic weakness in the Western position. Not only was it a source of continuing friction within the Western camp; it also affected Western relations with Asian countries like India, which were even more inclined to give Communist China its way; and it facilitated Communist efforts to divide the free world with reference to the possibility of fruitful negotiations between East and West. Indeed, the situation had such obvious advantages for the Communists that Moscow, at least, might be plausibly suspected of finding the denial of the Chinese demands more profitable than their satisfaction would have been. Each important Communist move, whether in the Far East or on the broader international plane, appeared to have as one of its main purposes the aggravation of these differences between Asia and the West and between the United States and its allies.

Although the United States stood virtually alone among the great powers in opposing the entire Chinese Communist program, that did not mean that our country possessed a clear-cut policy of its own for dealing with the China problem. Resistance to Chinese Communist claims of every nature was strongly endorsed at that period by leaders of both political parties and by the most articulate sections of national public opinion. Yet even the new administration, which had taken office on a platform of uncompromising hostility to Communism in general and Far Eastern Communism in particular, appeared to be in some uncertainty as to how far these hostile sentiments should be followed in practice. Secretary Dulles had told the Senate Foreign Relations Committee that the tie between China and Moscow was "an unholy arrangement" whose continuance we could not "tolerate." [7] In discontinuing any restraints on the gov-

[7] Above, p. 17.

ernment of President Chiang Kai-shek, who openly aspired to reconquer the Chinese mainland and whose armed forces were maintained and equipped by the United States, we seemed to be underlining our total, unlimited opposition to Chinese Communism. Various other actions during the year seemed to reflect a similar attitude. On the other hand, our readiness to resume the armistice negotiations in Korea as soon as the opportunity was offered suggested that we did not, after all, seek the elimination of Chinese Communism or even the forcible expulsion of the aggressors from Korea, but would content ourselves with a settlement based more or less on the existing *status quo*.

Precisely because our participation in armistice negotiations seemed to imply a willingness to leave the Communists in undisturbed enjoyment of their present holdings, the spectacle of the talks at Panmunjom had been especially distasteful to those Americans who thought it preferable to try to dislodge them even at the cost of a considerably greater military effort. General James A. Van Fleet, the retiring Eighth Army commander, objected in February 1953 that the commencement of armistice negotiations in the summer of 1951 had deprived us of a military victory which was actually within reach at that time. The United Nations forces, he implied, still had the capacity to launch a successful ground offensive, though evidently not without substantial reinforcement.[8] General MacArthur's views on seeking a clear-cut victory by extending the scope of military action were well known and frequently expressed,[9] and General Clark was to indicate in a book published after the armistice that he too had held similar opinions even though he had felt bound to defer to contrary instructions from Washington and recognized that a decisive victory would require greatly increased resources.[10]

President Eisenhower, however, had been elected by the American people not to intensify the Korean war but to end it if possible. General Clark later reported that when the President-elect visited Korea in December 1952 he had been

[8] *New York Times*, February 10 and 11, 1953.
[9] Cf. above, p. 67.
[10] Clark, *op. cit.*, 220 and *passim*.

so intent on seeking an "honorable truce" that he had not even inquired about the possibility of achieving "victory" through intensified military action.[11] However he may have felt about long-run relations with Communist China, the President's immediate approach to Far Eastern issues seemed to be guided by three relatively simple objectives: (1) to seek an end to the fighting on terms which would satisfy the requirements of national morality and make possible a reduction of American military commitments; (2) to avoid measures that would cost us the support of our allies, whose help he considered useful in Asia and indispensable in Europe; and (3) to avoid compromising with "principle" by making any concessions to the Chinese Communists other than by ceasing to conduct active hostilities against them. These, roughly, were the same objectives that had guided the previous administration; and the new President soon found that he was constrained to follow approximately the same course as his predecessor. Being unwilling either to intensify the military pressure in any decisive way or to seek a peace through political bargaining, he could only fall back upon such measures of limited effectiveness as the "unleashing" of Chiang Kai-shek and the tightening of restrictions on strategic trade with the China mainland. Beyond that, there was nothing to do except to hold firm and hope that the enemy would change his mind.

Even if that happened—as it did a scant twenty-three days after Stalin's death—there would remain the dangers inherent in Communist China's political claims, its determination to get possession of Formosa, and its probable ambitions in Southeast Asia. Indeed, the conclusion of a Korean armistice was likely to render these problems even more acute, since it would free the Chinese armies for possible activity elsewhere and would also strengthen support abroad for Communist political aspirations. The former of these dangers, at any rate, was clearly foreseen in Washington. As President Eisenhower said in his address of April 16: ". . . any armistice in Korea that merely released aggressive armies to attack elsewhere would be a fraud. We seek, throughout Asia

[11] *Ibid.*, 233, 236, 239.

as throughout the world, a peace that is true and total." [12] As for Chinese political aims, the United States was to remain silent or negative. Yet despite its unwillingness to bargain and its avowed skepticism regarding Communist intentions, Washington apparently hoped that its desire for "true and total" peace in Asia would be respected by the Communist powers. The preparations it made to meet the alternative possibility were still limited in scope and by 1954 were to seem rather inadequate to meet the situation created by Communist aggressiveness.

1. THE KOREAN ARMISTICE

The Korean armistice negotiations occupy a special place in the annals of the East-West struggle as the first contact between the opposing camps to produce substantial results since the termination of the Berlin blockade in 1949. Although the motivations of the Communist negotiators remain obscure in many particulars, sufficient documentation is available from the Western side to illuminate both the principal issues in dispute and some of the main considerations affecting later developments in the Far East.[13]

When negotiations had been suspended on the insistence of the United States in October 1952, the two teams of conferees at Panmunjom—one representing the United Nations Command, the other the commanders of the "Korean People's Army" and the "Chinese People's Volunteers"—had already reached a general understanding on three of the four main aspects of the proposed armistice agreement. First, a military demarcation line was to be established along the line of contact of the opposing forces at the time the armistice was signed; each side was to withdraw two kilometers from this demarcation line, thus creating a demilitarized zone four kilometers wide. Second, the execution of the detailed armistice arrangements was to be overseen by (a) a

[12] *Documents on American Foreign Relations, 1953,* 31; cf. also the U.S.-French statement of March 28, above, pp. 35-36.

[13] See especially Clark, *op. cit.,* 240-297; "Special Report of the Unified Command on the Armistice in Korea," U.N. Document S/3079, August 7 (in *Department of State Bulletin,* XXIX, August 24, 1953, 246-251); and "La Situation en Corée," *Chronique de politique étrangère,* VII, January 1954, 18-80.

Military Armistice Commission, composed of officers of the United Nations and Communist forces, and (b) a Neutral Nations Supervisory Commission consisting of four officers from so-called neutral nations, two of which would be designated by each side. (Sweden and Switzerland were the choices of the United Nations; the enemy eventually selected Czechoslovakia and Poland after the Unified Command had made it clear that it would not accept the U.S.S.R. as a "neutral" nation.) Third, the two sides would recommend to the governments concerned that within three months after the armistice became effective a "political conference" of both sides should be held "to settle through negotiation the questions of the withdrawal of foreign forces from Korea, the peaceful settlement of the Korean question, etc." [14]

It was on the fourth point, "Arrangements Relating to Prisoners of War," that the two sides still found themselves wide apart. The United Nations Command held about 132,000 prisoners of war and civilian internees, including some 20,700 Chinese, while the enemy had admitted to holding the remarkably low total of 11,559 prisoners of war of all nationalities, including 3,198 Americans. Both sides had agreed that an exchange of prisoners should be completed within two months of the armistice; but difficulty had arisen from the discovery that more than one-third of the prisoners held by the United Nations actually did not *want* to be exchanged. Some 34,000 Koreans and 14,500 Chinese [15] had actually convinced the United Nations Command that they would go so far as physically to resist repatriation and therefore could not be returned to their Communist masters except by force. The Communists, professing disbelief in a state of affairs so humiliating for them, insisted that all prisoners must be repatriated without exception. But the United Nations command, strongly backed by Washington, had

[14] Special Report of the Unified Command, October 18, 1952, in *Documents on American Foreign Relations, 1952*, 310-317.

[15] Figures as of April 22, 1953 from *Department of State Bulletin*, XXVIII, May 25, 1953, 758. The total for Koreans resisting repatriation apparently includes civilian internees not listed in U.N. Command figures, which give a somewhat different breakdown of prisoner preferences. Cf. *The United States in World Affairs, 1952*, 181-185, 290 and *Documents on American Foreign Relations, 1952*, 318-321.

taken the humanitarian position that no prisoner would be returned who did not choose to go voluntarily. A great deal of ingenuity had been devoted by the Unified Command and other interested parties to seeking a solution that would save the Communists' faces while still permitting the unwilling Chinese and Korean prisoners to avoid repatriation. All such proposals, however, had been summarily rejected by the Communists—including a plan worked out by India and approved (with modifications) by the General Assembly in December 1952 under which those prisoners who refused repatriation would be removed from the control of the Unified Command and placed in neutral custody until their future was settled by the post-armistice political conference or by the United Nations.[16]

The Communists Yield a Point

There the matter rested from December 14, 1952, when the Communists spurned the General Assembly plan, until March 30, 1953, when Premier Chou En-lai suddenly proposed that those prisoners who were, as he put it, "afraid" to return home in view of "the intimidation and oppression of the opposite side" should be "handed over to a neutral state" and given "explanations" by their own side in order to ensure a "just" solution and permit the conclusion of an armistice agreement.[17] This did not mean that the Communists were bowing to the United Nations position on the issue. Chou En-lai explicitly stated that his government and that of North Korea continued to adhere to their previous viewpoint. But it did mean that they were admitting, for the first time, that the attitudes expressed by the prisoners constituted a real problem and necessitated special measures. In offering to place the unwilling prisoners temporarily in neutral custody, they came close to accepting the principle of the General Assembly resolution they had rejected a few months earlier. If the Communists were really working, as Chou said, "for the speedy realization of an armistice in Korea and

[16] *The United States in World Affairs, 1952,* 335-342; General Assembly Resolution 610 (VII), December 3, 1952, in *Documents on American Foreign Relations, 1952,* 374-377.

[17] *Department of State Bulletin,* XXVIII, April 13, 1953, 526-527; cf. above, p. 122.

. . . a peaceful settlement of the Korean question," a procedure was now available by which those ends could be readily achieved.

The nominal occasion for Chou En-lai's statement was the belated acceptance by the Communists of a proposal from the Unified Command—a proposal periodically put forward since December 1951, but hitherto ignored by the enemy—to effect an exchange of sick and wounded prisoners of war in accordance with standard international practice.[18] Action undertaken under this proposal was technically quite separate from the question of exchanging healthy prisoners after an armistice, but would nevertheless provide an opportunity to gauge Communist good faith while preparations were being made to resume the armistice negotiations themselves in accordance with Chou En-lai's offer. The exchange of sick and wounded prisoners—called "Little Switch" to distinguish it from the projected general prisoner exchange or "Big Switch"—was carried out in reasonably good order between April 20 and May 3 and resulted in the return of 6,670 prisoners by the United Nations Command and 684 by the Communists—the latter group including 471 Koreans and 149 Americans. Although the proceedings were somewhat marred by the calculated ingratitude displayed by prisoners released by the Unified Comand, more serious problems arose in connection with those sick and wounded prisoners who were not returned at all. The United Nations Command had made known from the first that it would return only *willing* prisoners, the others being held for later disposition. But the Communists, while claiming to have returned *all* of their sick and wounded prisoners who were fit to travel, had obviously failed to do so and returned only those prisoners who were in a presentable condition. They were definitely known to be withholding at least 234 non-Koreans and 141 Koreans who were fully qualified and fit for return. This deception, together with the tales of mistreatment brought back by American captives, was enough to disillusion any in the

[18] Letter of General Clark, February 22, and Communist reply, March 28, *ibid.*, April 6, 1953, 494-495. The record of subsequent negotiations on this issue appears *ibid.*, April 13, 1953, 528; April 20, 1953, 570-574, 576; April 27, 1953, 609-610; XXIX, September 28, 1953, 423-425; and in Clark, *op. cit.*, 241-247.

United States who had hoped the Communists were turning over a new leaf.[19]

The Prisoner Debate Resumed

In the meantime, the full armistice delegations had resumed their meetings at Panmunjom on April 26 [20] and begun discussing the detailed Communist proposal for dealing with those prisoners who refused to be repatriated. The Communists, it appeared, still did not admit that there could be prisoners from their side who really did not want to return; but they were willing to take a little time (up to six months) to free the recalcitrants from their "apprehensions" through the "explanations" which they proposed to give to the detained men while the latter were held by a neutral state.[21] To judge by later developments, what the Communists really desired was an opportunity to "brainwash" their men by the same methods they had employed so successfully with some of their American prisoners. It was to require six full weeks, from April 26 to June 8, to whittle down their proposals to a shape the United Nations Command felt able to accept. Even then, the Communists were given such extensive rights of access to and pressure upon the unwilling captives that many observers feared the latters' rights would be inadequately protected. General Clark was so impressed by the extent of the concessions approved in Washington as to express the opinion that "the Republicans were ready to go further than the Democrats to achieve a truce." [22]

The Communists, on the other hand, seemed in much less of a hurry to consummate the truce talks than United Nations quarters had hoped. Their initial proposal, which provided for physical transfer of the 48,000-odd nonrepatriate prisoners to the territory of some unnamed, Asian neutral state (not Switzerland, as proposed by the United Nations), had been wholly unacceptable to the Unified Command; but

[19] For the story of "Little Switch" cf. *Department of State Bulletin,* XXIX, September 28, 1953, 425-427 and Clark, *op. cit.,* 249-256, 258, 260.
[20] Preliminary negotiations are documented in *Department of State Bulletin,* XXVIII, April 13, 1953, 528; April 20, 1953, 575-576; May 11, 1953, 686-687.
[21] Letter of the Communist commanders, April 9, *ibid.,* April 20, 1953, 575-576; text of Communist proposal, April 26, *ibid.,* May 11, 1953, 687.
[22] Clark, *op. cit.,* 258.

it was not until May 7 that they came up with an alternative, apparently inspired by the General Assembly plan, which after further modification was to provide the basis of the armistice agreement. Instead of a single neutral custodian for the prisoners, this second Communist proposal provided for a five-country Neutral Nations Repatriation Commission, representing Poland, Czechoslovakia, Switzerland, Sweden, and India, which would take charge of the prisoners on the spot and hold them during four months of "explanations."

On May 13 the United Nations proposed a number of amendments to this plan, the most important being a suggestion that matters be simplified by releasing outright the 34,000 nonrepatriate Koreans and releasing the nonrepatriate Chinese at the end of a sixty-day explanation period.[23] But despite its practical advantages, this idea took little account of Communist sensibilities. It proved especially offensive to General Nam Il, the chief North Korean delegate, who promptly "blew up" and thereafter abandoned negotiation in favor of propaganda tirades. Disorders broke out once again among Communist-controlled prisoners in the United Nations prisoner of war camp on Koje Island, off South Korea, resulting in three deaths. Various United Nations members, including Canada, Great Britain, and India, also made known their misgivings about a proposal which departed in important respects from the General Assembly resolution.[24]

This was a period, it will be remembered, during which relations among the Western powers were under severe strain as a result of various incidents connected with the changing international climate. When General Clark advised Washington that it was time to bring matters to a head, he was instructed to yield on the matter of the Koreans and on various other points, while standing firmly on the principle that no force or intimidation should be used against unwilling prisoners. But he was also authorized, in case the Com-

[23] Material on the Panmunjom negotiations through May 15 appears in *Department of State Bulletin,* XXVIII, May 11, 1953, 687-689; May 18, 1953, 726-730; May 25, 1953, 755-757; XXIX, September 28, 1953, 426-428.

[24] Cf. *Chronique de politique étrangère,* VII, January 1954, 41-42.

munists rejected his final offer and made no constructive proposals of their own, to break off the negotiations and "to carry on the war in new ways never yet tried in Korea." What these "new ways" were, General Clark was still not at liberty to disclose when he published his book a year later; presumably they were still being held in reserve in case the armistice broke down.[25]

At all events, there was to be no need for recourse to novel methods of warfare at this stage. The "final" United Nations offer, put forward on May 25, was accepted by the Communists in all essentials on June 4 and led to the signature of agreed "Terms of Reference" for the Neutral Nations Repatriation Commission on June 8. Briefly, they provided that the five-nation neutral commission, with India serving as umpire and furnishing the necessary armed custodial forces, would establish its headquarters within the demilitarized zone and take charge of all nonrepatriate prisoners within sixty days after the armistice became effective. Thereafter, for a period of ninety days, a limited number of "explaining representatives" from the prisoners' countries of origin would be given the opportunity to meet with them under specified conditions in order to explain to them their rights and "their full freedom to return home to lead a peaceful life." The disposition of any prisoners who did not exercise their right of repatriation during this period would thereafter be considered by the post-armistice political conference, which was given a further thirty days to reach a final decision in the matter. If no decision was reached within this period (i.e., within a maximum of 180 days after the armistice), the remaining prisoners would revert to civilian status and be given their freedom, and the neutral commission itself would be dissolved within a month.[26]

President Rhee Protests

During the latter part of these negotiations, the Unified Command had worried less over the attitude of the Commu-

[25] Clark, *op. cit.*, 266-267; cf. the comment by Mr. Dulles, on p. 211, above, and the statement by the President, May 26, in *Department of State Bulletin*, XXVIII, June 8, 1953, 816.

[26] *Ibid.*, June 22, 1953, 866-868; excerpts in *Documents on American Foreign Relations, 1953*, 293-297. Cf. Clark, *op. cit.*, 276-278, and below, pp. 387-389.

nists than over that of the government of the Republic of Korea and its President, Syngman Rhee. This venerable patriot, whose devotion to the cause of Korean unity commanded the respect of all his American associates, had never sympathized with the United States and United Nations policy of seeking an armistice on the existing battle line. For him, nothing less would be satisfactory than the complete expulsion of the invaders from Korea and the unification of the entire country under the government he headed. It was true that the United Nations also desired the establishment of a "unified, independent and democratic Korea"; but its military action under the Security Council resolution of 1950 was aimed only at "repelling the aggression and restoring international peace and security in the area." Thus the United States and the United Nations were prepared to conclude an armistice which would leave the country divided and its southern, non-Communist portion exposed to at least a possibility of renewed invasion whenever its adversaries might choose. To Dr. Rhee this prospect was intolerable; and he very nearly succeeded in preventing its effectuation. For weeks this one old man—fully supported, as it seemed, by the South Korean National Assembly and the population at large—was to keep the world in suspense and confound the intentions of both East and West as he battled to save his devasted country from an undesired armistice.

In opposing the policies of the United States and the Unified Command, President Rhee could count on various practical advantages in addition to his personal force and the natural reluctance of the United States to leave South Korea to its fate. The army of the Republic of Korea, whose responsibilities had been extended in line with Washington's new policy of transferring as much of the military burden as possible to Korean shoulders, was now actually holding two-thirds of the allied battle line. While supposedly subject to the orders of the Unified Command, the R.O.K. troops would undoubtedly be responsive to any contrary directives originating with the Korean President. Logistical and tactical arrangements were such that it would be extremely difficult, if not impossible, to disentangle R.O.K. and United Nations forces. Should Dr. Rhee refuse to cooperate in the armistice arrangements—should he insist, as he threatened to do, on continuing the war independently of the United Nations—it was plain that an exceedingly unpleasant situation would be created. Fighting alone, the R.O.K. would clearly be doomed to a crushing defeat which would nullify the achievement of the United Nations over the past three years. It would be difficult for the United States to look on at such a debacle; it might be even more difficult to disengage and evacuate the American and other United Nations units in case Dr. Rhee's actions brought on a resumption of hostilities.

As early as April 24, the Korean Government had given official notice to the United States that it planned to withdraw its forces from the United Nations Command in case an armistice was concluded which permitted Chinese Communist troops to remain in any part of Korea. In subsequent conversations with General Clark, and in public declarations, Dr. Rhee added that he would not permit the transfer of nonrepatriate Korean prisoners of war to a neutral country, that he would not allow Communist "explainers" to operate in Korean Republic territory, and that he would not permit Indian troops to enter his country in any capacity. To avoid this, he said, he might himself release the nonrepatriate Korean prisoners (who were guarded by R.O.K. security guards) on his own responsibility "without involving the UN Command." General Clark, who for months had personally favored release of the nonrepatriates as the most effective way of settling an almost insoluble diplomatic problem, renewed his recommendation to Washington that at least the Korean prisoners be released to civilian status when the armistice went into effect. A precedent, he pointed out, had been provided by the Communists themselves early in the war when they "released" some 50,000 South Koreans for the purpose of drafting them into the Communist armies.[27]

Although the United States Government rejected a proposal so likely to upset negotiations with the Communists, it was nevertheless prepared to go to extraordinary lengths to induce President Rhee to accept the armistice arrangements. On the assumption that guarantees of the existing territory of the Korean Republic might induce him to re-

[27] *Ibid.*, 261-266.

nounce the demand for immediate liberation of all Korea, he was informally offered a variety of advantages: (1) a sixteen-nation pledge (already under consideration) to maintain the armistice agreement against the Communists; (2) American assistance in building up the R.O.K. Army to twenty divisions, with appropriate air and naval strength; (3) a billion-dollar economic rehabilitation program; and (4) assurances of special vigilance by United States forces until peace was firmly established. To these benefits was presently added the promise of a mutual defense pact similar to those the United States had concluded with the Philippines and with Australia and New Zealand.[28] The pledge of a mutual defense pact and of continued economic aid, as well as of political support in seeking the unification of Korea by peaceful means, was repeated in a personal letter which President Eisenhower addressed to the Korean President on June 6 and in which he explained that "we do not intend to employ war as an instrument to accomplish the world-wide political settlements to which we are dedicated." [29]

The Prisoners Released

But the delegations at Panmunjom were already approaching the completion of their task, and President Rhee, whose government was now boycotting the negotiations, was still protesting that he could "never" accept the armistice. Personal contact, it appeared, would be essential if his objections were to be overcome. President Eisenhower suggested that President Rhee come to Washington; President Rhee, declining, asked that Secretary Dulles be sent to him in Seoul instead. As an interim measure it was arranged that Walter S. Robertson, Assistant Secretary of State for Far Eastern Affairs, should pay Dr. Rhee an urgent visit.[30] But before Mr. Robertson could board a plane, the Korean President proceeded to carry out his threat to release the Korean nonrepatriates, thus setting at naught the elaborate preparations made for their handling under the armistice agreement. On the night of June 17-18, Korean guards act-

[28] *Ibid.*, 268-276.
[29] *Documents on American Foreign Relations, 1953*, 303-305.
[30] Clark, *op. cit.*, 279.

ing on orders from President Rhee opened the gates at four detention camps and allowed 25,000 Korean detainees to walk out to freedom. Another 2,000 were released during the next few days; although 971 escapees were recaptured, only 9,000 Koreans remained in custody, under American guard.[31] Expressions of dismay poured in from many parts of the free world. General Clark protested that this was a "direct violation" of his authority and the "unilateral abrogation" of a personal commitment by President Rhee; R.O.K. authorities assured him that the sole reason for proceeding in secret was "to cause as little embarrassment as possible to the United Nations Command."[32]

The effect of this sensational development, which happened to coincide with the anti-Communist riots in East Berlin, was to throw grave doubt on the prospects for an armistice. For once the Communists could hardly be blamed if they suspected a trick, despite the protestations of innocence immediately transmitted to them by the United Nations Command. Even if the latter's good faith was accepted, the action taken by elements under its command gave point to the questions which were now put to General Clark by the North Korean and Chinese commanders (Kim Il Sung and Peng Teh-huai):

"Is the United Nations Command able to control the South Korean Government and Army?

"If not, does the armistice in Korea include the Syngman Rhee clique?

"If it is not included, what assurance is there for the implementation of the armistice agreement on the part of South Korea?"

While awaiting their answer, the Communists demanded that the United Nations immediately undertake the impossible task of rounding up over 25,000 escapees who had already faded into the Korean landscape, and give firm assurances that such incidents would not recur.[33] Meanwhile the Panmunjom negotiations were recessed, Communist propa-

[31] *Ibid.*, 279-281.

[32] *Ibid.*, 279-282; *Department of State Bulletin*, XXVIII, June 29, 1953, 905-909.

[33] *Ibid.*, 905-907.

ganda enjoyed a field day, and active fighting continued. Everything now hinged on whether the Communists wanted an armistice sufficiently to swallow this new frustration. If not, they had a fully sufficient pretext for dropping the negotiations. If they did, they would have to accept the fact that most of the Korean nonrepatriates were irretrievably lost.

There also remained the necessity of reconciling President Rhee to any armistice that might be concluded. Luckily, his success in freeing the Korean prisoners made him somewhat more amenable to persuasion on other points, notwithstanding his continued talk of fighting on alone and his insistence that the armistice terms as drawn eliminated the possibility of unification and spelled "sure death for the Korean nation." [34] Assistant Secretary Robertson arrived in Korea on June 25, the third anniversary of the war, and conferred with President Rhee for a fortnight. While the well-disciplined Korean masses tearfully demonstrated outside the presidential mansion, the American representative gradually won Rhee's promise not to "obstruct" the implementation of the armistice even though he could not be brought to sign it. Dr. Rhee may have been influenced in part by the realization that his army had no independent sources of gasoline and other essentials. But in addition to inducements previously offered, such as a mutual security pact and military and economic aid, the Korean President apparently won an important new concession with reference to the political conference which was supposed to meet within three months of the armistice. Dr. Rhee had expressed a well-founded skepticism as to the results of this consultation: "Personally, I do not believe that the Communists will agree, at a conference table, to what they have never been made to agree to on the battlefield." [35] The United States itself was of much the same opinion; and Mr. Robertson now agreed with Dr. Rhee that both governments would withdraw from the conference—or "try to end" it "as a sham and a hostile trick"—if it failed to

[34] Letter to President Eisenhower, June 19, in *Documents on American Foreign Relations, 1953*, 306-308.
[35] *Ibid.*

make progress toward its announced objectives within ninety days.[36]

The Armistice Concluded

With this understanding in prospect and with the Unified Command still suffering some 900 casualties a day in heavy fighting, General Clark addressed a letter to the Communist commanders on June 29 in which he urged that the armistice arrangements be brought to a conclusion despite the manifest impracticability of recapturing the escaped Koreans. Concerning the future cooperation of the Republic of Korea, he could only say that his command and the interested governments would "make every effort" to obtain it, and that he proposed where possible to "establish military safeguards to insure that the armistice terms are observed." Meanwhile preparations were made to turn over the entire front to the R.O.K.'s should Rhee insist on continuing the fight. The Communists, while professing dissatisfaction with General Clark's offers, agreed on July 7 to resume negotiations in the second week of July; shortly thereafter they launched a final offensive, their heaviest in more than two years, which penetrated United Nations lines to a depth of seven miles, killed 14,000 United Nations troops (mostly Koreans), and left a permanent bend in the military demarcation line which formed part of the armistice agreement. Still taking their time, they refused to conclude matters until the Unified Command had promised to observe the armistice and deny support to the R.O.K. even if the latter should undertake aggressive action after the armistice was signed.[37]

Various special arrangements were required to make the armistice less unpalatable to the South Korean Government. To meet Dr. Rhee's refusal to admit Indian troops to South Korean territory, it was necessary to locate the entire prisoner repatriation operation within the four-kilometer-wide demilitarized zone, building special camps at a cost of over

[36] Clark, *op. cit.*, 286-288; Rhee-Robertson communiqué, July 11, in *Documents on American Foreign Relations, 1953*, 308-309; Robertson broadcast, July 17, in *Department of State Bulletin*, XXIX, July 27, 1953, 101-102; Dulles statements, July 22 and 28, *ibid.*, August 3, 1953, 141 and August 10, 1953, 177.

[37] *Ibid.*, July 13, 1953, 46-47 and July 20, 1953, 73-74; Clark, *op. cit.*, 289-292.

THE FAR EAST, 1953

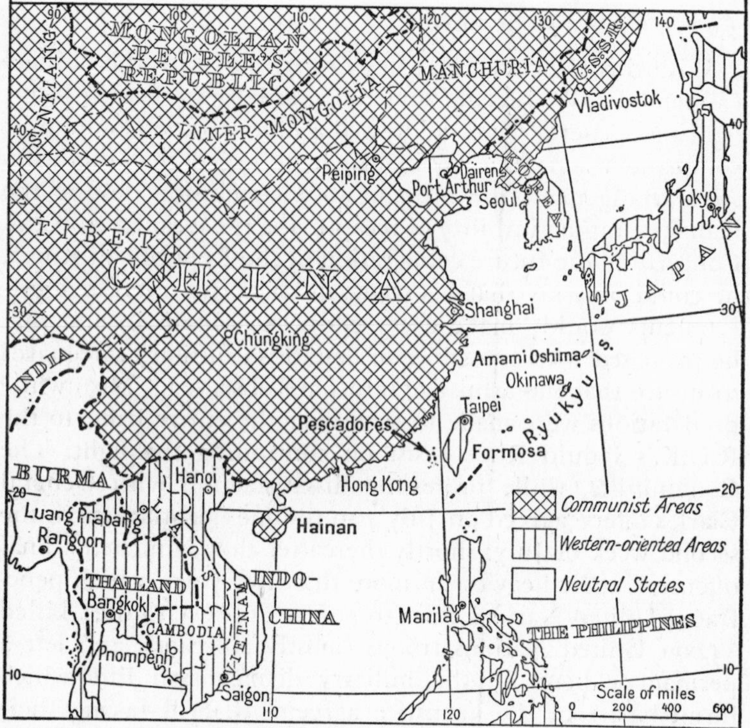

Communist Areas
Western-oriented Areas
Neutral States

THE KOREAN ARMISTICE

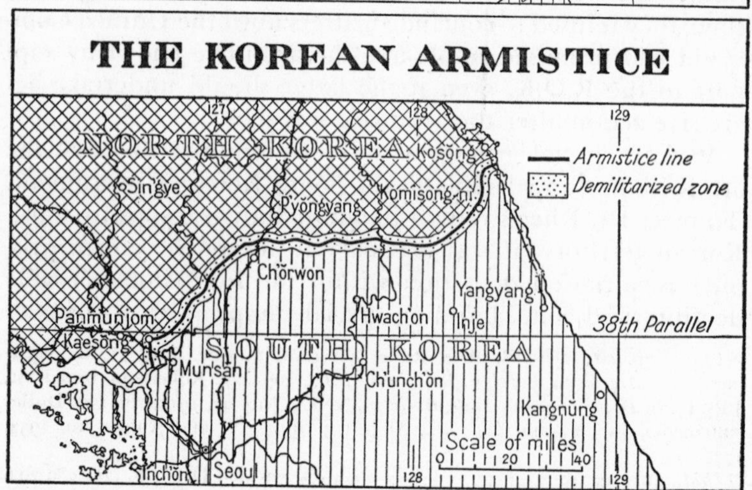

$7 million, moving the nonrepatriates from remote areas of South Korea, and making preparations to ferry in some 5,000 Indian guard troops by helicopter. When everything was at last in readiness, the Communists raised a final obstacle by refusing to sign the armistice in the presence of Republic of Korea representatives. Thus the signing ceremonies on July 27 had to be spread between three separate sites, the armistice building at Panmunjom and the headquarters of the two commands. But eventually all thirty-six documents were duly signed and at 10 P.M. on July 27 the guns were stilled.[38]

Thus ended, after three years and thirty-two days of fighting and more than two years of negotiation, the military phase of a conflict whose impact on modern civilization had been too strong and too varied to be adequately assessed by any contemporary. Some of the direct costs of the war could be approximated, among them the 300,000 South Korean and 155,000 United Nations casualties,[39] one and one-half to two million enemy casualties, perhaps a million other lives lost in South Korea and three million in North Korea. Under the armistice agreement the Korean Republic would gain some 1,500 square miles of territory—small compensation for the uprooting of two and one-half million refugees, five millions of destitute, 600,000 houses destroyed, and devastation estimated at anywhere from one to four billion dollars.[40] The monetary cost of the war to the United States was later estimated at $18 billion, exclusive of service pay.[41] Less easy to calculate was the moral and psychological damage sustained not only by the immediate victims but by all whose

[38] *Ibid.*, 292-296, 299. The text of the armistice agreement appears in *Department of State Bulletin*, XXIX, August 3, 1953, 132-140; for a summary of the major provisions cf. *Documents on American Foreign Relations, 1953*, 289-293.

[39] The "Special Report of the Unified Command on the Armistice in Korea" (U.N. Document S/3079, August 7, 1953, reprinted in *Department of State Bulletin*, XXIX, August 24, 1953, 246-251) sets U.S. casualties at about 141,000 and those of the other 15 participating U.N. members at about 14,000. The final U.S. casualty toll as printed in *U.S. News & World Report*, November 12, 1954, p. 4, was 142,091, including 23,300 killed, 105,785 wounded, and 24 missing.

[40] Statements of Assistant Secretary Robertson, July 17, and Secretary Dulles, July 26 and 27, in *Department of State Bulletin*, XXIX, July 27, 1953, 102; August 3, 1953, 132; August 10, 1953, 176.

[41] H. Struve Hensel, Assistant Secretary of Defense, in *New York Times*, April 16, 1955.

interests and emotions had in one way or another become involved in the struggle. And it was quite impossible as yet to balance these negative results against the positive achievement of the free world in successfully and unitedly repelling the Communist aggression without either extending the area of hostilities or sacrificing any fundamental principle. The worth of that historic achievement (to which was added the establishment of a new principle of political asylum for prisoners of war) was still in the balance, and could only be judged by the use the free nations might be able to make of their success. Repelling the aggression was only a part of the task the United Nations had set itself. There still remained the perhaps more difficult problem of "restoring international peace and security in the area."

2. TOWARD A FAR EASTERN CONFERENCE

In accepting an armistice which left them predominant in Northern Korea but gained them neither the control of South Korea, the satisfaction of their broad political claims, nor even the unconditional repatriation of their prisoners of war, the Communists acknowledged that like the United Nations they lacked the combination of strength and resolve that would have been needed if the Korean war was to be forced to a successful military conclusion. Perceiving that the United States under its new leadership planned neither to intensify the war nor to swerve from the nonrecognition policy laid down under President Truman, they had apparently concluded that it was time to seek an orderly liquidation of the war by conceding the main point still in dispute and permitting the prisoner issue to be resolved along lines favored by the United Nations Assembly. Whether or not this decision was directly encouraged from Moscow, it fitted in well with the new trend in Communist world policy inaugurated by Stalin's successors. Cessation of hostilities in Korea would contribute substantially to what seemed the general Communist aim of permitting a moderate relaxation of world tension. At the same time it would relieve the Communist governments in the Far East from the strain of active hostilities, provide Communist China with a defensive buffer in North Korea, and leave it free to pursue its broad objectives in the Far East by other means. The terms of the armistice, particularly the provision relating to a political conference, would afford ample opportunity to bring Communist Chinese aims to world attention and promote the divisive influence which they generally exerted in the free world. The cessation of military pressure in Korea, if the armistice was carried out, would free their hands for possible new ventures in the direction of Formosa or Southeast Asia.

For the United Nations powers, these were serious disadvantages. In addition, the armistice in Korea and the resultant letup in military preparations entailed a danger of possible economic dislocations in the United States, in Western Europe, and especially in Japan, where the Korean war had come to the rescue of a badly unbalanced national economy. In most non-Communist countries, however, these dangers seemed greatly outweighed by the sheer advantage of liquidating a war which entailed daily sacrifices and an ever-present danger of wider hostilities. So greatly was the armistice welcomed in most of the free nations that only limited precautions were taken against some of the perils inherent in the new situation it created.

Implementing the Armistice

From the United Nations point of view, the first and most obvious danger to be provided against was the possibility that the Communists might renew the war in Korea at some future time when they had caught their breath and the vigilance of the free nations had relaxed. Rather elaborate safeguards had been prepared against this particular eventuality, some of them built into the armistice itself and some of them embodied in supplementary understandings. From the very beginning, the Unified Command had insisted that the armistice must be based on a defensible military line, must forbid the reinforcement of troops in Korea, and must provide for adequate supervision and inspection to guard against the possibility of surprise attack.[42] Provisions designed to satisfy these requirements were incorporated in the armistice agreement of July 27.

[42] *The United States in World Affairs, 1951,* 145.

But since arrangements inside of Korea afforded only partial protection against aggressive preparations that might equally well be carried out on adjacent Chinese territory, it had been deemed necessary to reinforce these safeguards by a formal warning on the part of the sixteen nations participating in the United Nations action. As early as January 1952, the sixteen governments had agreed to make clear in a declaration to be issued after the signature of an armistice that if there were an unprovoked renewal of the aggression they would offer prompt and united resistance.[43] Accordingly, on July 27, within hours of the signature at Panmunjom, representatives of the sixteen governments in Washington signed a declaration[44] in which they not only affirmed their determination to carry out the armistice and to seek in good faith a settlement of the Korean problem but also voiced the following warning:

"We affirm, in the interests of world peace, that if there is a renewal of the armed attack, challenging again the principles of the United Nations, we should again be united and prompt to resist. The consequences of such a breach of the armistice would be so grave that, in all probability, it would not be possible to confine hostilities within the frontiers of Korea."

In other words the United Nations, which had so scrupulously limited the area of hostilities for more than three years, would not again refrain from carrying the war to Communist China itself. They also warned against new aggressions elsewhere, thus seconding the admonitions contained in the French-United States declaration of March 28, President Eisenhower's address of April 16, and the statement of the Big Three Foreign Ministers of July 14:[45]

"Finally, we are of the opinion that the armistice must not result in jeopardizing the restoration or the safeguarding of peace in any other part of Asia."

[43] Special Report of the Unified Command, August 7, in *Department of State Bulletin*, XXIX, August 24, 1953, 247.

[44] *Documents on American Foreign Relations, 1953*, 432-433; signed by Australia, Belgium, Canada, Colombia, Ethiopia, France, Greece, Luxembourg, Netherlands, New Zealand, Philippines, Thailand, Turkey, Union of South Africa, U.K., and U.S., and made public on August 7 in the Special Report of the Unified Command cited above.

[45] Cf. above, pp. 35-36, 129, and 190.

As often happened at such moments, the peace of Asia was made to look particularly tenuous by a pair of airplane incidents which rudely interrupted the general rejoicing. Shortly after the armistice was signed on July 27, but some hours before it went into effect, an American fighter plane on a combat mission over North Korea shot down a Soviet aircraft—presumably the same plane which the Soviet Government later claimed had been shot down on that day 100 miles inside Chinese territory while carrying fifteen passengers and six crew members, all of whom perished.[46] Two days later a United States Air Force plane on "a routine navigational training mission over the Sea of Japan" was attacked by Soviet MIG-15 fighters and shot down forty miles off the Soviet coast, the copilot being rescued by an American ship while other surviving members of the seventeen-man crew were apparently picked up by Soviet vessels in the vicinity. True to its invariable practice in such cases, the Kremlin asserted that the plane had violated Soviet territory near Vladivostok, opened fire on the Soviet fighters, and disappeared out to sea. All knowledge of the crew was denied.[47] Presumably those who survived had joined the growing number of Americans who faced indefinite captivity in Soviet labor camps.

For many American families the principal merit of the armistice had been the prospect of reunion with those of their men who had survived the rigors of imprisonment by the North Korean and Chinese Communists. Operation "Big Switch," the general exchange of prisoners of war, began at Panmunjom on August 5 and was completed without serious incident on September 6. The numbers of men to be exchanged had altered somewhat from earlier estimates, mainly

[46] Soviet note, July 31, and U.S. reply, August 1, in *Department of State Bulletin*, XXIX, August 10, 1953, 179; U.S. announcement and Soviet note, August 11, *ibid.*, August 24, 1953, 237; XXX, March 15, 1954, 410-412. It should be noted that the Soviet protest was not made until after the July 29 incident described below, and that the United States disclaimed knowledge of any attack by American aircraft outside of Korea. For further correspondence in 1954 cf. *ibid.*, March 15, 1954, 408-412.

[47] Soviet notes, July 30 and August 4, and U.S. notes, July 31 and August 4, *ibid.*, XXIX, August 10, 1953, 179 and August 17, 1953, 206-207. For further correspondence in 1954 cf. *ibid.*, XXX, March 15, 1954, 408-410; XXXI, December 6, 1954, 857-862.

because of the recent fighting, but prisoners held for repatriation by the Unified Command still outnumbered those acknowledged by the Communists by nearly six to one. In all, the United Nations repatriated 75,799 prisoners (70,159 North Koreans and 5,640 Chinese) and the Communists gave up 12,760, including 7,850 Koreans, 3,597 Americans, 945 British, and 228 Turks. Most prominent of the returning Americans was General William F. Dean, captured in 1950, whose modesty and quiet heroism relieved the sickening tale of Communist inhumanity on which all accounts of returning prisoners agreed. Of prisoners still refusing repatriation, the United Nations retained temporary custody of 22,600 Koreans and Chinese while the enemy held 359 personnel of the United Nations Command, including 23 Americans, who allegedly did not wish to be returned. Even now not all United Nations prisoners were accounted for. Apart from those murdered in captivity,[48] the Unified Command had evidence that 3,404 of its men (including 944 Americans) had definitely been in enemy custody but were not returned. All rights to insist on the repatriation of every single United Nations prisoner were reserved, but there seemed no way of enforcing them short of a renewal of the war which had only just been halted. The question was destined to remain as a permanently disturbing influence in American-Chinese relations.

The Rhee-Dulles Agreement

The next big step in implementing the armistice would be the transfer of the nonrepatriates from both sides to the custody of the Neutral Nations Repatriation Commission as a preliminary to the scheduled "explanations" by representatives of the respective commands.[49] Meanwhile there had been significant developments in connection with other phases of the armistice settlement. Early in August Secretary Dulles had paid his delayed visit to South Korea and reached agreement with President Rhee on the various inducements

[48] The number of persons tortured or massacred by the Communists was estimated in a report of the War Crimes Division of the U.S. Army in Korea (October 28, 1953) at 11,622 military personnel (including 6,113 Americans), 176 Korean police, 17,176 Korean civilians, and 2 European priests.

[49] Cf. below, pp. 387-389.

by which the latter was to be reconciled to not upsetting the armistice agreement. A draft mutual defense treaty was initialed on the spot; [50] the pledges of immediate and automatic reaction to any breach of the armistice by the Communists were renewed; plans for the billion-dollar economic rehabilitation program were carried forward; and views were exchanged concerning the proposed build-up of R.O.K. land, air, sea forces. Equally important with these longer-range commitments was the confirmation of the understanding already reached concerning the forthcoming political conference. Once again it was agreed that the conference would be given ninety days in which to make progress toward "the peaceful unification of historic Korea as a free and independent nation." During this period President Rhee agreed "to take no unilateral action to unite Korea by military means." If at the end of ninety days the two governments agreed that the conference had made no progress but was being improperly exploited by the Communists, they would be "prepared to make a concurrent withdrawal" and to "consult further" regarding the attainment of their common aim.[51]

It did not require an expert to perceive the complete lack of enthusiasm with which the Republic of Korea looked forward to this political conference which was nominally supposed to effect a peaceful settlement of the Korean question. A few days after Secretary Dulles had left, President Rhee predicted that during the next several months his government could expect "to be vilified, slandered, insulted and denounced in every vile form their [the Communists'] spiteful ingenuity can invent." Though respect for the United States and other friends abroad had induced the Republic of Korea "to postpone for a time" its own plans, Dr. Rhee insisted that "it is our wish and determination to march north at the earliest possible time"; and he apologized to "our North Korean brethren" that it had become necessary "to delay their ultimate salvation another few months." [52]

[50] Cf. below, p. 249 f. The press of business in Washington prevented a bipartisan Senate delegation from accompanying Secretary Dulles to Seoul for the negotiation of the treaty.

[51] Joint Statement, Seoul, August 8, in *Documents on American Foreign Relations, 1953,* 309-311.

[52] Address of August 15, *ibid.,* 298-302.

What Kind of Conference?

Without sharing Dr. Rhee's enthusiasm for a renewal of the war, the United States was equally pessimistic about the forthcoming conference. The bare idea of a meeting in which Communist China would be a participant was profoundly distasteful to the American Government, which had consented to this feature of the armistice terms only for the purpose of excluding political matters from the armistice negotiations themselves. Official Washington was well aware that the mere holding of a conference would not solve any political issue, in Korea or elsewhere. The questions of "the withdrawal of all foreign forces from Korea, the peaceful settlement of the Korean question, etc."—to quote the language of the armistice document—would not be settled unless some at least of the parties to the dispute were prepared to modify the stands they had maintained throughout the war. But the United States had no plans for modifying its position: it had no intention of withdrawing its support from Syngman Rhee's government, and no thought of trying to purchase Chinese concessions by taking a "new look" at Peking's political claims.[53] So far as Washington knew, the Communist governments also had no plans for yielding any of the advantages which the armistice agreement conferred on them. Thus the only certain result of a conference would be an enhancement of Communist China's diplomatic status and a flood of Communist propaganda aimed at denigrating the Republic of Korea and dramatizing what the Communists would undoubtedly try to present as the "obstructionist" position of the United States.

Unless the matter was carefully handled, moreover, there was a possibility that when the conference met the United States might actually find itself in a minority position, outnumbered by governments which took a less unfavorable view of Chinese Communist pretensions. To minimize this danger it seemed important that the conference be set up in

53 "I think I have made it clear," said Mr. Dulles on July 28, "I would not be prepared on behalf of the United States to try to buy the unity of Korea at the price of a concession which would involve bringing Communist China into the United Nations and, above all, into the Security Council." *Department of State Bulletin*, XXIX, August 10, 1953, 177.

such a way as to limit the range of discussion and ensure that the United States and South Korean viewpoints were given maximum weight. But the relevant paragraph of the armistice agreement (paragraph 60) was decidedly vague in regard to the actual composition and functioning of the conference. Technically, indeed, paragraph 60 was no more than an agreed recommendation by the two military commands "to the governments of the countries concerned on both sides." The substance of this recommendation was that:

> "within three (3) months after the Armistice Agreement is signed and becomes effective [i.e., not later than October 28, 1953], a political conference of a higher level of both sides be held by representatives appointed respectively to settle through negotiation the questions of the withdrawal of all foreign forces from Korea, the peaceful settlement of the Korean question, etc."

Nothing was said about how or by whom the conference should be convoked, nor about who precisely should be invited to participate, although the Unified Command had said that its recommendation would be made "to the United Nations as well as to the Republic of Korea" and that "et cetera," in its view, did not include matters outside of Korea.[54]

Up to the time of the armistice the United States had apparently given little thought to the interpretation of his language. Secretary Dulles had said more than once that he supposed the United Nations would be represented by a delegation chosen by the General Assembly, and that the United States did not exclude the possibility that non-Korean questions would also be taken up.[55] The South Korean Assembly, however, took a less liberal view. On August 3, the day before Mr. Dulles' arrival in Seoul, it unanimously resolved that no nations should be allowed to take part in the conference except those which had participated in the Korean war; that the duration of the conference should be limited to three months; and that no scheme of Korean unification should be entertained which would "violate the

[54] Fortieth Report of the U.N. Command on Operations in Korea, February 16-29, 1952 (U.N. Document S/2619), *ibid.*, XXVI, June 23, 1952, 999.

[55] Statements of June 15 and July 21, *ibid.*, XXVIII, June 29, 1953, 908 and XXIX, August 3, 1953, 141.

sovereignty of the Republic of Korea"—in other words, prevent the absorption of North Korea by the existing South Korean Government.[56] Some part of these demands was reflected in the Rhee-Dulles declaration of August 8, and other portions were presently adopted as formal United States policy. But serious disagreements were ahead, both with the Communists and with other free nations—disagreements so serious, in fact, that it was to be not three months but nine before any conference could meet that remotely resembled the one provided for in the Korean armistice.

The General Assembly Decides

The obvious forum for a matter of this sort was the General Assembly of the United Nations, which had recessed in April with the intention of resuming its consideration of the Korean question on notification that an armistice had been signed.[57] By the time the Assembly reconvened on August 17, the United States and other governments had had time to reflect more fully on the implications of paragraph 60 and to arrive at sharply differing conclusions. The United States had made up its mind to keep the proceedings as fully under its own control as possible; a good many other governments had made up their minds to try to dilute the influence of the United States in the hope of thereby improving the prospect that the conference would arrive at some measure of real agreement. Symbolic of the difficulties to come was a preliminary disagreement on the scope of the Assembly's responsibility in the matter. Assembly President Lester B. Pearson of Canada took the view that it was up to the Assembly to make all arrangements for the conference, while Mr. Lodge maintained for the United States that the Assembly's only function was to select the participants who would represent the free world. The fundamental issue, however, was not who should sponsor the conference but what kind of a conference should be held. Was it to be simply a new confrontation of the same hostile parties that

56 *Chronology of International Events and Documents,* IX, No. 15, July 23-August 5, 1953, 477.

57 Above, p. 66. A brief account of the Assembly's deliberations in the final part of the Seventh Session appears in *Chronique de politique étrangère,* VII, January 1954, 57-64.

had faced each other across the table at Panmunjom for the last two years and familiarized themselves *ad nauseam* with each other's points of view? Or should the line-up be modified in such a way as to veil these differences and possibly circumvent them?

Prime Minister Nehru of India had crystallized the issue in saying that what was needed was "more a round-table conference than an across-the-table conference" and that it "should approach matters rather informally and not in a rigid way." In other words, Mr. Nehru implied, the participants should sit not as belligerents but as parties having a common interest in seeking peaceful solutions of Far Eastern problems. This view seemed to be shared in some degree by Great Britain and by many of the other non-Communist countries; Selwyn Lloyd of the United Kingdom said that the political conference should be "a true conference and not a negotiation between two sides." Mr. Vyshinsky, too, seemed greatly attracted by the notion of a round-table conference, and undertook to propose the inclusion of a whole series of countries which had taken no direct part in the war: India, Poland, Sweden (or Czechoslovakia), Burma, Egypt, Indonesia, Mexico, and Syria, as well as the U.S.S.R. itself. By this method (which was endorsed in messages from China and North Korea), Mr. Vyshinsky obviously hoped to conjure up a majority which would be unfavorable to the United States position and would force this country into a minority even if it was unable to impose decisions unacceptable to the American Government. It would be unfair to suggest that Mr. Vyshinsky's objective was shared by the non-Communist advocates of a round-table conference; yet they must have hoped that this device would at least make it easier for the two principals—the United States as well as Communist China—to modify positions which might be found to stand in the way of a wider pacification.

Perceiving, however, that any such arrangement would necessarily weaken American influence within the political conference, the United States elected to stand firmly upon the letter of the armistice agreement, with its unequivocal reference to "a political conference . . . of both sides." This country, Mr. Lodge explained, had "adhered to paragraph

60, with its concept of two sides, because it is one of the few definite things in this whole picture"; if there was a desire for agreement, "a conference of both sides can reach agreement as readily as any other arrangement." For the United States, therefore, the form of the conference was not an issue. The only question remaining was, what particular countries should represent the United Nations "side"; and the answer of the American Government was, "those among the Member states *contributing armed forces* which desire to be represented, together with the Republic of Korea." Only those countries which had actively joined in repelling the aggression, in the United States view, had any justifiable claim to be represented at a conference whose purpose was to clear up the situation which the aggression had created. These, of course, were precisely the countries which were least inclined to neutralism and therefore would be most likely to side with the United States on any matters under discussion; and the United States had also taken the initiative in proposing a modified "veto" rule whereby no government participating on the United Nations side would be bound by any decision or agreement to which it did not individually adhere. In addition, Mr. Lodge took the view that the conference should confine itself strictly to the Korean question. If a prospect for fruitful discussion of other issues should develop, he said, this might well call for "another conference with different participants." [58]

Although the draft resolution which embodied these views was sponsored by fifteen of the sixteen United Nations which had sent troops to Korea, it afforded only a partial reflection of the sentiments existing within that group. Notwithstanding this country's opposition, there had been considerable partiality among the other delegations for a round-table type of conference or, at least, for the inclusion in the conference of certain additional countries which not only were interested in the Far East but might conceivably have something positive to contribute. The Soviet Union and India, in particular, had seemed to several governments to be ap-

[58] Statement to the First Committee, August 18, in *Department of State Bulletin*, XXIX, August 31, 1953, 284-285 (emphasis supplied); fifteen-power draft resolution (U.N. Document A/L.151/Rev.1, August 17), *ibid.*, 287.

propriate participants: the former as an acknowledged leader in the Communist world and the only great power which the American formula might leave unrepresented; the latter as a leading Asian state which had avoided commitments to either power group but had always stood ready to mediate between them and had, moreover, been of material assistance in finding a solution to the prisoner-of-war question. No full agreement on these matters had been reached among the sixteen powers before the Assembly opened, with the result that their differences were now aired on the floor of the Assembly itself.

Concerning the U.S.S.R., the United States did not insist on its exclusion from the conference but merely stipulated that if it attended at all it must attend as a member of the Communist "side," together with Communist China and North Korea. Moscow might pretend to have been a "neutral" in the Korea conflict, but the United States was not deceived and saw no reason for others to deceive themselves. Had not Mr. Vyshinsky himself admitted that his government had sold armaments to Communist China, a declared aggressor? [59] And who had supplied the aggressors with the seventy-five MIG fighters which had been shot down by the United Nations in the single month of June 1953? At Panmunjom, the United States had successfully resisted the attempt to include the U.S.S.R. among the "neutral" nations which were to supervise the Korean armistice, and there was no desire to find it masquerading as a "neutral" at the political conference. The most this country would concede was that the U.S.S.R. might take part in the conference if "the other side" desired it. A resolution in this sense was therefore introduced by Australia, New Zealand, Denmark, and Norway.

The proposed participation of India presented a thornier problem. Although President Syngman Rhee professed to consider India as no better than a Communist state, its government was widely respected in other non-Communist lands and the United States could not oppose its representation without risking widespread international disapprobation as

[59] Statement to the First Committee, March 2, *ibid.*, XXVIII, March 16, 1953, 420.

well as serious offense to the Nehru government. Yet this country had never been satisfied of Mr. Nehru's complete impartiality as between the two camps, especially in matters involving Communist China. In his anxiety to merit the confidence of Peking, the Indian Prime Minister seemed often to do less than justice to the point of view prevailing in Washington. If India came to the conference, it would undoubtedly begin by raising the question of Chinese representation in the United Nations, the very issue the United States was least anxious to discuss. After that it would be difficult to keep the debate within comfortable bounds; and, said Mr. Lodge: "If . . . we have a conference which becomes a catch-all for every problem in the world or even every problem in the Far East, it will probably lead to little more than 'sound and fury signifying nothing.' "[60] At an early stage, therefore, the United States let it be known that it was under no circumstances prepared to envisage the participation of India in the political conference.

The Indian Government itself took pains to point out that it had not sought representation in the conference and desired to participate only if it could be of use—a protestation which did not conceal the fact that it would be seriously affronted if its participation was not found useful. India, moreover, had powerful sponsors, including not only the United Kingdom (which was disinclined to offend another member of the Commonwealth) and the Communist bloc (which openly rejoiced at this new cleavage among the non-Communist powers) but also a large number of Asian states and several members of the Western coalition. Despite the known opposition of the United States, a formal proposal to invite India's participation was sponsored by Australia, Canada, and New Zealand as well as Great Britain; and the widespread sympathy it aroused made it clear that this was to be the chief issue as far as the General Assembly was concerned. Mr. Lodge said what he could by way of compliment to India, and emphasized that the United States would want India to "play a central and constructive role" in any later, general consultations on Far Eastern matters. The prospects for holding such consultations, however,

[60] *Ibid.*, XXIX, August 31, 1953, 285.

would depend on the attitude of the Communists at the forthcoming Korean conference; and in that conference, Mr. Lodge suggested. India had less reason to participate than various other nonparticipating countries such as Japan and Nationalist China. Apart from other considerations, he explained, the United States felt that in view of "the known attitude of the Republic of Korea" the participation of India could only jeopardize the success of the conference.[61]

This logic was only partially convincing to other delegates. When the First Committee voted on the invitation to India on August 27, it was found that twenty-seven governments favored it to only twenty-one who adhered to the American position; eleven governments abstained and India did not vote. Supporting the invitation were four Commonwealth delegations together with twelve Asian-African, three Scandinavian, and two Latin American countries as well as Yugoslavia and the five governments of the Soviet bloc. Opposing it were the United States, Nationalist China, Greece, Pakistan, and seventeen Latin American states. Even among the sixteen nations that had sent troops to Korea, five favored the invitation while only three opposed it and eight abstained. Although the pro-Indian majority was politically impressive, however, it fell short of the two-thirds majority which would be required if the resolution was to be approved in plenary session. The Indian delegate, V. K. Krishna Menon, therefore requested that the matter not be brought to a final vote. "What we are trying to do is not to add to the heat of any battle," he said—an attitude which Mr. Lodge termed both "generous" and "statesmanlike."

While India and various other countries nursed their injured feelings,[62] the full Assembly proceeded on August 28 to dispose of the other pending proposals on conference membership. The fifteen-power resolution, calling for participation on the United Nations side of "those among the Member States contributing armed forces which desire to be represented, together with the Republic of Korea," was approved by 43 votes to 5, with ten abstentions; the recom-

[61] Statement in the First Committee, August 25, *ibid.*, September 14, 1953, 362.

[62] On the Indian reaction cf. below, pp. 313-314.

mendation that the U.S.S.R. participate "if the other side desires it" was passed by 55 to 1 (Nationalist China), with one abstention. The United States was commissioned "to arrange with the other side for the political conference to be held as soon as possible, but not later than 28 October 1953, at a place and on a date satisfactory to both sides"; and the Secretary-General was requested to acquaint the Communist governments with the Assembly's views.[63] After the Soviet proposal for a conference with wider participation had been defeated by 42 to 5, with two abstentions, the Assembly went on to record by a large majority its tribute to those who had died resisting aggression in Korea.[64] Thereafter the Seventh Session of the Assembly, which had begun on October 14, 1952, was formally declared closed.

Before the votes were taken, Mr. Vyshinsky had warned that the "two-sided" conference officially favored by the Assembly was unlikely to be acceptable to the Communist governments. Presentation of the Assembly's proposals "as an ultimatum," he said, would "wreck the forthcoming conference before it opened." [65] It was certainly true that the Chinese and North Korean Communists—quite apart from the question of "face" involved—had little incentive to go into the type of conference envisaged by the Assembly resolutions. There was little they could expect to gain from a conference of two sides in which they would be segregated on one side while the other side was dominated by the United States. Their negative answer to the Assembly's proposals, when it was made public on September 13, would show that they expected greater gains from continuing the argument and trying to get a reversal of the Assembly's decision. But these later exchanges can be more advantageously considered in connection with the general problem of East-West negotiations as it developed in the later months of 1953.[66] In the meantime some attention must be devoted

[63] Resolution 711 (VII), August 28, 1953, in *Documents on American Foreign Relations, 1953*, 433-435.
[64] Resolution 712 (VII), August 28, 1953.
[65] General Assembly *Official Records, Seventh Session, First Committee*, August 26, 1953 (U.N. Document A/C.1/SR.624), 763.
[66] Cf. below, pp. 389-394.

to the broader Far Eastern picture as influenced by the Korean armistice.

3. BOLSTERING THE "DEFENSIVE PERIMETER"

In his address of April 18 on the first ninety days of the new administration, Secretary Dulles had taken pains to stress the increased importance which the whole Far East was receiving in American policy calculations, as well as the integrated nature of current problems throughout the area:

"You can see, as others have seen, that a new order of priority and urgency has been given to the Far East. Further, it has been made clear that we consider that our Eastern friends, from Japan, Korea, and Formosa to Indochina and Malaya, face a single hostile front, to be met with a common purpose and growing cooperation as between the component parts of freedom.

"This means that the Communists in the Far East can no longer count on winning by shifting their strength and by focusing attack on one or another free-world position that is isolated from the others. The Communist strategy, based on a contiguous land mass, is now confronted by a growing free-world unity based upon the peninsular positions and offshore island chain now controlled by the free peoples of Asia." [67]

This concept of Asian interdependence was stressed once again in an important address which Secretary Dulles delivered to the American Legion on September 2. "We do not make the mistake of treating Korea as an isolated affair," he said. "A single Chinese-Communist aggressive front extends from Korea on the north to Indochina in the south. The armistice in Korea, even if it leads to a political settlement in Korea, does not end United States concern in the western Pacific area." To make clear the extent of this concern and remove any doubts that might be lingering in the minds of potential aggressors, Mr. Dulles intimated that there were areas in the Far East where the United States, under certain circumstances, might again feel compelled to resort to military action—where, as he said, an aggressor who failed to exercise proper self-control "may face a hard fight, perhaps a losing fight." One such area was South Korea itself, which,

[67] *Department of State Bulletin,* XXVIII, April 27, 1953, 605.

Mr. Dulles pointed out, would henceforth be protected not only by the United Nations Charter (as in 1950) but also by the pending United States-Korean security treaty and by the sixteen-nation pledge of July 27.[68] This last declaration meant, according to Mr. Dulles' interpretation, that if the Communists renewed the war they could no longer count on a "privileged sanctuary" behind the Yalu River in Manchuria. Furthermore, the Secretary continued, a similar situation existed with respect to Indochina:

> "There is the risk that, as in Korea, Red China might send its own army into Indochina. The Chinese Communist regime should realize that such a second aggression could not occur without grave consequences *which might not be confined to Indochina.* I say this soberly in the interest of peace and in the hope of preventing another aggressor miscalculation." [69]

For practical purposes, however, there still remained considerable differences between an area like Korea, which the United States and fifteen other governments were explicitly pledged to defend, and a country like Indochina which nominally remained a French responsibility and in which the extent of prospective United States or other assistance was still by no means clear. South Korea, over the past two or three years, had come to occupy a status not dissimilar to that of Japan, Formosa, the Philippines, and similar positions which the United States considered vital to its own strategic interests in the Pacific. In effect, it constituted one more addition to that "defensive perimeter" which Dean Acheson had defined early in 1950 [70] and which had since been tacitly extended to include the island of Formosa and the Pescadores. Though not geographically a part of the "offshore island chain," it had both a similar strategic function in relation to the Asian continent and a similar political orientation in relation to Asian Communism. Thus the United States apparently intended to treat it henceforward as one of the elements in the general system of Pacific security which

[68] Above, p. 234.

[69] *Department of State Bulletin,* XXIX, September 14, 1953, 339-342 (emphasis supplied).

[70] *The United States in World Affairs, 1949,* 463; cf. Secretary Dulles' remarks on the strategic importance of Korea, January 27, in *Department of State Bulletin,* XXVIII, February 9, 1953, 213.

had been in process of formation since the conclusion of the Japanese Peace Treaty and the security treaties with Australia, New Zealand, the Philippines, and Japan in 1951. Indochina, on the other hand, had still to be treated primarily as a part of the general problem of Southeast Asia, where the vastly different military and political conditions had thus far prevented the establishment of any comparable defense arrangements.

America's Newest Ally

The new role envisaged for the Republic of Korea was clearly imprinted on the mutual defense treaty which Secretary Dulles and President Rhee had initialed at Seoul on August 8. The stated purpose of the parties was virtually identical to that expressed in the 1951 security treaties: ". . . to strengthen their efforts for collective defense for the preservation of peace and security *pending the development of a more comprehensive and effective system of regional security in the Pacific Area.*" In terms strongly reminiscent of the 1951 treaties, the two governments agreed to consult together if the political independence and security of either was threatened by external armed attack, and to maintain and develop, "separately and jointly, by self-help and mutual aid," their capacity to deter armed attack. Each recognized that an armed attack on the other party in the Pacific area, either in territories it already controlled or in others (such as North Korea) that might lawfully come under its administration at a later date, would be "dangerous to its own peace and safety"; and each promised that it would "act to meet the common danger in accordance with its constitutional processes." The United States would have the usual right to dispose land, air and sea forces "in and about" the territory of the Republic of Korea as might be determined by mutual agreement. Of more than routine importance, in view of the warlike dispositions of President Rhee's government, was the mutual undertaking of the parties to settle their international disputes by peaceful means and "to refrain in their international relations from the threat or use of force in any manner inconsistent with the purposes of the

United Nations, or obligations assumed by any Party toward the United Nations." [71]

Although the treaty was to remain in force indefinitely, it had been made clear to President Rhee that it could not go into effect until the normal processes of ratification had been completed, and that in view of the adjournment of Congress this could probably not occur until early 1954.[72] Meanwhile there was much else to do if South Korea was to be restored to a condition that would not invite further aggression. Most urgent was the task of commencing the rehabilitation of the country's prostrated economic life. President Rhee and Secretary Dulles had envisaged a program of three to four years' duration which would involve the expenditure of approximately $1 billion in United States funds—subject, of course, to appropriation by the Congress. As an initial step, President Eisenhower had asked Congress on the very day of the armistice to authorize the expenditure of up to $200 million which would be saved through the cessation of hostilities.[73] The sum requested was made available with minimum delay,[74] and by late August some half-dozen ships were carrying rice, barley, cotton, and other aid supplies from United States ports. By the end of the year, $50 million of the initial total had been allotted and substantial amounts of relief goods and fertilizers had arrived in Pusan harbor.[75]

Economic aid to Korea was a many-sided undertaking, involving complementary efforts by the Foreign Operations Administration, the Department of Defense, the Unified

[71] Text in *Documents on American Foreign Relations, 1953*, 312-313 (emphasis supplied). The treaty omits the customary provision for reporting by the parties to the U.N. Security Council in case of action against aggression.

[72] The treaty was signed in Washington on October 1, 1953; it was approved by the Senate with an understanding on January 26, ratified by the President on February 5, and entered into force on November 17, 1954.

[73] Message of July 27 (H. Doc. 215, 83d Cong., 1st Sess.), in *Department of State Bulletin*, XXIX, August 10, 1953, 193-194. This and subsequent recommendations were based on the report of a special economic mission to Korea headed by Dr. Henry J. Tasca, a summary of which appears in *Documents on American Foreign Relations, 1953*, 313-320.

[74] Supplemental Appropriation Act, 1954 (Public Law 207, 83d Congress, approved August 7, 1953).

[75] *Report to Congress on the Mutual Security Program*, December 31, 1953 (Washington, G.P.O., 1954), 42. For further details cf. "United States Economic Assistance to Korea, 1945–1954," *Department of State Bulletin*, XXXII, February 21, 1955, 296-300.

Command, and the United Nations Korean Reconstruction Agency (UNKRA), which itself delivered $30 million worth of supplies and equipment to Korea during 1953. To coordinate these various programs and develop effective arrangements with the Korean Government, C. Tyler Wood of Mr. Stassen's agency was appointed Economic Coordinator and Unified Command representative on the Combined Economic Board which had been set up in agreement with the Koreans in 1952. In December, a new agreement on the policies and operations of this body laid down a set of principles designed to ensure that all economic assistance funds would be used for the maximum benefit of the Korean people. Total economic support expenditures from all sources programmed for the fiscal year 1953–54 exceeded $400 million; the UNKRA program amounted to $85 million for 1953–54 and $110 million for 1954–55, although contributions to date by United Nations members other than the United States had fallen far short of the approved targets and it remained questionable how much of the United Nations program could be carried out.[76]

Still, these plans, coupled with a continuing build-up of the R.O.K. military forces, tended to engender an optimistic tone reminiscent in some ways of the situation that had prevailed in South Korea in early 1950. Signs of progress had then been so numerous that Mr. Dulles, visiting Korea on behalf of President Truman and Secretary of State Acheson, had talked of "peaceful influences which will disintegrate the hold of Soviet communism on your fellows to the north and irresistibly draw them into unity with you." [77] At that time, the Communist leaders had cut short any such peaceful threat to their hold on North Korea by making war on the

[76] *Report to Congress on the Mutual Security Program*, December 31, 1953, 42-43; Combined Economic Board Agreement for a Program of Economic Reconstruction and Financial Stabilization, December 14, 1953, in *Department of State Bulletin*, XXX, January 11, 1954, 65-67; statement by Henry Ford II, U.S. Representative to the General Assembly, December 2, *ibid.*, XXIX, December 28, 1953, 904-908. During 1953 the General Assembly adopted two resolutions urging contributions to Korean relief and rehabilitation: Resolution 701 (VII), March 11, in *Documents on American Foreign Relations, 1953*, 435-436; and Resolution 725 (VIII), December 7, text in *Department of State Bulletin*, XXIX, December 28, 1953, 908.

[77] *The United States in World Affairs, 1950*, 187.

budding South Korean Republic. This time, too, they appeared to be taking no chances. True, they gave no sign of wanting to renew the war; but as the United States moved to help stricken South Korea to its feet, the Communist powers moved, too, to tighten their grip on a reviving North Korea.

Premier Malenkov announced on August 8 that the Soviet Government had determined to allocate one billion rubles (officially $250 million) "for restoration of Korea's ruined economy." [78] Six weeks later the North Korean leaders were in Moscow, winding up negotiations on the utilization of the funds and on the "further developing and strengthening" of their "friendly" relations with the U.S.S.R.[79] Communist China, not to be outdone, entertained the North Korean leaders in Peking in November and undertook to fortify the "traditional and indestructible friendly relations between the Chinese and Korean peoples" with a reconstruction gift of eight trillion yuan ($317 million) as well as an agreement on economic and cultural cooperation and promises of technical assistance and other benefits.[80] Although both Moscow and Peking professed confidence that Korea would soon be peacefully unified, the immediate aim seemed to be a strengthening of Communist control over North Korea which would tend to perpetuate the division of the country just as it had done in Germany. This would be true whether the two powers were working in complete harmony or, as seemed possible, were engaged in a competition for the dominant influence in Korean affairs.

The Republic of China on Formosa

President Syngman Rhee had long been ambitious to play a role in an anti-Communist alliance of Asian states, a project he had discussed with President Chiang Kai-shek as far back as 1949 and continued to broach at intervals despite the fact that his own government's relations with some im-

[78] *Documents on American Foreign Relations, 1953,* 137.

[79] Soviet-North Korean communiqué, September 20, *ibid.,* 157-159.

[80] TASS summary of the Chinese Communist-North Korean negotiations of November 14-22, *ibid.,* 159-161; text of agreement in *New York Times,* November 25, 1953.

portant Asian states, notably Japan, were not of the best.[81] In November 1953, fortified by the signature of his new treaty with the United States, Dr. Rhee flew to Formosa and joined the Nationalist President in a statement reiterating their joint determination "to carry on the fight against Communist aggression until those of our brethren who have been enslaved are restored their liberty." Both countries, the two presidents declared, stood firmly united in the determination "to mobilize all our moral and material forces to defeat the aggressors in Asia." Urging all the free countries of Asia "to organize a united anti-Communist front," they called for the backing of such an alignment by "other freedom-loving nations" and particularly by Pacific countries like the United States.[82] On his return to Seoul, Dr. Rhee confirmed that he and President Chiang were negotiating an alliance, but refused to say whether Chinese Nationalist troops would be used in Korea if fighting there should resume.[83]

Although Nationalist China had as yet no mutual security treaty with the United States, its situation resembled that of South Korea in various essential respects. In both cases a strongly anti-Communist government, supported by the United States for a combination of idealistic and strategic reasons, claimed to speak for a nation which it controlled only in part but hoped to liberate in full. In both cases, moreover, there existed the same fundamental ambiguity as to the nature and ultimate implications of United States support. Nominally, American military and economic assistance was designed only to enable the two governments to defend the territories they presently controlled; yet President Rhee and President Chiang Kai-shek did not conceal—in fact, they openly proclaimed—their determination not only to protect their present territories but also to wrest full control of the respective countries from their present Communist rulers at the earliest opportunity. With these aspirations the United States was clearly in sympathy; yet it hesitated, apparently, to underwrite them at the risk of what might turn into a

[81] Cf. Clark, *op. cit.*, 154-167.
[82] Joint statement, November 28, in *Documents on American Foreign Relations, 1953*, 341-342.
[83] *New York Times*, November 29, 1953.

general war. President Rhee had been restrained by a mutual security pact from attempting the immediate conquest of North Korea, and there were rumors at about the same time that President Chiang, despite the "unleashing" order of a few months before, had been induced to promise that he would make no intensified military move against Communist China without first consulting the United States. But these reports were denied by Vice Admiral Joseph P. Clark, commander of the Seventh Fleet, who said that no American permission was needed for Chinese Nationalist attacks—although, he added, the United States was not encouraging a mainland invasion, and would presumably be asked for assistance before any such attempt was made.[84]

Although "Return to the Mainland" was the fundamental theme of all Nationalist China's internal and external relations, the obstacles to a successful reinvasion of continental China were in reality so formidable that without stronger United States backing than was available at present there seemed little serious chance of its being attempted. Opposing the half-million men in Chiang's armed forces (his army numbered around 300,000) was a Communist military force of upward of five million. Whatever the internal weaknesses of Communist China, whatever the true sympathies of the mainland Chinese after four years or more of Communist repression, such an enterprise would be foredoomed as long as the United States withheld its full support. Conceivably such support might one day be provided as the result of a change of policy in Washington, a new act of aggression by Communist China, or a successful move by Chiang Kai-shek to force Washington's hand. Even in 1953 there were developments that could point toward a reinvasion of continental China, such as the strengthening with United States encouragement of the Nationalist positions on Quemoy, Matsu, and other small coastal islands just off the China mainland.[85] But from the American point of view the immediately important task was to preserve Formosa itself as a non-Communist Chinese outpost, a beacon of hope for

[84] *Ibid.*, August 19 and 23, 1953.

[85] Richard H. Rovere, "Letter from Washington," *New Yorker*, XXXI, No. 11, April 30, 1955, 105-106.

freedom-loving Chinese on the mainland and overseas, and an essential link in the chain of strategic offshore islands.

It was primarily for this reason, presumably, that the administration had followed up its January order "unleashing" the Nationalist forces with a marked increase in American military assistance (including delivery of the first jet aircraft under the Mutual Defense Assistance Program) and a stepping-up of the training program supervised by the American Military Assistance Advisory Group under Major General William C. Chase. Up-to-date equipment and arms had been reaching Formosa for some time under an aid program amounting to some $300 million annually, about two-thirds of which went toward military and one-third toward economic assistance. Contributing to the intensified rate of deliveries of military matériel in 1953 were the high productive levels reached by American munitions producers and the cutback in requirements for Korea. In the economic field, as in each year since 1950, American assistance in 1953 comprised at least half of the total funds allotted to the Far East.[86]

A principal shortage on Formosa was a lack of manpower for use as replacements and additions to the armed forces. In 1953, by a fortunate set of circumstances, some 24,000 Chinese Nationalist troops (and 5,000 dependents) were transferred to Formosa after three years' internment in Indochina, and over 2,000 Chinese troops were evacuated to the island from North Burma.[87] In addition, about 14,000 Chinese prisoners of the Korean conflict who had refused repatriation to Communist China were due to arrive from Panmunjom once the Neutral Nations Repatriation Commission had finished its work. These new arrivals would accentuate the strain placed on the Formosan economy by Chiang's disproportionately large military establishment. There was, however, a governmental four-year plan in existence which was designed to make the island economically self-supporting. Based on annually decreasing amounts of

[86] Foreign Operations Administration, *Allotments, Authorizations and Paid Shipments, Data as of November 30, 1953* (Washington, F.O.A., March 1, 1954), 24.

[87] Cf. below, p. 281.

American aid during the period 1953–1956, it aimed at solving the four major problems of financing the military budget, raising production levels, overcoming the trade deficit, and combating inflationary pressures.[88]

The political support which accompanied American material aid was emphasized during 1953 by the raising of the United States representation in Formosa to Embassy status under Ambassador Karl L. Rankin, as well as by the successful upholding of the Nationalist claim to represent China in all organs of the United Nations. Internally, plans were laid by the Nationalist government to conduct the first legislative and presidential elections to be held in Nationalist-controlled territory since 1947. Originally scheduled for 1953, the elections were later postponed for a year because of the lack of a quorum in the Legislative Yuan, the body which elected the President and Vice-President. Perhaps inevitably, democratic processes were conducted under difficulties in Formosa. In one of the main political developments of the year, K. C. Wu, the American-trained and highly respected governor of the island, resigned in April following a dispute with Premier Chen Cheng. Subsequently, from his exile in the United States, he was to charge the Nationalist government with authoritarian practices directly contrary to the democratic principles of Sun Yat-sen.[89] But whatever the justice of this indictment, Formosa was one of those countries whose strategic position was considered too important to the United States and the free world to permit this country to indulge in a rigid insistence on democratic purity.

New Hope for the Philippines

In the Philippines, 220 miles farther along the island chain, the United States had the gratification in 1953 of witnessing a clean-cut victory for political democracy which also promised to strengthen the over-all position of the free world in the Far East. The most important event of the year for the Philippine Republic was the election in November of Ramón Magsaysay for a four-year term as President. Mag-

[88] Cf. *Department of State Bulletin,* XXVIII, March 23, 1953, 438-439.
[89] *New York Times,* February 28 and March 15, 1954.

saysay was that rare thing in Asian politics, a popular leader who combined inexhaustible energy and clear-headed anti-Communism with genuine concern for social justice and popular welfare. Had there been more men of his type in the countries of East and Southeast Asia, the democratic cause in that area would not perhaps have been in such perilous straits. Magsaysay's effective work as Secretary of Defense in breaking the back of the Communist-led Hukbalahap movement through a combination of military, social, and economic measures had early attracted the favorable notice of the United States, which could only nominally conceal its preferences after Magsaysay bolted his own party and came out as the Nationalist presidential candidate against the incumbent Liberal, President Elpidio Quirino.[90] On a smaller scale, the ensuing contest recalled the September election in Germany, except that here the choice was primarily one between an effective, democratic form of anti-Communism and an anti-Communism inhibited by a weight of corruption and special interests. Magsaysay's two-to-one victory on November 10 seemed a striking vindication of the soundness of popular judgment in this corner of the Pacific. Especially gratifying were the generally orderly character of the elections and the apparent indifference of the electorate to President Quirino's attempt to brand his opponent as an "American" candidate.

Shortly before the election, an American spokesman had defined this country's long-range objectives in relation to the Philippines in terms of "the development of a democratic nation, stable in government and economy, friendly toward the United States, and cooperative with the United Nations." [91] Magsaysay's election seemed clearly to be a step in this direction. His inaugural address on December 30 gave evidence of real determination to improve living conditions and eliminate the remaining Huk resistance, even if he disappointed some American observers by his tendency to shy away from suggestions that he assume the leadership of an

[90] For President Eisenhower's expression of interest in the election as "a vital test of democracy" (November 6), see *Department of State Bulletin*, XXIX, November 16, 1953, 676-677.

[91] James D. Bell, Officer in Charge, Philippine Affairs, *ibid.*, October 19, 1953, 523-525.

Asian anti-Communist alliance.[92] As in most other countries allied with the United States, improvement of internal conditions would require a combination of local effort with international economic measures which would have to be concerted primarily with this country. Especially important in Filipino eyes was a revision of the United States-Philippine trade agreement of 1946, whereby the tariff concessions granted the infant republic on the occasion of its independence were to be gradually withdrawn beginning in July 1954. Proposals in this field were submitted to Washington by the Philippine Government in May, but the only action taken upon them was their referral to a special committee which was expected to correlate its recommendations with those of the Randall Commission on Foreign Economic Policy.[93] Meanwhile the military aid agreement between the two governments, which raised no fundamental policy question for the United States, was extended for a five-year period.

For historical reasons, the Philippines had been an object of special solicitude to the United States even before the postwar concepts of the "defensive perimeter" and the "off-shore island chain" were formalized. Since the conclusion of the Japanese Peace Treaty and the United States-Philippine Mutual Defense Treaty in 1951, however, the status of the republic had become assimilated in some respects to that of other countries with which the United States had negotiated mutual security treaties on that same occasion: Australia and New Zealand on one side, and Japan itself on the other. With Japan, the Philippines were still nominally in a state of war, owing to the refusal of the Philippine legislature to ratify the Peace Treaty in the absence of a satisfactory settlement of Philippine reparation claims. While awaiting the solution of this and other issues that still divided its Pacific friends, the United States continued to buttress the broad framework of security pacts which seemed to be increasingly relied upon in Washington as the main guarantee of peace and security in the Pacific area.

[92] Cf. the suggestion of Senator Knowland (November) in *Documents on American Foreign Relations, 1953,* 131-132.

[93] *Department of State Bulletin,* XXIX, September 7, 1953, 316-318.

The ANZUS Meeting

The so-called ANZUS powers, the signatories of the Australia-New Zealand-United States security treaty of 1951, held but one formal consultation during 1953. This was a regularly scheduled meeting of the ANZUS Council, comprising the Secretary of State and the Australian and New Zealand Ministers of External Affairs, together with ranking military representatives of the three governments. No positive decisions of importance were announced, apart from a statement approving continuing consultation among the three powers at the military level. More noteworthy were two negative conclusions on which the three ministers announced their agreement, namely: (1) that none of the three governments should consider "under present circumstances" the recognition of Communist China or the admission of its representatives to the United Nations; and (2) that the defense of the Pacific area would not be strengthened by attempting to enlarge the membership of the pact.[94] This second point reflected the continued opposition of the United States to the inclusion of Great Britain in the ANZUS treaty as desired by Prime Minister Churchill, who had earlier proposed that not only the United Kingdom but also France and Thailand be brought in as the nucleus of a Southeast Asian defense pact along the lines of the North Atlantic Treaty. Six months later, when the Indochina situation had flamed into crisis, the United States was to try hard, though unsuccessfully, to form just such a combination to deal with Communist aggression in Southeast Asia. In September 1953, however, a variety of factors—among them Britain's recognition of Communist China, the reluctance of the United States to assume definite commitments for the defense of Hong Kong, Malaya, and Indochina, and the unwillingness of this country to give ANZUS the appearance of an alliance of "colonial" powers—sufficed to rule out any expansion of the existing pact.

94 Communiqué, September 10, in *Documents on American Foreign Relations, 1953*, 321-323.

4. JAPAN FALLS IN LINE

Among the numerous countries concerned with Pacific security, Japan occupied a unique position by virtue not only of its intrinsic importance as a factor in the Far Eastern balance of power but also of historical reasons which sharply limited its role in the current defense of the free world. South Korea and Nationalist China, Australia, New Zealand, and the Philippines had recently been threatened or engulfed by Japanese aggression, but were also fully alive to the menace of Communist imperialism; Japan, on the other hand, had still to be convinced of its duty to its former enemies and victims in the world struggle against Communism. In dealing with the Korean and Chinese governments, the United States had at times to dampen their military ardor and dissuade them from reckless adventures; with Japan, the problem was rather one of persuading a disarmed and reluctant nation to make at least a minimum contribution to its own and the common defense. Thus the most important development of the year 1953—the second year of Japan's reemergence as an independent nation—was the decision of the Japanese Government to implement former promises and initiate a policy of gradual rearmament in close collaboration with the United States. This decision, if carried out, would clearly represent a major turning point in the internal and external development of the new Japan and an important influence on Far Eastern history for generations to come.

Relations between the United States and Japan were naturally not confined to the concept of partnership in the defense of the Western Pacific. Illustrative of the cordial over-all relationship which had been reestablished between the two countries were the celebration, with appropriate ceremonies on both sides of the Pacific, of the one hundredth anniversary of Commodore Perry's opening of Japan; the informal tour of the United States by Crown Prince Akihito; and the important visit to Tokyo of Vice-President Nixon in November. In a major policy statement on this latter occasion, the Vice-President expressed the opinion that Japan's defense forces "must be increased eventually" and that the United States had made "an honest mistake" in 1946 in insisting that Japan disarm. In 1953, he declared, we must change our opinion; and he assured Japan of American assistance in developing its defense forces.[95] Similar statements were made at intervals through the year by such authorities as Secretary Dulles, Air Force Secretary Harold E. Talbott, and General John E. Hull, who succeeded General Clark as United States Commander-in-Chief in the Far East in October.

The principal impetus in favor of Japan's rearmament arose from the obvious fact that a threat of Communist aggression still existed in the Far East. To the United States, Japan represented on the one hand a prime object of Communist ambitions and on the other perhaps the most stable, easily defensible, and productive country in the area—one with a technical competence, industrial capacity, and manpower potential which were of outstanding importance to the free world's defense posture. In his first radio address as Secretary of State,[96] Mr. Dulles called attention to the presence of Soviet forces in islands just two miles north of Hokkaido and identified Japan as one of the primary objectives of the Communists in their Korean aggression. To most Americans, such facts seemed sufficient in themselves to bring Japan into equal partnership with the other non-Communist allies.

The feeling that Japanese and American interests coincided was reinforced by numerous indications of Communist hostility toward Japan, among them a series of Soviet violations of the air space over Hokkaido which prompted Tokyo and Washington to warn in January 1953 that further incursions would bring joint Japanese-United States steps to repel intruding aircraft.[97] Similar conclusions seemed to arise from the painfully slow repatriation of Japanese held on the Communist mainland since World War II, an estimated 265,000 of whom were dead or missing while 85,000 were still to be repatriated; and there was also a Communist threat inside Japan from an effective underground leader-

[95] *Department of State Foreign Policy Briefs,* III, December 4, 1953.

[96] Cf. above, pp. 20-21.

[97] *Department of State Bulletin,* XXVIII, January 26, 1953, 134-135; cf. also Clark, *op. cit.,* 130-131.

ship and the presence of a considerable number of pro-Communists among intellectuals, students, and the large Korean minority in the country.

In at least partial recognition of these dangers, the Japanese Government itself had undertaken through the United States-Japanese Mutual Security Treaty of 1951 a clear-cut verbal commitment to begin providing for its own defense.[98] Yet for many Japanese, the impact of hostile Communist actions was dulled by various contrary influences, including the effects of an active and continuous campaign of Communist Chinese and Soviet blandishments. Communist propaganda laid heavy stress on the prospects for Japan of trade with the Asiatic mainland and on the already popular ideal of a neutral Japan functioning as a kind of Switzerland of the Far East. Occasionally there were signs of ostensible Communist good will, such as the repatriation in 1953, after eight years' internment, of some 6,000 Japanese from Communist China and about 2,000 from Soviet Russia as well as the return from Siberia of more recently detained Japanese fishermen and their craft.

Added to these external factors were the psychological complexities of Japan's own attitude toward the question of rearmament and the re-creation of those armed forces which had been "forever" renounced in Article 9 of the postwar Japanese Constitution. With fresh memories of their defeat in the Pacific and of the antimilitarist emphasis in postwar occupation policy, many Japanese felt reluctant to see their country committed to a program of remilitarization which might expose it to attack in a third world war or possibly to a revival of pre-surrender authoritarian political patterns. The constitutional prohibition on armed forces, originally laid down with American encouragement, served as an important weapon to neutralist and anti-American elements, particularly on the extreme Left.

It was significant, moreover, that anti-American sentiment actually tended to increase during 1953, partly as the result of the retention by the United States of extraterritorial rights, the stationing of American troops in the country, the continued American use of many buildings in heavily popu-

[98] *The United States in World Affairs, 1951,* 198-199.

lated areas, the preemption of large rural tracts which in some cases deprived farmers of badly needed land, and the offshore firing exercises which interfered with Japanese fishing activities. A poll conducted by the newspaper *Asahi* in mid-1953 showed that almost half those queried favored the withdrawal of American troops from Japan while only 27 percent approved their presence, in contrast to 48 percent a year earlier.[99]

Implications of the April Elections

This rather widespread opposition both to rearmament and to the presence of United States forces was at least partially reflected in the election for the lower house of the Japanese Diet on April 19. A considerable effort had been made by the United States to conciliate Japanese opinion through such moves as the negotiation of a treaty of friendship, commerce and navigation restoring Japan to a most-favored-nation position (April 2)[100] and a State Department declaration (April 15) that in its "great concern" for the stability of the Japanese economy the United States expected to maintain its expenditures in Japan "at a relatively high level" for at least the next two years.[101] Yet although conservative and generally pro-American elements led by Prime Minister Shigeru Yoshida's Liberal Party obtained 66 percent of the popular vote and a combined (if somewhat unstable) total of 310 out of 466 seats, the greatest gains were registered by the Socialists, who opposed rearmament. Socialist strength was increased by 20 to a new total of 138 (72 Left and 66 Right Socialists), 14 of the new seats being captured by candidates of the strongly neutralist Left Socialist faction. The greatest losses, 12 and 15 seats respectively, were sustained by the conservative Progressives and New Liberals (led by Ichiro Hatoyama), both of them groups which had favored early and rapid rearmament. Despite

[99] *New York Times,* September 7 and 8, 1953.

[100] *Department of State Bulletin,* XXVIII, April 13, 1953, 531; XXIX, August 3, 1953, 160-162. The U.S. Senate gave its consent to ratification with a reservation on July 21 (Executive O, 83d Cong., 1st Sess.) and the treaty entered into force, following Japanese ratification, on September 30. *Ibid.,* October 19, 1953, 525-526.

[101] *Ibid.,* XXVIII, April 27, 1953, 611.

Yoshida's victory, therefore, an important effect of the elections was the apparent repudiation of any immediate, large-scale rearmament effort.[102]

Balancing this rather widespread resistance to American policy was the recognition by many Western-oriented Japanese that the presence of American forces was not only an assurance of continuing moral and material support from the United States but a valuable source of income to Japanese manufacturers and merchants, and therefore to Japan's entire economy. Furthermore, the generosity and cooperativeness of the Americans were not unnoticed in times of crisis such as the disastrous early summer floods in Kyushu, when United States forces came forward with emergency assistance and aided in the rescue activities. Premier Yoshida himself appeared as convinced a partisan of rearmament and of the American connection as Chancellor Adenauer did in Germany. Yet without a more reliable majority in the lower house he could not risk an all-out struggle to amend the constitution, which would require a two-thirds vote of both houses plus an affirmative majority of Japan's electors in a special referendum or election.

Aside from constitutional difficulties, moreover, the cost of any rearmament program posed an additional dilemma. During the economic boom created by the Korean war, Japan had lived beyond its means and run up a yearly trade deficit of some $750 million, only partially offset by American military procurement and United Nations troop expenditures in connection with Korean operations. Now Japan was being asked to increase its defense outlays at the very time when this windfall was likely to disappear as a result of the Korean armistice. United States Ambassador John M. Allison warned on June 23 that the Japanese trade deficit in 1953 could reach "the very large figure of $1,150 million" and reduce foreign exchange reserves by as much as $350 million even after the crediting of "special" dollar receipts.[103]

[102] Cf. *New York Times,* April 27, 1953.

[103] Address on "U.S. Views on the Japanese Economy," *Department of State Bulletin,* XXIX, July 13, 1953, 35-38.

Rearmament Plans and Projects

Even within these political and economic limitations, however, it was certainly possible for Japan to make a beginning toward provision for its own future security. The country already possessed the nucleus of a future army in the National Safety Force, a kind of national police which was scheduled to be built up to an authorized strength of 110,000 by the end of 1953. In late September Premier Yoshida reached an agreement with Mamoru Shigemitsu, leader of the conservative Progressive party, permitting a change in the law whereby the National Safety Force would be converted into a "National Self-Defense Force" authorized to oppose direct aggression.[104] Meanwhile plans for further expansion were under active consideration. In mid-June it was reported that private surveys of Japan's armament industries had resulted in proposals for an eight-year arms program costing $1 billion a year, half of which was to be provided by the United States, and an eight-year build-up of Japan's armed forces to a total of 300,000 men with naval vessels and military aircraft. Other sources spoke of an official Japanese plan for a five-year build-up of the armed forces to 200,000 men.[105] Shortly thereafter, Secretary Dulles indicated that "tentative thinking" in Washington envisaged a Japanese security force of about 350,000 men organized into approximately ten divisions. The decision, he stressed, was one for the Japanese Government and people to make; but State Department officials indicated that other allied signatories of the Japanese Peace Treaty had offered no objection when informed of these figures.

Conditions and Inducements

Although the United States was planning to allocate $115 million in military aid to Japan under the 1953–54 Mutual Security Program, its immediate expectations regarding a Japanese defense contribution were clearly modest. Late in June Ambassador Allison assured the Japanese Foreign Minister (Katsuo Okazaki) in response to specific questions that acceptance of this amount would not obligate Japan to send

[104] *New York Times,* September 28, 1953.
[105] *Ibid.,* June 13 and 14, 1953.

troops abroad or to use them for any purpose except self-defense.[106] With this assurance, the Foreign Minister was prepared to open negotiations for the requisite mutual security assistance agreement—though only on the further stated understanding that (1) the primary purpose of United States aid was to ensure Japan's internal security; (2) Japan's defense forces would be built up only "in a manner consistent with her political and economic stability"; and (3) Japan would assume no new military obligations beyond those contained in the United States-Japan Security Treaty.[107]

Negotiations for this agreement, which envisaged the establishment of an American Military Assistance Advisory Group to "assist and guide" the development of Japan's defense forces, were commenced on July 15 but not completed until after prolonged and "arduous" negotiations which were finally brought to a successful conclusion on March 8, 1954.[108] Meanwhile the United States offered various additional proofs of its confidence in and good will toward the new Japan. In August Secretary Dulles, stopping in Tokyo after his conference with President Rhee, announced that the United States planned to return to Japan the small group of islands known as the Amami Oshima, situated between Okinawa and the Japanese island of Kyushu, which the United States was holding together with the rest of the Ryukyu Islands in accordance with the Japanese Peace Treaty. This promise was carried out on Christmas Eve, although many Japanese were disappointed that the United States asserted at the same time its intention of holding the rest of the Ryukyu chain "so long as conditions of threat and tension exist in the Far East." [109]

A still clearer proof of American respect for Japan's independence and sovereignty was the negotiation in late September of a protocol relating to criminal jurisdiction over United States military personnel and their families in Japan. Signed on September 29, this agreement, which amended the

[106] *Ibid.*, June 28, 1953.
[107] *Ibid.*, July 16, 1953.
[108] *Department of State Bulletin*, XXX, April 5, 1954, 518-520; text *ibid.*, 520-525, and in *Documents on American Foreign Relations, 1954*, 332-339.
[109] *Department of State Bulletin*, XXIX, August 17, 1953, 208; XXX, January 4, 1954, 17.

United States-Japanese administrative agreement of 1952, assigned to Japan at its discretion criminal jurisdiction over American personnel for crimes committed against non-Americans outside of line of duty and off American-held property. Japan was thus placed on a par in this respect with NATO countries in which American forces were stationed, and was incidentally put in a position to claim similar rights over personnel of other United Nations forces.[110]

Economic Prospects

Of even greater practical importance, perhaps, was the assistance the United States was willing to give toward maintaining Japan's economic viability in the face of dwindling trade, the poorest rice crop in nineteen years, and the expense of the projected defense program. As President Eisenhower had so often pointed out, military defenses were of little value unless they rested on sound economic foundations. In Japan's case, the pertinence of this observation was even more obvious than in that of the United States and the other NATO powers which were so carefully protecting their economies against excessive military strain. With Japan, moreover, there was a special problem resulting from its absolute dependence on foreign trade and its somewhat ambiguous situation in relation to the Communist bloc. Relying on the persuasions of the United States, Japan's government had aligned itself with with the West and turned its back on any possibilities of immediate *rapprochement* with Communist China or the U.S.S.R. Yet within Japan there was continuing pressure on the part of business and other groups for the reopening of commercial relations with Communist Asia. If Japan was unable to find an adequate place in the trading system of the non-Communist world, this pressure might easily become irresistible. And trade with the Communist East, many outsiders felt, would expose the country to Communist political influence which might in time imperil its Western orientation.

It was against this background that Assistant Secretary

110 *Ibid.*, XXIX, November 2, 1953, 595-598; cf. above, p. 170, and the comments by Foreign Minister Okazaki (October 29) in *Documents on American Foreign Relations, 1953*, 336-337.

Robertson held a series of informal conferences during October with Hayato Ikeda, former Japanese Finance Minister, who paid a visit to Washington as the personal representative of Prime Minister Yoshida. Although no binding agreements were reached, foundations were laid for an over-all, coordinated American-Japanese defense and economic aid program. The main points of the "understanding" reached by the conferees were: (1) recognition of "the necessity of increasing Japan's self-defense forces in order to protect her from possible aggression, and to reduce the United States burden related to the defense of Japan"; (2) acknowledgment of "constitutional, economic, budgetary and other limitations which will not allow the immediate building of Japan's self-defense forces to a point sufficient for Japan's defense"; (3) an expression of American willingness, subject to congressional authorization, "to assist Japan in developing the Japanese forces by supplying major items of military equipment for the land, sea and air forces which Japan raises"; and (4) agreement "that a reduction in Japan's contribution to the support of United States forces should be considered from time to time in the light of the development of Japan's own forces," and that "the withdrawal of the United States forces from Japan would be effected as the Japanese forces develop the capability to defend their country." [111]

Other matters discussed on this occasion included the prospective allocation to Japan of $50 million in surplus food products under the Mutual Security Act, the necessity for maintaining "a high level of controls" over trade with Communist China, and the importance of "vigorous efforts on the part of Japan to resist inflation." The conferees also noted that Japan was receiving an electric power loan of $40 million from the International Bank and a series of short-term Export-Import Bank credits (totaling $160 million during the year) to finance Japanese imports of American raw cotton.[112] The communiqué was silent on the crucial

[111] Communiqué, October 30, *ibid.*, 339-341.

[112] *Ibid.*, cf. *Department of State Bulletin*, XXVIII, May 11, 1953, 681-682; June 22, 1953, 878; XXIX, November 16, 1953, 676; XXX, January 11, 1954, 57-58.

question of Japan's export trade and its dependence on the reduction of trade barriers by the United States and other free world countries. Any decisive action by the United States in this matter would presumably have to await the recommendations of the Randall Commission. But meanwhile the United States was strongly supporting Japan's application for provisional association with the contracting parties to the General Agreement on Tariffs and Trade (GATT), which was approved in October at the organization's Eighth Session in Geneva,[113] thus partially realizing an objective whose full accomplishment was still opposed in 1953 by Great Britain, Canada, and other trading nations.

Ugly memories of World War II still hampered Japan's attempts to reestablish an economic position in the free world and particularly in Southeast Asia, where many authorities considered the nation's best opportunities to lie. In October, Foreign Minister Okazaki made a trip to the Philippines, Indonesia, and Burma, three formerly Japanese-occupied countries whose sentiments toward their late conqueror, he reported, were still far from cordial although they seemed "to be improving from year to year." Formal diplomatic relations with the three countries had not yet been restored, and there was still no agreement as to the extent of the reparations obligations which Japan was pledged to fulfill under the Treaty of Peace.[114]

Relations with the Republic of Korea, too, were seriously strained by various issues growing out of the two countries' wartime and prewar experience. Notable among the sources of recurrent friction were the activities of the large Korean element in Japan and the objections of President Rhee's government to Japanese fishing in the neighborhood of the Korean peninsula. The quest for fishing grounds also involved Japan in continual incidents with Communist China and the U.S.S.R., and provided a somewhat lesser source of contention with Australia. Such difficulties epitomized the plight of a nation which had made enemies of so many countires on whom its future survival directly depended. As the

113 *Ibid.*, XXIX, October 12, 1953, 495-496; XXX, February 1, 1954, 155-156; *Documents on American Foreign Relations, 1953*, 337-338.

114 Okazaki speech, October 29, *ibid.*, 333-334.

year ended, however, it seemed clear that Japan had on balance become more firmly committed to the free world and would gradually begin to make more adequate provision for its own self-defense, even though the scope and pace of its efforts would necessarily represent a compromise between what American officials thought desirable and what the Japanese considered to be their needs and capacity.

5. THE THREAT TO SOUTHEAST ASIA

As the outlook for a Korean armistice gradually brightened, American and world attention had shifted increasingly to another critical area whose long-time involvement in anti-Communist hostilities had been somewhat overshadowed by the scale and violence of the Korean conflict. People remembered that the war in Indochina was in its seventh year, that Malaya had been riven by guerrilla warfare since 1948, and that Burma had never fully succeeded in quelling the insurrectionary activities of a variety of Communist and racial minority groups. Note was taken of the interrelations between these widely separated theaters of conflict, and of the unpleasant possibility that improvement in one area might be matched by deterioration in another. President Eisenhower declared on April 16 that the Communists' professed desire for peace should mean not only a Korean armistice and political discussions but also,

> "no less importantly, an end to the direct and indirect attacks upon the security of Indochina and Malaya. For any armistice in Korea that merely released aggressive armies to attack elsewhere would be a fraud." [115]

Although the fate of Southeast Asia depended on many of the same factors as did that of South Korea, Formosa, and other areas exposed to Communist aggression, there were also essential differences. The very idea of an anti-Communist struggle was not accepted here as it was, in varying degrees, by the countries of the United States "defensive perimeter." The basic phenomenon in Southeast Asia was not so much a struggle for or against Communism as a more or

[115] *Ibid.*, 31; cf. above, pp. 128-130.

less unrelated series of struggles for national independence, over which the Communists had gained different degrees of control in different countries of the area. This general preoccupation with independence, moreover, tended to align popular feeling against the Western powers far more than against the Communists, thus rather obscuring the issues which were most important in Western eyes.

In other respects, too, the situation here was less clear-cut than farther north. Since some countries in the area were already independent while others were still in colonial status or only partially independent, there was no single set of authorities which could be mobilized in support of any common aim. An outside power like the United States was at a peculiar disadvantage in trying to mediate between the conflicting aims and rival sensibilities of indigenous leaders, colonial administrations, and European governments. Nor was the military situation in Southeast Asia consistent with normal strategic and tactical concepts. In Indochina, and to an equal extent in Burma and Malaya, there was no clearly recognizable "front" or military demarcation line. The front was "everywhere," in the cities hardly less than in the jungles and paddy fields. Warfare was endemic over large tracts of country and was carried on by guerrilla tactics of infiltration and terrorism much more than in organized battles.

The Indochina Problem

By reason of its strategic position and the intensity of the conflict which had been raging within its borders for the last half-dozen years, it was generally recognized that French Indochina—divided since 1949 into the three semi-independent states of Vietnam, Laos, and Cambodia—held the key to future developments in Southeast Asia as a whole. Much would be heard a few months later of the so-called "falling domino" theory according to which the fall of Indochina might be expected to bring about the fall of the remaining countries of Southeast Asia in rapid succession. But long before this critical stage was reached, world attention had begun to center on Indochina and, in particular, on two vital questions. First, would the Chinese Communists, after their disengagement in Korea, intensify the help they were already giving the Vietminh insurgents in the form of weapons and equipment, training, and bases for supply and operations? Second, what arrangements would be made for perfecting the independence of the three Indochinese states and getting them to participate more effectively in the effort which France was making, with increasing American and other allied support, to save them from falling under Communist domination? The answers would be influenced not only by the growing commitments of the United States and Communist China in the area but also by the growing restiveness of nationalist elements within the Associated States and the mounting war weariness of many groups in France.

The broadening scope of the Indochina problem had been illustrated during the spring of 1953 by the Vietminh invasion of Laos, the westernmost of the three Associated States, which up to that time had escaped direct involvement in the war. Acting in the name of an imaginary "free Lao" movement, the invading forces had threatened the ancient Laotian capital of Luang Prabang and driven southward toward the borders of Thailand before rain and resistance halted their offensive and occasioned their retreat into northeastern Laos.[116] This rather alarming incident, which noticeably heightened French distaste for the whole Indochina war, was partially responsible for the subsequent series of allied statements expressing solidarity with the French and warning the Communists against new adventures.[117]

Yet the effectiveness of such warnings remained uncertain because the conditions of the Indochina struggle were such that Communist China might well be able to intensify its clandestine support of the rebels without committing any overt act of intervention. Even without the Chinese, moreover, there was still the Vietminh itself to be dealt with; and the tough Vietminh fighters commanded by the shadow government of Ho Chi Minh were notoriously not men who would be frightened by political declarations issued in distant capitals. There was an obvious need to grapple with

[116] Cf. above, p. 66.

[117] Cf. especially the U.S.-French communiqué of March 28, the NATO communiqué of April 25, the tripartite (U.S.-U.K.-French) statement of July 14, and the 16-nation declaration of July 27 (above, pp. 35-36, 167, 190, 234).

the problem at close quarters. More and more, in fact, the French and their allies seemed to be faced with one simple alternative: either to negotiate a settlement with the Communists (which would mean giving them at least a part of the advantages they would surely demand), or to develop more effective means of warfare in the hope of eventually bringing the resistance under firm control.

Program for Victory

Although French minds were running increasingly in the direction of a negotiated settlement,[118] the United States was all for more effective military action and was able, for the time being, to carry its ally along with it. In Washington's view, a program of effective resistance had several elements. Outside intervention in support of the rebels was to be discouraged primarily by calling attention to such risks as were suggested by Secretary Dulles in his speech of September 2: "The Chinese Communist regime should realize that . . . a second aggression could not occur without grave consequences which might not be confined to Indochina."[119] Within Indochina itself, the solution was seen in a more vigorous direction and prosecution of the war against the Vietminh, based on (1) increased material aid from the United States, and (2) increased participation and support by the native populations of the Indochinese states. This in turn was to be ensured by promptly completing the transfer of governmental authority from the French administration to the governments of the Associated States. By giving the people of Vietnam, Laos, and Cambodia real independence, it was hoped to make possible a corresponding expansion of their national armies, a definitive victory over the Vietminh, and the return of all or most of the French expeditionary force to Europe—a movement which would have the further advantages of strengthening the NATO forces in the European theater and giving France less reason to fear the rearmament of Western Germany.

[118] For discussion of this aspect at the time of the "Little Bermuda" conference in July, cf. "La Conférence de Washington," *Chronique de politique étrangère*, VI, September 1953, 616-619.

[119] Above, p. 248.

Most of the elements of such a program were actually in the process of creation during the summer of 1953, although still awaiting completion and systematization in a formal agreement. In response to American urgency, French military authorities were developing plans to press the war against the Vietminh to a successful termination and political experts were at work on measures to transfer full sovereignty to the Associated States. In the Pentagon Building, meanwhile, studies were being made "to determine how and to what extent" the United States might be able to contribute "matériel and financial support" to the achievement of the two countries' joint objectives.[120] By September these studies had progressed far enough to be brought before the National Security Council and, with its approval, to become the basis of a firm agreement with France.

The projected revitalization of the war effort in Indochina is destined to remain inseparably connected with the name of General Henri-Eugène Navarre, formerly Chief of Staff of NATO land forces in Central Europe, who arrived in Saigon in May as Commander of French Union Forces in Indochina. General Navarre's advent resulted in a prompt upturn of local morale and within four months eventuated in a plan to increase vastly the recruitment and training of Vietnamese troops and to bring about a successful conclusion of the war in two years. The so-called Navarre Plan called for the training of nearly 125,000 Vietnamese troops by 1955 and an increase in the number of their light battalions to 54 by the end of 1953 and to 135 by 1955. This increase would raise the strength of Franco-Vietnamese forces to 250,000 French and 300,000 domestic troops, as opposed to an estimated Vietminh strength of 300,000 to 400,000. With these forces, as Secretary Dulles later explained, it was hoped "to break the organized body of Communist aggression by the end of the 1955 fighting season and thereby reduce the fighting to guerrilla warfare which could, in 1956, be met for the most part by national forces of the three Associated States." [121]

120 U.S.-French communiqué, March 28, in *Documents on American Foreign Relations, 1953,* 270.

121 Statement to the House Foreign Affairs Committee, April 5, in *New York Times,* April 6, 1954.

Encouraged by the report of an American military mission which visited Indochina early in the summer under Lieutenant General John W. O'Daniel,[122] the National Security Council decided that this program merited United States backing and recommended that the $400 million in United States funds already earmarked for Indochina for the fiscal year 1953–54 be increased by an additional $385 million, to be made available before the end of 1954. This increment, which would bring the total United States contribution for 1954 to more than half the total cost of the war, was officially pledged in an agreement with France announced on September 30.[123] France, as its part of the understanding, expressed its firm resolve (1) to carry out its announced intention of "perfecting" the independence of the Associated States, and (2) "to make every effort to break up and destroy the regular enemy forces in Indochina" and carry out the plans for increasing the forces of the Associated States. French forces in Indochina were also to be temporarily increased (though without "any basic or permanent alteration of the French Government's plans and programs for its NATO forces") through the removal of two colonial infantry regiments from France's NATO divisions as well as transfer of the French battalion from Korea.

France and the Associated States

By far the most difficult aspect of this undertaking was the attempt to enlist the support of the Vietnamese and other Indochinese populations by completing the status of independence which France had for years been slowly and hesitantly preparing to grant them. Two principal difficulties were involved, over and above the natural reluctance of the French to surrender the advantages they had gained through almost a century of activity in Indochina. First, independence in itself offered no guarantee of a pro-Western attitude, as the example of other recently emancipated states like Indonesia showed. Second, the state of war and the comparative political inexperience of the local populations made a

[122] *Department of State Bulletin*, XXIX, June 29, 1953, 909.

[123] Joint communiqué, September 30, in *Documents on American Foreign Relations, 1953*, 350-351.

full transfer of authority to them a particularly risky expedient under the prevailing circumstances. There remained a wide gulf between the ambitions of Indochinese nationalists and the prevailing French opinion as to the degree of independence which could and should be granted. Nevertheless, dissatisfaction with the existing state of affairs in the Associated States had become so intense and general that the necessity for some further action was unmistakable.

On July 3, the new Laniel government in Paris therefore declared that the time had come to adapt France's existing agreements with the Associated States, concluded in 1949, "to the position which they have succeeded in acquiring, with her full support, in the community of free peoples." In view of the progress made by the Associated States during the past four years, the French declaration continued, there was "every reason to complete [their] independence and sovereignty" by transferring to them the powers France had hitherto retained—nominally in their own interests—in view of the perilous circumstances of the war. Accordingly, it was now France's purpose "to invite each of the three Governments to agree with it on the settlement of questions which each of them may deem necessary to raise in the economic, financial, judicial, military and political fields." The objective, the declaration made clear, was not to set the three states adrift, but rather "to strengthen the friendship which unites France and the Associated States within the French Union." [124] Whether the prospect of permanent membership in the French Union would satisfy that section of nationalist opinion in the Associated States which had thus far stood aloof from France as well as the Communists, time alone would determine.

Of the separate negotiations which France now undertook with delegations of the three governments, the easiest proved to be those with the Kingdom of Laos, the state in which independence sentiment was least fully developed. By a "Treaty of Amity and Association," signed in Paris on October 22,[125] France recognized Laos as "a fully independent and sovereign state" and Laos reaffirmed its membership in the

[124] French Government declaration, July 3, *ibid.*, 347-348.
[125] *Ibid.*, 348-350.

French Union and its decision to sit in the High Council of that association as well as to make all its resources available for the common defense. Subsidiary questions were left to be settled in separate conventions.

Cambodia proved more difficult to deal with, partly because its comparative immunity from Vietminh harassment inclined it toward a neutralist position and partly because of the demonstratively independent attitude of its King, Norodom Sihanouk, who had already made one spectacular exit from his capital of Pnompenh in the attempt to enforce his demands for full independence. No full treaty was signed with Cambodia in 1953, but an agreement concluded in October gave the King virtual command of all troops, including French forces, in the state.

Difficulty with Vietnam

The central question in Indochina, however, concerned the status of Vietnam, by far the largest and most populous of the three states and the one most thoroughly permeated with Vietminh influences. Here the French had to contend not with a king who was a nationalist symbol, as in Cambodia, but with native independence groups many of whom regarded their nominal Chief of State, the ex-Emperor Bao Dai, as little more than a French puppet. In September, while Bao Dai and Premier Nguyen Van Tam conferred in Paris with French officials, a serious crisis arose in Saigon with the issuance of an uncompromising statement by five nationalist organizations demanding complete and unequivocal freedom from France. Premier Tam hastened back to Vietnam and on October 16 convened a national congress to nominate delegates for the forthcoming French-Vietnamese negotiations—only to see the congress repudiate both Bao Dai and France by rejecting participation in the French Union "in its present form" and demanding to be transformed into a constituent assembly so that it might draft a national charter limiting Bao Dai's powers.

These events caused consternation in Paris. On October 21 the French cabinet called on the Vietnamese to state clearly whether or not they intended to remain in the French Union after the war; a week later, M. Laniel told the

Assembly he had warned the Vietnamese that France itself would feel free to quit the war if Vietnam questioned "the conception of the French Union." Although the Vietnam Government replied on November 14 that it had decided to remain in the French Union, there was little certainty that this stand reflected majority nationalist opinion. In the meantime, on October 28, the Assembly had adopted by 315-251 a resolution which endorsed the policy of developing the armed forces of the Associated States "to the point where they will gradually be able to replace the French troops"; stipulated "that the defense and independence of the Associated States be realized within the French Union"; and called on the government not only to assure "a fair balance in the efforts and sacrifices made by the free nations in different parts of the world" but also to do "everything possible to achieve a general peace in Asia by negotiations."

Since membership in the French Union threatened to become the sticking point in French-Vietnamese negotiations, President Vincent Auriol undertook to restate and clarify some basic concepts at the annual meeting of the High Council of the French Union in Paris on November 27-29. The three Associated States, M. Auriol declared, were independent, sovereign, and equal with France in rights and duties; and he defined the function of the High Council in terms of a coordinating body rather than in terms of the advisory role it had been assigned by the 1946 French Constitution. A similar restatement had been included in the French-Laotian treaty of October 22. Although all four of the governments involved agreed on this definition, it was not clear how it would be reconciled with the provisions of the French Constitution; nor had any solution been discovered by the end of the year. Quite possibly, however, the point might remain an academic one.

In undertaking to sponsor the Navarre Plan and the independence negotiations, the French Government had made it rather clear that this was the last big effort France would be prepared to undertake in Indochina on its own responsibility. If it failed, the only alternative (unless the United States chose to commit its own armed forces to the struggle) would be to negotiate with the Communists. Sentiment in favor of this approach continued to increase in France, even in official quarters: as early as September 25, Deputy Foreign Minister Maurice Schumann had suggested that negotiations for peace in Indochina should be conducted at the Eighth United Nations General Assembly, which had just convened in New York. The prospect for any such negotiations, however, would depend largely on the general status of East-West relations and the still unclarified outlook regarding the Korean political conference and a possible high-level meeting with the Russians. Meanwhile, as the flow of American arms to Indochina gradually increased, the Vietminh awaited the termination of the rainy season and the opportunity for new assaults on the precarious independence of the Associated States. Its resourcefulness and determination were to be demonstrated once again before the end of the year.[126]

Other Southeast Asian Trends

The other countries of Southeast Asia experienced no comparable crisis during 1953, though all of them were adversely affected by the drop in world market prices of tin, rubber, and rice, and pressure mounted in Burma and Indonesia for increased trade with Communist China. In contrast to Indochina's difficult situation, Malaya and Burma were able to record distinct improvement in the sphere of internal security and stability, largely because Communist tactics in those areas were shifting from guerrilla warfare to political action—a method less productive of immediate embarrassment, though perhaps not less dangerous in the long run.[127] In Indonesia, which was not directly threatened from outside, no similar improvement in internal conditions was visible; extremists and separatists continued to oppose the authority of the central government at Jakarta. Thailand stood out as the principal bright spot in the area, maintaining close relations with the United States and supporting the American position in the United Nations even on issues which found most Asian and African states aligned against this country.

[126] Cf. below, pp. 451-453.

[127] Cf. the statement of Malayan High Commissioner Sir Gerald Templer, May 18, in *Documents on American Foreign Relations, 1953*, 342-347.

Chinese Troops in Burma

Aside from the continuing threat of Communist-supported aggression, Southeast Asia's principal diplomatic problem in 1953 arose out of the continued presence in Burma of some 12,000 refugee Chinese Nationalist troops who had been driven over the border from Yunnan Province in 1949 and had remained to harass the country under the nominal leadership of the Chinese Nationalist General Li Mi. For three years the Burmese Government had been vainly attempting to persuade or compel these troops, some of whom had acquired Burmese wives and families, to leave the country. By 1953 there were indications that some of the Chinese were in touch with dissident Burmese elements and were coordinating their guerrilla activities with those of the rebellious Karen tribesmen.[128] The Chinese, 6,000 of whom were reportedly organized in regular units while the remainder were guerrillas, lived off the land, reputedly trafficked in opium and other contraband, and were sufficiently well supplied to maintain their limited military capabilities in face of Burmese countermeasures.

Internationally, these troops posed a problem that involved not only Burma but also the Peking regime, the Republic of China, Thailand, the United States, and the United Nations. The Chinese Communists had more than once offered to wipe out the Li Mi force if Burma would only give the word. The Formosa authorities disclaimed any control over the refugee troops, but the Burmese Government charged that they were actually "directed and supported by the Government of Formosa." [129] Thailand's involvement resulted from an alleged two-way traffic in military supplies and opium across the Thai-Burmese border, and from General Li Mi's reported periodic presence in Bangkok. American interest stemmed especially from Burmese allegations that some Americans had unofficially helped to train and arm the Chinese guerrillas—allegations that were eagerly taken up and embroidered upon by Communist propaganda. The widespread belief in Burma that the

[128] *New York Times,* January 15, 1953.
[129] *Ibid.,* March 27, 1953.

United States had at least acquiesced in a Chinese policy of sustaining guerrilla forces on Burmese soil was producing a progressive deterioration in United States-Burmese relations. Washington, for its part, desired an amicable settlement both because of its friendship and support for the principal parties involved and because the only beneficiaries of the impasse were the disruptive forces in Southeast Asia, principally the Communists.

The United Nations became involved in the matter when the Burmese Government introduced in the General Assembly on March 25 a formal complaint of aggression against the Chinese Government on Formosa. With rare unanimity the Assembly voted 59 to 0 (China abstaining) to condemn the presence of the foreign forces in Burma and called for their immediate withdrawal or internment.[130] During the debate on the issue, both the Chinese and American delegates stated that their governments were trying to persuade the offending forces to give up the Burma campaign. Largely on American initiative, discussions were later held in Bangkok among representatives of Burma, Nationalist China, Thailand, and the United States, resulting in October in an agreement whereby 2,000 Chinese and their dependents would be withdrawn from Burma. Despite several hitches, by early December 2,258 refugees had been air-lifted to Formosa in planes of General Claire L. Chennault's Civil Air Transport. At the year's end, further negotiations were planned in Bangkok on Chinese initiative to remove additional refugees who wished to depart, and the Chinese Government was pledged to disown all who refused to leave.[131]

Dissatisfaction in Burma over the position of the United States on this issue weakened the Burmese Government's resistance to internal pressures aimed at closer relations with the Communist bloc and noninvolvement with the United

[130] Resolution 707 (VII), April 23, in *Documents on American Foreign Relations, 1953*, 429-430.

[131] By Resolution 717 (VIII), adopted December 8, 1953, the General Assembly reaffirmed its April resolution, expressed concern about the difficulties experienced in disarming the troops who remained in Burma, asked that no assistance be given them, urged continuation of their evacuation, noted with appreciation the conduct of the evacuation by the U.S. and Thailand, and requested Burma to report on the situation as appropriate.

States. Such pressures were at least partially responsible for an official decision to discontinue the United States economic aid program, thus closing out at least temporarily an activity which had brought Burma $30 million in technical and other economic assistance.[132] Indonesia, on the other hand, while refusing to assume the obligations that went with military assistance from the United States, proved willing to sign a new agreement providing for the continuance of strictly economic aid.[133] In other respects, however, Indonesia was even more insistent than Burma on stressing its "neutral" and implicitly anti-American position, accrediting an ambassador and concluding a trade agreement with Peking and repeatedly abstaining in General Assembly votes adverse to the Soviet bloc. At home, deep factional divisions paved the way for the formation in July of a Nationalist coalition cabinet, headed by Ali Sastroamidjojo, which included no Communists but displayed an alarming complaisance toward Communist activity as well as a rather limited capacity for dealing with Indonesia's serious internal problems.

Economic Development Efforts

Somewhat removed from the lights and shadows of day-to-day politics, efforts to strengthen Southeast Asia's economic foundations and improve its living standards went quietly forward, primarily within the loose framework of the British Commonwealth's Colombo Plan for Economic Development in South and South-East Asia. The second annual report of the Colombo Plan, prepared at a meeting of the fourteen-nation Consultative Committee (attended by United States observers) in New Delhi on October 13-17,[134] noted that development expenditure in the area was increasing despite a general decline in export earnings and national incomes. Total public expenditures on development had grown from £345 million in 1951–52 to £429 million in 1952–53 and a planned £528 million in 1953–54. By far the greatest part of this expenditure, however, was taking place in India and Pakistan. Southeast Asia as such accounted for less than a

[132] *Department of State Bulletin,* XXVIII, April 13, 1953, 530.
[133] *Ibid.,* February 9, 1953, 220.
[134] Summary in *Documents on American Foreign Relations, 1953,* 323-333.

fourth of the total, and Indochina, especially Vietnam, where the need was presumably most urgent, had been prevented by the exigencies of war from making anything more than the barest beginnings.

A fundamental limit on the pace of development in the region was imposed by the necessity for outside financial assistance, principally from the United Kingdom and the United States; and American aid, in particular, was limited by domestic considerations as well as by Korean reconstruction needs and the heavy demands of the military assistance program in Formosa and Indochina. This was one of the cases in which the United States, having assigned a clear priority to combating Communism in its purely military manifestations, did not feel able to put forth a comparable effort against the economic and social conditions in which Communism had shown a tendency to flourish.

The disadvantages inherent in this order of priority were not unrecognized in Washington, where it was conceded that "Asians . . . expect a great deal more from the American people than expressions of sympathy and of support for their struggles for independence." [135] But economic aid, even if more abundantly available, would have been only a part of the answer to Southeast Asia's problems. Vice-President Nixon, returning late in the year from a world tour which had taken him into most parts of non-Communist Asia, told of discovering not only "a great well of friendship for America" but also the existence of "millions of people who honestly believe in their hearts that the United States is just as great a threat to the peace as is the Soviet Union and Communist China." Did you ever stop to think what the people of Asia want?" he asked.

> "Well, they want independence. They want economic progress. They want freedom of choice as to their culture, religion, and their economic systems. And they want fundamental recognition of their equal dignity as human beings."

And the Vice-President quoted what he had been told by "a very wise and a very young king—the King of Thailand":

[135] Address by Assistant Secretary Robertson, October 9, in *Department of State Bulletin*, XXIX, October 19, 1953, 520.

"He was speaking about the needs of Thailand, a country which is threatened from Communist subversion within and possible Communist aggression at any time, of course, from without. He said they needed military assistance, they needed economic assistance, and they needed understanding. And significantly enough, he told me that understanding was the most important of the three." [136]

[136] Broadcast talk, December 23, 1953, *ibid.*, XXX, January 4, 1954, 10-14.

CHAPTER FIVE

THE WORLD BETWEEN

STILL SOMEWHAT apart from the open conflicts of the Far East and the active, urgent diplomacy of Europe stretched the vast reaches of Southern Asia, the Middle East, Africa, and Latin America. One-third of the world's population inhabitated these "in-between" areas. By choice or accident they were of the "free world"; yet few of them, with the important exception of the Latin America peoples, could be said to belong either to "East" or "West" in the political sense which had become current since World War II. The whole expanse from East Bengal to Chile constituted a world by itself—in many ways an "uncommitted world," as Adlai Stevenson, among others, pointed out after a post-campaign trip through much of the area.[1] Despite their obvious dissimilarities, these nations held in common various attitudes of the utmost significance in contemporary world affairs—a general indifference to "cold war" issues"; keen resentment of the phenomena of "colonialism" and "racial discrimination," especially as practiced by Western governments; and acute preoccupation with the need to remedy their own poverty and the industrial underdevelopment to which they often ascribed it. Among the peoples of these nations were numbered many millions of the poorest mortals alive. Population pressure on resources and land was an almost universal problem. If a further decline in standards of living was to be averted in the years ahead, the same problems had everywhere to be faced and solved: higher yields to be won from agriculture, and factories, dams, bridges, houses, high-

[1] Address of September 15, in *Documents on American Foreign Relations, 1953*, 120-121.

ways, and railroads to be built. And everywhere, as the President's brother, Dr. Milton Eisenhower, wrote of Latin America, the leaders of these countries had the same attitude: "[they] want greater production and higher standards of living, and they want them *now.*" [2]

This mood of impatience, coupled as it usually was with a deep mistrust of the "imperialist" powers of Europe and North America, presented the Western governments with one of their most urgent and baffling problems. In Western eyes, many of these lands were menaced both by Soviet imperialism and by the tendency of the local peoples to grasp uncritically at new economic and social solutions and political beliefs. Some areas were directly threatened by Communism, among them one or two that lay as remote from the seats of Communist power as Guatemala and British Guiana. But of more immediate importance in most places were locally generated currents that sometimes rose to storm intensity and threatened to destroy such barriers as existed against Communist advance. These were the dynamic local nationalist movements which flourished almost everywhere, however varied they might appear in their surface manifestations and however frequently they operated at cross purposes with one another. Among their representatives were the half-famished street demonstrators of Tehran; the followers and some of the opponents of General Muhammad Nagib in Egypt; the supporters of General Juan D. Perón in Argentina; the Mau Mau terrorists in Kenya; the proudly sensitive intellectuals of India; the Afrikaner Nationalists of the Union of South Africa, and the nation-builders of Israel.

Over three continents on which the United States considered it imperative to maintain some measure of peace and stability, as a bar to Communist penetration and a guarantee of unhindered access to raw materials, these nationalist movements produced frequent threats of explosion, open violence, and revolts. Where it could not avert such developments, Washington sought at least to prevent their exploitation by Communist forces either locally or from Moscow and Peking. Beyond the negative goal of keeping Communism out, moreover, the United States was moved by

[2] Report to the President, November 18, *ibid.*, 383-384; cf. below, p. 330 ff.

a genuine desire to see all these regions transformed, so far as possible, into healthy and prosperous sections of the free world. Americans, as Secretary Dulles said on May 29 on his return from a survey trip to the Near East and South Asia in company with Mutual Security Director Stassen, wanted these nations "to live together in amity and peace" so that they might "move on to a healthy national life which will accept the responsibilities, and add to the strength, of the free-world community." [3]

The very fact that Mr. Dulles and Mr. Stassen could find time, so shortly after their induction into office, to spend twenty days in regions never before visited by an incumbent Secretary of State showed the importance which the new administration attached to a group of countries which had thus far refused any firm alignment with the West. And the Dulles-Stassen mission, which ventured into countries as far afield as India and Pakistan, was but one among many manifestations of American interest, official and unofficial. Vice-President Nixon, Senator Knowland, and Mr. Stevenson all touched India, Pakistan, and other points in the course of world tours. The retiring Ambassador to India, Chester Bowles, drew on his experience to offer advice in lectures, magazine articles, and a book.[4] The President sent Eric Johnston to the Middle East late in the autumn to promote a plan for the development of the Jordan Valley. A congressional delegation journeyed to South Africa to witness progress in the Union's uranium extraction program. Dr. Milton Eisenhower made a widely publicized survey of the needs and problems of the South American republics, whose formal political alignment with this country did not always mean firm attachment to the United States position in hemisphere or world affairs.

In its determination to effect radical improvements in the state of some of these "neglected" areas, the Eisenhower administration faced an accumulation of difficulties which had been piling up throughout the postwar period. In the Near East and Southern Asia, as Mr. Dulles pointed out shortly before his departure, "Western, and even American, prestige

[3] *Department of State Bulletin,* XXVIII, June 8, 1953, 804.

[4] Chester Bowles, *Ambassador's Report* (New York, Harper, 1954, 425 p.)

. . . has been deteriorating steadily, and the situation requires urgent and decisive remedial measures." [5] On his return he listed some of the more intractable problems: "The Suez base dispute between Egypt and Britain; the uneasy armistice and economic warfare between Israel and the Arab states; the problems of Arab refugees; the India-Pakistan dispute over Kashmir; the prevalence of poverty." [6] Others, omitted presumably because the Secretary's tour had not taken him to these countries, were Iran's dispute with Britain over the affairs of the expropriated Anglo-Iranian Oil Company; the restless independence movements in Tunisia and Morocco; the upsurge of African nationalism south of the Sahara; and the steadily increasing Communist influence in Guatemala and possibly other parts of the Western Hemisphere.

Each of these problems was complex in the extreme, but their most frustrating characteristic was the way they interlocked. Any hope of improving the miserable lot of the Arab refugees in the Near East was blocked by the Arab-Israeli impasse. Any hope for a workable Middle East defense system foundered on Egypt's demand for unconditional evacuation of the British forces protecting the Suez Canal zone. Any hope of adding to the strength of nations farther east, as a possible alternative to a Middle East defense plan, was similarly thwarted—in Iran by the political turmoil resulting from the oil crisis, in Pakistan by the wrangle with India over Kashmir and other matters. Indeed, the interlocking repercussions ranged still farther. For France's troubles in North Africa helped sap the nation's will toward European unity and effective action in Indochina. And in Guatemala the problem of Communist influence adversely affected United States relations with all the American republics below the Rio Grande.

The attempt to grapple with these difficulties was complicated in 1953 by certain new tendencies related to the governmental changes which had occurred in Washington and Moscow. So far as the ever-present possibility of Communist

[5] Statement to congressional committees on the Mutual Security Program, May 5, in *Department of State Bulletin,* XXVIII, May 25, 1953, 738.
[6] *Ibid.,* June 8, 1953, 804.

aggression in Asia was concerned, the relaxation of international pressures which followed the death of Stalin provided at least a temporary breathing space during which the likelihood of overt hostiliities receded and Moscow contented itself for the most part with reassuring gestures of the same type which it was using so effectively in Europe. As already noted, the Kremlin's territorial and other claims against Turkey were ostentatiously withdrawn in the course of the summer.[7] Diplomatic relations with Israel, which Moscow had broken off in February at the height of the anti-Semitic agitation accompanying the "doctors' plot," were restored in July on Israel's promise that it would "not take part in any alliance or agreement which has aggressive designs on the Soviet Union."[8] Premier Malenkov, in his speech of August 8, overflowed with good will toward all the neighbors of the Soviet Union, from Turkey to Pakistan and India.[9] Moscow's general policy, clearly, was to refrain from open interference in an area whose internal quarrels already threatened the foundations of international order and precluded the development of an effective anti-Communist policy.

If the absence of Soviet pressure offered the United States and its allies an unusual opportunity to place relations with the "uncommitted" countries of the Middle East and Southern Asia on a more satisfactory basis, this country also faced a notable handicap which was especially important in areas where so many problems were basically economic in character. In nearly all of the remedial programs put forward for these economically underdeveloped countries, large-scale American economic aid in one form or another stood out as one of the basic and indispensable ingredients. Despite the commitment of the new administration to governmental economy, moreover, the importance of action to raise living standards and assist general economic development in Asia, Africa, and Latin America was authoritatively recognized in Washington. "No nation," Secretary Dulles

[7] Above, p. 137. The U.S.S.R. continued, however, to object to visits to the port of Istanbul by naval vessels of the U.S., U.K., and other countries. Cf. *Documents on American Foreign Relations, 1953,* 166-169.

[8] *Ibid.,* 163-165.

[9] *Ibid.,* 138-140.

observed in his testimony on the Mutual Security Program, "can long survive as a citadel of self-indulging privilege surrounded by massed human misery and despair." [10] A special advisory committee of eight distinguished private citizens, reporting to Mr. Stassen on the principles of a United States foreign development program, insisted "that our interest in these areas is not a short-run emergency policy and that the United States must accept continuing responsibilities in today's interdependent world." [11]

But Congress, as in past years, showed no great inclination to aid these areas with "masses of money." Although the appropriation for economic and technical assistance in the Near East, South Asia, and Africa for the fiscal year 1953–54 was somewhat increased as compared with the year preceding, total appropriations were reduced and lagged considerably behind those provided for Europe and for other parts of Asia, such as Formosa and Indochina, where military assistance was regarded as urgent. The aggregate funds available for the Mutual Security Program throughout the Near East, South Asia, and Africa during the fiscal year amounted to $574 million for military aid (mostly to Greece and Turkey) and $424 million for economic assistance and technical cooperation [12]—not large sums for an area which, as Mr. Dulles pointed out, contained "about one-fourth of the world's population" and represented "about one-half of the people of the world who are still free of Communist domination." [13] Total aid for the year to India and Pakistan, with a combined population of some 450 million persons, was about $100 million. Small military aid grants went to Iran

[10] Statement to the House Ways and Means Committee, May 4, in *Department of State Bulletin,* XXVIII, May 25, 1953, 743.

[11] *Documents on American Foreign Relations, 1953,* 72-79; cf. *Department of State Bulletin,* XXIX, July 6, 1953, 16-17.

[12] *Report to Congress on the Mutual Security Program,* December 31, 1953 (Washington, G.P.O., 1954), 25. For further details see especially the third installment of Harry N. Howard, "The Development of United States Policy in the Near East, South Asia, and Africa During 1953," *Department of State Bulletin,* XXX, February 22, 1954, 274-281; March 1, 1954, 328-333; March 8, 1954, 365-371. This article offers a detailed exposition, from the State Department point of view, of much of the subject matter of the present chapter. For a briefer review, cf. Richard H. Sanger, "American Policy in the Middle East During 1953," *ibid.,* February 8, 1954, 209-214.

[13] Address of June 1, *ibid.,* XXVIII, June 15, 1953, 831.

and to some Latin American countries. Otherwise the accent was on technical assistance, refugee relief, and strictly limited funds for economic development.

Aid alone, whether large or small, was only one of the means at the disposal of the West in its attempt to transform these areas into participating members of a free world community. Diplomacy, information programs, and the cultivation of mutual understanding were other means. For the most part, it was work that had to be done on a country-by-country basis—a single formula for three continents in the midst of dynamic events had not been and presumably could not be devised. Meanwhile, from India and Pakistan to Syria and Spanish America, the nations of "the world between" were playing an increasing role in world affairs and at times directly influencing the fluctuating fortunes of the East-West struggle—as could be seen, for example, in the General Assembly vote on the Korean political conference.[14]

One serious danger to the Western position in these areas was averted during 1953 through the overthrow of a fanatically anti-Western government in Iran. The prospects for a settlement of Egypt's account with the West likewise underwent some improvement, as did the chances for construction of a defensive barrier stretching across Southern Asia from Turkey to Pakistan. Balancing these achievements were a further deterioration of the situation in French North Africa, complete lack of progress toward eliminating the sore spots in Kashmir and the Palestine area, a tightening of the Communist grip on Guatemala, and, perhaps most important, a perpetuation of the profound political and psychological differences that separated the United States from India and alienated the Western powers as a group from many of the "uncommitted" peoples.

1. THE ARAB STATES AND ISRAEL

From Scandinavia to Greece and Turkey, the NATO powers had succeeded in erecting a defensive shield which, despite many weaknesses, offered a considerable measure of protection against any forward military thrust by Soviet

[14] Cf. above, p. 245.

Communism. Eastward and southward from Turkey, there were as yet no comparable defenses. Given the military weakness of the Arab states and their neighbor Iran, the defense of the Middle East rested almost entirely on the small British contingents in Iraq and Jordan, the larger British garrison of the Suez Canal base, and the retaliatory threat of American air power based in Libya and elsewhere in the Mediterranean. In 1951, a Western offer to join with Egypt and neighboring countries in establishing a Middle East Defense Organization which might take over the responsibility for the Suez base as well as the general defense of the area had been angrily repudiated by the Egyptians, who insisted that the British must unconditionally evacuate Egyptian territory before any alternative arrangements could even be considered. While this problem remained unsettled, there was little possibility of putting the defense of the Middle East on firmer foundations. Even the attempt to strengthen the local defense forces of the Arab countries by giving them modern armaments and equipment could not go forward on any scale because of the danger that any armaments brought into the area would be used by the Arab states not to defend themselves against outside aggression but to renew their 1948–1949 war against Israel, a country to which all of the Arab governments and peoples remained implacably hostile.

Egypt and the United Kingdom

The Eisenhower administration took office with a determination to do what it could to settle these perennial problems and clear the ground for a workable regional defense system. Washington observers thought they could discern some basis for optimism in the course of recent political developments in Egypt, the richest and most influential of the Arab states, which held the keys to a settlement of the Suez base issue and whose example might well prove decisive in Arab relations with Israel. The revolutionary government of General Muhammad Nagib, which had overthrown the Egyptian dynastic and parliamentary system in the course of 1952, had shown some tendency to take a realistic view of Middle Eastern problems and might possibly be induced to cooperate with the West once its rule was consolidated. The process of internal consolidation went rapidly forward during the first half of 1953. A "liberation festival" was held in January to celebrate the first six months of the new regime, and a "Liberation Front" was formed to replace the ousted and discredited political parties. On June 18, Egypt formally became a republic when General Nagib deprived the infant King Fuad II of his royal title and assumed the presidency. Foreign observers were impressed by the dedication of the new leaders and the progress made toward abolishing corruption and implementing land reform.

As the year wore on, however, two things became increasingly evident. General Nagib, for all his popular appeal, seemed, after all, to be little more than a "front" man for a small group of revolutionary army officers led by Lieutenant Colonel Gamal Abdel Nasser. It was to these other, less conspicuous figures, perhaps, that the authoritarian aspects of the new regime were primarily to be attributed—political arrests and trials, and such fascist-type slogans as "unity, discipline, work." Secondly, the balance of political forces in the country was such that its political leaders could not, even if they wished, ignore the violently nationalistic passions which a long succession of earlier governments had fostered in the Egyptian masses. In this atmosphere, progress toward a settlement with Great Britain could not be rapid; progress toward a settlement with Israel was nil.

Stripped of its emotional aspects, the Anglo-Egyptian dispute had two main elements, both concerned with the termination of a legal relationship which had existed for more than seventy years but which in recent decades had become increasingly intolerable to Egyptian opinion. One was the British occupation of the Suez Canal zone under the Anglo-Egyptian treaty of 1936; the other, the British position in the Sudan under the Anglo-Egyptian condominium agreement of 1899.[15] In 1951, the then Egyptian government had brusquely denounced both of these instruments, thus putting Egypt legally in the wrong while leaving the British effectively in control. But the former Egyptian government had since been removed; and in the fall of 1952 the gov-

[15] For a detailed account, cf. "Problèmes égyptiens," *Chronique de politique étrangère*, VI, September 1953, 658-689.

ernment of General Nagib had taken the initiative in suggesting to the British that discussion of the future of the Sudan be renewed. With some encouragement from the United States, negotiations were continued and now led to an agreement making definitive provision for the future of the Sudan and its people.

This agreement, signed in Cairo on February 12, 1953,[16] provided for (1) a transitional period of not more than three years during which the administration of the Sudan would be carried on by the British Governor-General with the aid of a Sudanese parliament and a mixed commission of Sudanese, Egyptian, British, and Pakistani nationals; and (2) the election, after the end of the transitional period, of a constituent assembly whose duty would be to frame a constitution and "to decide the future of the Sudan as one integral whole" by either "choosing to link the Sudan with Egypt in any form" or "choosing complete independence." In Great Britain, the second of these alternatives was held to include the possibility of the Sudan's association with the Commonwealth, while Cairo expressed the view that Commonwealth membership was excluded. As a practical matter, however, the prospects for a choice in favor of Commonwealth membership by the native Sudanese were slight. Election of the Sudanese Parliament took place in November and December, under the supervision of a mixed electoral commission which included one American member. When the results were tallied, the pro-Egyptian National Union party had won a majority in the lower house and half the seats in the senate, effectively defeating the pro-independence or Umma party. The most likely outcome of the entire process, apparently, would be the fulfillment—perhaps under some international safeguards—of Egypt's long-standing demand for the "unity of the Nile Valley" under Egyptian rule.

The Suez Base Dispute

Ambassador Jefferson Caffery, who represented the United States in Cairo, had played an active role in encouraging the diplomatic discussions that led to the Sudan accord and took

16 Text in *Documents on American Foreign Relations, 1953,* 357-364.

a similar part in bringing Egyptians and British together to renew negotiations on the Suez Canal base issue. The British would have preferred direct American participation in these discussions, but Washington was reluctant to involve itself too deeply and remained on the sidelines in deference to the wishes of the Egyptians.[17] On April 27, General Nagib and Foreign Minister Mahmud Fawzi of Egypt sat down with Ambassador Sir Ralph Stevenson and General Sir Brian Robertson of Great Britain to try to hammer out a definitive agreement. At issue was the fate of perhaps the largest military depot in the world, comprising some $1.5 billion worth of workshops and supplies lying in a zone three miles wide and sixty-five miles long on the west side of the Canal.

Great Britain, which was maintaining a garrison of 80,000 men in the base at a yearly cost of over £50 million, had long since announced its readiness to withdraw its forces whenever the Egyptians should be ready to take over in orderly fashion the responsibilities inherent in the custody of so vital a strategic position. The British, however, still were not prepared to bow to Egypt's demand for what General Nagib called "total and unconditional evacuation of our territory." This demand the Egyptians now reiterated; and within a fortnight the talks had reached a dead end.[18] "We have washed our hands" of the negotiations, General Nagib asserted. "Independence . . . can be achieved only by sacrifice and blood."

Just at this moment Mr. Dulles and Mr. Stassen arrived in Cairo on their survey tour, the former bearing a pistol given him by President Eisenhower for presentation to the Egyptian Chief of State. Although the United States was doing its best to promote a settlement agreeable to both parties and had taken care to avoid any appearance of forming a common front with the British, the effect produced by the presidential gesture at such a strained moment illustrated better than anything else could have done the pitfalls with which Middle Eastern politics abounded. Suspicions

[17] Statement by Sir Winston Churchill, May 11, in *Parliamentary Debates, Weekly Hansard,* House of Commons, May 11, 1953, 891.

[18] Cf. the statements by Sir Winston Churchill (May 11) and General Nagib (May 19), printed in part in *Documents on American Foreign Relations, 1953,* 365-369.

were easily aroused in this area, and General Eisenhower's token—the gift of one military man to another—proved an all too apt symbol for the many critics of American policy in the Middle East. Pictures of General Nagib and the pistol turned up on the front pages of British tabloids, illustrating complaints of alleged American partiality for Egypt. Israeli commentators thought the pistol was pointed at them. In Egypt itself one magazine asked:

"Mr. Dulles, what are we supposed to think you mean? Are you asking Nagib to start shooting at the British in Suez or are we to understand that we must preserve public order by gunfire in our nation—which, after all, is a democracy? Or is it the idea that our President needs a revolver to protect himself . . . ?"

Although Mr. Dulles exerted himself in Cairo and elsewhere to underline this country's preference for rational and nonviolent solutions, his insistence on the compatibility of Egyptian and British interests failed to allay the mounting tension in and around the Canal zone. Incidents multiplied, and nonessential Britishers once more began to leave the country. By July, when the British placed a military cordon around the town of Ismailia to search for a missing Royal Air Force enlisted man allegedly kidnaped by the Egyptians, tension and Egyptian bitterness reached the pitch of previous years.

But eventually the incident was smoothed over and negotiations resumed on an informal basis, continuing intermittently through the late summer and autumn. Great Britain, it appeared, was prepared to withdraw its troops from the base but wished to leave 4,000 technicians to care for the equipment until Egyptians could be trained to man the installations. Egypt was said to be seeking a three-year or five-year limit on this training period, while Britain asked an interval of up to ten years for the transfer. A point of national pride was also involved, since Egypt insisted that the British technicians must wear civilian clothes while Britain wished them to remain in uniform. More fundamental were differences over the conditions under which British or other foreign troops might return to the base in an emergency. Egypt was said to be willing to permit their reentry in the event of war or in the event that the Arab League decided that there was a threat of war. Britain wanted specific guarantees on this point and, it was reported, desired an advance understanding that an attack on a Middle Eastern country outside the Arab League, such as Iran, would constitute an emergency calling for the reoccupation of the base.

Here the dispute rested at the end of the year, with final agreement still ten months away. When Prime Minister Churchill met with the President and Premier Laniel in Bermuda at the beginning of December, he "made it clear . . . that there was no prospect of any modification" in the British position. British action, he assured the House of Commons, "will be based on a careful and faithful study of the merits of the problem, and will not be dictated either by the violence of our foreign enemies or by the pressure of some of our best friends"—an obvious reference to the United States.[19]

While holding out to the last for a settlement that could be considered acceptable in a political as well as a practical sense, Great Britain was already engaged in shifting the center of gravity of its Middle East defenses to what it hoped would be less vulnerable ground. Unfortunately the island of Cyprus, selected as the main alternative to the Suez base, was also the center of an indigenous nationalist movement—in this case, a movement for political union with Greece—which was almost as intense, if not yet as powerful, as the one that was driving the British from Egypt. Future years might tell whether Britain would be more successful in harmonizing its defense arrangements with the demands of majority local sentiment in Cyprus than it had been in Egypt during the era now drawing to a close.

"New Look" at Palestine

From Egypt, Mr. Dulles and Mr. Stassen had gone on to Israel, the focal point of Middle Eastern tension ever since the new Jewish state had been brought to life, largely under

[19] *Parliamentary Debates, Weekly Hansard,* House of Commons, December 17, 1953, 580. On the Bermuda conference cf. below, pp. 425-428. The Anglo-Egyptian agreement on the Suez Canal base, signed October 19, 1954, appears in *Documents on American Relations, 1954.*

American patronage, in 1948.[20] Superficially, the feud that divided Israel from the neighboring Arab states was concerned with a multitude of interrelated technicalities arising out of the armistice agreements of 1949. Most conspicuously at issue were the status of the armistice lines which still existed in place of fixed and accepted international boundaries; the distressing plight of 865,000 Arab refugees from within Israel's frontiers; and the unsettled status of Jerusalem, now split between Jordan and Israel. At bottom, however, the Palestine situation reflected an incompatibility as stubborn as that between the Communist and free worlds—one that defied the best efforts of men of good will who felt that peace between these neighboring peoples was more important than any of the local considerations so important to them and their governments.

In this area United States policy, which had sometimes been criticized on the score of alleged partiality to Israel, underwent discernible changes. Secretary Dulles, in a speech of June 1 reporting on his Middle Eastern tour,[21] laid the basis for new points of emphasis in American relations with the nations of this region. "The United States," he said, "should seek to allay the deep resentment against it that has resulted from the creation of Israel." He declared that the Arab peoples were "more fearful of Zionism than of communism," and that they feared "lest the United States become the backer of expanionist Zionism." At the same time he took note of Israeli fears that the Arabs might try to push them into the sea, and reaffirmed the tripartite declaration of May 25, 1950, in which Britain, France, and the United States had pledged joint action should any state violate the frontiers and armistice lines of the area.[22] To this he added:

"We cannot afford to be distrusted by millions who should be sturdy friends of freedom. They must not further swell the ranks of Communist dictators. The leaders in Israel themselves agreed with us that United States policies should be impartial so as to

[20] A treaty of friendship, commerce and navigation between the U.S. and Israel, signed in Washington August 23, 1951, was approved by the Senate July 21, 1953 (Executive R, 82d Cong., 1st Sess.) and entered into force April 3, 1954.

[21] *Department of State Bulletin,* XXVIII, June 15, 1953, 831-835.

[22] Text reprinted *ibid.,* 834.

win not only the respect and regard of the Israeli but also of the Arab peoples. . . . Israel should become a part of the Near East community and cease to look upon itself, or be looked upon by others, as alien to this community." [23]

The Banat Ya'qub Incident

Given concessions on both sides, Mr. Dulles thought that integration of Israel in the Middle Eastern community should not be impossible. But mutual concessions did not come any more readily during 1953 than they had done in previous years. On the contrary, there occurred a succession of crises which if anything heightened rather than lessening the tensions of the area. Early in the autumn a serious dispute arose over Israel's construction of a hydroelectric project on the Jordan River at Banat Ya'qub in the demilitarized zone between Israel and Syria. On September 21 Syria asked the Israeli-Syrian Mixed Armistice Commission to halt the work, charging that the project would violate the armistice agreement by drying up 12,000 acres of Syrian land through diversion of Jordan waters. General Vagn Bennike, chief of staff of the United Nations Truce Supervision Organization, called on September 23 for a cessation of operations until the dispute could be resolved, but Israel refused to comply. More drastic and probably more effective, though widely criticized at home as well as in Israel, was the action of the United States in withholding an allotment of Mutual Security funds to Israel while that country was acting in defiance of the United Nations. On October 20 Secretary Dulles disclosed that an allocation to Israel under the recent Mutual Security Act had been deferred for nearly a month "in view of the problems which exist in that area between the United Nations and Israel." [24]

Syria meanwhile had carried the question to the Security Council, where Israel announced on October 27 that it had decided to suspend work pending an urgent examination of

[23] Mr. Dulles also expressed sympathy with the purposes of the U.N. General Assembly resolutions calling for the internationalization of Jerusalem; and the U.S. refused to move its embassy from Tel Aviv when Israel transferred its foreign ministry and other government offices to Jerusalem in July. Cf. *ibid.*, XXIX, July 20, 1953, 82; August 10, 1953, 177-178.

[24] *Ibid.*, XXIX, November 2, 1953, 589-590.

the matter by the United Nations. Next day Mr. Dulles recommended that the grant of approximately $26 million already earmarked for Israel be made available, since the "impediment" to this assistance had been removed.[25] When the Security Council got around to considering the question at the end of the year, the United States joined with Britain and France in supporting a resolution (ultimately vetoed by the U.S.S.R.) which called for continued interruption of the project while General Bennike sought a mutually acceptable reconciliation of interests.[26] Chances for such a reconciliation admittedly remained tenuous at best.

The Qibiya Incident

A far more incendiary crisis had meanwhile arisen over armed incidents along the Israeli-Jordanian border. This frontier, a line drawn hastily by truce negotiators in 1949 in such a way that it cut through towns and separated villagers from their lands, was the site of constant illicit crossings. Raids and counter-raids became more frequent in 1953. On the night of October 12-13 a Jewish mother and her two children were killed in their sleep on the Israeli side of the border. Two nights later (October 14-15) an armed force of about 250 Israelis raided the Jordan village of Qibiya, killing fifty-three Arab men, women, and children and destroying forty houses. General Bennike later reported to the United Nations that his observers had been unable to find evidence as to who had committed the earlier outrages; but he established that the Qibiya raid had been carried out by well-trained Israeli soldiers equipped with small arms, mortars, bangalore torpedoes, and incendiary and demolition bombs.

News of this incident occasioned "grave concern" to Secretary Dulles, Foreign Secretary Eden, and Foreign Minister Bidault, who were meeting in London and decided to request an urgent session of the Security Council on the whole

[25] *Ibid.*, November 16, 1953, 674-675.

[26] U.N. Document S/3151/Rev. 1, December 21, printed, with related statements, *ibid.*, XXX, January 11, 1954, 59; for prior discussion cf. *ibid.*, XXIX, November 9, 1953, 649. The resolution was vetoed by the U.S.S.R. on January 22, 1954.

problem of armistice enforcement.[27] General Bennike was hastily summoned to the United Nations and assured the Security Council on October 27 that violation of the Israeli-Jordanian armistice line had been "almost constant." In the ensuing debate the Arab spokesmen did their best to keep the discussion concentrated on the Qibiya affair, in which Israeli seemed most clearly at fault. Israel, on the other hand, while denying General Bennike's contention that regular Israeli military units had been involved in the raid, tried to focus attention on the general problem of border tension, Israel's geographic vulnerability, and its continuing exposure to "political warfare, economic blockade, the absence of peace as an article of policy [and] threats of violent invasion." It was a fact, said Jordan's representative, that the Palestine situation had become "as grave as it was in 1948"—although he took an opposite view of the causes of the difficulty and held that "only by putting an end to Israeli warlike actions will security be restored and tranquility prevail in the area."

Having heard the arguments on both sides, the United States joined with Britain and France in sponsoring a resolution which expressed "the strongest censure" of the "retaliatory action at Qibiya taken by armed forces of Israel" as inconsistent with the parties' obligations under the armistice agreement and the United Nations Charter. It called upon Israel "to take effective measures to prevent all such actions in the future," and, noting also the problem of infiltration from Jordan to Israel, requested the former country to "continue and strengthen" the measures which, according to its representative, were already being taken to prevent such crossings.

Ambassador Abba Eban of Israel objected to the resolution because it did not call on the governments concerned to negotiate a settlement of questions outstanding between them. On November 23 Israel had asked the United Nations Secretary-General to call a meeting of the Israeli and Jor-

[27] Communiqué, October 18, in *Documents on American Foreign Relations, 1953,* 215; cf. the State Department announcement of October 18 in *Department of State Bulletin,* XXIX, October 26, 1953, 552. Jordan had appealed to the Security Council two days earlier.

danian representatives at the United Nations, in conformity with Article XII of the armistice agreement, for direct negotiations to prevent a further impairment of peace. Partially to meet this objection, a paragraph was added to the draft resolution requesting the Chief of Staff of the Truce Supervision Organization to report to the Security Council within three months as to compliance with the General Armistice Agreements, taking into account any agreement reached as the result of Israel's request for a meeting with Jordan.[28]

In this form the resolution was adopted on November 24 by nine affirmative votes, with Lebanon and the U.S.S.R. abstaining. Lebanon's abstention reflected the Arab contention that the resolution was not strong enough since it lacked reference to compensation to Jordan or punishment of the perpetrators of the Qibiya raid. The parallel abstention of the Soviet Union conformed to what seemed a gradually developing tendency to cultivate the favor of the Arab states and thus encourage their resistance to Western aims in the area.

The Johnston Mission

Such diplomatic fencing, though unavoidable in the circumstances, did little to solve the basic problems of the area. Arab hostility to an isolated Israel continued; the plight of the Arab refugees in the bordering countries remained as miserable as ever;[29] a settled peace for the region appeared distant. One potentially promising development occurred, however, in the agreement of both Israel and the Arab states to consider a plan for unified development of the Jordan River Valley. Originally proposed by the United Nations Relief and Works Agency for Palestine Refugees and enthusiastically espoused by the United States Government, this project owed something to the example of the Tennessee Valley Authority in the United States; if accepted, it

[28] U.N. Document S/3139/Rev. 2, November 24, in *Documents on American Foreign Relations, 1953,* 427-429.

[29] By Resolution 720 A (VIII), November 27, 1953, the General Assembly decided to continue the U.N. Relief and Works Agency for Palestine Refugees in the Near East through June 1955, with a relief budget of $25 million for 1953–54 and a tentative budget of $18 million for 1954–55 in addition to its $200 million projects fund established in 1952.

might also perform a function analogous to that of the Schuman Plan in overcoming political rivalries by the creation of a common economic interest—in this case, the distribution of Jordan River water for irrigation and reclamation. In October and November, Eric Johnston visited the Near East as special representative of the President and managed to persuade Jordan, Syria, Lebanon, Egypt, and Israel to overcome their initial misgivings sufficiently to study the plan in preparation for further conversations.[30] Only time would tell whether this approach would prove more fruitful in the long run than sterile debates over the enforcement or nonenforcement of military armistice agreements which thus far were the only formal impediment to the renewal of full-scale fighting.

2. THE "NORTHERN TIER" AND INDIA

Considering the heartbreaking difficulty of the Arab-Israel situation, it was not surprising that the United States should have turned with something like relief to the more northerly belt of countries that lay between the Arab world and the sources of Soviet aggression. Secretary Dulles, alluding to the concept of a Middle East Defense Organization in his speech of June 1, described such a project as "a future rather than an immediate possibility." Many of the Arab League countries, he observed, were "so engrossed with their quarrels with Israel or with Great Britain or France" that they paid little heed to "the menace of Soviet communism." However, he said, "there is more concern where the Soviet Union is near. In general, the northern tier of nations shows awareness of the danger. There is a vague desire to have a collective security system"—a desire, he might have added, which he had done what he could to encourage in the course of his talks in Middle Eastern capitals. Such a security association, however, could not be imposed from without but, as Mr. Dulles pointed out, must grow from within "out of a sense of common destiny and common danger." In the meantime, the Secretary suggested, the United States could usefully "help

[30] See especially Mr. Johnston's broadcast of December 1, in *Department of State Bulletin,* XXIX, December 28, 1953, 891-893.

strengthen the interrelated defense of those countries which want strength, not as against each other or the West, but to resist the common threat to all free peoples." [31]

Of the countries that lay near the southern borders of the U.S.S.R., such a definition would clearly apply to Turkey, possibly to Iraq, and most probably to Pakistan, which had given various proofs of sympathy for the Western position despite its preoccupation with Kashmir and other local issues. Afghanistan's qualifications were more doubtful. The least suitable candidate for substantial American aid, however, and the primary obstacle to any "interrelated defense," was the Iranian government headed by Prime Minister Mohammad Mosaddeq and sustained by the enthusiasm of Moslem fanatics and the calculations of the Communist-led Tudeh party. While this key country refused accommodation with the West and neglected its defenses against Communism both within and without, the value of any defense arrangements concluded with other countries of the region would remain problematical.

Clearing Skies in Iran

Fortunately the Iranian problem was on the way to at least provisional solution—notwithstanding the fact that prospects had never been blacker than in the early part of 1953, when anti-Western agitation in that country had been running so high that a visit by the Secretary of State would have been unthinkable. All efforts to resolve Iran's dispute with Britain over the assets of the Anglo-Iranian Oil Company, nationalized in 1951, had proved fruitless. The British legal boycott on the marketing of Iranian petroleum, which was backed both by the Western governments and by Western oil interests fearful of the precedent set by Iran's unilateral action, effectively barred use of the country's one great resource for earning foreign exchange. As a consequence, the Iranian economy was nearly derelict and political life chaotic. It was only a matter of time, many observers felt, before the intransigence personified by Premier Mosaddeq would produce still more tragic results, quite possibly entailing the accession of the Tudeh party to governmental control.

[31] *Ibid.*, XXVIII, June 15, 1953, 835.

Such had been the situation at the beginning of 1953; yet by the end of the year a startling change had taken place. Dr. Mosaddeq had been swept from office and tried and convicted of treason. In his place as Prime Minister was a general, Fazullah Zahedi, backed by the constitutional monarch, Shah Mohammad Reza Pahlevi, and by the United States. In the turbulent sequence of mass demonstrations, the Shah had demonstrated stronger popular appeal than either the aged Dr. Mosaddeq, the Tudeh, or the uneasy combination of the two. And despite continued manifestations of Iranian nationalism, at the end of the year negotiations on the oil question had once again become a distinct possibility.

A complex sequence of events preceded this reversal. Dr. Mosaddeq, who had contemptuously rejected the proposals for settlement of the oil problem submitted to him in 1952 by President Truman and Prime Minister Churchill,[32] had entertained a hope of securing more liberal terms from the new American administration. As early as January 9, even before Mr. Eisenhower took office, he had addressed himself to the President-elect with a plea for support and a complaint against Washington's alleged tolerance of "the endeavors of the British to strangle Iran with a financial and economic blockade." He received a prompt reply assuring him of the new President's impartiality in the dispute,[33] but was not encouraged to expect a change of policy. A considerably modified version of the Truman-Churchill offer which was laid before him a few weeks later by Ambassador Loy Henderson failed to win his consent despite its endorsement by Mr. Dulles and Mr. Eden in terms suggesting that no further concessions would be forthcoming.[34]

[32] *The United States in World Affairs, 1952,* 234. For a detailed discussion cf. "Les Événements d'Iran," *Chronique de politique étrangère,* VI, November 1953, 765-803.

[33] Dr. Mosaddeq's letter and Mr. Eisenhower's reply of January 10, in *Department of State Bulletin,* XXIX, July 20, 1953, 76-77.

[34] Communiqué, March 7, in *Documents on American Foreign Relations, 1953,* 248. An important feature of the unpublished proposals presented on February 20 was the idea of replacing the Anglo-Iranian Oil Company by an international consortium of oil companies which would be set up to buy oil from Iran's nationalized industry (*New York Times,* February 21, 1953). This was the basis of the agreement ultimately announced on August 5, 1954; cf. *Documents on American Foreign Relations, 1954,* 383-388.

With his international position thus unchanged, Dr. Mosaddeq faced inevitable difficulties in grappling with the shifting forces at home. A first crisis had occurred as early as January when he sought continuance of his special powers to legislate by decree. Pro-Mosaddeq demonstrations induced the Iranian parliament to renew the Premier's emergency powers, but not before Dr. Mosaddeq had clashed with one of his principal supporters, Ayatollah Kashani, the nationalist Moslem mullah and speaker of the Majlis. February brought victory in a new trial of strength with the Shah after the Premier had denounced the palace for alleged intrigues with foreign interests concerned in the oil situation. The young monarch announced that he would abdicate, but retracted after several days of pro-Shah and pro-Mosaddeq street demonstrations. The strength of the illicit Tudeh party was instrumental in keeping the Premier in office; the army, however, manifested a degree of loyalty to the Shah which Dr. Mosaddeq subsequently tried to overcome by replacing key officers with his own men—an undertaking which was to lead directly to his downfall.

In March the Premier issued his final rejection of the Anglo-American oil proposal, denouncing it as a "form of plunder." Unable, however, to cope with the deteriorating economic situation, he addressed a new plea to President Eisenhower on May 28 in which he pointed out that as the result of the British boycott, Iran was "now facing great economic and political difficulties" that could have serious consequences. On June 29 the President replied that the people and Government of the United States, despite their friendly feelings for Iran, felt "that it would not be fair to the American taxpayers for the United States Government to extend any considerable amount of economic aid to Iran so long as Iran could have access to funds derived from the sale of its oil and oil products if a reasonable agreement were reached with regard to compensation whereby the large-scale marketing of Iranian oil would be resumed." In closing, the President noted the concern reflected in Dr. Mosaddeq's letter "at the present dangerous situation in Iran" and said he sincerely hoped "that before it is too late, the Government of Iran will take such steps as are in its power to prevent a further deterioration of that situation."[35]

By this time Dr. Mosaddeq was close to his ultimate test. In April he had sought parliamentary approval of a bill making him commander-in-chief of the army in place of the Shah. Riots, arrests, and parliamentary disorders became common. Unable to secure passage of his army bill, the Premier called on July 19 for the dissolution of the Majlis or second chamber. Tudeh support became bolder. A new Soviet ambassador to Tehran had been appointed, and Russian-Iranian diplomatic discussions on "all questions" were under way.[36] On July 28 Secretary Dulles expressed "great concern" over the growing activities of the Tudeh party and its toleration by the Iranian Government, developments which he said made it "more difficult for the United States to grant assistance to Iran."[37]

As part of the Premier's plan to supersede the Majlis, a plebiscite was held on August 2. Voting was nonsecret, the Tudeh was out in force, and Dr. Mosaddeq received 99.4 per cent of the votes. On August 15 he announced the dissolution of the Majlis; but, on the same day, the Shah signed decrees abruptly dismissing Dr. Mosaddeq from office and appointing in his place General Fazullah Zahedi, a veteran army officer once banished by the British during World War II for pro-Nazi leanings. Delivery of the Shah's decrees set off forty-eight hours of rioting, with mobs shouting "death to the Shah" and toppling over statues of the monarch and his father. The Shah and his Queen flew to Iraq, then to Rome. But on August 19 the tide turned. The lower ranks of the army, turning against their pro-Mosaddeq officers, quelled both left-wing and nationalist supporters of the ousted Premier and gave pro-Shah demonstrators a free hand. The mobs swept through government buildings and looted and burned Dr. Mosaddeq's home in his absence. By night, General Zahedi was in control and the Shah was preparing to fly back to Iran. The next day Dr. Mosaddeq, clad

[35] *Department of State Bulletin,* XXIX, July 20, 1953, 74-76.
[36] Cf. the comments of Prime Minister Malenkov, August 8, in *Documents on American Foreign Relations, 1953,* 138.
[37] *Department of State Bulletin,* XXIX, August 10, 1953, 178.

in his familiar pajamas, surrendered to arrest. The Zahedi regime immediately began rooting out Mosaddeq supporters, arresting Tudeh leaders, and seizing arms caches.

This overturn spelled a dramatic reversal in Iran's international orientation as well as its internal arrangements. To the Russians, who had so recently been congratulating themselves on what looked like an irresistible drift toward the Soviet camp, the Shah's coup was a "provocational" maneuver dictated by "American imperialists." To most Americans, the fall of Mosaddeq seemed more like a direct intervention of Divine Providence—although it was later to be claimed that agents of the Central Intelligence Agency had also had a hand in the affair, and that the United States itself had hand-picked General Zahedi as Dr. Mosaddeq's successor.[38]

At all events, Washington was in a receptive mood when the new Prime Minister, appealing to President Eisenhower for urgent aid on August 26, pointed out that Iran's treasury was empty and its foreign exchange exhausted but stated that the new government would pursue a policy of "eliminating such [international] differences as may exist." President Eisenhower immediately promised "sympathetic consideration of Iran's needs," and on September 5 the White House announced that Iran would receive an emergency grant of $45 million for "immediate economic assistance." In Tehran, meanwhile, arrangements were completed to make available to Iran $23.4 million in regular technical assistance funds during the fiscal year 1953–54.[39] In October Herbert Hoover, Jr., recently appointed State Department adviser on world petroleum affairs, went to Iran to take up once again the discussion of the oil question; and on December 5 Iran and Great Britain announced that they had decided to resume diplomatic relations without delay and thereafter to "proceed at the earliest mutually agreed mo-

38 Richard and Gladys Harkness, "America's Secret Agents: The Mysterious Doings of CIA," *Saturday Evening Post,* CCXXVII, No. 19, November 6, 1954, 66, 68; *New York Times,* April 9, 1955.

39 *Department of State Bulletin,* XXIX, September 14, 1953, 349-350. The letters exchanged between Premier Zahedi and President Eisenhower on August 26 appear also in *Documents on American Foreign Relations, 1953,* 369-371.

ment to negotiate a settlement of the oil dispute . . . on the basis of justice and equity." [40]

Iran began to settle down. The Shah's land reform program, sidetracked by Dr. Mosaddeq, was reinstated, and in October the monarch celebrated his thirty-fourth birthday by distributing royal land holdings to 1,600 peasants. There was renewed talk of the long dormant seven-year development program. New elections for the Majlis were announced for 1954. Dr. Mosaddeq was indicted for treason and, after a trial marked by six weeks of the familiar weeping and histrionics, was sentenced on December 21 to three years in solitary confinement.

The sum total of these dramatic events was not a clean victory for Western hopes of a free, strong and democratic Iran. Premier Zahedi spent his first four and one-half months in office ruling, of necessity, as a strong man. Solution of the oil dispute was as yet by no means assured. The Tudeh party, many observers felt, was down but not necessarily out. There were scores of political, economic, and social problems ahead. But at least the Iranian log jam had been broken. The drift toward chaos and Communism in one vital sector of the free world had been arrested. Not many developments in 1953 justified so large a measure of self-congratulation in Washington and throughout the Western world.

Rapprochement with Pakistan

The other countries of the "northern tier" experienced no such breathtaking reversals during 1953, although Turkey continued to solidify its international position, primarily through its friendship treaty with Greece and Yugoslavia,[41] and Pakistan continued its slow gravitation into the defensive orbit of the West through intensified contacts with Turkey and the beginnings of an understanding which would qualify it as a recipient of American military aid. There were two principal difficulties in the way of Pakistan's inclusion in an effective regional defense arrangement. One was the economic and political instability which continued to plague

[40] *Ibid.*, 371.
[41] Cf. above, pp. 203-205.

this six-year-old Moslem state, arbitrarily cut out from the body of the Indian subcontinent in the form of two completely detached territories separated by a thousand miles of Indian territory. The other, and more serious, was the bitter feud with India which made it impossible to strengthen Pakistan without running the risk of upsetting the balance of power in the subcontinent and further alienating the Government of India from the policies of the United States and its allies.

Superficially, alliance with Pakistan appeared to offer limited advantages to the West, apart from those inherent in its geographic position and the military spirit of its population. Through January, February, and March the country was disturbed by rioting and disorders inspired by both Communist and Moslem extremists. The continuance of a two-year drought resulted in a wheat deficit estimated at 1.5 million tons. Behind the scenes of the slow-moving Constituent Assembly, a sharp political struggle was going forward between rival interest groups whose power was rooted respectively in West and East Pakistan. On April 17 the Governor General, Ghulam Mohammad, dismissed Prime Minister Khwaja Nazimuddin as "entirely inadequate to grapple with the difficulties facing the country" and appointed Mohammad Ali, one of the younger Moslem League leaders and Pakistan's Ambassador to the United States, as his successor.

The new leader, installed in time to receive Mr. Dulles and Mr. Stassen on their visit to Karachi, followed up earlier pleas to the United States for wheat and received a quick response which was all the more sympathetic in view of the mounting difficulties this country had begun to face in disposing of its wheat surpluses. President Eisenhower asked Congress on June 10 to authorize an immediate grant to Pakistan of up to 700,000 tons from surplus wheat stocks held by the Commodity Credit Corporation, the local currency value of which would be set aside for development purposes within Pakistan; an additional 300,000 tons, he suggested, might be made available later on either a grant or a loan basis. Fifteen days later the necessary legislation had been enacted and signed and the first shipload was on its way.[42] In 1951 a loan to India had been approved for similar purposes, but not with the same cordiality and dispatch.[43]

The Kashmir Deadlock

In taking office as Prime Minister, Mr. Ali had said he would "welcome opportunities to discuss with the Western powers the immediate restoration of peace in this part of the world, including the Middle East."[44] Unfortunately the deadlock over Kashmir, the prime obstacle to restoration of peace in that part of the world, remained as firm as at any time since the fighting stopped in 1949. In June, however, Prime Ministers Ali and Nehru met at the Coronation in London and agreed to hold a private conference on Pakistani-Indian tensions at Karachi at the end of July. There they settled some problems in connection with the Bengal border and agreed to meet again in September.

Such cordiality, a novelty in the relations of the two states, was destined for early impairment. In August a crisis occurred in Kashmir when Sheikh Mohammad Abdullah, the Moslem leader who had been prime minister of the Indian-held portion of the state, was overthrown and arrested on charges of plotting Kashmir's independence—a surprising accusation, since he had previously favored accession to India. Abdullah was now replaced by Bakshi Ghulam Mohammad, another Moslem who was considered more firmly pro-Indian. Despite denials from New Delhi, Pakistan not unnaturally looked upon Abdullah's ouster as an Indian-engineered coup. As tension mounted, a new meeting between the two Prime Ministers was arranged and Mr. Ali went to New Delhi on August 16. By August 20 they had smoothed over the immediate difficulty and agreed to appoint a joint committee to iron out preliminary issues concerning the long-delayed Kashmir plebiscite; in addition, they committed themselves to name a mutually agreeable neutral plebi-

42 Presidential message, June 10, in *Documents on American Foreign Relations, 1953*, 371-374; Public Law 77, 83d Congress, approved June 25, 1953; further documentation in *Department of State Bulletin, passim.* For additional details on U.S.-Pakistan relations cf. "Les États-Unis et le Pakistan," *Chronique de politique étrangère*, VII, May 1954, 360-372.

43 Cf. *The United States in World Affairs, 1951*, 256-258.

44 *New York Times*, April 19, 1953.

scite administrator by April 30, 1954.[45] This understanding, however, failed to remove the deep-rooted sting from the Kashmir situation. The year ended with another deadlock: the joint committee could not agree on the old question of the number of troops to be retained on the Indian and Pakistani sides of the cease-fire line when and if the elusive plebiscite was held. Kashmir, no less than Palestine, continued to threaten the peace of free Asia and make enemies of those who needed to be friends if their freedom was to be put on solid foundations.

India and Aid to Pakistan

The later stages of the Kashmir negotiation in 1953 were vastly complicated by news of discussions between Pakistan and the United States concerning military aid—discussions which seemed to the principals a logical response to existing world conditions, but were viewed in India as a direct encroachment on Asia's right to remain aloof from world power antagonisms. Mr. Nehru's government had special grounds for disliking a policy which not only ran counter to its general theories on world affairs but also threatened to undermine its own military position and general influence in Asia. As early as 1952, India had expressly warned Pakistan that any step toward association with a Middle East defense organization would be viewed as an unfriendly act. India clearly did not relish the notion of Pakistan's emergence either as a leader of Moslem opinion or as a member of a pro-Western defense group; still less did it welcome any move that affected the balance of forces among the 450 million people of the subcontinent. The thought of Pakistan accepting alignment with the West and receiving military aid recalled tragic instances of Hindu-Moslem bloodshed and, from the Indian point of view, contained the elements of a serious psychological crisis.

Had the United States been less firmly committed to its world-wide strategic program, or had India been somewhat less unsympathetic to American views on the "cold war," this country might have hesitated to take a step which threatened to complete the breach of confidence which had

45 *Ibid.*, August 21, 1953.

been developing with the largest democracy in Asia. As things stood, however, Indian-American relations were already in a condition that made many Americans doubtful whether it was really possible to continue taking Indian susceptibilities into account. Throughout the year, the atmosphere between New Delhi and Washington had vacillated between "strained" and "improved," reaching a comparative high in the spring when Mr. Dulles, returning from his visit to the Indian capital, paid tribute to Nehru's "calm demeanor and lofty idealism," [46] and a relative low in August when the United States so resolutely opposed Indian participation in the Korean political conference.[47]

The maneuvers which took place on that occasion at the United Nations called forth one of Mr. Nehru's sharpest criticisms of the American position in world affairs. Addressing the lower house of the Indian parliament on September 17,[48] the Indian Prime Minister recalled that India had been excluded from the prospective conference essentially by the votes of the United States and seventeen Latin American countries. An "Asian question," he observed, had been decided, in contradiction to the desires of "nearly the whole of" Europe and Asia, by "some people who really are not concerned with this question so intimately." "Somehow," he added, "it is not realized by many of the great powers of the world that the countries of Asia, however weak they might be, do not propose to be ignored, do not propose to be bypassed, and certainly do not propose to be sat upon." He commented upon the "narrow approach which considers everything in terms of black or white—'those with us or those against us' "—which, he said, takes on "an element of dogmatic fervor" resembling "the old unfortunate bigoted approach of religion which brought about the wars of religion in the past, with not even the saving graces which religion sometimes had provided in the past." And he declared that the "strong" policy of "threatening everybody" adopted by

[46] Speech of June 1, in *Department of State Bulletin,* XXVIII, June 15, 1953, 833.

[47] Cf. above, pp. 243-245.

[48] *Documents on American Foreign Relations, 1953,* 374-381.

some nations indicated "great immaturity in political thinking or understanding."

This was typical Nehru, and, while the burden of the complaint was certainly directed against the United States, some of the generalities about a "bigoted approach" could also be applied to the Communist world. It represented an outlook far different from that held in Washington; and yet this difference by itself did not suffice to account for the growing crisis in Indian-American relations. One mitigating influence was the fact that Washington, following its victory at the United Nations, indicated that it would not continue to bar Indian representation at the Korean conference if, once such a meeting had started on a two-sided basis, the participants decided to extend an invitation to New Delhi. The United States also made other conciliatory gestures. The State Department, even while rounding up the August vote in the General Assembly, had published a pamphlet praising Indian democracy and noting points of agreement as well as disagreement between the two countries.[49] Later the United States supported the successful candidacy of Madame Vijaya Lakshmi Pandit, Mr. Nehru's sister, over more pro-Western figures as president of the Eighth General Assembly. The two nations differed profoundly on one great issue—the admission of Peking to representation in the United Nations—but the ultimate test posed by that question still lay ahead.

Military Aid Discussions

To Indians the matter of American aid to Pakistan was more immediate and pressing, and it was over the growing prospect of action in this field that the bitterest feelings arose. It was characteristic of the atmosphere of Indian-United States relations that Washington, in deciding to pursue discussions with Pakistan to a conclusion, neglected either to foresee or to provide against the inevitable adverse reaction in India. Indians, like everyone else, were left to guess at the facts from circumstantial evidence and newspaper speculation, which increased in volume from September onward. In that month the Pakistani Commander-in-Chief,

[49] *India: A Pattern for Democracy in Asia* (Department of State Publication 5095, Washington, 1953).

General Mohammad Ayub Khan, paid a visit to Ankara in company with the Minister of Defense and from there went on to Washington. Almost simultaneously, members of the House Armed Services Committee arrived in Karachi on an unannounced four-day visit. Indian apprehensions were thoroughly aroused by these movements. The negotiations, it was generally believed, involved not only the inclusion of Pakistan in a Middle East defense pact and the granting of substantial American military aid but also, most probably, the granting of air bases in Pakistan for use by American forces.

The tension occasioned in India by these reports was so great that the possibility of war between India and Pakistan was discussed quite openly. The storm did not reach full violence, however, until mid-November, when it became known that Pakistan's Governor-General had gone to the United States for medical treatment and had used the opportunity to confer on defense matters with President Eisenhower, Secretary Dulles, and other American authorities. On November 15, Prime Minister Nehru declared that any such action as the granting of military aid to Pakistan would "affect the whole structure of things throughout the area." His sharp reaction threw a note of caution into official American comment. Secretary Dulles on November 17 denied that any negotiations were going on "at present," and next day the President himself declared at his press conference that the United States

> "would be most cautious about doing anything that would create unrest and disaster or failure or hysteria in the neighboring nation, say, in India. . . . The fact is the Administration's effort would be to produce a friendship with that entire subcontinent and not with just one group." [50]

Although these declarations had a decidedly disconcerting effect in Karachi, they failed to reassure New Delhi. Indian leaders began an intense campaign of pressure against Pakistan, threatening that the latter's alignment with the United States would prejudice the success of the scheduled conferences on Kashmir. At the same time Indian diplomacy

[50] *New York Times,* November 19, 1953.

throughout the world neglected no possibility of isolating Pakistan and trying to prevent the consummation of the agreement. These efforts were powerfully abetted by the U.S.S.R. and Communist China, both of which made official protests in Karachi against the proposed pact. Moscow, said the Soviet note, could not be "indifferent" to activities having "a direct bearing on the security of the Soviet Union"—the customary formula which the Soviet Government was wont to advance whenever any neighbor state in Asia attempted to strengthen its security in association with the West.[51]

In discussions in the Indian parliament, Nehru and his principal associates did their best to keep popular indignation against the United States and Pakistan within bounds. Although the idea of an aligment with the Soviet Union had been freely bandied about in unofficial quarters, Nehru reemphasized his determination to keep India's hands free. He spoke gratefully of American aid to his country, and even emphasized that if the United States was offering military aid to Pakistan it was not from any hostility to India itself. But despite this studied moderation he made it clear that the plan had profoundly affected India's position and attitude toward the United States. Military equipment coming into the hands of Pakistan on the scale discussed in the newspapers would be more than sufficient to overturn the balance of military strength entirely in favor of Pakistan. India's position in the tug-of-war over Kashmir would be jeopardized, and India would lose the position of preponderance it had established throughout the non-Communist East—especially if Pakistan went on to ally itself with a powerful Middle East bloc. In addition, Pakistan's association with the United States might tend to attract the Soviet lightning which Nehru had striven so hard to keep away from the subcontinent, thus increasing the danger of India's involvement in a general war.

A corollary to these considerations was the prospect that India would become engaged in an arms race with Pakistan,

[51] The Soviet note of November 30 and Pakistan's firm but courteous reply of December 18 appear in *Documents on American Foreign Relations, 1953,* 169-170.

with consequent disruption of its five-year economic development plan. To many Indians (and to not a few Americans) this plan, which called for a capital expenditure of about $4.2 billion by 1956, was a bulwark against Communism at least as important as a guard at the Khyber pass. The United States itself was contributing substantially to Indian economic development through technical assistance and other means.[52] The administration fully subscribed to the view that the race for economic and social progress between India and Communist China would have wide repercussions on the choice of other countries between the methods of freedom and those of the police state. As the President's comments showed, moreover, the United States was well aware of India's objections to the involvement of any part of the subcontinent in Western defense arrangements. But this, in American eyes, was no reason to pass up the opportunity to gain a willing ally in Southern Asia. Nehru, Americans had been assured, was not, after all, "the Voice of Asia" but merely "a voice in Asia"—and, moreover, the proponent of a policy which some at least considered "very naive." [53]

Furthermore, the immediate intentions of the United States in regard to Pakistan were by no means so far-reaching as had been rumored. The Indian Government was officially assured on December 23 that the current conversations involved neither bases nor a military alliance, but were concerned only with the question of whether to establish a military assistance program in Pakistan on similar lines to those already in effect in Iran and elsewhere.[54] Such a program, it seemed, ought not to give serious offense to India, yet would surely be helpful in bolstering the defensive arc that ran from Japan to the Mediterranean. All in all, the advantages of the program seemed definitely to outweigh the risks. As the year closed, there was no longer much doubt that Paki-

[52] For details cf. H. N. Howard in *Department of State Bulletin,* XXX, March 8, 1954, 368-369, and *Report to Congress on the Mutual Security Program,* June 30, 1953, 44-46.

[53] Address of Senator Knowland, November 1953, in *Documents on American Foreign Relations, 1953,* 129-130.

[54] *New York Times,* December 24, 1953; cf. also the President's announcement of February 25, 1954 in *Documents on American Foreign Relations, 1954,* 373-374.

stan would be relied upon henceforth as one of the keystones in the "northern tier."

3. AFRICAN MEDLEY

Strongly as India and Pakistan disagreed on the problems of the subcontinent and its relation to the East-West struggle, there were other important issues on which they tended to agree with each other and, indeed, with most nations of Asia and the "uncommitted world." Most conspicuous among these areas of agreement was an issue which in Asian eyes loomed even larger than the "cold war" between East and West—the issue of so-called colonialism and racial discrimination, embracing all those situations from Indonesia to Morocco in which peoples who at an earlier period had come under European control were now striving to assert their independence against the "imperialist" powers of the West. To this order of questions belonged not only Egypt's and Iran's differences with the United Kingdom and the efforts of the Indochinese states to achieve complete independence from France, but also the acute problems arising from similar demands on behalf of the indigenous populations in French North Africa as well as numerous racial and political frictions in other portions of the African continent. To such problems the Asian countries were accustomed to address themselves with a unity and a fervor quite unfamiliar in the West. Far different from the vague interest of most Americans in the liberation of "captive peoples" in Eastern Europe was the uncompromising determination of Asian governments to achieve the "liberation" of those peoples whom they looked upon as the unwilling captives of Western colonialism in Africa and Asia.

French North Africa

With the possible exception of Indochina, the most powerful explosions of this sentiment in 1953 took place in connection with the ever-growing nationalist ferment in France's North African protectorates of Tunisia and Morocco. The issue posed by this agitation was one in which the United States felt no less directly concerned than in the tensions of the Middle East proper, since North Africa, despite its immunity from threats of Soviet invasion, was an important deployment area of the Strategic Air Command as well as a vital element in the position of a major ally. Even more sharply than in the Middle East and in Asia, moreover, the United States was faced with the embarrassing demand that it make a choice between encouragement of those indigenous nationalist movements which seemed to represent the "wave of the future" in North Africa and the support of a European colonial power whose interests were directly threatened by the uncompromising character of the demand for independence.

Secretary of State Dulles, returning from the middle East at the beginning of summer, had expressed the view that recent United States policy in this matter had "become unnecessarily ambiguous," and had seemed to suggest that in future this country would more actively promote "an orderly development of self-government" for dependent territories.[55] Confronted with the concrete issues of French North Africa, however, the United States still chose to support the French even at the cost of rising unpopularity in the Arab-Asian world.

Affairs in Tunisia, which had been turbulent throughout most of 1952, proved much calmer in 1953 despite continuing differences between the French administration and the Neo-Destour (New Constitution) party, which was recognized as the most responsible and on the whole the most moderate of Tunisian opposition elements. There was some violence in April and May while municipal elections were being held; the balloting was boycotted by the nationalists. On July 1 Prince Azzedine Bey, pro-French heir presumptive to the Bey of Tunis, was fatally shot by assassins; but by October the protectorate was quiet enough for the new Resident-General, Pierre Voizard, to announce relaxation of some of the restrictions imposed during the disorders of the previous year.

Morocco, with its complicated racial pattern involving both Arab and Berber elements in addition to the French

[55] Address of June 1, in *Department of State Bulletin*, XXVIII, June 15, 1953, 833-834.

colonial population, was the scene of a sharp struggle between indigenous factions which culminated in a virtual French *coup d'état* and in grave offense to nationalist opinion throughout the Arab-Asian world. The Moroccan Sultan, Sidi Mohammed Ben Youssef, who had been installed by the French a quarter of a century earlier but who in recent years had veered increasingly toward the nationalism of the Istiqlal (Independence) party, found himself not only at odds with the French but directly challenged by the staunchly pro-French Berber Pasha of Marrakesh, Haj Tihami al-Mezauri al-Glawi. After months of tension during which the Sultan vainly sought French support,[56] al-Glawi in August assembled a conclave of religious and feudal leaders, vowing to oust the Sultan. Rather late in the proceedings the French remonstrated with the Berber leaders, but the conclave formally relieved the Sultan of his religious powers and duties and designated his uncle, Sidi Mulay Mohammed Ben Arafa, as the new Imam or defender of the faithful and thus as legitimate sovereign. Although stripped of the religious position on which his leadership rested, the Sultan refused to yield, and there were bloody encounters between the two factions in Moroccan cities.

On August 20, as the embattled tribesmen converged on Rabat, the French intervened with lightning speed and ordered the Sultan deposed. With an armored column surrounding the imperial palace, the French Resident-General, Augustin Guillaume, informed the Sultan of his dismissal and sent him off to exile in Corsica. Next day Mulay Mohammed was installed as Sultan, and Paris announced that "the French Government intends that the new investiture should open an era of profound political, economic and social reforms." But the first reforms, announced on September 2, were not regarded by the nationalists as profound. They consisted in the Sultan's signing away most of his temporal powers, while the French announced the creation of a new series of courts and consultative committees to take over the functions of government. Real power, it appeared, would continue to rest with the French Resident-General.

[56] Cf. the documents printed in *Documents on American Foreign Relations, 1953*, 353-357.

Reaction in the United Nations

These events created a tremendous sensation throughout the Arab and Asian states and led the fifteen-nation Arab-Asian bloc in the United Nations to request an urgent meeting of the Security Council to consider a situation which, it was claimed, constituted "a danger to international peace and security." To this charge both the French and other delegations reacted in the Security Council with arguments already familiar from past discussions. France continued to insist that Morocco was legally under French jurisdiction and therefore not within the competence of the United Nations. Spokesmen for the Asian-Arab bloc, led by Pakistan and Lebanon, asserted that the drive to remove the Sultan was a minority one, probably aided by the French, and that the dispute was international in character because of the treaty relationships governing Morocco's status as well as a former decision of the General Assembly that it was competent to treat the issue. This view, however, was contested not only by Great Britain, which was accustomed to resist such claims on principle, but also by the United States. On a similar issue relating to Tunisia sixteen months earlier, this country had antagonized both sides by abstaining from voting.[57] This time the American delegation unequivocally supported the French stand. "It must be obvious to anybody who looks at the facts candidly," said Ambassador Lodge, "that the situation in Morocco does not endanger international peace and security." [58] On a final vote on September 3 the Council decided by a 5-5 vote not to consider the Arab-Asian complaint. The tally showed Chile, China, Lebanon, Pakistan, and the U.S.S.R. in favor while Colombia, Denmark, France, the United Kingdom, and the United States were opposed and Greece abstained.

Defeated in its attempt to obtain Security Council consideration, the Asian-Arab bloc brought both the Moroccan and the Tunisian disputes before the General Assembly at its Eighth Regular Session in the autumn; but here, too, resolutions scoring French policy in the two protectorates

[57] *The United States in World Affairs, 1952,* 245-246.

[58] Statement to the Security Council, August 27, in *Department of State Bulletin,* XXIX, September 7, 1953, 325.

failed to achieve the necessary two-thirds majorities. United States delegates, while stressing American sympathy for independence movements in general, reiterated the view that the situations did not threaten world peace and expressed the hope that increasing self-government in the territories would come as the result of bilateral negotiations between the French and Moroccan and Tunisian authorities. This line of reasoning was authoritatively set forth in the course of the Assembly session in a speech by Henry A. Byroade, Assistant Secretary of State for Near Eastern, South Asian and African Affairs, which was later described as "the first major statement of U.S. policy on colonialism to be made in many years":

"The United States Government believes that this complicated problem must be resolved primarily by the parties concerned. There is always a danger that the injection of outside influence into a situation of this kind will make it worse. It is difficult for us as a Nation to understand the extreme emotions on either side. We know of the delicate problem that the Government of France confronts in view of the large French population in this area. We agree that the local system of government in North Africa needs change before it can cope with present world conditions or guarantee social progress. We have important security interests in the strength of the French nation, as well as deep friendship for the French people. We also have a firm policy of supporting the right of dependent peoples to self-determination. We, therefore, understand the desire of the Tunisians and Moroccans for self-government.

"It is no secret that these problems confront America with a dilemma. The present situation therefore calls frankly for a middle-of-the road policy which will permit us to determine our position on practical issues on their merits as they arise. We greatly hope for progress on a bilateral basis with resultant easing of tensions. We do not rule out United Nations discussion if it appears that United Nations discussion can contribute positively to a satisfactory solution. This is one of the many situations in which it is not our interest to 'choose sides' for the sake of choosing sides. Our fundamental interests can be served only by an arrangement which is mutually satisfactory to both the French and the North Africans." [59]

[59] Address of October 31, *ibid.*, November 16, 1953, 659; comment *ibid.*, XXX, February 8, 1954, 212.

Following a precedent established in 1952, France withdrew altogether from the debates in the General Assembly on the ground that the United Nations was attempting to interfere in the domestic affairs of a member state. Other delegations which stayed to debate the resolutions proposed by the Arab-Asian bloc felt called upon to insist on important changes before the drafts were brought to a vote. The original thirteen-power resolution on Morocco had recommended such strong measures as the termination of martial law, the establishment of democratic institutions through free elections based on universal suffrage, and the consummation of Morocco's complete sovereignty and independence within five years. As approved by the First Committee on October 19, however, the resolution merely imputed to the people of Morocco a right to "complete self-determination," appealed for a reduction of tension, and urged that the Moroccans be given the "free democratic political institutions" to which they were entitled.[60] But even this language, which the committee approved by a vote of 31 to 18 (with the United States opposed and nine delegations abstaining), failed to survive the more rigorous scrutiny of the plenary session on November 3.

A similar fate awaited the Arab-Asian resolution on Tunisia, although the First Committee went further toward meeting the wishes of the sponsors and approved a text recommending "that all necessary steps be taken to ensure the realization by the people of Tunisia of their right to full sovereignty and independence."[61] Adopted in Committee by a vote of 29 to 22 (with the United States opposed and five abstentions), the resolution mustered 31 votes to 18 and ten abstentions but failed to gain the necessary two-thirds majority in the plenary session on November 11.

Once again the Arab-Asian states had lost their case in the United Nations—which did not mean, unfortunately, that the North African problem was any closer to solution or that the frictions it engendered were in any wise allayed. It only meant that the suppressed discontent in the protectorates

60 Text from U.N. Document A/2526, October 22, in *Documents on American Foreign Relations, 1953,* 430.

61 Text from U.N. Document A/2530, October 28, *ibid.,* 431.

would continue and that next year's eruption would be that much stronger. Meanwhile Secretary Dulles offered public assurance that the United States was "pushing for self-government more than appears on the surface," had "not forgotten we were the first colony to win independence," and had "not given a blank check to any colonial power." [62]

South of the Sahara

In Africa south of the Sahara the ferment of nationalism, racial tension, and economic development continued without, on the whole, involving the United States in international controversies on the high policy level. In parts of the emergent African continent these diverse forces gave rise to head-on clashes between different elements and produced such alarming manifestations as the disorders of Kenya and the internal strife of the Union of South Africa. Elsewhere, notably in British West Africa, they proved at least momentarily reconcilable and added momentum to the orderly progress toward self-government.

The official American role in African affairs remained relatively narrow during 1953. A limited amount of United States aid went into key projects designed to alleviate one of the continent's most pressing economic needs, the shortage of transportation. American interests were also involved in the development of Africa as a source of strategic materials. An undisclosed amount of uranium ore continued to flow to Western nations from the Belgian Congo, the free world's primary source of this material. The Union of South Africa also embarked on a program to recapture uranium in conjunction with gold mining operations, and a delegation from the Joint Congressional Committee on Atomic Energy, led by Senator Bourke B. Hickenlooper, inspected the Union's new installations in September.

Otherwise official Washington was cast in the role of an interested observer. There was much to observe, mainly in the British colonial territories. The French and Portuguese colonies were politically quiescent, and the Belgian Congo was primarily concerned with booming economic activities.

[62] Address to the Congress of Industrial Organizations, Cleveland, November 18, in *Department of State Bulletin,* XXIX, November 30, 1953, 743.

But on the British squares of the African checkerboard a notable succession of new moves occurred.

In West Africa, the Gold Coast underwent another year of increased self-government without a major hitch, and Prime Minister Kwame Nkrumah announced that he would seek to replace the three remaining Britons in his cabinet with Africans in 1954. Nigeria, less known to Americans but possibly more important in view of its population of 30,000,000 and its status as the largest remaining dependency in the British Empire, ran into difficulties. Its complex federal constitution, adopted in 1951 with the aim of reconciling the divergent views of its three main areas, reached a point of breakdown and serious violence between different native groups occurred in May. Nigerian political leaders traveled to London and in August came to agreement on the principles of a revised federal system to be embodied in a new constitution.[63]

East Africa continued to be the scene of Britain's most dismaying colonial troubles. The Mau Mau secret society among the Kikuyu tribe of Kenya bathed fellow Africans in murder and terror, continuing the disorders that had broken out in the fall of 1952. Although the avowed aim of the Mau Mau was to drive Europeans from Kenya, its main victims were Africans, less than a score of white settlers being killed during the year. The worst incident took place on March 27 when a Mau Mau moonlight raiding party slaughtered 150 inhabitants of a Kikuyu village. The rebellion led to full-scale guerrilla warfare, but toward the end of the year reinforced British troops appeared to be making headway in restoring order. In April the colonial administration successfully prosecuted Jomo Kenyatta, leader of the chief Kikuyu political movement, the Kenya African Union, on charges of organizing the Mau Mau society. A Communist background for some of Kenyatta's activities was suspected but could not be proved. European settlers inclined to view the Mau Mau movement as a form of African atavism, but colonial officials regarded land hunger, detribalization, and

[63] *Report by the Conference on the Nigerian Constitution* (Cmd. 8934, London, 1953, 23 p.)

lack of economic opportunities as the main problems to be attacked once "the emergency" was over.

Another East African crisis arose at the end of November when the Colonial Office deposed Mutesa II, young Cambridge-educated hereditary ruler (Kabaka) of the Buganda province of Uganda Protectorate, on grounds of noncooperation with the British colonial authorities. The incident brought spirited debate in the British House of Commons as well as unrest in the protectorate and unfavorable references in the United Nations.

Central Africa, too, was a source of differences over British colonial policy. After four years of conferences and controversy, London finally approved the creation of a Central African Federation embracing Northern and Southern Rhodesia and Nyasaland. Proposed as a spur to the economic development of the three territories, the plan met with objections on the ground that African inhabitants of both Northern Rhodesia and Nyasaland opposed a link with Southern Rhodesia, where effective government was in the hands of white settlers. The Federation constitution, which went into effect October 23, included a number of safeguards for African rights and a measure of African representation, without, however, overcoming the fears of indigenous leaders. Sir Godfrey Huggins, veteran leader of Southern Rhodesia and the foremost advocate of federation, became Prime Minister of the new unit. In December his Federal party, pledged to a program of increasing racial partnership, won a clear-cut electoral victory over the Confederate party, which had espoused a form of racial separation similar to the *apartheid* system embraced by the neighboring Union of South Africa.

South Africa and the United Nations

In the Union itself, political strife continued unabated notwithstanding the striking electoral success of Dr. Daniel F. Malan's Nationalist party, which emerged from the elections of April 15 with an increased majority and relatively firm assurance of another five years in office. *Apartheid* as an aim and a doctrine thus appeared well entrenched as part of the Union's way of life, even if the practicability of a complete separation of races in South Africa's rapidly expanding industrial economy remained to be demonstrated. The previous year's civil disobedience campaign by the African National Congress faded out in 1953, but the potential for racial explosion remained.

As in past years, South Africa received its customary quota of censure at the United Nations on the issues of treatment of the Union's Indian population, its general racial policy, and its refusal to conclude a trusteeship agreement for South West Africa. The only new note in these controversies was the Union's offer to negotiate a treaty with the United States, Britain, and France, outside the United Nations, on the future administration of the South West African mandate. These countries were singled out because of their role as the former Allies of World War I and therefore, in the Union's view, logical heirs to the League of Nations and the mandate system. But such an arrangement would have been of doubtful legal validity and wholly contrary to the current trend of world political sentiment, especially among the "anticolonial" countries. A majority of the Eighth General Assembly, including the United States, continued to feel that the only reasonable solution of the South West African problem was to place the territory under the trusteeship system. On November 28, over the lone negative vote of South Africa, the Assembly approved a "solemn appeal" to the Union to reconsider its position in this sense; it also reiterated six similar proposals adopted during the past seven years, and set up a new seven-member committee to give the matter further examination on behalf of the United Nations.[64]

The more dramatic issues relating to racial policy within the Union of South Africa itself found some governments, including the United States, more hesitant to join in condemning the Union Government. Their reservations resulted from a mixture of legal scruples, doubts as to the effectiveness of outside pressure, reluctance to offend an important friendly government, and unwillingness to set a precedent for United Nations involvement in matters of primarily domestic interest. Nevertheless the United States did not offer formal opposition to Assembly action as it did in

[64] Resolution 749 (VIII), November 28, 1953. For a statement of the U.S. position see *Department of State Bulletin*, XXIX, December 7, 1953, 805-806.

the cases of Morocco and Tunisia. Once again South Africa's treatment of its non-white populations was deplored in the name of the entire Assembly, albeit by comparatively small majorities and with no prospect that the policies of the Union Government would be brought into conformity with the Assembly's official views.

In 1952, in the course of its continuing attempts to ameliorate the treatment of persons of Indian origin in South Africa, the Assembly had set up a three-man good offices commission to assist in negotiations which it hoped to set on foot between India, Pakistan, and the Union. South Africa, however, had refused to cooperate with the commission, arguing that the United Nations effort constituted an invasion of its domestic jurisdiction. At most, it offered to pursue negotiations with India and Pakistan outside the United Nations framework. Nevertheless the Assembly adopted at its Eighth Session, by 42 votes to 1 (South Africa) with seventeen abstentions, a seventeen-nation resolution asking the commission to continue its work, report to the next session on any progress made, and formulate recommendations which might lead to a peaceful settlement. Concurrently, South Africa was urged once again to refrain from applying its Group Areas Act, which provided the legal basis for segregating persons of Indian origin.[65]

On the more general question of South African racial policies and conflicts, another three-man commission set up by the 1952 Assembly had been equally unsuccessful in gaining South African cooperation. Nevertheless it had produced a trenchant report condemning the *apartheid* doctrine as "scientifically false, extremely dangerous to internal peace and international relations . . . and contrary to 'the dignity and worth of the human person'," and had asserted that the situation in South Africa was daily becoming "more explosive and more menacing to international peace and to the foreign relations of the Union of South Africa." [66] The rejoinder of the South African delegate, G. P. Jooste, was

[65] Resolution 719 (VIII), November 11, in *Documents on American Foreign Relations, 1953,* 439-440. The U.S. voted affirmatively.

[66] General Assembly *Official Records, Eighth Session,* Supplement 16 (U.N. Documents A/2505 and A/2505/Add.1), October 3, 1953, 116, 118.

equally trenchant. The commission's statement, he charged, "was completely unwarranted, extremely dangerous and irresponsible, and was little short of an incitement to revolt, with the added implication that such a revolt would have the sympathy and support of the United Nations."

Undismayed, the Assembly adopted on December 8 a resolution commending the commission and asking it to continue its study, report to the next session, and suggest measures to alleviate the situation.[67] This time, however, the affirmative vote was only 38, with 11 negative votes and eleven abstentions. The other colonial powers joined South Africa in opposing the resolution, while the United States abstained in company with Turkey, Nationalist China, and a mixed group of Scandinavian and Latin American states. Such a course, perhaps, was unlikely to gain the United States great popularity in any quarter. But it at least acknowledged that there were problems in this part of the world for which no ready-made solution had yet been discovered.

4. FRIENDS WE TAKE FOR GRANTED

Nearer home, among the twenty Latin American states, the United States faced issues not too dissimilar in some ways to those of the Middle East and Africa. The problems of the Western Hemisphere, however, were not only more familiar in their general terms but differed from those of the older continents in that they arose in an area which was considerably more wealthy on a per capita basis and in which industrialization was well under way. Yet here, too, the same basic differences of outlook could be found. While the United States still looked on the inter-American system primarily as a bulwark against foreign aggression and internal subversion and sought to give it an increasingly anti-Communist emphasis, Latin Americans more and more viewed it as an instrument for assuring what to them were the far more urgent goals of economic cooperation and financial help. Secure, they thought, behind the shield of United States military power, they were primarily concerned with

[67] Resolution 720 (VIII), December 8, 1953.

their own economic problems. With few exceptions, their attitude on the "cold war" could be described in terms that varied from "neutral" to "isolationist."

For several years before 1953, students of the Latin American scene had noted a gradual swelling in the tide of anti-United States feeling through which the nationalism of republics below the Rio Grande found its most characteristic expression. Accentuated by a growing and one-sided economic dependence on the United States, and in some cases manipulated by Communists for their own ends, this trend had reached proportions alarming to the soberest observers in both North and South America. During the 1952 presidential campaign in the United States, Republicans had made much of these adverse currents and had freely taken the Truman administration to task for its alleged "policy of neglect."

In his very first nationwide broadcast, Secretary Dulles had promised to develop better understanding with an area which, he implied, we were sometimes too prone to "take for granted."[68] More concretely, President Eisenhower, in his Pan American Day address on April 12, announced that he was sending his brother, Dr. Milton Eisenhower, as his personal representative to visit "a number of these great Republics." The special envoy, said the President, would be directed to "take careful stock of the economic and social conditions now prevailing throughout our continent" and to "report on ways to be recommended for strengthening the bonds between us and all our neighbors in this Pan American Union."[69]

Economic Problems

From the point of view of Latin American opinion, no gesture could have been more happily conceived. For in Latin America, too, the advent of a new administration in Washington had signified a turning point. The direction of this region's economic and political life would be heavily influenced, as in the past, by policies shaped in the United

[68] Broadcast talk, January 27, in *Department of State Bulletin*, XXVIII, February 9, 1953, 214-215.

[69] *Ibid.*, April 20, 1953, 563-564.

States. Particularly crucial, in Latin American eyes, was the policy the incoming administration would adopt in the critical field of trade and raw materials. The slackening of the Korean war boom had caused a decline in world prices of copper, tin, cotton, and other raw materials which caught Latin American producers with stocks for which no markets could readily be found. Having expanded production to meet temporary war needs, a number of governments were looking to the United States to take their backlog of strategic materials for its stockpile or to conclude long-term contracts for the purchase of their current output at advantageous prices. Meanwhile, partly as a means of improving their bargaining position with the United States and partly because of genuine interest in new markets, some Latin American countries were lending an attentive ear to Communist proposals for trade in nonstrategic and even strategic materials—notwithstanding Washington's known objections to such shipments.

Not less important to the future of the hemisphere, and therefore not less deserving of attention by the presidential emissary, were deeper trends which likewise affected the prospects for Latin American development and growth. One little publicized development of recent years had been the impressive increase in productivity achieved by the Latin American countries as a group. But this gain, however significant in itself, was largely overshadowed by their explosive population growth, which was proceeding at a rate at least twice the world average. The area's population, already approximately equal to that of Canada and the United States combined, seemed likely to reach the half-billion mark by the end of the century. At the same time the average Latin American was being educated to desire standards of living approaching those of Western Europe or even the United States. A race was on between the desire for higher standards and the development of means for attaining them. This tension lay at the root of the prevalent social unrest in Latin America and helped to account for many of the political events which had bedeviled recent inter-American relations. It was a subject on which Dr. Eisenhower would certainly hear a great deal in every country he visited.

The Eisenhower Mission

Accompanied by a group of governmental experts, the presidential envoy left Washington on June 23. There were, of course, twenty independent states in Latin America, but limitations of time confined the visit to the ten South American republics. On July 29 the group was back in Washington.

> "In those thirty-six days we held friendly and informative discussions with the Presidents and cabinet ministers of the ten republics of an entire continent. We talked with their leaders of agriculture, industry, finance, labor and education. We visited factories, homes, farms, and schools. In all, we traveled about 20,000 miles and met with several thousand persons, individually or in groups.
>
> "Everywhere our mission was greeted with friendliness and understanding. . . . Exceptional courtesy was the rule everywhere. A few efforts by communists to mar the cordiality of the welcome were conspicuously futile. . . ." [70]

This, however, was only the beginning of Dr. Eisenhower's task. There still remained the formidable job of "synthesizing our data," "crystallizing our views," and coordinating any policy recommendations with the interested government departments and agencies. Meanwhile, Latin American affairs did not stand still. Indeed, in certain areas they continued to develop in directions that were nothing short of alarming.

Political Trends

One feature of the Latin American scene which had unavoidably impressed the Eisenhower party was the remarkable prevalence of nondemocratic political trends—or, in the more tactful language of Dr. Eisenhower's report, the "uneven success" with which different countries had been struggling "toward democratically-functioning republican forms of government." Such a country as Uruguay could be cited as one that justly took pride in "the advanced development of its political democracy." If Dr. Eisenhower saw no need to mention negative examples, it was partly because there were so many possibilities to choose from but more especially be-

[70] Report of the Eisenhower mission, November 18, *ibid.*, XXIX, November 23, 1953, 695.

cause the most notorious backsliders—Perón's Argentina and the Guatemalan regime of President Jacobo Arbenz Guzmán —were already in the mind of everyone interested in Latin American affairs. The Guatemalan and particularly the Argentine situation had for some time past been engaging public attention throughout the Americas; and the growing Communist influence on the "reform" government of the former country, together with Argentina's aggressive bid for continental leadership on an anti-United States platform, were to entail familiar discomforts for Washington under the new administration as they had done under the old. Although Guatemala was probably as far to the left and the Peronist regime as far to the right as is conceivable in Latin American politics, there were also important elements common to both countries, the most conspicuous being nationalism with a pronounced anti-United States tinge and a drive for "economic independence" which expressed itself in marked antipathy to United States economic enterprise. Events in both countries offered a continuing demonstration of the fact that extremism, whether of the Right or Left, inevitably took on an anti-United States flavor in the absence of any strong competing influence.

Red Threat in Guatemala

Guatemala, a country whose long-time subjection to military dictatorship had been happily terminated in 1944 but which had since experienced a gradual leftward drift under the successive presidencies of Juan José Arévalo (1944–1950) and Jacobo Arbenz Guzmán (1950–1954), confronted Washington with what was doubtless the year's most baffling problem in hemisphere relations. Involved were not only the old question of expropriation of foreign-owned properties by nationalistic Latin American governments but also the fact that this particular government had clearly fallen under Communist influence and was serving increasingly as an instrument of the Communist conspiracy in the Western Hemisphere. The chief immediate target of the Guatemalan Government was a private corporation, the United Fruit Company, which had for some years been an object of official hostility and in March 1953 was confronted with the loss of extensive reserve lands under an agrarian reform law providing for the expropriation, with compensation, of unused lands. Later in the year, similar pressure was applied against the company-controlled railway and the electric power company.

For the "benefits" allegedly resulting from these measures against "foreign imperialist monopolies," credit was claimed by Guatemala's strong Communist element, which by this time was known to control important sectors of Guatemalan life such as the official press and radio, organized labor, and the local machinery of land distribution. While Latin American specialists conceded that land reform in Guatemala was overdue and that there was a need for improved labor policy on the part of foreign companies, the "constant harassment" to which the United Fruit Company had been subjected was largely a Communist tactic. On August 28 the State Department sent Guatemala a sharply worded note labeling the expropriation of United Fruit Company lands as discriminatory (the 234,000 acres expropriated represented the great bulk of the entire 377,000 acres alienated to date under the land reform law) and criticizing as grossly inadequate the $600,000 settlement offered the company in long-term, nonnegotiable agrarian bonds.[71]

For the United States, however, Guatemala's arbitrary action against the American companies was but one of many factors in a complex and delicate situation. Even more serious in the long run was the thriving base of operations and propaganda that the country now offered the international Communist movement in the center of the Americas. Throughout the year President Arbenz, an army man and no Communist himself, continued to insist that his regime was not dominated by the extreme leftists. But outside observers were less impressed by these claims than by Guatemala's consistent tendency to support the Communist "line" in hemisphere and world affairs and by such actions as the government's withdrawal in April from the five-nation Organization of Central American States—ostensibly because it had been made the target of hostile propaganda and agressive conspiracies launched in other countries, but more prob-

[71] *Ibid.*, September 14, 1953, 357-360.

ably because it desired to avoid debate on an anti-Communist resolution which El Salvador planned to present at a forthcoming meeting.

Charges and countercharges also flew between Guatemala and the United States. Spruille Braden, former Assistant Secretary of State for Inter-American affairs, in an address at Dartmouth College on April 3 described Guatemala as a "beachhead of international communism" and censured the State Department for its "inaction" in the matter.[72] Voices were raised for economic sanctions in the form of an embargo on Guatemala's coffee exports. In reply, Guatemala protested to the United Nations that elements in the United States and Central America were threatening to intervene in its internal affairs. As the situation continued to deteriorate, the State Department itself became more outspoken. On October 14 John Moors Cabot, then Assistant Secretary, stated that Guatemala was "openly playing the Communist game" and warned that it could expect no "positive cooperation" from this country. On the contrary, he asserted, it was "our right and duty" to answer "years of wanton attacks on this country and its citizens from official Guatemalan sources."[73]

The situation was clearly not one whose continuance the United States could comfortably endure; yet it was also one for which no easily available remedy was at hand. To other Latin American governments, Guatemala's vagaries, if such they were, had been rather less disturbing. With the exception of Guatemala's immediate neighbors, most Latin Americans were either indifferent to events in that country or sympathetic with the Guatemalan revolution and committed to similar radical reforms in their own countries. Any unilateral action against Guatemala by this country would be likely to touch off charges that the United States was violating solemn pledges of nonintervention in the internal affairs of a sister republic—a principle which for Latin Americans constituted the basis of the inter-American system. The most immediate danger of the Guatemalan situation, some observers thought, lay in the possibility that Communist at-

72 "The Communist Threat in the Americas," *Vital Speeches*, XIX, May 1, 1953, 432-437.

73 *Department of State Bulletin*, XXIX, October 26, 1953, 555-556.

tacks would goad the United States into some arbitrary action which would set all Latin America by the ears. Yet should international Communism be allowed to pursue a flagrantly interventionist course behind the protection of the nonintervention principle? Mr. Braden had maintained that failure to intervene to stem the rise of Communism was itself a form of intervention—in the Communists' favor.

Another possible approach—and the one that was ultimately adopted—would be to bring the question of Communism in Guatemala before the Organization of American States at its Tenth Conference, scheduled for March 1954 in Caracas, Venezuela. But this, too, presented hazards in view of the generally complacent attitude of the other American republics. In contrast to prevailing United States views, an important non-Communist sector of Latin American opinion, strongly represented in political, intellectual, and free trade-union circles, continued to believe that in reality the concept of American freedom was as seriously threatened from the totalitarian Right as from the totalitarian Left. These quarters failed to attach as much significance as the United States to the fact that while other Latin American dictatorships were products mainly native to the Western Hemisphere, the Communist streak in the Guatemalan regime was a foreign importation. Thus, although a resolution on the question was proposed by the United States for the agenda of the Caracas Conference, it was anticipated at the time that the conference would hardly go beyond a general anti-Communist declaration without specific recommendations or enforcement measures.

The novel problem of dealing with Communism in the Americas was further complicated by an outcropping in British Guiana which suggested that the evil was spreading. On October 9 the British Government intervened drastically to suspend the colony's five-month-old constitution, vest the governor with emergency powers, and reinforce troops, acting in the stated belief that a Communist coup engineered by the People's Progressive Party might be in the offing.[74] That group, campaigning on a program of land reform,

[74] Cf. the statement of the British Colonial Office, dated October 3, in *Documents on American Foreign Relations, 1953,* 399-402.

labor legislation, and more freedom from Britain, had won a bare popular majority in the April elections and embarked on a campaign of agitation which was aided by the control of eighteen out of twenty-four elective seats in the House of Assembly. While the United States approved the British action as removing a possible threat to hemisphere security, the Latin American countries were uniformly critical regardless of the coloration of their internal politics. Their attitude was partly inspired by doctrinaire opposition to colonialism, particularly in the Americas, and was strongly reinforced by remembrance of the territorial claims which various Latin American states had put forward to British possessions in the Western Hemisphere.

Argentine Crossroads

While the relations of the United States with Guatemala deteriorated, those with the Argentine dictatorship seemed at times about to undergo marked improvement. President Perón, though a man of undoubted totalitarian proclivities, was scarcely more a Communist than was Generalissimo Franco in Spain. In the early months of the Eisenhower administration, he seemed more than half inclined to exploit this important advantage and to try to initiate a more friendly policy than he had found it worth while to pursue during the Truman era. There were some indications that his regime's anti-United States propaganda campaign would be muted, and in March certain legislative processes were initiated with the announced objective of creating a favorable climate for foreign investment. A setback occurred in May, when the government suspended the licenses of the three United States news agencies operating in Buenos Aires in token of its annoyance over the critical tone of the United States press. But Dr. Eisenhower's mission, when it arrived a few weeks later, was deeply impressed by the warmth of its reception as well as by Perón's omission to demand loans and other concessions as the price of his friendship. In October, in a speech intended for foreign consumption while on a state visit to Paraguay, Perón openly praised President Eisenhower and lauded the ideal of hemisphere solidarity.

If Perón's regime was veering away from the anti-United

States attitude it had consistently maintained in past years, the explanation undoubtedly was to be sought in the difficulties of Argentina's domestic situation rather than in any special affection for the Eisenhower administration. The fact was that Argentina was in the throes of a serious internal crisis, brought on primarily by almost a decade of adventurist economic policies which had fostered industrialization at the expense of agriculture. In 1950–1952 conditions had been further aggravated by drought which had seriously affected the country's cattle and grain exports and its balance-of-payments position. At home, a severe price inflation, combined with rising unemployment and unaccustomed food scarcities, aroused open revolt in the ranks of the General Confederation of Labor, hitherto Perón's militant supporter. During the spring the regime had experienced its most difficult moment in years, marked by a wave of bombings in the capital, a wild night of arson following an explosion in the Plaza de Mayo on April 15, and numerous arrests of opposition leaders, intellectuals, and businessmen.

As in the past, the search for a permanent solution to Argentina's economic problem was made more difficult by the nationalist tenor of the regime. Perón attempted to meet the crisis on two fronts: a campaign to curtail imports and check inflation, and a drive for trade agreements featuring Argentina's high-priced wheat. By November, fourteen "compensation agreements" had been concluded with European countries and South American neighbors. Although their practical effect remained doubtful, certain of these pacts reflected long-range political as well as purely commercial objectives. Most publicized but not necessarily most important was the Argentine-Soviet agreement signed on August 5, providing for an exchange of Argentine agricultural products for Soviet manufactured items as well as a substantial Soviet credit for the purchase of transportation, oil-field, power and other capital equipment.

Within South America itself, Argentina exploited its advantages as a wheat exporting country to conclude agreements for "economic union" with Chile and Paraguay that, at least on paper, would have far-reaching effects. The "Act of Santiago," signed during Perón's state visit to Chile in

February, aimed at increasing the exchange of Chilean minerals for Argentine foodstuffs by reforming customs and exchange regulations, coordinating production, and developing transportation and communications facilities between the two countries. But whether the treaty finalized in July would actually be implemented was another question; similar proposals in the past had led nowhere. Agreement with Paraguay was likewise reached with comparative dispatch, thanks largely to that landlocked country's heavy dependence on Argentine capital, supplies, and transportation. Ecuador, headed like Chile by a pro-Perón government, also signed up; but Bolivia and Uruguay remained aloof, and Peru went so far as to conclude in August an agreement for economic cooperation with Brazil which was interpreted as a countermove.

To those familiar with the attitudes and policies of Argentine nationalism, these moves seemed intended not only to alleviate a difficult economic situation but to assert Argentina's "natural leadership" in the southern part of the hemisphere. They fell into a pattern with other Peronist activities: the obtrusive "anti-Yankee" and isolationist or "third-position" propaganda still disseminated by Argentine embassies and broadcasts; the dummy Latin American labor organization, ATLAS, which Perón had created in late 1952 to oppose both the Communist-controlled labor body and the democratic labor organization which was supported by the United States and the International Confederation of Free Trade Unions; and finally, the "socialist international" which was set up toward the close of 1953 to sponsor a congress of "socialist" parties in Buenos Aires.

Yet it remained questionable how far such devices could arrest the internal decay of the regime. Economic conditions had failed to improve significantly, and labor and army support continued to drift away. Foreign loans and investments would be badly needed if the regime was to gain a new lease on life. Thus it seemed not unlikely that the trend toward more agreeable relations with the United States, inaugurated at the time of the Eisenhower mission, would be further emphasized during the period ahead.

Mexico, Brazil, and Chile

Although Argentina and Guatemala together furnished the most extreme examples of isolationism, anti-Yankeeism, and the drive for "economic independence," such attitudes were by no means confined to those two countries. The struggle to harmonize long-term aspirations with present-day realities was especially difficult for those countries like Brazil, Chile, Mexico, Uruguay, and Costa Rica which had well-established democratic traditions. With such countries the United States enjoyed generally good relations, signalized during 1953 by President Eisenhower's participation with President Adolfo Ruiz Cortines of Mexico in the dedication of the Falcón Dam on the Rio Grande on October 19.

Yet even a country so friendly to the United States as Brazil was resentful of what Brazilians considered this country's failure to follow through on promises of financial assistance. Brazil's short-term commercial debt owing in the United States alone was estimated in the spring at more than $400 million; at such a rate the $300 million loan that the Export-Import Bank extended in March would prove only a stopgap.[75] The economic issue intruded into the debate over the long-delayed ratification of the military assistance pact concluded with the United States in 1952, which the Brazilian Congress belatedly approved on May 3. The obvious need for drastic economic readjustment led in June to cabinet changes and the appointment of former Foreign Minister Oswaldo Aranha as Finance Minister. But the new cabinet appeared unable to act unitedly to pull Brazil out of its economic morass. The Aranha plan for "making the family live within its income" found little favor in any quarter. Aranha himself was reported to be disgruntled with the United States. The army was at loggerheads with the new Labor Minister, João Goulart, over the latter's demagogic promises to Brazilian workers—who were also being courted by Luiz Carlos Prestes, the famous Communist leader, from his hide-out. As Brazil's essential imports continued to eat up its supply of dollars, pressure increased even from conservative

75 *New York Times,* May 1, 1953.

quarters for resumption of trade and perhaps diplomatic relations with the Soviet bloc.

In Chile, President Carlos Ibañez del Campo did not carry out his implied campaign threats of 1952 to repudiate the country's military agreement with the United States and resume relations with the U.S.S.R. But this threat continued to hang in the background of negotiations with Washington for the disposal of Chilean copper holdings. In November the talks were broken off in protest against the insistence of the United States on the cessation of discriminatory treatment of United States copper-producing companies (whose taxes and foreign exchange payments were helping to finance the Chilean development program), as well as a prohibition on deliveries of Chilean copper to Communist countries. Anti-United States feeling ran high when these "conditions" became known, and it was fanned by Communists who had a virtual monopoly on the labor press.

Bolivia and Costa Rica

Bolivia was in a separate category. In contrast to the trend over much of Latin America, the recently installed government of President Víctor Paz Estenssoro was proving itself to be not merely nationalistic but essentially democratic and desirous of effecting genuine reforms. But Bolivia was feeling the pinch of declining world prices for its high-cost tin exports, and was further plagued by the question of compensation for former stockholders of its nationalized tin industry. A three-year contract for one-half the country's annual tin output was concluded early in the year with a British group representing the former mineowners, but although the United States agreed to take one year's supply of Bolivian tin concentrates at world market prices, the Reconstruction Finance Corporation reportedly refused to enter into a long-term purchasing agreement on the ground that this country's stockpile was adequate. Bolivian pride in the fact that British smelters were buying their tin in Bolivia for the first time was clouded by the fear of famine, for future sales might not cover the cost of the country's essential food imports. The situation was only temporarily alleviated by President Eisenhower's action in October in making available $5 million worth of surplus United States wheat, together with $4 million in special economic aid and an extra $2 million in technical assistance funds for agricultural expansion.[76] Harassed by opponents on the Right and the extreme Left, some of them inside the government party itself, Bolivia's President on one occasion found himself in the embarrassing position of saying to his own group, "We cannot afford a social revolution."

A not dissimilar case was that of the Central American republic of Costa Rica, although here the momentary outlook was much more favorable. With coffee prices booming, Costa Rica was poised for a crusade to "prove that democracy can solve the problem of underdeveloped countries," as President José Figueres put it after an overwhelming majority of Costa Rican voters, with women voting for the first time, elected his self-styled "socialist" government to power on July 26. The new President's views on the role of foreign capital aroused considerable speculation concerning the future of United Fruit Company operations in Costa Rica; Figueres had made it clear that the company would be asked to renegotiate its contract to provide a 50-50 division of profits. Whether the company would oppose this move, which might set off a chain reaction in other countries in which it operated, and whether Costa Rica would adopt Guatemalan tactics in reprisal, were open questions—as was Washington's position in the controversy.

Relations with the Dictatorships

Fewer problems were presented to the United States by the countries with authoritarian governments, several of which were buoyed up by favorable terms of trade and a certain stability made possible by censorship and the suppression of opposition parties. Old-line dictatorships, like those in the Dominican Republic and Nicaragua, and the newer military governments of Peru and Venezuela maintained fairly consistent records of cooperation with the United

[76] *Department of State Bulletin,* XXIX, July 20, 1953, 82; October 19, 1953, 518-519; November 2, 1953, 584-586; December 14, 1953, 822; *Report to Congress on the Mutual Security Program,* December 31, 1953 (Washington, G.P.O., 1954), 55.

States. Their controversial politics to one side, they were administrations dedicated to the welfare of business and industry. Peru under General Manuel Odría was in fact held up as a model of the free economy to other Latin American republics. But the decline in prices of cotton, sugar, and minerals—important Peruvian exports—cast a shadow over the future, threatening the stability of the currency; and Venezuela's spectacular prosperity was menaced by agitation within the United States to curb imports of foreign crude oil.

That Colombia and Cuba exhibited less stability could perhaps be attributed to the fact that in these countries strong-man government had interrupted a process of evolution toward democratic functioning. Colombia presented the paradox of a country experiencing a *coup d'état* in the midst of an unprecedented economic boom sustained by its coffee revenues. A move by Conservative President Laureano Gómez to introduce a fascist-type corporative congress induced the army to abandon an old hands-off tradition and take power in a bloodless coup on June 13. The United States promptly recognized the new government of Lieutenant General Gustavo Rojas Pinilla, which made a start toward pacifying the country, relaxing censorship, and encouraging the Liberal opposition to resume an active role in politics.

Affairs in Cuba, however, took an opposite course. Following a coup by opposition leaders in Oriente province in July, elections were postponed for the third time since General Fulgencio Batista seized power in March 1952. Constitutional guarantees were suspended and a drastic public order law was imposed, along with a period of censorship. That the unrest had not been eliminated was apparent in December when the United States indicted former President Carlos Prío Socarrás in Florida on the charge of conspiracy to violate the Neutrality Act by shipping arms to Cuba, presumably for the use of his adherents.

The Eisenhower Report

It was amid such varied developments that the long-awaited report of the Eisenhower mission was submitted on

November 18.[77] The analytical portions of the document were presented as a consensus of the views of Dr. Eisenhower and representatives of the Departments of State, Commerce, and the Treasury; the concluding recommendations, however, lacked this warranty and were presented as the personal views of the President's brother. Although the report ranged over the entire field of inter-American relations, achievements, and problems, it gave most attention to economic factors on the dual ground that (a) "essential cooperative processes" were working well in most other fields, and (b) economic relations were both the central problem of the hemisphere and the one in which the United States position was most widely misunderstood. "Economic cooperation," it said, "is unquestionably the key to better relations between the United States and the Latin American Republics. Everything else, no matter how important, must take a secondary place, at least in the absence of war."

While the mission had noted the heartening advances of recent years and appeared sympathetic to Latin American aspirations for further development, it was critical of certain features of economic planning and of budgetary, fiscal, and credit policies in the Latin American states. It stressed the need of balance between industrial and agricultural development, criticized the idea of "industrialization for its own sake," and called for the free play of market forces. Prevention of inflation—the "maintenance of honest money"—was identified as a vital contribution to sound development, unpopular though the necessary measures would be.

Acknowledging that "South America's need for capital . . . is difficult to exaggerate," the report repeated the familiar contention that "The major part of this capital must come from local earnings," with foreign private capital playing an "important complementary role." Note was taken of the considerable credits furnished to Latin American countries by the Export-Import Bank and the International Bank, and of the willingness of these institutions to provide "reasonable" support in the field of power development under carefully specified conditions. At several points, the

[77] Text in *Department of State Bulletin,* XXIX, November 23, 1953, 695-717; excerpts in *Documents on American Foreign Relations, 1953,* 382-399.

Latin Americans were reproved for actions tending to frighten off potential investment and told that in the field of private as well as public lending, certain things would have to be done to attract the investor. Assurances would have to be given of reasonable profit on the enterprise, of opportunity to remit earnings, and, not least, of guarantees against "creeping expropriation."

It was perhaps foreordained that so temperate an analysis of economic problems and differences would not please everybody either in Washington or Latin America. As for Dr. Eisenhower's personal recommendations for "strengthening economic cooperation," they went considerably further than certain Washington agencies believed wise, even though they fell considerably short of Latin American demands. Stressing the "trade, not aid" theme, Dr. Eisenhower gave top priority among his recommendations to the adoption of a stable and consistent United States trade policy, "with a minimum of mechanisms permitting the imposition of increased tariffs or quotas." Even more controversial was his second recommendation, the establishment of a "long-range basic-material policy" which would permit purchases of certain "imperishable" materials for an enlarged United States stockpile at times when the prices of such materials were declining. On the burning question of economic aid and investment, Dr. Eisenhower again set the premium on private investment, with a suggestion that existing United States tax laws be studied with a view to alleviating the so-called "double taxation" of American companies operating in Latin America. He also, however, advanced the controversial recommendation that the United States continue to make loans "on a substantial scale" for the foreign currency costs of "sound" development projects where private financing was not available and the borrower was demonstrably a good credit risk. A considerable concession to the Latin American viewpoint, this recommendation collided with one of the basic tenets of the United States Treasury, which opposed the use of the Export-Import Bank as a vehicle for developmental loans and whose opposition to this line of thought may well have contributed to the delay in issuing the report.

Another suggestion concerned possible grants of food to Latin American countries from United States surplus stocks "in very unusual circumstances," as when normally heavy importers of food found themselves unable to buy because of balance-of-payments difficulties. This recommendation was closely related to the $5 million food grant made to Bolivia in October. Dr. Eisenhower also recommended that the United States stand ready to furnish technical advice directly to Latin American countries, as well as expanding the "effective" technical cooperation program already in existence and giving continued support to the technical cooperation agencies of the United Nations and the Organization of American States.

While reaction to the report of the President's delegate was generally favorable both in the United States and in Latin America, his economic analysis and the good will plainly animating the conclusions were considered more valuable than his observations on the political situation. Few observers of the Latin American scene could wholeheartedly endorse the optimistic statement that "Most American nations which still have degrees of feudalism and dictatorship are moving gradually toward democratic concepts and practices." In respect to Communist influence, Dr. Eisenhower said that conquest of Latin America would not occur by direct assault but rather by infiltration and the "undermining of free institutions one by one." He deplored ultranationalism as a "regressive influence, fostered by Communist agitators whose support is sometimes accepted by non-Communist political leaders for reasons of temporary political advantage"—a plain reference to Guatemala. But there was no reference to Latin American dictatorships as a field for Communist operations or a brake on hemisphere cooperation. Nor was there any direct reference to Argentina, even though several passages seemed to advocate a more normal relationship with that country.

As for the practical consequences of the Eisenhower report, not much could come of its recommendations before the United States had defined its general foreign economic policy, at least in broad outline. Like so many other aspects of United States foreign relations, the problem identified as the key to inter-American affairs would have to await the report of the Randall Commission early in 1954 before even a preliminary move could be made toward its solution. Latin Americans were already looking forward to the Caracas Conference in 1954 as an opportunity to acquaint themselves more definitely with the long-run intentions of their powerful neighbor in the economic field. But if Washington, too, looked forward to the Caracas meeting, it was not as a forum for economic discussions—for which the United States might not even then be fully prepared—but as an opportunity to mobilize inter-American sentiment against the Communist threat as exemplified in Guatemala.

As so often happened, in focusing on an acute manifestation of the Communist virus in a particular area the United States was finding itself unable to give full attention to those general conditions which might involve the health of the free world in an even more fundamental sense. The critical situations which had been developing in such diverse places as Guatemala, British Guiana, Indochina, and French North Africa might have been less threatening if the governments concerned had given more thought to their emerging problems at an earlier date. It was to be hoped that other countries of "the world between" would not be plunged in crisis at some future date simply because their problems had failed to show an acute Communist tinge in 1953.

CHAPTER SIX

THE SHADOW OF THE H-BOMB

THE DATE August 8, 1953 marks one of those rare occasions on which the outlook of a whole generation of human beings is revolutionized almost literally from one day to the next. Try as we may, we of the free world are unlikely to recapture fully the sense of comparative security that all of us enjoyed up to the moment when Premier Malenkov revealed that the Soviet Union had learned to manufacture the hydrogen bomb. As he paused in the reading of his lengthy report to the Supreme Soviet, Stalin's successor seemed to take positive delight in shattering our complacency. "It is well known," he declared (to the "stormy, long unabating applause" of the assembled delegates),

> "that abroad the advocates of war have long cherished illusions of United States monopoly of production of the atomic bomb. However, history has shown that this was a profound illusion. The United States has long since ceased to hold a monopoly of production of atomic bombs. Recently the transoceanic opponents of peace found a fresh consolation. The United States possesses a weapon more powerful than the atomic bomb, it has a monopoly of the hydrogen bomb, if you please. This, evidently, would have been some consolation for them if it corresponded to reality. But this is not so. The government considers it necessary to report to the Supreme Soviet that *the United States has no monopoly of production of the hydrogen bomb.*"[1]

Naturally, Americans and most other people hoped that the Soviet Premier was lying or at least exaggerating. If so,

[1] *Documents on American Foreign Relations, 1953,* 144-145 (emphasis supplied).

he would not be the first dictator to try to mask the weakness of his regime with flamboyant claims of nuclear achievement. Malenkov's statement, Mr. Dulles commented on August 12, could only be accepted "with some skepticism," since we had "no independent evidence" to support it. But the supporting evidence was to be forthcoming within hours after Mr. Dulles spoke. According to a statement released some days later by the Atomic Energy Commission, the Soviet Union actually conducted an "atomic test" on the very morning of Mr. Dulles' statement. Information about it reached the Commission that same night. Subsequent information indicated that the test "involved both fission and thermonuclear reactions" [2]—or, presumably, as *Pravda* announced in less recondite language, that the U.S.S.R. had exploded a hydrogen bomb with a strength "many times greater than the power of atomic bombs." Eleven days later the Atomic Energy Commission revealed that there had been still another fission (atomic) explosion "in Russian territory" on August 23, adding that no further announcements would be made unless "intelligence" indicated "information of greater interest."

Evaluation of these startling details was left to a public unguided except by such light as was obtainable from scientific and military sources outside the American government. Gradually, two main facts trickled into general consciousness, one alarming, the other somewhat comforting. The detonation of a thermonuclear or hydrogen device by the U.S.S.R. not only made that country a greater international menace than ever before but went far to disprove its supposed scientific backwardness; indeed, there were indications that in some respects it was actually ahead of the United States and had used certain techniques which could not have been obtained by espionage because they had not yet been developed in this country.[3] But although it was

[2] *Department of State Bulletin,* XXIX, August 24, 1953, 236-237.

[3] Chairman Lewis L. Strauss of the Atomic Energy Commission stated on March 31, 1954: "In August of last year the Russians also tested a weapon or device of a yield well beyond the range of regular fission weapons and which derived a part of its force from the fusion of light elements. There is good reason to believe that they had begun to work on this weapon substantially before we did." *Ibid.,* XXX, April 12, 1954, 548.

clear that the Soviet Government now could produce explosions of practically limitless force, this ability did not of itself put it on an equality in nuclear warfare with the United States and the free world. As yet the U.S.S.R. had no stockpile of atomic or hydrogen weapons at all commensurate with those available to the United States; nor did it possess means of delivery in any way comparable to those of the United States Strategic Air Command with its worldwide chain of bases. To develop a respectable stockpile of hydrogen weapons and a fleet of long-range aircraft or missiles capable of delivering the weapons on American or other free world targets would presumably be the work of several years. Meanwhile the basic elements of the world military situation would remain, provisionally, what they had been before: a Communist superiority in ground strength and conventional weapons, balanced for the time being by an allied (principally American) superiority in nuclear weapons and strategic air power.

But this state of affairs, which had afforded reasonable protection to the key democratic countries throughout the postwar period, would henceforth be strictly temporary. Unavoidably, it seemed, the present military balance would soon be giving way to a different and much less comfortable balance, a kind of "balance of terror" in which not merely one side, but both sides would possess a nuclear capability sufficient to wreak wholesale destruction on the other in one swift, deadly operation. When that time came it would not make so much difference who had the larger stockpile, the bigger air force, or the greater industrial capacity to back it up. The decisive question might well be who would strike the first blow, since the first blow with nuclear weapons might quite possibly decide the outcome of the conflict. At the very least, it would almost certainly inflict heavier damage than either side had experienced in any previous war. And, if this reasoning was sound, there was no necessity for the Soviet Union to try to overtake the West in the atomic arms race. It needed only to develop a capability sufficient to strike one conclusive blow—to "saturate" or inflict intolerable damage upon a respectable number of vital enemy targets. With such a capability, it could either gamble on a quick victory or it could use the threat of nuclear devastation to paralyze the nuclear forces of the West, thus providing an opportunity for its superior conventional forces to advance into the critical areas of free Europe and Asia. And of its ability to attain such a capability there was no longer much room for doubt.

These unpleasing prospects happened to develop at a particularly critical moment in the evolution of United States policy, of the North Atlantic community, and of the relations between East and West. When the Soviet detonation occurred, the Eisenhower administration had been in office for almost seven months, the Malenkov government for five; the armistice in Korea was less than a month old. The first effervescence occasioned by the governmental changes in Washington and Moscow had subsided, but no new international pattern had clearly emerged. The treaty establishing the European Defense Community was still unratified, and the question of a possible four-power meeting to deal with the German and Austrian problems or with international tensions generally was still unresolved. Discussions looking to a Far Eastern political conference under the Korean armistice had scarcely begun. The basic reviews of United States policies in the military and economic fields were still in their earliest stages. Over all these undertakings, as indeed over the general tone and temper of public life throughout much of the world, the bad news from Moscow was to cast a shadow of deep uncertainty and uneasiness.

The earliest and perhaps the most authoritative assessment of the Soviet achievement would presumably be that of the new United States Joint Chiefs of Staff, who began work in August under the chairmanship of Admiral Arthur W. Radford. Their first duty, it had been said, would be to take a "new look" at the whole range of United States defense problems, as the administration had promised in presenting its defense estimates for the fiscal year now beginning.[4] According to Defense Secretary Charles E. Wilson, the new Joint Chiefs would review the entire military planning of the administration and "consider all aspects of defense—strategic plans, forces, missions, weapons, readiness levels,

[4] Cf. above, p. 83.

and mobilization reserves." Obviously, to do this they would have to consider also the international aspects of American defense, including the commitments and capabilities of the United States and its allies, the prospects for a strengthened ground defense of Western Europe aided by German divisions, and especially the implications of the latest Soviet military developments for all phases of allied defense planning.

If Russia's hydrogen blast thus found the United States at a critical turning point in its global military relationships, it caught the North Atlantic alliance at perhaps an even more significant moment. The NATO Council meeting in April[5] had sanctioned a "stretch-out" of the rearmament program but had left unresolved a number of other questions equally vital to the future of the Atlantic community. Among these unclarified issues were the prospects for E.D.C. and German rearmament, the relationship of E.D.C. to a possible settlement of the German question through negotiation with the Russians, and, most important of all, the future role of the United States itself in European and NATO affairs. The first months of the Eisenhower administration had been filled with verbal assurances of solidarity with Western Europe, mingled with expressions of impatience over the slow materialization of E.D.C. But except for the "defense stretch-out" decided upon at Paris—which was based mainly on decisions already taken by the governments concerned—there had as yet been few indications as to just how, and how far, the United States intended to share actively in the interests and concerns of its NATO allies. The "new look" and the Randall Commission studies on foreign economic policy would doubtless be helpful in estimating the trend of future American action. But meanwhile Europeans had grown as impatient over the apparent irresolution of the United States as the latter had become with their hesitations. The European mood was not improved by the revelation that the U.S.S.R., with whose government the United States had seemed so reluctant to seek negotiated settlements, could now make weapons capable of eliminating organized life in any country of Europe.

[5] Above, pp. 166-168.

The United States itself was clearly not unimpressed by the effects of this development on the world balance of power and, indeed, on the prospects for world civilization and human survival. Various new lines of action initiated by the administration testified to its genuine concern over the threat of nuclear extermination, as well as to an apparently continuing hope that the peril might still be exorcised by the adoption of some suitable political or military formula. Even in the matter of negotiations with the Communist states, Washington began to behave in a manner that seemed rather less implacable than when it had believed itself to hold a monopoly of thermonuclear weapons. The U.S.S.R., for its part, seemed rather less anxious to engage in serious negotiations than before, either because its self-confidence had been bolstered by the new discovery or, possibly, because of a sense of political insecurity related to the struggle for power within the Soviet leadership and to indications of popular unrest at home. By late 1953, however, both leading powers had so far modified their positions that prospects for an East-West diplomatic meeting of some sort looked much more real than they had appeared at any time during the spring. Before the end of the year a series of procedural concessions by both sides had paved the way for the meeting which eventually took place in Berlin early in 1954, thus initiating a dramatic new chain of events which would affect all parts of the world through 1954 and subsequently.

1. FUSION BOMB AND "NEW LOOK"

On the basis of knowledge available to the public, it would be quite impossible to present a detailed and accurate account of what has so often been called the "new look" at United States defense problems. One of the less wholesome aspects of military affairs in these early years of the atomic age was the degree to which significant information was withheld from ordinary citizens, congressmen, and even executive officials either because it might be of value to a potential enemy or because it could not be grasped without more specialized technical and scientific training than most Americans possessed. How far the prevailing ignorance on atomic matters, in particular, was unavoidable and how far it resulted merely from an excess of official caution or indifference, could not be accurately appraised in the existing state of public ignorance. What was clear was that national policies of decisive importance to every citizen were now being framed on the basis of military and scientific calculations over which the citizen had no control and which even his elected representatives had to accept largely on faith. Even the substance of policy was likely to be conveyed in the form of condensed slogans which sounded impressive in the abstract but whose application to real situations was not always easy to visualize.

About the best we can do with the "new look," therefore, is to try to analyze one or two of the authoritative statements made about it in the light of some of the problems that must have come under review by the new defense planners, and to search for some of the probable implications with respect to the general world position of the United States. After making due allowance for the complexities of the subject and the effects of unresolved differences of opinion within the government and the defense establishment, we shall find that the net effect of the entire process was to confirm and intensify that special emphasis in defense planning which had already been evident in the first defense budget of the new administration and to some extent even in those of its predecessor: the tendency, namely, to entrust the nation's physical safety primarily to the deterrent or retaliatory capabilities of strategic air power equipped with nuclear weapons, as the form of defense supposedly most efficacious as well as most economical under modern conditions. The end result, as approved on December 19 by the National Security Council and the President, was succinctly described by Secretary Dulles in a famous address on January 12, 1954. The objectives of American world policy, he explained, were to be sought henceforth "by placing more reliance on deterrent power and less dependence on local defensive power." Local defenses would remain important, but would be "reinforced by the further deterrent of massive retaliatory power." "The basic decision was to depend primarily upon a great capacity to retaliate, instantly, by means and at places of our choosing." Thus we should be able "to get, and share, more basic security at less cost." [6]

Hedged with qualifications though it was, the underlying significance of this shift of emphasis was clear enough. Since the last war, American defense policy had always rested on a combination of two separate types of military power, both equally directed, in the last analysis, at deterring or repelling any armed attack by the Soviet Union and/or its Communist allies. One was the application of local military power, in conjunction with allied and friendly governments, in areas directly threatened by Communist attack; the other was the air-atomic weapon, which was held in reserve and presumably would be used only if the Communist powers were rash enough to precipitate direct hostilities. Up to 1953, the principal emphasis had been on local military power applied in key areas under NATO and similar arrangements; air-atomic power was the ultimate deterrent which was relied on to keep Communist aggressiveness within bounds, but was considered by this country and its allies as too formidable a weapon to be invoked except in the last extremity. But under the "new look,"apparently, this emphasis was to be reversed. The United States would depend "primarily" upon its air-atomic or retaliatory power; local defense forces would be relegated to second place, and would be relied upon mainly in special situations where our retaliatory power might not be fully effective. By placing primary reliance on "national airpower" and keeping it "superior to that of any other nation in the world," [7] it was hoped not only to deter aggression but also to reduce the military budget and the number of men under arms.

The most striking feature of this "new look" program was the fact that it was *not* a reply to Soviet possession of the hydrogen bomb or, indeed, to any other aspect of the international military situation. Its sponsors repeatedly pointed out that its whole inspiration was economic rather than military in character. Its starting point, Admiral Radford himself explained, had been the President's April directive

[6] Address to the Council on Foreign Relations, January 12, in *Documents on American Foreign Relations, 1954,* 9-10.
[7] Address by Admiral Radford, December 14, *ibid., 1953,* 66.

to base defense planning on the "long pull" rather than the "year-of-crisis" concept, thus ensuring that the nation would be kept strong economically as well as militarily.[8] For the "long pull," air-atomic power was considered more economical than any other form of national military power.

But there was also another factor, less explicitly identified but perhaps not less compelling than concern for the national finances. This was the strong and widespread desire to limit the use of American manpower for defense purposes. President Eisenhower himself voiced the national feeling in this respect in the course of a discussion of the "new look" philosophy early in 1954:

> "I hear people say 'bigger Army.' Now, our most valued, our most costly asset, is our young men. Let's don't use them any more than we have to." [9]

From a political and emotional standpoint, much of the appeal of the "new look" undoubtedly lay in its implied promise of lessened demands on the individual citizen both as a taxpayer and as a potential combatant.

The official contention that economic factors necessitated a reorientation of the defense program was not fully supported by independent studies of national defense economics. An important analysis released in October by the National Planning Association [10] put forward the conclusion that the current rate of defense spending was not only well within the capacity of the American economy but could actually be increased by 30 to 40 percent without excessive economic strain. According to this study, an annual expenditure of $70 billion to $75 billion on "major national security programs" (compared with a current expenditure of around $53 billion) would require neither wartime controls, substantial tax increases, nor major deficit financing. The precise figure, the report's sponsors asserted, should be fixed "on the basis of clear military and political strategic needs in the light of the international situation; and not on the basis of assumed economic limits that are not present." These con-

[8] *Ibid.*, 63-64; cf. above, pp. 81-82.

[9] Press conference statement, March 17, in *New York Times*, March 18, 1954.

[10] Gerhard Colm, *Can We Afford Additional Programs for National Security?* (New York, National Planning Association, 1953, 70 p.)

clusions, however, were claimed to be valid only under one essential condition:

"Any such programs, however, could be executed only if the people were convinced that the effort was needed for the survival of the nation and if they fully accept the consequences."

In 1953 that condition did not exist, either before or after Mr. Malenkov's announcement. Consequently, the military authorities were informed that they would have to get along with less money. Their answer was that if existing United States military commitments were to be maintained (or even increased, as seemed to be the case in the Far East) they had no choice but to base their planning on the fullest exploitation of the nation's air-atomic capability.

Implications of the "New Look"

How did a program avowedly inspired by the desire to economize the nation's material and human resources fit into a world situation dominated by a rivalry of great powers in which the most devastating weapons were or soon would be available to the leading contenders on both sides? To attempt a systematic answer would be to anticipate discussions which did not get fairly under way in this country until some of the implications of the "new look" strategy had been more fully brought as the result of Secretary Dulles' address of January 12, 1954. In the meantime certain tentative considerations suggested themselves in the light of disclosures which were being made from time to time throughout the autumn by sources close to the Pentagon Building. How sharply the conclusions were to be drawn in this field of unknown quantities depended on how seriously the United States intended to stake its future on the single card of its air-atomic power and how far the "new look" doctrine as made known to the public represented either a passing phase or a necessary oversimplification.

The obvious merit of the "new" strategy lay, of course, in its frank acceptance of the fact that air-atomic power was one department of military strength in which the United States had already attained a high level of preparedness and in which its capabilities seemed likely to go on increasing more or less indefinitely. This was undoubtedly a field in which American resources and industrial and scientific prowess conferred special advantages. This country's lead in the development of atomic weapons and in the capacity to deliver them had all along been a decisive element—very possibly *the* decisive element—in the postwar security of the United States and the free world. With its growing stockpile of nuclear weapons, its expanding Air Force and Naval aviation, its numerous bases in North America, Greenland, Great Britain, the Mediterranean, the Middle East, and the Pacific, there was little doubt of its ability to inflict the heaviest kind of punishment on any aggressor country. As this capability continued to grow, it might well deter the most cynical Communist from thoughts of aggression. How could world peace be better secured than by concentrating in the hands of a peace-loving nation like the United States the capacity to inflict inconceivable damage on any aggressor?

Yet there were from the first certain obvious limitations on the sufficiency of this method for protecting United States interests. Five or six years before, the United States had already possessed what for that time was a great capacity for atomic retaliation. Yet this capability had not prevented China from going Communist; it had not prevented the Communist aggression in Korea; nor had the nuclear weapons then available been found useful in prosecuting the Korean war, despite the urgency with which certain congressmen had pressed their use on the Defense Department. On the other hand, the United States had found itself seriously underequipped in many departments of conventional strength and had felt compelled to embark on a major over-all expansion of its armed forces which was only now being completed.

Perhaps Korea was a special case, of a kind that would not recur because the United States now possessed better nuclear weapons and felt fewer inhibitions about using them. Some such line of thought had certainly been implicit in Secretary Dulles' warnings to the Chinese Communists since the Korean armistice.[11] Nevertheless, the Korean experience suggested that there were situations in which atomic retaliation

[11] Cf. above, pp. 247-248.

as such was not the most useful form of military counteraction. It was difficult to be sure that there might not be other "little wars" on the Korean model which would have to be fought, if at all, by more conventional methods. Our military task, as Admiral Radford himself pointed out, was complicated by the fact that two distinct requirements were imposed on us: "We must be ready for tremendous, vast retaliatory and counteroffensive blows in event of a global war, and we must also be ready for lesser military actions short of all-out war." [12] But if it was still necessary to contemplate the possibility of these lesser military actions, we should clearly be imprudent if we were to rely on air-atomic power to the extent of unduly weakening ourselves in other lines.

The suggestion was occasionally heard that the United States could undertake to deal with any local aggression of this kind by threatening to retaliate against the country supporting it. To quote Mr. Dulles again, aggression by the Chinese Communist army in Indochina "could not occur without grave consequences which might not be confined to Indochina." [13] The difficulty was that aggression might easily occur in such places as Indochina *without* the direct participation of Communist China or any other Communist power. We have already seen what perplexity was occasioned by the Vietminh invasion of Laos in the spring of 1953.[14] Suppose that invasion were repeated; it would be a clear case of aggression, yet against whom or what was the United States to retaliate? Against Ho Chi Minh's jungle hideout, or against Peking or Moscow? Americans could not be sure just what effect atomic or hydrogen bombardment would produce on the sprawling economy of a country like China or the U.S.S.R., but they did know that an atomic or hydrogen bomb dropped over a thickly populated area would kill a very great number of their fellow creatures. Presumably they would not want this to happen every time there was some local aggression carried out on a minor scale at the instigation of persons unknown. But just where was the line to

[12] Address of December 14, in *Documents on American Foreign Relations, 1953*, 63-64.
[13] Speech of September 2, cited above, p. 248.
[14] Cf. above, pp. 66, 212.

be drawn? Was there not a danger that the Communists would exploit our humane feelings by stimulating one or perhaps a whole series of local aggressions, "brush fires," or "little Koreas," too inconsequential to be dealt with by massive retaliation, yet too serious to be effectively dealt with either by local forces or by our own reduced regular military establishment?

A far more potent limitation, moreover, would presently affect our ability to use the air-atomic weapon if indeed it was not already doing so. This was the nuclear capability of the Soviet Union itself, recently enhanced by the development of a hydrogen bomb and, presumably, by parallel advances in the design of long-range aircraft and guided missiles. No doubt the U.S.S.R. lagged far behind the United States in its over-all air-atomic capability. But the significant point was that even if it did lag behind it would still be in a position before long to inflict grave damage on the United States or any other country in the northern hemisphere. And, to quote the retiring chairman of the Atomic Energy Commission (Gordon R. Dean): "It does us no good to reach the point where we would be able to wipe out an enemy twenty times over if he reaches the point where he can wipe us out just once." [15]

If there was to be war with the Soviet Union, would we be the first to strike, and to strike with such devastating effect as to eliminate the possibility of Soviet attack on us? It seemed unlikely; yet, if not, the Soviet nuclear potential would tend to neutralize ours and in effect deprive us of the advantages we had promised ourselves from it. We might find ourselves unable to use our superior air-atomic power, not necessarily because of any moral scruples but simply because to do so would invite the enemy to use his own inferior but still formidable power against us or our allies. A war fought by two countries, or two coalitions, with

[15] *New York Times*, June 26, 1953; cf. the statement of Admiral Lewis L. Strauss, Mr. Dean's successor (*ibid.*, August 22, 1953): "It is idle to assume that it is beyond the capabilities of our potential enemies to develop atomic weapons with a tremendously destructive capacity. . . . It is also a fallacy to assume that a stockpile of atomic weapons in our hands is in itself any longer a complete deterrent to aggressive action." See also the President's statement of December 8, quoted below, p. 431.

nuclear weapons would entail a prospect of destruction which might be judged out of proportion to any advantage either side might hope to gain from it.[16] In that case both sides might hesitate to resort to nuclear bombardment. A kind of "atomic stalemate" would develop in which the atomic armories of the two sides would cancel each other out and the emphasis would shift back to conventional forces as the primary element of usable military strength. Where would this leave the United States if we had meanwhile made the mistake of overdeveloping our atomic capability at the expense of our conventional strength?

These were some of the thoughts that inevitably presented themselves when one tried to examine critically the little that was publicly known in this complex and highly secret field. There were, of course innumerable qualifications and distinctions to be borne in mind: the differing potentialities of tactical and strategic atomic weapons; the possibility that one side or both would tend to exploit the bomb as a means of political pressure rather than as a military weapon; the comparative importance of different types of weapons and forces in long and short wars; the possibility of some new and better defense against nuclear attack; the prospects for perfection of pilotless bombers and missiles which might break through any defense. Yet none of these considerations seemed to overcome the disparity between the apparent trend of the international military situation and the apparent trend of United States defense policy. The Soviet hydrogen bomb, presumably the major military development of 1953, was the one which had left the least perceptible imprint on the "new look" strategy. Ostensibly that strategy was designed for the "long pull," not merely for the few years during which the United States was expected to retain its present nuclear advantage. Yet it seemed to make no explicit allowance for the probability that this advantage might be doomed to early disappearance. Followed to its logical

16 "We may anticipate a state of affairs in which two Great Powers will each be in a position to put an end to the civilization and life of the other, though not without risking its own. We may be likened to two scorpions in a bottle, each capable of killing the other, but only at the risk of his own life." J. Robert Oppenheimer, "Atomic Weapons and American Policy," *Foreign Affairs,* XXXI, July 1953, 529.

conclusion, it seemed, the "new look" might leave the United States with a great capacity to fight an offensive war with nuclear weapons, and an insufficient capacity to fight any other war with which circumstances and our enemies might confront us.

Practical Beginnings

Probably, however, the "new look" would not be followed out to what seemed at the moment its logical conclusions. Admiral Radford, in his authoritative exposition of the program, emphasized that the initial phase was considered to extend only to mid-1957 and that the Joint Chiefs of Staff had

"no preconceived ideas as to what our Armed Forces will look like a decade from now. . . . Improved guided missiles, atomic-powered ships and aircraft, an enlarged family of weapons, and new applications of electronics, all will have their effects and will be reflected in the evolution of our combat units."

For the present, he said, the Joint Chiefs had proposed a program which was designed to meet a variety of objectives —to "provide for the security of the United States; . . . deter aggression in consonance with the concept of collective security with our Allies in Europe and the Far East; and . . . provide the basis for winning a war—an all-out war or a limited war—if war is forced upon us." It was agreed, he said, "that our plans and programs cannot be developed by the United States for ourselves alone" but "must be worked out in cooperation with our Allies, with full recognition of their problems." If this was true, it might mean a considerably diminished emphasis on retaliatory power, which Europeans in particular considered a highly unsatisfactory solution of *their* problems, in favor of old-fashioned area defense.

Finally, Admiral Radford gave an indication that the United States' own defenses against nuclear attack might be given more adequate consideration than they had received in the past: "We want to see continental defense programming continue on an orderly basis, with phased increases in forces and facilities, to improve our defenses against bombing attack." [17] He thus appeared to take a middle position in one of the year's bitterest controversies, in which the pleas of atomic scientists and others for greatly expanded continental and civil defense efforts had been sharply resisted by partisans of the strategic offensive as well as by advocates of governmental economy.

For the next fiscal year, at any rate, economic considerations would definitely dominate the defense budget and result in an appreciably lower level of defensive expenditure —perhaps around $44.8 billion in 1954–55 as compared with something like $48.7 billion in 1953–54. The Air Force and related activities, however, would receive a larger than usual share of this reduced "cake," in line with the new emphasis on "the creation, maintenance, and full exploitation of modern air power." [18]

The personnel strength of the armed forces was also to be reduced. In December it became known that Defense Secretary Wilson, overriding protests which centered in the Army and its new Chief of Staff, General Ridgway, had ordered the three services to reduce their manpower by about 10 percent over the next eighteen months, bringing down the total numbers in uniform from about 3,500,000 to 3,100,000. The cuts would not be strictly proportionate, since the Air Force was due to add men while the Army, Navy, and Marines lost them.[19] In the following fiscal year it was hoped to reduce the total number in uniform well below the three-million level.

Whether or not this reduction in the active forces would be compensated by an expansion of the Reserves, as recommended by the distinguished private citizens who made up the National Security Training Commission,[20] had not yet been decided; nor was it apparent as yet how far, if at all, the need for ground forces might be reduced by the availability of the new atomic canon and other "tactical" atomic weapons. Some said the new weapons would require fewer

[17] Address of December 14, in *Documents on American Foreign Relations, 1953,* 63-66. Cf. below, p. 419.

[18] Budget message of the President for the fiscal year 1955, in *New York Times,* January 22, 1954.

[19] *Ibid.,* December 10, 1953.

[20] *Ibid.,* December 15, 1953.

men, others said more. Already, however, the administration was preparing to proceed with that "disengagement" from "overextended military commitments" which had all along been one of its prime objectives. Contrary to widespread rumors,[21] this process was initiated not in Europe but in the Far East—in the very country, in fact, with which the United States had just concluded a new mutual security treaty. On December 26 President Eisenhower announced that two United States Army divisions were soon to be withdrawn from Korea as part of a broad program of reduction of American ground strength, made possible by the increased capabilities of the Republic of Korea forces and the fact that "our growing national air power possesses greater mobility and greater striking force than ever before." [22]

The H-Bomb and World Policy

In one sense, even the best-conceived national defense program was bound to remain highly unsatisfactory now that man's destructive powers had so far outrun any foreseeable possibilities of defensive counter-action. The state of affairs crystallized by Mr. Malenkov's announcement lent added weight to what President Truman had pointed out in January: that war today was "a very different thing from what it used to be" and in fact "might dig the grave not only of our Stalinist opponents, but of our own society." [23]

President Eisenhower, too, now began to refer more frequently to a problem which many experts felt was still dangerously underestimated by the public. "We know," he said in an address on October 6, "that our former unique physical security has almost totally disappeared before the long-range bomber and the destructive power of a single bomb. . . . In its wake we see only sudden and mass destruction, erasure of cities, the possible doom of every nation and society." Two days later, in an official statement, he confirmed reports that the Soviets possessed "a stockpile of atomic weapons of conventional types" and that the August 12 explosion, involving thermonuclear reaction, "was produced by

[21] Cf. below, pp. 370-371.
[22] *Department of State Bulletin,* XXX, January 4, 1954, 14.
[23] Above, p. 13.

a weapon, or the forerunner of a weapon, of power far in excess of the conventional types." "We therefore conclude," he said, "that the Soviets now have the capability of attack on us, and such capability will increase with the passage of time." [24] Concerning possible plans for dealing with this situation, the President said only that our own atomic strength was "large and increasing steadily." But, he said, "It is my hope, my earnest prayer, that this country will never again be engaged in war." And he referred to the advances being made in the development of peacetime atomic power "and the other benign uses of atomic energy" as evidence of the "constructive goals" we had set for ourselves.

Here, perhaps, was suggested the most promising line of endeavor that was open to the United States in the circumstances. With the advent of nuclear and then thermonuclear power, war had reached a degree of destructiveness that virtually nullified its utility as an instrument of policy in the old sense. The very idea of "national defense" seemed rather out of date in a world where a single bomb might inflict casualties comparable to those of any previous war. The only rational policy, the President seemed to feel, was to try to create conditions in which wars would not have to be fought. The "new look," in so far as its fundamental aim was to deter potential aggressors, was one effort aimed in this general direction; but there were others that might conceivably prove not less effective. One such was the quest for international disarmament through the United Nations, still blocked at the moment by the U.S.S.R.'s adherence to positions adopted in the Stalin era, but perhaps still capable of being reinvigorated—though the decision of the United States to increase its own reliance on atomic weapons would not make it easier to join in outlawing such weapons by international agreement. Another possibly constructive line of action was the attempt to eliminate specific international differences which might lead to war in Europe or the Far East. A third was the familiar endeavor to maintain and develop the over-all strength of the non-Communist world, as an essential accompaniment to any measures aimed

[24] Text of address and statement from *Department of State Bulletin,* XXIX, October 19, 1953, 507-508.

at direct restraint of the Communist powers. A fourth concerned the peaceful uses of atomic energy and the possibilities of an international partnership for atomic development such as the President was later to propose to the United Nations.[25] In none of these matters could we count on such a degree of success as to obviate the dangers inherent in the international military trend. Yet none of them could be safely neglected by a nation which still hoped to avoid inflicting or suffering thermonuclear retribution.

2. THE EUROPEAN IMPACT

As Russia's discovery of the hydrogen bomb revolutionized the long-term defense problems of the United States, it likewise ushered in a critical phase in the life of Western Europe and in the relations between Western Europe and the United States. The European members of NATO, lying some thousands of miles closer to Soviet-controlled territory than their transatlantic allies, had even more reason than the latter for misgivings over the trend toward greater and greater reliance on bigger and bigger nuclear weapons. Consciousness of their direct exposure to atomic attack was one of the reasons why Europeans so frequently behaved in a manner that Americans, with their less developed sense of peril, found hard to understand. It very largely accounted for their emotional revulsion against anything that suggested atomic warfare; their eagerness to explore every possible avenue for reducing international tension and promoting East-West settlement; their dislike of such venturesome American moves as those connected with the "rollback" or "liberation" policy and the "unleashing" of Chiang Kai-shek; the susceptibility of some of them to manipulation by the Communist "peace" movement, with its versatile propaganda directed against the atomic policies of the United States and the Atlantic alliance.

Every indication that the United States was placing increased dependence on atomic weapons was a source of widespread distress and dismay in Europe. To Europeans it seemed that this tendency not only made atomic war more

[25] Cf. below, pp. 428-433.

difficult to avoid but also reduced their protection against direct invasion by Communist armies. They were well aware of the antithesis in American thinking between local defense and the concept of a mobile striking force consisting primarily of atomic bombers. The greater the emphasis on the mobile striking force, it seemed to them, the less there would probably be on local ground defense. As applied to Europe, this could easily mean reduction or removal of the six American divisions on the Continent and retreat to some kind of "peripheral" defense plan based on Great Britain, Spain and Portugal, and perhaps Greece and Turkey. From such positions the United States might, of course, return one day to "liberate" those parts of Europe which had meanwhile fallen under Soviet occupation; but no European could forget the image conjured up by France's Premier Henri Queuille in 1949: "You would be liberating a corpse."

Although the tendencies inherent in the "new look" were thus bound to cause concern in Europe, the effects were perhaps more speedily visible in the political than in the strictly military realm. In military matters, NATO's European command under General Gruenther was still working along on the basis of decisions reached at the April Council meeting [26] and still awaiting the ratification of the E.D.C. treaty and the beginning of German rearmament. General Gruenther—who felt that NATO was not strong enough to prevent the Russians from overrunning Europe, but that it could at least compel them to bring in reinforcements from the U.S.S.R. before attacking with reasonable certainty of success—was going out of his way to insist that the hydrogen bomb was no reason for neglecting the defense of Europe along conventional lines.[27] For the moment the chief interest in NATO revolved not around the hydrogen bomb but around the question of tactical atomic weapons and their possible usefulness in compensating for Soviet superiority in manpower. There had been signs of late that Congress might be asked at its next session to amend the Atomic Energy Act of 1946

[26] Above, pp. 166-168.

[27] Address of October 8, in *Department of State Bulletin,* XXIX, November 9, 1953, 633-637.

so that our allies could be provided with sufficient data in this field to enable them to plan more realistically.

The Outlook for E.D.C.

If strategic planning under NATO seemed relatively little affected by the latest developments, the same cannot be said concerning the prospects for bringing the European Defense Community into being. It is true that the hydrogen bomb and the "new look" brought no relaxation in the pressure on behalf of E.D.C. on the part of the United States and Great Britain, which did not themselves intend to participate; but they did almost certainly contribute to the growing emotional resistance on the part of certain prospective participating countries, especially France. This resistance did not arise primarily from reasoned doubts about the military value of E.D.C. in the hydrogen bomb age. It arose, rather, from a growing disinclination to follow the lead of the United States at a time when this country seemed increasingly bent on adopting courses unrelated or even antithetic to the interests of its European allies.

With the victory of Chancellor Adenauer and his pro-E.D.C. coalition on September 6,[28] France had once more emerged as the most doubtful factor in the entire European situation, the country whose action might spell success or failure for the whole project of European consolidation.[29] Awareness of this decisive role did not, however, incline French political circles to be overhasty in acting on the fifteen-month-old E.D.C. treaty. As Germany grew stronger, the prospect of intimate association with that country grew less and less attractive. Each hint of a conciliatory tendency in Moscow was eagerly examined, while each sign of impatience in Washington seemed to produce the opposite of the desired effect. France, said Foreign Minister Bidault on October 29, would accept certain limitations of its sovereignty but would do so by its own sovereign decision and not under pressure from a foreign government.

[28] Above, pp. 199-201.

[29] Of the six countries concerned, only Western Germany completed action on the E.D.C. treaty in 1953. The treaty was approved by the Dutch Second Chamber on July 23 and by the Belgian Chamber of Deputies on November 26.

Of the three broad conditions laid down by Premier Mayer in January as a preliminary to ratification of E.D.C., the first, the revision or "clarification" of the treaty by new protocols, had been substantially fulfilled.[30] The second, a closer association with Great Britain, was on the way to realization in the form of a special protocol or treaty by which the United Kingdom would undertake not to withdraw its troops from the Continent without first consulting the E.D.C. members.[31] The third, a definitive understanding with Germany concerning the European status of the Saar, might also be within reach now that the Adenauer government had renewed its popular mandate and was showing eagerness to resume negotiations. Still another impediment to French action had meanwhile been removed by the agreement of the United States to shoulder a larger part of the financial burden of the Indochina war.[32] Yet with the near-fulfillment of their original conditions, those Frenchmen who opposed the treaty seemed only concerned to find new pretexts for delaying action. On September 20 the Radical Socialists, a party which included both advocates and opponents of E.D.C., laid down a whole new set of conditions for ratification, among them the stipulation that the new unified European army must be democratically controlled by a new supranational organization.[33]

As always, signs of hesitation in France called forth expressions of impatience abroad which, instead of spurring the French to action, seemed only to redouble their obstinate caution. Sir Winston Churchill exploded on October 10 in a speech to the Conservative party conference at Margate. Germany, he said, would have to be rearmed, with or without E.D.C.:

[30] Above, p. 160.

[31] *New York Times,* September 17, 1953. This was the basis of the "Association Agreement" between the U.K. and the six E.D.C. powers which was signed April 13, 1954, and is printed in *Documents on American Foreign Relations, 1954.*

[32] Above, p. 275.

[33] This condition had particular reference to the efforts of the six governments to draft a basis for a European Political Community as envisaged by the E.D.C. treaty. (Cf. above, p. 162.) These efforts were carried forward at meetings of Deputy Foreign Ministers in Rome (September 22–October 9) and of Foreign Ministers in The Hague (November 26-28); see their communiqués in *Documents on American Foreign Relations, 1953,* 208-210.

"If E.D.C. should not be adopted by the French, we shall have no choice in prudence but to fall in with some new arrangement which will join the strength of Germany to the western allies through some rearrangement of the forces of N.A.T.O." [34]

Chancellor Adenauer, reviewing the world situation before the new Bundestag on October 20, was carefully conciliatory in all his references to France. But, he said, the German people, who had given such an unqualified endorsement to the principle of European integration,

"would be filled with profound disappointment if the entry into force of the whole set of treaties—which includes the Bonn Conventions—were to be ever further delayed. After having done everything to pave the way for ratification, they would not understand it if they were not at last to enjoy the status of independence. I hope that abroad this state of mind of the German people will be appreciated and taken into account." [35]

France and the "New Look"

These carefully pondered statements received less attention in France—and in Europe generally—than an apparently unrehearsed remark of Defense Secretary Wilson in a Washington press conference on October 19. Reports concerning the "new look," especially its tendencies toward economy and increased reliance on air-atomic power, had already caused some apprehension in Europe that the United States was veering away from its continental military commitments toward a policy of peripheral defense. This impression was greatly strengthened when Secretary Wilson revealed that he, at least, was seriously considering the possibility of reducing United States troop commitments abroad and implied that the availability of new weapons might lessen the need to station American troops overseas in future. The important thing about NATO, he said, was not that the United States should maintain "x" number of divisions in Europe, but that everyone should be aware of our determination to protect the free world and to be in any fight from the beginning.[36] To Europeans, habituated as they were to exaggerate

[34] *Chronology of International Events and Documents,* IX, No. 20, October 8-21, 1953, 643.
[35] *Documents on American Foreign Relations, 1953,* 273.
[36] *New York Times,* October 20, 1953.

the significance of casual utterances across the Atlantic, this sounded like a confirmation of the numerous press reports which had indicated that the net effect of the "new look" would be to leave Europe to defend itself without direct assistance while the United States withdrew its troops and fell back on its air-atomic capability.

To counteract the resulting wave of consternation, Secretary Dulles went out of his way to deny "the spate of rumors to the effect that we are contemplating a withdrawal of our troops." [37] President Eisenhower himself declared that there was "no plan for reduction of any combat forces of the United States anywhere," and drew attention to the growing role of the nation's overseas air bases.[38] General Ridgway redoubled his efforts to disabuse public opinion at home of the notion that tactical atomic weapons could take the place of ground troops.

So far as France was concerned, however, the effect had already been produced; and it was kept alive by continuing unofficial discussion in the United States of possible troop withdrawals within a couple of years—perhaps before the 1956 elections.[39] On October 30 the Council of the Republic asked the French Government to seek further guarantees before accepting the European army, and on November 24, in a general foreign affairs debate in the Assembly, Prime Minister Laniel said that both Great Britain and the United States would be asked for assurance that their forces would remain on the Continent during E.D.C.'s first years. In addition, he reiterated his former stipulations that the Assembly would not be asked to ratify the treaty until the question of the Saar, the additional protocols, and the agreement with Great Britain had been satisfactorily disposed of.

M. Laniel was about to depart with M. Bidault for the long-delayed meeting with President Eisenhower and Prime Minister Churchill, which was scheduled to take place in Bermuda at the beginning of December.[40] Before he left, on November 27, the National Assembly voted its confidence

[37] Statement of October 27, in *Department of State Bulletin*, XXX, November 9, 1953, 632; see also *New York Times*, October 21, 1953.

[38] Press conference statement, October 28, *ibid.*, October 29, 1953.

[39] Cf. *Le Monde*, Paris, November 5, 1953.

[40] Cf. below, pp. 428-433.

in the government's foreign policy by 275 to 244. This victory would have been more impressive if it had not been made possible by the abstention of eighty-five ex-Gaullists who had expressly dissociated themselves from support of the E.D.C. concept.

Crisis in Southeastern Europe

Although it was France's hesitation to ratify E.D.C. that gained the largest headlines, Italy, too, had emerged as a potential stumbling block to the E.D.C. project. As we have already noted, there was a tendency on the part of Italian statesmen to make ratification of E.D.C. dependent on a satisfactory settlement of the Trieste question, a matter which in Italian eyes loomed considerably larger in significance than E.D.C. itself.[41] This tendency was in no way diminished by the critical situation which arose in October as the result of an Anglo-American attempt to cut the Gordian knot of Trieste and hand over the Italian-speaking parts of the Free Territory (Zone A) to Italy while awarding the remainder (Zone B) to Yugoslavia.

This plan, sound in substance but almost disastrous in execution, originated in the "great concern" with which both Washington and London had viewed the deteriorating relations between Italy and Yugoslavia. The various proposals for a settlement of the Trieste issue which had been put forward by the two claimants having been "reciprocally rejected," Great Britain and the United States declared that they saw "no alternative but to bring the present unsatisfactory situation to an end." Being unprepared, they said, to continue their responsibility for administering Zone A, they announced on October 8 that they had decided "to terminate the Allied Military Government, to withdraw their troops, and having in mind the predominantly Italian character of Zone A to relinquish the administration of that Zone to the Italian Government." Yugoslavia already exercised full administrative control of Zone B; thus the two governments expected, they said, that the step they were taking would "lead to a final peaceful solution," "contribute to stabilization of a situation which has disturbed Italo-Yugo-

[41] Cf. above, pp. 206-207.

slav relations during recent years," and "provide the basis for friendly and fruitful cooperation between Italy and Yugoslavia, which is as important to the security of Western Europe as it is to the interests of the two countries concerned." [42]

The only serious defect of this plan, whose essential principles did not differ greatly from those of the settlement eventually reached a year later,[43] was the fact that it was disclosed without the agreement or apparently even the knowledge of the Yugoslav Government. Tito was undisguisedly furious; so were a great many other Yugoslavs whose patriotic atachment to Trieste was independent of their sentiments toward their own government. Anti-British and anti-American demonstrations broke out in Belgrade on a scale unknown in recent years. If Italy moved troops into Zone A to replace the Anglo-Americans, said Tito, Yugoslavia would consider it an act of aggression. To make the situation even more embarrassing, the U.S.S.R. undertook to try to bring the matter before the Security Council as a "threat to the peace"—a move which was warded off on October 20 by nine votes to one, though not before Mr. Vyshinksy had threatened that Moscow would never countenance a solution in Trieste that was reached without its participation.[44]

The Foreign Ministers of the Big Three had scheduled one of their periodic meetings in London on October 16-18. Taken by surprise, they added the Trieste situation to a prickly agenda which also included the U.S.S.R., Germany, Austria, Korea, Indochina, and the Qibiya massacre in Palestine.[45] Back in Washington two days later, Secretary Dulles said that no formal proposal had yet been made, but that it was believed that a conference of the Big Three with Italy and Yugoslavia "could be a useful step in putting the Trieste matter into its proper perspective." By putting it into its

[42] Anglo-American announcement, October 8, in *Documents on American Foreign Relations, 1953,* 282-283. For details cf. "La Question de Trieste," *Chronique de politique étrangère,* VII, May 1954, 303-312.

[43] Italian-Yugoslav agreement, October 5, 1954, in *Documents on American Foreign Relations, 1954,* 191-195.

[44] U.S. statements made in the Security Council on October 15 and 20 appear in *Department of State Bulletin,* XXIX, November 2, 1953, 609-610.

[45] Tripartite communiqué, October 18, in *Documents on American Foreign Relations, 1953,* 215-216.

proper perspective, he said, he meant subordinating it to "the development of a sound strategic plan for the defense of South Europe." [46]

But Tito declared that he would attend such a meeting only if the Western powers withdrew their declaration of October 8; while Italy, on the contrary, insisted that it would attend only on the basis of the October 8 declaration. The task of Solomon, commented the London *Economist* on October 23, "was child's play compared with that confronting the Allies in Trieste." Italian nationalist riots in Trieste city, which killed several persons and injured hundreds during the first week of November, supported this opinion. But once again the tension presently slackened off when it became clear that no move would be made by any party to change the existing situation. Before December closed there had been a reciprocal withdrawal of troops from the Italo-Yugoslav frontier and both governments had consented to meet with the Big Three. It was still uncertain whether a basis for agreement could be found, however; and meanwhile Britain and the United States were forced to continue their occupation of Zone A, the defense of southeastern Europe remained as fragmentary as before, and Italy's position added one more note of uncertainty to the future of that most elusive of political creations, the European Defense Community.

To some Americans, these setbacks in the southeastern European area might seem compensated by their government's simultaneous success in negotiating an agreement with Greece which provided for the development and joint use of certain airfields and naval facilities in accordance with "approved NATO plans." The general form and purport of this agreement, signed in Athens on October 12,[47] was comparable to that of the United States-Spanish defense agreement of September 26. It added another link to the chain of United States bases which were or soon would be available to this country to implement the deterrent-retaliatory

[46] Statement of October 20, in *Department of State Bulletin,* XXIX, November 2, 1953, 589.

[47] Text *ibid.,* December 21, 1953, 863-864; on the U.S.-Spanish agreement, cf. above, p. 208

strategy of the "new look." How far such facilities could substitute for solid understanding among the peoples of Europe, and between Europe and the United States, depended on how far the "new look" strategy offered a valid alternative to the development of a stronger and more self-confident Atlantic community.

Psychological and Economic Frictions

In any survey of general conditions in the Atlantic community during the second half of 1953, it must be admitted that the over-all political or psychological relationship between the United States and its allies left a great deal to be desired. Even General Gruenther spoke cautiously during this period of a "slight increase" in anti-American sentiment in Europe, adding that it was "not significant" but that he did find "an increasing concern whether or not we Americans as a people have the necessary maturity to lead the world through this critical struggle." [48]

Adlai Stevenson, whose range of observation was not limited by official position, drew a considerably sharper picture in the nonpartisan address which he delivered about the same time on his return from a six months' trip around the world:

"There is uncertainty abroad about America and our objective. . . . Many think we are intemperate, inflexible and frightened. . . .

"Also, like ourselves, proud nations resent any real or suspected interference in their domestic affairs. Nor can they reconcile our exhortations about the peril with deep cuts in our defense budget. And everywhere people think they recognize the dominant mood of America in what is called 'McCarthyism,' now a world-wide word. Inquisitions, purges, book-burning, repression and fear have obscured the bright vision of the land of the free and the home of the brave.

". . . There is an uneasy feeling that the U.S. is showing signs of economic nationalism, of a drift towards no trade and no aid. . . .

". . . There is anxiety lest the shaping of our policy may be slipping from the respected hands of President Eisenhower into

[48] Address of October 8, in *Department of State Bulletin,* XXIX, November 9, 1953, 636.

the hands of men less concerned with strengthening our alliances abroad than with appeasing our isolationists at home." [49]

Two elements, in particular, were common to almost every European criticism of the United States: dissatisfaction with this country's posture in the "cold war," which will be considered more specifically in the following section, and discontent with its attitude in economic matters, which requires an additional word of comment here. As we have already observed, the United States could not be reproached in 1953 with following any very distinct policy in international economic affairs, since all major decisions in this field had been put off until the Randall Commission completed its studies. But we have also noted that this postponement of major policy decisions, in conjunction with a declining foreign aid program and a general tendency toward political and economic "disengagement," tended in itself to aggravate the dilemma of free world countries which needed to buy from the United States but, to do so, had also to sell to this country.[50] As 1953 went on, the evidence of a congressional revulsion against foreign economic aid grew stronger; by November, Foreign Operations Director Stassen was constrained to promise a substantial reduction in military aid and the elimination, with certain exceptions, of economic aid to Europe during the next fiscal year.[51] Meanwhile there were no compensating signs of the lowering of United States trade barriers. What did become evident were the first indications of that economic "downturn," "recession," or "rolling readjustment" in the United States which was to occasion a noticeable decline in economic activity, including imports, during the winter of 1953–1954.

Interestingly enough, Western European economies were not nearly so much affected by this development as had seemed probable in the light of earlier experiences such as the United States recession of early 1949. Despite a marked falling off in this country's demand for imports, the fears of

[49] Chicago address, September 15, in *Documents on American Foreign Relations, 1953,* 120-127.

[50] Cf. above, pp. 94-96.

[51] *New York Times,* November 26, 1953. The exceptions named were Spain, Greece, Turkey, and France (for Indochina).

balance-of-payments difficulties and deflationary pressures in world markets proved unfounded for the most part. General international trade continued to expand, and European countries made some progress toward recapturing their prewar share of world markets. European industrial production remained on the upgrade; exports to nondollar countries increased all through 1953, and those to the United States remained high until near the end of the year. Thus most European countries actually were able to increase their gold and dollar reserves and to finish the year in a more flourishing condition than they had begun it. This improvement was accompanied by a significant increase in real wages and living standards; even the cautious specialists of the United Nations Economic Commission for Europe discerned signs of a "hesitant" recovery. The fact that all this could be accomplished in the absence of specific action by the United States bore witness, on the one hand, to the solid progress achieved in earlier years toward the rebuilding of the European and world economy; and, on the other, to the important continuing role of United States military expenditures of all kinds as a source of dollars which helped compensate for the lack of a coherent international economic policy on the part of this country.[52]

These favorable trends, however, would not be fully apparent until the statistics had been collated and analyzed after the end of the year. What was clearly evident during the summer and autumn of 1953 was that the Europeans themselves were facing a struggle for markets which promised to be all the more bitter because of their limited success in securing a foothold in the American market. Germany and Japan in particular, being unhampered as yet by any rearmament burden, were making heavy inroads in the markets of the Near East, Latin America, Southeast Asia, and even North America, to the special detriment of Britain, France, and other NATO countries. But in the absence of

[52] Cf. "World Trade and Production in 1953–54," *Federal Reserve Bulletin*, XL, October 1954, 1033-1040; *Report to Congress on the Mutual Security Program*, December 31, 1953 (Washington, G.P.O., 1954), 16-18; and, for more details, the *Economic Survey of Europe in 1953* (U.N. Publication 1954. II. E. 2, Geneva, 1954).

American tariff reductions, efforts at increasing exports to the dollar area were generally far from successful.

The great, perhaps exaggerated, hopes which many Europeans still attached to a liberalization of American trade policies were sharply illustrated at Geneva at the eighth session of the Contracting Parties to the General Agreement on Tariffs and Trade (GATT), which took place from September 17 to October 24. All leading representatives emphasized the importance attached by their governments to the review of foreign economic policy proceeding in the United States. A statement by Peter Thorneycroft, President of the British Board of Trade, summed up the European point of view:

> "Any attempt to cure the chronic unbalance which exists today is doomed to failure this side of a fundamental change in American commercial policy. A large range of potential exports to America are faced with tariff rates 50 percent, 60 percent, or even more. There are notorious difficulties of customs valuation which vastly increases the real burden of tax. There is the Buy American Act. . . . Mr. Howe [Canada's Minister of Trade and Commerce] has indicated the crucial importance for all of us of the United States policy. I agree with him." [53]

But since the United States as yet *had* no policy, there was not much GATT could do except agree to mark time until a policy was adopted. The principal decision reached at Geneva was to give effect to a suggestion from this country by extending existing tariff schedules and concessions—the fruit of earlier rounds of multilateral negotiations—until July 1, 1955. In addition, the delegates considered several technical questions relative to tariff modifications and several complaints against United States import restrictions and export subsidies, particularly on agricultural products; and they agreed, again at the instance of the United States, to admit Japan as an unofficial and temporary partner with the right to attend but not vote at GATT meetings.[54]

[53] Quoted by Grover W. Ensley, Staff Director, in a memorandum of November 6, 1953 to the Joint Congressional Committee on the Economic Report entitled *Observations on Economy of Western Europe: Report on GATT Sessions at Geneva and Statistical Meetings at Rome*, 9.

[54] Cf. above, p. 269; and, for details, see "Results of Eighth Session of Contracting Parties to GATT," *Department of State Bulletin*, XXIX, November 16, 1953, 677-680.

As the months slipped by and the prospect for American action receded into the mists of another election year, European hopes gave way to increasing frustration and disillusionment. As often happened, it was the British, as the principal trading partners of the United States, who were most outspoken; but their Ambassador, Sir Roger Makins, might have been speaking for all Europeans when he described the situation of the European countries in a speech to the National Foreign Trade Convention in New York:

"For the moment they are holding the line and trying to make small advances. But they cannot break out on their own. Time presses upon us in these matters and we cannot, any of us, stand still indefinitely. If we do not seize the chances of moving forward when they are presented to us, we may find that the force of circumstances will compel us to move reluctantly back." [55]

The clear implication was that unless the United State did really move forward toward trade liberalization, the European countries would be forced to move backward toward trade discrimination, bilateralism and autarky. This, indeed, appeared to be a real and ominous prospect as 1953 drew to a close.

The East-West Trade Problem

A theoretical alternative to this disagreeable prospect lay in the possibility of increased Western European trade with areas behind the Iron Curtain. Expansion of East-West trade was continually urged by Moscow and Peking both because they wanted Western goods and because they knew it was one of the most delicate issues within the Western coalition. As we have seen, the question of what types of Western goods could properly be shipped to the Communist world had caused political irritation among the democracies far in excess of any practical consequences resulting from the limited East-West trade that had been carried on during the past few years. From a realistic standpoint, moreover, there was room for considerable skepticism as to the ability of the Communist bloc states to export commodities needed by the West in exchange for the Western industrial prod-

[55] Associated Press dispatch, New York, November 18, 1953.

ucts, machine tools, and precision instruments which they needed to develop their economies. Yet with United States aid declining and American tariff barriers not being lowered, European exporters were bound to keep the possibilities of Communist trade under consideration, and the Russians could hardly fail to exploit the situation propagandistically even if they could not fully exploit it economically. In April, Communist representatives had made a very businesslike impression at a Geneva trade conference sponsored by the United Nations Economic Commission for Europe. The subsequent shift to a policy emphasizing consumers' goods production throughout the Soviet bloc seemed likely to create still greater opportunities for Western enterprise, some of which at least might well escape the international ban on exports of strategic commodities.

Yet no over-all increase in East-West trade took place during 1953; on the contrary, Western trade with the U.S.S.R. and its European satellites actually declined as compared with 1952, and trade with Communist China increased but slightly.[56] Moscow, however, was obviously proposing to keep the issue alive in 1954, and there were signs that it had lost none of its explosive potentialities on the American political front.[57] In September Mr. Stassen, in a periodic report on his agency's administration of strategic trade controls, called attention to the many misconceptions prevailing on the subject and their harmful effects in the free world:

"In Western Europe, for example, it is not rare to encounter the notion that a vast increase in East-West trade is dangling just beyond the horizon; that if the Western nations would only reach out and grasp this horn of plenty it would rid them of unemployment, raise their living standards, solve most of the problems growing out of their shortage of dollars, and put the

[56] According to the Foreign Operations Administration, free world exports to the U.S.S.R. and its European satellites declined from $1,153 million in 1952 to $1,070 million in 1953, while exports to Communist China increased only from $268 million to $280 million during the same years. Imports from the U.S.S.R. and the satellites were $1,242 million in 1952 and $1,146 million in 1953; imports from Communist China, $366 million in 1952 and $425 million in 1953. *East-West Trade Trends: Mutual Defense Assistance Control Act of 1951 (the Battle Act)—Fourth Report to Congress, Second Half of 1953* (Washington, G.P.O., 1954), 89.

[57] Cf. below, pp. 422-424.

world on the road toward lasting peace; and that the only obstacle to this fulfillment is the restrictions imposed upon trade by the Western countries. All this is a myth, for the chief deterrent to peaceful trade has been the policies of the Soviet Union.

"In the United States, on the other hand, the notion is held by some people that our allies are shipping military items to the Soviet bloc, and some have the idea, besides, that *all* East-West trade is an evil in itself, unpatriotic, disgraceful, no different from wartime 'trading with the enemy,' and ought to be abolished; and that the United States could and should 'get tough' about East-West trade, regardless of the disrupting effect it would have on the Mutual Security Program. All this, too, is a mythical view because it bears no relation to the hard facts." [58]

Such clarifications were helpful to those who sought to maintain a broad perspective on world issues and to resist the torrents of interested propaganda from many sources. Important, however, as strategic trade controls had become in the general economic life of the free world, they were primarily significant as a reflection of the long-continued political antagonism between East and West. Their future, and indeed the economic future of the free world generally, would be shaped primarily by the course of East-West political relations and the success or failure of the great powers in working out some method for reducing their mutual hostility and distrust—or, failing that, of learning to live with it.

3. EAST-WEST PROBING OPERATIONS

By the autumn of 1954, the problem of general relations among the great powers had been reduced for the time being to a set of specific issues relating to (a) a post-armistice political conference on the Far East and (b) a possible four-power conference on Germany and Austria. Negotiations relating to the Far Eastern conference had been entrusted by the General Assembly to the United States, acting in the interest of the United Nations as well as in its own interest and that of the Republic of Korea. In the negotiations relat-

[58] *World-Wide Enforcement of Strategic Trade Controls: Mutual Defense Assistance Control Act of 1951 (The Battle Act)—Third Report to Congress, First Half of 1953* (Washington, G.P.O., 1953), 23.

ing to Europe, the three Western powers continued to act as a unit in the running exchange of diplomatic notes with the U.S.S.R. which had been initiated after the Washington Conference in July.[59] Although the two colloquies were carried on by some of the same parties and sometimes overlapped or merged, the issues at stake can be better understood if they are considered separately.

Dialogue with Moscow (Continued)

In their notes to the Soviet Union of September 2, delivered in Moscow shortly before the West German election, the three Western governments had urged that a meeting of Foreign Ministers of the Big Four on Germany and Austria be convened at Lugano on October 15. Had the Soviet Government been genuinely anxious to come to an agreement on the German and Austrian issues and thus perhaps pave the way toward a larger détente, such a meeting would have provided an entirely suitable opportunity. It is even possible that a four-power meeting held in the early autumn, after the Soviet H-bomb announcement and Dr. Adenauer's victory in the German election, would have found the United States more ready to take the Kremlin's peculiar viewpoint into account than it had appeared to be at an earlier period. Secretary Dulles, addressing the new session of the General Assembly on September 17, not only stressed America's readiness "to explore ways to end the present tension" but offered assurances that the United States had no plans for "exporting revolution" or "inciting . . . violence" behind the Iron Curtain. "We can understand the particular desire of the Russian people to have close neighbors who are friendly," he said. ". . . The United States does not want to see Russia encircled by hostile peoples." [60] Apparently there was even a disposition in Washington at this time to consider the idea of some kind of nonaggression pact such as Prime Minister Churchill had suggested in May and Chancellor Adenauer, among others, had continued to advocate. "We want to get ideas," said Mr. Dulles.

[59] Cf. above, pp. 187-198 and 245-246.

[60] *Documents on American Foreign Relations, 1953*, 37, 40-41. On the General Assembly session cf. below, pp. 394-407.

"In all these matters we are working with a very great sense of urgency. We are trying to be imaginative, to find new solutions, realizing that the stakes are greater now than perhaps they have ever been before in history." [61]

To judge by appearances, however, no such conciliatory tendencies swayed the councils of the Soviet Government, which seemed in no haste whatever to take advantage of Washington's new mood.[62] If anything, Soviet policy toward the outside world seemed rather to have hardened than softened during the late summer and autumn of 1953. Perhaps this was the result of confidence bred of the hydrogen bomb discovery; perhaps it reflected a mood of caution induced by the successive miscarriages of Soviet policy in Germany and strengthened by the Western insistence on free all-German elections as a necessary preliminary to any broader German settlement. When the Kremlin replied to the Western note on September 28, therefore, it took no notice of the invitation to meet in mid-October. Instead it reiterated the argumentation contained in its earlier notes and repeated its wholly unpalatable proposal to hold two separate diplomatic meetings, both at the Foreign Ministers' level, in addition to the prospective political conference on the Far East. One of these, it will be recalled, was to be a five-power conference, including Communist China, on "measures to lessen tension in international relations"; the other, a four-power conference on Germany which, however, would discuss *all aspects* of the German problem rather than limiting itself to the question of free elections. As for Austria, the U.S.S.R. still seemed disinclined to consider the matter of a state treaty at a special conference but said it was

[61] Press conference statement, October 6, in *Department of State Bulletin*, XXIX, October 19, 1953, 528.

[62] The U.S.S.R. did respond favorably to a reminder from the State Department (September 11) of its long-standing obligation to return 186 borrowed U.S. naval craft in connection with a settlement of its wartime lend-lease indebtedness to this country. But although the Soviet Ambassador declared on October 20 that his government was "prepared henceforth to cooperate for purposes of a swift and definitive settlement of all matters relating to the lend-lease accounts," procedural disagreements prevented any progress before the end of the year. For details cf. *ibid.*, XXIX, September 21, 1953, 391; XXX, January 11, 1954, 44-47 and April 12, 1954, 563.

willing to continue discussions through normal diplomatic channels.[63]

Though it was already too late to hold a meeting in mid-October, the Big Three believed they detected some embarrassment in these evasions and determined to renew the pressure for an early encounter on Western terms. Messrs. Dulles, Eden, and Bidault, at their meeting in London on October 16-18, approved a new note to the U.S.S.R. in which the three governments stressed their interest in a frank exchange of views on Germany and Austria and again proposed a meeting of Big Four Foreign Ministers in Lugano, this time for November 9. As to the proposed five-power conference on general international tensions, they said they were always ready to discuss such matters under suitable conditions; but they implied that there was no need for a special conference along the lines proposed in view of the projected political conference on Korea, the discussions which had meanwhile been getting under way at the United Nations General Assembly, and the continuing availability of normal diplomatic channels.[64]

These arguments, though unquestionably valid, omitted to mention what was perhaps the decisive factor in the Western attitude, the unwillingness of the United States to join in a conference with Communist China. It was precisely this aspect of the Western position, however, that the Kremlin chose to belabor most heavily in the reply to the Western note which it released on November 3. This communication seemed clearly aimed at creating embarrassment for Western policy rather than at forwarding the solution of diplomatic problems. Offering no modifications of earlier Soviet proposals, it merely undertook to support them with lengthy criticisms of Western policy in all parts of the world. The denial of "China's legitimate rights," it said, was perpetuating international tension and would not be rectified merely by Chinese participation in the Korean political conference. As for Germany, ratification and implementation of the E.D.C. agreements would make the reunification of the country "impossible" and a four-power meeting "pointless."

[63] Soviet note, September 28, *ibid.*, XXIX, October 26, 1953, 548-550.
[64] U.S. note, October 18, *ibid.*, 547-548.

Though its language was somewhat vague, the Kremlin seemed actually to suggest that discussion on Germany should be deferred until two wholly improbable events had come to pass: namely, until (1) the Western powers had renounced the E.D.C. policy, and (2) a five-power conference on international tensions had been convened and begun to produce results.[65]

To such a communication no Western government could respond with much warmth. "The Soviet Government," said the American reply, concerted as usual with those of Britain and France and delivered in Moscow on November 16, "must be well aware that such demands are totally unacceptable." The Soviet price for a conference, it said, appeared to entail nothing less than "a defenseless Western Europe" and the abandonment by the Western powers "of all their plans to safeguard their own security." Considering that the U.S.S.R. had for the third time in four months ignored the invitation "to discuss the most urgent international problems," the Western governments could only conclude "that the Soviet Government does not wish at the present time to enter into any negotiations which might have positive results." Their previous invitation was left open, but with no apparent expectation that it would be accepted.[66] Nine days later, in separate communications on Austria, they reemphasized their desire to settle at least this question and offered to discuss "any Soviet proposal . . . which does not raise extraneous issues" either at the Foreign Ministers' or the Deputies' level or through diplomatic channels.[67]

This was perhaps the lowest ebb of the hopes for a four-power meeting since the death of Stalin. In the United Nations, Vyshinsky had repeatedly lashed out at America's alleged aggressive intentions and restated the familiar Stalinist formula for disarmament. In Moscow, Marshal Voroshilov had commemorated the October Revolution

[65] Soviet note, November 3, *ibid.*, November 30, 1953, 745-748.

[66] U.S. note, November 16, *ibid.*, 745.

[67] U.S. note, November 25, in *Documents on American Foreign Relations, 1953*, 239-240. To remove any misunderstanding it was explicitly stated that the so-called short treaty for Austria, to which the U.S.S.R. continued to object, had been withdrawn by the Western governments in their note of August 17. Cf. above, p. 196.

in terms equally reminiscent of the days of Stalin: "The filthy, unbridled, slanderous campaign against the U.S.S.R. and other peace-loving countries does not cease but has been intensified."[68] Discouraged by such developments, Prime Minister Churchill, who had repeated his proposal for a top-level conference as lately as September 28, admitted that the prospects for such negotiations were dim. President Eisenhower, too, found the Soviet attitude frustrating and remarked that the note of November 3 suggested an intention "to create as many difficulties as possible."[69] "The Soviet rulers," said Secretary Dulles, "have retreated into a diplomatic defensive. The free world now has the diplomatic and moral initiative."[70]

Paradoxically, however, it was just at this moment that the Soviet attitude on the question underwent one of its periodic mutations, either because of a shift of influence within the Soviet governing clique or, more probably, because Mr. Molotov and the Soviet Foreign Office reckoned that more was to be gained from keeping the discussion alive than from allowing it to lapse. On November 26 a new Soviet note was presented to the Western representatives in Moscow which for the first time implied a willingness to join in a four-power meeting without preliminary conditions. The form of the Soviet capitulation—if such it was—was typically ungracious. All the familiar Soviet arguments about the world situation, the position of China, and the E.D.C. were repeated with the usual harshness if not at quite the usual length. If a four-power meeting was held, Moscow warned, the opportunity would be used to propose the early convocation of a five-power meeting including Communist China. Nothing specific was said about the ground that might be covered by a four-power meeting, except that there would be no preliminary conditions. The significant point, however, was the expression of willingness to hold such a

[68] *New York Times,* November 7, 1953.

[69] Press statement, November 4, in *Department of State Bulletin,* XXIX, November 16, 1953, 670.

[70] Mr. Dulles interpreted the Soviet evasions as a sign not of strength, but of fear: "They dare not admit of a prospect of greater liberty anywhere behind the Iron Curtain, lest restiveness increase everywhere behind that curtain." Address of November 18, *ibid.,* November 30, 1953, 744.

meeting at all. The U.S.S.R. even offered the concrete suggestion that it be held in Berlin.[71]

As the State Department immediately pointed out, the Soviet note made no concessions of substance. Even the procedural concessions that Moscow seemed to be offering could be easily attributed to such Machiavellian aims as the influencing of the French debate on E.D.C. and the allaying of the disappointment occasioned in Europe by its last previous communication. Nevertheless the State Department promised that the new note would "receive the most serious study and consideration." The prospective Bermuda meeting between President Eisenhower and the British and French heads of government, it noted, would provide an opportunity for early consultation among the countries principally concerned.[72]

Back to Panmunjom

Negotiations looking toward a Far Eastern political conference had meanwhile been proceeding independently, and with equally doubtful prospects of success. Here, at least, one important point was already agreed upon by most of the parties concerned—namely, that a conference should definitely take place, with Korea and possibly other matters on its agenda. But the prospect of convening such a conference by the October 28 deadline specified in the armistice agreement had rapidly receded; and even if it were eventually held, the likelihood of its leading to constructive results could not be considered great in view of the differing aims of the prospective participants and the multiple frictions which the Korean situation continued to generate.

The most serious of these,[73] apart from the progressive

[71] Soviet note, November 26, *ibid.*, December 21, 1953, 853-854; excerpts in *Documents on American Foreign Relations, 1953*, 227-229.

[72] Statement of November 27, in *Department of State Bulletin*, XXIX, December 7, 1953, 786; cf. below, pp. 427-428.

[73] A minor incident occurred on September 21 when a defecting North Korean pilot surrendered his MIG-15 aircraft to U.N. authorities, apparently without knowing that the Unified Command some months earlier had offered a reward of $100,000 for the first MIG brought into the U.N. lines. Acting on information supplied by the pilot, the U.N. Command on October 12 formally complained that the Communists had moved military aircraft into North Korea in violation of the armistice agreement. A general summary of Korean developments during this period appears in *Chronique de politique étrangère*, VII, January 1954, 64-80.

revelation of Communist atrocities and the uncertain status of 3,421 prisoners of war (944 Americans) not returned or accounted for by the enemy,[74] arose out of the armistice provisions relating to the 23,000 prisoners of war held by the two sides who had refused to be returned to their former commands. During September these unenviable men—22,604 Chinese and North Koreans held by the United Nations and 359 personnel of the United Nations Command held by the Communists—had been concentrated in the demilitarized zone under the custody of the Neutral Nations Repatriation Commission and its Indian custodial forces. There they were now to be subjected to the first stage of the multiple ordeal prescribed for them by the terms of reference incorporated in the armistice agreement—exposure to the ministrations of "explaining representatives" from their former governments (limited to seven explainers per thousand prisoners) who would be permitted (during specified hours, and in the presence of accredited observers)

"to explain to all the prisoners of war . . . their rights and to inform them of any matters relating to their return to their homelands, particularly of their full freedom to return home to lead a peaceful life. . . ." [75]

From September 24, when the Neutral Nations Repatriation Commission assumed full custody of the prisoners, to January 22, 1954, when the responsibility of the commission came to an end, the situation regarding nonrepatriate prisoners continued as the world's prime source of international irritation. Almost nothing was satisfactory about the procedure, unless perhaps it was the quiet efficiency with which the excited and unruly prisoners were handled by General K. S. Thimayya, the Commission chairman, and the 2,800 unarmed riflemen constituting the Custodial Force, India. Although it was felt by the Unified Command that the Indians tended at first to be unnecessarily deferential to the

[74] In addition, 33 American civilians were being held in Chinese Communist jails despite repeated State Department efforts in their behalf. Departmental announcement, October 9, in *Department of State Bulletin,* XXIX, October 26, 1953, 551-552.

[75] Terms of reference of the Neutral Nations Repatriation Commission, June 8, in *Documents on American Foreign Relations, 1953,* 295.

Communist viewpoint, their exposure to Communist tactics was felt to be having a useful educational effect.[76] But there was constant wrangling between the Communists, the Unified Command, and the Repatriation Commission over the detailed conditions of the explanation sessions, which did not get under way until October 14 and even thereafter remained subject to constant interruptions.[77]

The greatest surprise of the early explaining sessions, apart from the fact that some few of the prisoners turned over by the United Nations actually did decide to return to Communism, was the vehement resistance of the anti-Communist majority to the whole procedure. The average Korean or Chinese prisoner was prepared to stamp, shout, sing, almost anything but listen. Among the first batch of 500 Chinese interviewed, only ten were willing to be repatriated. As for the North Koreans, the first 1,000 of them simply refused to appear for explanations. The Communists demanded that they be brought in by force; the Indians refused. Not until the end of October did the North Koreans agree to meet the explainers at all. When they did, they were prevented with difficulty from physically attacking their Communist countrymen.

Correspondence with Peking

While these turbulent scenes were being enacted in Panmunjom, the question of a political conference was once again under discussion in Washington and at the United Nations. In August the General Assembly had decided to endorse the United States preference for a "two-sided" conference which would be confined to nations participating directly in the Korean war—plus the U.S.S.R. if "the other side" desired it.[78] Pursuant to this decision, the United States had conferred with its fifteen cobelligerents and South Korea and, with their concurrence, had sent off a message to Peking

[76] Mark W. Clark, *From the Danube to the Yalu* (New York, Harper, 1954), 324-325.

[77] For details see the *Reports of the Neutral Nations Repatriation Commission,* 9 September 1953 to 21 February 1954, and *Report of the United Nations Command on the Operations of the Neutral Nations Repatriation Commission,* printed as U.N. General Assembly *Official Records, Eighth Session,* Supplements 18 and 19 respectively; also below, pp. 448-450.

[78] Above, pp. 245-246.

and Pyongyang on September 5 (using Swedish diplomatic channels, since this country had none of its own) suggesting that the conference begin on October 15 and be held in San Francisco, Honolulu, or Geneva.[79] A parallel might be seen here with the note of September 2 in which the three Western powers had proposed a meeting with the U.S.S.R. at Lugano, also on October 15;[80] and there was also a parallel to be found in the evasive tactics employed by the Communist governments. Like Moscow, Peking and Pyongyang instead of accepting the proposal made to them took the position that a different kind of conference altogether was required.

The official Chinese Communist and North Korean replies to the United Nations, delivered on September 13 and 14, went all the way back to the notion of a "round-table" conference with neutral participation—which had been rejected by the General Assembly—and proposed that the whole matter be reconsidered by the Assembly at its Eighth Session, which was to open in New York on September 15.[81] This proposal was strongly supported by Mr. Vyshinsky when the Assembly convened, but gained little backing from other delegations and was rejected on September 22 by a vote of 40 to 8, with ten abstentions.

Meanwhile the United States had dispatched a new communication to the Communist governments in which it pointed out that the General Assembly had already made its decision and once again proposed a conference at San Francisco, Honolulu, or Geneva beginning October 15. A supplementary communication a few days later, phrased in the same conciliatory terms as Mr. Dulles' address to the General Assembly,[82] emphasized that the United States was "most anxious to facilitate the work of the conference," suggested that the question of neutral participation could still be taken up at the conference itself, and offered to send a represent-

[79] The official announcement of the Washington meeting on September 2 appears in *Department of State Bulletin,* XXIX, September 14, 1953, 361. The text of the U.S. communication of September 5 seems not to have been published but is authoritatively described *ibid.,* September 28, 1953, 422.

[80] Above, p. 198.

[81] U.N. Documents A/2469 and A/2476, September 13 and 15, 1953.

[82] Above, p. 382.

ative to meet with the Communists for preliminary negotiations at any one of the proposed conference sites. No reply to these messages having been received, the United States on October 8 sent off a third message pointing out that an early expression of Communist views was essential if the conference was to meet on time, and that there could be no reason for balking if the Communists intended to carry out the armistice recommendations at all.[83]

To these three communications the Communists replied on October 10 that despite their extreme disgust with the way the matter had been handled thus far, they were willing to appoint representatives for preliminary discussions with the United States. But these discussions, they maintained, should settle not only the time and place of the conference but also its *composition* (which the General Assembly considered already settled), and should take place in Panmunjom rather than at any of the sites suggested by the United States. Despite this unamiable tone, the United States in a reply released two days later offered only such limited objection to these proposals as was inseparable from its insistence on a "two-sided" conference. The Communists, similarly, continued in a further message of October 19 to insist that their stand on the composition of the conference was the only correct one, but also contrived to make it clear that this difference would not be allowed to stand in the way of preliminary negotiations. Thus by October 21 an American representative—Arthur H. Dean, Secretary Dulles' former law partner, whom the President had designated as Special Ambassador for the Korean conference—was actually on his way to Panmunjom. The discussions there, Mr. Dulles pointed out, would deal only with arrangements and not with substantive matters.[84]

Up to this point, Peking and Washington had shown a rather unusual willingness to compromise on matters which were, to be sure, nonessential as far as their basic positions were concerned but were not without significance from the

[83] Texts released September 18, September 23, and October 8, in *Department of State Bulletin,* XXIX, September 28, 1953, 422; October 12, 1953, 486; October 19, 1953, 526-527.

[84] *Ibid.,* October 26, 1953, 550-551; November 2, 1953, 590-591.

point of view of "face." But the question of the actual composition of the conference was a considerably more vital one because, as already pointed out, the choice of the participants would largely determine what results, if any, the conference was going to produce. All technicalities aside, that was the reason why the Communists still insisted upon a "round-table" conference packed with countries favorable to their viewpoint; that was the reason why the United States adhered so steadfastly to the notion of a conference of "two sides," in which the United States point of view would be vigorously represented and could not be challenged except by the other "side"—which would be the side of the recognized aggressors. This, furthermore, was the reason why the Panmunjom preliminary negotiations, though arranged with such deceptive ease, became deadlocked practically from the moment of their commencement on October 26 and remained almost continuously in that status until they were broken off by Mr. Dean on December 12.

Another Korean Deadlock

The particular form assumed by this deadlock was that of a dispute about the agenda for the talks Mr. Dean had come to hold with his Communist opposites. The North Korean and Chinese Communist delegates wanted to begin by settling what to them was the wide-open question of the composition of the political conference; Mr. Dean and his advisers wanted to begin by discussing the time and place of the conference—it was supposed to have begun by October 28—and to leave the matter of composition until later. Mr. Dean upheld his position with "great skill, resourcefulness, and patience"; the Communists upheld theirs with "a wooden inflexibility" [85] which was not less effective. Eventually, at Mr. Dean's suggestion, the issue was turned over to technical advisers who on November 14 came up with an elaborate compromise formula providing, in effect, that all matters could be discussed simultaneously but that no single point would be settled until every other point was settled.

[85] Statement of Secretary Dulles, November 3, *ibid.*, November 16, 1953, 666; for details cf. further *ibid.*, November 16, 1953, 666-670; December 7, 1953, 788-789.

On this basis, the discussion of the matters which had brought the delegates to Panmunjom could at least begin; but the likelihood of actual agreement on them was not much advanced. A few limited concessions were offered by each side and rejected by the other: Mr. Dean suggested that the addition of neutrals to the conference might be considered *after* a Korean settlement had been reached provided the course of discussions made it desirable; the Communists suggested that neutrals might participate without vote, the actual decisions being made by the belligerents acting according to the rule of unanimity. In essence, however, each side remained firmly wedded to its own view, and willing to participate in a political conference only if it took the essential form on which that side had insisted all along. By late November, the Communists were still displaying an attitude of which Mr. Dulles had remarked weeks earlier:

"I think that one cannot . . . take a confident view that they really want to have a conference. Certainly they are going about it in a queer way if they do." [86]

If the Communist negotiators at Panmunjom had shown a more convincing interest in holding a conference, it would presumably have been because they hoped to gain greater advantages from a conference than they were able to draw from the continuance of the existing state of affairs. But such a conference as the United States was willing to agree to offered them only limited inducements because it would be set up in such a way that no decision could be reached that did not have United States approval. What that meant could be guessed from the continued insistence of American authorities on the principle of a "free" Korea and from their unwavering opposition to Chinese Communist political aims.[87] The most to which the United States might possibly

[86] Statement of November 3, in *Department of State Bulletin*, XXIX, November 16, 1953, 666. See further below, pp. 446-448.

[87] On October 15, the opening day of the Eighth General Assembly, Mr. Dulles proposed and the Assembly adopted by 44-10-2 the usual resolution postponing for that year any consideration of the problem of China's representation in the U.N. Mr. Dulles emphasized that the limitation of his proposal to the current year "should not be interpreted as indicating any expectation on the part of the United States to change its position after the current year." *Department of State Bulletin*, XXIX, September 28, 1953, 412-413.

have agreed was a tentative plan, discussed in September with certain United Nations members, whereby a free, reunified, and independent Korea from which foreign forces had been withdrawn would be neutralized under some kind of international guarantee.[88] Such a plan, if approved by Washington and Seoul and buttressed with suitable safeguards, might have provided a reasonable basis for the settlement of the Korean problem, despite the difficulty of reconciling it with the provisions of the recent United States-Korean mutual defense treaty. For the Communists, however, it would have represented a setback too important to be accepted in the absence of countervailing advantages to which the United States would have found it impossible to agree.

Confronted with this meager prospect, the Chinese Communist negotiators and their North Korean coadjutors evidently found it more profitable to continue dragging out the talks at Panmunjom on procedural matters than to accept a diplomatic defeat by agreeing to a conference on American terms. In that respect they were proving even more stubborn than the Russians, who had now agreed to meet with the Big Three at Berlin despite the rejection of most of their preliminary conditions.[89] But the Chinese Communists had an important advantage over the Russians in their dealings with the West. The Russians had already reached the limits to which they could hope to expand their influence and control without risking a head-on clash with the Western powers. The Chinese Communists, despite the many warnings they had received from Western capitals, had not yet reached such a limit. They were soon to show that where diplomacy failed they could still find means of promoting their interests by political warfare and even armed force.[90]

4. THE EIGHTH GENERAL ASSEMBLY

In arguing against the Soviet proposal for a special five-power conference on international tensions, the Western

[88] *New York Times*, September 25 and 26, 1953.
[89] Above, pp. 386-387.
[90] Cf. below, pp. 451-453.

powers had pointed out that numerous facilities were already available for East-West discussion and had drawn special attention to the potentialities of the United Nations General Assembly as a forum for the consideration of international questions. To this reminder Moscow had retorted in language hardly flattering to the United Nations. "It is impossible," it said, "to acknowledge this reference as in any degree well founded." From the beginning of its existence, the Kremlin recalled, the United Nations had been concerning itself with disarmament and other questions related to international peace. Yet solutions had not been found; the armaments race, far from being arrested, was continuing at an accelerated rate, while "weapons of mass destruction" were becoming "ever more destructive and dangerous, especially with the appearance of the hydrogen bomb." [91]

The fact that the United Nations had found no solution for these admittedly pressing problems was not, of course, primarily the fault of the world organization. It was the fault of the differences in aims and viewpoint which divided the Communist governments from those of the free world. At bottom, it reflected the apparent inability or unwillingness of Communists to cooperate with non-Communists on any basis which the latter could consider fair or reasonable. Granting, however, that the U.S.S.R. itself was primarily responsible for the limited achievement of the United Nations in its most vital area of endeavor, Moscow still had good reason to dislike the institution and to prefer that serious diplomatic business be transacted elsewhere. From the point of view of the Soviet Union, with only one seat out of eleven in the Security Council and only five sure votes out of sixty in the General Assembly, its interests were seriously underrepresented. Admittedly it could not be compelled by the United Nations to do anything it did not choose to do voluntarily; but it also could not compel the United Nations to adopt its own viewpoint except in the rare instances when its wishes happened to coincide with those of the majority of United Nations members. Of late

[91] U.S. note, October 18, and Soviet reply, November 3, in *Department of State Bulletin,* XXIX, October 26, 1953, 548 and November 30, 1953, 746.

the United States had lost a good deal of its own former influence in the United Nations, especially in the General Assembly. The U.S.S.R., however, had never had much influence to lose. It still regarded the United Nations as a good place to make trouble for its opponents, but not, ordinarily, as a good place for serious discussion of real issues.

These were among the reasons why the Eighth Session of the General Assembly, which met in New York from September 15 to December 9, 1953,[92] witnessed few developments of outstanding significance despite the crucial importance of the period at which it met. By far the most important event of the session was the disclosure on December 8 of President Eisenhower's plan for international participation in the peaceful development of atomic energy. This, however, took place after the main business of the Assembly had been completed, and must be reserved for consideration in our final chapter.[93] In other respects the Assembly's transactions had a depressingly routine character, only slightly mitigated by the presence of Mme. Pandit of India as the first woman occupant of the presidential chair. As at earlier sessions, the attention of the delegates was by no means monopolized by the great conflict between East and West. The claims of underdeveloped and anticolonial countries for increased attention to their special concerns occupied their full share of committee and plenary debates.[94] Neither in this field nor in the more familiar sectors of the East-West conflict, however, were there new developments in any way comparable to those occurring during the same period in Washington, London, Paris, Moscow, and Peking.

The United States Position

Since this was the first new session of the Assembly to meet since the advent of the Eisenhower administration, there was

[92] The Assembly recessed on December 9 and thereafter met only to dissolve itself on September 20, 1954. A convenient summary of its activities at the Eighth Session appears in *International Organization,* VIII, February 1954, 49-116. For texts of resolutions, see General Assembly *Official Records, Eighth Session,* Supplement 17 (New York, 1954).

[93] Cf. below, pp. 428-433.

[94] Colonial and related issues considered by the Assembly are discussed above at pp. 321-324 and 327-329.

considerable curiosity as to the spirit in which the United States intended to join in the Assembly's work. The general demeanor of the United States, both in the Assembly and elsewhere, had been characterized in recent months by a degree of resoluteness in the pursuit of American objectives that had not always been compatible with regard for the interests and sensitivities of other nations. Even the normally pro-American *Economist* of London had been moved to remark in its issue of August 22 that "some recent American actions . . . would seem nicely calculated to transfer to the United States the reputation for mulishness that has so long —and so rightly—been enjoyed by the Soviet Union."

By September, however, there were signs that the State Department was reverting to a milder, more "diplomatic" approach. The new tone was reassuringly present in Mr. Dulles' address in the Assembly's opening general debate:

> ". . . We shall state as clearly as possible what we deem to be the just and right solution of the problems we shall here encounter. We do not think that the United States ought to be ambiguous about the problems of our time. But also we adhere to the basic United States belief expressed in our Declaration of Independence that we owe 'a decent respect to the opinions of mankind.' We are ready to learn from others. Also we recognize that our views may not always prevail. When that happens we shall no doubt regret it, but we shall not sulk. We shall try to accept the result philosophically, recognizing that we have no monopoly of wisdom or virtue, also that sometimes the passage of time alone provides the final verdict." [95]

This proved to be a reasonably accurate description of the attitude the United States was to adopt on the one potentially explosive issue that directly concerned its own relationship to the United Nations: the status of United States citizens employed by the United Nations, particularly with respect to loyalty and security considerations as interpreted by the United States Government. Since the discussion of this matter at the Assembly's spring session,[96] interested Americans had been considerably irritated by a ruling handed

95 Statement in plenary session, September 17, in *Documents on American Foreign Relations, 1953,* 34-35.
96 Cf. above, pp. 50-51.

down by the United Nations Administrative Tribunal in the case of the twenty-one staff members of United States nationality who had been dismissed by Secretary-General Lie in 1952 in view of their refusal to testify to United States authorities regarding their alleged Communist affiliations. On September 1 the tribunal, sitting in Geneva, found that in eleven of these cases the dismissals had been illegal and ordered the employees concerned to be reinstated or financially compensated. Total compensation for the entire group was eventually fixed at $179,420.

Without echoing the angry terms in which some highly placed Americans denounced this action,[97] the United States mission to the United Nations was resolutely opposed to accepting this disposition of the case. The Administrative Tribunal's action, it claimed, was vitiated by numerous errors; the Assembly was under no obligation to accept its ruling; the financial awards were exorbitant and ought not to be paid. This view, however, was not widely held by other delegates to the Assembly, many of whom were still considerably embarrassed by the conflict between their own views of legality and the strong contrary convictions of the United States. Luckily, a device was at hand for postponing action until the issue had somewhat cooled off. Late in the session, by 41 votes to 6 (with the United States and twelve other delegations abstaining), the question of the Assembly's obligations was referred to the International Court of Justice for an advisory opinion.[98] Meanwhile the United States joined with the majority in sponsoring amendments to the staff regulations and the statute of the Administrative Tribunal which would make it more difficult for such cases to arise in future.[99]

In no other instance did the United States find it necessary to assert with full vigor a point of view so little congenial to

[97] Cf. *New York Times,* September 5, 1953.

[98] Resolution 785 (VIII), December 9, 1953. For a statement of the U.S. position see the speech by Delegate James P. Richards in the Fifth (Administrative and Budgetary) Committee, November 19, in *Department of State Bulletin,* XXIX, December 21, 1953, 873-875. The International Court ruled against the U.S. contention on July 13, 1954; for details cf. *American Journal of International Law,* XLIX, January 1955, 6-9.

[99] Resolutions 781 (VIII) and 782 (VIII), December 9, 1953.

the views of the Assembly as a whole. The matter of budgetary assessments, a source of considerable friction in earlier years, was finally brought into order by limiting the United States assessment to one-third of the total United Nations budget, in conformity with a policy laid down at earlier sessions.[100] Among other controversial issues, the question of human rights still remained in an unsettled state following the submission of the new United States "action program" in the spring.[101] On colonial and related matters, the United States incurred some criticism from the "anticolonial" bloc for its stand on the issues of Tunisia, Morocco, and South Africa,[102] but was able to claim the Assembly's endorsement for its own action in according full self-government to the Commonwealth of Puerto Rico.[103] On the United Nations Children's Emergency Fund, it joined in the unanimous vote to drop the word "Emergency," retain the symbol UNICEF, and continue the fund on a permanent basis—though without obligation to contribute.[104]

International Development

Little was accomplished toward healing one major breach which existed between the so-called underdeveloped countries and the developed countries, including the United States. Despite its initiative in sponsoring the Point Four program and its participation in various technical assistance and cooperation programs through the United Nations and

100 By Resolution 765 (VIII), November 27 (printed in part in *Documents on American Foreign Relations, 1953,* 416-418), the U.S. assessment toward the $47,479,600 budget for 1954 was reduced to 33.33 percent and that of the U.S.S.R. was raised to 14.15 percent, exclusive of the small assessments of Byelorussia and the Ukraine.

101 Cf. above, pp. 54-55. By a series of resolutions adopted on November 28, the Assembly asked the Human Rights Commission to consider the U.S. proposals at its 1954 session as well as continuing its work on the draft covenants on human rights.

102 Cf. above, pp. 321-324, 327-329.

103 By Resolution 748 (VIII), November 27 (in *Department of State Bulletin,* XXIX, December 14, 1953, 841-842), the Assembly recognized that Puerto Rico had ceased to be a non-self-governing territory for purposes of the submission of information under Article 73(e) of the Charter. For background cf. *ibid.,* XXVIII, April 20, 1953, 584-589; XXIX, September 21, 1953, 393-398.

104 Resolution 802 (VIII), October 6, 1953 (in *Documents on American Foreign Relations, 1953,* 443-444). The U.S. contribution to UNICEF for 1953 was $9,814,333.

otherwise, this country was widely regarded within the underdeveloped world as too niggardly in making a portion of its wealth available for the promotion of economic development in less favored countries. During 1953 this feeling was somewhat intensified on the one hand by the much-publicized emphasis of the Eisenhower administration on governmental economy and, on the other, by the superficially contrasting decision of the U.S.S.R. and Poland to join on a small scale in the United Nations technical assistance program. World conditions being what they were, a Soviet offer of four million rubles (nominally $1 million) for 1953 was more impressive to some people than even the American pledges of $12,767,145 for 1953 and $13,861,809 for 1954,[105] representing some 60 percent of the entire United Nations program.

Nor was the United States able to generate much enthusiasm for its long-standing contention that the investment capital needed for economic development must come primarily from local and foreign private sources rather than from governments or international lending institutions. The Assembly did adopt one declaration which at least recognized the importance of private investment in economic development and thus, in the United States view, undid some of the harm occasioned by its negative stand in the previous year.[106] The main emphasis, however, was again placed on grandiose international projects which the United States felt unable to encourage: an International Finance Corporation to participate in equity investments and make loans directly to private enterprises in underdeveloped countries, and a Special United Nations Fund for Economic Development to make grants in aid and long-term, low-interest loans to underdeveloped countries. Concerning the first of these projects the United States continued to maintain a neutral attitude. Concerning the second, it recalled President Eisenhower's speech of April 16 in which he had indicated that world-wide disarmament was a prerequisite to large-scale constructive use

105 Figures from *US Participation in the UN: Report by the President to the Congress for the Year 1953* (Department of State Publications 5459, Washington, 1954), 109; cf. *United Nations Bulletin,* XV, August 1, 1953, 101.

106 Resolution 724 (VIII), part C (II), December 7, 1953; cf. *The United States in World Affairs, 1952,* 369-371.

of the world's resources.[107] Only under circumstances such as those indicated in the President's speech, said the American delegation, would the United States be likely to find itself in a position to contribute to a United Nations development fund.[108]

Under these circumstances the Assembly "refrained from pressing for action . . . beyond a point acceptable to the United States and other developed countries," [109] and contented itself with calling for further study of the two projects. In addition, both the developed and the underdeveloped countries joined in a declaration affirming their readiness to ask their peoples,

"when sufficient progress has been made in internationally supervised world-wide disarmament, to devote a portion of the savings achieved through such disarmament to an international fund, within the framework of the United Nations, to assist development and reconstruction in under-developed countries." [110]

This, no doubt, was a rather remote prospect—probably even more remote than the prospect of economic development through peaceful uses of atomic energy which President Eisenhower was to spread before the Assembly on December 8.[111] Like the Eisenhower "atoms-for-peace" plan, however, it stressed the way in which man's whole future on earth had come to depend on the progress of the armaments race and of the general East-West struggle, in which the competition in the new super-weapons constituted the most dangerous element.

Disarmament Once More

Of the various "East-West" issues considered by the Assembly at its Eighth Session, that of disarmament was one of the most familiar and certainly the most crucial in terms of its direct bearing on human destiny. Debates on other dead-

[107] Cf. above, p. 130.

[108] Cf. the statement by James D. Zellerbach in the Second (Economic and Financial) Committee, November 23, in *Department of State Bulletin,* XXIX, December 14, 1953, 839.

[109] *US Participation in the UN, 1953,* cited, 118.

[110] Resolution 724 (VIII), December 7, 1953, printed in part in *Documents on American Foreign Relations, 1953,* 444-447.

[111] Cf. below, pp. 428-433.

locked issues, such as the question of United Nations membership, served equally well to register the present state of East-West tension and the readiness or unreadiness for compromise of the principal contenders. The debate on disarmament possessed additional significance in that its outcome would have an immediate effect, positive or negative, on the course of the armaments race between East and West. Cooperation by the Soviet Union in a practical system of disarmament under the United Nations had been one of the tests of Soviet intentions enumerated by President Eisenhower in his address of April 16.[112] Any progress in this direction achieved during the Assembly session would be looked upon by most people as promoting the cause of peace and tending to mitigate the arms competition. Conversely, an obvious lack of progress in the General Assembly would remove one more of the restraints that might still be operating to reduce the chances of an armed collision among the great powers.

As a practical matter, however, any progress the Assembly might make in this field was entirely dependent on the attitude of the big powers themselves, who alone held the key to any solution of the impasse brought about by their conflicting stand on the matter. The nature of the deadlock was simple and familiar. Both sides—the U.S.S.R. and the Western powers—professed to favor disarmament, but only under conditions which would not result in placing their side at a relative disadvantage. The primary demand of the West was that disarmament must be subject to effective international inspection and control, thus protecting the free nations against the possibility of evasions and violations by their untrustworthy adversary. The U.S.S.R., while refusing to subject itself to this sensible procedure, sought to embarrass the West by calling instead for immediate disarmament in certain selected categories (abolition of weapons of mass destruction, and a one-third reduction in conventional armaments) which would have left it unquestionably the world's strongest military power. At the spring session of the General Assembly, the usual impasse had reappeared.[113] Subsequent developments, however, including the change of "line"

[112] *Documents on American Foreign Relations, 1953,* 32-33; cf. above, p. 129.
[113] Cf. above, pp. 118-119, 123-124.

in the U.S.S.R. and especially the wider availability of the hydrogen bomb, made it seem possible that the autumn session might have more encouraging results. "The destructive power inherent in matter," Mr. Dulles had told the Assembly, "must be controlled by the idealism of the spirit and the wisdom of the mind. They alone stand between us and a lifeless planet." [114]

Most delegates wholeheartedly agreed; Mr. Vyshinsky, unhappily, was not among them. Where Mr. Dulles had emphasized the willingness of the United States to consider any disarmament proposals that met the fundamental test of providing effective safeguards, Mr. Vyshinsky had nothing to offer but the old demand for the unconditional prohibition of atomic, hydrogen, and other "mass destruction" weapons, a one-third reduction in the armed forces of the Big Five within a year, and the elimination of military, air, and naval bases in the territories of other states. In reiterating this time-honored proposal it is uncertain whether or not Moscow had taken into account the fact that the adoption of the "new look" strategy in the United States would make it more difficult than ever for this country to accept a plan that patently aimed at nullifying its all-important air-atomic capability. At any rate, the repetition of the Soviet proposals under the new circumstances now obtaining suggested that even with the H-bomb at their disposal the Soviet leaders had not lost sight of the advantages conferred by their strength in conventional armaments.

Since the great powers continued to disagree so radically, there was nothing the Assembly as such could do except to exhort them to stop disagreeing and come to some kind of an understanding, "as the existence of civilization itself may be at stake." The fourteen-power resolution, cosponsored by the United States, in which Assembly views were eventually set forth was chiefly notable for its emphasis on keeping the discussion going in the hope that "recent international events" might still "create a more propitious atmosphere" for reconsideration of the question. The United Nations Disarmament Commission, which consisted of the eleven mem-

114 Address to the plenary session, September 17, in *Documents on American Foreign Relations, 1953*, 36.

bers of the Security Council plus Canada, was asked to continue its efforts and report back not later than September 1, 1954. Allowance was also made for the possibility that direct talks among the big powers under United Nations auspices might be helpful: the Disarmament Commission was invited to "consider the desirability of establishing a subcommittee consisting of representatives of the Powers principally involved, which should seek in private an acceptable solution and report to the Disarmament Commission as soon as possible." [115] Fifty-five delegations supported the resolution when it came before the plenary session on November 28; the five Soviet bloc states abstained, and there were no opposing votes. The suggestion for private disarmament talks, if acted upon—as it presumably would be—would establish still another forum for direct East-West discussions, side by side with the proposed Big Four conference and the Korean political conference.[116]

Other East-West Issues

Assembly discussion of other East-West issues produced additional acrimony but perhaps even fewer positive results. The old deadlock among the Big Five over the admission of new members still persisted; all the Assembly could do was to establish another Committee of Good Offices (Egypt, the Netherlands, and Peru) to consult with members of the Security Council "with the object of exploring the possibilities of reaching an understanding." [117] Two questions of high emotional significance growing out of the Korean war were also discussed at length. The impartial investigation of the Communist "germ warfare" charges against the United States, ordered by the previous Assembly,[118] had not taken place because of the noncooperation of the Communist gov-

[115] Resolution 715 (VIII), November 28 (*ibid.*, 425-427). For details of the debate cf. *Department of State Bulletin*, XXIX, December 14, 1953, 829-838.

[116] The competing Soviet resolution on "Measures to avert the threat of a new world war and to reduce tension in international relations" (U.N. Document A/L.168, November 27, *ibid.*, 834) was defeated in paragraph-by-paragraph voting in the First Committee on November 27 and in plenary session on November 30.

[117] Resolution 718 (VIII), October 23 (*Documents on American Foreign Relations, 1953*, 418-419).

[118] Cf. above, p. 121.

ernments; but the United States was now in a position to present evidence from returning prisoners of war which fully confirmed the falsity of the charges.[119] In addition, the United States undertook to acquaint the Assembly with details of the shocking atrocities committed by North Korean and Chinese Communist forces against United Nations prisoners of war in Korea, and cosponsored the resolution in which the Assembly expressed its grave concern at and condemnation of these inhuman practices—which, it said, violated international law and basic standards of conduct and morality and were an affront to human rights and the dignity and worth of the human person.[120] Of more routine interest was another resolution, likewise cosponsored by the United States, deploring on similar grounds the use of forced labor systems such as were known to exist in several countries of the free world as well as the Communist bloc.[121]

Prospects for Charter Review

Amid their preoccupation with these and similar matters of current interest, many delegates were beginning to look forward to the basic reconsideration of the United Nations Charter which was scheduled to occur in 1955. Article 109 of the Charter adopted in 1945 provided that a general conference of United Nations members for the purpose of reviewing the Charter could be called at any time by a two-thirds vote of the Assembly and a vote of any seven members of the Security Council; if no such conference had been held previously, the proposal to call one should definitely be discussed by the Assembly at its Tenth Session, which would be held in 1955. Here, it seemed, was still another possibility for

119 Cf. the statement of U.S. Delegate Charles W. Mayo to the First Committee, October 26, in *Department of State Bulletin,* XXIX, November 9, 1953, 641-647. The only action formally taken on this issue—by Resolution 714 (VIII), November 3, 1953, approved by 47-0-12—was the referral to the Disarmament Commission of a Soviet draft resolution, introduced with the obvious aim of confusing the issue, calling for universal accession to or ratification of the Geneva Protocol of June 17, 1925 prohibiting bacterial weapons.

120 Resolution 804 (VIII), December 3, 1953, adopted by 42-5-10.

121 Resolution 740 (VIII), December 7, 1953, adopted by 40-7-12; text and excerpts from debate in *Department of State Bulletin,* XXIX, December 21, 1953, 865-873. The Assembly also adopted on December 7, 1953 Resolution 741 (VIII) reiterating earlier appeals for the repatriation of all World War II prisoners of war; text *ibid.,* December 28, 1953, 904.

getting around some of the deadlocks and frustrations that had developed in eight years of operating under the old Charter. No government was wholly satisfied with the United Nations as it stood. Every government would soon have the opportunity to suggest improvements. As a preliminary measure the Assembly decided, after extensive discussion, to ask the Secretary-General to begin immediately to prepare documentation for study by the member states.[122]

This decision was opposed only by the five delegations of the Soviet bloc, which took the position that the plan to hold a Charter Review conference was actually an American conspiracy to revise the Charter to their governments' disadvantage. This negative attitude could not in itself prevent the holding of a review conference, but it promised badly for the success of any conference that might be held. However desirable it might be to modify the Charter, no modification could be effected without the approval and ratification of two-thirds of the membership, including all of the Big Five. Thus the Soviet Union had a veto on Charter amendments, and would presumably use it to block any amendment it did not like. Just what amendments would be proposed by other powers could not be foreseen. Secretary Dulles, while admitting the anachronistic character of the existing "pre-atomic-age charter," had said frankly that the United States had not yet made up its mind on specific revisions.[123] But since so much of the existing discontent with the United Nations related to those provisions that enabled the Soviet Union to frustrate the will of the free world majority, it was fairly certain that these would be precisely the provisions that many people would wish to alter—and which the U.S.S.R., to judge by all past performance, would defend with all the tenacity of which it was capable.

If things worked out in that way, the deadlock already existing in so many organs of the United Nations would speedily reappear in the Charter Review conference. In that case the United States and its friends might find themselves

[122] Resolution 796 (VIII), November 27, adopted by 54-5-0; text *ibid.*, December 28, 1953, 909.

[123] Address of August 26 and related comments, *ibid.*, September 7, 1953, 310-311 and September 14, 1953, 343.

forced to choose between keeping the old Charter, with all its imperfections, and reorganizing the United Nations without the Communist states. Quite a number of Americans would, no doubt, have welcomed a prospect of getting rid of such objectionable fellow members. It is to be presumed, however, that the majority of the American public endorsed the view of their government that in a world of superweapons it was desirable to have at least one organization where we could regularly talk even to our chief adversaries.

With the adoption on December 7 and 8 of resolutions on Korean reconstruction and on Burma,[124] the Assembly reached the end of its scheduled business except for tying up various loose ends and listening to the important address which President Eisenhower was to deliver on his return from the Bermuda conference. That address was to open up some interesting new perspectives, but would require no immediate action. The only remaining question before the Assembly was how and when it should reconvene; and that depended mainly on the progress of negotiations relating to Korea, still not quite at their last gasp despite the lack of agreement at Panmunjom. There was a general feeling that in view of the delicate situation in Korea and the various deadlines affecting the prisoners of war, the Assembly should keep the matter under observation and that some latitude must be left to its chairman, Mme. Pandit. Also on December 8, therefore, the Assembly declared itself recessed and called on Mme. Pandit to reconvene it—provided only that the majority of the member states concurred—on her own initiative or that of any member state growing out of developments in Korea.[125] By this step the Assembly quite unwittingly removed itself from the further consideration of Korean matters and, in effect, left the entire responsibility for international affairs during the next ten months in the hands of those powers which continued to exercise the decisive influence on prospects for war or peace.

124 Above, pp. 251 n. and 288 n.

125 Resolution 716 (VIII), December 8, approved by 55-0-5. A final meeting of the Assembly was held on December 9.

CHAPTER SEVEN
DECEMBER HARVEST

THE MONTH of December 1953 was a much more active period in international affairs than the corresponding month of 1952. At that time, the machinery of world politics had slowed to a virtual standstill while awaiting the installation of the Eisenhower administration and the disclosure of its international purposes. By December 1953, those purposes seemed reasonably well defined. If the final outcome of the Republican experiment in national and world leadership could not yet be forecast with certainty, there was on hand a voluminous record of international action which testified to the gradual clarification of Republican thinking on world affairs and made possible at least a provisional definition of the basic ideas by which American foreign policy was being guided. In general, these ideas appeared to differ far less from those of the preceding administration than might have been expected from a study of the 1952 campaign literature. The heat of eleven months of international politics had vaporized more than one well-turned campaign slogan. What remained was, on the whole, a national policy rather than a party policy—a policy whose expression and emphasis were strongly influenced by party considerations, but which in essence continued to reflect basic national opinion to approximately the same extent as before 1953.

This national, bipartisan, or supra-partisan quality was perhaps more evident in relation to the fundamental aims of the new administration than in the particular methods by which it had chosen to pursue them. The aims could be roughly characterized by some such formula as "peace without appeasement"—this phrase being understood to imply the avoidance of any surrender or concession, verbal or otherwise, to Communists. The influence of this underlying conception could be seen in a whole series of actions and policy declarations by which the United States had demonstrated that, despite its sympathy for the 600 million victims of Communism outside the U.S.S.R. and its belief in their ultimate liberation, it planned no overt action aimed at upsetting the present Communist control in Europe or Asia. Chiang Kai-shek had been "unleashed," but had been offered no support in reinvading the Chinese mainland; Syngman Rhee had been given a mutual defense treaty, but strongly discouraged against breaking the Korean armistice. Three months after the June 17 uprising in Berlin, Mr. Dulles had given the world a virtual assurance that the United States, while trusting with undiminished confidence in the power of freedom, had no intention of fomenting revolution behind the Iron Curtain.[1]

All of this seemed closer to the old, allegedly discredited policy of "containment" than to the new policy of "liberation" that was to have replaced it. Not less noteworthy, however (though equally rooted in the traditions of the pre-1953 period) was the refusal of the United States Government to envisage any type of concessions to the Communist governments other than that of leaving them, provisionally, in relatively undisturbed possession of the areas they presently controlled. "We should never, as the price of admission to a conference, abandon basic positions and programs in Asia or Europe"—this point Secretary Dulles emphasized repeatedly. The captive peoples must be made to realize "that they are not forgotten, that we are not reconciled to their fate, and, above all, that we are not prepared to seek safety for ourselves by a bargain with their masters which will confirm their captivity." [2] Communist China must remain excluded from the United Nations, even if this prevented the unity of Korea.[3] German rearmament through the European Defense Community must continue to take pre-

[1] Address to the U.N. General Assembly, September 17, in *Documents on American Foreign Relations, 1953,* 40; cf. above, p. 382.

[2] Address by Secretary Dulles, November 18, in *Department of State Bulletin,* XXIX, 744.

[3] Above, p. 238 n.

cedence over any plan of German unification through negotiations with the U.S.S.R. We did not wish to fight the Communist governments, but neither did we wish to make peace with them on any but our own terms—terms which would, unquestionably, have involved something like a renunciation of their basic principles of existence. How fully most Americans understood the nature of Soviet society and the real seriousness of the Communist threat might still be a moot question. There was, at any rate, no disposition to underrate the moral and political differences between the two camps or to delude ourselves with dreams of gaining Soviet friendship.

In the means by which it sought to implement this broad policy of avoiding both war and concessions, the Eisenhower administration had adopted a somewhat novel emphasis, even while still relying essentially on tools and techniques inherited from its predecessor. It certainly shared the misgivings of the past administration about premature negotiation with the principal adversary government. While not refusing to consider the possibility of negotiations on specific issues, it was disposed to insist on strong preliminary gurantees of "good faith" and, meanwhile, to place more reliance on the military strength of the free world than on its moral superiority or diplomatic adroitness. Secretary Dulles, like Secretary Acheson, clearly thought it preferable for the non-Communist nations to establish a "position of strength" before venturing on serious negotiations. If there was a significant difference in approach between the two, it lay in the energy with which Secretary Dulles from his first day in office had devoted himself to the effort to develop a particular kind of "position of strength" in Europe and Asia. This special approach, consistent no doubt with the dominant outlook in Congress and the Republican party, combined clear-cut emphasis on the element of *military* strength with what might seem a rather diminished concern for those economic, social, and psychological factors which had weighed so heavily with the past administration.

In this central effort to erect a position of military strength as the basis for future relations with the Communist bloc, the Eisenhower administration appeared to think in terms of a rather clear-cut division of labor and responsibility as between the United States and those other non-Communist countries which were more directly threatened by Communist attack. In Europe, the Middle East, South and East Asia, a constantly increasing emphasis was placed on regional security pacts, designed, by legal commitment backed up where possible by military forces, to seal off critical areas against Communist penetration. It is no exaggeration to say that the preeminent objective of United States policy in 1953, building on any foundations that might be discoverable and usable, was to get such a system of local or regional security pacts established and in operating condition. Mr. Dulles had made it plain that our policy in Europe stood or fell with the materialization of the European Defense Community. The Trieste problem, similarly, must be settled for the specific reason that it stood in the way of "a sound strategic plan for the defense of South Europe."[4] Identical considerations accounted for our efforts to promote settlements in Egypt and Iran and our growing solicitude for the military condition of Pakistan. The primary object of our various favors to Japan was admittedly to induce that country to undertake more of the responsibility for its own defense —always pending "the development of a more comprehensive system of regional security in the Pacific area."

This effort to encourage more active measures of coordinated defense in Europe and Asia had been accompanied by a perceptible tendency toward limiting the involvement of the United States itself in such regional defense efforts, and concentrating rather on the development of deterrent and retaliatory power as embodied in our stockpile of nuclear weapons, our Strategic Air Command, and our world-wide network of strategic air bases. While professedly dictated primarily by the determination to reduce military expenditure in the interest of national solvency, this change of emphasis in our national military policy also tended to bring it into closer alignment with the particular trend of thought on military matters of which Secretary Dulles himself had been one of the persuasive exponents.[5] Reliance on our own deter-

[4] Above, pp. 373-374.

[5] Cf. above, p. 79.

rent or retaliatory power did not, of course, imply indifference to local defense of threatened areas, for which the United States retained important direct responsibilities, especially in Western Europe. It did, however, imply some limitation on the over-all strength of United States ground forces and perhaps naval forces, and a readiness to withdraw such forces from outlying areas, as in Korea, as rapidly as local replacements became available. Remarks like those of Secretary Wilson[6] suggested that even in Europe there might be a disposition to limit the commitment of American forces as new weapons were perfected and deterrent-retaliatory power increased—especially if the Western European countries failed to meet their own commitment under the over-all Western defense plans.

This tendency toward at least partial disengagement from the direct defense of the non-Communist countries was accompanied by what seemed a perceptibly decreased concern with their nonmilitary needs—with trade, with economic development, with the fostering of a sense of common interests and purposes transcending the immediate concern with world Communism. An important and instructive example was provided by our relations with India, whose progressive psychological alienation from this country had been climaxed precisely by the decision to extend the American-sponsored network of security pacts into the Indian subcontinent.[7] This is not to say that the Indian attitude was justified, or the official American attitude unjustified, in terms of the realities of the world situation. The fact remains, however, that in its quest for a particular type of military security within the framework of a particular type of over-all policy, the United States was sometimes led to neglect or even violate other interests which to the parties concerned were equally or more compelling. This was a weakness in American world policy which eleven months under a new administration had sufficed to illuminate without as yet suggesting any practical remedy.

Whether the policies thus briefly described would be adequate to achieve the national objective of "peace without

[6] Above, pp. 370-371.
[7] Cf. above, pp. 312-318.

appeasement" would depend on how well they functioned (a) as a deterrent to Communist aggression, (b) as a protection to countries threatened with such aggression, and (c) as a source of material and spiritual health and strength to the free world—both for its own sake and for the sake of those captive millions whose ultimate hope was said to lie in "deeds which confront the Soviet world with living examples of how a free society works creatively to advance human welfare."[8] It would also depend on the degree of consistency and stability with which these national policies were pursued in the face of continuing evidence of dissent on the part of certain elements—presumably minority elements—in the United States itself.

No full answers to these questions could be expected in the immediate future, but some further clarifications were to be forthcoming before 1953 was ended. The month of December brought further evidence that the United States Government envisaged no concessions to Communism but would also make no substantive concessions to those at home who sought to divert it from a policy of fundamental concord with its allies. It brought a strong reiteration of United States insistence on the consummation of the European Defense Community, coupled with an implied suggestion that disappointment of our hopes in this respect might lead to a further disinvolvement in European affairs. Most important, perhaps, it brought in President Eisenhower's "atoms-for-peace" plan an attempt to formulate an original and constructive approach to some of the most urgent international problems of the atomic age.

1. LEADERSHIP BUT NOT COERCION

To outside observers, one of the most confusing features of American foreign policy was the fact that so many of this country's actions and pronouncements were subject to varying interpretations depending on what line of American thought about foreign policy matters they were assumed to reflect. Despite the broad agreement on the principle of

[8] Address by Secretary Dulles, November 18, in *Department of State Bulletin*, XXIX, November 30, 1953, 744.

"peace without appeasement," so many conflicting views were constantly being voiced within the United States and even within the dominant party that almost any specific action could be viewed in more than one light. The "unleashing" of Chiang Kai-shek had been a case in point, and by no means an isolated one. Officially presented as a rectification of an error of the past administration, it was widely viewed—and in some influential quarters welcomed—as the initiation of a much more active campaign of military and/or economic pressure against Communist China. Yet these expectations had not been borne out by later developments. A few months later, the "unleashing" action could be more truly evaluated as a gesture whose primary significance had lain in the field of domestic politics and which otherwise had aimed, at most, not at reopening the battle for China but rather at encouraging the Chinese Communists to make peace in Korea. The original announcement had elated activists and alarmed quietists all over the world. Not until much later, when the sense of the President's announcement had been filled out by concrete (if limited) measures of implementation, could one venture a conclusion as to what lay behind it and what its real tendency had been.

This, moreover, had been only the first of many instances in which American leaders had spoken words or taken actions which might appear at one time internationalist and at another almost isolationist in character but which later proved not to signify any important modification of substantive policy. And there were also instances, of which the whole doctrine of the "new look" was an example, in which the adoption of a given line of policy was inconclusive in itself because it could later receive either a peaceful or a bellicose turn, an isolationist or an internationalist tendency, dependent on what influences and what frame of mind might then be predominant in the government. That was why Europeans and many others kept such an anxious watch on the political scene in the United States and particularly on the internal differences that continued to manifest themselves within the majority party. On the resolution of those differences would very probably depend not only the future of American politics as such but the whole content of United

States policy and thus the whole nature of United States participation in world affairs. The real meaning of American policy declarations, and of plans like those associated with the "new look," could not be adequately assessed until it was known whether they would be carried out in the same spirit of moderate internationalism that had prevailed officially through most of 1953 or in the more peremptory and nationalistic spirit that animated some critics of the official line.

The Subversives Issue Again

That grave differences over the policy to be adopted toward Communism at home and abroad continued to perplex the United States during 1953 was a fact impossible to overlook as conveniently at the time as has been the case in recent chapters of this volume. The death of Senator Taft, whose misgivings about NATO and the United Nations had inspired the most significant dissenting statement of early 1953,[9] had resulted not in a collapse of the quasi-isolationist sentiment of which he had been a spokesman but rather in a coalescence of much of this sentiment with the more novel and, as some felt, less responsible tendencies associated with Senator McCarthy. With Mr. Taft no longer on the scene, Mr. McCarthy emerged as the most prominent representative of right-wing dissent on all domestic and foreign matters in any way related to Communism. In line with this change of personalities, the domestic and foreign aspects of America's anti-Communist struggle had tended to become increasingly intertwined in the texture of domestic politics. International affairs, in the practice of the Wisconsin Senator and his adherents, were no sacrosanct area reserved to diplomats and specialists but were subject to the same rules and procedures they had developed in connection with the search for Communists at home.

The undoubted popularity of this approach with a section of the American public had made it difficult for the administration to admit in public how widely its own position differed in most respects from that of the McCarthy wing. It seemed obvious that President Eisenhower and Secretary Dulles were less than appreciative of the Senator's occasional

[9] Above, pp. 70-71.

ventures into the diplomatic sphere. Yet there was no apparent desire within the administration to bring on an open conflict; and it was clearly not by its design that a chain of events was now inaugurated which ultimately led to a clear-cut repudiation of Mr. McCarthy's foreign policy views by Secretary Dulles and by the President himself. Equally unintended, no doubt, were the sharp repercussions of these developments on the national foreign relations.

The story of this important episode begins on Tuesday, November 3, when congressional and local elections in various parts of the United States resulted in scattered victories for Democratic candidates. The President's reaction was characteristically military: "I have lost skirmishes before," he said. But some of his politically minded advisers expressed the view that one factor in the Republican setback had been an insufficient emphasis on the theme of "Communists in government," which, though particularly associated with Senator McCarthy, had benefited many another Republican candidate in the national election of the year before. True, the new administration had thus far discovered fewer Communists in government than it apparently expected. A report of the Civil Service Commission on four months' operations under the new security system instituted in May had listed only 863 dismissals and 593 resignations on any type of security grounds, with no indication that any individual had been accused as a Communist or Communist agent.[10] But if these figures were relatively unimpressive in a Federal establishment of nearly 2,500,000, there were in the files individual cases from past years whose political potency was still largely unexploited.

One of these was the case of the late Harry Dexter White, a one-time key official of the Treasury Department who had been appointed in 1946 to the position of United States Executive Director of the International Monetary Fund, had resigned that post in 1947, and had died in 1948 after having publicly denied charges of participation in a wartime Communist espionage ring. Three days after the election, on November 6, 1953, Attorney General Herbert Brownell, Jr. in the course of a speech in Chicago made the startling

[10] *New York Times*, October 24, 1953.

assertion that President Truman had nominated White for the International Fund post even after "White's spying activities for the Soviet Government were reported in detail by the F.B.I. to the White House." White, he said, "was known to be a Communist spy by the very people who appointed him to the most sensitive and important position he ever held in Government service." [11]

This, undoubtedly, was a serious charge; but as usually happened in such cases, neither Mr. Brownell's original allegation, Mr. Truman's prompt denial, nor the subsequent restatements and clarifications of the two principals could be documented in sufficient detail to establish a fully satisfactory historical record. That the White appointment had been a serious administrative error seemed scarcely open to doubt; but whether the Truman administration had deliberately taken risks with the national security or had acted from inadvertence or even from cautious calculation was less clear. By themselves the published facts were inconclusive; they could only be interpreted in the light of one's individual estimate of the personalities involved. Not less important than the evaluation of this long-past incident, however, was the immediate revival nationally and internationally of the whole furor over the question of Communism and of Communist and anti-Comunist tactics in the United States. The commotion reached heights as yet unknown when Mr. Truman was subpoenaed to appear before the House Un-American Activities Committee, refused in deference to his conception of the rights and immunities of the presidency, but denied the charges made against him in a radio and television address (November 16) in which he made the further statement that "the present Administration has fully embraced, for political advantage, McCarthyism." [12]

The consequence of this allusion was to make Senator McCarthy the central figure in a quarrel with whose beginnings he had had no direct connection. In the meantime, however, the repercussions of the affair had begun seriously to affect the international climate. The implied attack on the loyalty

[11] *Ibid.,* November 7, 1953. The Executive Directors of the I.M.F. are not international civil servants but national representatives.

[12] *Ibid.,* November 17, 1953.

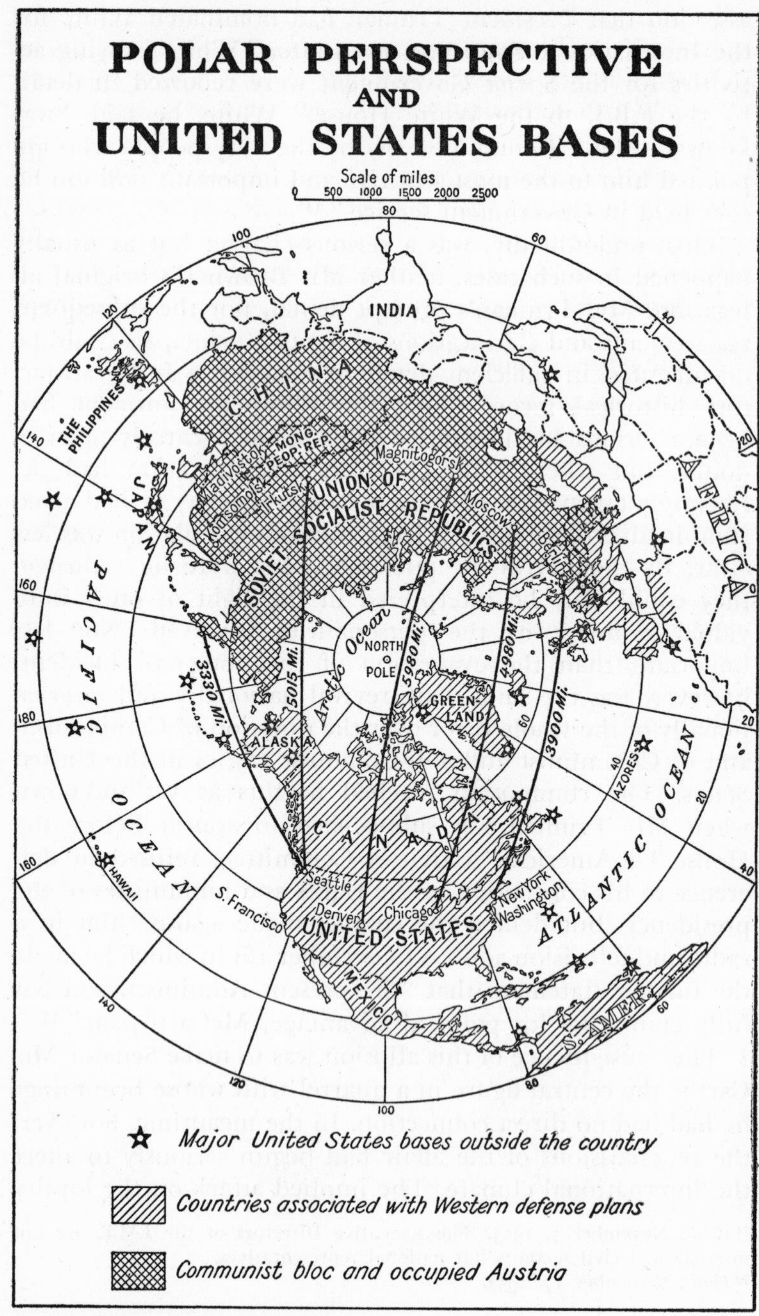

By permission of *The New York Times*

of a former President, especially the President who had sponsored the Truman doctrine and similar anti-Communist policies, was not widely commended abroad. The comment of the British Laborite *Daily Herald* of November 12 was fairly typical: "It would be better . . . for the reputation of the United States throughout the world, if this wildest of all the witch hunts is called off." In addition to this generally unfavorable response, particular difficulties developed in relations with the country which had long been recognized as our closest and in some ways most important neighbor.

Trouble with Canada

To the many permanent factors which enjoin a close and cordial understanding between the United States and Canada, a new and highly persuasive one had recently been added by the Soviet acquisition of the hydrogen bomb. The shortest distances from Soviet bases to North American population centers lay across the Arctic wastes and Canada. However backward this country's own preparations for coping with an enemy attack by nuclear weapons, it had immediately become clear that continental defense, in terms of an integrated plan for the defense of the whole North American continent, would henceforth represent a matter of the highest urgency for both nations. A joint radar network, the so-called Pinetree Chain, had been under construction not far from the Canadian-United States border for three or four years; but in October 1953, advisers of both governments had concluded that "additional early warning" must be provided "by the establishment of a further radar system generally to the north of the settled territory in Canada." [13] In November President Eisenhower, in the course of a visit to Ottawa to repay an earlier visit of Prime Minister St. Laurent, joined the latter in stressing "the importance of effective methods for joint defense, especially in the light of evidence of increasing technical capability of direct attack on both countries by weapons of great destructive power." [14]

[13] Statement by the Secretary of Defense, April 8, 1954, in *Department of State Bulletin*, XXX, April 26, 1954, 639.

[14] Joint communiqué, November 14, in *Documents on American Foreign Relations, 1953*, 404-405; on the visit of Canadian leaders to Washington in May 1953 cf. above, p. 66 n.

While in Ottawa the President also addressed the Canadian House of Commons and expatiated at some length on "the friendship, the sense of partnership, that for generations has been the hallmark of the relations between Canada and the United States." [15] Yet within a few days this historic friendship was to be clouded by an incident of unusual seriousness, one that vividly illustrated the difficulties faced by the United States in trying to reconcile its internal anti-Communist policies with the maintenance of a working partnership with other independent states. Involved were both the national sovereignty of Canada, so often recognized on both sides as basic to all cooperation between the two countries, and the national dignity of an important fellow democracy. The threat to both—for as such it was regarded by most Canadians and by some Americans—arose directly from the activities of a United States congressional committee in pursuit of further information on the Harry Dexter White case.

An initial jolt to the Canadians occurred three days after the President's Ottawa visit when data purporting to have been derived from official Canadian sources were made available to the Subcommittee on Internal Security of the Senate Judiciary Committee by the Director of the Federal Bureau of Investigation. The Canadian Government promptly protested the unilateral release of this hitherto classified information—which, incidentally, was later shown to have originated not with Canadian authorities but with a security officer of a third friendly power. More serious difficulties arose when the committee, headed by Senator William E. Jenner of Indiana, announced its wish to question a Canadian citizen, Igor Gouzenko, a former code clerk in the Soviet Embassy in Ottawa who had offered to provide information on espionage rings supposedly still operating in the United States. The Canadian Government at first refused

[15] Address of November 14, in *Department of State Bulletin*, XXIX, November 30, 1953, 735-738. Current expressions of this sense of partnership included the establishment on November 12 of a Joint Board of Engineers for the St. Lawrence power project (*ibid.*, 739; for background, cf. *ibid.*, November 23, 1953, 724-725) and of a Joint Committee on Trade and Economic Affairs which included the Secretaries of State, Treasury, Agriculture, and Commerce and their Canadian opposites (*ibid.*, 739-740).

this request on the ground that Gouzenko had already told all he knew. But the committee insisted; its requests were duly transmitted to Ottawa by the State Department; and, after considerable irritation had been vented on both sides of the border, arrangements were eventually made for committee representatives to interview Gouzenko under protective arrangements so strict as almost to recall those set up for the "explanations" to nonrepatriate prisoners of war in Korea.[16]

In the opinion of the committee chairman, the testimony eventually given by Mr. Gouzenko on January 4, 1954 was "both valuable and informative." [17] The primary significance of the affair, however, lay not so much in any new "leads" given the committee as in the mutual exasperation resulting from the conflict of United States and Canadian viewpoints. The difference was well exemplified in contrasting statement by Senator Alexander Wiley, Chairman of the Foreign Relations Committee, and Lester B. Pearson, Canadian Minister of External Affairs. Senator Wiley, noting what he termed a "widening gulf" between American and allied views in security matters, declared on November 21 that "whether or not foreign reactions improve or worsen, our United States investigations are not going to be stopped by anything." Speaking in New York two days later, Mr. Pearson, who had had the mortification of hearing his own political outlook questioned in some American circles, suggested that even an "occasional traitor in any one of our countries" would do security less harm than "suspicion and lack of mutual trust can do the cooperation and unity of the coalition on which our security must largely rest." [18]

Enter Senator McCarthy

This bilateral difference between the United States and Canada was now inflated to multilateral dimensions as the

[16] Diplomatic correspondence and related documents, November 19–December 3, *ibid.*, December 7, 1953, 789-792 and December 14, 1953, 812-813.

[17] *Testimony of Former Russian Code Clerk Relating to the Internal Security of the United States* (S. Doc. 5, 84th Cong., 1st Sess., Washington, 1955), 1.

[18] Statements of Sen. Wiley and Mr. Pearson in *New York Times,* November 22 and 24, 1953, respectively.

result of the intervention of Senator McCarthy, who had meanwhile demanded and received radio and television time to answer Mr. Truman's reference to "McCarthyism." In a speech delivered on November 24, Mr. McCarthy not only elaborated his familiar views on "Trumanism" and Communists in government but also expressed keen dissatisfaction with some aspects of the Eisenhower administration's performance in both domestic and foreign affairs. He did not, he said, share a hope expressed by President Eisenhower that domestic Communism would have ceased to be an issue by the time of the 1954 elections. There were still people on the Federal payroll who, in his estimation, ought not be there. But "the foulest bankruptcy of the Democratic Administration" which his party, he said, had failed to liquidate was the continued captivity of "some 900 American young men known to have been prisoners of the Communists in Korea" but still unaccounted for and therefore, presumably, "being brainwashed, starved or murdered behind an Iron or Bamboo Curtain."

The Republicans, said Senator McCarthy, had inherited this situation rather than creating it; but they were now responsible for its proper handling. "Now what are we going to do about it? Are we going to continue to send perfumed notes, following the style of the Truman-Acheson regime?" The Senator professed to favor more vigorous methods; he would "use all the power of this nation" to rescue the 900 captives, and felt that "we must regain our national honor regardless of what it costs." The procedure recommended for dealing with this problem was apparently based on a threefold assumption that (a) Communist China was kept alive only by its seaborne trade with the West, that (b) this trade could be effectually halted by energetic action on the part of the United States, and that (c) the importance of halting it outweighed any other considerations:

"We can deal a death blow to the war-making power of Communist China. We can, without firing a single shot, force the Communists in China to open their filthy Communist dungeons and release every American. We can blockade the coast of China, without using a single ship, a single sailor or a single gun. . . .

"We can handle this by saying to our Allies: If you continue to ship to Red China, while they are imprisoning and torturing American men, you will get not one cent of American money.

"If we do that, my good friends, this trading in blood-money will cease. No question about that." [19]

This program, which presupposed a willingness to part company with our major allies in the Far East if not all over the world, was put forward at a moment when the administration was preparing to concert policy with those allies at the forthcoming Bermuda conference. It was not the first statement of its kind, but it was the sharpest and, therefore, the most unequivocal challenge to the broad principles of international policy the administration had so often invoked. In its tone even more than in its specific content, it seemed to challenge the whole notion of a foreign policy based on common interests, and to set up in its place a new scale of priorities in which the interests peculiar to this country would be given absolute preponderance over any interests which this country happened to share with other nations.

The Administration Replies

This time, the administration's response was unequivocal even if Senator McCarthy was not directly named. "I welcome constructive criticism," Secretary Dulles told his news conference on December 1. "But [this] criticism . . . attacks the very heart of U.S. foreign policy." The fact that it was to our interest to assist certain countries did not, he said, "give us the right to try to take them over, to dictate their trade policies, and to make them our satellites." We did not want "weak or subservient allies." Not only were we dependent on them in a material sense but we, and they, recognized that cooperation was possible only on the basis of "mutual respect and friendship." "We do not propose to throw away those precious assets by blustering and domineering methods." These principles had been agreed upon with President Eisenhower before Mr. Dulles took office; and, said the Secretary, they still stood.[20]

These principles, moreover, were reaffirmed next day by President Eisenhower himself, in terms which left no doubt

[19] *Ibid.*, November 25, 1953.

[20] *Department of State Bulletin,* XXIX, December 14, 1953, 811-812.

that he was repudiating the McCarthy program in domestic as well as foreign affairs. Not only did he reaffirm the view that Communism would not be an issue in 1954; he asserted that the next election would hinge on "whether or not the Congress enacts a progressive, dynamic program enhancing the welfare of the people of our country." "Unless," he said, "the Republican Party can develop and enact such a program for the American people, it does not deserve to remain in power"—a sentiment which he declared was held by the vast majority of Republicans. As for the statements of Secretary Dulles, he not only endorsed them but had this to add:

> "The easiest thing to do with great power is to abuse it, to use it to excess. This most powerful of the free nations must not permit itself to grow weary of the processes of negotiation and adjustment that are fundamental to freedom. If it should turn impatiently to coercion of other free nations, our brand of coercion, so far as our friends are concerned, would be a mark of the imperialist rather than of the leader." [21]

In themselves these comments professed to offer no solution to the problem of missing American personnel in the Far East; but they did establish a perspective more broadly adjusted to the ramifications of what was, as President Eisenhower reminded his hearers, a world struggle of "freedom versus communism"—an issue which, he declared, "dominates all other considerations of our times"; "a life and death matter . . . the struggle of the ages." [22]

The presidential statement failed to alter the opinions of Senator McCarthy, who flatly reasserted them next day (December 3) before the television cameras and urged all Americans who shared his views about the "blood trade" to write or telegraph the President. Some thousands of messages poured in on the White House, more than half of them apparently favoring the McCarthy stand. More important, however, than this proof of Senator McCarthy's national following was the clear-cut reiteration by the heads of the administration that American policy would continue, despite such contrary opinion, to be conducted in what Secretary Dulles had called "a spirit of justice, forbearance and mag-

[21] *Ibid.*
[22] *Ibid.*

nanimity." Such an assurance meant a good deal in the uncertain atmosphere of the free world in late 1953. It would assist greatly in the assessment of some existing military and diplomatic policies of the United States. It would also be helpful in surmounting some of those "marginal disagreements" which, Mr. Dulles warned, still persisted—even though, as he hastened to add, they presented "no reason for sacrificing friendship by attempting to coerce; the more so because the attempt would be fruitless." [23]

2. BERMUDA AND "ATOMS FOR PEACE"

Seldom if ever has a meeting among the heads of great governments been so long planned, so anxiously awaited, surrounded with such secrecy, and produced so little visible result as the Bermuda meeting between President Eisenhower, Prime Minister Churchill, and Premier Laniel which took place, after many postponements, on December 4-7, 1953. The original motive for this unprecedented encounter among the leaders of the Western Big Three had been the need to concert a common policy in face of the change of "line" in Moscow and the widespread clamor, official and unofficial, for negotiations with the new Soviet leaders. That need, however, had been very largely fulfilled by the "Little Bermuda" conference held in Washington in July.[24] By the time the three heads of government were themselves ready to assemble, negotiations looking toward the establishment of contact with the Russians on the Foreign Ministers' level were already well advanced and little more was required except to fix definitely the place and date of a conference to be devoted primarily to the German and Austrian questions.[25] What remained for the three leaders and their Foreign Ministers was to examine their policies in common, reaffirm their unity concerning those points on which they were in agreement, and try to minimize the effects of their disagreements on those points concerning which no full agreement was possible.

[23] *Ibid.*
[24] Above, pp. 186-191.
[25] Cf. above, pp. 386-387.

Accomplishments at Bermuda

In the foreshortened view of history, the Bermuda conference will always be overshadowed by the plan for international participation in developing the peaceful uses of atomic energy which President Eisenhower unrolled before the United Nations General Assembly immediately on his return to the United States. That plan, however, was not an outgrowth of the Bermuda meeting but the fruit of long-continued consultation within the United States Government itself. So far as the Bermuda discussions were concerned, the only definite action announced was the approval of the three powers' replies to the latest Soviet note. Other accomplishments were mainly of an intangible nature. In their final communiqué the three statesmen declared that their meetings had "reinforced our solidarity, strengthened our resolve, and fortified our hopes." Sir Winston Churchill, who had personally been most anxious for "long, intimate, secret talks" with President Eisenhower but had not seemed overly cordial to the French visitors, later told the House of Commons that "We had some good talks," adding that the results "should . . . manifest themselves not so much in words as in policy and action and improved relations as the months go by." [26]

Most notable in the official declaration of the conference was not the recapitulation of well-established Allied policies —maintenance of united strength, development of NATO and a united Europe including E.D.C., restoration of more normal conditions in the Far East, and so on—but the comparatively relaxed tone of the entire pronouncement. There was even an unaccustomed suggestion that world conditions had actually improved: "If the danger of aggression now appears less imminent, we attribute this to the mounting strength of the free world and the firmness of its policies." Although the three statesmen did not neglect to include a reference to the captive peoples, its terms were more than usually restrained:

[26] Communiqué, December 7, in *Documents on American Foreign Relations, 1953,* 216-218; Churchill's account in *Parliamentary Debates, Weekly Hansard,* House of Commons, December 17, 1953, 579-588.

"We cannot accept as justified or permanent the present division of Europe. Our hope is that in due course peaceful means will be found to enable the countries of Eastern Europe again to play their part as free nations in a free Europe."

The three governments, said their leaders, intended to "lose no opportunity for easing the tensions that beset the world and for reassuring all nations that they have no cause to fear that the strength of the West will be invoked in any cause of wrongful violence." Such, they said, was the spirit in which they were preparing to meet with the Soviet Union on Germany and Austria; such, they implied, was also the spirit in which they continued to seek, as an immediate policy objective, the convening of the political conference provided for in paragraph 60 of the Korean armistice agreement.

Rather paradoxically, it was less than a week after this declaration that the President's special representative at Panmunjom found it necessary to break off his talks with Chinese and North Korean Communists in protest against their vilification of the United States.[27] The negotiations with the U.S.S.R., however, were destined for smoother sailing, despite Moscow's embarrassing insistence on the need for a five-power conference with Communist China as well as a four-power conference on Germany. President Eisenhower in his press conference of December 2—the same in which he so pointedly stressed his disagreement with Senator McCarthy—had shown sufficient coolness to this last idea to suggest the possibility of sharp disagreement with the French and British leaders at Bermuda. It was presumably Sir Winston Churchill, who had gone to Bermuda as strongly convinced as ever of the necessity for East-West consultations, who won unanimous assent to the view that this mainly theoretical difference ought not to be allowed to provoke an allied split or a breakdown in the negotiations with Moscow. Thus the Western notes, approved in Bermuda and delivered in Moscow on December 8, waived what was essentially the last obstacle to a four-power meeting by intimating that Mr. Molotov would not be prevented from bringing up at that meeting the subject of a five-power conference if he chose

[27] Cf. below, p. 448.

to do so. In this way the track was cleared for the conference of Big Four Foreign Ministers which eventually met in Berlin on January 25, 1954.[28]

There were other matters taken up at Bermuda on which agreement was less easily reached. The outlook for E.D.C. was found to be still highly problematical, despite Sir Winston's assurance that British troops would be kept on the Continent "at least as long as the American troops were kept there"—a pledge whose value naturally depended on the not wholly clarified intentions of the United States itself. The Prime Minister was disconcerted at learning that there seemed to be no possibility of agreement on any alternative line of action, such as the establishment of a separate German army, in case the E.D.C. project fell through: the question of what then would happen, he found, had "become for the time being unanswerable." Equally unsusceptible of clarification at the moment were "such questions as trade with China, recognition of the Chinese Communist Government, the admission of China to the United Nations organization, Korean problems and . . . such awkward personalities as Syngman Rhee and Chiang Kai-shek." But some reason was found for optimism about Trieste; and although the Prime Minister refused to modify his position on the Egyptian question, important understandings were reached concerning the exchange of additional information on atomic matters between Britain and the United States within the limits sanctioned by existing American law.[29]

The "Atoms-for-Peace" Plan

But the outstanding event of the conference was one that deserves to be recorded in Sir Winston's own words:

"After the President's arrival, in one of our earliest talks, he informed me of his intentions to deliver a speech to the United

[28] In their notes of December 8 (U.S. text in *Documents on American Foreign Relations, 1953,* 230) the Western powers suggested that the meeting begin January 4, 1954 in the Allied Control Council building in Berlin. Replying on December 26, Moscow proposed that the opening date be deferred to January 25 and that the meeting place be settled by the four High Commissioners in Berlin; to this the Western powers agreed on January 1, 1954. Texts in *Department of State Bulletin,* XXX, January 11, 1954, 43-44.

[29] Churchill account, cited; on Egypt, cf. above, p. 297.

Nations on a new proposal for the future of atomic energy for industrial or for peaceful purposes. He gave me a copy of this document upon which the policy of many months of American thought in the highest circles had been concentrated. [After study of the document] I wrote to the President saying I welcomed his proposal, as I thought it ended a long period of deadlock and might afford an opportunity for contact with the Soviets on the highest level. I suggested one or two alterations, not of course in the theme but in the preliminary and surrounding matter. I discussed with the President, but I was not aware when he left Bermuda what alterations he would make"—

and the Prime Minister went on to ridicule press reports in which he had been charged "on the one hand . . . with trying to prevent the President from making his speeech and, on the other, with having largely written it for him."

What was to be the nature of this famous address of December 8, which Sir Winston regarded "as one of the most important events in world history since the end of the war"? Like most major acts of statecraft, it would be several things at once. From the standpoint of United States "psychological strategy," it would be America's answer—presented, significantly, to the body that most nearly approximated a representative assembly of the human race—to those who claimed that the United States, in its preoccupation with the military aspects of the East-West struggle and the development of its national air-atomic capability, had lost sight of humanity's larger interest in the maintenance of peace and in the creation of a life of abundance for mankind.[30] From an individual and party standpoint, it would be the Republican equivalent to President Truman's Point Four program, put forward as a "dramatic highlight" to the inaugural address of 1949 and immediately acclaimed as one of the most statesmanlike proposals of the decade if not of the century. From the standpoint of the perils of the atomic age, it would represent the administration's response to long-continued pressure for "Operation Candor"—for revealing the truth about the new weapons and their implications for the future of

[30] The significance of the "atoms-for-peace" plan as "unquestionably the best idea in the cold war so far" was authoritatively brought out by the assistant director of the U.S. Information Agency in testimony before a House Appropriations subcommittee, summarized in *New York Times,* April 13, 1955.

civilization. Finally and perhaps most important, from the standpoint of the atomic armaments race it would offer a shift of emphasis which would not of itself resolve the disarmament deadlock, but which would open up the possibility of a kind of flanking movement whereby it might be possible to develop the mutual confidence through which alone the disarmament deadlock might ultimately be resolved.

The President's Address

As the last important occasion of the General Assembly session, the presidential address provided a hopeful addendum to the Assembly's own deliberations in regard to disarmament and economic development.[31] Aside from introductory civilities, it fell into three parts: (1) an indication of the destructive power of modern atomic weapons, (2) a reiteration of the peaceful aims of the United States, and (3) a specific proposal for the formation of an International Atomic Energy Agency to receive contributions of uranium and fissionable materials from participating countries for allocation to peaceful uses.

The section on the perils of the modern atom, based necessarily on the President's detailed knowledge of United States atomic capabilities, was as frightening to those with a little imagination as anything that had thus far been revealed from official sources:

"Atomic bombs today are more than 25 times as powerful as the weapons with which the atomic age dawned, while hydrogen weapons are in the ranges of millions of tons of TNT equivalent.

"Today, the United States' stockpile of atomic weapons, which, of course, increases daily, exceeds by many times the explosive equivalent of the total of all bombs and all shells that came from every plane and every gun in every theatre of war in all of the years of World War II.

"A single air group, whether afloat or land-based, can now deliver to any reachable target a destructive cargo exceeding in power all the bombs that fell on Britain in all of World War II."

[31] Above, pp. 399-404. The full text of the address appears in *Documents on American Foreign Relations, 1953,* 45-52.

While he made no attempt to relate these potentialities to the strategy of the "new look," the President went on to emphasize that no degree of superiority in this field could provide a nation with any permanent or absolute guarantee of safety.

". . . Even a vast superiority in numbers of weapons, and a consequent capability of devastating retaliation, is no preventive, of itself, against the fearful material damage and toll of human lives that would be inflicted by surprise aggression. . . . Even against the most powerful defense, an aggressor in possession of the effective minimum number of atomic bombs for a surprise attack could probably place a sufficient number of his bombs on the chosen targets to cause hideous damage."

To any such attack on the United States, the President emphasized, the reaction would be "swift and resolute," and of such force that "an aggressor's land would be laid waste." But this, he went on, was not the true purpose and hope of the United States, which wanted "to be constructive, not destructive," to bring about "agreements, not wars, among nations," and "to help us move out of the dark chamber of horrors into the light." It was for this reason, said the President, that we had agreed to a four-power meeting with the Russians; that we would "bend every effort of our minds to the single purpose of emerging from that conference with tangible results toward peace"; that we would "never say that the peoples of Russia are an enemy with whom we have no desire ever to deal or mingle in friendly and fruitful relationship." It was for this reason, likewise, that the United States welcomed the Assembly's recent suggestion that a solution to the disarmament impasse be sought in private talks among the powers principally involved. Not only were we "instantly prepared" to join in such talks; we should carry into them "a new conception."

"The United States would seek more than the mere reduction or elimination of atomic materials for military purposes.

"It is not enough to take this weapon out of the hands of the soldiers. It must be put into the hands of those who will know how to strip its military casing and adapt it to the arts of peace.

"The United States knows that if the fearful trend of atomic military buildup can be reversed, this greatest of destructive forces can be developed into a great boon, for the benefit of all mankind."

What the President proposed was not a fresh approach to the problem of disarmament as such, on which the United States position apparently remained unchanged. The "new conception" involved a supplementary effort whereby the United Nations, in addition to its efforts to solve the disarmament problem, would also sponsor an experiment in the peaceful application of atomic energy under international auspices—an experiment that would have "the great virtue that it can be undertaken without the irritations and mutual suspicions incident to any attempt to set up a completely acceptable system of world-wide inspection and control." Due precautions would be taken to prevent the misapplication of the fissionable and other materials which the participating nations would allocate—in quantities that would undoubtedly be small at first—to the international agency. But a hopeful picture was painted of the benefits that could flow from the scheme:

"Experts would be mobilized to apply atomic energy to the needs of agriculture, medicine, and other peaceful activities. A special purpose would be to provide abundant electrical energy in the power-starved areas of the world. Thus the contributing powers would be dedicating some of their strength to serve the needs rather than the fears of mankind."

Thus far the rationale of the scheme appeared plain enough. Not quite so easy to grasp was the connection which the President's exposition appeared to establish between (a) the allocation of limited amounts of fissionable material for peaceful purposes, and (b) a reduction in the peril of atomic destruction. The supplies of fissionable material available to the leading powers were not likely to be so scanty that even a considerable diversion to peaceful uses would significantly reduce the amounts available for military use. On the contrary, the recent expansion of the United States atomic energy program, and the successful development of a "breeder" process for increasing the quantity of fissionable material even as it was consumed, promised a supply of atomic fuel sufficient for all foreseeable needs.[32] Thus it was not quite easy to see all that the President had in mind when he described the specific plan which, in his opinion, should be drawn up by "the powers principally involved"—including, "of course," the Soviet Union:

"I would be prepared to submit to the Congress of the United States, and with every expectation of approval, any such plan that would:

"First—encourage world-wide investigation into the most effective peacetime uses of fissionable material, and with the certainty that they had all the material needed for the conduct of all experiments that were appropriate;

"Second—begin to diminish the potential destructive power of the world's atomic stockpiles;

"Third—allow all peoples of all nations to see that, in this enlightened age, the great powers of the earth, both of the East and of the West, are interested in human aspirations first, rather than in building up the armaments of war;

"Fourth—open up a new channel for peaceful discussion, and initiate at least a new approach to the many difficult problems that must be solved in both private and public conversations, if the world is to shake off the inertia imposed by fear, and is to make positive progress toward peace."

But no minor obscurity in this dramatic program could disguise its potential importance. "As I meditated on the President's proposals," said Sir Winston Churchill,

"limited though they are in scope, and shrouded in technicalities as they are for laymen, I could not help feeling that we were in the process of what might prove to be a turning point in our destiny. I fervently hope that the Soviet Government will not ignore this beam of light through much darkness and confusion. I am sure of the sincerity and altruistic good will by which it was inspired, and I trust that they will advance with confidence, to which their own strength entitles them, along a path which certainly leads in the direction of expanding the welfare and calming the fears of the masses of the people of all the world." [33]

[32] Cf. Gordon Dean, *Report on the Atom* (New York, Knopf, 1953), 126-127, 178-181.

[33] Address of December 17, cited.

The U.S.S.R. Responds

It was undoubtedly the Soviet reaction which would primarily determine whether the "atoms-for-peace" plan was to be a true turning point in human destiny or only another milestone on the road toward mutual annihilation. A day before the Eisenhower speech, the Soviet Foreign Office had been specially alerted to its importance by a visit from Ambassador Bohlen. Would Mr. Malenkov's government embrace the unprecedented opportunity that was now offered it to develop at least one cooperative relationship with the countries of the free world, or would it treat the Eisenhower plan with the same derision that Stalin's government had accorded the Point Four program? The Malenkov regime had at least come around, four years late, to participating in a limited way in international technical assistance activities under the United Nations. Would it be more forthright in supporting the Eisenhower project? The first reactions of Mr. Vyshinsky and the Moscow radio were definitely unencouraging; but within four days Mr. Molotov had at least promised to give the matter "serious attention," and on December 21 the Soviet Government released a lengthy recapitulation of its own views which contained elements that Secretary Dulles was able to pronounce "hopeful." [34]

The Eisenhower proposal, according to Moscow, was seriously objectionable in that it failed to coincide with the well-known Soviet views on disarmament and "in its present form . . . neither stops the growing production of atomic weapons nor limits the possibility of using these weapons." The correct procedure, as always, in the Soviet view, was to begin with "the unconditional prohibition of atomic and hydrogen weapons" under "strict international supervision" —a procedure which, it was claimed, would make it possible to devote "not a certain part, but the entire mass of atomic materials" to peaceful purposes. Nevertheless, true to its unswerving pursuit of a "peace-loving" policy, the Soviet Government declared itself willing to take part in the "confidential or diplomatic conversations" proposed by President Ei-

[34] *Department of State Bulletin,* XXIX, December 21, 1953, 851 and XXX, January 4, 1954, 9-10.

senhower in connection with his project. In doing so it would expect to receive the "necessary clarification" of the Eisenhower proposal and would insist on simultaneous consideration of its own plan for the outlawing of weapons of mass destruction.[35]

Thus was opened still another potential channel of communication among the great powers. In addition to the forthcoming Berlin conference on Germany and Austria, there were now scheduled or in prospect a political conference on Korea, private meetings on disarmament under the United Nations, and private conferences—which apparently would be held separately from the disarmament conversations—on the "atoms-for-peace" plan. All this was in addition to the five-power conference on international tensions which the U.S.S.R. continued to advocate. There would be no lack of available facilities if Moscow was desirous, during the coming year, of doing its share to make possible a settlement of the issues which thus far had prevented a genuine reduction of tension such as it claimed to be seeking.

3. E.D.C. OR "AGONIZING REAPPRAISAL"?

In the atmosphere of pleased anticipation engendered by the enunciation of the "atoms-for-peace" plan, it was not to be expected that so routine an event as the Twelfth Ministerial Session of the North Atlantic Council, which took place in Paris on December 14-16, should attract much public attention or receive specially favorable notice on the part of Western opinion. If anything, the Council meeting and related events had the effect of dampening the optimism that followed the Bermuda meeting and the President's speech. Those occasions had been largely concerned with such hopeful prospects as conciliation and the settlement of East-West differences. The NATO meeting, on the contrary, was chiefly concerned with maintaining and developing the strength of the West as an essential protection against aggression and an essential preliminary to any understanding with the Communist bloc. This encounter of fourteen dif-

[35] *Ibid.*, January 18, 1954, 80-82; also printed in *Documents on American Foreign Relations, 1954*, 462-466.

ferent teams of Foreign, Defense, and Finance ministers, the first since April, was a reminder that important differences of opinion still existed concerning the means by which Western strength should be developed as well as the nature and timing of any discussions with the U.S.S.R.

The NATO Council

The chief nominal business of this Council meeting was to confirm and ratify the "long-haul" concept for NATO's military build-up which had received preliminary approval at the April session.[36] Since this involved a reduction rather than an intensification of the exertions involved in NATO's defense effort, agreement could be reached with a minimum of friction. Unlike Secretary Acheson, Secretary Dulles was not pressing the allied governments for greater material efforts, and General Gruenther was able to appraise the recent progress and the existing state of affairs affecting his command in much more optimistic terms than either of his two predecessors. The reduced military goals for 1953, it appeared, had been "completely met for the land forces and to a substantial extent for the naval and air forces." Support units had increased by 40 percent, and aircraft by 30 percent, within the past year; the total land forces directly available to NATO now totaled "some 100 divisions—both active and reserve—in varying states of combat readiness." Lord Ismay's annual report showed that the aggregate defense expenditure of the fourteen allies in 1953 had amounted to $65.6 billion, or 10 percent more than in 1952. ($51.9 billion of this amount was American, $2.1 billion Canadian, and $11.6 billion European expenditure.) Nearly $3 billion in American military supplies had been sent to Europe during the year, bringing the total of such shipments (exclusive of shipments to Greece and Turkey) to $5.7 billion. No fewer than 120 airfields and a large signal communication network developed under the infrastructure program were already in use. Still another reason for optimism was the announcement of Defense Secretary Wilson that Congress was definitely going to be asked to amend the Atomic Energy Act so that appropri-

[36] Cf. above, pp. 166-168.

ate atomic intelligence and weapons could be made available to NATO.[37]

It was against this encouraging background that the Council proceeded to adopt "firm force goals for 1954, provisional goals for 1955, and planning goals for 1956." The 1954 goals were said to envisage "some increase in the numerical strength of existing NATO forces"—specifically, an increase of 5 percent in army divisions, 25 percent in aircraft, and 15 percent in naval vessels—and, as usual, "a very substantial improvement in their quality and effectiveness." Special attention was to be given "to the continuing provision of modern weapons of the latest types," and the Military Committee was directed to continue its long-term reassessment of "the most effective pattern of military forces," paying due regard to what could be learned about the effects of new weapons. Agreement was reached on additional military construction totaling $251 million (£90 million), constituting the first installment of the three-year, "Fifth Slice" infrastructure program discussed in April. Half the money would be used for fuel pipelines and storage systems and the remainder for naval facilities, signals and communications, additional airfields, navigational aids, and military headquarters.

Once again, the Council emphasized the continuing nature of the threat to the Western world and the probability that the NATO forces would have to be maintained in top condition over a period of years "so that, in the event of attack, they can act as a shield behind which the full strength of the member countries can be rapidly mobilised." But it was the political rather than the military implication of this effort that seemed to be of most interest to European delegates at this time when East-West negotiations seemed definitely in prospect. The equilibrium that NATO was seeking to establish, said Belgium's Foreign Minister, Paul van Zeeland, was, after all, only an intermediate aim of Western policy.

[37] Final communiqué, December 16, in *Documents on American Foreign Relations, 1953,* 203-205; further details in Lord Ismay, *NATO: The First Five Years, 1949–1954* (n.p., n.d.), 107-108, 118; *Report to Congress on the Mutual Security Program,* December 31, 1953 (Washington, G.P.O., 1954), 12-15; "Activités dans le cadre du Traité de l'Atlantique Nord," *Chronique de politique étrangère,* VII, March 1954, 166-181.

The essential objective was the reopening of negotiations, and this should be steadily pursued even while rearmament was going on. M. Bidault, who presided, was equally emphatic on the urgency of East-West conversations.

As had so frequently happened before, however, United States representatives seemed only partially to share this dominant preoccupation. Having so recently brought forth both the "atoms-for-peace" plan and the strategy of the "new look" (Admiral Radford's public exposition of the "new look" concept was made on December 14, the opening day of the Council session),[38] United States policy seemed for the present to have exhausted its powers of innovation. Secretary Dulles did indeed accept the Council's unaccustomed conclusion "that Soviet armed aggression in Europe is less likely today than it seemed several years ago," as well as its finding that "the Soviet threat persists and probably will long persist." [39] He, too, seemed anxious to exploit the opportunities thus afforded; but his prime interest was plainly concerned not with East-West relations as such but with the need to mend that serious fissure in the Western position that was associated with the nonmaterialization of the European Defense Community.

Mr. Dulles on E.D.C.

When the Eisenhower administration had assumed office nearly eleven months earlier, it had surveyed the difficulties surrounding the E.D.C. project and decided to commit its own vast prestige in support of the undertaking. Secretary Dulles had warned that in the absence of "effective unity" soon, there would have to be "a little rethinking" of American policy toward Western Europe; Congress had underlined the warning by adopting the "Richards Amendment" making half of the military aid appropriation for Europe for 1953–54 contingent on adoption of E.D.C.[40] In the intervening period, some of the obstacles to E.D.C. had collapsed while others had been reinforced. In Washington, the admin-

[38] Cf. above, pp. 355 ff.

[39] Statement to the Council, December 14, in *New York Times*, December 15, 1953.

[40] Above, pp. 20-21 and 90.

istration had presumably considered whether it should still insist on E.D.C. or investigate the possibility of attaining the same or similar objectives by other means. But no alternatives had been brought to light at Bermuda; and Mr. Dulles now made clear in his principal statement to the NATO Council that if alternatives had in fact been considered, they had been rejected in favor of continued endorsement of E.D.C. Indeed, he implied that if there was any alternative at all it was the drastic one of a reversal in American policy toward Europe.

The Secretary of State avoided the word "reversal" in his formal declaration, which was communicated to the press immediately after its delivery to the Council.[41] He used instead the words "agonizing reappraisal"—a phrase which Sir Winston Churchill judged "most formidable" [42] and which, of course, in practice meant virtually the same thing. The need, said Mr. Dulles, was "for Europe to move onward to more complete and organic forms of union." "Treaties between sovereign states" and "mere promises for the future" were not enough. If the E.D.C. was established, he intimated, the fear that the United States would "abandon military support of Europe" would be "baseless"; and he quoted a passage from the Bermuda communiqué to the effect that establishment of E.D.C. would "ensure intimate and durable cooperation between the United Kingdom and United States forces and the forces of the European Defence Community on the Continent of Europe."

But the opposite possibility was less pleasingly delineated:

"If, however, the European Defense Community should not become effective; if France and Germany remain apart, so that they would again be potential enemies, then indeed there would be grave doubt whether Continental Europe could be made a place of safety.

"That would compel an agonizing reappraisal of basic United States policy."

If the Defense Community did not soon come into being, Mr. Dulles went on, "different and divisive forces" might

[41] Text in *New York Times*, December 15, 1953.

[42] *Parliamentary Debates, Weekly Hansard*, House of Commons, December 17, 1953, 583.

take command. "These separatist forces will also be found in the United States."

"It may never again be possible for integration to occur in freedom, although it might be that West Europe would be unified, as East Europe has been unified, in defeat and servitude."

In a press conference following the Council meeting the Secretary added a number of important details: [43]

"The [United States] Government was not at the moment making any plans on the supposition that E.D.C. would fail. If it did fail it would call for a fundamental reappraisal of United States policy.

". . . The United States is not interested primarily in the E.D.C. as a means of getting any fixed number of German divisions. At present it is interested in trying to create a situation so that the Western countries will not commit suicide. If they decide to commit suicide they may have to commit it alone.

". . . [A reappraisal of United States policy] would not involve abandonment or repudiation of United States obligations under the NATO Treaty. It would involve some rethinking of how to implement that treaty.

". . . If events compelled what he referred to as an 'agonizing reappraisal' one of the elements that would be considered in that reappraisal would be the disposition of United States forces"—

the implication being that American divisions would be withdrawn from Germany and that the United States would most probably revert to a "peripheral" strategy whereby our role in European defense would be limited to the threat of air strikes against the industrial heart of the U.S.S.R.[44]

As on several earlier occasions, Mr. Dulles' bluntness evoked varying reactions, warmer among those who shared his opinions and coolest among those whom he appeared to

[43] *New York Times,* December 15, 1953.

[44] In a speech to the National Press Club on December 22 (*Department of State Bulletin,* XXX, January 4, 1954, 3-7), Mr. Dulles stated definitely that in the event of a rejection of E.D.C. it would be necessary to "reexamine" the so-called "forward strategy" in Western Europe, which he defined as "a plan . . . to defend the entire area of the prospective E.D.C. countries rather than to contemplate from the beginning the abandonment of advanced positions in Germany, which might make the rest [of Europe] untenable." (The bracketed words, omitted from the official text, appear in the recorded version printed in *New York Times,* December 23, 1953.)

be directly criticizing. France, as the principal delinquent in regard to E.D.C., appeared least appreciative—partly, perhaps, because Mr. Dulles' observations happened to precede by three days the commencement of a French presidential election and thus recalled another pronouncement made on the eve of the German election in September.[45] During the NATO Council meeting there was more than one sign of disagreement between the Secretary of State and M. Bidault, who laid considerable emphasis on the need for still stronger NATO guarantees of E.D.C. (backed, of course, by the United States) if the project was to be made palatable to French parliamentary opinion.

For Europeans, the hint of possible reversion to a peripheral strategy was underlined by the simultaneous disclosures about the "new look" strategic policy with its increased reliance on atomic weapons and curtailment of armed manpower. Mr. Dulles, said the *Manchester Guardian,* seemed to be implying "that if there is to be no German contribution through the European Defence Community, then almost the whole structure of European defence must be torn down." [46] Europe, so it seemed, had reached a turning point. Unless it could resolve itself in favor of the E.D.C. and thus assure itself of continued American support, the pressure on the United States to limit its interest and participation in European defense might, after all, become irresistible.

President Eisenhower, according to authoritative sources, was fully in accord with the views put forward by the Secretary of State. A White House release of December 23 described a briefing presented by the latter at a meeting of the National Security Council:

". . . The President was informed concerning the prospects of bringing into being the European Defense Community, a matter which has long been of deep concern to him. He considers this the only practical proposal for ending permanently the recurrent strife between France and Germany, provoked twice in our own generation by German militarism, and of creating a solid core at the center of the NATO structure. The President shares the view which had been expressed to the Coun-

[45] Cf. above, p. 199.
[46] *Manchester Guardian Weekly,* December 18, 1953.

cil by Secretary Dulles, that failure soon to consummate the EDC would confront the United States with the necessity of reappraising its basic policies as regards Europe."[47]

France Chooses a President

Debate on E.D.C. in the French National Assembly had by now been deferred until early in the new year. The scheduling of the Berlin conference had offered a new argument to those Frenchmen who held that no final action should be taken on E.D.C. until the possibility of an accommodation with the Russians had been more thoroughly explored. In the meantime, the process of choosing a successor to President Vincent Auriol, whose seven-year term was to end January 17, 1954, provided another demonstration of the difficulty Frenchmen experienced in achieving working agreement in political matters even when foreign policy issues were not directly involved. Disagreement over the choice of a President was in some ways less serious than an ordinary cabinet crisis, since the presidential functions in France were only remotely concerned with day-to-day policy. Yet the prolonged deadlock which now occurred in the French Parliament (the National Assembly and the Council of the Republic, meeting in joint session at Versailles) before the elimination of Premier Laniel and the election of Senator René Coty, a dark horse candidate of the Independent party, on the thirteenth ballot on December 23 could not be dissociated from all the other signs of weakness which France had exhibited during the year. To some foreigners it seemed a crowning proof of French incapacity to face the demands of the postwar period—something that in itself would justify the kind of "agonizing reappraisal" Mr. Dulles had talked about.

To a good many Frenchmen, too, this performance seemed almost the last gasp of the political system of the Fourth Republic as it had developed since the exclusion of the Communists from the government in 1947. The next stage in French affairs, now only a few months away, would be the emergence of a quite novel type of governmental policy under an as yet untried leader, Pierre Mendès-France. Thus

[47] *Department of State Bulletin*, XXX, January 4, 1954, 7.

far M. Mendès-France, who had figured in June as one of the unsuccessful candidates for the premiership now held by M. Laniel, was chiefly known as a long-standing advocate of negotiations to liquidate the war in Indochina and thus begin the process of bringing France's commitments into closer relationship to the nation's real strength. Within a few months he was to have his chance to see what negotiation with the Communists would accomplish. Before that happened, however, the world was to witness in Indochina the collapse of still another French enterprise, one to which the United States had seemingly begun to attach as much importance as it did to the consummation of E.D.C. itself.

It was paradoxical that France, in some respects the least dependable member of the Atlantic coalition, had become so vitally essential to the most urgent United States policy objectives in both Europe and Asia. In Europe, it held the key to the establishment or collapse of the European Defense Community; in Asia, it was the irreplaceable executor of the much-advertised Navarre plan for the termination of the war in Indochina and the blocking of the last unprotected corridor open to Chinese Communist expansion.

4. STORM SIGNALS IN ASIA

Despite anxiety over the future of E.D.C. and the trend of American policy in Europe, the prevailing mood of the West as 1954 approached was one of considerable optimism. In his principal public report on the NATO meeting, Secretary Dulles reiterated as his own the view of the NATO Council that "the danger of open military aggression from Soviet Russia was less than it had been a year or two before." NATO's growing power, coupled with rising internal pressures and discontents within the Soviet bloc, had produced a condition in which, he said, the Soviet leaders seemed to recognize that "it would be reckless for them to engage in general war." The coming year would be "a year for great decision."

> ". . . There lie ahead European unity, a possible recession of the horror of atomic warfare, and a beginning of an ending of the unnatural division of Europe.

"In Korea we look forward to the first year of peace since 1949.

"The problems are many and grievous, but our hopes are high . . ." [48]

If there was a conspicuous omission in this brief survey of world prospects, it was the lack of reference to the expansionist ambitions and aggressive proclivities of Communist China—tendencies which had already led the United States to take such extraordinary measures for the protection of the Republic of Korea, Formosa, and Indochina. Needless to say, these dangers had not been forgotten in the State Department. As Assistant Secretary Robertson had pointed out not long before,[49] "We in the Far Eastern Bureau are constantly reminded by the Peiping radio exactly how the Communists regard us and what they have in mind for Asia. . . . This is our daily fare." Militarily, he recalled, the Communists had "by far the largest ground forces in the Far East," including the Soviet divisions in Eastern Siberia and the Maritime Provinces, the "several million troops" of Communist China, and the "additional hundreds of thousands" of North Korea and the Vietminh; and there were also the "formidable" air forces of Communist China and North Korea and the "exceedingly large" Soviet submarine fleet based on Vladivostok.

In estimating the Communist menace, moreover, Mr. Robertson had observed that "we must not fail to bear in mind that the Communists are able to switch from one method of attack to an entirely different method as the situation seems to warrant." Such a tactical reversal, indeed, had appeared to him to be in process at that very time:

"Once more, except in Indochina, the Communists seem to be relying on propaganda and political weapons and on identifying themselves with popular movements. For everywhere, the military attacks launched by the Communists since 1948 have been decisively repelled—except in Indochina, where, however, we believe the tide is now turning."

Even in Indochina, the initiation of the Navarre plan had offered grounds for anticipating that the long-standing Viet-

[48] Address of December 22, *ibid.*, 7.

[49] Address of December 2, *ibid.*, XXIX, December 14, 1953, 814-818.

minh threat might soon be eradicated once for all. Mr. Dulles, in his Paris press conference on December 14, had voiced a hope that hostilities there would be successfully concluded in the course of 1954.[50]

Elsewhere, the threat of Communist aggression did not appear sufficiently grave to interfere with the gradual redeployment of United States forces involved in the "new look" program. The armies of the Republic of Korea and the Republic of China were growing daily more proficient in handling the weapons and equipment supplied to them under the United States military assistance program. The Strategic Air Command was always ready to implement the various warnings extended to Communist China to the effect that renewed aggression would invite retaliation that might not be localized in character. On December 26 President Eisenhower was ready to disclose that United States ground forces in Korea would be "progressively reduced as circumstances warrant," beginning with the two Army divisions which would shortly be returned to the United States.[51] In making this announcement, the President emphasized that United States forces in the Far East would "be maintained at appropriate levels to take account of [the United Nations pledge to Korea] and to fulfill the commitments which the United States has undertaken in that area, and which are vital to the security of the United States. These forces will feature highly mobile naval, air, and amphibious units." The action being taken, said the President, "does not impair our readiness and capacity to react in a way which should deter aggression and, if aggression should nevertheless occur, to oppose it with even greater effect than heretofore." [52]

There were, to be sure, a few dark spots in this otherwise pleasing picture. For one thing, if the Communists were indeed switching from a policy of military expansion to one of political and psychological penetration, it was questionable how well the free world was equipped to resist such an attack, particularly in the "soft" areas of Southeast Asia. Nonmilitary methods for resisting Communist expansion had

[50] *New York Times,* December 15, 1953.
[51] Above, p. 364.
[52] *Department of State Bulletin,* XXX, January 4, 1954, 15.

not loomed large in recent Washington planning. The transfer of real power from the French to the governments of the Associated States of Indochina had not yet been consummated; neutralist and even anti-Western tendencies still had the upper hand in countries like Burma and Indonesia; economic progress under the Colombo Plan and similar projects had not yet raised Asian living standards to a point where the average individual could feel that he had much stake in preserving the existing order.

Furthermore, there had as yet been no resolution of the basic political conflict in the Far East between the ambition of Communist China to extend its power and influence and the determination of the United States, supported in varying degrees by its allies, to block or reverse the tide of Communist expansionism. As long as that conflict remained, it was unlikely that the Peking government would passively cooperate in Western plans for consolidating the *status quo* in the Far East. It might be restrained by threats of retaliation from openly breaking the peace in areas like Korea, the Straits of Formosa, or Indochina. It could hardly be expected to neglect any opportunities that might present themselves for aggrandizement that could be carried out without resorting to open aggression.

Korean Finale

Developments at Panmunjom, though seemingly involving no threat of a renewal of the Korean war, had taken a course that underlined the irreconcilability of Chinese Communist and American aims. At Bermuda the Big Three had declared that the "immediate object" of their policy was "the convening of the political conference provided for in the Korean Armistice agreement." This, they had said, "would provide the means for reaching a peaceful settlement of the Korean question and for making progress in restoring more normal conditions in the Far East and South East Asia."[53] But at Panmunjom, Mr. Dean and his Communist opposites had quite failed to resolve their deadlock over the question whether they were there to arrange a conference of the two

[53] Communiqué, December 7, in *Documents on American Foreign Relations, 1953,* 218; cf. above, p. 427.

belligerent sides, as stipulated by the United States with the endorsement of the General Assembly, or a conference encompassing other shades of opinion as desired by the Communists. Mr. Dean summed up the situation in these words:

"Time and place are relatively easy. As to time, we are agreeable to any date so long as there is adequate time to prepare the necessary facilities, transport the delegations, etc. As to place, we say Geneva, the Communists say New Delhi, and we could probably agree on Beirut, or Colombo or Kandy or Nuwara Eliya in Ceylon.

"The meat of the coconut is the composition. Who will attend the conference—who will be bound by agreements reached?" [54]

On this point there was as yet no sign of agreement.

Emulating the tactics employed by the United Nations armistice delegation at Panmunjom a few months earlier,[55] Mr. Dean put forward on December 8—one day after the Bermuda conference—a "package proposal" designed, as he said, "to stop the other side's byplay as to neutrals and further the early convening of the conference." [56] By its terms the political conference would be convened in Geneva four to six weeks after the termination of the preliminary talks. The principle of a two-sided conference of the belligerents (and the U.S.S.R.) would be maintained, but it was provided that other nations which were "actually working" or had "current experience" in Korea and were "currently familiar with its problems" (meaning principally India) could be "invited by both sides to attend and take part . . . without vote on either of the two sides." Such governments would be entitled to express their views on any item of the agenda that was up for discussion, but could not introduce "formal motions or proposals"; and no representative at the conference could "speak on any topic not on the agenda and then only in the order on the agenda."

Whether or not Mr. Dean had been instructed to regard this as a "final" proposal has not been disclosed. Apparently,

[54] Address of December 21, in *Department of State Bulletin,* XXX, January 4, 1954, 16.

[55] Above, pp. 222-223.

[56] Address of December 21, cited. The proposal (circulated as U.N. Document A/2628, December 11) is printed in *Department of State Bulletin,* XXIX, December 21, 1953, 877-878.

however, it went as far in the direction of Communist views as the United States felt able to go, and its nonacceptance by the Communists was soon followed by the breaking off of negotiations, technically on a separate issue. Mr. Dean's account follows:

"At the meeting on December 10 [actually December 12], 1953, in an uninterrupted 5¾-hour session, the Chinese delegate, Huang Hua, after several warnings from me accused the United States of America of perfidy or deliberate treachery in connection with the release of prisoners by President Rhee . . . on June 17-18. . . . I told him that his statement was false—that my Government was not guilty of perfidy and unless he withdrew the charge I would treat the meetings as in indefinite recess. He repeated the charge. And I withdrew in protest. To my mind it is quite sufficient. If I had not, the Communists would have broadcast far and wide that a representative of the United States Government had admitted the charge of perfidy." [57]

Not surprisingly, the Communists charged the United States with having deliberately sought a pretext to break off the conversations; and similar charges were brought against the Communists by the United States. Mr. Dean returned home for Christmas, leaving word that his deputy would be available to resume negotiations if the Communists chose to retract their statement. Obviously, however, there was scant prospect of an agreement even if the talks were renewed. As matters turned out, the issue was left in abeyance until it was taken up again under different auspices at the Berlin conference early in 1954.

In the meantime the "explanation" machinery set up for the supposed benefit of nonrepatriate prisoners of war had sputtered and backfired violently without ever getting fully into motion, due mainly to the efforts of the Communist explainers to disguise their almost complete lack of success in persuading their men to go home. As the ninety-day explanation period approached its scheduled termination on December 23, the vast majority of the 22,604 nonrepatriates turned over by the Unified Command had not even been interviewed; of the 3,200-odd who had been subjected to explaining sessions, no more than a handful (90 Chinese and 47

[57] Address of December 21, cited. On the prisoner release cf. above, pp. 226-227.

Koreans) had chosen to return to Communism.[58] This vindication of free ideals was somewhat soured, however, by the recalcitrance of those prisoners, including twenty-three Americans and one Britisher, who were held by the Communists and insisted on staying where they were. Only seven Koreans out of 335, and two Americans out of the twenty-three, chose to be repatriated despite the persuasive efforts of their own countrymen.

Like everything else related to prisoners of war, the causes of the breakdown of the explanations were a matter of sharp disagreement. A majority report of the Neutral Nations Repatriation Commission, submitted by Poland, Czechoslovakia, and India on December 28, ascribed the uncooperative behavior of prisoners turned over by the Unified Command to pressure from "the former detaining side," especially the authorities of South Korea. A minority report signed by Sweden and Switzerland minimized this factor and generally supported the views of the Unified Command.[59] One of the few agreeable notes in the entire debacle was the praise extended to the Indian custodial troops by General John E. Hull, who had succeeded General Clark as United Nations Commander:

"In their unique and sensitive mission these officers and men have demonstrated an almost unprecedented capacity for military firmness and humane restraint. Their rigid adherence to mandate imposed upon them by the terms of reference has earned them the plaudits of all fairminded nations of the world. . . ." [60]

Despite objections from the Communists, the explanation sessions were terminated on schedule on December 23; but a graver problem loomed in connection with the armistice stipulation that the future of the remaining nonrepatriates

58 Some additional prisoners exercised their option to be repatriated without explanation, bringing the total number repatriated through January 22, 1954 to 188 Koreans and 440 Chinese. *Report of the United Nations Command on the Operation of the Neutral Nations Repatriation Commission* (U.N. General Assembly *Official Records, Eighth Session,* Supplement 19), 13.

59 *Reports of the Neutral Nations Repatriation Commission,* 9 September 1953 to 21 February 1954 (U.N. General Assembly *Official Records, Eighth Session,* Supplement 18).

60 Statement of December 23, 1953, in ***Department of State Bulletin,* XXX,** January 18, 1954, 90.

must now be settled by the political conference within a thirty-day period ending January 22, 1954. Since no political conference had as yet so much as been scheduled, the majority of the Neutral Commission took the view that the armistice provisions could not be implemented and the matter must be referred back to the two military commands for further consideration. This opinion, which coincided with the view expressed by Prime Minister Nehru of India, was sharply disputed by the United States. The terms of reference said plainly that any prisoners whose status was still undetermined at the expiration of the designated period would revert to civilian status; and this provision, General Hull pointed out, was "fixed and does not depend on the holding of any political conference." Accordingly he gave notice that in the opinion of the Unified Command, at the end of thirty days (i.e., as of January 23) the prisoners still in custody of the Neutral Commission would be "free to move to destinations of their choice." [61]

There was a possibility here of further trouble, both with India as the leading member of the Neutral Commission and the actual custodian of the detainees and with the Communist governments as the defeated claimants to over 7,700 Korean and nearly 14,500 Chinese prisoners of war. No one doubted that if they were actually set free on January 23, most of these prisoners would accept the invitations already issued to them to proceed to South Korea and Formosa respectively. Those who were still fit would probably wind up before long in the armed forces of the two anti-Communist republics—a conclusion against which the Communist side had been striving from the beginning. It was not likely, however, that the Communists would go so far as to resume hostilities over this issue, especially at a moment when more tempting opportunities were opening up elsewhere. By the end of the year it seemed probable that January 23, 1954 would mark the end of the prisoners' vicissitudes and the final vindication of the new right of asylum for prisoners of war which had been so steadfastly upheld by the United States on behalf of the United Nations.

[61] Letter to Gen. Thimayya, December 28, *ibid.*, 91.

Indochina Prelude

Developments in Indochina during these weeks were much less reassuring. As the new fighting season got under way, the Vietminh insurgents, undeterred by the Navarre plan and the many warnings of the Western powers to Communist China, seemed if anything to be intensifying the pressure against the French and the Associated States on both the political and military levels. In doing so they undoubtedly were relying on the sympathy and clandestine support of Communist China, which would now be even better able to help since its own hands were no longer tied in Korea. In addition, the Vietminh could also take advantage of growing war weariness in the State of Vietnam and especially in France, where the desire to seek an end of the war by negotiation had continued to grow amid the quarreling over E.D.C., North Africa, and French internal politics. The strain of the war on France had been much heavier than was sometimes realized; according to one later compilation, French Union casualties in Indochina through 1953 totaled 157,793, including 57,586 dead or missing in action. The growing restiveness of French opinion was reflected in Premier Laniel's remark to the Council of the Republic on November 12. France, he said, sought "any honorable solution" to the Indochina war; no more than the Americans in Korea would it "require . . . an unconditional surrender of the enemy to negotiate with him." [62]

Such a statement could almost be construed as an invitation to the Vietminh to negotiate; and it was soon answered by a typically indirect but none the less unmistakable "peace feeler" put forward in the name of Ho Chi Minh, the Vietminh leader, in his self-conferred capacity as president of the "Democratic Republic of Vietnam." Replying on November 29 to five questions submitted by a Swedish newspaper, Ho declared that if the French Government had learned its lesson and wanted "to declare a truce and reach a negotiated settlement of the Indochina question," his government and people were "prepared to discuss the French proposal." But the French, he warned, would first have to cease hostilities,

[62] *New York Times,* November 13, 1953.

and any truce would have to be "based on genuine respect . . . for the independence of Vietnam"—presumably the same kind of "independence" that was enjoyed by North Korea, East Germany, and other Communist appanages. He also hinted broadly that the French would do well to resist the efforts of "American imperialism" to supplant them in Indochina and subject them to German "militarism" in Europe.[63]

This rather one-sided proposal, repeated over the Vietminh radio through most of December, increased the agitation in French and Vietnamese political circles. In Paris the reaction was somewhat mixed, and the government insisted that the proposals must be made through official channels if they were to be taken seriously. Premier Nguyen Van Tam of Vietnam, supported by Chief of State Bao Dai, still adhered to his frequently expressed view that the most satisfactory peace would be achieved by defeating the Vietminh in combat, and that truce talks could be considered only if the enemy gave the most serious guarantees in advance. But Premier Tam was himself about to fall a victim to Vietnam's increasing political instability, the product of internal confusion aggravated by an increasingly unsatisfactory military situation in the northern delta area. His cabinet resigned on December 17 after Bao Dai had rejected his proposals for general elections, governmental reorganization, and an ultracautious approach to peace negotiations. Vietnam, Tam had said, required a stable government and a popularly elected national assembly if it was to negotiate successfully either with France or with the rebels. Unfortunately, conditions were developing in a way that made these prerequisites look more remote than ever.

An even more disquieting aspect of the Vietminh strategy was revealed on December 23 with a new invasion of the Kingdom of Laos, the second of the year. A Vietminh force of some 20,000 regulars, after occupying a remote position on the frontier between Vietnam and Laos, proceeded to push its way straight across that narrow state to the Mekong River on the boundary between Laos and Thailand. Military maps showed that the Vietminh had thus succeeded in cutting Indochina in two at its narrowest point. In a military

[63] *Documents on American Foreign Relations, 1953,* 161-163.

sense, the movement was less immediately formidable than it may have appeared, though its long-range consequences, which included the establishment of a large French garrison in the isolated fortress of Dienbienphu, were to be intimately involved in the final collapse of 1954. Politically, the importance of the Vietminh action was difficult to overlook. When the Vietminh had first invaded Laos earlier in the year, there had been room for doubt as to whether the move was coordinated with over-all Communist strategy; [64] but under present conditions, such doubts were plainly untenable. True, there was no evidence as yet that Communist China itself was directly involved. Yet the step would hardly have been taken without at least the tacit sanction of the Peking authorities. Far Eastern Communism, it appeared, was still on the offensive despite the tightening of the ring surrounding it from Korea to Pakistan and Turkey.

When Secretary Dulles held his last press conference of the year on December 29, he was still disinclined to attach undue significance to the invasion. His judgment of the total situation, he said, was "not appreciably affected" by the Communist offensive, which he believed might have some relationship to the forthcoming conference in Berlin. "I do not believe that anything that has happened upsets appreciably the timetable of General Navarre's plan. There is no reason that I am aware of for anybody to get panicky about what has happened." As to its relation to the Vietminh "peace feelers," he pointed out that he had never placed much belief in their sincerity.

At the same time, however, Secretary Dulles made it clear that there was no disposition on the part of the United States to shirk the serious obligations it had undertaken in the Far East. The plan to withdraw two divisions from Korea (which had caused some misgivings in that country and elsewhere in the Far East) did not, he emphasized, entail any diminution in the total strength the United States would be able to bring to bear in the area. "Our power will, I believe, on net balance be greater than it has been heretofore." There was merely to be a change of emphasis in its composition and in the methods by which it might be projected:

[64] Cf. above, p. 212.

". . . instead of trying to meet any . . . new aggressions merely by land power of our own in Asia, there would be more reliance on sea and air power which would give us a greater choice." [65]

The applicability of such a system to the developing situation in Asia would be partially tested during the coming year by events that were even then in the making. Southeast Asia in particular had become, to a degree unforeseeable even a few months earlier, the nerve center of world politics. On the outcome of the current fighting would hinge to a large degree not only the future of the Associated States but the role of France on both sides of the globe, the fate of the European Defense Community, perhaps ultimately the chances of war or peace between the world's two great power blocs.

Meanwhile, there was room for gratification in the fact that 1953, full of excitement as it had been, had passed with no clash of superpowers, no recourse to nuclear weapons, and no surrender to Communism. In itself, no doubt, this achievement was inconclusive. New trends had been initiated in the year now closing which would exert their full influence only at a later date. Whether the first year post Stalin would represent a temporary respite or the beginning of a long-term improvement in the world situation would depend mainly on future developments—most conspicuously, perhaps, upon the role of the United States in world affairs, in 1954 and afterward.

[65] *Department of State Bulletin*, XXX, January 11, 1954, 42-43.

SELECTED BIBLIOGRAPHY

No annual bibliography of world affairs can list more than a fraction of the literature that constantly pours from the world's presses. The present selection, designed to provide a point of departure for both the student and the general reader, attempts to give due representation to all significant viewpoints but is necessarily limited to works that are both relevant and reasonably accessible. The decision for or against inclusion of particular titles has been governed solely by these criteria and not by agreement or disagreement with the views expressed. Additional materials of permanent interest will be found listed in earlier volumes of this series, and more extensive bibliographies are readily available in many of the specialized publications listed below. A number of representative American and foreign periodicals which specialize in international affairs are included as a reminder that much of the most illuminating current material in the field appears in this medium. Except as otherwise indicated, all official United States documents are distributed by the U.S. Government Printing Office (Washington 25, D.C.). United Nations publications are obtainable in the United States from the International Documents Service, Columbia University Press, New York 27, New York; official foreign documents, from the various foreign governments' information service offices in Washington and New York.

GENERAL

Periodicals

(See also regional headings)

American Journal of International Law. Washington, American Society of International Law, quarterly.

Aussenpolitik: Zeitschrift für Internationale Fragen. Stuttgart, Deutsche Verlags-Anstalt, bimonthly.

Bulletin of the Atomic Scientists. Chicago, Educational Foundation for Nuclear Science, monthly (September-July).

Chronique de Politique Étrangère. Brussels, Institut des Relations Internationales, bimonthly.

Current History. Philadelphia, Events Publishing Company, monthly.

Department of State Bulletin. Washington, Department of State, weekly.

The Economist. London, The Economist, weekly.

Europa-Archiv. Frankfurt am Main, Verlag Europa-Archiv, fortnightly.

Foreign Affairs. New York, Council on Foreign Relations, quarterly.

Foreign Commerce Weekly. Washington, Department of Commerce, weekly.

International Affairs. London, Royal Institute of International Affairs, quarterly.

International Conciliation. New York, Carnegie Endowment for International Peace, monthly except July and August.

International Organization. Boston, World Peace Foundation, quarterly.

Politique Étrangère. Paris, Centre d'Études de Politique Étrangère, quarterly.

Relazioni Internazionali. Milan, Istituto di Studi Internazionali, weekly.

The Reporter. New York, Fortnightly Publishing Co., fortnightly.

World Politics. Princeton, Center of International Studies, quarterly.

The World Today. London, Royal Institute of International Affairs, monthly.

General

PROBLEMS OF STABILITY AND PROGRESS IN INTERNATIONAL RELATIONS, by Quincy Wright. Berkeley, University of California Press, 1953, 392 p.

FOUNDATIONS OF THE WORLD REPUBLIC, by G. A. Borgese. Chicago, University of Chicago Press, 1953, 336 p.

HOW NATIONS SEE EACH OTHER: A Study in Public Opinion, by William Buchanan and Hadley Cantril. Urbana, University of Illinois Press, 1953, 229 p.

NATIONALISM AND SOCIAL COMMUNICATION, by Karl W. Deutsch. Cambridge, Technology Press, 1953, 292 p.

"Excesses of Self-Determination," by Clyde Eagleton. (*Foreign Affairs,* XXXI, July 1953, 592-604.)

DER DIPLOMATISCHE DIENST, by Richard Sallet. Stuttgart, Deutsche Verlags-Anstalt, 1953, 367 p.

THE WORLD AND THE WEST, by Arnold Toynbee. New York, Oxford University Press, 1953, 99 p.

PROBLEMS OF EAST-WEST SETTLEMENT, by W. W. Wade, F. W. Riggs and H. C. Gary. New York, Foreign Policy Association, 1953, 63 p. (Headline Series No. 101.)

Handbooks, Reference Works and Documents

POLITICAL HANDBOOK OF THE WORLD, 1953, edited by Walter H. Mallory and Joseph Barber. New York, Harper (for the Council on Foreign Relations), 1953, 233 p.

THE YEAR BOOK OF WORLD AFFAIRS, 1953. London, Stevens (for the London Institute of World Affairs), 1953, 427 p.

L'ANNÉE POLITIQUE, 1953, edited by André Siegfried, Édouard Bonnefous and J.-B. Duroselle. Paris, Presses Universitaires, 1954, 707 p.

STATISTICAL YEARBOOK, 1953. New York, United Nations, 1953, 578 p. (United Nations Sales No. 1953.XVII.9.)

DOCUMENTS ON INTERNATIONAL AFFAIRS, 1951, edited by Denise Folliot. London, Oxford University Press (for the Royal Institute of International Affairs), 1954, 698 p.

DOCUMENTS ON INTERNATIONAL AFFAIRS, 1952, edited by Denise Folliot. London, Oxford University Press (for the Royal Institute of International Affairs), 1955, 529 p.

DOCUMENTS ON AMERICAN FOREIGN RELATIONS, 1953, edited by Peter V. Curl. New York, Harper (for the Council on Foreign Relations), 1954, 458 p.

Recent History

THE WORLD BETWEEN THE WARS: From the 1918 Armistice to the Munich Agreement, by Quincy Howe. New York, Simon and Schuster, 1953, 797 p.

HISTOIRE DIPLOMATIQUE DE 1919 À NOS JOURS, by J.-B. Duroselle. Paris, Dalloz, 1953, 744 p.

THE UNDECLARED WAR, 1940–1941, by William L. Langer and S. Everett Gleason. New York, Harper (for the Council on Foreign Relations), 1953, 979 p. (Volume II of *The World Crisis and American Foreign Policy.*)

TRIUMPH AND TRAGEDY, by Winston S. Churchill. Boston, Houghton Mifflin, 1953, 800 p. (The sixth and final volume of *The Second World War.*)

SURVEY OF INTERNATIONAL AFFAIRS, 1939–1946: America, Britain and Russia, Their Co-operation and Conflict, 1941–1946, by William Hardy McNeill. New York, Oxford University Press (for the Royal Institute of International Affairs), 1953, 819 p.

PERPETUAL WAR FOR PERPETUAL PEACE: A Critical Examination of the Foreign Policy of Franklin Delano Roosevelt and Its Aftermath, edited by Harry Elmer Barnes. Caldwell, Idaho, The Caxton Printers, 1953, 679 p.

MY NAME IS TOM CONNALLY, by Senator Tom Connally (as told to Alfred Steinberg). New York, Crowell, 1954, 376 p.

ADVENTURES IN DIPLOMACY, by William Phillips. Boston, Beacon, 1953, 477 p.

SURVEY OF INTERNATIONAL AFFAIRS, 1951, by Peter Calvocoressi and Konstanze Isepp. London, Oxford University Press (for the Royal Institute of International Affairs), 1954, 513 p.

Economic Affairs

WORLD ECONOMIC REPORT, 1952–53. New York, United Nations, 1954, 156 p. (United Nations Sales No. 1954.II.C.1.)

ECONOMIC STABILITY IN A CHANGING WORLD, by John H. Williams. New York, Oxford University Press, 1953, 284 p.

WORLD POPULATION AND PRODUCTION: Trends and Outlook, by Wladimir S. Woytinsky and E. S. Woytinsky. New York, Twentieth Century Fund, 1953, 1340 p.

THE LIMITS OF THE EARTH, by Fairfield Osborn. Boston, Little, Brown, 1953, 226 p.

WORLD PRODUCTION OF RAW MATERIALS. London, Royal Institute of International Affairs, 1953, 104 p.

FINAL REPORT ON OPERATIONS OF THE INTERNATIONAL MATERIALS CONFERENCE, March 1 to September 30, 1953. Washington, International Materials Conference, 1953, 16 p.

YEARBOOK OF INTERNATIONAL TRADE STATISTICS, 1953. New York, United Nations, 1954, 481 p. (United Nations Sales No. 1954.XVII.3.)

WORLD TRADE POLICIES: The Changing Panorama, 1920–1953: A Series of Contemporary Periodic Surveys, by Henry Chalmers. Berkeley, University of California Press, 1953, 573 p.

A STUDY OF TRADE BETWEEN ASIA AND EUROPE. Geneva, United Nations, 1953, 146 p. (United Nations Sales No. 1953.II.F.3.)

THE STATE OF FOOD AND AGRICULTURE, 1953. Rome, Food and Agriculture Organization, 1953–1954, 2 parts.

OUR UNDERDEVELOPED WORLD, by L. Dudley Stamp. London, Faber, 1953, 187 p.

THE ECONOMIC IMPACT ON UNDER-DEVELOPED SOCIETIES: Essays on International Investment and Social Change, by Herbert S. Frankel. Oxford, Blackwell, 1953, 179 p.

PROBLEMS OF CAPITAL FORMATION IN UNDERDEVELOPED COUNTRIES, by Ragnar Nurske. New York, Oxford University Press, 1953, 163 p.

THE FUTURE OF UNDERDEVELOPED COUNTRIES: Political Implications of Economic Development, by Eugene Staley. New York, Harper (for the Council on Foreign Relations), 1954, 410 p.

INTERNATIONAL ECONOMIC ORGANISATIONS, by Charles H. Alexandrowicz. New York, Praeger (for the London Institute of World Affairs), 1953, 263 p.

Social and Cultural Problems

DEMOGRAPHIC YEARBOOK, 1953. New York, United Nations, 1953, 441 p. (United Nations Sales No. 1953.XIII.9.)

THE REFUGEE IN THE POSTWAR WORLD, by Jaques Vernant. New Haven, Yale University Press, 1953, 843 p.

THE FLOW OF THE NEWS: A Study by the International Press Institute. Zurich, International Press Institute, 1953, 266 p.

THE INTERNATIONAL LABOR MOVEMENT, by Lewis L. Lorwin. New York, Harper, 1953, 366 p.

Communism

FROM LENIN TO MALENKOV: The History of World Communism, by Hugh Seton-Watson. New York, Praeger, 1953, 377 p.

IMPERIAL COMMUNISM, by Anthony T. Bouscaren. Washington, Public Affairs Press, 1953, 256 p.

EUROPEAN COMMUNISM, by Franz Borkenau. New York, Harper, 1953, 564 p.

COMMUNIST CONSPIRACY, by Stephen King-Hall. New York, Macmillan, 1953, 239 p.

STUDY OF BOLSHEVISM, by Nathan C. Leites. New York, Free Press, 1953, 639 p.

THE ROSENBERG CASE: Fact and Fiction, by S. Andhil Fineberg. New York, Oceana Publications, 1953, 159 p.

UNITED STATES POLICY

General

THE AMERICAN APPROACH TO FOREIGN POLICY: The Gottesman Lectures, Upsala University, by Dexter Perkins. Cambridge, Harvard University Press, 1953, 203 p.

BEYOND CONTAINMENT, by William Henry Chamberlin. Chicago, Regnery, 1953, 412 p.

THE CHALLENGE TO AMERICAN FOREIGN POLICY, by John J. McCloy. Cambridge, Harvard University Press, 1953, 81 p.

DE ROOSEVELT À EISENHOWER: la politique étrangère américaine (1945–1952), by Jaques Freymond. Geneva, Droz, 1953, 160 p.

Organization and Operations

ADMINISTRATION IN FOREIGN AFFAIRS, by Arthur W. Macmahon. University, University of Alabama Press, 1953, 275 p.

CONGRESSIONAL RECORD. Washington, GPO, daily (during congressional sessions).

BUDGET OF UNITED STATES GOVERNMENT, Fiscal Year 1954. Washington, GPO, 1953, 1155 p. (House Document 16, 83d Congress.)

APPROPRIATIONS, BUDGET ESTIMATES, etc.: Statements, 83d Congress, 1st Session, January 3-August 3, 1953, Showing Appropriations Made. Washington, GPO, 1953, 563 p. (Senate Document 77, 83d Congress.)

DEPARTMENTS OF STATE, JUSTICE AND COMMERCE APPROPRIATION ACT, 1954 (Public Law 195, 83d Congress, approved August 5, 1953—H.R. 4974.)

Hearings: Subcommittee of House Appropriations Committee, Mar. 18-23, 1953, 2 pts.; Subcommittee of Senate Appropriations Committee, Apr. 20-27, 1953, 1680 p. (pp. 901-1618); Supplemental hearings, Subcommittee of Senate Appropriations Committee, May 15, 1953, 42 p. *Reports:* H. Rept. 341, Apr. 30, 1953, 29 p.; H. Rept. 342, May 1, 1953, 1 p.; S. Rept. 309, May 28, 1953, 30 p. *Conference report:* H. Rept. 868, July 17, 1953, 6 p.

DEPARTMENT OF STATE, NOMINATIONS AND APPOINTMENTS, HEARINGS:

on the Nomination of John Foster Dulles to be Secretary of State, Senate Foreign Relations Committee, Jan. 15, 1953, 32 p.; on the Nomination of James B. Conant to be U.S. High Commissioner to Germany, Senate Foreign Relations Committee, Feb. 2-3, 1953, 111 p.; on the Nomination of Walter Bedell Smith to be Under Secretary of State, Senate Foreign Relations Committee, Feb. 4, 1953, 39 p.; on the Nomination of Charles E. Bohlen to be U.S. Ambassador to the U.S.S.R., Senate Foreign Relations Committee, Mar. 2 and 18, 1953, 128 p.

UNDER SECRETARY OF STATE FOR ADMINISTRATION (Public Law 2, 83d Congress, approved February 7, 1953—S. 243.)

Hearings: House Foreign Affairs Committee, Jan. 28, 1953, 20 p. *Reports:* S. Rept. 10, Jan. 23, 1953, 4 p.; H. Rept. 5, Jan. 29, 1953, 4 p.

DEPARTMENT OF STATE, FILE SURVEY—

Hearings: Permanent Subcommittee of Senate Government Operations Committee, Feb. 4-20, 1953, 2 pts. *Report:* S. Rept. 836, (interim report, no date) 1953, 19 p.

DEPARTMENT OF STATE INFORMATION PROGRAM, VOICE OF AMERICA—

Hearings: Permanent Subcommittee of Senate Government Operations Committee, Feb. 16-Apr. 1, 1953, 10 pts. *Report:* S. Rept. 928, (no date) 1954, 14 p.

DEPARTMENT OF STATE INFORMATION PROGRAM CENTERS—

Hearings: Permanent Subcommittee of Senate Government Operations Committee, Mar. 24-July 14, 1953, 9 pts. *Report:* S. Rept. 879, Jan. 25, 1954, 24 p.

DEPARTMENT OF STATE OVERSEAS INFORMATION PROGRAM: Consolidated Report (with Staff Studies), S. Rept. 406, (no date) 1953, 209 p.

UNITED STATES INFORMATION AGENCY, ESTABLISHMENT—

Documents: Message from the President, June 1, 1953 (H. Doc. 156), 5 p.; Reorganization Plan No. 8 of 1953, June 1, 1953 (H. Doc. 158), 3 p. *Hearings:* House Government Operations Committee (on H. J. Res. 262), June 22-24, 1953, 219 p. *Report:* H. Rept. 844, July 16, 1953, 2 pts.

FOREIGN OPERATIONS ADMINISTRATION, ESTABLISHMENT—

Documents: Message from the President, June 1, 1953 (H. Doc. 156), 5 p.; Reorganization Plan No. 7 of 1953, June 1, 1953 (H. Doc. 157), 4 p. *Hearings:* House Government Operations Committee (on H. J. Res. 261), June 22-24, 1953, 1953, 219 p. *Report:* H. Rept. 843, July 16, 1953, 2 pts.

PARTICIPATION OF THE UNITED STATES GOVERNMENT IN INTERNATIONAL CONFERENCES, July 1, 1952-June 30, 1953. Washington, GPO, 1954, 240 p. (Department of State Publication 5334; International Organization and Conference Series I, 27.)

Legislation

REPUBLICAN CONGRESS SEVEN MONTHS' PROGRESS: Review of 83d Congress (Jan. 3-Aug. 3, 1953), by William F. Knowland of California, together with Summary of Legislation. Washington, GPO, 1953, 33 p. (Senate Document 75, 83d Congress.)

LEGISLATIVE REVIEW, EIGHTY-THIRD CONGRESS, FIRST SESSION: Statement by Lyndon B. Johnson. Washington, GPO, 1953, 3 p. (Senate Document 76, 83d Congress.)

"Record of 83rd Congress (First Session)," by Richard M. Boeckel. (*Editorial Research Reports,* II, August 4, 1953, 501-553.)

SURVEY OF ACTIVITIES OF THE COMMITTEE ON FOREIGN AFFAIRS, HOUSE OF REPRESENTATIVES (January 3, 1953-August 20, 1954). Washington, GPO, 1954, 75 p. (House Foreign Affairs Committee print, 83d Congress.)

TREATIES AND EXECUTIVE AGREEMENTS, POWER TO MAKE (S. J. Res. 1 and 43).
Hearings: Subcommittee of Senate Judiciary Committee, Feb. 18-Apr. 11, 1953, 1267 p. *Report:* S. Rept. 412, June 15, 1953, 2 pts.

"The Bricker Amendment and Authority over Foreign Affairs," by Arthur H. Dean. (*Foreign Affairs,* XXXII, October 1953, 1-19).

TRADE AGREEMENTS EXTENSION ACT OF 1953 (Public Law 215, 83d Congress, approved August 7, 1953—H.R. 5495.)
Document: Message from the President, Apr. 7, 1953 (S. Doc. 38), 2 p. *Hearings:* House Ways and Means Committee (on H.R. 4294), Apr. 27-May 19, 1953, 2028 p.; Statements on H.R. 5495 submitted to the Committee on Finance, United States Senate, and a summary of testimony on related provisions of H.R. 4294 before the House Committee on Ways and Means, June 1953 (Committee print, Senate Committee on Finance), 600 p. *Reports:* H. Rept. 521, June 9, 1953, 12 p.; H. Rept. 539 (on H. Res. 275), June 10, 1953, 1 p.; S. Rept. 472, June 26, 1953, 7 p. *Conference report:* H. Rept. 1089, Aug. 1, 1953, 6 p.

CUSTOMS SIMPLIFICATION ACT OF 1953 (Public Law 243, 83d Congress, approved August 8, 1953—H.R. 5877.)
Hearings: House Ways and Means Committee (on H.R. 5106), May 27-29, 1953, 227 p. *Reports:* H. Rept. 760, July 9, 1953, 48 p.; S. Rept. 632, July 24, 1953, 39 p.

MUTUAL SECURITY ACT OF 1953 (Public Law 118, 83d Congress, approved July 16, 1953—H.R. 5710.)
Documents: Message from the President, May 5, 1953 (H. Doc. 140), 3 p.; Basic Data Supplied by the Executive Branch (Committee print, House Foreign Affairs Committee and Senate Foreign Relations Committee), 113 p. *Hearings:* House Foreign Affairs Committee, Mar. 11-June 6, 1953, 1303 p. Senate Foreign Relations Committee (on S. 2128), May 5-29, 1953, 803 p. *Reports:* H. Rept. 569, June 16, 1953, two parts; S. Rept. 403 (on S. 2128), June 13, 1953, 84 p.; S. Rept. 444 (on S. 2128), June 18, 1953, 2 p. *Conference report:* H. Rept. 770, July 10, 1953, 21 p.

MUTUAL SECURITY APPROPRIATION ACT FOR FISCAL 1954 (Public Law 218, 83d Congress, approved August 7, 1953—H.R. 6391.)
Document: Message from the President, July 16, 1953 (H. Doc. 209), 5 p.

Hearings: Subcommittee of the House Committee on Appropriations, July 6-11, 1953, 737 p. *Reports:* H. Rept. 880, July 18, 1953, 13 p.; S. Rept. 645, July 25, 1953, 15 p. *Conference report:* H. Rept. 1056, July 30, 1953, 8 p.

DEPARTMENT OF DEFENSE APPROPRIATIONS, 1954 (Public Law 179, 83d Congress, approved August 1, 1953—H.R. 5969.)

Hearings: Subcommittee of House Appropriations Committee, Feb. 24-June 10, 1953, 792 p.; Subcommittee of Senate Appropriations Committee, May 19-July 10, 1953, 2 pts. *Reports:* H. Rept. 680, June 27, 1953, 64 p.; S. Rept. 601, July 17, 1953, 19 p. *Conference report:* H. Rept. 1015, July 28, 1953, 8 p.

Hearings on separate departments: (Army) Subcommittee of House Committee on Appropriations, Mar. 5-June 11, 1953, 1667 p.; (Air Force) Subcommittee of House Appropriations Committee, Mar. 6-June 13, 1953, 1051 p.; (Navy) Subcommittee of House Appropriations Committee, Mar. 3-June 8, 1953, 1088 p.

REFUGEE RELIEF ACT OF 1953 (Public Law 203, 83d Congress, approved August 7, 1943—H.R. 6481.)

Hearings: Subcommittee No. 1 of House Judiciary Committee (on H.R. 361), May 21-July 9, 1953, 246 p.; Subcommittee of Senate Judiciary Committee (on S. 1917), May 26-28 and July 1, 1953, 325 p. *Reports:* H. Rept. 974, July 27, 1953, 20 p.; S. Rept 629 (on S. 1917), July 23, 1953, 21 p. *Conference Report:* H. Rept. 1069, July 31, 1953, 11 p.

EMERGENCY FAMINE ASSISTANCE AUTHORITY (Public Law 216, 83d Congress, approved August 7, 1953—S. 2249.)

Document: Message from the President, June 30, 1953 (H. Doc. 202), 2 p. *Hearings:* Senate Agriculture and Forestry Committee, July 16, 1953, 59 p.; House Agriculture Committee (on H.R. 6016), July 22-24, 1953, 173 p. *Reports:* H. Rept. 983 (on H.R. 6016), July 27, 1953, 3 p.; S. Rept. 631, July 24, 1953, 3 p. *Conference Report:* H. Rept. 1070, July 31, 1953, 4 p.

PAKISTAN, EMERGENCY WHEAT GRANT FOR (Public Law 77, 83d Congress, approved June 25, 1953—S. 2112.)

Document: Message from the President, June 10, 1953 (H. Doc. 171), 3 p. *Hearings:* Senate Committee on Agriculture and Forestry, June 12, 1953, 64 p.; House Agriculture Committee (on H.R. 5659-5661), June 15-16, 1953, 89 p. *Reports:* H. Rept. 570 (on H.R. 5659), June 16, 1953, 4 p.; S. Rept. 404, June 13, 1953, 3 p.

INTERNATIONAL WHEAT AGREEMENT (S. Exec. H, 83d Cong., 1st Sess., ratified July 14, 1953.)

Hearings: Subcommittee of Senate Foreign Relations Committee, June 26, 1953, 59 p. *Report:* S. Exec. Rept. 4, 83d Cong., 1st Sess., July 8, 1953, 12 p.

NATO STATUS OF FORCES AND HEADQUARTERS AGREEMENTS (S. Exec. T and U, 82d Cong., 2d Sess., and B, 83d Cong., 1st Sess., ratified July 24, 1953.)

Hearings: Senate Foreign Relations Committee, Apr. 1, 7-8 and June 24, 1953, 3 pts. *Report:* S. Exec. Rept 1, 83d Cong., 1st Sess., Apr. 28, 1953, 19 p.

FRIENDSHIP, COMMERCE AND NAVIGATION TREATIES WITH ISRAEL, ETHIOPIA, ITALY, DENMARK, GREECE, FINLAND, GERMANY AND JAPAN (S. Exec. R, 82d Cong., 1st Sess., F, H, I and J, 82d Cong., 2d Sess., and C, N and O, 83d Cong., 1st Sess.)

Hearings: Subcommittee of Senate Foreign Relations Committee, July 13, 1953, 32 p. *Report:* S. Exec. Rept. 5, 83d Cong., 1st Sess., July 17, 1953, 11 p.

ENSLAVEMENT OF FREE PEOPLES, RESOLUTION—
Document: Message from the President, Feb. 23, 1953 (H. Doc. 93), 2 p.
Hearing: House Foreign Affairs Committee (on H. J. Res. 200 and similar pending measures), Feb. 26, 1953, 61 p.

Economic Policy and Foreign Aid

THIRTY-SEVENTH ANNUAL REPORT OF THE UNITED STATES TARIFF COMMISSION, 1953. Washington, GPO, 1953, 66 p. (House Document 278, 83d Congress.)

OPERATION OF THE TRADE AGREEMENTS PROGRAM: 6th Report, July 1952-June 1953. Washington, United States Tariff Commission, 1954, 252 p.

A TRADE AND TARIFF POLICY IN THE NATIONAL INTEREST, prepared by the Public Advisory Board for Mutual Security. Washington, Mutual Security Agency, 1953, 78 p.

MUTUAL DEFENSE ASSISTANCE CONTROL ACT OF 1951: Reports to Congress by the Director of the Foreign Operations Administration. 3d, World-wide Enforcement of Strategic Trade Controls, Sept. 27, 1953, 96 p.; 4th, East-West Trade Trends, May 17, 1954, 102 p. Washington, Foreign Operations Administration, 1953–1954.

SOVIET BLOC, CONTROL OF TRADE WITH—
Hearings: Permanent Subcommittee of Senate Government Operations Committee, Mar. 30-May 20, 1953, 2 pts. *Report:* S. Rept. 606, July 21, 1953, 57 p.

INTERNATIONAL TRADE POLICY ISSUES: Report by the Fletcher School of Law and Diplomacy. Washington, Chamber of Commerce of the United States, 1953, 68 p.

FOREIGN TRADE AND U.S. TARIFF POLICY: A Report on the Views of Leading Citizens in Twenty-five Cities, edited by Joseph Barber. New York, Council on Foreign Relations, 1953, 39 p.

"The Problem of Our Trade Balance," by Willard L. Thorp. (*Foreign Affairs,* XXXI, April 1953, 405-417.)

HISTORY OF THE OPERATIONS AND POLICIES OF THE EXPORT-IMPORT BANK OF WASHINGTON, by Hawthorne Arey. Washington, GPO, 1953, 175 p.

SEMIANNUAL REPORTS TO CONGRESS OF THE EXPORT-IMPORT BANK OF WASHINGTON: 16th, Jan.-June 1953, 79 p.; 17th, July-Dec., 1953, 79 p. Washington, Export-Import Bank of Washington, 1953–1954.

SEMIANNUAL REPORTS OF THE NATIONAL ADVISORY COUNCIL on International Monetary and Financial Problems: Oct. 1, 1952-Mar. 31, 1953, 66 p. (H. Doc. 214, 83d Cong.); Apr. 1, 1953-Sept. 30, 1953, 58 p. (H. Doc. 338, 83d Cong.).

SURVEY OF UNITED STATES INTERNATIONAL FINANCE, 1953, by Gardner Patterson, John M. Gunn, Jr. and Dorothy L. Swerdlove. Princeton, Princeton University Press, 1954, 317 p.

AID, TRADE AND THE TARIFF, by Howard S. Piquet. New York, Crowell, 1953, 358 p.

TRADE, AID OR WHAT?: A Report Based upon a Conference on International Economic Policy at the Merrill Center for Economics, Summer, 1953, by Willard L. Thorp. Baltimore, The Johns Hopkins Press, 1954, 239 p.

AMERICAN FOREIGN ASSISTANCE, by William Adams and Redvers Opie. Washington, Brookings, 1953, 615 p.

STRENGTHENING THE FREE WORLD ECONOMY, by Klaus Knorr. Princeton, Princeton University Press, 1953, 45 p. (Center of International Studies, Memorandum No. 3.)

REPORTS TO CONGRESS ON THE MUTUAL SECURITY PROGRAM: 4th, Aug. 17, 1953, 61 p.; 5th, Mar. 8, 1954, 65 p. (H. Doc. 226 and 337, 83d Cong.)

ECONOMIC STRENGTH FOR THE FREE WORLD: Principles of a United States Foreign Development Program—A Report to the Director for Mutual Security by the Advisory Committee on Underdeveloped Areas. Washington, Mutual Security Agency, 1953, 36 p.

CONCLUSIONS AND RECOMMENDATIONS OF THE INTERNATIONAL DEVELOPMENT ADVISORY BOARD. Washington, Foreign Operations Administration, 1953, 27 p.

THE MUTUAL SECURITY ACT AND OVERSEAS PRIVATE INVESTMENT: Preliminary Report of the Subcommittee on Foreign Economic Policy, Committee on Foreign Affairs, House of Representatives, June 3, 1953, 87 p. (Subcommittee print.)

Defense Policy and Atomic Energy Developments

SEMIANNUAL REPORTS OF THE SECRETARY OF DEFENSE (with semiannual reports of the Secretaries of the Army, Navy and Air Force): 5th, Jan. 1-June 30, 1953, 310 p.; 6th, July 1-Dec. 31, 1953, 55 p. Washington, Department of Defense, 1953–1954.

"Military Problems of the New Administration," by Walter Millis. (*Foreign Affairs,* XXXI, January 1953, 215-224.)

WINGS FOR PEACE, by Brigadier General Bonner Fellers. Chicago, Regnery, 1953, 248 p.

CAN WE AFFORD ADDITIONAL PROGRAMS FOR NATIONAL SECURITY? by Gerhard Colm and Marilyn Young. Washington, National Planning Association, 1953, 70 p. (Planning Pamphlets No. 84.)

REPORTS TO THE PRESIDENT BY THE DIRECTOR OF DEFENSE MOBILIZATION: 8th, The Job Ahead for Defense Mobilization, Jan. 1, 1953, 51 p.; 9th, Defense Mobilization, Oct. 1, 1953, 23 p.; Manpower Resources for National Security, Jan. 6, 1954, 70 p.

SEMIANNUAL REPORTS OF THE ATOMIC ENERGY COMMISSION: 14th, July 1953, 98 p.; 15th, Jan. 1954, 151 p. Washington, GPO, 1953–1954.

"Impact of Atomic Energy," edited by R. A. Dahl. (*Annals of the American Academy of Political and Social Science,* vol. 290, November 1953, 1-133.)

"The Hidden Struggle for the H-Bomb." (*Fortune,* XLVII, May 1953, 109-110, 230.)

"Atomic Weapons and American Policy," by J. Robert Oppenheimer. (*Foreign Affairs,* XXXI, July 1953, 525-535.)

REPORT ON THE ATOM: What You Should Know about the Atomic Energy Program of the United States, by Gordon Dean. New York, Knopf, 1953, 334 p.

ANNUAL REPORT [of the Federal Civil Defense Administration] FOR 1953. Washington, Federal Civil Defense Administration, 1954, 174 p.

The Information Program

SEMIANNUAL REPORTS OF THE SECRETARY OF STATE ON THE INTERNATIONAL INFORMATION AND EDUCATIONAL EXCHANGE PROGRAM: 11th, Jan. 1-June 30, 1953, 51 p.; 12th, July 1-Dec. 31, 1953, 26 p. (Department of State Publications 5284 and 5409; International Information and Cultural Series 34 and 35.) Washington, 1953–1954.

SEMIANNUAL REVIEW OF OPERATIONS BY THE UNITED STATES INFORMATION AGENCY: 1st, Aug.-Dec. 1953, 30 p. Washington, 1954.

REPORT ON OPERATIONS OF DEPARTMENT OF STATE (under Public Law 584, 79th Congress). Washington, GPO, 1953, 97 p. (House Document 115, 83d Congress.)

NINTH SEMIANNUAL REPORT OF UNITED STATES ADVISORY COMMISSION ON INFORMATION, February 1954. Washington, GPO, 1954, 21 p. (House Document, 311, 83d Congress.)

SEMIANNUAL REPORTS OF THE UNITED STATES ADVISORY COMMISSION ON EDUCATIONAL EXCHANGE: 10th, Jan. 1-June 30, 1953, 49 p.; 11th, July 1-Dec. 31, 1953, 10 p. (H. Doc. 294 and 355, 83d Cong.)

TRUTH IS OUR WEAPON, by Edward W. Barrett. New York, Funk and Wagnalls, 1953, 355 p.

Immigration Policy

WHOM WE SHALL WELCOME: Report of the President's Commission on Immigration and Naturalization. Washington, GPO, 1953, 319 p.

GOLDEN DOOR: The Irony of Our Immigration Policy, by John C. Bruce. New York, Random House, 1953, 244 p.

"The Refugee Relief Act of 1953," by Frank L. Auerbach. (*Department of State Bulletin,* XXIX, August 24, 1953, 231-235.)

UNITED NATIONS

(See also regional headings)

General

EVERYMAN'S UNITED NATIONS. 4th edition; New York, United Nations, 1953, 433 p. (United Nations Sales No. 1953.I.7.)

ANNUAL REVIEW OF UNITED NATIONS AFFAIRS, 1953, edited by Clyde Eagleton and Richard N. Swift. New York, Oceana Publications, 1954, 221 p.

IN THE CAUSE OF PEACE: Seven Years with the United Nations, by Trygve Lie. New York, Macmillan, 1954, 473 p.

U.N. TODAY AND TOMORROW, by Eleanor Roosevelt and William A. De Witt. New York, Harper, 1953, 236 p.

The United States and the United Nations

UNITED STATES PARTICIPATION IN THE UNITED NATIONS: Report by the President to the Congress for the Year 1953. Washington, GPO, 1954, 277 p. (Department of State Publication 5459, International Organization and Conference Series III, 100.)

UNITED NATIONS, INVESTIGATION OF ACTIVITIES OF U.S. CITIZENS EMPLOYED BY— *Hearings:* Subcommittee of Senate Judiciary Committee, Oct. 13-Dec. 17, 1952, Feb. 19, Apr. 27, Sept. 24-25, Oct. 2, 29 and Dec. 22, 1953, 695 p. *Reports:* 1st Report, Jan. 2, 1953 (Subcommittee print), 18 p.; S. Rept. 223, May 4, 1953, 10 p.

REPORT OF THE SECRETARY-GENERAL ON PERSONNEL POLICY. New York, United Nations, 1953, 39 p. (United Nations Document A/2364, dated 30 January 1953.)

Reports of United Nations Activities

UNITED NATIONS BULLETIN. New York, United Nations Department of Information, fortnightly.

YEARBOOK OF THE UNITED NATIONS, 1953. New York, United Nations, 1954, 906 p.

ANNUAL REPORT OF THE SECRETARY-GENERAL ON THE WORK OF THE ORGANIZATION, 1 July 1952-30 June 1953. New York, United Nations, 1953, 162 p. (United Nations General Assembly *Official Records, Eighth Session,* Supplement No. 1.)

RESOLUTIONS ADOPTED BY THE GENERAL ASSEMBLY AT ITS 7TH SESSION during the Period from 24 February to 23 April 1953. New York, United Nations, 1953, 5 p. (United Nations General Assembly *Official Records, Seventh Session,* Supplement No. 20A.)

RESOLUTIONS ADOPTED BY THE GENERAL ASSEMBLY AT ITS 7TH SESSION during the Period from 17 to 28 August 1953. New York, United Nations, 1953, 2 p. (United Nations General Assembly *Official Records, Seventh Session,* Supplement No. 20B.)

"The Seventh Assembly of the United Nations." (*World Today,* IX, June 1953, 265-276.)

"General Assembly." (*International Organization,* VII, May 1953, 243-254.) (Summary of actions of resumed 7th Session of the General Assembly, Feb. 24-Apr. 1, 1953.)

"General Assembly." (*International Organization,* VII, August 1953, 380-385.) (Summary of actions of resumed 7th Session of the General Assembly, Apr. 7-23, 1953.)

"General Assembly: Seventh Session." (*International Organization,* VII, November 1953, 511-519.) (Summary of U.N. action regarding Korea during the General Assembly's 7th Session.)

RESOLUTIONS ADOPTED BY THE GENERAL ASSEMBLY AT ITS 8TH SESSION during the Period from 15 September to 9 December 1953. New York, United Nations, 1954, 55 p. (United Nations General Assembly *Official Records, Eighth Session,* Supplement No. 17.)

"Issues before the Eighth General Assembly." (*International Conciliation,* No. 493, September 1953, 1-128.)

REPORT ON THE EIGHTH SESSION OF THE GENERAL ASSEMBLY OF THE UNITED NATIONS, prepared for the Committee on Foreign Affairs, House of Representatives, 83d Congress, 2d Session, pursuant to H. Res. 113, May 28, 1954. Washington, GPO, 1954, 376 p. (House Report 1695, 83d Congress.)

"General Assembly." (*International Organization,* VIII, February 1954, 49-116.) (Summary of actions of the first part of the 8th Session of the General Assembly, Sept. 15-Dec. 9, 1953.)

Political and Security

REPORT OF THE SECURITY COUNCIL TO THE GENERAL ASSEMBLY Covering the Period from 16 July 1952 to 15 July 1953. New York, United Nations, 1953, 32 p. (United Nations General Assembly *Official Records, Eighth Session,* Supplement No. 2.)

"The Arab-Asian States in the United Nations," by Harry N. Howard. (*Middle East Journal,* VII, Summer 1953, 279-292.)

SECOND REPORT OF THE DISARMAMENT COMMISSION. New York, United Nations, 1953, 163 p. (United Nations Disarmament Commission *Official Records,* Special Supplement No. 1.)

Economic and Social

REPORT OF THE ECONOMIC AND SOCIAL COUNCIL Covering the Period from 2 August 1952 to 5 August 1953. New York, United Nations, 1953, 143 p.

(United Nations General Assembly *Official Records, Eighth Session,* Supplement No. 3.)

WORLD AGAINST WANT: An Account of the U.N. Technical Assistance Programme for Economic Development. New York, United Nations, 1953, 80 p. (United Nations Sales No. 1953.I.27.)

REPORT ON A SPECIAL U.N. FUND FOR ECONOMIC DEVELOPMENT. New York, United Nations, 1953, 61 p. (United Nations Sales No. 1953.II.B.1.)

"Human Rights and the United Nations," by O. F. Nolde. (*Proceedings of the American Academy of Political Science,* XV, January 1953, 39-48.)

REPORT OF THE 9TH SESSION OF THE COMMISSION ON HUMAN RIGHTS. New York, United Nations, 1953, 248 p. (United Nations Economic and Social Council *Official Records, Sixteenth Session,* Supplement No. 8.)

"New U.S. Action Program for Human Rights," by Mrs. Oswald B. Lord. (*Department of State Bulletin,* XXIX, August 17, 1953, 215-222.)

REPORT OF THE AD HOC COMMITTEE ON FORCED LABOUR. New York, United Nations, 1953, 619 p. (United Nations Economic and Social Council *Official Records, Sixteenth Session,* Supplement No. 13.)

REPORT OF THE U.N. HIGH COMMISSIONER FOR REFUGEES [Covering the Period June 1952 to May 1953]. New York, United Nations, 1953, 26 p. (United Nations General Assembly *Official Records, Eighth Session,* Supplement No. 11.)

MEASURES FOR THE PEACEFUL SOLUTION OF THE PROBLEM OF PRISONERS OF WAR: Progress Report to the Secretary-General on the Work of the Ad Hoc Commission on Prisoners of War. New York, United Nations, 1953, 25 p. (United Nations Document A/2482, dated 8 September 1953.)

Trusteeship and Non-Self-Governing Territories

REPORT OF THE TRUSTEESHIP COUNCIL Covering the Period from 4 December 1952 to 21 July 1953. New York, United Nations, 1953, 138 p. (United Nations General Assembly *Official Records, Eighth Session,* Supplement No. 4.)

NON-SELF-GOVERNING TERRITORIES. New York, United Nations, 1953, 55 p. (United Nations Document ST/DPI/SER.A/73.)

Specialized Agencies

THE WORK OF FAO, 1952/53: Report of the Director-General. Rome, FAO, 1953, 46 p.

INTERNATIONAL BANK FOR RECONSTRUCTION AND DEVELOPMENT: 8th Annual Report, 1952–53. Washington, International Bank, 1953, 68 p.

THE INTERNATIONAL BANK FOR RECONSTRUCTION AND DEVELOPMENT, 1946–1953. Baltimore, Johns Hopkins Press, 1954, 273 p.

ANNUAL REPORT OF THE EXECUTIVE DIRECTORS [of the International Monetary Fund] for the Fiscal Year Ended 30 April 1953. Washington, International Monetary Fund, 1953, 160 p.

UNESCO REPORT TO THE UNITED NATIONS, 1952–53. New York, United Nations, 1953, 243 p.

REPORT OF THE ACTING DIRECTOR-GENERAL [of UNESCO] ON THE ACTIVITIES OF THE ORGANIZATION from November 1952 to April 1953. Paris, UNESCO, 1953, 82 p.

THE WORK OF WHO, 1953: Annual Report of the Director-General to the World Health Assembly and to the United Nations. Geneva, WHO, 1954, 190 p.

International Court of Justice

INTERNATIONAL COURT OF JUSTICE: Reports of Judgments, Advisory Opinions and Orders, 1953. Leyden, Sijthoff, 1954, 200 p.

YEARBOOK [of the International Court of Justice], 1952–1953. The Hague, International Court of Justice, 1953, 255 p. (International Court of Justice Sales No. 107.)

THE WESTERN COMMUNITY

General

FIRE IN THE ASHES: Europe in Mid-Century, by Theodore H. White. New York, Sloane, 1953, 405 p.

THE TEMPER OF WESTERN EUROPE, by C. Crane Brinton. Cambridge, Harvard University Press, 1953, 118 p.

"La Conférence de Washington (10-14 juillet 1953)." (*Chronique de Politique Étrangère,* VI, September 1953, 595-624.)

WHAT EUROPE THINKS OF AMERICA, edited by James Burnham. New York, John Day, 1953, 235 p.

Economic Problems

ECONOMIC SURVEY OF EUROPE SINCE THE WAR: A Reappraisal of Problems and Prospects. Geneva, United Nations, 1953, 385 p. (United Nations Sales No. 1953.II.E.4.)

ECONOMIC SURVEY OF EUROPE IN 1953, Including a Study of Economic Development in Southern Europe. Geneva, United Nations, 1954, 314 p. (United Nations Sales No. 1954.II.E.2.)

ECONOMIC COMMISSION FOR EUROPE: Annual Report (19 March 1952–18 March 1953). New York, United Nations, 1953, 37 p. (United Nations Economic and Social Council *Official Records, Sixteenth Session,* Supplement No. 9.)

ECONOMIC COMMISSION FOR EUROPE: Annual Report (19 March 1953-25 March 1954). New York, United Nations, 1954, 44 p. (United Nations Economic and Social Council *Official Records, Eighteenth Session,* Supplement No. 3.)

Western European Political and Economic Integration

"L'integration politique européenne." (*Chronique de Politique Étrangère,* VI, May 1953, 277-398.)

"Draft Constitution for a European Political Community," by Basil Karp. (*International Organization,* VIII, May 1954, 181-202.)

A RECORD OF PROCEEDINGS IN THE CONSULTATIVE ASSEMBLY IN RELATION TO THE DRAFT TREATY EMBODYING THE STATUTE OF THE EUROPEAN COMMUNITY. Strasbourg, Council of Europe, 1953, 306 p.

LA COMMUNAUTÉ EUROPÉENNE DU CHARBON ET DE L'ACIER, by Paul Reuter, Paris, Pichon et Durand-Auzias, 1953, 322 p.

LA COMMUNAUTÉ EUROPÉENNE DU CHARBON ET DE L'ACIER, Paris, Colin, 1953, 338 p.

DER SCHUMAN-PLAN: Eine Untersuchung im besonderen Hinblick auf die deutsch-französische Stahlindustrie, by Carl Hahn. Munich, Pflaum, 1953, 158 p.

EUROPEAN COAL AND STEEL COMMUNITY: Hearings before the Senate Committee on Foreign Relations, 83d Congress, 1st Session, June 4 and 5, 1953. Washington, GPO, 1953, 37 p. (Informal meeting of the Committee with members of the High Authority of the European Coal and Steel Community.)

L'EUROPE UNIE ET SA PLACE DANS L'ÉCONOMIE INTERNATIONALE, by André Philip. Paris, Presses Universitaires, 1953, 365 p.

L'INTÉGRATION ÉCONOMIQUE DE L'EUROPE, by Lucien de Saint-Grette. Paris, Presses Universitaires, 1953, 329 p.

LA COOPÉRATION ÉCONOMIQUE EUROPÉENNE, Paris, O.E.C.E., 1953, 189 p. (Fifth Annual Report of the O.E.E.C.)

OBSERVATIONS ON THE ECONOMY OF WESTERN EUROPE: Report on GATT Sessions at Geneva and Statistical Meetings at Rome. Washington, GPO, 1953, 26 p. (Memorandum from Grover W. Ensley to the Congressional Economic Report Joint Committee, November 6, 1953.)

"American Foreign Policy and European Integration," by Hajo Holborn. (*World Politics,* VI, October 1953, 1-30).

NATO and the European Defense Community

ESSAI DE STRATÉGIE OCCIDENTALE, by General P. É. Jacquot. Paris, Gallimard, 1953, 202 p.

THE NATO HANDBOOK. Paris, NATO, 1953, 55 p.

SECOND ANNUAL REPORT, SUPREME ALLIED COMMANDER, EUROPE (May 30, 1952-May 30, 1953). Paris, SHAPE, 1953, 28 p.

"Activités dans le cadre du traité de l'Atlantique nord: la conférence de Paris." (*Chronique de Politique Étrangère,* VI, November 1953, 744-759.) (Describes the 11th Ministerial Session of the North Atlantic Council, Apr. 24-26, 1953.)

"Activités dans le cadre du traité de l'Atlantique nord: la conférence de Paris." (*Chronique de Politique Étrangère,* VII, March 1954, 166-181.) (Describes the 12th Ministerial Session of the North Atlantic Council, Dec. 14-16, 1953.)

"Atlantikpakt und Europäische Verteidigungsgemeinschaft auf der 12. Tagung des Nordatlantikrates in Paris vom 14. bis 16. Dezember 1953," by Hermann Volle. (*Europa-Archiv,* IX, January 20, 1954, 6285-6294.)

"Die Umstellung der NATO auf eine Politik der 'Langen Sicht'," by Hermann Volle. (*Europa Archiv,* IX, February 5, 1954, 6321-6328.)

LA COMMUNAUTÉ EUROPÉENNE DE DÉFENSE: Étude analytique du traité du 27 mai 1952, by Jean Legaret and E. Martin-Dumesnil. Paris, Vrin, 1953, 275 p.

"The Mediterranean: Pivot of Peace and War," by W. Gordon East. (*Foreign Affairs,* XXXII, October 1953, 48-67.)

Individual Western-oriented Countries

THE REBIRTH OF AUSTRIA, by Richard Hiscocks. London and New York, Oxford University Press, 1953, 248 p.

ZWISCHEN BEFREIUNG UND FREIHEIT: Der Sonderfall Oesterreich, by Karl Gruber. Vienna, Ullstein, 1953, 326 p.

AUSTRIA'S INTERNATIONAL POSITION, 1938–1953: The Reestablishment of an Independent Austria, by Travers C. Grayson, Jr. Geneva, Droz, 1953, 317 p.

ECONOMIC RECONSTRUCTION OF AUSTRIA, 1945–52: Report on Postwar Developments, by Franz Heissenberger. Washington, Library of Congress, 1953, 153 p.

THE AUSTRIAN TREATY: A Case Study of Soviet Tactics. Washington, GPO, 1953, 16 p. (Department of State Publication 5012; European and British Commonwealth Series 43.)

FRANCE: Keystone of Western Defense, by Edgar S. Furniss, Jr. Garden City, Doubleday, 1954, 94 p. (Doubleday Short Studies in Political Science.)

FRENCH POLITICS: The First Years of the Fourth Republic, by Dorothy Pickles. London and New York, Oxford University Press (for the Royal Institute of International Affairs), 1953, 302 p.

"De la chute du gouvernement Mayer à l'avènement du cabinet Laniel." (*Chronique de Politique Étrangère,* VI, September 1953, 626-634.)

"The French Union: Concept, Reality and Prospects," by General Georges Catroux. (*International Conciliation,* No. 495, November 1953, 200-247.)

ITALY IN CRISIS, by Mario Einaudi. Toronto, Canadian Institute of International Affairs, 1953, 16 p. (Behind the Headlines, XIII, No. 3.)

"Les crises gouvernementales en Italie depuis les élections générales du 7 juin 1953, jusqu'à l'avènement du cabinet Scelba." (*Chronique de Politique Étrangère,* VII, May 1954, 292-302.)

THE UNITED STATES AND ITALY, by H. Stuart Hughes. Cambridge, Harvard University Press, 1953, 267 p.

"La question de Trieste." (*Chronique de Politique Étrangère,* VII, May 1954, 303-312.)

"Spain in Western Defense," by Lawrence Fernsworth. (*Foreign Affairs,* XXXI, July 1953, 648-662.)

THE PRICE OF FREEDOM: Greece in World Affairs, 1939–1953, by Dimitrios G. Kousoulas. Syracuse, Syracuse University Press, 1953, 221 p.

GREECE: A Political and Economical Survey (1939–1953), by Bickham Sweet-Escott. London, Royal Institute of International Affairs, 1954, 207 p.

The United Kingdom and British Commonwealth

(See also regional headings)

PARLIAMENTARY DEBATES. Weekly Hansard. London, H.M.S.O., weekly (during parliamentary sessions).

BRITAIN AND THE UNITED STATES: Problems in Cooperation, by Henry L. Roberts and Paul A. Wilson. New York, Harper (for the Council on Foreign Relations), 1953, 253 p.

"Britain and America: Common Aims, Different Opinions," by Clement R. Attlee. (*Foreign Affairs,* XXXII, January 1954, 190-202.)

ECONOMIC SURVEY FOR 1953. Cmd. 8800; London, H.M.S.O., 1953, 50 p.

BRITAIN IN THE WORLD ECONOMY, by Sir Dennis H. Robertson. London, Allen and Unwin, 1954, 92 p.

THE STERLING AREA AND THE DOLLAR PROBLEM, by Forrest Rogers. Toronto, Canadian Institute of International Affairs, 1953, 33 p. (Behind the Headlines, XII, No. 7.)

THE COMMONWEALTH IN ASIA, by Nicholas Mansergh. Toronto, Canadian Institute of International Affairs, 1953, 16 p. (Behind the Headlines, XIII, No. 2.)

THE COMMONWEALTH AND THE UNITED NATIONS, by Lionel Gelber. Toronto, Canadian Institute of International Affairs, 1953, 16 p. (Behind the Headlines, XIII, No. 5.)

THE GERMAN PROBLEM

GERMANY REPORTS. Bonn, Press and Information Office, 1953, 367 p.

GERMANY: Key to Peace, by James P. Warburg. Cambridge, Harvard University Press, 1953, 363 p.

RUSSLAND, DIE WESTMÄCHTE UND DEUTSCHLAND: Die sowjetische Deutschlandpolitik, 1943–1953, by Boris Meissner. Hamburg, Nölke, 1953, 372 p.

"Le problème de l'unification de l'Allemagne à la veille de la conférence de Berlin." (*Chronique de Politique Étrangère,* VII, January 1954, 5-17.)

"How Strong Is the New Germany?" by Percy Bidwell. (*Yale Review,* XLII, Summer 1953, 34-63.)

GOVERNING POSTWAR GERMANY, by Edward H. Litchfield and others. Ithaca, Cornell University Press, 1953, 678 p.

Berlin and the Soviet Zone

THE TERROR MACHINE: The Inside Story of the Soviet Administration in Germany, by Gregory P. Klimov. London, Faber, 1953, 400 p. (Translated from the German by H. C. Stevens.)

CLOSE CONTACT, by Brigadier C. H. Dewhurst. Boston, Houghton Mifflin, 1954, 173 p.

"Les événements de Berlin-Est des 16 et 17 juin 1953." (*Chronique de Politique Étrangère,* VI, September 1953, 635-640.)

DER 17. JUNI, by Arno Scholz and Werner Nieke. Berlin, Arani, 1953, 95 p.

THE SOVIET UNION AND ITS EUROPEAN SATELLITES

The U.S.S.R.

CURRENT DIGEST OF THE SOVIET PRESS. New York, Joint Commitee on Slavic Studies, weekly.

NEW TIMES. Moscow, *Trud,* weekly.

NEWS: A Soviet Review of World Events. Moscow, *Trud,* fortnightly.

RUSSIA: A History and an Interpretation, by Michael T. Florinsky. New York, Macmillan, 1953, 2 volumes.

THE DYNAMICS OF SOVIET SOCIETY, by W. W. Rostow and Alfred Levin. New York, Norton, 1953, 282 p.

OUR SECRET ALLIES: The Peoples of Russia, by Eugene Lyons. Boston, Little, Brown, 1953, 384 p.

RUSSIAN ASSIGNMENT, by Admiral Leslie C. Stevens. Boston, Little, Brown, 1953, 583 p.

THE RED CARPET, by Marshall MacDuffie. New York, Norton, 1955, 330 p.

HOW RUSSIA IS RULED, by Merle Fainsod. Cambridge, Harvard University Press, 1953, 575 p.

CURRENT SOVIET POLICIES: The Documentary Records of the 19th Communist Party Congress and the Reorganization after Stalin's Death, from the Translations of the *Current Digest of the Soviet Press,* edited by Leo Gruliow. New York, Praeger, 1953, 268 p.

CRISIS IN THE KREMLIN, by Maurice G. Hindus. Garden City, Doubleday, 1953, 319 p.

"La politique de l'U.R.S.S. depuis le décès de Staline." (*Chronique de Politique Étrangère,* VI, July 1953, 426-437.)

MALENKOV: Stalin's Successor, by Martin Ebon. New York, McGraw-Hill, 1953, 284 p.

WHAT NEXT IN RUSSIA? by Isaac Deutscher. New York, Oxford University Press, 1953, 230 p.

SOVIET ECONOMIC GROWTH: Conditions and Perspectives, edited by Abram Bergson. New York, Row, Peterson and Company, 1953, 368 p.

THE RED ARMY TODAY, by Louis B. Ely. 3d edition; Harrisburg, Military Service Publishing Company, 1953, 272 p.

SOVIET MILITARY DOCTRINE, by Raymond L. Garthoff. Glencoe, Illinois, Free Press, 1953, 605 p.

SOVIET POLICY IN THE FAR EAST, 1944–1951, by Max Beloff. New York, Oxford University Press (for the Royal Institute of International Affairs), 1953, 284 p.

"The Kremlin's Foreign Policy since Stalin," by Philip E. Mosely. (*Foreign Affairs,* XXXII, October 1953, 20-33.)

The European Satellites

NEWS FROM BEHIND THE IRON CURTAIN. New York, Committee for Free Europe, monthly.

FOR A LASTING PEACE, FOR A PEOPLE'S DEMOCRACY! Bucharest, Information Bureau of the Communist and Workers' Parties, weekly.

THE GREAT POWERS AND EASTERN EUROPE, by John A. Lukacs. New York, American Book, 1953, 878 p.

READINGS ON CONTEMPORARY EASTERN EUROPE, edited by C. E. Black. New York, National Committee for a Free Europe, 1953, 346 p. (Mid-European Studies Center Publication No. 11.)

"Russia's European Satellites," by W. T. Stone. (*Editorial Research Reports,* II, No. 18, November 4, 1953, 769-785.)

TENSIONS WITHIN THE SOVIET CAPTIVE COUNTRIES. Washington, GPO, 1953–1954, 6 pts. (Senate Document 70, 83d Congress.)

THE POLITICAL CONTROL OF CZECHOSLOVAKIA: A Study in Social Control of a Soviet Satellite State, by I. Gadourek. Leiden, Stenfert Kroese, 1953, 285 p.

POLAND: White Eagle on a Red Field, by Samuel L. Sharp. Cambridge, Harvard University Press, 1953, 345 p.

THE NEAR AND MIDDLE EAST

General

MIDDLE EAST JOURNAL. Washington, Middle East Institute, quarterly.

EVOLUTION IN THE MIDDLE EAST: Reform, Revolt and Change—A Series of Addresses Presented at the Seventh Annual Conference on Middle East Affairs, Sponsored by the Middle East Institute, March 6-7, 1953, edited by S. N. Fisher. Washington, Middle East Institute, 1953, 97 p.

THE MIDDLE EAST IN THE WAR, by George Kirk. New York, Oxford University Press (for the Royal Institute of International Affairs), 1953, 521 p.

THE MIDDLE EAST, 1945–1950, by George Kirk. New York, Oxford University Press (for the Royal Institute of International Affairs), 1954, 338 p.

MIDDLE EAST DILEMMAS: The Background of United States Policy, by J. C. Hurewitz. New York, Harper (for the Council on Foreign Relations), 1953, 273 p.

A SURVEY OF AMERICAN INTERESTS IN THE MIDDLE EAST, edited by Frances C. Mattison. Washington, Middle East Institute, 1953, 140 p.

"The Development of United States Policy in the Near East, South Asia and Africa during 1953," by Harry N. Howard. (*Department of State Bulletin,* XXX, February 22, 1954, 274-281; March 1, 1954, 328-333; March 8, 1954, 365-371.)

"American Policy in the Middle East during 1953," by Richard H. Sanger. (*Department of State Bulletin,* XXX, February 8, 1954, 209-214.)

"Strategic Problems of the Middle East," by G. F. Eliot. (*Middle Eastern Affairs,* IV, October 1953, 313-323.)

SUMMARY OF RECENT ECONOMIC DEVELOPMENTS IN THE MIDDLE EAST, 1952–53: Supplement to World Economic Report. New York, United Nations, 1954, 128 p. (United Nations Sales No. 1954.II.C.2.)

RURAL RECONSTRUCTION IN ACTION: Experience in the Near and Middle East, by H. B. Allen. Ithaca, Cornell University Press, 1953, 204 p.

The Palestine Problem and Israel

WHAT PRICE ISRAEL, by Alfred M. Lilienthal. Chicago, Regnery, 1953, 282 p.

ISRAEL BETWEEN EAST AND WEST: A Study in Human Relations, by Raphael Patai. Philadelphia, Jewish Publication Society of America, 1953, 348 p.

DEMOCRATIC BULWARK IN THE MIDDLE EAST: A Review and Analysis of Israel's Social, Economic and Political Problems during the Period from 1948 to 1953, by Joseph Dunner. Grinnell, Grinnell College Press, 1953, 41 p.

"The Impact of Immigration on Israel," by E. Samuel. (*Political Quarterly,* XXIV, July-September 1953, 272-284.)

"The Arab-Israel Frontier," by Elizabeth Monroe. (*International Affairs,* XXIX, October 1953, 439-448.)

"The United Nations Conciliation Commission for Palestine: Establishment and Definition of Functions," by J. C. Hurewitz. (*International Organization,* VII, November 1953, 482-497.)

U.N. CONCILIATION COMMISSION FOR PALESTINE: 13th Progress Report (for the Period from 28 November 1952 to 31 December 1953). New York, United Nations, 1954, 11 p. (United Nations Document A/2629, dated 4 January 1954.)

REPORT DATED 23 OCTOBER 1953 BY THE CHIEF OF STAFF OF THE TRUCE SUPERVISION ORGANIZATION Submitted to the Secretary-General for the Security Council. New York, United Nations, 1953, 25 p. (United Nations Document S/3122, dated 23 October 1953.)

ANNUAL REPORT OF THE DIRECTOR OF UNITED NATIONS RELIEF AND WORKS AGENCY FOR PALESTINE REFUGEES IN THE NEAR EAST Covering the Period 1 July 1952 to 30 June 1953. New York, United Nations, 1953, 27 p. (United Nations General Assembly *Official Records, Eighth Session,* Supplement No. 12.)

The Arab States

THE ARAB WORLD: Past, Present and Future, by Nejla Izzedin. Chicago, Regnery, 1953, 424 p.

MOSLEMS ON THE MARCH: People and Politics in the World of Islam, by F. W. Fernau. New York, Knopf, 1953, 329 p. (Translated from the German by E. W. Dickes.)

"The Intellectual Impact of Communism upon Contemporary Islam," by Kenneth Cragg. (*Middle East Journal,* VIII, Spring 1954, 127-138.)

"The Arab League: An Experiment in Regional Organization," by Mahomed Shafi Agwani. (*India Quarterly,* IX, October-December 1953, 355-366.)

THE EMERGENCY OF MODERN EGYPT, by J. S. Badeau and R. H. Nolte. New York, Foreign Policy Association, 1953, 62 p. (Headline Series No. 98.)

"Problèmes égyptiens." (*Chronique de Politique Étrangère,* VI, September 1953, 658-689.)

"Lands A-thwart the Nile," by Derwent Whittlesey. (*World Politics,* V, January 1953, 214-241.)

A HISTORY OF MODERN EGYPT AND ANGLO-EGYPTIAN RELATIONS, 1800–1953, by John Marlowe (pseud.). New York, Praeger, 1954, 440 p.

"The Anglo-Egyptian Question," by Randolph Gherson. (*Middle East Journal,* VII, Autumn 1953, 456-483.)

DOCUMENTS CONCERNING CONSTITUTIONAL DEVELOPMENT IN THE SUDAN and the Agreement between the Government of the United Kingdom . . . and the Egyptian Government concerning Self-Government and Self-Determination for the Sudan, February 17, 1953. Cmd. 8767; London, H.M.S.O., 1953, 70 p.

REPORT OF THE SUDAN ELECTORAL COMMISSION, Khartoum, December 13, 1953. Cmd. 9058; London, H.M.S.O., 1954, 24 p.

THE SUEZ CANAL IN WORLD AFFAIRS, by Hugh J. Schonfield. New York, Philosophical Library, 1953, 174 p.

"The Suez: International Roadway," by André Siegfried. (*Foreign Affairs,* XXXI, July 1953, 605-618.)

IRAQ, 1900 TO 1950: A Political, Social and Economic History, by Stephen H. Longrigg. London, Oxford University Press, 1953, 446 p.

"Lebanon's Popular Revolution," by G. Britt. (*Middle East Journal,* VII, Winter 1953, 1-17.)

Iran

LANDLORD AND PEASANT IN PERSIA, by A. K. S. Lambton. New York, Oxford University Press, 1953, 401 p.

THE ANGLO-IRANIAN OIL DISPUTE OF 1951–1952, by Alan W. Ford. Berkeley, University of California Press, 1954, 348 p.

OIL DIPLOMACY: Powderkeg in Iran, by Nasrollah Saifpour Fatemi. New York, Whittier, 1954, 405 p.

ABADAN: A First-hand Account of the Persian Oil Crisis, by Norman Kemp. London, Wingate, 1953, 270 p.

"Les Événements d'Iran." (*Chronique de Politique Étrangère,* VI, November 1953, 765-803.)

"The Beginnings of Point IV Work in Iran," by F. S. Harris. (*Middle East Journal,* VII. Spring 1953, 222-228.)

AFRICA

General

AFRICAN AFFAIRS. London, Royal African Society, quarterly.

STRUGGLE FOR AFRICA, by Vernon Bartlett. London, Muller, 1953, 251 p.

AFRICA: A Study in Tropical Development, by L. Dudley Stamp. New York, Wiley, 1953, 568 p.

SUMMARY OF RECENT ECONOMIC DEVELOPMENTS IN AFRICA, 1952–53: Supplement to the World Economic Report. New York, United Nations, 1954, 83 p. (United Nations Sales No. 1954.II.C.3.)

L'INDUSTRIALISATION DE L'AFRIQUE, by I. du Jonchay. Paris, Payot, 1953, 344 p.

North Africa

RÉVOLUTION AU MAROC, by Robert Montagne. Paris, Éditions France-Empire, 1953, 415 p.

LES AFFAIRES DE LA TUNISIE ET DU MAROC DEVANT LES NATIONS UNIES, by G. Day. Paris, Pedone, 1953, 134 p.

"Libya after Two Years of Independence," by William H. Lewis and Robert Gordon. (*Middle East Journal,* VIII, Winter 1954, 41-53.)

THE ECONOMIC AND SOCIAL DEVELOPMENT OF LIBYA. New York, United Nations, 1953, 170 p. (United Nations Sales No. 1953.II.H.8.)

Central and Southern Africa

LA BELGIQUE ET LE CONGO AU MILIEU DU XXE SIÈCLE, by V. Lefèbvre, Charleroi, Imprimerie Provinciale, 1953, 639 p.

SOUTHERN RHODESIA, NORTHERN RHODESIA AND NYASALAND: The Federal Scheme Prepared by A Conference Held in London in January 1953. Cmd. 8754; London, H.M.S.O., 1953, 45 p.

GOLD COAST REVOLUTION: The Struggle of An African People from Slavery to Freedom, by George Padmore. New York, British Book Centre, 1953, 272 p.

"Kenya: the Land and Mau Mau," by Derwent Whittlesey. (*Foreign Affairs,* XXXII, October 1953, 80-90.)

THE NEW WEST AFRICA, edited by Basil Davidson and Adenekan Ademola. London, Allen and Unwin, 1953, 181 p.

Union of South Africa

"The South African General Election, 1953," by T. W. Price. (*Parliamentary Affairs,* VI, Summer 1953, 258-268.)

REPORT OF THE U.N. COMMISSION ON THE RACIAL SITUATION IN THE UNION OF SOUTH AFRICA. New York, United Nations, 1954, 166 p. (United Nations General Assembly *Official Records, Eighth Session,* Supplement No. 16.)

TREATMENT OF PEOPLE OF INDIAN ORIGIN IN THE UNION OF SOUTH AFRICA: Report of the U.N. Good Offices Commission. New York, United Nations, 1953, 16 p. United Nations Document A/2473, dated 17 September 1953.)

QUESTION OF SOUTH WEST AFRICA: Report of the Ad Hoc Committee on South West Africa to the General Assembly. New York, United Nations, 1953, 18 p. (United Nations Document A/2475, dated 16 September 1953.)

"South Africa: A Land Divided against Itself," by Z. K. Matthews. (*Yale Review,* XLII, June 1953, 513-528.)

ASIA AND THE FAR EAST

General

FAR EASTERN SURVEY. New York, American Institute of Pacific Relations, fortnightly.

PACIFIC AFFAIRS. New York, Institute of Pacific Relations, quarterly.

ASIA AFLAME, by Ebed Van der Vlugt. New York, Devin-Adair, 1953, 294 p.

ASIAN NATIONALISM AND THE WEST, edited by William L. Holland. New York, Macmillan (for the Institute of Pacific Relations), 1953, 449 p.

" 'Neutralism' in Asia," by Robert A. Scalapino. (*American Political Science Review,* XLVII, March 1954, 49-62.)

Economic Affairs

ECONOMIC SURVEY OF ASIA AND THE FAR EAST, 1953. Bangkok, United Nations, 1954, 161 p. (United Nations Sales No. 1953.II.F.8.)

ANNUAL REPORT OF THE ECONOMIC COMMISSION FOR ASIA AND THE FAR EAST, 15 February 1953-19 February 1954. New York, United Nations, 1954, 39 p. (United Nations Economic and Social Council *Official Records, Seventeenth Session,* Supplement No. 3.)

India, Pakistan and South Asia

INDIA QUARTERLY: A Journal of International Affairs. New Delhi, Indian Council of World Affairs, quarterly.

AMBASSADOR'S REPORT, by Chester Bowles. New York, Harper, 1954, 425 p.

INDIA AND THE AWAKENING EAST, by Eleanor Roosevelt. New York, Harper, 1953, 229 p.

THE UNITED STATES AND INDIA AND PAKISTAN, by W. Norman Brown. Cambridge, Harvard University Press, 1953, 308 p.

INDIA, PAKISTAN AND THE WEST, by Percival Spear. 2d edition; New York, Oxford University Press, 1953, 251 p.

"The Kashmir Dispute after Six Years," by Josef Korbel. (*International Organization,* VII, November 1953, 498-510.)

FIFTH REPORT TO THE SECURITY COUNCIL BY THE UNITED NATIONS REPRESENTATIVE FOR INDIA AND PAKISTAN. New York, United Nations, 1953, 44 p. (United Nations Document S/2967, dated 27 March 1953.)

THE STRUGGLE FOR KASHMIR, by Michael Brecher. Toronto, Ryerson, 1953, 211 p.

AFGHANISTAN: A Study of Political Developments in Central and Southern Asia, by W. K. Fraser-Tytler. Revised edition; London, Oxford University Press, 1953, 348 p.

PARLIAMENTARY GOVERNMENT IN SOUTHERN ASIA: A Survey of Developments in Burma, Ceylon, India and Pakistan, 1947–1952, by Sydney D. Bailey. New York, Institute of Pacific Relations, 1953, 100 p.

REPORT OF THE SPECIAL STUDY MISSION TO PAKISTAN, INDIA, THAILAND AND INDOCHINA . . . of the Committee on Foreign Affairs, House of Representatives, 83d Congress, 1st Session, Pursuant to H. Res. 113. Washington, GPO, 1953. 104 p. (House Report 412, 83d Congress, 1st Session.)

China

MODERN CHINA'S FOREIGN POLICY, by Werner Levi. Minneapolis, University of Minnesota Press, 1953, 399 p.

CHINA AND THE WORLD, by Tillman Durdin and Robert Aura Smith. New York, Foreign Policy Association, 1953, 63 p. (Headline Series No. 99.)

THE CHINA TANGLE: The American Effort in China from Pearl Harbor to the Marshall Mission, by Herbert Feis. Princeton, Princeton University Press, 1953, 455 p.

FIFTY YEARS IN CHINA, by John Leighton Stuart. New York, Random House, 1954, 346 p.

THE ECONOMIC RESOURCES AND DEVELOPMENT OF FORMOSA, by N. S. Ginsburg. New York, Institute of Pacific Relations, 1953, 58 p.

THE GREAT PEACE: An Asian's Candid Report on Red China, by Raja Hutheesing. New York, Harper, 1953, 246 p.

OUT OF RED CHINA, by Liu Shaw-tong. New York, Duell, 1953, 269 p.

GOVERNMENT AND ADMINISTRATION IN COMMUNIST CHINA, by S. B. Thomas. New York, Institute of Pacific Relations, 1953, 153 p.

"The 'Three Anti' and 'Five Anti' Movements in Communist China," by T. H. E. Chen and W. H. C. Chen (*Pacific Affairs,* XXVI, March 1953, 3-23.)

MOSCOW AND CHINESE COMMUNISTS, by Robert Carver North. Stanford, Stanford University Press, 1953, 315 p.

Japan

CONTEMPORARY JAPAN. Tokyo, Foreign Affairs Association of Japan, quarterly.

THE NEW JAPAN, by Royden Dangerfield. New York, Foreign Policy Association, 1953, 62 p. (Headline Series No. 102.)

THE GREAT SEDUCTION: Red China's Drive to Bring Free Japan behind the

Iron Curtain, by Richard L-G. Deverall. Tokyo, International Literature Printing Company, 1953, 427 p.

"Japanese Election Results Reconsidered," by N. Ukai. (*Pacific Affairs,* XXVI, June 1953, 139-146.)

"The Future of the Ryukyus," by Joseph W. Ballantine. (*Foreign Affairs,* XXXI, July 1953, 663-674.)

JAPAN'S NATURAL RESOURCES AND THEIR RELATIONS TO JAPAN'S ECONOMIC FUTURE, by Edward A. Ackerman. Chicago, University of Chicago Press, 1953, 680 p.

JAPAN AND AMERICA TODAY, by Edwin O. Reischauer and others. Stanford, Stanford University Press, 1953, 166 p.

THE FAR EASTERN COMMISSION: A Study in International Cooperation, 1945 to 1952. Washington, GPO, 1953, 239 p. (Department of State Publication 5138; Far Eastern Series 60.)

Korea

"Korea: Collective Measures Against Aggression," by Leland M. Goodrich. (*International Conciliation,* No. 494, October 1953, 64 p.)

THE UNITED STATES AND THE KOREAN PROBLEM: Documents, 1943–1953. Washington, GPO, 1953, 168 p. (Senate Document 74, 83d Congress, 1st Session.)

THE QUESTION OF KOREA, 1950–1953. New York, United Nations, 1954, 44 p. (United Nations Department of Information Background Paper No. 79.)

"La situation en Corée." (*Chronique de Politique Étrangère,* VII, January 1954, 18-80.)

REPORT OF THE UNCURK. New York, United Nations, 1953, 21 p. (United Nations General Assembly *Official Records, Eighth Session,* Supplement No. 13.)

SPECIAL REPORT OF THE UNIFIED COMMAND ON THE ARMISTICE IN KOREA. New York, United Nations, 1953, 51 p. (United Nations Document S/3079, dated 7 August 1953.)

MILITARY ARMISTICE IN KOREA and Temporary Supplementary Agreement, Signed at Panmunjom, Korea, July 27, 1953, Entered into Force, July 27, 1953. Washington, GPO, 1953, 127 p. (Department of State Publication 5197; Treaties and Other International Acts Series 2782.)

DECISION IN KOREA, by Rutherford M. Poats. New York, McBride, 1954, 340 p.

FROM THE DANUBE TO THE YALU, by General Mark W. Clark. New York, Harper, 1954, 369 p.

GENERAL DEAN'S STORY, by Major General William F. Dean. New York, Viking, 1954, 305 p.

SUBSTITUTE FOR VICTORY, by John Dille. Garden City, Doubleday, 1954, 219 p.

I WAS A CAPTIVE IN KOREA, by Philip Deane. New York, Norton, 1953, 253 p.

QUESTION OF ATROCITIES COMMITTED BY THE NORTH KOREAN AND CHINESE COMMUNIST FORCES AGAINST U.N. PRISONERS OF WAR IN KOREA: Letter dated 26 November 1953 from the U.S.A. Representative to the U.N. New York, United Nations, 1953, 166 p. (United Nations Document A/2563.)

KOREAN WAR ATROCITIES—

Hearings: Subcommittee of Senate Permanent Subcommittee on Investigations, Dec. 2-4, 1953, 3 pts. *Report:* S. Rept. 848, Jan. 11, 1954, 27 p.

REPORT OF THE AGENT GENERAL OF THE U.N. KOREAN RECONSTRUCTION AGENCY for the Period 15 September 1952 to 30 September 1953. New York, United Nations, 1953, 29 p. (United Nations General Assembly *Official Records, Eighth Session,* Supplement No. 14.)

Southeast Asia

REPORT ON INDOCHINA, by Bernard Newman. London Hale, 1953, 245 p.

L'OPÉRATION INDOCHINE, by Jacques Dinfreville. Paris, Éditions Internationales, 1953, 183 p.

LE DRAME INDOCHINOIS, by General Jean Marchand. Paris, Peyronnet, 1953, 247 p.

INDOCHINA: Report of Mike Mansfield on Study Mission to the Associated States of Indochina, Vietnam, Cambodia, and Laos. Washington, GPO, 1953, 12 p. (Committee print, Committee on Foreign Relations, United States Senate, 83d Congress, 1st Session.)

SOME ASPECTS OF SIAMESE POLITICS, by John Coast. New York, Institute of Pacific Relations, 1953, 58 p.

"Communalism and Communism in Malaya," by F. G. Carnell. (*Pacific Affairs,* XXVI, June 1953, 99-117.)

PUBLIC ADMINISTRATION IN MALAYA, by S. W. Jones. New York, Oxford University Press (for the Royal Institute of International Affairs), 1953, 229 p.

ECONOMICS AND ECONOMIC POLICY OF DUAL SOCIETIES AS EXEMPLIFIED BY INDONESIA, by J. H. Boeke. New York, Institute of Pacific Relations, 1953, 319 p.

THE EIGHTH YEAR OF A FREE NATION, 1952–1953: Republic of Indonesia. New York, Information Office of the Republic of Indonesia, 1953, 38 p.

"The 1953 Philippine Presidential Elections," by Willard H. Elsbree. (*Pacific Affairs,* XXVII, March 1954, 3-15.)

"Philippine Economic Progress," by J. A. Storer. (*Far Eastern Survey,* XXII, July 1953, 89-95.)

THE SOUTH SEAS IN TRANSITION, by W. E. H. Stanner. Sydney, Australasian Publishing Company, 1953, 464 p.

SPECIAL STUDY MISSION TO SOUTHEAST ASIA AND THE PACIFIC: Report by Walter H. Judd and others. Washington, GPO, 1953, 107 p. (House Foreign Affairs Committee print, 83d Congress, 2d Session.)

The ANZUS Powers

"New Zealand and the New Pacific," by L. K. Munro. (*Foreign Affairs,* XXXI, July 1953, 634-647.)

"Anzac Dilemma," by F. L. W. Wood (*International Affairs,* XXIX, April 1953, 184-192.)

WESTERN HEMISPHERE

General

ANNALS OF THE ORGANIZATION OF AMERICAN STATES. Washington, Pan American Union, quarterly.

INTER-AMERICAN ECONOMIC AFFAIRS. Washington, Institute of Inter-American Studies, quarterly.

THE STATE OF LATIN AMERICA, by Germán Arciniegas. New York, Knopf, 1952, 416 p.

REPORT ON THE ACTIVITIES OF THE ORGANIZATION OF AMERICAN STATES, 1948–1953. Washington, Pan American Union, 1953, 229 p.

ECONOMIC SURVEY OF LATIN AMERICA, 1953. New York, United Nations, 1954, 262 p. (United Nations Sales No. 1954.II.G.1.)

ECONOMIC COMMISSION FOR LATIN AMERICA: Fifth Annual Report, 15 February 1952-25 April 1953. New York, United Nations, 1953, 56 p. (United

Nations Economic and Social Council *Official Records, Sixteenth Session,* Supplement No. 3.)
ECONOMIC COMMISSION FOR LATIN AMERICA: Sixth Annual Report, 26 April 1953-10 February 1954. New York, United Nations, 1954, 24 p. (United Nations Economic and Social Council *Official Records, Seventeenth Session,* Supplement No. 2.)
REPORT TO THE PRESIDENT: UNITED STATES-LATIN AMERICAN RELATIONS. Washington, GPO, 1953, 23 p. (Department of State Publication 5290; Inter-American Series 47; Report of the President's Special Ambassador, Milton S. Eisenhower.)
THE U.S. AND LATIN AMERICA, by H. L. Matthews and L. T. Holmes. New York, Foreign Policy Association, 1953, 62 p. (Headline Series No. 100.)

Mexico, Central America, the Caribbean

THE ECONOMIC DEVELOPMENT OF MEXICO. Baltimore, Johns Hopkins Press (for the International Bank for Reconstruction and Development), 1953, 392 p.
THE CARIBBEAN: Contemporary Trends, edited by Alma Curtis Wilgus. Gainesville, University of Florida Press, 1953, 318 p.
THE BRITISH HONDURAS-GUATEMALA DISPUTE, by L. M. Bloomfield. Toronto, Carswell, 1953, 234 p.

South America

THOSE PERPLEXING ARGENTINES, by James K. Bruce. New York, Longmans, Green, 1953, 349 p.
PERÓN'S ARGENTINA, by George I. Blanksten. Chicago, University of Chicago Press, 1953, 478 p.
YANKEE DIPLOMACY: U.S. Intervention in Argentina, by O. Edmund Smith, Jr. Dallas, Southern Methodist University Press, 1953, 182 p.
LE BRÉSIL: Structure sociale et institutions politiques, by Jacques Lambert. Paris, Colin, 1953, 166 p. (Cahiers de la Fondation nationale des sciences politiques No. 44.)
COLOMBIA: A General Survey, by W. O. Galbraith. New York, Royal Institute of International Affairs, 1953, 140 p.
STUDY OF THE PROSPECTS OF INTER-LATIN AMERICA TRADE (Southern Zone of the Region). New York, United Nations, 1954, 134 p. (United Nations Sales No. 1953.II.G.4.)

Canada

SPRINGS OF CANADIAN POWER: A Chatham House Information Paper. London, Royal Institute of International Affairs, 1953, 59 p.
CANADA: A Story of Challenge, by J. M. S. Careless. New York, Cambridge University Press, 1953, 432 p.
CANADA AND THE FAR EAST, 1940–1953, by H. F. Angus. Toronto, University of Toronto Press, 1953, 121 p.
"Canada's Northern Horizon," by L. B. Pearson. (*Foreign Affairs,* XXXI, July 1953, 581-591.)
CANADA'S FOREIGN POLICY: A Look at the Record, by G. M. Craig. Toronto, Canadian Institute of International Affairs, 1953, 16 p. (Behind the Headlines, XIII, No. 4.)

CHRONOLOGY OF WORLD EVENTS

JANUARY 1–DECEMBER 31, 1953

In any such general chronology as this the selection of events to be included is necessarily somewhat arbitrary. Primary emphasis has been placed on listing the most significant international agreements, statements of policy, changes of government, and general elections, which are entered wherever possible under appropriate regional or organizational headings. The reader who desires a more detailed chronology has a choice of several convenient compilations, among which mention may be made of the *Chronology of International Events and Documents* (London, Royal Institute of International Affairs, fortnightly) and chronologies included in *Current History* (Philadelphia, Events Publishing Company, monthly) and in the *World Almanac and Book of Facts* (New York, New York World-Telegram and Sun, annual).

THE UNITED STATES

Jan. 3-Aug. 4. The Republican-controlled 83d Congress holds its First Session.

Jan. 7. President Harry S. Truman submits to Congress his final State of the Union message.

———. A resolution to modify the constitutional provisions relating to the treaty-making power is introduced in the Senate by Senator John W. Bricker.

Jan. 9. President Truman submits to Congress a revised budget calling for expenditures of $78.6 billion in the fiscal year 1953–54.

Jan. 20. General of the Army Dwight D. Eisenhower is inaugurated as 34th President of the United States.

Jan. 21. The Senate confirms the nomination of John Foster Dulles as Secretary of State.

Jan. 30-Feb. 9. The Secretary of State and the Mutual Security Director (Harold E. Stassen) tour Western European capitals to discuss common problems.

Feb. 2. President Eisenhower delivers in person his first State of the Union message and announces that the U.S. Seventh Fleet will no longer prevent Nationalist Chinese attacks on the Communist-held mainland.

Mar. 7. Senate Republican leaders decide to defer action on a resolution condemning Soviet "perversion" of wartime agreements leading to "enslavement" of free peoples.

Mar. 27. Charles E. Bohlen is confirmed as Ambassador to the U.S.S.R. by a 74-13 vote of the Senate.

Mar. 30. Mutual Security Director Stassen clashes with Senator Joseph R. McCarthy over the latter's activities in the field of East-West trade.

Apr. 30. The President announces that he will recommend cuts in defense spending to gear the military budget to long-term strategic planning.

May 8. The report of a special cabinet committee recommending participation with Canada in developing the Great Lakes-St. Lawrence Seaway is approved by the Cabinet.

May 9-29. The Secretary of State and the Director for Mutual Security tour eleven countries in the Near and Middle East and Southern Asia.

May 13. Senator McCarthy denounces former British Prime Minister Clement R. Attlee on the Senate floor.

May 26. Senator Robert A. Taft urges the administration to do what it can to negotiate a truce in Korea and, if unsuccessful, to act independently of the U.N. in the Far East. The President repudiates (May 28) any "go-it-alone" policy.

June 19. The convicted spies, Julius and Ethel Rosenberg, are executed at Sing Sing Prison.

June 25. Legislation authorizing delivery of up to 100 million tons of surplus wheat as famine relief to Pakistan is signed by the President.

July 14. The President ratifies the International Wheat Agreement for the United States. The agreement (signed in Washington April 13) enters into force for all parties on July 15.

July 15. The Senate approves the NATO Status of Forces Agreement, which enters into force Aug. 23.

July 16. The President signs the Mutual Security Act of 1953.

July 22. The President announces his support of a substitute for the Bricker resolution on the treaty-making power, introduced by Senator William F. Knowland. Further action on the issue is postponed to the next congressional session.

July 31. Senator Robert A. Taft dies at the age of 63.

Aug. 1. The Mutual Security Agency is superseded by the Foreign Operations Administration under Mr. Stassen, and the International Information Administration of the State Department is replaced by a separate United States Information Agency under Theodore C. Streibert.

Aug. 1. The President signs the $34.4 billion defense appropriation bill for the fiscal year 1953–54.

Aug. 7. The President approves a one-year extension of the Trade Agreements Act; the Refugee Relief Act to admit 214,000 nonquota immigrants on an emergency basis; the $4.5 billion Mutual Security Appropriation Act for fiscal year 1953–54; an act authorizing gifts of up to $100 million in surplus agricultural commodities; and a Supplemental Appropriation Act carrying $200 million for Korean rehabilitation.

Aug. 8. A Customs Simplification Bill is signed by the President.

Aug. 14. Clarence B. Randall is appointed chairman of the Commission on Foreign Economic Policy established by the Trade Agreements Extension Act.

Aug. 15. Admiral Arthur W. Radford succeeds General Omar N. Bradley as Chairman of the Joint Chiefs of Staff. Other new members of the Joint Chiefs of Staff are General Nathan F. Twining, Chief of Staff of the Air Force (June 30); General Matthew B. Ridgway, Chief of Staff of the Army (Aug. 15); and Admiral Robert B. Carney, Chief of Naval Operations (Aug. 17).

Sept. 3. An Operations Coordinating Board is established to ensure effective implementation of decisions of the National Security Council.

Oct. 6-Dec. 14. Vice President Richard M. Nixon tours nineteen Far Eastern and Middle Eastern countries as the President's personal representative.

Oct. 19. Defense Secretary Charles E. Wilson suggests that new weapons may enable the U.S. to reduce its overseas troop commitments.

Oct. 28. The President states that there is no plan for reduction of U.S. combat forces anywhere.

Nov. 3. The Democrats make scattered gains in Congressional and local elections.

Nov. 6. Attorney-General Herbert Brownell, Jr., asserts that President Truman appointed a known Communist spy to high official position in 1946. Mr. Truman publicly repudiates the charge Nov. 16.

Nov. 24. Senator McCarthy challenges the administration's policy of sending "perfumed notes" to countries trading with Communist China. The President rejects a policy of coercion in a statement on Dec. 3.

Dec. 19. The President and the National Security Council approve budget estimates submitted by the Joint Chiefs of Staff for military spending in fiscal years 1954–57, thus endorsing the "new look" in military planning.

THE WESTERN COMMUNITY

The "Big Three"

July 10-14. The Foreign Ministers of the U.S., U.K. and France meet in Washington and agree on a new approach to the U.S.S.R. on the German and Austrian questions.

Oct. 16-18. The three Foreign Ministers meet in London to discuss current questions.

Dec. 4-7. The President of the U.S. and the Prime Ministers of the United Kingdom and France meet in Bermuda and agree to accept the latest Soviet proposal for a four-power conference.

The North Atlantic Treaty Organization

Mar. 15. The NATO Mediterranean Command is activated with Admiral Earl Mountbatten as Commander-in-Chief and headquarters at Malta.

Apr. 23-25. The North Atlantic Council holds its eleventh Ministerial Meeting in Paris and approves a "long-haul" concept for Western defense.

June 10. The second annual report of the Supreme Allied Commander in Europe describes NATO's European command as "still critically weak to accomplish its mission."

July 10. General Alfred M. Gruenther assumes his duties as Supreme Allied Commander, Europe, replacing General Matthew B. Ridgway. Other new designations include Admiral William M. Fechteler, Commander-in-Chief, Allied Forces, Southern Europe; Marshal Alphonse-Pierre Juin, Commander-in-Chief, Allied Forces, Central Europe; and General Lauris Norstad, Air Deputy.

Dec. 14-16. The North Atlantic Council holds its twelfth Ministerial Meeting in Paris and hears Secretary Dulles refer to a possible "agonizing reappraisal" of U.S. policy toward Europe.

European Coal and Steel Community, European Defense Community, and European Political Community

Jan. 7-10. The Ad Hoc Assembly of the Coal and Steel Community meets at Strasbourg and transforms itself into an Assembly for a European Political Community.

Feb. 10. The European Coal and Steel Community commences effective operation with the entry into force of the common market for coal. The common market for steel becomes operative May 1.

Feb. 24-25. The Foreign Ministers of the six participating governments meet at Rome.

Mar. 6-10. The Assembly for a European Political Community meets at Strasbourg and adopts the text of a draft treaty for a political community.

Mar. 24. The Interim Committee of the European Defense Community approves the text of six additional protocols to the treaty submitted by France. The protocols are accepted by the member governments Apr. 24 and made public June 18.

May 12-13. The six Foreign Ministers meet in Paris. Further meetings are held in Baden-Baden, Aug. 7-8, and in The Hague, Nov. 26-28.

Organization for European Economic Cooperation

Mar. 23-24. The Council of the O.E.E.C. meets and decides to continue the European Payments Union until June 30, 1954.

Oct. 29-30. The Council meets to plan removal of quantitative restrictions on European and dollar imports.

The Council of Europe

Jan. 14-17. The Consultative Assembly meets in special session at Strasbourg.

May 6-7. The Committee of Ministers meets at Strasbourg to consider ways for tightening relations between the Council and other European organizations.

May 8-13. The Consultative Assembly meets to urge a speed-up in drafting the constitution of a European political community and other steps leading to unification.

Sept. 14-26. The Consultative Assembly meets to request negotiations on the Saar, a conference on Germany and Austria, and a mutual security pact with the U.S.S.R.

Dec. 11-12. The Committee of Ministers meets in Paris to sign a series of social and economic conventions and urge settlement of the Saar issue and a four-power conference on Germany and Austria.

Great Britain and the Commonwealth

(See also regional headings)

Jan. 5-9. *United Kingdom*—Prime Minister Winston Churchill confers with President-elect Eisenhower and President Truman in New York and Washington.

Mar. 4-7. *United Kingdom*—Foreign Secretary Anthony Eden and Chancellor of the Exchequer R. A. Butler discuss Anglo-U.S. political and economic relations with American officials in Washington.

Apr. 24. Prime Minister Churchill is created a Knight of the Garter and becomes Sir Winston Churchill.

June 2. Elizabeth II is crowned "by the Grace of God, of the United Kingdom of Great Britain and Northern Ireland and of her other Realms and Territories Queen, Head of the Commonwealth, Defender of the Faith."

June 3-9. The Commonwealth Prime Ministers meet in London.

Nov. 23. The Queen and the Duke of Edinburgh begin a six-month tour of the Commonwealth.

France

Jan. 7. René Mayer (Radical) obtains a vote of investiture from the National Assembly, ending a cabinet crisis which began with the resignation of Antoine Pinay on Dec. 23, 1952. Georges Bidault (M.R.P.) is Foreign Minister.

Jan. 28. The E.D.C. Treaty and the Contractual Agreements with Germany are submitted to the National Assembly.

Mar. 25-28. Premier Mayer, Foreign Minister Bidault and other high offcials discuss common problems with U.S. officials in Washington.

May 20. The Governments of France and the Saar sign a convention giving the Saar political autonomy and providing for economic union with France.

May 21. The Mayer government resigns on a vote of no confidence on the issue of "special powers" to deal with the economic situation.

June 26. Joseph Laniel (Independent) receives an Assembly vote of investiture as Prime Minister. M. Bidault is again Foreign Minister.

Aug. 6-28. A series of strikes occurs in various public services.

Nov. 27-29. The High Council of the French Union meets in Paris.

Dec. 23. René Coty (Independent Conservative) is elected President of the Republic on the thirteenth ballot.

Italy

June 7-8. Parliamentary elections give 303 seats in the Chamber of Deputies to the center party coalition (262 seats to the Christian Democrats) and 287 seats to the opposition parties (143 to the Communists and 75 to the left-wing Socialists). In the Senate the coalition wins 125 of a possible 237 seats.

June 29. The government of Premier Alcide De Gasperi resigns. A new De Gasperi government is formed July 15.

July 28. The De Gasperi government loses a vote of confidence (282-263).

Aug. 24. A predominantly Christian Democratic cabinet headed by Giuseppe Pella is approved by the Chamber of Deputies.

The German Federal Republic

(See also East-West Relations)

Jan.14. British authorities arrest seven ringleaders in a neo-Nazi movement accused of infiltrating the Free Democratic, German, and all-German Bloc (Refugee) parties.

Feb. 27. By a series of agreements signed in London, Germany accepts a settlement of its foreign indebtedness. The U.S. and Germany sign in Bonn an agreement establishing procedures for validation of German dollar bonds.

Mar. 19. The Bundestag approves the E.D.C. treaty by a vote of 224-165; the Contractual Agreements are approved by 226-164.

Apr. 7-9. Federal Chancellor Konrad Adenauer discusses German problems with American officials in Washington.

May 15. The Bundesrat approves the E.D.C. treaty and the Contractual Agreements by a vote of 23-15.

June 3. The U.S. and the German Federal Republic sign an agreement reviving the 1923 Treaty of Friendship, Commerce and Consular Rights. It is approved by the U.S. Senate July 21 and enters into force Oct. 22.

June 10. The Bundestag approves a program for free all-German elections, formation of an all-German government, and negotiation of a peace treaty.

Sept. 6. In elections to the Bundestag the government coalition wins 307 seats

(Christian Democrats 244; Free Democrats, 48; German party, 15) while the opposition parties hold 180 seats (Social Democrats, 150; All-German Bloc, 27; Center party, 3).

The Benelux Countries

July 23. The Second Chamber (lower house) of the Netherlands Parliament votes 75-11 for ratification of the E.D.C. treaty.

Nov. 26. The Belgian Chamber of Representatives votes 148-49 to approve ratification of the E.D.C. treaty.

Dec. 22. Premier Pierre Dupong of Luxembourg dies. He is succeeded Dec. 28 by Joseph Bech, who retains the Army and Foreign Affairs portfolios.

The Scandinavian Countries

Feb. 13-21. The Nordic Council, attended by representatives of all Scandinavian governments except Finland, meets in Copenhagen.

May 19. The Foreign Ministers of Norway, Denmark, Sweden and Iceland meet in Oslo.

Aug. 31-Sept. 1. The Foreign Ministers of Denmark, Norway and Sweden confer in Stockholm.

Denmark

Apr. 21-22. General elections give the Social Democrats 61 seats, the Agrarians 33, the Conservatives 26, and the remaining parties 29. The Social Democrats refuse to form a government and the incumbent coalition government of Prime Minister Erik Eriksen agrees to remain in office.

June 5. A new constitution which abolishes the upper house of the Parliament and changes the law of succession to the throne is approved by the King.

Sept. 22-Oct. 6. General elections held under the new constitution put the Agrarian party out of office, and the Social Democrats form a minority government under Hans Hedtoft.

Norway

Oct. 12. The Labor party remains in power following general elections which give it 78 seats to 26 for the Conservatives and 46 for the other parties.

Iceland

June 28. A new Parliament is elected, the Independence party winning 21 seats, the Progressives 16 and the remaining parties 15. Premier Steingrimur Steinthorsson (Progressive) resigns, and Olafur Thors (Independent) heads a coalition government, Sept. 13.

Finland

Nov. 4. The government of Premier Urho K. Kekkonen resigns and is succeeded (Nov. 18) by a non-party government of experts headed by Sakari Tuomioja.

Portugal

Nov. 8. The National Union party wins all 120 seats in elections to the National Assembly.

Spain

Sept. 26. The United States and Spain sign agreements at Madrid for construction of American bases and economic and military aid to Spain.

Austria

(See also East-West Relations)

Feb. 22. A general parliamentary election gives the People's and Socialist parties 74 and 73 seats, respectively, in the lower house. Minor parties hold 18 seats. Chancellor Leopold Figl (People's party) forms a new cabinet Feb. 28.

Apr. 1. A coalition government headed by Julius Raab (People's party) replaces the Figl government.

June 10. The Soviet High Commissioner in Austria is named first Ambassador of the U.S.S.R. in Vienna.

July 30. The Soviet Government informs Austria that it will pay its own occupation costs commencing Aug. 5.

Greece, Turkey, and Yugoslavia

Jan. 12. The Yugoslav National Assembly approves a new constitution to replace the Soviet-type constitution of 1946. Marshal Josip Broz Tito is elected first President of the Republic (Jan. 14) by the National Assembly.

Feb. 28. A tripartite treaty of friendship and collaboration is signed at Ankara by Greece, Turkey and Yugoslavia.

Oct. 12. A U.S.-Greek agreement for development and joint use of airfields and naval facilities is signed in Athens.

Trieste

Oct. 8. The U.S. and U.K. announce a decision to withdraw their occupation forces from Zone A and turn it over to Italy. The decision remains unimplemented because of tension between Yugoslavia and Italy.

Oct. 20. The U.N. Security Council rejects a Soviet proposal to consider the Trieste situation as a threat to peace.

THE SOVIET UNION AND THE EUROPEAN SOVIET BLOC

The U.S.S.R.

Jan. 13. TASS announces the uncovering of an alleged American- and British-sponsored Jewish doctors' plot against the lives of Soviet leaders.

Mar. 6. Official announcement is made of the death of Premier J. V. Stalin on Mar. 5. Georgi M. Malenkov takes over as Chairman of the Council of Ministers, Vyacheslav M. Molotov replaces Andrei Y. Vishinsky as Foreign Minister. Molotov, Lavrenti P. Beria (Minister of Internal Affairs), Marshal Nikolai A. Bulganin (Minister of Defense) and Lazar M. Kaganovich (without portfolio) are named First Deputy Chairmen of the Council of Ministers. Marshal Kliment Y. Voroshilov replaces Nikolai M. Shvernik as Chairman of the Presidium of the Supreme Soviet.

Mar. 14. Premier Malenkov resigns from the Secretariat of the Central Committee of the Communist Party, which is headed by Nikita S. Khrushchev. (Announced Mar. 20.)

Apr. 4. The 15 doctors arrested in the "Jewish plot" are released by the Ministry of Internal Affairs and their accusers are taken into custody.

July 10. The dismissal of Beria is announced together with his arraignment on treason charges before the Soviet Supreme Court.

Aug. 8. Addressing the Supreme Soviet, Premier Malenkov announces increased budgetary allocations to consumer goods, light industry and agriculture, stresses the theme of peaceful coexistence between states with different systems, and claims that the U.S. no longer possesses a monopoly of hydrogen bomb production.

Aug. 12. A thermonuclear (hydrogen) explosion takes place in Soviet territory. (Announced Aug. 20.)

Sept. 12. Khrushchev is named First Secretary of the Communist Party's Central Committee.

Dec. 23. Beria and six associates are sentenced to death by the Supreme Court of the U.S.S.R. and shot.

Czechoslovakia

Mar. 10. A U.S. fighter plane is shot down over Germany by two Czechoslovak aircraft.

Mar. 14. President Klement Gottwald dies following his return from Stalin's funeral in Moscow. Antonín Zápotocký is elected (Mar. 21) to succeed him, and Viliám Široký replaces Zápotocký as Premier.

May 15-16. William N. Oatis is pardoned by President Zápotocký for his alleged espionage activities and released from prison after serving a two-year term. The U.S. Government lifts (June 5) many of the restrictions imposed in retaliation for Mr. Oatis' imprisonment.

June 1. Rioting in Plzeň and other centers is curbed by mass arrests.

Hungary

May 17. Elections give 98.2 percent of the total vote to the Hungarian Popular Front for Independence.

July 3. Mátyás Rákosi is replaced by Imre Nagy as Prime Minister, and a radical change in the three- and five-year plans of the government is announced.

The "German Democratic Republic"

May 28. Vladimir Semyenov is appointed Soviet High Commissioner in the Soviet Zone of Germany, replacing the Soviet Control Commission under General Vassily I. Chuikov.

June 17. A strike originating in the building trades in East Berlin in protest to a decree of the G.D.R. on labor conditions gets out of regular police control. Russian tanks and troops are required to subdue the uprising, and a state of siege is proclaimed and maintained until July 12.

June 22. The government announces a reform program to meet many of the demands of the rioters.

July 11. A U.S. request for negotiations to arrange for distributing $15 million worth of food in the Soviet Zone is refused by the Soviet Foreign Minister.

July 27-Aug. 16. The first phase of the direct distribution of U.S. food parcels to East Germans in Berlin is completed with a total delivery of some 2,600,000 parcels.

Aug. 21-22. An East German-Soviet economic and political agreement announced in Moscow purports to ease the occupation regime in the Soviet Zone.

Oct. 7. Wilhelm Pieck is unanimously reelected President of the G.D.R.

The World Communist Movement

June 15-20. The World Peace Council meets in Budapest and issues an appeal for easing international tensions through negotiation.

Nov. 24-28. The World Peace Council holds a session in Vienna and adjourns without passing any resolutions.

EAST-WEST RELATIONS

Feb. 6, 9. The Austrian Treaty Deputies hold two meetings in London and adjourn *sine die* because of the Soviet Deputy's refusal to discuss either of the existing treaty drafts.

Mar. 15. Addressing the Supreme Soviet, Premier Malenkov declares that East-West differences can be settled by peaceful means.

Apr. 1. Foreign Minister Molotov endorses a Chinese Communist-North Korean proposal to resume armistice negotiations in Korea.

Apr. 16. Addressing the American Society of Newspaper Editors in Washington, President Eisenhower outlines ways in which the U.S.S.R. could demonstrate its peaceful intent.

Apr. 25. *Pravda* publishes a lengthy, point-by-point reply to President Eisenhower's peace program (Apr. 16), casting doubts on the "sincerity" of the proposals.

Apr. 28. The U.S.S.R. suggests a "Big Five" peace pact (to include the "Big Four" and Communist China).

May 11. In a general review of British world policy before the House of Commons, Prime Minister Churchill calls for a meeting with the Russians "at the highest level."

May 24. A *Pravda* article favors many of the suggestions made by the British Prime Minister on May 11 but rejects the concept of a new "Locarno" settlement in Eastern Europe.

May 25. The U.S.S.R. refuses on technical grounds to participate in a new meeting of the Austrian Treaty Deputies in London.

June 11. The Western Powers ask the Soviet Government to specify the text of an Austrian treaty which it is prepared to discuss.

July 15. Following the Washington conference of Foreign Ministers, the Western powers propose a conference with the U.S.S.R. on the problems of Germany and Austria.

July 19. The U.S.S.R. publicly renounces its territorial demands on Turkey.

July 30. The U.S.S.R. repeats its demand that the Western powers withdraw the proposed abbreviated treaty for Austria.

Aug. 4. Replying to the Western note of July 15, the U.S.S.R. asks that the proposed conference on Germany and Austria consider ways of reducing general international tension and that Communist China participate.

Aug. 15. In a new note on Germany the U.S.S.R. proposes a German peace conference, formation of a provisional all-German government, holding of all-German elections and alleviation of German economic burdens.

Aug. 17. The Western powers agree to drop the abbreviated treaty for Austria provided the U.S.S.R. raises no extraneous issues to obstruct conclusion of a treaty.

Aug. 28. The Soviet Government rejects the conditions in the Western powers' proposals of Aug. 17 and suggests that any further negotiations on an Austrian treaty be conducted through regular diplomatic channels.

Sept. 2. The Western powers, replying to the Soviet notes of Aug. 4 and 15, propose a foreign ministers' conference on Germany to meet at Lugano on Oct. 15.

Sept. 28. Replying to the Western powers' note of Sept. 2, the U.S.S.R. repeats its demand for a five-power conference on international tensions as well as a four-power conference on Germany.

Oct. 18. The Western powers propose a meeting of the four foreign ministers at Lugano on Nov. 9.

Nov. 3. The Soviet Government repeats its demand for Communist China's participation in any forthcoming conference and urges the formation of an all-German government to precede any other action on Germany.

Nov. 16. The Western powers reject the conditions outlined in the Soviet note of Nov. 3 and repeat the invitation extended in their note of Oct. 18.

Nov. 25. The Western powers offer to discuss with the Russians any version of the Austrian Treaty they may prefer and through any medium the Soviet Government wishes to suggest.

Nov. 26. The Soviet Government agrees to take part in a conference on Germany with no prior conditions. Subsequent exchanges lead to the scheduling of a conference to be held in Berlin in January 1954.

Dec. 21. The U.S.S.R. expresses willingness to confer on peaceful uses of atomic energy as proposed by President Eisenhower in an address of Dec. 8 to the U.N. General Assembly.

NEAR AND MIDDLE EAST

Arab League

Mar. 28. The Arab League Council admits Libya to membership in the League.

Apr. 4-10. The Council of the Arab League holds its 20th regular session at Cairo.

Aug. 25-Sept. 9. The Foreign and Defense Ministers of the member states hold military and political talks in Cairo.

Israel and the Palestine Problem

Feb. 9. A bomb is exploded in the Soviet Legation at Tel Aviv and leads to a break in diplomatic relations (Feb. 12) between Israel and the U.S.S.R.

June 9. Major General Vagn Bennike of Denmark is named to succeed Lieutenant General William E. Riley as Chief of Staff of the U.N. Truce Supervision Organization.

July 6, 15. The Israeli and Soviet Foreign Ministers exchange notes effecting a resumption of diplomatic relations.

July 12. The Israeli Foreign Ministry is transferred from Tel Aviv to Jerusalem. The U.S. Department of State announces (July 11) that the U.S. will maintain its Embassy at Tel Aviv.

July 21. The U.S. Senate approves the U.S.-Israeli Treaty of Friendship, Commerce and Navigation (signed at Washington, Aug. 23, 1951). The treaty is ratified by the President Dec. 18 and enters into force Apr. 3, 1954.

Sept. 23. General Bennike requests Israel to discontinue work on the Banat

Ya'qub hydroelectric project. Following a suspension by the U.S. of economic aid funds allocated to Israel (announced Oct. 20), Israel announces compliance in the U.N. Security Council Oct. 27.

Oct. 15. An Israeli raid on the village of Qibiya in Jordan leads to passage by the U.N. Security Council (Nov. 24) of a resolution censuring Israel.

Dec. 7-9. Prime Minister David Ben-Gurion resigns and a new government coalition of all except the extremist parties assumes responsibility with former Foreign Minister Moshe Sharett as Prime Minister.

Egypt, the Sudan and Suez

Jan. 17. Following the dissolution of all political parties (Jan. 16) General Muhammad Nagib is given sovereign authority to July 23, 1953.

Feb. 11. The government decrees a three-year period of provisional monarchy and sets up a "provisional parliament" composed of government members and the 13 members of the "Council of the Revolution."

Feb. 12. The United Kingdom and Egypt sign at Cairo an agreement on the future of the Sudan.

Apr. 27-May 6. Unfruitful talks on the Suez base issue between British representatives and Egyptian officials are held in Cairo and broken off by the Egyptian Government.

June 18. General Nagib proclaims the end of the monarchy and the establishment of a republic with himself as President and Prime Minister.

Nov. 2-30. Elections are held throughout the Sudan, giving the National Unionist party a majority of the seats in both the Senate and House of Representatives. Five university seats are decided Dec. 10.

Iraq

Jan. 17. The first direct parliamentary election in Iraq's history results in a victory for followers of former Premier Nuri al-Sa'id.

Jan. 24. The government of Nur al-Din Mahmud resigns and is succeeded (Jan. 29) by one headed by Gamil al-Madfai.

Lebanon

Apr. 28. The government of Premier Khalid Shehab resigns and is succeeded (May 1) by one headed by Saeb Salem.

Syria

July 10. Brigadier Adib Shishakli is elected President of the Republic with 86.6 percent of the popular vote, and amalgamates the Prime Minister's office with that of President.

Saudi Arabia

Nov. 9. The death of King Ibn Saud brings to the throne his eldest son, Saud Ibn Abdul Aziz.

Iran

Jan. 19. The Majlis votes to extend for one year the plenary powers of Premier Mohammad Mosaddeq.

Mar. 20. Anglo-American proposals (Feb. 20) for settling the oil controversy are rejected by the Mosaddeq government.

June 29. President Eisenhower informs Premier Mosaddeq that the U.S. cannot increase aid to Iran while the oil dispute with Britain remains unsettled.

Aug. 15. The Shah dismisses Premier Mosaddeq and appoints a new government headed by General Fazullah Zahedi. In the ensuing disorders the Shah temporarily leaves the country.

Aug. 19-20. General Zahedi is swept into power and Dr. Mosaddeq is arrested, clearing the way for the Shah's return.

Sept. 5. The White House announces the allocation of $45 million in emergency aid to Iran.

Nov. 8-Dec. 21. Dr. Mosaddeq is tried and found guilty of treason. He is sentenced to three years' solitary confinement.

Dec. 5. The United Kingdom and Iran resume diplomatic relations (broken off Oct. 22, 1952).

AFRICA

Tunisia

July 1. Prince Azzedine Bey, the heir apparent, is assassinated in Tunis.

Sept. 2. Pierre Voizard replaces Jean M.-F. de Hauteclocque as French Resident-General.

Nov. 11. The U.N. General Assembly rejects a compromise draft resolution on the status and future of Tunisia.

Morocco

Aug. 20. Sultan Sidi Mohammed Ben Youssef is deposed by French authorities and exiled. A new Sultan, Sidi Mulay Mohammed Ben Arafa, is installed Aug. 21.

Sept. 3. The U.N. Security Council rejects (5-5-1) a proposal of the Arab-Asian bloc to discuss the situation in Morocco as a threat to peace.

Nov. 3. A compromise proposal on Moroccan independence adopted in the U.N. General Assembly's First Committee (Oct. 19) fails to pass in plenary session.

Ethiopia

May 22. The U.S. and Ethiopia sign in Washington a mutual defense assistance agreement.

Oct. 8. The Treaty of Amity and Economic Relations between the U.S. and Ethiopia (signed Sept. 7, 1951; ratified by the President Aug. 4, 1953) enters into force.

British Africa

Feb. 5-8. *Kenya*—The Government extends emergency conditions to the entire Kikuyu tribal area and appoints an Emergency Council to advise the Governor.

July 30-Aug. 22. *Nigeria*—A conference of representatives of political groups in Nigeria is held in London and drafts recommendations for changes in the constitution of the territory.

Oct. 23. *Central African Federation*—The Federal Constitution becomes operative.

Nov. 30. *Uganda*—The Government of Uganda deposes the Kabaka of Buganda for failure to live up to his treaty obligations.

Union of South Africa

Apr. 15. General elections give 94 seats (a gain of 9) to the Nationalist party, 57 to the United party, 4 to the Labor party, with 4 remaining seats to be contested at a later date.

Nov. 11-Dec. 8. The U.N. General Assembly reaffirms its stand on the treatment of persons of Indian origin in South Africa (Nov. 11), South Africa's obligation in regard to the territory of South West Africa (Nov. 28), and South African racial policies (Dec. 8).

SOUTH AND SOUTHEAST ASIA

Economic and Social

Jan. 6-12. The Asian Socialist Conference meets at Rangoon and sets itself up as a permanent organization.

Oct. 13-17. The Colombo Plan Consultative Committee holds its fifth meeting in New Delhi.

India, Pakistan and the Kashmir Problem

Apr. 17. Pakistan's Governor-General, Ghulam Mohammad, dismisses Prime Minister Khwaja Nazimuddin and appoints Mohammad Ali to succeed him.

July 25-27. The Prime Ministers of India and Pakistan discuss common problems in Karachi.

Aug. 7-9. A government crisis in Kashmir results in the dismissal of Prime Minister Sheikh Mohammad Abdullah and the appointment of the former Vice-Premier (Bakshi Ghulam Mohammad) as his successor.

Aug. 16-20. The Prime Ministers of Pakistan and India discuss the Kashmir problem in New Delhi and agree on steps to prepare a plebiscite to be held before April 30, 1954.

Sept. 17. Addressing the Indian Parliament, Prime Minister Jawaharlal Nehru criticizes the barring of India from the Korean political conference and the continued lack of representation of Communist China in the U.N.

Nov. 2. The Pakistani Constituent Assembly recommends the designation of Pakistan as "the Islamic Republic of Pakistan" and the adoption of a system of cabinet government responsible to a parliament.

Nov. 5. Governor-General Ghulam Mohammad of Pakistan visits with President Eisenhower in Washington, reviving speculation over plans for granting the U.S. military base rights in Pakistan in exchange for military matériel.

Ceylon

Oct. 12-13. Prime Minister Dudley Senanayake resigns and is succeeded by a government headed by Sir John Kotelawala.

Indochina

Apr. 12. The Kingdom of Laos is invaded by 40,000 Vietminh troops.

May 8. General Henri-Eugène Navarre is named Commander-in-Chief of French Union forces in Indochina.

June 14-20. The King of Cambodia goes into brief exile in Thailand to dramatize his country's demands for complete independence.

July 3. The French Government issues a declaration promising negotiations to complete the independence of the Associated States within the French Union.

Sept. 9. The U.S. National Security Council recommends to President Eisenhower the spending of $385 million additional aid for use by the French in Indochina. Negotiations with the French Government to implement this decision are concluded Sept. 30.

Oct. 17. France and Cambodia sign agreements allocating military command responsiblities among their respective forces in Indochina.

Oct. 22. Laos and France sign in Paris a Treaty of Amity and Association and a series of conventions transferring authority to the Laotian Government and assuring Laotian independence within the French Union.

Nov. 14. Replying to a French inquiry (Oct. 21), the Vietnamese Government indicates its intention of keeping Vietnam in the French Union after the conclusion of hostilities.

Nov. 20. The Vietminh base at Dienbienphu is seized by French and Vietnamese parachute troops.

Nov. 29. An interview with Ho Chi Minh, President of the "Democratic Republic of Vietnam," is made public indicating the Vietminh's readiness to negotiate a cease-fire with French officials. The Vietminh offer is repeated Dec. 10 and 14.

Dec. 23. Communist forces numbering 20,000 reinvade Laos and reach the Mekong River frontier with Thailand Dec. 26.

Burma

Mar. 17. The Foreign Ministry informs the U.S. that it desires to discontinue American economic aid as of June 30.

Apr. 23. A resolution urging the internment or evacuation of Chinese forces in Burma is adopted by the U.N. General Assembly.

Oct. 31. It is announced that 2,000 of the Chinese forces in Burma have agreed to repatriation and (Nov. 4) that the U.S. has assumed the responsibility for airlifting the repatriates to Formosa. The operation is successfully conducted, Nov. 7-Dec. 10.

Dec. 8. The U.N. General Assembly reaffirms its interest in the evacuation of Chinese Nationalist troops.

Indonesia

Jan. 12. The U.S. and Indonesia conclude an agreement whereby American military grants-in-aid are to be replaced by direct Indonesian purchases. Technical and economic aid is continued on a grant basis.

June 3. The coalition cabinet of Dr. Wilopo resigns.

July 30. Formation of a nationalist coalition cabinet under Dr. Ali Sastroamidjojo is announced.

Philippines

July 1. The Philippine Government's request for renegotiation of the July 4, 1946 U.S.-Philippine Trade Agreement is tabled pending recommendations by the Commission on Foreign Economic Policy.

Nov. 10. The Nationalist party's candidate, Ramón Magsaysay, wins the presidential election over the incumbent President Elipidio Quirino (Liberal) by 2.8 million to 1.2 million votes. He is inaugurated Dec. 30.

EAST ASIA AND THE PACIFIC

Aircraft Incidents

Mar. 15. Two Soviet MIG fighters fire on an American RB-50 weather patrol plane over the North Pacific.

July 27. A U.S. fighter plane downs a Soviet aircraft over North Korea. The U.S.S.R. claims on July 31 that the attack occurred over Chinese territory.

July 29. Soviet fighters shoot down a U.S. training plane over the Sea of Japan. The U.S.S.R. disclaims knowledge of survivors.

The Anzus Powers

Sept. 9-10. The ANZUS (Australia-New Zealand-U.S.) Council meets in Washington.

China

Jan. 5-6. The Chinese Communists' first five-year plan is officially launched.

Feb. 21. Speaking at Dairen, Chinese Communist Prime Minister Chou En-lai charges the U.S. with using germ warfare and extending the war in Korea, sponsoring Nationalist raids on the mainland and converting Japan into an American military base.

Feb. 24. The Chinese Nationalist Legislature votes to repudiate the Sino-Soviet agreement of 1945 granting the U.S.S.R. special rights in Outer Mongolia, Dairen and Port Arthur.

Oct. 15. The U.N. General Assembly decides not to consider the problem of Chinese representation during 1953.

Korea

Jan. 6-8. President Syngman Rhee confers with Japanese officials in Tokyo on means of improving Korean-Japanese relations.

Jan. 28. The U.N. Command publishes an intelligence report accusing the Communist negotiators at Panmunjom of masterminding prisoner-of-war riots at Koje, Cheju and Pongam.

Feb. 8. The U.N. Command announces that the Korean Army is to be increased from 12 to 14 divisions.

Feb. 11. General Maxwell D. Taylor succeeds General James A. Van Fleet as Commander of the U.S. Eighth Army in Korea.

Feb. 22. The U. N. Commander repeats an earlier proposal to the Chinese and North Korean commanders for immediate exchange of sick and wounded prisoners.

Feb. 24. The U.N. Command issues a formal denial of germ warfare charges revived by the Peking radio.

Mar. 28. The Chinese and North Korean commanders agree to an exchange of sick and wounded prisoners of war and propose a resumption of formal armistice negotiations.

Apr. 18. The U.N. General Assembly unanimously approves a resolution terminating further consideration of the Korean problem pending the conclusion of an armistice.

Apr. 20-May 3. An exchange of sick and wounded prisoners of war is carried out at Panmunjom.

Apr. 23. The U.N. General Assembly approves a resolution to establish a commission to investigate Communist charges of use of germ warfare in Korea.

Apr. 26. Armistice negotiations are resumed at Panmunjom.

June 8. An agreement on prisoners of war is signed at Panmunjom by representatives of the U.N. and Communist commands and is subsequently incorporated in the armistice agreement.

June 17-18. With the connivance of the Republic of Korea Government, 25,000 Korean prisoners of war are permitted to escape. Armistice negotiations are recessed.

June 25-July 11. The U.S. Assistant Secretary of State for Far Eastern Affairs (Walter S. Robertson) confers with President Syngman Rhee in Seoul and obtains his promise not to obstruct implementation of the armistice agreement.

July 27. The 16 nations contributing to the U.N. effort in Korea sign in Washington a declaration (made public Aug. 7) threatening an extension of the conflict outside of Korea should the armistice be broken.

——. The armistice agreement is signed at Panmunjom by representatives of the U.N. Command and of the Korean People's Army and Chinese People's Volunteers.

Aug. 4-8. The U.S. Secretary of State confers with President Rhee in Seoul.

Aug. 5-Sept. 6. The U.N. and Communist Commands exchange prisoners of war at Panmunjom.

Aug. 8. A U.S.-Korean mutual defense treaty is initialed at Seoul. It is subsequently signed in Washington Oct. 1.

Aug. 28. The U.N. General Assembly adopts a resolution on the proposed Korean political conference, providing for participation of U.N. members contributing armed forces and also of the U.S.S.R. "if the other side desires it."

Sept. 5. The U.S. in a message to the Chinese Communist and North Korean governments suggests that a political conference convene Oct. 15 in San Francisco, Honolulu, or Geneva.

Sept. 9. The U.N. Command asks the Communist Command to account for 3,409 prisoners not returned in the exchange.

Sept. 11-19. The Prime Minister, Foreign Minister and other high officials of the Korean People's Democratic Republic conclude economic agreements with the U.S.S.R. in Moscow.

Sept. 13-14. Communist China and North Korea demand that the question of a political conference be reconsidered by the U.N. General Assembly at its Eighth Session. The Assembly rejects this proposal Sept. 22.

Sept. 18, 23. The U.S. releases further messages to the Communist governments regarding the political conference.

Sept. 21. A MIG 15 aircraft is surrendered to U.N. authorities in Korea by its North Korean pilot.

Sept. 24. The Custodial Force, India assumes temporary responsibility for prisoners refusing to be repatriated.

Oct. 6. General John E. Hull, named by President Eisenhower Sept. 11 to replace General Mark W. Clark, takes over as Supreme Commander of U.S. and U.N. Command forces in the Far East.

Oct. 6-21. Korean and Japanese officials hold a second series of unsuccessful talks in Tokyo on Japanese fishing rights and Korean-Japanese relations in general.

Oct. 10. Replying to a further U.S. message of Oct. 8, the Communists agree to hold preliminary discussions regarding a political conference. Details are settled by a further exchange of messages on Oct. 12-19.

Oct. 12. The U.N. Command charges that the Communists have moved military aircraft into North Korea in violation of the armistice agreement.

Oct. 14-Dec. 23. Explanation conferences with prisoners of both sides refusing repatriation are held under the supervision of the Neutral Nations Repatriation Commission.

Oct. 26. Procedural discussions relating to the political conference are begun by U.S. and Communist negotiators at Panmunjom.

Nov. 14-22. North Korean authorities negotiate with the Chinese Communist government at Peking agreements on economic and cultural collaboration.

Nov. 28. President Rhee and President Chiang Kai-shek issue a joint statement at Taipei affirming their unity in the struggle against Communism.

Dec. 3. Following disclosure by the U.S. Government of the extent of Communist mistreatment of prisoners in the Korean conflict, the U.N. General Assembly passes a resolution expressing "grave concern" over the atrocities.

Dec. 12. Procedural discussions at Panmunjom are broken off by the U.S. delegate following Communist charges of U.S. "perfidy."

Dec. 14. The U.S. and Korea sign at Seoul an agreement for a program of economic reconstruction and financial stabilization in Korea.

Dec. 26. President Eisenhower announces the prospective withdrawal of two American divisions from Korea.

Japan

Jan. 13, 16. Japan and the U.S. exchange notes on measures to discourage future violation of Japanese air space by foreign aircraft.

Feb. 23. Japanese and Chinese Red Cross Societies' representatives in Geneva negotiate an agreement for repatriation of 30,000 former Japanese prisoners in China.

Apr. 2. The U.S. and Japan sign at Tokyo a Treaty of Friendship, Commerce and Navigation. The treaty is approved by the U.S. Senate July 21 and enters into force Sept 30.

Apr. 19. General elections to the lower house of the Diet return 199 Liberals, 76 Progressives, 66 Right-wing Socialists, 72 Left-wing Socialists and 35 (Hatoyama splinter) Liberals, with 18 seats to the remaining parties.

May 19. The Diet again approves Shigeru Yoshida (Liberal) as Prime Minister.

July 15. Negotiations are commenced in Tokyo for a U.S.-Japanese mutual security assistance agreement (concluded Mar. 8, 1954).

Aug. 8. Following talks with Japanese officials in Tokyo, the U.S. Secretary of State announces that the U.S. will arrange for the return of the Amami Oshima island group to Japanese sovereignty.

Sept. 27. The Prime Minister and the leader of the opposition reach agreement on the conversion of the national safety force into a national self-defense force of 250,000 men.

Sept. 29. The U.S. and Japan sign a protocol at Tokyo defining Japanese jurisdiction over U.S. military personnel.

Sept. 29-Oct. 15. Foreign Minister Katsuo Okazaki visits the Philippines, Indonesia and Burma to discuss reparations and normalization of relations.

Oct. 5-30. Hayato Ikeda, personal representative of the Prime Minister, discusses future defense and economic relations with American officials in Washington.

Oct. 26. U.N. and Japanese representatives sign an agreement in Tokyo regarding Japanese criminal jurisdiction over U.N. military personnel.

Nov. 19. The Japanese and Soviet Red Cross Societies sign an agreement for repatriation of Japanese prisoners of war in the U.S.S.R.

Oct. 28. Japan is accepted for provisional membership in the General Agreement on Tariffs and Trade.

Dec. 24. The U.S. concludes arrangements with Japan in Tokyo for return of the Amami Oshima to Japanese sovereignty.

THE WESTERN HEMISPHERE

Feb. 9-21. The Inter-American Economic and Social Council holds its Third Extraordinary Meeting at Caracas.

Apr. 20-May 9. The Inter-American Council of Jurists holds its second meeting at Buenos Aires.

May 11-16. The Caribbean Commission holds its sixteenth meeting at Paramaribo.

June 23-July 29. Dr. Milton S. Eisenhower, the President's Special Ambassador, tours 10 South American countries on a fact-finding mission. His report is submitted to the President Nov. 18.

Argentina

Feb. 20-26. President Juan D. Perón pays a state visit to Chile, and agreements providing for economic union of the two countries result.

Apr. 15-16. An attempt on the life of President Perón results in rioting by his supporters and numerous arrests.

Sept. 30-Oct. 3. President Perón pays a state visit to Paraguay and calls for unity of the Americas against common dangers.

Brazil

May 3. The military assistance agreement concluded with the U.S. in 1952 is approved by the Brazilian Congress.

June 15. Oswaldo Aranha becomes Finance Minister in a cabinet reshuffle.

Chile

Mar. 1. General elections return a majority for the opposition in both houses of the Parliament.

Bolivia

Oct. 6. President Eisenhower authorizes the allocation of $5 million in agricultural commodities for famine relief, together with $4 million in special economic aid and increased technical assistance funds.

Colombia

June 13-18. General Gustavo Rojas Pinilla heads an Army coup that results in the deposition of President Laureano Gómez and his replacement by a junta of 13 officers with Rojas Pinilla as President.

Ecuador

Dec. 12. Ecuador joins the Argentine-Chilean economic union.

Paraguay

Feb. 15. Federico Chávez (National Republican) is reelected President to serve a five-year term.

Aug. 14. Paraguay joins the Argentine-Chilean economic union.

Venezuela

Jan. 9. The Constituent Assembly approves Colonel Marcos Pérez Jiménez as provisional President and subsequently (Apr. 19) elects and inaugurates him as constitutional President for a five-year term. A bicameral National Congress selected by the Constituent Assembly is installed for a five-year term effective Apr. 19.

Costa Rica

July 26. General elections return José Figueres (National Liberation) as President (inaugurated Nov. 8) and give the National Liberation party 30 of the 45 seats in the Congress.

Cuba

July 26-28. A revolt instigated by followers of ex-President Carlos Prío Soccarás leads the government to make mass arrests and suspend constitutional rights for a ninety-day period.

Dominican Republic

Mar. 6. A bilateral military assistance agreement with the U.S. is signed in Washington.

Guatemala

Jan. 16-18. Elections to 32 of the 56 seats in Congress are held, returning 28 leftist candidates.

Feb. 6. Four members of the Supreme Court (including the Chief Justice) are removed by a vote of the Congress for their legal opinions against the government's expropriation policies.

Aug. 28. The U.S. formally protests the legal position assumed by the Guatemalan Government in expropriating property of the United Fruit Company.

Oct. 6. The U.S. proposes consideration of "intervention of international communism in the American republics" at the Tenth Inter-American Conference, meeting in Caracas in 1954.

Panama

Sept. 28-Oct. 7. President Antonio Remón Cantera pays a state visit to the U.S.

Mexico

Oct. 19. President Eisenhower and President Adolfo Ruiz Cortines of Mexico dedicate the Falcón Dam on the Rio Grande.

British Guiana

Apr. 30. Elections under a new constitution give the leftist People's Progressive party 18 of the 24 elective seats in the House of Assembly.

Oct. 6. The British Government sends troops and suspends the Constitution (Oct. 9) to prevent a possible coup by the People's Progressive party.

Canada

May 7-8. Prime Minister Louis St. Laurent and Minister for External Affairs Lester B. Pearson hold discussions with American officials in Washington.

Aug. 10. The Liberal party is returned to power with 171 of the 265 seats in the House of Commons, a loss of 22.

Nov. 12. The U.S. and Canada agree to establish a joint U.S.-Canadian Committee on Trade and Economic Affairs and a Joint Board of Engineers for the St. Lawrence power project.

Nov. 13-14. President and Mrs. Eisenhower pay a state visit to Canada.

Nov. 19-Dec. 3. A series of exchanges takes place between the U.S. and Canadian governments regarding a proposed interview with Igor Gouzenko by members of a U.S. Senate subcommittee in connection with its investigation of Soviet spy systems in the U.S.

UNITED NATIONS

(See also regional headings)

Secretariat

Apr. 10. Dag Hammarskjold of Sweden is installed as Secretary-General, replacing Trygve Lie of Norway, pursuant to his election Apr. 7 by the General Assembly.

Sept. 1. The Administrative Tribunal votes indemnities for eleven U.S. citizens dismissed from the Secretariat and recommends the reinstatement of four of them.

General Assembly

Feb. 24-Apr. 23. The Assembly holds the second part of its Seventh Regular Session under the presidency of Lester B. Pearson of Canada, and adopts the following resolutions among others:

Mar. 17—Urging contributions for Korean relief and reconstruction.
—Continuing the Collective Measures Committee.
—Urging release of interned Greek soldiers.
Apr. 1—Reaffirming Charter provisions on the character of the Secretariat.
Apr. 8—Continuing the work of the Disarmament Commission.
April 18—Suspending the session pending Korean developments.
Apr. 23—Calling for evacuation and internment of Chinese Nationalist troops in Burma.
—Calling for an impartial investigation of Communist "germ warfare" charges.

Aug. 17-28. The Assembly holds the third part of its Seventh Regular Session to consider the post-armistice situation in Korea and adopts a resolution on membership in the Korean political conference.

Sept. 15-Dec. 9. The Assembly holds the first part of its Eighth Regular Session under the presidency of Mme. Vijaya Lakshmi Pandit of India, and adopts the following resolutions among others:

Oct. 6—Continuing the U.N. Children's Fund (UNICEF).
Oct. 23—Establishing a negotiating committee on U.N. membership.
Nov. 11—Continuing the committee on treatment of Indians in South Africa.
Nov. 27—Recognizing the non-self-governing status of Puerto Rico.
—Envisaging preparations for a Charter Review conference.
—Continuing the U.N. Relief and Works Agency for Palestine Refugees.
—Making assessments toward the 1954 budget.
Nov. 28—Requesting continued effort by the Disarmament Commission.
—Requesting further work by the Human Rights Commission.
—Establishing a new committee on South West Africa.
Dec. 3—Deploring Communist atrocities in Korea.
Dec. 7—Asking contributions for Korean reconstruction.
—Calling for further studies of economic development.
—Deploring the practice of forced labor.
—Calling for repatriation of World War II prisoners.
Dec. 8—Condemning South African racial policies.
—Calling for evacuation of Chinese Nationalist troops in Burma.
Dec. 9—Requesting a court opinion on the authority of the Administrative Tribunal.

Dec. 8. President Eisenhower outlines a program for peaceful uses of atomic energy and indicates the measures the U.S. would be prepared to take in this direction.

Security Council

(See also Trieste, Palestine and Morocco entries)

Oct. 5. The General Assembly elects Turkey, Brazil and New Zealand to membership on the Security Council as replacements for Greece, Chile and Pakistan.

Economic and Social Activities

Feb. 6-14. The Economic Commission for Asia and the Far East holds its ninth session at Bandung.

Mar. 3-18. The Economic Commission for Europe holds its eighth session in Geneva.

Mar. 31-Apr. 28. The Economic and Social Council holds its fifteenth session in New York.

Apr. 7-June 1. The Commission on Human Rights holds its ninth session in Geneva.

Apr. 9-17. The Economic Commission for Latin America holds its fifth session at Rio de Janeiro.

Apr. 13-18. The Economic Commission for Europe holds an East-West Trade Conference at Geneva.

May 11-29, Aug. 25-Sept. 15. The Ad Hoc Commission on Prisoners of War holds its fourth session in Geneva.

June 30-Aug 8. The Economic and Social Council holds its sixteenth session in Geneva. Three final meetings are held in New York Nov. 30, Dec. 1 and Dec. 7.

Nov. 12-13. The Fourth U.N. Technical Assistance Conference is held in New York.

Trusteeship and Non-Self-Governing Territories

Jan. 19. The U.S. informs the U.N. Secretary-General that as a result of the entry into force (June 30, 1952) of the constitution of the new Commonwealth of Puerto Rico, the U.S. will cease transmitting information on Puerto Rico under Article 73 (e) of the U.N. Charter.

June 16-July 31. The Trusteeship Council's twelfth session is held in New York.

Specialized Agencies

May 5-22. The Sixth Assembly of the World Health Organization meets in Geneva.

June 4-27. The International Labor Organization's 36th Annual Conference takes place in Geneva.

July 1-4. The Second Extraordinary Session of the UNESCO General Conference is held in Paris.

Sept. 9-12. The Boards of Governors of the International Bank and International Monetary Fund hold their eighth annual session in Washington.

Sept. 17-Oct. 24. The Contracting Parties to the General Agreement on Tariffs and Trade hold their eighth session at Geneva.

Nov. 23-Dec. 11—The Seventh General Conference of the Food and Agriculture Organization is held in Rome.

INDEX